Lecture Notes in Computer Science 13656

More information about this series at https://link.springer.com/bookseries/558

Yuan Xu · Hongyang Yan · Huang Teng ·
Jun Cai · Jin Li (Eds.)

Machine Learning for Cyber Security

4th International Conference, ML4CS 2022
Guangzhou, China, December 2–4, 2022
Proceedings, Part II

 Springer

Editors
Yuan Xu
School of Computing and Informatics
University of Louisiana at Lafayette
Lafayette, IN, USA

Huang Teng
Institute of Artificial Intelligence
and Blockchain
Guangzhou University
Guangzhou, China

Jin Li
Institute of Artificial Intelligence
and Blockchain
Guangzhou University
Guangzhou, China

Hongyang Yan
Institute of Artificial Intelligence
and Blockchain
Guangzhou University
Guangzhou, China

Jun Cai
Guangdong Polytechnic Normal University
Guangzhou, China

ISSN 0302-9743   ISSN 1611-3349 (electronic)
Lecture Notes in Computer Science
ISBN 978-3-031-20098-4   ISBN 978-3-031-20099-1 (eBook)
https://doi.org/10.1007/978-3-031-20099-1

This Springer imprint is published by the registered company Springer Nature Switzerland AG
The registered company address is: Gewerbestrasse 11, 6330 Cham, Switzerland

Preface

The Fourth International Conference on Machine Learning for Cyber Security (ML4CS 2022) was held in Guangzhou, China, during December 2–4, 2022. ML4CS is a well-recognized annual international forum for AI-driven security researchers to exchange ideas and present their works.

The conference received 367 submissions. Committee accepted 100 regular papers and 46 short papers to be included in the conference program. It was single blind during the paper review process, and there are two reviews per paper at least. The proceedings contain revised versions of the accepted papers. While revisions are expected to take the referees comments into account, this was not enforced and the authors bear full responsibility for the content of their papers.

ML4CS 2022 was organized by Guangdong Polytechnic Normal University, Pazhou Lab, and Sun Yat-sen University. The conference would not have been such a success without the support of these organizations, and we sincerely thank them for their continued assistance and support.

We would also like to thank the authors who submitted their papers to ML4CS 2022, and the conference attendees for their interest and support. We thank the Organizing Committee for their time and effort dedicated to arranging the conference. This allowed us to focus on the paper selection and deal with the scientific program. We thank the Program Committee members and the external reviewers for their hard work in reviewing the submissions; the conference would not have been possible without their expert reviews. Finally, we thank the EasyChair system and its operators, for making the entire process of managing the conference convenient.

September 2022

Xiaochun Cao
Jin Li
Jun Cai
Huang Teng
Yan Jia
Min Yang
Xu Yuan

Organization

General Chairs

Xiaochun Cao	Sun Yat-sen University, China
Jin Li	Guangzhou University, China
Jun Cai	Guangdong Polytechnic Normal University, China
Teng Huang	Guangzhou University, China

Program Chairs

Yan Jia	Peng Cheng Laboratory, China
Min Yang	Fudan University, China
Xu Yuan	University of Louisiana at Lafayette, USA

Track Chairs

Machine Learning Based Cybersecurity Track

Wei Wang	Beijing Jiaotong University, China
Yu-an Tan	Beijing Institute of Technology, China

Big Data Analytics for Cybersecurity Track

Xuyun Zhang	Macquaire University, Australia
Wenchao Jiang	Guangdong University of Technology, China

Cryptography in Machine Learning Track

Xinyi Huang	Fujian Normal University, China
Joseph K. Liu	Monash University, Australia

Differential Privacy Track

Changyu Dong	Newcastle University, UK
Tianqing Zhu	University of Technology Sydney, Australia

Data Security in Machine Learning Track

Zheli Liu   Nankai University, China
Zuoyong Li   Minjiang University, China

Adversarial Attacks and Defenses Track

Qian Wang   Wuhan University, China
Kai Chen   Institute of Information Engineering, Chinese
                                   Academy of Sciences, China

Security and Privacy in Federated Learning Track

Lianyong Qi   Qufu Normal University, China
Tong Li   Nankai University, China

Explainable Machine Learning Track

Sheng Hong   Beihang University, China

Security in Machine Learning Application Track

Tao Xiang   Chongqing University, China
Yilei Wang   Qufu Normal University, China

AI/Machine Learning Security and Application Track

Hao Peng   Zhejiang Normal University, China

Workshop Chair

Wei Gao   Yunnan Normal University, China

Publication Chair

Di Wu   Guangzhou University, China

Publicity Chair

Zhuo Ma   Xidian University, China

Steering Committee

Xiaofeng Chen	Xidian University, China
Iqbal Gondal	Federation University, Australia
Ryan Ko	Waikato University, New Zealand
Jonathan Oliver	Trend Micro, USA
Islam Rafiqul	Charles Sturt University, Australia
Vijay Varadharajan	University of Newcastle, Australia
Ian Welch	Victoria University of Wellington, New Zealand
Yang Xiang (Chair)	Swinburne University of Technology, Australia
Jun Zhang (Chair)	Swinburne University of Technology, Australia
Wanlei Zhou	Deakin University, Australia

Program Committee

Silvio Barra	University of Salerno, Italy
M. Z. Alam Bhuiyan	Guangzhou University, China
Carlo Blundo	University of Salerno, Italy
Yiqiao Cai	Huaqiao University, China
Luigi Catuogno	University of Salerno, Italy
Lorenzo Cavallaro	King's College London, UK
Liang Chang	Guilin University of Electronic Technology, China
Fei Chen	Shenzhen University, China
Xiaofeng Chen	Xidian University, China
Zhe Chen	Singapore Management University, Singapore
Frédéric Cuppens	IMT Atlantique, France
Changyu Dong	Newcastle University, UK
Guangjie Dong	East China Jiaotong University, China
Mohammed EI-Abd	American University of Kuwait, Kuwait
Wei Gao	Yunnan Normal University, China
Dieter Gollmann	Hamburg University of Technology, Germany
Zheng Gong	South China Normal University, China
Zhitao Guan	North China Electric Power University, China
Zhaolu Guo	Chinese Academy of Sciences, China
Jinguang Han	Queen's University Belfast, UK
Saeid Hosseini	Singapore University of Technology and Design, Singapore
Chingfang Hsu	Huazhong University of Science and Technology, China
Haibo Hu	The Hong Kong Polytechnic University, Hong Kong
Teng Huang	Guangzhou University, China
Xinyi Huang	Fujian Normal University, China

Wenchao Jiang	Guangdong University of Technology, China
Lutful Karim	Seneca College of Applied Arts and Technology, Canada
Hadis Karimipour	University of Guelph, Canada
Sokratis Katsikas	Open University of Cyprus, Cyprus
Neeraj Kumar	Thapar Institute of Engineering and Technology, India
Kangshun Li	South China Agricultural University, China
Ping Li	South China Normal University, China
Tong Li	Naikai University, China
Wei Li	Jiangxi University of Science and Technology, China
Xuejun Li	Anhui University, China
Kaitai Liang	University of Surrey, UK
Hui Liu	University of Calgary, Canada
Wei Lu	Sun Yat-sen University, China
Xiaobo Ma	Xi'an Jiaotong University, China
Fabio Martinelli	IIT-CNR, Italy
Ficco Massimo	Second University of Naples, Italy
Weizhi Meng	Technical University of Denmark, Denmark
Vincenzo Moscato	University of Naples, Italy
Francesco Palmieri	University of Salerno, Italy
Fei Peng	Hunan University, China
Hu Peng	Wuhan University, China
Lizhi Peng	Jinan University, China
Umberto Petrillo	Sapienza University of Rome, Italy
Lianyong Qi	Qufu Normal University, China
Shahryar Rahnamayan	University of Ontario Institute of Technology, Canada
Khaled Riad	Guangzhou University, China
Yu Sun	Guangxi University, China
Yu-An Tan	Beijing Institute of Technology, China
Zhiyuan Tan	Edinburgh Napier University, UK
Ming Tao	Dongguan University of Technology, China
Donghai Tian	Beijing Institute of Technology, China
Chundong Wang	Tianjin University of Technology, China
Ding Wang	Peking University, China
Feng Wang	Wuhan University, China
Hui Wang	Nanchang Institute of Technology, China
Jianfeng Wang	Xidian University, China
Jin Wang	Soochow University, China

Licheng Wang	Beijing University of Posts and Telecommunications, China
Lingyu Wang	Concordia University, Canada
Tianyin Wang	Luoyang Normal University, China
Wei Wang	Beijing Jiaotong University, China
Wenle Wang	Jiangxi Normal University, China
Sheng Wen	Swinburne University of Technology, Australia
Yang Xiang	Swinburne University of Technology, Australia
Run Xie	Yibin University, China
Xiaolong Xu	Nanjing University of Information Science & Technology, China
Li Yang	Xidian University, China
Shao-Jun Yang	Fujian Normal University, China
Zhe Yang	Northwestern Polytechnical University, China
Yanqing Yao	Beihang University, China
Xu Yuan	University of Louisiana at Lafayette, USA
Qikun Zhang	Beijing Institute of Technology, China
Xiao Zhang	Beihang University, China
Xiaosong Zhang	Tangshan University, China
Xuyun Zhang	Macquarie University, Australia
Yuan Zhang	Nanjing University, China
Xianfeng Zhao	Chinese Academy of Sciences, China
Lei Zhu	Huazhong University of Science and Technology, China
Tianqing Zhu	China University of Geosciences, China

Track Program Committee - AI/Machine Learning Security and Application

Hao Peng (Chair)	Zhejiang Normal University, China
Meng Cai	Xi'an Jiaotong University, China
Jianting Ning	Singapore Management University, Singapore
Hui Tian	Huaqiao University, China
Fushao Jing	National University of Defense Technology, China
Guangquan Xu	Tianjin University, China
Jun Shao	Zhejiang Gongshang University, China

Contents – Part II

AMAD: Improving Adversarial Robustness Without Reducing Accuracy

Yujie Lin[1], Ximeng Liu[1(✉)], and Nan Jiang[2]

[1] College of Computer and Data Science, Fuzhou University, Fuzhou 350108, China
snbnix@gmail.com
[2] Department of Internet of Things, East China Jiao Tong University University,
Nanchang 330013, China
jiangnan@ecjtu.edu.cn

Abstract. The data augmentation method has been demonstrated as a ploy for enhancing model accuracy and adversarial robustness. However, it is well known that the traditional data augmentation methods have limited ability to defend against adversarial attacks. The most effective way to defend against adversarial attacks is still adversarial training. In addition, the trade-off between classification accuracy and robustness in adversarial training is also a popular research direction. In this paper, we propose a more effective method to combine one mixup algorithm with adversarial training to further enhance the robustness and accuracy of the model. Specifically, we align images in the feature space before the adversarial training. This method adds the features of another image on the basis of retaining the outline of one image. The images are trained by adversarial attack afterward. To verify the effectiveness of our method, we compare several other adversarial training methods. The experiments show our method achieves significant robustness and accuracy gains. Especially, our method makes an impressive trade-off between robustness and accuracy.

Keywords: Mixup · Data augmentation · Adversarial training

1 Introduction

Deep neural network (DNN) is becoming increasingly popular and successful in many machine learning tasks. It is widely applied in many areas, including image recognition. Despite its success, the adversarial perturbations are easy to deceive the classifier of DNN. Although these deceptions are not enough to deceive human vision, they can decrease the accuracy of the model's classification. Therefore, many researchers have turned attention to the defense against these adversarial perturbations. Adversarial training has become a popular research area in this environment. Researchers utilize the images which have added these perturbations to train the classifier to improve the robustness of the model. These methods of adding perturbations include rotation, cropping,

Y. Xu et al. (Eds.): ML4CS 2022, LNCS 13656, pp. 1–14, 2023.
https://doi.org/10.1007/978-3-031-20099-1_1

flipping, gray variation, adding noise, etc. These methods are essentially data augmentation methods, which can produce many new training examples. With the emergence of more adversarial attack algorithms, the effect of these methods becomes very restricted.

Goodfellow et al. [1] propose the adversarial training, which generates adversarial examples through the adversarial attack algorithm to train the classifier. Adversarial training is a more effective way to enhance the robustness of the model at present. In fact, the essence of adversarial training is also a data augmentation method. It adds the generated adversarial examples to the training set so that the model can learn the adversarial examples during training. Unfortunately, the improvement of robustness brought by adversarial training is generally accompanied by a decrease in recognition accuracy of natural examples, which means that the model may have to choose between robustness and accuracy. Therefore, the need for exploring better data expansion methods and better training strategies is urgent.

Mixup is a data augmentation method proposed by Zhang et al. [2], but it is different from the ordinary data augmentation method. It mixes two or more images in the input space or feature space. Mixup has been demonstrated to be an effective method to enhance the robustness of the model against adversarial attacks. Nevertheless, the initial mixup algorithms are superimposed in the input space, which is commonly unnatural. Lately, more mixed methods have begun to mix two or more images in their feature space. The effect of these methods is usually better than methods of operating in the input space. Therefore, whether these mixup algorithms can be combined with other methods to generate more different enhancement examples to enhance the robustness of the model is of great research significance. It is valuable to explore whether these methods are complementary in essence.

In this paper, we propose a new idea of adversarial training named aligned mixup and adversarial training (AMAD), which preprocesses the training set with an improved mixup algorithm and then uses the mixed data set as the training set for adversarial training. Through AMAD, more training-meaningful examples can be created, which is different from the conventional addition of random perturbations, and our generated samples are purposeful. The purpose of our generate examples is to preserve the posture or texture of one image while adding the texture or posture of another one. This method can effectively improve the classification accuracy of the model and slightly improve the robustness. Afterwards, we introduce the new images to adversarial training to enhance the robustness. Our method makes an impressive trade-off between the robustness and classification accuracy. AMAD improves the robustness of the model without reducing the classification accuracy; while enhancing the classification accuracy, it does not lose the robustness. In addition to testing AMAD in simple networks, we also apply AMAD to larger capacity networks. Moreover, we also evaluate AMAD's ability to deal with stronger adversarial attacks. We test AMAD on two classic image classification data sets and find that AMAD achieves accuracy improvement and robustness gain in most cases.

2   Related Works

2.1   Data Augmentation

Data augmentation is a method of utilizing limited data to extend the data set. It can decrease the dependence of the model on parameters and enhance the robustness of the model. Traditional data augmentation methods are predominantly geometric changes, including rotation, clipping, flip, gray variation, scaling, translation, etc. These methods are to alter the absolute position of the object in the original image without changing the semantic features to generate new data. After that, the data augmentation of color transformation appears, including adding noise, blurring, filling, etc. These methods enhance the generalization ability of the model to a certain extent.

Lately, researchers have turned their attention to two or more images. Cutout [3] randomly removes a small part of the original image based on retaining the most information to generate new data, which enhances the model's ability to recognize the occluded target. Mixup [2] fused the two images in proportion to decrease the model's memory of damaged labels and enhances the robustness against adversarial examples. Samplepairing [4] superimposes the average value of pixel values in two images. Cutmix [5] randomly fills the area pixel values of other data based on retaining most of the information of the original image. Manifold mixup [6] extends the input data mixing to the output mixing of the intermediate hidden layer. Saliencemix [7] adds significance analysis based on Cutmix so that the clipping area is only a significant area. In addition to adding significance analysis, Puzzlemix [8] also adds some complex and delicate optimization operations. Co-mixup [9] mixes the significant regions of multiple samples based on Puzzlemix. Stylemix [10] flexibly blends the contents and styles of different images to generate various data samples. Alignmix [11] mixes the pose and texture of different images to generate more disturbing images to achieve a better training effect. Augmix [12] generates more realistic images by blending images generated by other mixing methods. Almost all of these hybrid data augmentation algorithms based on mixup can enhance the robustness and classification accuracy of the model to a certain extent.

In addition, there are many unsupervised data augmentation methods, such as GAN [13], Autoaugment [14], Trivial Augment [15], etc. These data augmentation strategies generate high-quality images with strong robustness after training, but they often cost a lot. Most of them are not appropriate to be combined with other data augmentation strategies such as adversarial training, so they are not mentioned in this paper.

2.2   Adversarial Training

The defense methods against adversarial examples can be divided into data preprocessing, adversarial example detection, and adversarial training. The idea of data preprocessing and adversarial example detection is comparable in essence. They are both methods of processing adversarial examples directly. However, they are not necessarily efficient. There is always the case that the adversarial example is successfully input into the target model. Hence, it is particularly essential to enhance the robustness of the model itself, and adversarial training is currently the most effective way. The basic idea of adversarial training is to add the adversarial examples to the training data set to train the model, which could make the model attain the defense ability. Goodfellow et al. [1] proposed the fast gradient sign method (FGSM) and firstly proposed that training the model with adversarial examples can reduce the classification error rate of the model to adversarial examples. This discovery has become the prototype of the adversarial training method. Subsequently, Madry et al. [16] specified the concept of adversarial training while proposing the projected gradient descent (PGD). They use the adversarial examples generated by the PGD attack method to train the model. This training method is PGD adversarial training.

With the continuous development of related research, some problems of adversarial training gradually appear, such as high training cost, difficulty with balancing the robustness and accuracy of the model, and so on. The main idea of the fast adversarial training method named FreeAT proposed by Shafahi et al. [17] is to directly generate new adversarial examples by using the gradient information generated by the training of old adversarial examples, to decrease the computational overhead of generating examples. Unlike FreeAT, the FreeLB method proposed by Zhu et al. [18] does not obtain new gradient information through the training of adversarial examples. They directly get new gradient information from the old gradient information, thus reducing the gradient calculation steps. Trades proposed by Zhang et al. [19] divides the robustness error into two parts: natural error and boundary error, and balances the classification accuracy of natural data and the robustness of the model. Mart proposed by Wang et al. [20] uses regularization to optimize the error judgment of robustness to improve adversarial training. It is noteworthy that many adversarial training ideas are improved based on PGD adversarial training. Nowadays, PGD adversarial training is still the most popular research method of adversarial defense.

3   Aligned Mixup and Adversarial Training

3.1   Preliminaries

We first define some symbols in the mixup operation. We use lowercase characters (x), uppercase characters $(\mathbf{A})$, and italic characters (A) to represent vectors, sets, and the matrix. Suppose we have a training set, including images and labels, and these data are from the unknown underlying distribution D. In the adversarial training setting, $J(\theta, x, y)$ is the cross-entropy loss function of the neural network, where θ represents the model parameters.

For the mixup data Augmentation method, we follow the setting in [11]. An encoder network (F) maps the image x to the feature tensor. And ε is a regularization parameter.

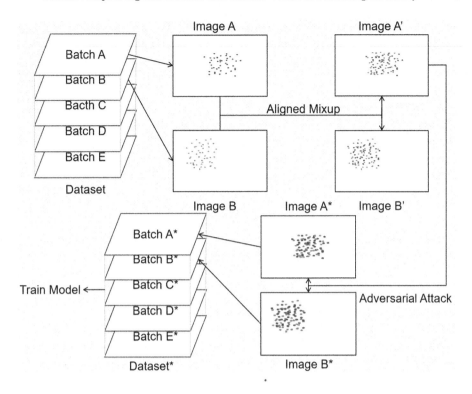

Fig. 1. The training process. Firstly, image A and B from two batches in the dataset are aligned and mixed to generate images A' and B'. Then these generated images are used to generate adversarial samples A*, B*. Lastly, the dataset composed of these adversarial samples is used to train the model.

3.2 Proposed Training Method

As shown in Fig. 1, the training method we proposed is to mix the data sets first and then conduct adversarial training on the mixed data sets. Before mixing the image, we need to process the feature tensor of the image. The mixup method we utilize is different from the traditional mixup methods. Instead of combining or filling two images, we map the feature tensor of one image to another. It makes the generated image more natural and substantial.

Let $\mathbf{A}_1=F(x_1)$ and $\mathbf{A}_2=F(x_2)$ be the feature tensor of images x_1 and x_2, and convert them into $c \times r$ matrices A_1 and A_2 by flattening the spatial dimension, where c is the number of channels and r is the spatial resolution. Let M be the cost matrix composed of paired distances:

$$m_{ij} = \|a_i - a_j\|^2 \tag{1}$$

Subsequently, a $r \times r$ matrix P is used for a transformation. The sum of elements in each row and column is $1/r$, and the elements represent the joint probability of the feature tensor matrix in space. We use it to minimize the pairwise distance by image features through entropy regularization:

$$P' = \arg\min_{P}\langle P, M\rangle - \varepsilon H(P) \tag{2}$$

where $H(P)$ is the entropy of P and M is the cost matrix composed of paired distances. Then the matrices A_1 and A_2 transformed by the characteristic tensor are aligned through the assignment matrix $R = rP'$. The element r_{ij} in R represents the probability that the column a_i of A_1 maps the column a_j of A_2. Thus, the aligned matrix is:

$$\widetilde{A}_1 = A_2 R^{\mathsf{T}} \tag{3}$$

$$\widetilde{A}_2 = A_1 R \tag{4}$$

Then $\widetilde{A}_i$ is transformed into feature tensor $\widetilde{\mathbf{A}}_i$ by extending the spatial dimension. Finally, $\widetilde{\mathbf{A}}_i$ mixed with the feature tensor $\mathbf{A}_i$:

$$\mathrm{mix}_\lambda(\mathbf{A_i}, \widetilde{\mathbf{A}}_i) = \lambda\mathbf{A_i} + (1-\lambda)\widetilde{\mathbf{A}}_i \tag{5}$$

where $\lambda \in (0,1)$ is the mixing factor calculated from $\mathrm{Beta}(\alpha, \alpha)$.

Of course, mixing all the original data sets will considerably increase the training time, but it can make the trained model have better classification accuracy while having similar robustness. We also consider setting a mixing proportion parameter $\mu \in (0,1)$, which represents the data set after aligned mixup as:

$$x' = \lambda x_{mix} + (1-\lambda)x_{clean} \tag{6}$$

where x' represents the image in the data set after mixing processing, x_{mix} represents the image after mixing processing, and x_{clean} represents the original image without mixing processing.

As for the adversarial training method, we apply the classical adversarial attack algorithms PGD [16]. PGD is an improved algorithm based on FGSM. FGSM is essentially a gradient-rising algorithm. By moderately changing the input, the predicted value of the output is very different from the actual value. FGSM implements a one-step update along the gradient direction of the loss function to enhance the loss in the most abrupt direction. The specific formula is as follows:

$$x^* = x + \epsilon \cdot \mathrm{sign}(\nabla_{\mathbf{x}} J(\theta, \mathbf{x}, \mathbf{y})) \tag{7}$$

where ϵ is the perturbations size, and $\epsilon \cdot \mathrm{sign}()$ limits the perturbations size to a certain range. Because FGSM is a one-step method to generate adversarial examples, its premise is that the loss function is linear or at least locally linear. If the loss function is not linear, the increasing direction of the gradient is not necessarily the optimal direction. This means that the model may fail in defense after FGSM adversarial training, while the attack samples are adversarial samples generated by complex multi-step attacks.

To solve the linear hypothesis problem in FGSM, we consider PGD adversarial training. Compared with one iteration of FGSM, PGD adopts the strategy of

---

Algorithm 1: Aligned Mixup and Adversarial Training

Input: images $x_1, \ldots, x_n \in \chi$; label $y_1, \ldots, y_n \in Y$; encoders F;
transport matix P; regularization coefficient ε;

Input: epochsT; pertubationboundβ; adversarialstepsizeδ;
PGDsteps m; radiusα; interpolation factor λ

1 **for** $i = 1, \ldots, n$ **do**
2      $A_i = F(x_i)$;
3      $A_i \leftarrow$ ToMatrix (A_i); //Reshape feature tensor to a c × r matrix
4      $M \leftarrow m_{ij} = \|a_i - a_j\|^2$; //Calculate the cost matrix
5      $P' = \arg\min_P \langle P, M \rangle - \varepsilon H(P)$;
6      $R = rP'$;
7      $\widetilde{A}_1 = A_2 R^\mathsf{T}, \widetilde{A}_2 = A_1 R$;
8      $\widetilde{A}_i \leftarrow$ ToTensor $(\widetilde{A}_i)$; //Reshape matrix to feature tensor
9      $\text{mix}_\lambda(A_i, \widetilde{A}_i) = \lambda A_i + (1 - \lambda)\widetilde{A}_i$;
10 **end**
11 **for** $t = 1, \ldots, T$ **do**
12   **for** $i = 1, \ldots, n$ **do**
13          $\delta = 0$ *or* $\delta = \text{Uniform}(-\beta, \beta)$; //randomly initialized
14   **for** $j = 1, \ldots, m$ **do**
15              $\delta = \delta + \epsilon \cdot \text{sign}(\nabla_\delta J(\theta, x_i + \epsilon, y_i))$;
16              $\delta = \max(\min(\delta, \alpha), -\alpha)$;
17   **end**
18          $\theta = \theta - \nabla_\theta J(\theta, x_i + \epsilon, y_i)$; //Update model
19   **end**
20 **end**

---

multiple iterations and one small step at a time. It calculates the perturbations according to the gradient through repititive forward and backward propagation and limits the current perturbation to a certain range. The specific formula is as follows:

$$x_0^* = x \tag{8}$$

$$x_{t+1}^* = \prod_{x+S}(x_t^* + \epsilon \cdot \text{sign}(\nabla_x J(\theta, x_t^*, y))) \tag{9}$$

The function is to map the perturbation back to the specified ranges S when the perturbation exceeds a certain range. Since only a small step is taken at a time, the local linearity assumption is basically established. After multiple iterations, we can achieve the optimal solution. Then, the generated adversarial examples are used for adversarial training, which is usually transformed into a robustness optimization problem:

$$\min_\theta \sum_i \max_{\delta \in S} J(\theta, x_i + \delta, y) \tag{10}$$

where δ is the perturbation, S is the set of perturbations, and θ is the model parameter. The inner layer is a maximization process, and $\max J()$ is the optimization goal, i.e., to confirm the perturbation that maximizes the loss function. In short, the added perturbation should confuse the neural network as much as possible. The outer layer is the minimization formula for optimizing the neural network, i.e., we minimize the loss while the perturbation is regular. In short, it is to make the model have certain robustness and be able to adapt to this perturbation.

Since adversarial training takes a lot of time, we consider some methods to accelerate the adversarial training, such as label smoothing and logit squeezing [21], learning rate adjustment [22], mixed-precision calculation [23], random perturbation and step size [24], Jacobi regularization [25], etc. However, these accelerated training methods will also optimize the training effect of the model when they improve the training speed. In order not to affect the training effect as much as possible, we use random initialization perturbation [26]. We set a non-zero initial perturbation to accelerate the adversarial training by avoiding the non-smooth region near the data points. Our training process is summarized in Algorithm 1.

4   Experiments

To demonstrate our training method can enhance the classification accuracy and robustness, we have carried out a large number of experiments on the classical data sets MNIST [27] and CIFAR-10 [28]. To compare more intuitively, we compare different adversarial training methods in both black-box and white-box settings to evaluate the robustness. In addition, we also extend the experiment to a larger network to demonstrate the universality of our method.

4.1   Robustness Evaluation

In this section, we utilize the same experimental settings under the white-box and black-box threat models to verify the effect of our method.

MNIST Setup. We use a CNN with four convolution layers as the architecture of MNIST. All models are trained with SGD. The initial learning rate is 0.01 and the momentum is 0.9.

CIFAR-10 Setup. We use ResNet-18 [29] as the backbone architecture of CIFAR-10. All models are trained with SGD. The initial learning rate is 0.1, the momentum is 0.9, and the weight decay is 3.5×10^{-3}.

Experimental Setup. The maximum perturbation $\epsilon = 8/255$. The training attack starts at random and the step size is $\epsilon/4$. The PGD^{20} attack used in the test attack has random initial disturbance and the step size is $\epsilon/10$. We use the experimental setup in MART [20], and set the baseline as PGD adversarial training [16], TRADES [19], and MART [20].

Table 1. MNIST: White-Box robustness (%). Blue: second best.

Defense	Natural	FGSM	PGD^{20}
Madry	99.08	97.10	94.55
TRADES	**99.23**	96.62	94.51
MART	98.75	**97.74**	**96.39**
AMAD	98.97	97.50	95.83

Table 2. CIFAR-10: White-Box robustness (%). Blue: second best.

Defense	Natural	FGSM	PGD^{20}
Madry	84.44	61.89	47.55
TRADES	82.75	62.80	50.22
MART	83.05	65.60	55.54
AMAD	**86.64**	**65.76**	**56.42**

White-Box Attacks. We evaluate the robustness of all defense models to FGSM attack and PGD^{20} attack in MNIST and CIFAR-10. And "Natural" is used to represent the accuracy of natural images test to evaluate the trade-off between classification accuracy and robustness of each model. We summarize the results of our and other models under white-box attack in Table 1 and Table 2. As shown in Table 1, the performance of our method in MNIST is second only to MART, and the robustness against FGSM and PGD^{20} attacks is improved by 0.4% and 1.28% compared with Madry. As shown in Table 2, the improvement of our method in CIFAR-10 is more significant, and the response to FGSM and PGD^{20} attacks has increased by 3.87% and 8.87% respectively. Most importantly, the accuracy of recognizing natural images is 3.59% higher than that of MART. AMAD achieves the best performance in the case of no attack and two types of attacks of CIFAR-10. Noteworthily, our method can considerably enhance the accuracy of the model in recognizing natural images while attaining the same robustness as MART. Although our method does not achieve the best performance in MNIST, and the accuracy in recognizing natural images is only a little greater than mart, it achieves robustness close to MART.

Black-Box Attacks. We also evaluate the robustness of all defense models under black-box attacks in MNIST and CIFAR-10. The attack samples in MNIST are generated through a copy of the attack defense model. The attack samples in CIFAR-10 are obtained by attacking the more complex ResNet-50 model. We add the PGD^{10} attack to the black-box attack. We summarize the results of our and other models under black-box attack in Table 3 and Table 4. As shown in Table 3, the performance of our method in MNIST is second only to MART, and the robustness against FGSM and PGD^{20} attacks is 1.59% and 1.21% higher than Madry. Interestingly, AMAD is 0.06% more robust to PGD^{10} attacks than

Table 3. MNIST: Black-Box robustness (%). Blue: second best.

Defense	FGSM	PGD^{10}	PGD^{20}
Madry	96.12	95.73	95.47
TRADES	97.49	96.03	95.73
MART	**97.77**	96.96	**96.97**
AMAD	97.71	**97.02**	96.68

Table 4. CIFAR10: Black-Box robustness (%). Blue: second best.

Defense	FGSM	PGD^{10}	PGD^{20}
Madry	79.98	80.27	80.01
TRADES	81.51	81.71	81.48
MART	82.59	82.82	82.60
AMAD	**84.25**	**83.12**	**82.86**

MART. As shown in Table 4, in CIFAR-10, the improvement of our method is also more significant, and the response to PGD^{10} and PGD^{20} attacks is increased by 2.82% and 2.85% respectively. In addition, AMAD's robustness against FGSM attacks is 1.66% higher than that of MART. In MNIST, our method obtains the robustness improvement close to MART in black-box attack and obtains the highest robustness under PGD^{10} attack. Our method achieves the best performance under the three types of attacks in CIFAR-10.

4.2   Performance on WideResNet

In order to test our method in a large-capacity network, we utilize the same neural network architecture WideResNet-34-10 [30] as Madry [16]. In CIFAR-10, we evaluate the robustness of all defense models to FGSM and PGD^{20} white-box attacks. In Table 5, we summarize the results of our and other models under the white-box attack. As shown in Table 5, the robustness of AMAD against FGSM and PGD^{20} attacks is only 5.72% and 3.58% higher than Madry. But most importantly, the accuracy of AMAD in recognizing natural images is 2.38% and 5.51% higher than Madry and MART respectively. Although our method does not get the best performance in dealing with FGSM and PGD^{20}, it shows a strong ability in recognizing natural images. Noteworthily, compared with Madry, our method not only improves the classification accuracy but also improves the robustness. TRADES and MART enhance the robustness by decreasing the accuracy of normal samples. Our method can better balance the robustness and accuracy.

4.3 Performance to the Stronger Attack

To demonstrate that our approach also has the ability to cope with stronger attacks, we test different settings for CW_∞ attack. CW_∞ attack used is based on the L_∞ version of PGD-optimized CW. First, we test the ability of AMAD against CW_∞ attack in ResNet-18 with the settings in Sect. 4.1, then we follow the settings in Sect. 4.2 to test the white-box attack in WideResNet-34-10. In Table 6, we summarize the results of our and other models dealing with CW_∞ attack in various situations. For R-18 networks, AMAD should have 1.53% and 1.52% better robustness to CW_∞ attack (white-box) and CW_∞ attack (black-box) than Madry in MNIST, respectively, the robustness is only second to MART. In CIFAR-10, the robustness of CW_∞ attacks should be improved by 5.06% (white-box) and 2.32% (black-box), respectively, compared with Madry. Among them, under black-box attack, the robustness is even 0.42% higher than that of MART. For WideResNeet-34–10 networks, AMAD should be 1.95% more robust to CW_∞ attack (white-box) in CIFAR-10 than Madry. Overall, AMAD is only behind MART in most cases, higher than Madry and TRADES, and even better than MART in some cases. This demonstrates AMAD's ability to respond to stronger attacks.

4.4 Analysis

Obviously, AMAD's improvement in dealing with MNIST is not as good as CIFAR-10. Since MNIST is a digital data set, the characteristics of each number are quite diverse. The training value of the mixed image is reduced, which leads to the loss of accuracy in identifying natural images. Nevertheless, AMAD can still bring robustness when dealing with adversarial attacks. Because the feature mixing we utilize can enhance the robustness to a certain extent, we can still get good robustness. The performance of AMAD in CIFAR-10 is outstanding because the image features in CIFAR-10 are abundant. Utilizing the mixup method can get more meaningful error examples, which can considerably improve the accuracy of the model in identifying natural images, and the robustness gain brought by the mixup method and adversarial training can complement each other.

Table 5. CIFAR10: White-Box robustness (%) on WideResNet. Blue: second best.

Defense	Natural	FGSM	PGD^{20}
Madry	87.30	56.10	51.36
TRADES	84.15	64.66	54.92
MART	84.17	**67.51**	**57.96**
AMAD	**89.68**	62.82	54.94

Table 6. Robustness (%) to CW$_\infty$ attack. Blue: second best.

Setting	White-box			Black-box	
Network	R-18		W16-8	R-18	
Dataset	MNIST	CIFAR-10	CIFAR-10	MNIST	CIFAR-10
Madry	94.25	45.98	50.52	96.34	80.85
TRADES	94.05	48.26	51.70	97.30	82.05
MART	**96.12**	**54.90**	**54.55**	**98.46**	82.75
AMAD	95.78	51.04	52.47	97.86	**83.17**

Compared with the white-box results, AMAD is as robust as other methods in black-box results. The attacker knows nothing about the target model, in this case, in addition to adversarial training, the mixup method can also achieve better robustness, which makes our method more adaptable under black-box attacks.

Nevertheless, in large-capacity networks, the ability of our mixup method to enhance robustness is reduced, which results in AMAD not getting the best performance against adversarial attacks in WideResNet-34-10. Though, in large-capacity networks, the mixup method still has a strong ability to enhance the accuracy of natural image recognition, which considerably improves AMAD's ability to recognize natural images.

AMAD still performs well against the stronger CW$_\infty$ attack. Because our mixup approach is similar to CW attacks in that the smaller the gap between the generated sample and the original one. As shown in Fig. 2, there are two examples of the image generated by our mixup method. We expect the generated images

Image A$_1$ Image A$_2$ mix$_\lambda$(A$_1$, $\tilde{A}_1$)   mix$_\lambda$(A$_2$, $\tilde{A}_2$)

Fig. 2. Examples of mixup processing generation. A$_1$ and A$_2$ are the original images, and mix$_\lambda$(A$_1$, $\tilde{A}_1$) and mix$_\lambda$(A$_2$, $\tilde{A}_2$) are the images generated after mixing.

to be very close to the original images, which makes our samples for adversarial training more significant, so AMAD still has a strong ability under CW_∞ attack.

5 Conclusion

In this paper, we investigate the trade-off between robustness and accuracy and discover that adversarial training enhances robustness by decreasing the accuracy of normal samples. Based on this discovery, we design a defense method integrating mixup processing and adversarial training, which is called AMAD. This method not only improves the robustness but also does not reduce the accuracy. Experimental results demonstrate the effectiveness of our proposed method, and our method is universal in both simple and complex network architectures.

Acknowledgements. This work is supported by the National Natural Science Foundation of China (No. 62072109, No. U1804263) and Natural Science Foundation of Fujian Province (No. 2021J06013).

References

1. Goodfellow, I.J., Shlens, J., Szegedy, C.: Explaining and harnessing adversarial examples. arXiv preprint arXiv:1412.6572 (2014)
2. Zhang, H., Cisse, H., Dauphin, Y.N., Lopez-Paz, D.: mixup: beyond empirical risk minimization. arXiv preprint arXiv:1710.09412 (2017)
3. DeVries, T., Taylor, G.W.: Improved regularization of convolutional neural networks with cutout. arXiv preprint arXiv:1708.04552 (2017)
4. Inoue, H.: Data augmentation by pairing samples for images classification. arXiv preprint arXiv:1801.02929 (2018)
5. Yun, S., et al.: CutMix: regularization strategy to train strong classifiers with localizable features. In: Proceedings of the IEEE/CVF International Conference on Computer Vision, pp. 6023–6032 (2019)
6. Verma, V., et al.: Manifold mixup: better representations by interpolating hidden states. In: International Conference on Machine Learning, pp. 6438–6447. PMLR (2019)
7. Uddin, A.F.M., et al. SaliencyMix: a saliency guided data augmentation strategy for better regularization. arXiv preprint arXiv:2006.01791 (2020)
8. Kim, J.-H., Choo, W., Song, H.O.: Puzzle mix: exploiting saliency and local statistics for optimal mixup. In: International Conference on Machine Learning, pp. 5275–5285. PMLR (2020)
9. Kim, J.-H., Choo, W., Jeong, H., Song, H.O.: Co-mixup: saliency guided joint mixup with supermodular diversity. arXiv preprint arXiv:2102.03065 (2021)
10. Hong, M., Choi, J., Kim, G.: StyleMix: separating content and style for enhanced data augmentation. In: Proceedings of the IEEE/CVF Conference on Computer Vision and Pattern Recognition, pp. 14862–14870 (2021)
11. Venkataramanan, S., Avrithis, Y., Kijak, E., Amsaleg, L.: AlignMix: improving representation by interpolating aligned features. arXiv preprint arXiv:2103.15375 (2021)

12. Hendrycks, D., Mu, N., Cubuk, E.D., Zoph, B., Gilmer, J., Lakshminarayanan, B.: AugMix: a simple data processing method to improve robustness and uncertainty. arXiv preprint arXiv:1912.02781 (2019)
13. Goodfellow, I., et al.: Generative adversarial nets. In: 27th Proceedings Conference on Advances in Neural Information Processing Systems (2014)
14. Cubuk, E.D., Zoph, B., Mane, D., Vasudevan, V., Le, Q.V.: AutoAugment: learning augmentation policies from data. arXiv preprint arXiv:1805.09501 (2018)
15. Müller, S.G., Hutter, F.: TrivialAugment: tuning-free yet state-of-the-art data augamentation. In: Proceedings of the IEEE/CVF International Conference on Computer Vision, pp. 774–782 (2021)
16. Madry, A.,Makelov, A., Schmidt, L., Tsipras, D., Vladu, A.: Towards deep learning models resistant to adversarial attacks. arXiv preprint arXiv:1706.06083 (2017)
17. Shafahi, A., et al.: Adversarial training for free! In: 32nd Proceedings of the Conference on Advances in Neural Information Processing Systems (2019)
18. Zhu, C., Cheng, Y., Gan, Z., Sun, S., Goldstein, T., Liu, J.: FreeLB: enhanced adversarial training for natural language understanding. arXiv preprint arXiv:1909.11764 (2019)
19. Zhang, H., Yu, Y., Jiao, J., Xing, E., El Ghaoui, L., Jordan, M.: Theoretically principled trade-off between robustness and accuracy. In International Conference on Machine Learning, pp. 7472–7482. PMLR (2019)
20. Wang, Y., Zou, D., Yi, J., Bailey, J., Ma, X., Gu, Q.: Improving adversarial robustness requires revisiting misclassified examples. In: International Conference on Learning Representations (2019)
21. Shafahi, A., Ghiasi, A., Huang, F., Goldstein, T.: Label smoothing and logit squeezing: a replacement for adversarial training? arXiv preprint arXiv:1910.11585 (2019)
22. Smith, L.N., Topin, N.: Super-convergence: very fast training of residual networks using large learning rates. In: ICLR (2018)
23. Micikevicius, P., et al.: Mixed precision training. arXiv preprint arXiv:1710.03740 (2017)
24. Tramèr, F., Kurakin, A., Papernot, N., Goodfellow, I., Boneh, D., McDaniel P.: Ensemble adversarial training: attacks and defenses. arXiv preprint arXiv:1705.07204 (2017)
25. Jakubovitz, D., Giryes, R.: Improving DNN robustness to adversarial attacks using jacobian regularization. In: Ferrari, V., Hebert, M., Sminchisescu, C., Weiss, Y. (eds.) ECCV 2018. LNCS, vol. 11216, pp. 525–541. Springer, Cham (2018). https://doi.org/10.1007/978-3-030-01258-8_32
26. Wong, E., Rice, L., Kolter, J.Z.: Fast is better than free: revisiting adversarial training. arXiv preprint arXiv:2001.03994 (2020)
27. LeCun, Y., Bottou, L., Bengio, Y., Haffner, P.: Gradient-based learning applied to document recognition. Proc. IEEE **86**(11), 2278–2324 (1998)
28. Krizhevsky, A., et al.: Learning multiple layers of features from tiny images (2009)
29. He, K., Zhang, X., Ren, S., Sun, J.: Deep residual learning for image recognition. In: Proceedings of the IEEE Conference on Computer Vision and Pattern Recognition, pp. 770–778 (2016)
30. Zagoruyko, S., Komodakis, N.: Wide residual networks. arXiv preprint arXiv:1605.07146 (2016)

Multi-party Secure Comparison of Strings Based on Outsourced Computation

Xin Zhang[✉], Chao Shan, and Yunfeng Zou

State Grid Jiangsu Marketing Service Center, State Grid Jiangsu Electric Power
Co. Ltd., Nanjing, China
sankchang@126.com

Abstract. Data is an important production factor in the era of digital economy. Privacy computing can ensure that data providers do not disclose sensitive data, carry out multi-party joint analysis and computation, securely and privately complete the full excavation of data value in the process of circulation, sharing, fusion, and calculation, which has become a popular research topic. String comparison is one of the common operations in data processing. To address the string comparison problem in multi-party scenarios, we propose an algorithm for secure string comparison based on outsourced computation. The algorithm encodes the strings with one hot encoding scheme and encrypts the encoded strings using an XOR homomorphic encryption scheme. The proposed algorithm achieves efficient and secure string comparison and counts the number of different characters with the help of a cloud-assisted server. The proposed scheme is implemented and verified using the new coronavirus gene sequence as the comparison string, and the performance is compared with that of a state-of-the-art security framework. Experiments show that the proposed algorithm can effectively improve the string comparison speed and obtain correct comparison results without compromising data privacy.

Keywords: Privacy-preserving computation · Outsourced computation · String comparison · One-hot encoding · XOR homomorphic encryption

1 Introduction

The development of Internet technology has made data an important factor of production and brought huge socio-economic benefits. As people continue to pay attention to data privacy, countries starting legislation to protect data security. The law and the awakening of people's privacy awareness have prevented organizations or enterprises from directly collecting and sharing data. Furthermore,

Supported by the Scientific and Technological Project of State Grid Jiangsu Electric Power Co., Ltd (No. J2021038).

Y. Xu et al. (Eds.): ML4CS 2022, LNCS 13656, pp. 15–30, 2023.
https://doi.org/10.1007/978-3-031-20099-1_2

when the data of each organization or enterprise are stored and maintained independently of and isolated from each other, the usefulness of the data becomes extremely limited. As an interdisciplinary technology system that includes cryptography, data science, artificial intelligence, and other fields, privacy-preserving computation can effectively break the barrier of "data islands" and establish joint query, statistics, and modeling of data from multiple parties under the premise of guaranteeing data confidentiality to realize the zero-sum game of data value mining and privacy preservation.

Secure multi-party computation (MPC), which was first proposed by Yao in 1982, is a key technology in privacy-preserving computation [1]. MPC enables a group of mutually untrusted parties to collaboratively compute a given function without revealing their respective private input and output, achieving secure computation process. As a subject of great importance in the international cryptographic circle, many scholars have devoted themselves to studying the basic theory and practical development of MPC [2]. MPC has been widely used in the fields of data mining [3], email filtering [4], and machine learning [5].

String comparison is one of the basic operations in privacy computing and plays an important role in many fields. In the bioinformatics field, biological sequences such as DNA and protein sequences, can be perceived as strings composed of basic characters. By comparing biological sequences, and identifying the similarities between sequences, the functional, structural, and evolutionary information in biological sequences can be obtained. In the field of the information security system defense, the feature code of each file is calculated and compared with the feature code in the virus database to determine whether the file carries a virus in a virus detection system. In addition, with the development of information technology, a large amount of data containing character text types are stored in computer devices in the form of electronic documents. String comparison is of great importance in the analysis of text data and information retrieval.

Traditionally, string comparison is often based on a character set in which the characters are arranged in any order to form a string. Then, two or more strings are compared to determine whether the strings are identical, and the different characters between the strings are counted. Generally, a certain character set may contain dozens or even hundreds of characters. For example, more than 80,000 Chinese characters exist. However, in specific fields, the number of characters in the string to be compared is limited, and encoding all characters will undoubtedly cause a great waste of system resources. For example, in the field of bioinformatics, DNA sequences often contain a very limited number of characters. DNA sequence comparison is a key step in analyzing biological sequences to understand the structure, function, and evolution of DNA sequences and the traditional coding method will cause a serious decrease in comparison efficiency.

In this paper, we propose an algorithm for the multi-party secure comparison of strings in an outsourcing setting that can efficiently compare strings and count the number of different characters between the strings. To verify the efficiency of the scheme, we compare our scheme with those proposed in [6,7]. The experimental results show that the scheme proposed in this paper can perform string comparison tasks well in specific scenarios, such as gene sequence comparison, and significantly outperforms other existing schemes in terms of efficiency and accuracy.

2   Related Work

The string secure comparison problem can be converted into a secure computation of Hamming distance. Hamming distance is widely used for binary string comparison, where the Hamming distance between two strings is defined as the number of different characters in the same location. Protocols for calculating the scalar product between two vectors using homomorphic encryption with semi-honest security were proposed in [8,9]. If the elements in vector are represented in binary form, the protocol is equivalent to implementing the secure computation of the Hamming distance. Secure approximation protocols for Hamming distance computation were proposed in [10,11], which require the communication overhead of $O(\sqrt{l})$, where l is the string length. Indyk $et\ al.$ [12] improved the communication efficiency based on these two works. However, these above works are only secure against semi-honest adversaries. Jarrous $et\ al.$ [13] proposed a oblivious transfer based secure protocol for computing the Hamming distance against malicious adversaries and proved the application of this protocol in different aspects such as string comparison and symmetric privacy information retrieval. Yasuda $et\ al.$ [14]proposed a method to pack a feature vector into a single ciphertext for secure and efficient Hamming distance computation based on somewhat homomorphic encryption. Ge $et\ al.$ [15] proposed a simple and efficient architecture for string comparison to simulate Hamming distance computation using Memristors. In recent years, Khan $et\ al.$ [16] implemented string comparison on a quantum computer using the Hamming distance algorithm to speed up the comparison when comparing one string against many strings.

Secure comparison of strings can be achieved through basic primitives in MPC [17]. The problem of binary string comparison was solved earlier by Hazay and Lindell [18], who used the oblivious pseudorandom function (OPRF) and the Naor-Reingold pseudorandom function. However, the protocol has only one-sided simulatability for malicious security. Privacy-preserving DNA search matching using Oblivious Automata Evaluation was implemented by [19], where one party owns a finite state machine and the other party holds a DNA sequence. Mohassel $et\ al.$ [20] proposed an efficient protocol for oblivious deterministic finite automaton (DFA) evaluation, which also can achieve the secure comparison of strings. Kang $et\ al.$ [17] designed a secure protocol that can determine whether two strings are equal or not through Goldwasser-Micali XOR homomorphic encryption algorithm, and further constructed an efficient string pattern matching protocol based on the BMH algorithm. Kolesnikov $et\ al.$ [21] proposed an efficient secure string equality test protocol under the semi-honest security model based on the oblivious transfer extension.

Pattern matching problems can be seen as a special case of string secure comparison, so the underlying construction in pattern matching schemes can often be used to design string comparison protocols. Gennaro *et al.* [22] proposed an efficient protocol for securely computing approximate pattern matching based on oblivious automata evaluation and solved this problem with full security in the face of malicious adversaries. The protocol utilizes the Knuth-Morris-Pratt (KMP) algorithm [23] to implement pattern matching. Yasuda *et al.* [24] designed a secure approximate pattern matching protocol using somewhat homomorphic encryption with unlimited operation types but supporting only a limited number of both additions and multiplications on encrypted data. Faust *et al.* [25] provided the first protocol for the pattern matching problem in the cloud. The protocol is shown to be simulation-based secure in the presence of semi-honest and malicious adversaries.

3 Preliminary

Before introducing the proposed scheme, we first introduce the relevant basics, including string comparison, secure outsourcing computation, the Goldwasser-Micali cryptosystem [26], and the security model. Table 1 lists the symbols used in the paper and the definitions to help in understanding the formulas and algorithms.

Table 1. Table of notations

Symbols	Meaning
T	Text string
p	Pattern string
h	Length of T
l	The length of the binary form m and p
S	Substring of T
τ	Threshold
m^j	String of the party P_j
m_i	The i-th bit of the binary form m
m^j_{onehot}	The one-hot encoding string of m^j
n	The number of partys
w	The number of character type
ρ	one-hot encoding string length
$num_{j,k}$	The number of different characters between in m^j and m^k
$Array_j$	Array to store encrypted one-hot encoding strings
$Result_{j,k}$	$Array_j$ Calculated by bitwise multiplication with $Array_k$

3.1 String Comparison and Hamming Distance

String sequence comparison, one of the basic operations of computer character manipulation, plays an important role in information search and text pattern matching. In terms of the sequence comparison, the Hamming distance is one of the most commonly used similarity metrics. The sequence comparison problem and the Hamming distance are defined as follows.

Definition 1. Given the strings m and m', string sequence comparison is the process of determining whether m and m' are equal or satisfy the given similarity threshold τ.

Definition 2. Hamming distance: Given two strings of equal length(i.e., m and m'), the Hamming distance between m and m' is the number of different characters at the same location.

3.2   Goldwasser-Micali Cryptosystem

The Goldwasser-Micali (GM) cryptosystem is the first probabilistic public key encryption scheme and proven secure under standard encryption assumptions. Based on the quadratic residue assumption, the GM cryptosystem consists of three algorithms: key generation, encryption and decryption.

Key Generation: Randomly generate two large prime numbers b and c and computes $N = bc$; q is a quadratic nonresidue of modulo b and modulo c. The public key is (N, q), and the private key is (b, c).

Encryption: Randomly generate $r_i \in Z_N$ satisfying $gcd(r_i, N) = 1$ and computes $Enc(m_i) = q^{m_i} r_i^2 (\bmod N)$, here m_i denotes each bit of a message m.

Decryption: Given private key (b, c), compute $Enc(m_i)/b$ and $Enc(m_i)/c$ for each cipher $Enc(m_i)$. If $Enc(m_i)/b = Enc(m_i)/c = 1$, then $m_i = 0$; otherwise, $m_i = 1$.

In addition, the GM cryptosystem has the XOR homomorphism property, that is, $Enc(m_1) \times Enc(m_1) \times \cdots \times Enc(m_l) = Enc(m_1 \oplus m_2 \oplus \cdots \oplus m_l)$.

3.3   Secure Outsourcing Computation

In Fig. 1, it illustrates the secure outsourcing computation process in two scenarios. Given limited computing and storage resources, the traditional local computing model has been unable to meet the current demand. In the outsourcing scenario, the data owner outsources data to a cloud service provider, who then computes the acquired data and returns the computation results to the data owner. However, cloud service providers might snoop and attempt to access the private data uploaded by the data owner, even maliciously compromise the correctness and integrity of the computation results. Therefore, the secure outsourcing of computation is extremely important.

3.4   Security Model

In this paper, we mainly consider the protocol under the semi-honest security model where the corrupted party honestly follows the protocol and works with the honest party to accomplish a certain computational task. Meanwhile, the malicious party can attempt to infer some information about the private input of the honest party by observing the messages obtained from the protocol.

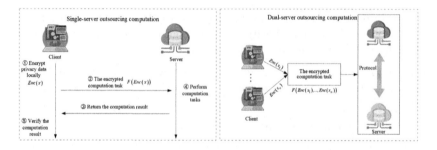

Fig. 1. The process of secure outsource computation

4 Outsourcing Secure Computation Scheme

4.1 Efficient String Comparison

To achieve efficient string comparison, we adopt the one-hot encoding method, which takes advantage of the statistical feature that a character is encoded with only one bit of "1" and the rest as "0". Therefore, the location of "1" after encoding must be different for any two different characters (Table 2 shows the encoding process of the one-hot encoding). Given the one-hot encoding of two different characters, the number of "1" must appear in the result of the XOR operation in pairs. The number of different characters between the two strings is counted based on the appearance of the number "1" in the result and the frequency of appearance.

Table 2. Example of one-hot encoding representation

Characters to be encoded	one-hot encoding (length w)
Character 1	$000\cdots001$
Character 2	$000\cdots010$
Character 3	$000\cdots100$
$\cdots$	
Character w	$100\cdots000$

In the privacy-preserving scenario, n clients are considered, and each party holds a string m^j with length l, $1 \leq j \leq n$. The clients want to collaboratively compute to obtain the comparison information between two strings without revealing the information of their respective strings, including 1) whether the two strings are identical, and 2) the number of different characters if they are different. Considering the outsourcing scenario, we adopt the GM public key encryption system. First, the client transmits the encrypted data to the server, and then the server performs the calculation under the ciphertext and returns the computation result to the client.

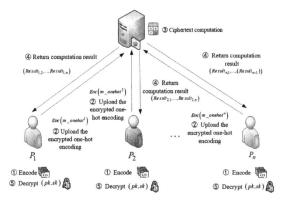

Fig. 2. Outsourcing secure multi-party string comparison

Due to the XOR's homomorphism of the GM cryptosystem, he result of the computation is equivalent to performing an XOR operation on the original plaintext and then encrypting it. The server performs the computation on the ciphertext after accepting the one-hot encoded string encrypted by the client. Given that the GM public key encryption scheme is a probabilistic encryption system, the existence of random numbers during encryption makes the encryption result completely different even for the same message, so the server cannot obtain any information about the client string. To prevent malicious clients from acquiring plaintext information from other honest parties, the server must shuffle the result of the per-bit computation and then return it to the client. The client receives the computation result with the order of the ciphertext completely shuffled and would thus fail to decrypt and restore the plaintext, but the statistical characteristics of the result are retained, that is, the numbers of 1 and 0 are unaffected by the shuffle. This process allows each client to obtain the result of the comparison between any two strings without revealing any information about the plaintext of the strings. We provide the detailed Algorithm for our scheme in appendix.

The entire comparison process is divided into three phases, the encoding and encryption phase of the client, the ciphertext computation phase of the server, and the decryption phase of the client to obtain the result. Figure 2 shows the process of the comparison.

Encoding and Encryption Phase. Suppose that n clients each hold a string of length l and the number of character types w. Each client first encodes the string uniquely so that it looks like $m_{onehot} = m_1 m_2 \ldots m_\rho$, where $m_i = 0, 1$ and $\rho = w \times l$. Then, each client P_i encrypts the encoded bit string bit by bit $Enc(m_i)$ using the GM public key encryption scheme, resulting in an array of length ρ $Array_i$, which holds the ciphertext of each bit. Finally, the client sends the array to the server.

Computation Phase. After collecting the arrays sent by each client, the server multiplies each pair of arrays $(Array_j, Array_k)$ by the location of the elements to obtain a new array of results.

$$Results_{j,k} = Enc(m_1^j) \times Enc(m_1^k), \ldots, Enc(m_\rho^j) \times Enc(m_\rho^k)$$

From the XOR homomorphism of the GM key encryption scheme, we obtain

$$Enc(m_i^j) \times Enc(m_i^k) = Enc(m_i^j \oplus m_i^k)$$

At this point, to prevent the client from recovering valid information from the original string, the elements in $Result_{j,k}$ will be scrambled and reordered $Shuffle(Result_{j,k})$ and returned to the client.

Decryption Phase. After the client P_j receives array $Result_{j,k}$, it decrypts the elements of the array one by one to obtain $m_i^j \oplus m_i^k$. However, at this time, the client can only obtain the statistical characteristics of 0 and 1 in the decryption result and not the i-th bit of the original character of P_k by decoding nor the location information of the character because the order of the array has been shuffled. According to the number of digit 1s in the decryption result, the number of different characters in m^j and m^k can be obtained as follows: for any two different character encodings, two digit 1s will appear in the result of the XOR operation, so the number of digit 1s is twice the number of different characters.

4.2   Security Analysis

The clients and servers involved in our scheme are semi-honest parties. To prove the security of the scheme, we adopt the ideal/realistic simulation paradigm: a scheme is secure if, for any semi-honest party, the information obtained by the party in the process of execution according to the scheme can be simulated by its own input and output, and the sequence of messages obtained is indistinguishable from the sequence of messages obtained by the actual process.

First, the correctness of the scheme is proven. The server performs a multiplication operation based on the encrypted string $Enc(m_{onehot}^j)$ uploaded by the party. Owing to the XOR homomorphism of the GM encryption scheme, the result of the computation is equivalent to two strings being XOR operated then encrypted directly, so that the party decrypts the result of the ciphertext computation returned by the server to determine whether the two strings are equal and counts the number of different characters if they are not equal. Therefore, the scheme has correctness. Second, the privacy of the scheme is proven through a simulator. Considering the security model of the scheme in which the outsourced server and the arbitrary client are not colluding with each other, the proof is performed in two cases.

(1) When the outsourcing server is corrupted by adversary $\mathcal{A}$ in the real scenario, an adversary (simulator) exists in the ideal world, which uses the input and output of adversary $\mathcal{A}$ to simulate the view of the adversary.

During the execution of the realistic scenario, the outsourcing server has no input and output and receives messages as $Enc(m^j_{onehot})$, which constitutes its $view$, which can be simulated by $Simulator_1$ as follows: for $Enc(m^j_{onehot})$, $1 \leq j \leq n$, the simulator randomly selects the string m^j and encodes it using one-hot encoding, encrypts it with the public key, and computes ciphertext $Enc(m^j_{onehot})$ as $view'$.

The following shows that the above simulated message sequence $view'$ is computationally indistinguishable from the real message sequence $view$ obtained by the outsourcing server in the real scenario. Obviously, the only difference between the two view distributions is the generation of the cipher-text, where the ciphertext of the real scenario outsourcing server comes from the client and is generated by the client based on its own input, while during the simulation, the simulator randomly selects the string and encrypts it. The indistinguishability of the views is the direct result of the semantic secu-rity of the homomorphic encryption algorithm used in this paper. Therefore, the adversary cannot distinguish the way the ciphertext is generated in the two view distributions, and the two views mentioned above have indistin-guishability. The scheme is secure in the case in which the outsourcing server is corrupted.

(2) When the client is corrupted by adversary $\mathcal{A}$, $Simulator_2$ existing in the ideal world uses the input and output of adversary $\mathcal{A}$ to simulate the view of the adversary. The client receives no message other than input m^j and output $Result_{j,k}$ during the execution of the scheme. Thus, during ideal simulation, given the adversary's input and output, the simulator can simulate a view that is indistinguishable from the real execution, so our scheme is secure in the case in which the client is corrupted.

4.3 Application Scenario: Gene Data Comparison

As of April 2022, the cumulative number of confirmed cases of COVID-19 world-wide has exceeded 400 million and is still soaring at a rate of 1.5 million new cases per day. In the post-epidemic era, the genomic evolution analysis of COVID-19 provides comprehensive and effective data to support the comprehensive assess-ment of epidemic risk, initiate public health response, and formulate medical countermeasures.

The routine process of virus evolution analysis can be generally divided into several steps, namely, obtaining sequences, sequence screening, sequence comparison, constructing evolution, and interpreting evolutionary trees. Among them, sequence computation refers to the computation of the degree of differ-ence between gene sequences, and the degree of difference is generally measured by the p-distance index, which is the ratio of the number of different characters to the length of characters between two strings. This index directly reflects the degree of difference between two sequences, which is the basis for constructing the evolutionary tree, and the result of the comparison directly determines the accuracy of the evolutionary tree.

The proposed privacy-preserving string computation scheme can efficiently and correctly compare viral genomic data without disclosing private data information and further construct evolutionary trees on the basis of the comparison results, thus realizing efficient privacy-preserving virus evolutionary analysis and providing strong data support for formulating effective medical countermeasures.

5   Experiments Analysis

5.1   Data Sources

The test data used in this article was obtained from the gene sequences of COVID-19 in China's National Gene Bank (https://db.cngb.org/gisaid/). Genetic mutations include mutations, insertions, deletions, and recombination of gene points, so each gene contains a slightly different number of bases. In this paper, the gene sequence of COVID-19 was first aligned using the Mafft software, which is the most authoritative and accurate sequence alignment software in the bioinformatics industry. Then, 100 gene sequences were randomly selected as the test data of this protocol, and the number of gene sequences selected for each experiment was increased in turn to test the robustness of the protocol. The bases contained in these 100 gene data are A, T, C, G,-, where - indicates that the base is missing at that location, and each gene sequence contains 500 bases (containing deletions). Table 3 shows the amount of test data per set.

Table 3. Test data

The total number of genes	The number of genes	Length of per gene/bit
10	5	500
20	10	500
40	20	500
100	50	500

5.2   Data Encoding

Gene sequence comparison essentially counts the number of different bases between two gene sequences. Traditional privacy computing technology for genetic sequence comparison can prevent the leakage of private data but increases the complexity of computation and communication, resulting in the reduction of the comparison efficiency. This paper adopts the method of one-hot encoding of strings and then performs the XOR operation to determine whether the two strings are the same through the statistical of the number of "1" in XOR operation result and count the number of different characters in the case of two different strings.

The test data contains five different bases, and each base is encoded as a 5-bit long binary string. Each binary string contains four "0" and one "1", and different bases correspond to "1" in different locations. Table 4 shows the base encoding results.

Table 4. Base encoding

A	10000
T	01000
C	00100
G	00010
–	00001

5.3 Test Environment

Considering the limitations of ordinary users' computing power, we build a string secure sharing and comparison framework based on secure outsourcing computation and outsource complex computing tasks to cloud servers with sufficient computing resources. Two cloud servers with the same configuration as the computing party and two personal PCs with the same configuration as the client are used in the tests of [6,7]. In our scheme, one cloud server with the same configuration is used as the computing party and two identical PCs are used as the client. The ECS configuration is Intel(R) Core(TM) i7 @ 3.6 GHz and 32G of RAM. Ordinary users have Intel(R) Core(TM) i5 @ 2.3 GHz and 8G of RAM.

5.4 Performance

For different numbers of gene sequences, this experiment tests the runtime and communication traffic of the server. The experimental results show that the proposed scheme exhibits superior performance in terms of time and communication traffic. Table 5 shows the test results of our scheme.

Table 5. Test result

The number of client genes	Length of gene/bit	Time/min	Communication/MB
5	500	3.68	2.86
10	500	7.5	5.71
20	500	16	11.43
40	500	23	22.86
50	500	36	45.71

To demonstrate the efficiency of the scheme, it is compared with the current efficient general-purpose secure MPC protocols. In brief, these general secure MPC protocols are used to implement the secure comparison of strings, and then the effectiveness of the scheme is studied in comparison with this one. For

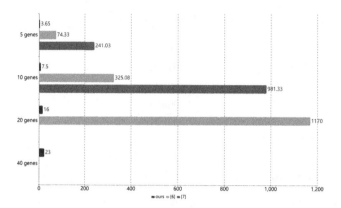

Fig. 3. Time comparison of three schemes

this purpose, the latest secure MPC protocol framework, MP-SPDZ [27], was used to instantiate the relevant computation protocols. MP-SPDZ is a complete and comprehensive secure MPC protocol framework, which can implement more than 30 secure MPC protocols and their variants (mainly in terms of computation domain and security), supporting Boolean type, arithmetic type circuits and multiple security models. And before that nearly all publicly available secure multi-party computation protocol frameworks were limited to one security model and computational domain (e.g., finite domain). Meanwhile, compared with these frameworks, MP-SPDZ has superior performance and can simulate real environments.

We used the MP-SPDZ framework to instantiate the protocols proposed in [6,7]. Subsequently, we performed the security comparison of strings and then compared the results with the present scheme. Although the efficiency of the proposed protocols in [6,7] is not as good as the current state-of-the-art privacy-preserving schemes, experiments revealed that among the secure MPC protocols that can be implemented in MP-SPDZ, those proposed in [6,7] have the best performance in string matching. Therefore, the proposed scheme is experimentally compared with those in [6,7]. The experiments show that the efficiency of the proposed algorithm in gene sequence comparison is significantly superior to the other two schemes.

Table 6 shows the runtime of the schemes proposed in [6,7] instantiated with the MP-SPDZ framework on the test data. Figure 3 shows the run time of our scheme in comparison with those in [6,7] on the test data.

Table 6. Running time of [6,7]

The number of gene/stripes	[6]/min	[7]/min
5	74.33	241.03
10	325.08	981.33
20	1170	–
40	–	–

6   Conclusion

In this paper, we propose a novel secure outsourced comparison of strings scheme that can achieve the secure comparison of strings in specific scenarios. The scheme can efficiently determine whether two strings are identical and count the number of different characters if they are not identical by using the one-hot encoding of strings and then performing the XOR operation. The GM public key encryption scheme is used to protect the private data of the honest client. In addition, we use the gene sequence of COVID-19 as the test data and compare the proposed scheme with the instantiated protocols of [6,7] for string comparison using the MP-SPDZ framework. Our scheme is suitable and efficient for application scenarios with few character types, such as gene sequence comparison. The length of the encoding will increase with the number of character types, resulting in the decrease in the efficiency of the scheme. Therefore, performing efficient and secure string comparison under multiple character types will be our next research, and on this basis, we will explore other secure and efficient string pattern matching schemes.

A   Appendix

Algorithm 1 Algorithm for secure multi-party string comparison in outsourcing scenarios

---

Input: Client $P = P_1, P_2, \ldots, P_n$, $M = m^j | j \in [1, n]$, $length(m^j) = l$, m^j indicates that P_j holds a string of length l

Output: matrix $A^{n \times n}$ with the number of different characters of m^j and m^k $num_{j,k}$

function CLIENT-SIDE EXECUTION

for m^j *in* M **do**

   Initialization m_onehot^j

   for e *in* m^j **do**

      $e_o nehot \leftarrow encode(e)$

      m_onehot^j concatenate $e_o nehot$ // initialize the original string as a one-hot encoded bit string $Array_j$ to hold the ciphertext of each bit

   for *each bit* e_i *(*$i \in 1, 2, \ldots, \rho$*,*ρ*is the length of* $m_o nthot^j$ *)* *in* m_onehot^j **do**

      $Enc(e_i)$

      Store $Enc(e_i)$ in the array $Array_j$ // Store the bit string in the array $Array_j$ by bit encryption

   $Array_j \rightarrow Servers$

function SERVER-SIDE EXECUTION

Receive($Array_1, Array_2, \ldots, Array_n$)

for *each pair(*$Array_j, Array_k$*) of Arrays* **do**

   Initialize the result array $Result_{j,k}$

   for i *in* $[1, \rho]$ **do**

      Calculate $Array_j[i] \times Array_k[i]$

      Store calculation results in $Result_{j,k}$

   shuffle($Result_{j,k}$) // rearrange the result array randomly

   $Result_{j,k} \rightarrow Client$

function CLIENT-SIDE EXECUTION

for p *in* P **do**

   Receive $Result_{j,k}$

   for *each* $Result_{j,k}$ **do**

      $num_{j,k} = 0$

      for *each res in* $Result_{j,k}$ **do**

         if *Dec(res=1)* **then**

            $num_{j,k} = num_{j,k} + 1$

         $num_{j,k} = num_{j,k}/2$ // Each two 1s represents a different person

   Based on all $num_{i,j}, i, j = 1, 2, \ldots, n$, generate the matrix $A^{n \times n}$

References

1. Yao, A.C.: Protocols for secure computations. In: 23rd Annual Symposium on Foundations of Computer Science (SFCS 1982), pp. 160–164. IEEE (1982)
2. Zhao, C., et al.: Secure multi-party computation: theory, practice and applications. Inf. Sci. **476**, 357–372 (2019)

3. Himeur, Y., Sohail, S.S., Bensaali, F., Amira, A., Alazab, M.: Latest trends of security and privacy in recommender systems: a comprehensive review and future perspectives. Comput. Secur. **118**, 102746 (2022)

4. Suresh, A.: Mpcleague: robust MPC platform for privacy-preserving machine learning. arXiv preprint arXiv:2112.13338 (2021)

5. Zheng, W., Deng, R., Chen, W., Ada Popa, R., Panda, A., Stoica, I.: CEREBRO: a platform for {Multi-Party} cryptographic collaborative learning. In 30th USENIX Security Symposium (USENIX Security 2021), pp. 2723–2740 (2021)

6. Keller, M., Orsini, E., Scholl, P.: Mascot: faster malicious arithmetic secure computation with oblivious transfer. In: Proceedings of the 2016 ACM SIGSAC Conference on Computer and Communications Security, pp. 830–842 (2016)

7. Keller, M., Pastro, V., Rotaru, D.: Overdrive: making SPDZ great again. In: Nielsen, J.B., Rijmen, V. (eds.) EUROCRYPT 2018. LNCS, vol. 10822, pp. 158–189. Springer, Cham (2018). https://doi.org/10.1007/978-3-319-78372-7_6

8. Goethals, B., Laur, S., Lipmaa, H., Mielikäinen, T.: On private scalar product computation for privacy-preserving data mining. In: Park, C., Chee, S. (eds.) ICISC 2004. LNCS, vol. 3506, pp. 104–120. Springer, Heidelberg (2005). https://doi.org/10.1007/11496618_9

9. Wright, R., Yang, Z.: Privacy-preserving Bayesian network structure computation on distributed heterogeneous data. In: Proceedings of the tenth ACM SIGKDD International Conference on Knowledge Discovery and Data Mining, pp. 713–718 (2004)

10. Feigenbaum, J., Ishai, Y., Malkin, T., Nissim, K., Strauss, M.J., Wright, R.N.: Secure multiparty computation of approximations. In: Orejas, F., Spirakis, P.G., van Leeuwen, J. (eds.) ICALP 2001. LNCS, vol. 2076, pp. 927–938. Springer, Heidelberg (2001). https://doi.org/10.1007/3-540-48224-5_75

11. Freedman, M.J., Nissim, K., Pinkas, B.: Efficient private matching and set intersection. In: Cachin, C., Camenisch, J.L. (eds.) EUROCRYPT 2004. LNCS, vol. 3027, pp. 1–19. Springer, Heidelberg (2004). https://doi.org/10.1007/978-3-540-24676-3_1

12. Indyk, P., Woodruff, D.: Polylogarithmic private approximations and efficient matching. In: Halevi, S., Rabin, T. (eds.) TCC 2006. LNCS, vol. 3876, pp. 245–264. Springer, Heidelberg (2006). https://doi.org/10.1007/11681878_13

13. Jarrous, A., Pinkas, B.: Secure hamming distance based computation and its applications. In: Abdalla, M., Pointcheval, D., Fouque, P.-A., Vergnaud, D. (eds.) ACNS 2009. LNCS, vol. 5536, pp. 107–124. Springer, Heidelberg (2009). https://doi.org/10.1007/978-3-642-01957-9_7

14. Yasuda, M., Shimoyama, T., Kogure, J., Yokoyama, K., Koshiba, T.: Packed homomorphic encryption based on ideal lattices and its application to biometrics. In: Cuzzocrea, A., Kittl, C., Simos, D.E., Weippl, E., Xu, L. (eds.) CD-ARES 2013. LNCS, vol. 8128, pp. 55–74. Springer, Heidelberg (2013). https://doi.org/10.1007/978-3-642-40588-4_5

15. Ge, N., et al.: An efficient analog hamming distance comparator realized with a unipolar memristor array: a showcase of physical computing. Sci. Rep. **7**(1), 1–7 (2017)

16. Khan, M., Miranskyy, A.: String comparison on a quantum computer using hamming distance. arXiv preprint arXiv:2106.16173 (2021)

17. Kang, J., Li, S., Yang, X., et al.: Secure multiparty string matching computation. J. Cryptol. Res. **4**(3), 241–252 (2017)

18. Hazay, C., Lindell, Y.: Efficient protocols for set intersection and pattern matching with security against malicious and covert adversaries. In: Canetti, R. (ed.) TCC 2008. LNCS, vol. 4948, pp. 155–175. Springer, Heidelberg (2008). https://doi.org/10.1007/978-3-540-78524-8_10

19. Frikken, K.B.: Practical private DNA string searching and matching through efficient oblivious automata evaluation. In: Gudes, E., Vaidya, J. (eds.) DBSec 2009. LNCS, vol. 5645, pp. 81–94. Springer, Heidelberg (2009). https://doi.org/10.1007/978-3-642-03007-9_6

20. Mohassel, P., Niksefat, S., Sadeghian, S., Sadeghiyan, B.: An efficient protocol for oblivious DFA evaluation and applications. In: Dunkelman, O. (ed.) CT-RSA 2012. LNCS, vol. 7178, pp. 398–415. Springer, Heidelberg (2012). https://doi.org/10.1007/978-3-642-27954-6_25

21. Kolesnikov, V., Rosulek, M., Trieu, N.: SWiM: secure wildcard pattern matching from OT extension. In: Meiklejohn, S., Sako, K. (eds.) FC 2018. LNCS, vol. 10957, pp. 222–240. Springer, Heidelberg (2018). https://doi.org/10.1007/978-3-662-58387-6_12

22. Gennaro, R., Hazay, C., Sorensen, J.S.: Text search protocols with simulation based security. In: Nguyen, P.Q., Pointcheval, D. (eds.) PKC 2010. LNCS, vol. 6056, pp. 332–350. Springer, Heidelberg (2010). https://doi.org/10.1007/978-3-642-13013-7_20

23. Knuth, D.E., Morris, Jr. J.H., Pratt, V.R.: Fast pattern matching in strings. SIAM J. Comput. 6(2), 323–350 (1977)

24. Yasuda, M., Shimoyama, T., Kogure, J., Yokoyama, K., Koshiba, T.: Secure pattern matching using somewhat homomorphic encryption. In: Proceedings of the 2013 ACM Workshop on Cloud Computing Security Workshop, pp. 65–76 (2013)

25. Faust, S., Hazay, C., Venturi, D.: Outsourced pattern matching. In: Fomin, F.V., Freivalds, R., Kwiatkowska, M., Peleg, D. (eds.) ICALP 2013. LNCS, vol. 7966, pp. 545–556. Springer, Heidelberg (2013). https://doi.org/10.1007/978-3-642-39212-2_48

26. Goldwasser, S., Micali, S.: Probabilistic encryption. J. Comput. Syst. Sci. **28**(2), 270–299 (1984)

27. Keller. M.: MP-SPDZ: a versatile framework for multi-party computation. In: Proceedings of the 2020 ACM SIGSAC Conference on Computer and Communications Security, pp. 1575–1590 (2020)

Highway: A Super Pipelined Parallel BFT Consensus Algorithm for Permissioned Blockchain

Zui Luo[1], Chang Chen[1], and Wangjie Qiu[1,2(✉)]

[1] Institute of Artificial Intelligence and Blockchain, Guangzhou University, Guangzhou, China
[2] Beijing Advanced Innovation Center for Future Blockchain and Privacy Computing, Beihang University, Beijing, China
`wangjieqiu@buaa.edu.cn`

Abstract. Blockchain technology has recently received widespread attention from academia and industry, and its application scenarios have expanded from digital currency to all walks of life. However, as a crucial component of the blockchain, the poor performance and scalability of the current Byzantine Fault Tolerance (BFT) consensus algorithms severely limit the development of the blockchain. To cope with this dilemma, we propose Highway, a parallel optimized high-performance BFT consensus algorithm that supports decentralized management. Our algorithm is a state machine replication protocol based on a partial synchrony model. Our approach has an 18×–50× throughput improvement over HotStuff and can reach millions of throughput at 1000 Mbps networks.

Keywords: Consensus · Blockchain · Byzantine fault

1 Introduction

Consensus algorithms are used to achieve multiple replica consistency, which can be divided into Byzantine Fault Tolerance (BFT) and Crash Fault Tolerance (CFT). In traditional distributed systems, consensus algorithms widely respond to crash faults to improve the availability of the system, such as Paxos [9] and Raft [15]. The concept of BFT was first proposed by Lamport et al. [11]. Proof-of-work [4] based BFT consensus algorithms, such as Bitcoin [13], Ethereum [1], Conflux [12], etc., can achieve good robustness and safety in large scale networks, but they consume a lot of energy and perform poorly. Because networks' safety and performance issues of small scale, the permissioned blockchain generally chooses the voting-based schemes. The first synchronization protocol for Byzantine fault tolerance was proposed by Pease et al. [16]. Castro and Liskov proposed PBFT [2], which is an efficient leader-based BFT consensus algorithm. The complexity of PBFT to reach agreement on a proposal is $O(n^2)$. Because the linear message complexity of HotStuff [20] and Fast-HotStuff [7] is based on

This work was funded by grants from the National Key Research and Development Program of China (Grant No. 2021YFB2700300).

Zyzzyva [8] and SBFT [6], they have a great advantage over PBFT in large scale
networks. Besides chained HotStuff [20] uses pipelining to improve consensus
performance.

Some recent research attempts to improve performance and achieve significant throughput gains, such as Kauri [14] and Mir-BFT [18,19]. But Kauri has a
large reconfiguration overhead when the leader switches, and only supports stable leaders, which reduces fairness and has the problem of Byzantine oligarchy.
Mir-BFT uses multiple leaders to achieve agreement on multiple batches in parallel, which can achieve extremely high throughput. However, we observe that
this approach leads to an increase in latency as different batches would compete
for bandwidth.

In this paper, our contributions are as follows: ① A super pipelined parallel
consensus algorithm is proposed, named Highway, which has excellent performance and is friendly to large scale. ② The safety and liveness of the algorithm
are proved. ③ A decentralized dynamic reconfiguration method is proposed. ④
The algorithm is implemented using Go and sufficiently evaluated.

2   System Model

We assume the system has a fixed set of $n = 3f + 1$ replicas (nodes), indexed
by $i \in \mathbb{N}$, where $\mathbb{N} = \{1, \ldots, n\}$. The adversary set $\mathbb{F} \subset \mathbb{N}$ has up to $f = |\mathbb{F}|$
Byzantine nodes. Our protocol provides ordering services, and it is based on
the state machine replication (SMR) model [10,17]. Based on FLP theory [5],
we adopt the partial synchrony model [3]: assuming that the latency of each
message has an unknown but bounded global stabilization time (GST). $H(m)$
is used to represent the hash digest of the message m. For the node i, let $\langle m \rangle_{\sigma_i}$
indicate the message m signed with private key σ_i, and let $\langle m \rangle_{\Sigma_\mathbb{I}}$ indicate the
aggregated signature for $\{\langle m \rangle_{\sigma_i} \mid i \in \mathbb{I}\}$.

3   Highway

3.1   Preliminaries

The Workflow. ① Multiple clients continuously request operations (or transactions) to the consensus nodes. ② Consensus nodes use the protocol to determine
the global unique execution order of the operations for all nodes. ③ After the
operation is executed, the consensus nodes return the result to the client.

Basics of the Protocol. In each term (height), the leader packages the newly
received operations into a *block* as a proposal and broadcasts it to all nodes. After
receiving the block, the node will vote to the leader. When the leader receives
$2f + 1$ votes, it will aggregate these votes into a *quorum certificate* (QC) and
then broadcast it to all nodes. Each QC can represent that the block has been
confirmed once by the consensus system. Highway use two-phase commit and

super pipeline, and its commit conditions are described Sect. 3.2. The upper-level server executes the committed blocks sequentially, and the execution is asynchronous without blocking the consensus processes.

Highway uses pipelining based on HotStuff, and the current term of voting is equivalent to the second term of voting for the previous term. Further, our approach decouples proposal and voting, supporting multiple proposal processes in super pipeline parallel and voting processes in pipeline parallel. As shown in the Fig. 1, our approach is theoretically able to fetch better performance.

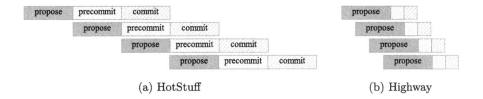

(a) HotStuff   (b) Highway

Fig. 1. Gantt chart of pipelined HotStuff and super pipelined Highway.

3.2 The Protocol

Notions
- h_p and h_v indicate the current propose-term and vote-term for the node.
- If $h_p \bmod n = i$ is true, node i is the propose-leader.
- If $h_v \bmod n = i$ is true, node i is the vote-leader.
- $\mathfrak{H}_h^b$ and $\mathfrak{H}_h^{qc}$ indicate a block and a QC with a term (height) of h. $\mathfrak{H}_h^b = \langle H(\mathfrak{H}_h^b.parent), h, \text{operations} \rangle_{\sigma_i}$, $\mathfrak{H}_h^{qc} = \langle \langle H(\mathfrak{H}_h^{qc}.parent), H(\mathfrak{H}_h^b), h \rangle_{\Sigma_1}, \mathbb{I} \rangle_{\sigma_i}$.
- b_{high}, qc_{high}, qc_{cmt} indicate the latest (maximum term) block, the latest QC and the committed QC, in local.

Propose
- For propose-leader i: Obtain N operations from the *cache pool* and combine them into a collection $\mathbb{L}$. If available operations are less than N, wait until timeout. Then pack the block: $\mathfrak{H}_h^b = \langle H(b_{\text{high}}), h, \mathbb{L} \rangle_{\sigma_i}$ and broadcast the message $\langle \text{BLOCK}, \mathfrak{H}_h^b \rangle$ to all replicas (including it self).
- For each replica: When the message $\langle \text{BLOCK}, \mathfrak{H}_h^b \rangle$ is received, if the block is legitimate and the parent of $\mathfrak{H}_h^b$ is accepted locally, accept it and if $h > h_p$ update $h_p := h + 1$ and $b_{\text{high}} := \mathfrak{H}_h^b$. If timeout occurs, update $h_p := h + 1$.

Vote
- For each replica i: If and only if vote-term h_v updates, send the vote message $\langle \text{VOTE}, \langle H(qc_{\text{high}}), H(\mathfrak{H}_{h_v}^b), h_v \rangle_{\sigma_i}, i \rangle$ to the current vote-leader. When the message $\langle \text{QC}, \mathfrak{H}_h^{qc} \rangle$ is received, if the QC is legitimate and the parent of $\mathfrak{H}_h^{qc}$ is accepted locally, accept it, and if $h > h_v$ update $h_v := h+1$ and $qc_{\text{high}} := \mathfrak{H}_h^{qc}$. If timeout occurs, update $h_v := h + 1$.

- For vote-leader i: If $n - f$ votes are received for same $\mathfrak{H}_h^{qc}$, $\mathfrak{H}_{h'}^b$ and h_v, then the signatures of the votes can be aggregated to produce $\mathfrak{H}_h^{qc} = \langle\langle H(\mathfrak{H}_{h'}^{qc}), H(\mathfrak{H}_h^b), h\rangle_{\Sigma_1}, \mathbb{I}\rangle_{\sigma_i}$, leader will broadcast $\langle QC, \mathfrak{H}_h^{qc}\rangle$ to all replicas (including itself).

Commit

- For each replica: If a new $\mathfrak{H}_h^{qc}$ is accepted and its parent is $\mathfrak{H}_{h'}^{qc}$, and if $h = h' + 1$, then commit all blocks corresponding to the path (branch) qc_{cmt} to $\mathfrak{H}_{h'}^{qc}$ and update $qc_{cmt} := \mathfrak{H}_h^{qc}$, The committed block will be executed sequentially and asynchronously.

Super pipelining

- Parallel parameter: The proposal is allowed to be ahead of the voting α for one term, and if it exceeds α term, it will block proposal progress, so there are at most α parallel proposal processes in the network.
- Communication optimization: propose-leader i will send block to other nodes one by one in order $i+1, i+2, \cdots, n-1, 0, 1, \cdots, i-1, i$. Because node $i+1$ is the propose-leader of the next term, if it receives the block first, it can immediately start proposing a block for the next term. Smaller block header, vote, and QC broadcast via gossip protocol for safety.

There is a normal case, as shown in Fig. 2a. When the node received $\mathfrak{H}_5^{qc}$ before, only block $\mathfrak{H}_1^b$ is committed because it is confirmed twice in succession by $\mathfrak{H}_1^{qc}$ and $\mathfrak{H}_2^{qc}$, while $\mathfrak{H}_2^b$ and $\mathfrak{H}_3^b$ do not satisfy the commit condition. When the node receives $\mathfrak{H}_5^{qc}$, blocks $\mathfrak{H}_2^b$ and $\mathfrak{H}_3^b$ can be safely committed.

3.3 Decentralize Reconfiguration

This module supports the definition of some management instructions define which can be used to define some scripts. Consensus nodes can initiate system transactions to invoke these scripts, and these transactions achieve agreement through the consensus algorithm, just like user transactions. Each path (branch) maintains a configuration *effective table*, and for each data entry (vote, QC, or proposal), it is processed using the version of the configuration corresponding to its height, as shown in Fig. 2b. For safety and liveness, additional requirement is needed for the protocol that the execution of the block containing the system transactions must be synchronized. This method can achieve the addition and remove of nodes at runtime, as well as the customization of event-triggered based scripts to manage the network automatically.

4 Safety and Liveness

Notation 1. $\mathfrak{H}_h^\chi.parent$ *represent the parent of* $\mathfrak{H}_h^\chi$, $\chi \in \{qc, b\}$, $h_{\mathfrak{H}_h^\chi}$ *represent the height of* $\mathfrak{H}_h^\chi$, *exist* $h \neq h_{\mathfrak{H}_h^\chi.parent} + 1$ *sometimes. Use the symbol "$\leftarrow$" to indicate the* **predecessor adjacent relationship**, *only if* $h_{\mathfrak{H}_h^\chi.parent} + 1 = h$, *then there exist* $\mathfrak{H}_h^\chi.parent \leftarrow \mathfrak{H}_h^\chi$. *Use the symbol "$\leftarrow\cdots-$" to represent the* **grandparent relationship**, *such as* $\mathfrak{H}_h^\chi.parent \leftarrow\cdots-\mathfrak{H}_h^\chi$, $\mathfrak{H}_h^\chi.parent.parent \leftarrow\cdots-\mathfrak{H}_h^\chi$. *Use the symbol "$\xleftarrow{\not{\;}}$" to indicate a* **conflict relationship** *(non-grandparent relationship), such as* $\mathfrak{H}_{h_1}^\chi \xleftarrow{\not{\;}} \mathfrak{H}_{w_1}^\chi$ *indicates that* $\mathfrak{H}_{h_1}^\chi \leftarrow\cdots-\mathfrak{H}_{w_1}^\chi$ *is not true.*

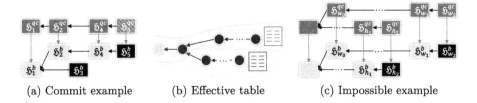

(a) Commit example   (b) Effective table   (c) Impossible example

Fig. 2. Examples.

4.1 Safety

According to the protocol, we can derive Lemma 1,2.

Lemma 1. *There is no QC of the same height.*

Lemma 2. *For any honest node, if $\mathfrak{H}_h^{qc} \leftarrow\!\cdots\!\text{-}\mathfrak{H}_w^{qc}$, the conclusion is $h < w$. In addition, if $\mathfrak{H}_w^b$ was executed, $\mathfrak{H}_h^b$ was executed earlier than $\mathfrak{H}_w^b$. If $\mathfrak{H}_h^b$ was not executed, then $\mathfrak{H}_w^b$ is not executed either.*

Theorem 1. *For any honest node, if $\mathfrak{H}_{h_1}^{qc} \xleftarrow{\cdots} \mathfrak{H}_{w_1}^{qc}$ ($h_1 \neq w_1$), then $\mathfrak{H}_{h_1}^b$ and $\mathfrak{H}_{w_1}^b$ cannot both be executed.*

Proof. Assumption: Relationship $\mathfrak{H}_{h_1}^{qc} \xleftarrow{\cdots} \mathfrak{H}_{w_1}^{qc}$ exists, $\mathfrak{H}_{h_1}^b$ and $\mathfrak{H}_{w_1}^b$ were all executed. Based on the assumptions and commit conditions of the agreement (refer to *commit* in Sect. 3.2), there is $\mathfrak{H}_{h_1}^{qc} \leftarrow \mathfrak{H}_{h_2}^{qc}$ and $\mathfrak{H}_{w_1}^{qc} \leftarrow \mathfrak{H}_{w_2}^{qc}$ simultaneously, as shown in Fig. 2c. Based on Lemma 1, let us assume that $h_2 < w_1$.

Let

$$\mathfrak{H}_{w_0}^{qc} = \arg\max_{\mathfrak{H}_x^{qc}}\{x \mid (x < h_1) \wedge (\mathfrak{H}_x^{qc} \leftarrow\!\cdots\!\text{-}\mathfrak{H}_{w_1}^{qc})\}.$$

Let $\mathfrak{H}_{w_0}^{qc} \leftarrow \mathfrak{H}_{w_1'}^{qc}$, obviously $w_1' > h_2$, because of Lemma 1. When $\mathfrak{H}_{h_2}^{qc}$ is generated, it means that there are at least $2f + 1$ nodes at $T_{\mathfrak{H}_{h_2}^{qc}}$ where $qc_{High} = \mathfrak{H}_{h_1}^{qc}$. For these nodes state $h_{qc_{High}} \geq h_1 > w_0$ is established, so there were at most $2f$ votes for $\mathfrak{H}_{w_0}^{qc}$. Therefore, $\mathfrak{H}_{w_1'}^{qc}$, $\mathfrak{H}_{w_1}^{qc}$, $\mathfrak{H}_{w_2}^{qc}$ will not be generated and $\mathfrak{H}_{w_1}^b$ could not be committed and executed. Contradictory to assumption.

Theorem 2. *For different honest nodes, the execution order of blocks is same.*

Proof. Assumption: There are two honest node i and node j, and there are two different blocks with inconsistent execution order: For block $\mathfrak{H}_h^b$ and $\mathfrak{H}_w^b$, node i executes $\mathfrak{H}_h^b$ first, then executes $\mathfrak{H}_w^b$, and node j execute $\mathfrak{H}_w^b$ before executing $\mathfrak{H}_h^b$. For node i according to Theorem 2 the relationship $\mathfrak{H}_h^{qc} \leftarrow\!\cdots\!\text{-}\mathfrak{H}_w^{qc}$ exists, which indicates $h < w$, and similarly for node j, $\mathfrak{H}_w^{qc} \leftarrow\!\cdots\!\text{-}\mathfrak{H}_h^{qc}$ exists, which indicates $w < h$, contradiction. Therefore, for different honest nodes, the order of block execution is always the same.

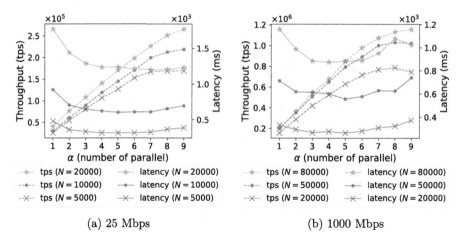

(a) 25 Mbps   (b) 1000 Mbps

Fig. 3. Parallelism for throughput and latency improvement. Running with 24 nodes, different batch size (N) of block.

4.2 Liveness

According to the assumption of a partial synchrony network, assuming a timeout Δ for each term and correcting it by exponential backoff, the system can always make progress as long as there are always $2f + 1$ correct nodes in the network.

Theorem 3. *After a limited time, a new block will always be executed or aborted.*

Proof. In the network of $n = 3f + 1$ nodes, there are $2f + 1$ honest nodes. According to the drawer principle, there are at least $f + 1$ adjacent honest node pairs. There are only 2 consecutive honest nodes, then there must exist $\mathfrak{H}_{h_1}^{qc} \leftarrow \mathfrak{H}_{h_2}^{qc}$, and the unexecuted blocks on the path $\mathfrak{H}_0^{qc} \leftarrow^{\cdots}\!- \mathfrak{H}_{h_1}^{qc}$ will be executed in order, and other blocks that are not on the path will be aborted. Even if f malicious nodes do attacks at the same time, the protocol can guarantee that any block will be committed or aborted within $2f + 1$ terms.

5 Evaluation

We have implemented Highway as a package using Golang. To avoid the overhead of responding to a massive concurrent request from clients, we embed the realization of the client request logic into the service program. In fairness, the experiment method is used in both Highway and HotStuff.

The experiments were deployed on simulated 24 nodes configured with a 4 core CPU and 16G of DRAM by Docker. Using Linux TC, we conducted experiments in two network environments for real deployment scenarios: 25 Mbps and 1000 Mbps bandwidth for global and national.

Table 1. Peak throughput limited to one second latency

Scale n (nodes)	25 Mbps			1000 Mbps		
	Throughput (tps)		Up	Throughput (tps)		Up
	HotStuff	**Highway**		**HotStuff**	**Highway**	
4	24000	460000	**19x**	71000	1276838	**18x**
8	12000	355000	**30x**	64000	1256250	**20x**
12	10000	287500	**29x**	57000	1300000	**23x**
16	8000	271250	**34x**	52000	1187500	**23x**
20	6000	255000	**43x**	54000	1027500	**19x**
24	5000	249242	**50x**	47000	1043750	**22x**
Loss	↓ 79%	↓ 45%	**1.7x**	↓ 34%	↓ 18%	**1.9x**

Highway running at $\lceil \frac{n}{3} \rceil$-parallel.

We tested the performance improvement from super piplining using different parallel stretchs as variables, and the experimental results are shown in Fig. 3: As the parallel stretch increases, the throughput increases significantly, while the delay becomes lower.

We compared the peak throughput of HotStuff and Highway in the presence of no more than 1 s of commit latency. The consensus network scale for this experiment is from 4 to 24 nodes. As shown in Table 1, the experimental results show that: ① At peak performance, our algorithm improves 18 to 50 times over HotStuff. ② Our approach is more friendly to large scale networks, that the performance degrades 1.7 to 1.9 times slower than HotStuff as the consensus network scale increases.

6 Conclusion

This paper proposes a super pipelined parallel high performance BFT consensus algorithm and a decentralized reconfiguration method, and provides detailed proof of safety and liveness. Our approach can achieve a throughput of one million within a second of latency while running at 1000 Mbps network without sharding, and it is more friendly to large scale networks.

References

1. Buterin, V., et al.: A next-generation smart contract and decentralized application platform. White Paper **3**(37) (2014)
2. Castro, M., Liskov, B., et al.: Practical byzantine fault tolerance. In: OSDI. vol. 99, pp. 173–186 (1999)
3. Dwork, C., Lynch, N., Stockmeyer, L.: Consensus in the presence of partial synchrony. J. ACM (JACM) **35**(2), 288–323 (1988)

4. Dwork, C., Naor, M.: Pricing via processing or combatting junk mail. In: Brickell, E.F. (ed.) CRYPTO 1992. LNCS, vol. 740, pp. 139–147. Springer, Heidelberg (1993). https://doi.org/10.1007/3-540-48071-4_10

5. Fischer, M.J., Lynch, N.A., Paterson, M.S.: Impossibility of distributed consensus with one faulty process. J. ACM (JACM) **32**(2), 374–382 (1985)

6. Gueta, G.G., et al.: SBFT: a scalable and decentralized trust infrastructure. In: 2019 49th Annual IEEE/IFIP International Conference on Dependable Systems and Networks (DSN), pp. 568–580. IEEE (2019)

7. Jalalzai, M.M., Niu, J., Feng, C., Gai, F.: Fast-hotstuff: a fast and resilient hotstuff protocol. arXiv preprint arXiv:2010.11454 (2020)

8. Kotla, R., Alvisi, L., Dahlin, M., Clement, A., Wong, E.: Zyzzyva: speculative byzantine fault tolerance. In: Proceedings of Twenty-first ACM SIGOPS Symposium on Operating Systems Principles.,pp. 45–58 (2007)

9. LAMPORT, L.: The part-time parliament. ACM Trans. Comput. Systt. **16**(2), 133–169 (1998)

10. Lamport, L.: Time, clocks, and the ordering of events in a distributed system. In: Concurrency: the Works of Leslie Lamport, pp. 179–196 (2019)

11. LAMPORT, L., SHOSTAK, R., PEASE, M.: The byzantine generals problem. ACM Trans. Program. Lang. Syst. **4**, 382–401(1982)

12. Li, C., et al.: A decentralized blockchain with high throughput and fast confirmation. In: 2020 USENIX Annual Technical Conference (USENIX ATC 2020), pp. 515–528 (2020)

13. Nakamoto, S.: Bitcoin: a peer-to-peer electronic cash system. Decentral. Bus. Rev. 21260 (2008)

14. Neiheiser, R., Matos, M., Rodrigues, L.: Kauri: Scalable BFT consensus with pipelined tree-based dissemination and aggregation. In: Proceedings of the ACM SIGOPS 28th Symposium on Operating Systems Principles, pp. 35–48 (2021)

15. Ongaro, D., Ousterhout, J.: In search of an understandable consensus algorithm. In: 2014 USENIX Annual Technical Conference (Usenix ATC 2014), pp. 305–319 (2014)

16. Pease, M., Shostak, R., Lamport, L.: Reaching agreement in the preDsence of faults. J. ACM (JACM) **27**(2), 228–234 (1980)

17. Schneider, F.B.: Implementing fault-tolerant services using the state machine approach: a tutorial. ACM Comput. Surv. (CSUR) **22**, pp. 299–319 (1990)

18. Stathakopoulou, C., David, T., Vukolic, M.: MIR-BFT: High-throughput BFT for blockchains. arXiv preprint arXiv:1906.05552 (2019)

19. Stathakopoulou, C., Pavlovic, M., Vukolić, M.: State machine replication scalability made simple. In: Proceedings of the Seventeenth European Conference on Computer Systems, pp. 17–33 (2022)

20. Yin, M., Malkhi, D., Reiter, M.K., Gueta, G.G., Abraham, I.: Hotstuff: BFT consensus with linearity and responsiveness. In: Proceedings of the 2019 ACM Symposium on Principles of Distributed Computing, pp. 347–356 (2019)

Overview of DDoS Attack Research Under SDN

Lei Guo[1], Shan Jing[1(✉)], and Chuan Zhao[1,2]

[1] School of Information Science and Engineering, University of Jinan, Jinan, China
{jingshan,ise_zhaoc}@ujn.edu.cn
[2] Quan Cheng Laboratory, Jinan, China

Abstract. Software Defined Network (SDN) has been developed and applied gradually in recent years. SDN decouples the data plane from the control plane to implement centralized control, improving network operation efficiency and simplifying network management. However, SDN is vulnerable to Distributed Denial of Service (DDoS) attacks, especially on the control plane, which affects the whole network. In this paper, DDoS attack detection and defense under SDN are comprehensively reviewed, mainly classified according to different detection methods. On this basis, different methods are analyzed and compared in detail, which involves the advantages and disadvantages of different methods, application scenarios and specific DDoS attack types targeted by the methods. After analyzing and comparing different kinds of methods, this paper also points out the current difficulties in the field of DDoS detection and defense under the SDN architecture, and provides ideas for future research.

Keywords: SDN · DDoS · Attack detection · Control plane

1 Introduction

In traditional computer networks, different devices support different network protocols. In order to achieve high performance forwarding of equipment, equipment manufacturers will use a specific embedded operating system. Therefore, limited by predefined commands, network administrators must manually convert advanced policies into low-level configuration commands and adapt to the constantly changing network environment [1]. In addition, network administrators also need to use very limited tools to complete some complex tasks. In terms of network security, common DDoS attack defense can only rely on conventional intrusion detection systems. Because these devices come from different vendors, this leads to poor scalability. Therefore, the management and performance adjustment under the traditional computer network brings challenges to the network administrator. If control and forwarding can be separated to program network control in a more flexible way, it will become simpler and more efficient to support multiple protocols and applications [2, 3]. Therefore, the emergence of SDN architecture makes up for the defects of traditional networks.

This section describes the SDN architecture and features of DDoS attacks. The emergence of SDN has brought impacts and changes to the traditional network security model, especially in the detection and defense of DDoS attacks, SDN has flexible advantages.

Y. Xu et al. (Eds.): ML4CS 2022, LNCS 13656, pp. 39–53, 2023.
https://doi.org/10.1007/978-3-031-20099-1_4

Different from the various security mechanisms in reviews [4] and [5], this paper focuses on the review of DDoS attack detection and defense methods under the SDN architecture, and classifies them by different DDoS detection methods. The methods investigated are concentrated in the last decade. The core connotation of the classification method is based on three DDoS detection methods, and it also involves new defense methods different from traditional blocking malicious traffic, which is the biggest difference between this review and the traditional review. The overall structure of this paper includes introduction, three kinds of DDoS detection methods (mathematical statistics, machine learning and new architecture), conclusion and future work.

1.1 Overview of SDN Architecture

The emergence and development of SDN broke the limitation of traditional network architecture. As Fig. 1 shows, it is not a specific technology or protocol, but rather an idea or framework. It completely separates control and forwarding. The control layer realizes centralized control, and the software is programmable. The forwarding layer realizes high-speed forwarding through hardware, and the control layer interacts with the forwarding layer through OpenFlow protocol [6, 7].

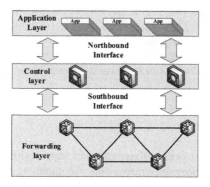

Fig. 1. SDN architecture

In SDN, the switches have no independent brain and only have the forwarding function. All path calculation strategies are executed in the controller. The flow tables are delivered to the switches through the OpenFlow protocol, and the switches rapidly forwards according to the flow table [8]. Compared with the distributed control of the traditional network, the controller under the SDN framework can dynamically formulate the corresponding strategy to deliver the flow table according to the real-time situation of the network, so the network performance can be greatly improved.

1.2 Introduction to DDoS Attacks

In DDoS attacks, attackers at different locations send malicious traffic to the target link to flood key nodes or links and occupy their resources, ultimately leading to the failure of legitimate users to obtain services [9]. Table 1 lists common DDoS attack types.

Table 1. Common DDoS attacks

Name	TCP/IP protocol layer	Resource consumption/cause exception	Whether to forge the source address	Intrusion target
SYN flood	Transport layer	Resource consumption	Yes	Key nodes
UDP flood	Transport layer	Resource consumption	Yes	Key nodes
ICMP flood	Network layer	Resource consumption	Yes	Key nodes
HTTP flood	Application layer	Cause exception	No	Key nodes
LFA	Network interface layer	Resource consumption	Yes	Key links

SYN flooding attack [10] is reflected in the three handshakes of TCP. Attackers generally send malicious SYN requests to the server by forging the source address, resulting in the failure of the victim server to establish a TCP connection with the legitimate user. UDP flooding attack [11] generally saturates the network by sending a large number of UDP packets to the victim server. ICMP flooding attack also sends a large amount of traffic to key nodes such as servers to saturate their networks. HTTP flooding attack [12] is reflected in the application layer, which can bypass the common firewall and affect the database resource scheduling of the victim nodes. Link flooding attack (LFA) [13] is different from the above DDoS attacks. Its attack targets are key links, bypasses the key nodes, and sends a large number of low-speed streams to multiple decoy servers by coordinating multiple attack bots, so as to drown the key links around the key nodes and block the communication between the key nodes and the outside world, and finally achieve the attack effect.

On the one hand, DDoS attacks pose a greater threat to SDN architecture. On the other hand, compared with traditional networks, SDN architecture has the characteristics of obtaining the whole network view and has great advantages in detecting DDoS attacks.

2   DDoS Attack Detection Based on Mathematical Statistics

This chapter mainly introduces the methods of DDoS attack detection using mathematical statistics, which can be divided into two categories. One is clearly proposed to judge whether the network traffic is abnormal by calculating the entropy of network traffic characteristics, and the other is to judge whether the traffic is abnormal by analyzing the traffic pattern. This method of analyzing the traffic pattern becomes more flexible and diverse than the method of calculating the entropy.

2.1   Detection Methods Based on Entropy

Entropy is used to measure the degree of chaos. In judging DDoS attacks, the change degree of various parameters of network traffic is expressed by calculating the entropy of traffic characteristics. The entropy referred to here is information entropy. The method of DDoS attack detection through information entropy is lightweight [14, 15]. Due to its low computational overhead, many researchers use entropy based methods to solve security problems [16, 17].

Because of the advantages of SDN, it can directly use the concept of flow tables in OpenFlow protocol to obtain traffic characteristics and make full use of its recording function, such as [18]. Sanguankotchakorn et al. [19] judged whether the traffic was abnormal by calculating the information entropy. In their research, they extracted the characteristics of the number of packets corresponding to the IP address and calculated the entropy. During the attack, the entropy decreases sharply to 0. During the normal traffic, the entropy ranges from 0.8 to 1.2. Therefore, the controllers determine whether to receive DDoS attack by calculating entropy in real time. When an attack is detected, the controllers send the corresponding blocking flow tables to switches for the source IP of malicious traffic. Sahoo et al. [20] used the Generalized Enterprise (GE) to detect low-speed DDoS attacks on the control layer. In order to improve the judgment efficiency, the GE was used as a measure to distinguish malicious traffic from legitimate traffic. The GE is the information entropy with parameter constraints. The above two methods focus on the feature extraction at the IP address level. Although the whole system was lightweight, the feature extraction was still relatively single. Kalkan et al. [21] paid attention not only to the entropy of the destination IP address, but also to the combination of IP address and TCP layer attributes. This method was also the first model to detect and mitigate DDoS attacks with joint entropy in SDN environment, which could mitigate new DDoS attacks against unknown.

The method of calculating entropy value to judge abnormal traffic is not only reflected in the conventional network environment, but also widely used in the Internet of Things environment. Kshira et al. [22] proposed a model applied in the Internet of Things scenario. The monitoring module mainly conducted coarse-grained judgment through computational entropy, and then conducted fine-grained classification through machine learning algorithm. The module for calculating entropy was consisted of a statistical monitor and an entropy estimator. The entropy of the destination address was calculated to roughly determine whether the traffic was malicious. The machine learning module was started for fine-grained classification. Similarly, the method [23] was not only judged by calculating entropy, but also combined with machine learning algorithm for final confirmation. This method is the mainstream method of DDoS attack detection and defense at present.

2.2 Detection Methods Based on Flow Pattern Analysis

The commonness of this kind of methods is to analyze the different behavior patterns between legitimate traffic and malicious traffic and distinguish them, so as to defend against malicious DDoS traffic. For example, most DDoS attackers might not directly attack key nodes. In order to prevent the traceability of defense mechanisms such as intrusion detection system, most malicious attackers would control the botnet as a springboard to attack. Multiple members of the same botnet had similar network traffic behaviors, including scanning packets and routing tracking packets. According to these characteristics, legitimate traffic and malicious traffic could be distinguished and defended [24].

Botminer [25] used this method to identify malicious traffic. The application assumed that hosts infected with the same botnet would show similar patterns at the network level, and these patterns were different from legitimate hosts. Therefore, the program would mark hosts with similar packets and bytes per second as potential threats.

The use of SDN architecture combined with traffic pattern analysis methods to provide network security solutions could be traced back to Shin et al. [26], who proposed a comprehensive framework called FRESCO for developing OpenFlow-based security applications. Jin et al. [27] proposed a mobile malware detection system based on real-time traffic analysis. The core of the algorithm was to detect hosts controlled by intruders by identifying similar communication sets. These sets included the same destination address and similar connection time. Although they were lightweight detection defense systems and had a good defense effect against unknown attacks, legitimate traffic might be easily identified as malicious traffic. In recent years, the flow pattern analysis as a detection method is shown in Table 2 below.

Table 2. Comparison of traffic pattern analysis methods

Name	Attack types	Deployment of plane	Application scenarios	Defense	Advantages
AEGIS	SYN Flood	Control plane	Conventional SDN	Blocking flow table	Simple and low overhead
VIST	Hybrid DDoS attack	Control plane/data plane	Conventional SDN	Nothing	Distinguish ddos traffic from flash crowd traffic
OMNeT++	SYN Flood	Control plane	5G	Blocking flow table	Low overhead
DDoS defense based on SDN/NFV	Hybrid DDoS attack	Control plane/data plane	Conventional SDN	Deploying filtering rules	High efficiency
SDNShield	SYN Flood	Control plane	Conventional SDN	Blocking flow table and virtualization software	Double-checking malicious traffic

AEGIS [28] was a method of traffic pattern analysis, and the system detected and defended against SYN flood attacks. The whole system architecture is shown in Fig. 2. The detection stage was divided into evaluation and analysis. Start the analysis module when the FOM value is less than 60. In the analysis module, the author divided exceptions into three types: IP spoofing, MAC spoofing and legitimate Flash Crowd. Flash Crowd was not a malicious attack traffic, similar to the legitimate but effective attack traffic of college students choosing courses. The detection of IP spoofing was determined by the MAC-IP table. If an attacker wanted to perform IP spoofing, one MAC would correspond to multiple IP addresses. In the defense phase, the attack flow was blocked by the flow table. Both MAC spoofing and Flash Crowd were detected at the same time. Based on the characteristics of both flow charts, one was continuous silky, the other was jagged. In the MAC spoofing defense phase, the blocking flow table were delivered. For Flash Crowd, alternative controllers were selected to alleviate the problem, and the author converts the alternative controller problem into knapsack problem. AEGIS was novel and could conduct real-time network analysis, but the detection was passive. Only when the performance of controllers started to decline, it could detect SYN flooding. Meanwhile, it only used the traffic chart to distinguish MAC spoofing from Flash Crowd, and the accuracy still needed to be improved.

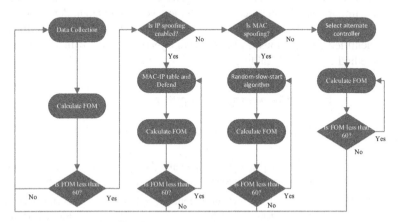

Fig. 2. AEGIS system architecture

Tu [29] proposed real-time analysis of network traffic behavior under SDN architecture to detect abnormal DDoS attack traffic, and the model was named VIST. Using the idea of edge computing, the information statistics module was deployed on edge switch. Features were extracted at the IP level to determine the number of new users and the number of old users. When a DDoS attack occurred, the number of new users was much larger than the number of old users. Similarly, Forland et al. [30] considered the characteristics of connection rate. For 5G network scenarios, due to the characteristics of 5G network, a large number of terminals would be connected. The detection system targeted SYN flood attacks. Based on the assumption that the connection attempt rate of malicious hosts was higher than that of benign hosts. The system sent a blocking flow table to the corresponding switch to block the detected malicious traffic. However, feature judgment of these two methods was relatively simple. Fischer [31] et al., combined with entropy calculation, preliminarily judged whether the traffic was attacked by calculating the entropy of destination address and destination port in the traffic. If the destination IP address and destination port increased rapidly in a short time, the entropy would decrease sharply. Once the attack was detected, the pattern generation module was started to further analyze the traffic and generate attack patterns, so as to distinguish the attack traffic from legitimate traffic. The pattern generation module could export rules describing attack traffic, and the controllers converted the corresponding attack rules into filtering rules, which were deployed on corresponding network nodes to alleviate DDoS attacks. Compared with [29] and [30], this method became more comprehensive and features judgment more comprehensive. Chen [32] et al. proposed the SDNShield scheme. Based on the network function virtualization technology, the scalability and ease of customization of virtualization software functions were utilized to protect the SDN control plane, and a two-level filtering scheme was adopted to protect the centralized SDN controller. There were three stages to the process. The first phase statistically identified legitimate flows with low complexity and overhead. The second phase of detection penetrated into the TCP handshake process to ensure the final legitimate flow. In the last stage, in order to prevent legitimate streams from always being discarded, remedial measures in the blacklist of discarded packets were proposed. This remedy was based on a research phenomenon that legitimate traffic often has many consecutive packets and lasts for a long time, while malicious traffic had only a small number of packets. This method could ensure that the majority of legitimate traffic was served while identifying and mitigating malicious traffic at multiple stages. Dalati et al. [33] proposed a tool named Network Gate to detect and filter malicious DDoS attack traffic. Based on packet specifications, such as the average packet size and the number of packets per second, the system used mathematical statistics to determine whether the current traffic is legitimate by setting thresholds.

3   DDoS Attack Detection Based on Machine Learning

Detection methods based on machine learning are widely used in traditional intrusion detection systems. In SDN architecture, machine learning algorithms are also applied to DDoS attack detection, such as Decision Tree, Support Vector Machine, Artificial Neural Network and Bayesian Network. Compared with the detection method based on mathematical statistics, the detection method based on machine learning can make decisions without external interference. Most system architectures based on machine learning detection methods are shown in Fig. 3 below. The data plane collects flow table information and sends it to the control plane through OpenFlow protocol. The control plane distinguishes legitimate traffic from malicious traffic through machine learning classification model and delivers flow table to the data plane through OpenFlow protocol for defense.

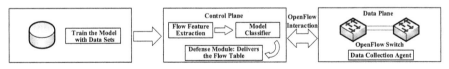

Fig. 3. Detection system architecture based on machine learning

Jin [34] and Jia [35] built a DDoS attack detection model based on SVM. The whole process of Jin's detection included flow state collection, feature extraction and classifier judgment. After feature extraction, a six-tuple eigenvalue matrix was constructed. In terms of source IP address speed change, when attacks occurred, a large number of attacks sent data packets by randomly forging IP addresses, and the number of source

IP addresses increased rapidly. In terms of source port speed, a large number of port numbers were generated randomly when a large number of attack requests occurred. The standard deviation of traffic packets was smaller than that of normal traffic packets to produce attack effect. Regarding the standard deviation of traffic bytes, in the event of an attack, to reduce packet load, the attacker would send smaller packet bits with a standard deviation less than normal traffic. With regard to flow velocity, in the event of an attack, the number of incoming flows per unit time increased dramatically and was significantly higher than normal. As for the ratio of interactive traffic entries to total traffic entries, when an attack occurred, the attacker could not use a large number of pseudo addresses in the source and target to respond, so the corresponding interactive flows and ratio would decrease. Finally, in the classifier judgment module, SVM was used to classify feature information to distinguish normal traffic from abnormal attack traffic. If the traffic information was collected within the interval of attack traffic, the status of the collected traffic would be marked as 1, indicating attack traffic, and the remaining normal traffic is marked as 0. SVM classifier was used to train the sample set. This method used SVM for classification and could achieve good classification effect through training of a small number of samples. However, it had low accuracy in detecting ICMP flood attacks, because its traffic lacked two features of source port and destination port. Dou [36] also adopted SVM classification algorithm for DDoS attack detection. Its innovation lay in that a single attack traceability scheme was proposed in the defense stage, and a multi-attack traceability method was proposed based on the scheme using K-means algorithm. Hannache et al. [37] proposed a neural network-based DDoS attack traffic detection classifier (TDC-NN) and designed a neural network with three hidden layers to distinguish normal traffic, SYN Flood, UDP Flood and ICMP Flood. Ujjan et al. [38] proposed a deep learning model named Stacked Autoencoders (SAE), which had three layers: input layer, hidden layer and output layer. The structure was similar to neural network, but different from CNN, DBN, DNN and other neural networks. SAE was simple in structure, short in training time, and unsupervised learning. Ma [39] also used neural network to train the detection model, and constructed a feature selection algorithm to select the optimal feature subset from the original network traffic to distinguish network traffic. Xiao [40] and others using KNN algorithm optimization to deal with the key characteristics to identify traffic flow was normal. It used the data structure based on index KD-Tree to hold the learning samples and made the KNN algorithm computational overhead big up, which had a higher detection rate and lower false detection rate. But it ignored the flow table in feature extraction rate changes. Dai et al. [41] improved this and proposed a random forest-based DDoS attack detection method. In addition to the average number of stream packets, the average number of stream bytes, the growth of source IP addresses and ports, the growth of stream entries was also added. And the random forest algorithm was used for classification detection, which could tolerate noise better and was not easy to appear over fitting. Table 3 compares the mainstream methods of DDoS attack detection based on machine learning technology.

Cui [42] et al. proposed an innovative method for feature calculation module and attack detection module. Entropy was used as the input feature of DDoS attack detection module for classification and judgment through SVM instead of traditional threshold setting judgment. On the DDoS defense module, the system created an IP blacklist.

Table 3. Comparison of DDoS attack detection methods based on machine learning

Method	Feature extraction/preprocessing	Detection algorithm	Defense
[34]	Network six-tuple	SVM	Nothing
[36]	IP entropy	SVM	Trace the source
[37]	OSI protocol features	Neural network	Firewall and ACL
[40]	Preprocessing with KD-Tree	KNN	Nothing
[41]	Network five-tuple	Random forests	Nothing
[42]	IP entropy	SVM	IP blacklist
[43]	Number of packets, number of bytes, and connection rate	Decision tree	Dynamic whitelist
[44]	Preprocessing with KD-Tree	SOM	Nothing

These destination IP addresses were all the IP addresses of key nodes under attack. The system discarded the traffic as long as the destination IP address was the IP address under attack. However, there were legitimate traffic among the discarded traffic. Therefore, the author calculated the probability of the packets visiting the attacked node as malicious packets. When the probability was low to a certain extent, the normal access of this stream was restored. Chen [43] et al. used Gini impurity to establish a decision tree model and used PEP algorithm for pruning operation to improve efficiency. In the mitigation module, the dynamic whitelist mechanism was introduced, which identified legitimate traffic to ensure normal communication between legitimate users and blocked illegal traffic that was not in the whitelist. There were three criteria for whitelisting. First, ensure that the flow was an interactive flow, that was, traffic coming and going. Second, ensure that there were more than a certain number of stream entries for the same source IP address. Third, the number of previous events on the source IP address exceeded a certain threshold. Although this method was innovative, in actual application scenarios, most traffic was legitimate traffic, but less illegal traffic. Therefore, the efficiency of using the whitelist mechanism would be reduced. Xu et al. [44] constructed a self-organizing mapping network based on entropy measurement (EMSOM), and then preprocessed the data using KD-tree. This operation was similar to the pruning operation of method [43], which could improve the classification efficiency and finally distinguished normal traffic from abnormal DDoS traffic. Shen [45] based on reinforcement learning, modeled DDoS defense through Markov Decision Process, designed corresponding actions to mitigate attacks using near-end strategy optimization algorithm, and improved training efficiency through reward shaping. The advantages of this method were reflected in the reinforcement learning algorithm, which was not limited by data sets and could optimize the model in real time. Ye [46] proposed an attack detection algorithm based on VAE for classification detection. In terms of mitigation, traffic control was carried out according to QoS, priority was set for different application flows, and application flow classification model was established to mitigate DDoS attack traffic. This method could mitigate DDoS attacks and set priorities for different service traffic.

4 DDoS Attack Detection Based on New Architecture

The new architecture referred to in this module is different from conventional DDoS detection and defense architectures based on machine learning methods, which are novel against DDoS attacks or use different technologies, such as cloud computing, edge computing, and network function virtualization.

In terms of DDoS attack types, Wang et al. [47] proposed LFADefender for LFA. Ahren et al. [48] first proposed the concept of LFA in the academic circle. The defense system proposed by Wang et al. has a good effect. The overall architecture of the system is shown in Fig. 4, which was mainly composed of four modules: target link selection module, link congestion monitoring module, traffic rerouting module and malicious traffic blocking module. The overall idea was to select critical links, deploy monitoring agents in advance, balance traffic load after detecting LFA, and block malicious traffic at last. The target link selection module selected key links based on traffic density. The link congestion monitoring module determined whether LFA occurred according to the packet loss rate, RTT, and available bandwidth. In the defense module, it did not block malicious traffic directly, but implemented load balancing through traffic rerouting, and finally considered blocking malicious traffic. The proposed method could quickly detect and eliminate LFA with low cost, but the cost of traffic reroute module was high, which made it possible for an attacker to change the target link faster before the reroute defense mechanism toke effect.

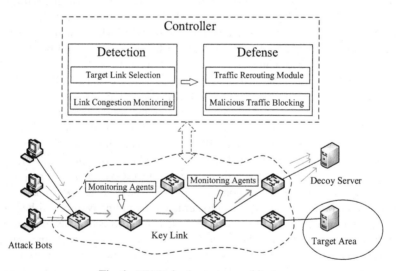

Fig. 4. LFADefender system architecture

Debroy et al. [49] detected and defended DDoS attacks in the cloud computing architecture combined with the advantages of SDN architecture. The detection was based on the traditional intrusion detection system. In terms of defense and resource migration, the controller migrated applications between virtual machine to achieve dynamic resource adjustment. The migration criteria toke into account the computing capacity, available network bandwidth, and attack history of the candidate virtual machine. The whole scheme optimized the frequency of migration and minimized the waste of network resources. Houda [50] and Sharma [51] et al. proposed a collaborative DDoS attack defense framework based on block chain under the Internet of Things. Zhou [52] et al. proposed a new defense framework to adapt to network data plane attacks and dynamically optimize defense strategies by taking advantage of the advantages of SDN. The defense mechanism could combine the key target defense with the network deception technology, confuse the attacker by spreading the camouflage information, and train the defense model through the method of game. Wu et al. [53] also used network spoofing technology. This paper proposed a DDoS defense method based on port and address hopping, which not only sent attack traffic to switches in time, but also delivered flow tables containing new virtual IP address and port mapping to switches where the attacked server was located. Finally, the server port and address hopping was realized to avoid DDoS attacks. Similarly, Zhang [54] et al. proposed the use of port hopping technology to alleviate attacks on SDN. In this method, ports were mapped randomly and dynamically to unused ports. As a result, attackers would be deceived and their attack costs would increase. Although the defense effect was better, using this technique consumed more resources. Bawany [55] et al. proposed a new adaptive framework to defend against DDoS attacks in smart cities. The framework was mainly composed of D-defense, A-Defense and C-defense modules, which respectively dealt with attacks on data plane, control plane and application layer. This method had a comprehensive defense level, covering three levels of SDN architecture. Ambrosin et al. [56] proposed the method LineSwitch, which was different from the conventional method and directly identified attacks in the data plane. The core of the method was to make the OpenFlow switch at the edge of the network act as a proxy for TCP connections, which forced the attacker to use real IP addresses to complete the three-way handshake process. Only hosts that had completed the handshake process can connect to the controller; otherwise, switches blacklisted, blocked and monitored them for a period of time to prevent attacks from spreading to the network. This method had a good detection effect and reduced the false detection rate. However, the detection process was reflected in the TCP three-way handshake. It toke a long time to separate the complete TCP three-way handshake and the efficiency was low.

Jeong et al. [57] integrated the combination of the different methods mentioned above. The author limited the influence of Denial of Service attacks by carrying out deep packet check on incoming traffic of controllers and scheduling and queuing traffic. The solution combined techniques such as checking incoming packets, scheduling requests, and redirecting streams. However, because the controllers must wait for the deep packet checking process before delivering the flow table, this caused a delay in the transmission of traffic in the switches to the destination address, resulting in packet delay. Similar methods included SDN-Guard [58] and flood-Guard [59]. In SDN-Guard, the author alleviated attacks through dynamic methods such as rerouting traffic, changing traffic rules, and combining multiple traffic rules. Flood-guard proposed a forward analyzer to analyze flow rules in flow tables and performed packet movement analysis in a circular manner. Other solutions used multiple virtual machines to detect and defend against DDoS attacks in the SDN environment. For example, in method [60], the author applied multiple virtual machines to isolate shared resources and monitored resource usage among shared hosts. Resources could be allocated and cancelled as needed to improve network flexibility and adaptability, especially during attacks, when more resources were available. In addition, if an attack occurred on one virtual machine, the system would isolate the virtual machine to prevent it from spreading to other virtual machines. Similarly, Bahman et al. [61] proposed a DDoS detection defense scheme named CoFence, which utilized network function virtualization technology. The core of the scheme was the cooperation between different domains of network function virtualization. When a domain based on network function virtualization was attacked, traffic was redirected to other domains to filter packets.

5   Conclusion and Future Work

Although the SDN architecture improves the overall efficiency of the network, security problems are exposed, especially the control plane is vulnerable to DDoS attacks. This paper summarizes and analyzes the current mainstream DDoS attack detection and defense methods. Although they are generally divided into three categories, the effective methods all involve more than one type. If the DDoS attack detection method based on mathematical statistics is not flexible, it is generally used in small-scale LAN scenarios. Most detection methods combine mathematical statistics and machine learning algorithms. Firstly, mathematical statistics are used to classify coarse-grained traffic, and then machine learning algorithm is used to classify fine-grained traffic to distinguish legitimate traffic from malicious traffic. The DDoS detection method based on the new architecture is not universal, but specific to a special scenario. Most detection algorithms are based on supervised machine learning, and the SDN architecture needs to be implemented, which has poor detection effect on unknown new DDoS attacks. Therefore, the detection of DDoS attacks under SDN in the future should focus on unsupervised machine learning algorithms and reinforcement learning algorithms. In terms of defense, the main methods are to set the blacklist and deliver the blocking traffic table. However, due to the limitation of detection algorithms, some legitimate traffic will be blocked. Therefore, a key point of defense against DDoS attacks in the future is to consider system performance while not affecting legitimate users.

Acknowledgment. This work was supported by National Natural Science Foundation of China (No. 62172258, 61702218, 61672262), Natural Science Foundation of Shandong Province (No. ZR2021LZH007, ZR2019LZH015), Shandong Provincial Key Research and Development Project (No. 2019GGX101028, 2018CXGC0706), Shandong Province Higher Educational Science and Technology Program (No. J18KA349), Project of Independent Cultivated Innovation Team of Jinan City (No. 2018GXRC002), Project of Shandong Province Higher Educational Youth Innovation Science and Technology Program (No.2019KJN028), Projects of Ministry of Education Industry-University Cooperation Education (No. 202101103019, 201901234008, 201901166007), and Project of Shandong Postgraduate Education Teaching Case (No. SDYAL20119).

References

1. Farhady, H., Lee, H.Y., Nakao, A.: Software-defined networking: a survey. Comput. Netw. **81**, 79–95 (2015)
2. Bera, P., Saha, A., Setua, S.K.: Denial of service attack in software defined network. In: 2016 5th International Conference on Computer Science and Network Technology (2017)
3. Bahaa-Eldin, A.M., Eldessouky, E.E., Dag, H.: Protecting openflow switches against denial of service attacks. In: International Conference on Computer Engineering and Systems (2017)
4. Mengmeng, W., Jianwei, L., Jie, C.: Software defined networks: security model, mechanism and research progress. J. Softw. **24** (2016)
5. Dayal, N., Maity, P., Srivastava, S., Khondoker, R.: Research trends in security and DDoS in SDN. Secur. Commun. Netw. **9**, 6386–6411 (2016)
6. Hongli, Z.: Application and implementation of SDN in cloud data center network. Inf. Technol. Informatiz., 173–175 (2021)
7. Bu, K., Yang, Y., Guo, Z.: Securing middlebox policy enforcement in SDN. Comput. Netw. **193**(4), 108099 (2021)
8. Cheng, H., Liu, J., Mao, J.: A compatible OpenFlow platform for enabling security enhancement in SDN. Secur. Commun. Netw., 1–20 (2018)
9. Patil, N.V., Krishna, C.R., Kumar, K.: SSK-DDoS: Distributed stream processing framework based classification system for DDoS attacks. Cluster Comput. **25**, 1355–1372 (2022)
10. Kumar, P., Tripathi, M., Nehra, A.: SAFETY: early detection and mitigation of TCP SYN flood utilizing entropy in SDN. IEEE Trans. Netw. Serv. Manag. **15**, 1545–1559 (2018)
11. Mamolar, A.S., Salva-Garcia, P., Chirivella-Perez, E.: Autonomic protection of multi-tenant 5G mobile networks against UDP flooding DDoS attacks. J. Netw. Comput. Appl. **145**, 1–12 (2019)
12. Raja Sree, T., Mary Saira Bhanu, S.: Detection of HTTP flooding attacks in cloud using fuzzy bat clustering. Neural Comput. Appl. **32**(13), 9603–9619 (2019). https://doi.org/10.1007/s00 521-019-04473-6
13. Merling, D., Lindner, S., Menth, M.: Robust LFA protection for software-defined networks. IEEE Trans. Netw. Serv. Manag. **18**, 2570–2586 (2021)
14. Rui, W., Jia, Z., Lei, J.: An entropy-based distributed DDoS detection mechanism in software-defined networking. In: IEEE International Conference on Trust, Security and Privacy in Computing and Communications (2015)
15. Wagner, A., Plattner, B.: Entropy based worm and anomaly detection in fast IP networks. In: IEEE International Workshops on Enabling Technologies: Infrastructure for Collaborative Enterprise (2005)
16. Yu, S., Zhou, W., Doss, R., Jia, W.: Traceback of DDoS attacks using entropy variations. IEEE Trans. Parallel Distrib. Syst. **22**, 412–425 (2011)
17. Kumar, K., Joshi, R.C., Singh, K.: A distributed approach using entropy to detect DDoS attacks in ISP domain. In: International Conference on Signal Processing (2007)
18. Braga, R., Mota, E., Passito, A.: Lightweight DDoS flooding attack detection using NOX/OpenFlow. In: The 35th Annual IEEE Conference on Local Computer Networks, pp. 10–14 (2010)
19. Sanguankotchakorn, T., Arugonda, S.K.: Hybrid controller for securing SDN from switched DDoS and ARP poisoning attacks. In: 2019 20th Asia-Pacific Network Operations and Management Symposium, pp. 1–6 (2019)
20. Sahoo, K.S., Puthal, D., Tiwary, M.: An early detection of low rate DDoS attack to SDN based data center networks using information distance metrics. Future Gener. Comput. Syst. **89**, 685–697 (2018)

21. Kalkan, K., Altay, L., Gür, G.: JESS: Joint entropy-based DDoS defense scheme in SDN. IEEE J. Sel. Areas Commun. **36**, 2358–2372 (2018)
22. Sahoo, K.S., Puthal, D.: SDN-assisted DDoS defence framework for internet of multimedia things. ACM Trans. Multimedia Comput. Commun. Appl. **16**, 1–18 (2020)
23. Yang, X., Han, B., Sun, Z.: SDN-based DDoS attack detection with cross-plane collaboration and lightweight flow monitoring. In: GLOBECOM (2017)
24. Yen, T.F., Reiter, M.K.: Traffic aggregation for malware detection. In: Proceedings of the 5th International Conference on Detection of Intrusions and Malware, and Vulnerability Assessment (2008)
25. Gu, G., Perdisci, R., Zhang, J.: BotMiner: clustering analysis of network traffic for protocol and structure-independent botnet detection. In: Proceedings of the 17th USENIX Security Symposium (2008)
26. Shin, S., Porras, P., Yegneswaran, V.: Modular composable security services for software-defined networks. In: Proceedings of Network and Distributed Security Symposium (2013)
27. Jin, R., Wang, B.: Malware detection for mobile devices using software-defined networking. In: 2013 Second GENI Research and Educational Experiment Workshop (2013)
28. Ravi, N., Shalinie, S.M., Lal, C.: AEGIS: Detection and mitigation of TCP SYN flood on SDN controller. IEEE Trans. Netw. Serv. Manag. **18**, 745–759 (2020)
29. Weiyang, T.: Research on DDoS attack detection method based on network abnormal behavior under SDN architecture. Central China Normal University (2021)
30. Frland, M.K., Kralevska, K., Garau, M.: Preventing DDoS with SDN in 5G. In: IEEE GLOBECOM (2019)
31. Bulbul, N.S., Fischer, M.: SDN/NFV-based DDoS mitigation via pushback. In: IEEE International Conference on Communications (2020)
32. Chen, K.Y., Junuthula, A.R., Siddhrau, I.K.: SDNShield: towards more comprehensive defense against DDoS attacks on SDN control plane. In: IEEE Conference on Communications and Network Security (2017)
33. Dalati, M.S., Meng, W., Chiu, W.Y.: NGS: mitigating DDoS attacks using SDN-based network gate shield. In: IEEE Global Communications Conference, pp. 1–6 (2021)
34. Jin, Y., Xiangyang, C., Jian, Z.: A DDoS attack detection method based on SVM in software defined network. Secur. Commun. Netw., 1–8 (2018)
35. Kun, J., Junnan, W., Feng, L.: DDoS detection and mitigation mechanism in SDN environment. J. Inf. Secur., 15 (2021)
36. Jian, D.: Research and application of DDoS attack detection and traceability technology based on SDN. Xidian University (2021)
37. Hannache, O., Batouche, M.C.: Neural network-based approach for detection and mitigation of DDoS attacks in SDN environments. Int. J. Inf. Secur. Priv. **14**, 50–71 (2020)
38. Ujjan, R., Pervez, Z., Dahal, K.: Towards sFlow and adaptive polling sampling for deep learning based DDoS detection in SDN. Future Gener. Comput. Syst. **111**, 763–779 (2019)
39. Jinxing, M.: Research on DDoS attack detection and defense based on spatio-temporal characteristics in software defined networks. Anhui University (2021)
40. Xiao, F., Ma, J., Huang, X.: DDoS attack detection based on KNN in SDN environment. J. Nanjing Univ. Posts Telecommun. Nat. Sci. **35**(1), 84–88 (2015)
41. Yougen, D., Qian, L.: A random forest based DDoS attack detection method under SDN architecture. Netw. Secur. Technol. Appl., 12–14 (2021)
42. Cui, J., Wang, M., Luo, Y.: DDoS detection and defense mechanism based on cognitive-inspired computing in SDN. Future Gener. Comput. Syst. **97**, 275–283 (2019)
43. Chen, Y., Pei, J., Li, D.: DETPro: a high-efficiency and low-latency system against DDoS attacks in SDN based on decision tree. In: IEEE International Conference on Communications (2019)

44. Xu, Y., Yu, Y., Hong, H.: DDoS detection using a cloud-edge collaboration method based on entropy-measuring SOM and KD-Tree in SDN. Secur. Commun. Netw., 1–16 (2021)
45. Jinfan, S.: Research on DDoS attack defense method based on reinforcement learning under SDN. Zhejiang University (2020)
46. Peng, Y.: A new DDoS attack protection system based on SDN. University of Electronic Science and Technology of China (2021)
47. Wang, J., Wen, R., Li, J.: Detecting and mitigating target link-flooding attacks using SDN. IEEE Trans. Depend. Secur. Comput. 16, 944–956 (2018)
48. Studer, A., Perrig, A.: The Coremelt attack. In: Backes, M., Ning, P. (eds.) ESORICS 2009. LNCS, vol. 5789, pp. 37–52. Springer, Heidelberg (2009). https://doi.org/10.1007/978-3-642-04444-1_3
49. Debroy, S., et al.: Frequency-minimal utility-maximal moving target defense against DDoS in SDN-based systems. IEEE Trans. Netw. Serv. Manag. 17, 890–903 (2020)
50. Houda, Z., Hafid, A., Khoukhi, L.: Co-IoT: a collaborative DDoS mitigation scheme in IoT environment based on blockchain using SDN. In: IEEE Global Communications Conference (2019)
51. Sharma, P.K., Chen, M.Y., Park, J.H.: A software defined fog node based distributed blockchain cloud architecture for IoT. IEEE Access 6, 115–124 (2017)
52. Zhou, Y., Cheng, G., Yu, S.: An SDN-enabled proactive defense framework for DDoS mitigation in IoT networks. IEEE Trans. Inf. Forensics Secur. 16, 5366–5380 (2021)
53. Hua, W., Tingzheng, C.: DDoS defense method based on address hopping in SDN environment. Cyberspace Secur., 17–22 (2020)
54. Zhang, L., Yi, G., Yuwen, H.: A port hopping based DoS mitigation scheme in SDN network. In: International Conference on Computational Intelligence and Security (2017)
55. Bawany, N.Z., Shamsi, J.A.: SEAL: SDN based secure and agile framework for protecting smart city applications from DDoS attacks. J. Netw. Comput. Appl. 145, 102381 (2019)
56. Ambrosin, M., Conti, M., Gaspari, F.D.: LineSwitch: tackling control plane saturation attacks in software-defined networking. IEEE/ACM Trans. Netw. 25, 1206–1219 (2017)
57. Jeong, S., Lee, D., Hyun, J.: Application-aware traffic engineering in software-defined network. In: Asia-Pacific Network Operations and Management Symposium (2017)
58. Maddu, J.S., Tripathy, S., Nayak, S.K.: SDNGuard: an extension in software defined network to defend DoS attack. In: IEEE Region 10 Symposium (2020)
59. Wang, H., Lei, X., Gu, G.: FloodGuard: a DoS attack prevention extension in software-defined networks. In: IEEE/IFIP International Conference on Dependable Systems and Networks (2015)
60. Mattos, D., Duarte, O.: XenFlow: seamless migration primitive and quality of service for virtual networks. In: IEEE Global Communications Conference (2015)
61. Rashidi, B., Fung, C., Bertino, E.: A collaborative DDoS defence framework using network function virtualization. IEEE Trans. Inf. Forensics Secur. 12, 2483–2497 (2017)

A Medical Image Segmentation Method Based on Residual Network and Channel Attention Mechanism

Sikai Liu(✉) ⓘ, Fei Wu ⓘ, Jinghong Tang ⓘ, and Bo Li ⓘ

School of Information Engineering, East China Jiaotong University, Nanchang 330013, China
2740104172@qq.com

Abstract. In the past years, semantic segmentation method based on deep learning, especially Unet, have achieved tremendous success in medical image processing field. However, due to the limitation of traditional convolution operations, Unet cannot realize global semantic information interaction. To address this problem, this paper proposes a deep learning model based on Unet. The proposed model takes the Residual network as the image feature extraction layer to alleviate the problem of gradient degradation and obtain more effective features. Besides, we add Squeeze-and-Excitation block to the encoder layer, which helps the whole network get the importance of each feature channel, and then improve the useful features and suppress the less useful features according to the importance, so as to improve the segmentation accuracy. According to the experiments on two medical image datasets, our method achieved better segmentation performance than other deep learning-based algorithms, which verified the effectiveness and efficiency of our method.

Keywords: Medical image · Segmentation · Residual network · Squeeze · Excitation

1 Introduction

Medical images play a vital role in medical treatment. At present, lots of medical images are still labeled manually, which suffers from a heavy workload and low accuracy. Therefore, manually annotated images are often not in line with the actual situation, which has a significant impact on the diagnosis. With the development of computer technology [1, 2], computers have been able to help researchers solve problems in various fields [3, 4]. It is a wise decision to use computers to improve the accuracy of medical image segmentation [5]. For example, computer-aided diagnosis can help doctors analyze medical images to better diagnose patients. However, there are many interferences in medical images, and traditional segmentation methods can't get accurate segmentation results [6]. Therefore, the deep learning method has attracted much attention in the field of medical image segmentation.

Recently, the convolutional neural network (CNN) has made great progress in the task of visual image recognition. Since 2012, there have been lots of networks based

© The Author(s), under exclusive license to Springer Nature Switzerland AG 2023
Y. Xu et al. (Eds.): ML4CS 2022, LNCS 13656, pp. 54–60, 2023.
https://doi.org/10.1007/978-3-031-20099-1_5

of CNN, such as VGG [7], GoogleNet [8] and so on. In 2014, FCN [9] was proposed, which transforms the full connection layer in CNN into a convolution layer, thus realizing pixel-level semantic segmentation. However, the segmentation effect of FCN is far from enough. To overcome this problem, Unet [10] was proposed, and made great progress in medical image segmentation. Its excellent performance is attributed to the following characteristics of medical image: Usually, the characteristic information of medical images is relatively simple, and there is no significant difference among the images. 2) Medical image datasets usually contain fewer data samples, and it is relatively difficult to obtain medical image data; 3) Compared with natural images, medical images have various modalities. Inspired by the success of Unet, many U-shaped networks have been proposed, such as Unet++ [11], R2Unet [12], Unet+++ [13], and ResUnet [14]. These networks inherited the topology of Unet and added network parameters, and achieved better results in various medical image segmentation tasks.

However, the past deep learning network framework still has limitations in the field of medical image segmentation, so we proposed a convolution neural network structure in this paper, which takes the Residual network as the feature extraction layer and introduces the channel attention module in the encoder layer. On the basis of Unet, our method can extract more image features and effectively solve the gradient problem in the training process. Compared with previous methods, the proposed model can extract more effective features and get higher segmentation accuracy.

2   Proposed Method

2.1   Network Structure

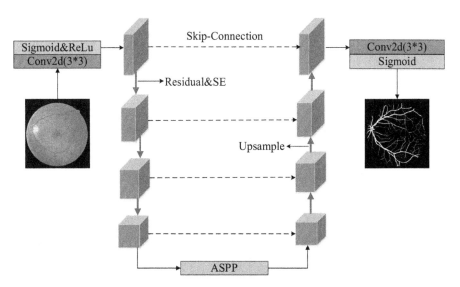

Fig. 1. The structure of proposed network.

In the proposed network in this paper, the encoder layer and the decoder layer include five down-sampling and five up-sampling, which are connected by a jump connection layer. Each downsampling operation is completed by a residual network and an SE module. Finally, the output features of the encoder will be transmitted to the decoder through Atrous Spatial Pyramid Pooling (ASPP) [15], which is improved based on spatial pyramid pooling [16]. In this paper, ASPP is used as an intermediary structure to connect the encoder layer and decoder layer in the whole architecture.

2.2 Squeeze and Excitation Block

The SE network [17] can help the network learn the feature weight according to the loss function to strengthen the weight of feature images in the training process. As a substructure, the SE block can be easily embedded into other classification or detection models. Although this increases the parameter size and calculation amount inevitably, it is still acceptable considering the effect. According to Fig. 1, we add SE network to the encoder layer of Unet, which extracts more medical image features of different scales for the decoder layer in the training process. The structure of the SE network is shown in Fig. 2.

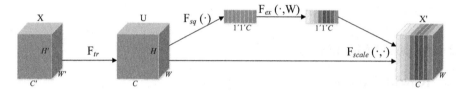

Fig. 2. The diagram of SE network

The main operation includes two parts, squeeze $\mathbf{F}_{sq}$ and excitation $\mathbf{F}_{ex}$. Convolution operation $\mathbf{F}_{tr}$ is performed on the input image before it is squeezed:

$$\mathbf{u}_c = \mathbf{v}_c * \mathbf{X} = \sum_{s=1}^{C'} \mathbf{v}_c^s * \mathbf{x}^s \tag{1}$$

Then, the squeeze operation $\mathbf{F}_{sq}$ is performed on $\mathbf{U}$ to make C feature maps a real number sequence of $1 \times 1 \times C$. The calculation process is expressed as:

$$\mathbf{z}_c = \mathbf{F}_{sq}(\mathbf{u}_c) = \frac{1}{W \times H} \sum_{i=1}^{W} \sum_{j=1}^{H} u_c(i,j) \tag{2}$$

Formula 2 means global average pooling. The result $\mathbf{z}_c$ Indicates the numerical distribution of C feature maps in this layer. Finally, the excitation operation $\mathbf{F}_{ex}$ is performed, which can capture the channel-wise dependencies fully. The calculation process is shown below:

$$s = \mathbf{F}_{ex}(\mathbf{z}, \mathbf{W}) = \sigma(\mathbf{W}_2 \delta(\mathbf{W}_1 \mathbf{z})) \tag{3}$$

2.3 Residual Network

The Residual network is used to overcome the degradation problem and improve the network performance. Figure 3 shows the components of the Residual network, it can be expressed as:

$$y_l = h(x_l) + F(x_l, w_l)$$
$$x_{l+1} = f(y_l) \tag{4}$$

In formula 4, x_l represents the input of the $l - th$ Residual unit; $F(*)$ is the Residual function; $f(y_l)$ is an activation function; $h(x_l)$ is an identity mapping function, and x_{l+1} represents the output of the $l - th$ Residual unit.

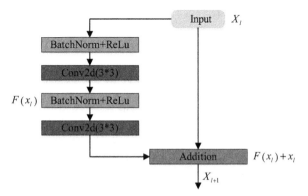

Fig. 3. The components of the Residual network.

3 Experiments

To verify the feasibility and effectiveness of our proposed method, the Liver dataset and the DRIVE dataset were selected for experiment. The Liver dataset contains 800 liver CT images, and the DRIVE dataset contains 40 eyeball images, all the images are resized into 224*224 pixels. We selected 80% of the slices as the training set, 10% as the test set, and 10% as the validation set.

3.1 Comparison with Other Methods

During the training period, all the models were trained for 150 epochs to achieve model fitting. On the two datasets, we selected dice coefficient (Dice), Intersection over Union (IoU) and Hausdorff Distance (HD) as evaluation indexes. The results are shown in Table 1 and Table 2.

Table 1. Compare results of Liver dataset with other methods.

Method	Unet [10]	Unet++ [11]	R2Unet [12]	ResUnet [14]	Ours
Dice (%)	85.21	88.42	84.18	89.36	**91.30**
IoU (%)	74.92	78.65	72.19	79.24	**80.27**
HD	4.70	4.35	4.93	4.18	**4.03**

Table 2. Compare results of DRIVE dataset with other methods.

Method	Unet [10]	Unet++ [11]	R2Unet [12]	ResUnet [14]	Ours
Dice (%)	78.60	77.89	78.27	77.31	**83.27**
IoU (%)	70.33	70.41	70.05	68.94	**73.72**
HD	5.07	5.26	5.14	5.38	**4.53**

The higher the Dice and IoU values are, the better the segmentation effect is, while the HD value is opposite. From Table 1 and Table 2 we can see, our method has achieved the best segmentation performance in both datasets.

According to the detailed numerical analysis, compared with the original network, our method improves the Dice value by 7.1%, the IoU value by 7.1%, and lowers the HD value by 14.3% on the Liver dataset; on the DRIVE dataset, our method improves the Dice value by 5.9%, the IoU value by 4.8% and lowers the HD value by 10.7%.

3.2 Ablation Study

In order to ensure the rigor of the experimental results, we have done ablation experiments on the proposed method with Liver dataset. The experimental results are shown in Table 3.

Table 3. Ablation study on proposed methods.

Method	Unet [10]	Unet+SE	Unet+Res	Ours
Dice (%)	85.21	86.43	88.70	**91.30**
IoU (%)	74.92	77.35	78.56	**80.27**
HD	4.70	4.42	4.24	**4.03**

According to Table 3 we can see, both Res and SE can improve the segmentation effect. From the detailed value, Res can bring more performance improvement than SE.

4 Conclusion

In this paper, we propose a deep learning network based on Unet, it takes the Residual network as the feature extraction layer, which effectively solves the problem of gradient disappearance in the training process. Besides, we introduce the channel attention module in the encoder layer, which helps the whole network extract more important features. In the experiments on the two datasets, our method all achieved better segmentation results than other deep learning methods.

Acknowledgments. This paper was supported by the National Natural Science Foundation of China Project No. 61863013.

References

1. Jiang, N., Duan, F., Chen, H., Huang, W., Liu, X.: MAFI: GNN-based multiple aggregators and feature interactions network for fraud detection over heterogeneous graph. IEEE Trans. Big Data (2021). https://doi.org/10.1109/TBDATA.2021.3132672
2. Jiang, N., Huang, D., Chen, J., Wen, J., Zhang, H., Chen, H.: Semi-direct monocular visual-inertial odometry using point and line features for IoV. ACM Trans. Internet Technol. **22**(1), 1–23 (2022)
3. Jiang, N., Gao, L., Duan, F., Wen, J., Wan, T., Chen, H.: SAN: attention-based social aggregation neural networks for recommendation system. Int. J. Intell. Syst. (2021). https://doi.org/10.1002/int.22694
4. Tu, B., Zhao, Y., Yin, G., Jiang, N., Zhang, Y.: Research on intelligent calculation method of intelligent traffic flow index based on big data mining. Int. J. Intell. **37**(2), 1186–1203 (2022). https://doi.org/10.1002/int.22665
5. Hua, S., Liu, Q., Yin, G., et al.: Research on 3D medical image surface reconstruction based on data mining and machine learning. Int. J. Intell. Syst. **37**, 4654–4669 (2021)
6. Zhang, Y., Zhao, Y., Yin, G., Guan, X., Zhong, M., Li, G.: Secure data stream transmission method for cell pathological image storage system. Int. J. Intell. Syst. **37**(2), 1552–1571 (2022). https://doi.org/10.1002/int.22685
7. Simonyan, K., Zisserman, A.: Very deep convolutional networks for large-scale image recognition. arXiv preprint arXiv:1409.1556 (2014)
8. Szegedy, C., Liu, W., Jia, Y., et al.: Going deeper with convolutions. In: Proceedings of the IEEE Conference on Computer Vision and Pattern Recognition, pp. 1–9 (2015)
9. Long, J., Shelhamer, E., Darrell, T.: Fully convolutional networks for semantic segmentation. In: Proceedings of the IEEE Conference on Computer Vision and Pattern Recognition, pp. 3431–3440 (2015)
10. Weng, W., Zhu, X.: Convolutional networks for biomedical image segmentation. IEEE Access (2015)
11. Zhou, Z., Siddiquee, M.M.R., Tajbakhsh, N., et al.: A nested U-Net architecture for medical image segmentation. arXiv, arXiv preprint arXiv:1807.10165 (2018)
12. Alom, M.Z., Yakopcic, C., Taha, T.M., et al.: Nuclei segmentation with recurrent Residual convolutional neural networks based U-Net (R2U-Net). In: NAECON 2018-IEEE National Aerospace and Electronics Conference, pp. 228–233 IEEE ()018
13. Huang, H., et al.: UNet 3+: a full-scale connected UNet for medical image segmentation (2020)
14. Zhang, Z., Liu, Q., Wang, Y.: Road extraction by deep Residual UNet. IEEE Geosci. Remote Sens. Lett. **15**(5), 749–753 (2018)
15. Chen, L.C., Papandreou, G., Kokkinos, I., Murphy, K., Yuille, A.L.: DeepLab: semantic image segmentation with deep convolutional nets, atrous convolution, and fully connected CRFs. IEEE Trans. Pattern Anal. Mach. Intell. **40**(4), 834–848 (2018). https://doi.org/10.1109/tpami.2017.2699184

16. He, K., Zhang, X., Ren, S., Sun, J.: Spatial pyramid pooling in deep convolutional networks for visual recognition. IEEE Trans. Pattern Anal. Mach. Intell. **37**(9), 1904–1916 (2015). https://arxiv.org/abs/1406.4729

17. Hu, J., Shen, L., Sun, G.: Squeeze-and-excitation networks. In: Proceedings of IEEE Conference on Computer Vision and Pattern Recognition (CVPR), pp. 7132–7141 (2018)

Performance Improvement of Classification Model Based on Adversarial Sample Generation

Qian Jiang, Jie Kang, and Zhendong Wu(✉)

Hangzhou Dianzi University, Hangzhou, China
{jqqzzz,wzd}@hdu.edu.cn

Abstract. The bad information in the network is often filtered by the neural network model, which is easy to be attacked by various adversarial samples. In order to improve the text filtering ability of the neural network model, it is necessary to make the filtering model learn more bad text feature information, especially the feature information that is not recognized by the filtering model at present. Therefore, having more abundant and diverse high-quality data set is one of the ideal methods to improve the accuracy of neural network filtering model. First of all, aiming at the generation of Chinese adversarial samples, we propose a method to generate semantically similar adversarial samples based on GPT2 model. At the same time, we put forward the mutation strategy by using three kinds of mutation methods (homophonic substitution, visual replacement and letters replaced), in order to extend the data set. So that we can improve the performance of classification models. After retraining the classifier with the expanded data set, the accuracy of the LSTM model of the classifier is improved from 82% to 93%.

Keywords: Chinese adversarial samples · Adversarial samples generation · GPT2 · LSTM · Performance improvement

1 Introduction

Adversarial samples are those generated by adding minor variations to the original sample. It can attack the model by reducing the accuracy of sample judgment. Adversarial sample technology was originally applied in the field of image. Szegedy et al. [13] first proposed an adversative sample generation method called box-constrained L-BFGS. By adding mutated data in the image, it can deceive the classification network, resulting in wrong output, but also maintain the high similarity between the mutated image and the original image, so that the human eye can not distinguish. Subsequently, Goodfellow et al. [7] proposed an adversative sample generation method, FGSM. This was one of the earliest image attacks, but its ideas are often borrowed from later fields of text adversarial.

Text antagonism refers to the interference of classifier judgment by adding variation to text. Compared with the image field, there are visible differences

Y. Xu et al. (Eds.): ML4CS 2022, LNCS 13656, pp. 61–74, 2023.
https://doi.org/10.1007/978-3-031-20099-1_6

between the adversarial text and the original text, and the adversarial sample also needs to meet the requirements of syntax and semantics. In addition, due to the discreteness of text, the mutation method also needs more elaborate design, and the generation method of image field cannot be directly applied to the text field. In 2017, Liang et al. [10] proposed TextFool method by referring to the idea of FGSM algorithm. Firstly, the contribution of words in the text to the classification results is calculated and the key words with the greatest influence on the classification results are screened out. Then the key words can be changed by inserting, modifying and deleting to deceive the classifier.

In the field of Chinese text adversarial sample generation, Wang et al. [17] put forward the Word Handing method in 2019. They used TF-IDF score and the effect of word sequence on confidence to extract key words in the text. Next, they took advantage of Chinese pinyin's characteristic of having multiple characters with one sound and used homophone substitution to generate antagonistic samples. In 2020, Li et al. [9] proposed a way to use pre-trained language model as a substitute generator to generate adversarial samples, using sentence fragments instead of words for substitution. In recent years, some other researchers [6] proposed to use generative adversarial network to generate adversarial samples. This makes the adversarial sample more natural and more syntactic and grammatical.

GPT model [11] is a classic pre-training model developed on the basis of Transformer model. Different from BERT model [1], GPT model does not adopt the encoder module of Transformer model, but adopts the stack of decoder modules. The GPT training process is divided into two stages: pre-training and fine-tuning. The first stage of pre-training is unsupervised training, and the second stage of fine-tuning is supervised training. GPT2 [12] is an upgraded version of GPT model, but the model structure is not much different, but a larger data set is used in training. Through training on 40GB large data sets, GPT2 model has higher generality and adaptability when applied to downstream tasks. And we have made considerable progress in applying deep neural networks to accurately control the generation of feature sequences [18–20].

In order to generate enough bad text samples that cannot be identified by the filtering model, we introduce the idea of confrontation. Mutating existing bad samples that can be identified produces text that still contains bad information in the eyes of humans, but cannot be detected by existing filtering models. Then, the generated adversarial samples are used to construct higher-quality data sets to train the filtering model and help the filtering model learn more features of undesirable information. So as to improve the performance of filtering model.

In the stage of undesirable text generation, we propose an adversarial sample generation model based on semantic similarity. Based on GPT2 model, this model automatically picks out important words in the input text and adds appropriate variations to generate bad text that cannot be filtered by the filtering model. This makes semantic extraction formally enter the era of pre-training model. In the generation process, due to the diversity of variant forms, each original statement can generate multiple adversarial texts at the same time, which greatly expands the bad text data set. At the same time, due to the GPT2 model's semantic control, the generated bad text has higher semantic consistency with the original text. Finally, we put forward using the generated adversarial samples to retrain the original filtering model, so as to achieve the goal of improving the model performance.

Our main contributions are as follows:

1. An adversarial sample generation model based on GPT2 is proposed. The semantic information is used to control the generation of adversarial samples, so that the generated adversarial samples can maintain high semantic consistency with the original samples.
2. Vocabulary mutation strategies are put forward. So that the generated counter sample is more in line with the form of today's network language, more authentic. Various variations enable each text to generate multiple adversarial samples, greatly enriching the bad text data set.
3. Propose the retraining classification model performance improvement method. The performance of the classification model can be improved effectively by expanding the data set.

2   Background

2.1   Adversarial Sample Attack Method

On the one hand, there are two common adversarial sample attack methods: white-box attack and black-box attack [2,14]. The key factor to distinguish white box attacks from black box attacks is whether the attack method needs to access the internal parameters of the classification model. On the other hand, adversarial sample attacks can also be divided into character level attacks and word level attacks according to different mutation locations. Character-level attacks mutate a character in a word, such as adding, deleting, or swapping positions. Word-level attacks mutate a word in the text by replacing or modifying it. Table 1 statistics the common methods of text adversarial sample attack.

In this paper, we adopt the black box adversarial sample generation method. Combined with our word-level mutation strategies, the adversarial sample can maintain a high semantic similarity with the original sample, while effectively bypassing the detection of classifier.

Table 1. Methods of text adversarial sample attack

Attack method	Attack Type	Attack task
HotFlip [4]	White-box, Character-level	Text classification
Ebrahimi [3]	White-box, Character-level	Machine translation
Tsai [15]	White-box, Word-level	Emotion classification
Deep WordBug [5]	Black-box, Character-level	Text classification
Jia [8]	Black-box, Word-level	Reading comprehension
Greedy [15]	Black-box, Word-level	Emotion classification

2.2 The Similarity Evaluation Index

While the adversarial sample can deceive the classifier model, it should minimize the influence of variation on people's reading, which means that it is necessary to maintain a high degree of semantic similarity between the adversarial sample and the original sample. For the measurement of semantic similarity, three indicators (Euclidean distance, Cosine similarity, Word Mover's Distance) [16] can be used to evaluate. In this paper, we use Word Mover's Distance to evaluate the semantic similarity.

Cosine similarity is the cosine of the Angle between two word vectors. The closer the cosine value is to 1, the higher the semantic similarity of the two words. The cosine similarity is shown as formula (1).

$$Cos\_Sim = \frac{\sum\limits_{i=1}^{n} x_i y_i}{\sqrt{\sum\limits_{i=1}^{n} x_i{}^2}\sqrt{\sum\limits_{i=1}^{n} y_i{}^2}} \tag{1}$$

3 Model Design

In order to generate a large number of adversarial samples for improving the performance of filtering model, we propose a model of adversarial sample generation based on GPT2. Since text is discrete, changes in data may not have corresponding text. So we cannot use the data level mutation, can only use text field mutation in the generated text adversarial samples. Considering the particularity of the text field, we propose a keyword location method based on GPT2 model and two new compilation strategies. The model process is shown in Fig. 1.

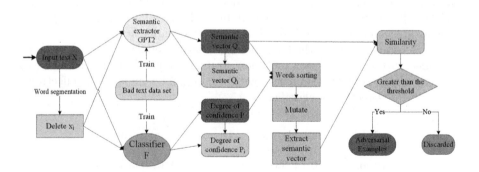

Fig. 1. Workflow of generating Chinese adversarial samples

The process can be described as follows:

1. Word segmentation for input text;
2. The pre-trained language model GPT2 is used to extract the semantic vector of the input text, denoted as Q;
3. The word x_i in the text is traversed. On the basis of deleting the word, the same GPT2 model is used to extract the semantic vector of the remaining text, which is denoted as Q_i;
4. Rank the importance of words in the text according to the similarity of Q_i and Q and the impact level of classification results;
5. Mutate the first K important words by mutating them to generate mutated texts;
6. The same GPT2 model is used to extract the semantic vector of the mutated text, and the similarity calculation is carried out with vector Q. If the similarity reaches the threshold, the output is the admissible sample.

3.1 Word Segmentation

If Chinese only uses a single character, there are many problems of unclear meaning expression. Therefore, words are chosen as the unit of text variation. In addition, there is no obvious distinguishing mark between Chinese words, so it is necessary to use a special algorithm for word segmentation. In Table 2, we compare the effects of Jieba word segmentation, Baidu LAC and Tsinghua THULAC, three mature word segmentation tools, in two data sets. According to the results, THULAC's overall word segmentation effect is best, which is more consistent with the human word segmentation form. Therefore, THULAC word segmentation algorithm is adopted in the experiment. For input text X, THULAC segmentation results in $\{x_1, x_2, ..., x_n\}$, where x_i is the i-th word after the word segmentation, which can contain one or more Chinese characters.

Table 2. Comparison of three word segmentation algorithms

Algorithms	Pku data set			Msr data set		
	Precision	Recall	F1	Precision	Recall	F1
Jieba	85.27	78.66	81.83	81.63	81.04	81.33
LAC	87.81	80.01	83.73	90.14	86.83	88.46
THULAC	92.24	92.33	93.43	83.38	87.86	85.56

3.2 Semantic Vector Extraction

We use GPT2 pre-training model for semantic vector extraction. Because the object to be used by the model is bad text, there is less learning of bad text in the model training stage. Therefore, we collected nearly 2W inappropriate texts from the Internet, including various forms of pornography, violence, sensitivity and so on. The collected data is cleaned and sorted into new bad text data sets. The GPT2 model is fine-tuned with this data set so that the model can fully learn the semantic characteristics of undesirable texts.

For the input text X, the trained GPT2 model G is used to extract the semantic vector Q of X, and Q is a multidimensional vector.

3.3   Sorting by Importance of Words

Iterate over each word in the text and calculate the word importance score. The word importance score was weighted by semantic impact and classification confidence.

Semantic impact score: Calculates the impact of words on the overall semantic meaning of the text. For text X, deletes the word X_i in X, and extracts the semantic vector Q_i using model G for the remaining text. The semantic impact degree of the word X_i is calculated by the formula (1).

$$S_i = 1 - \frac{QQ_i}{\| Q \|\| Q_i \|} \tag{2}$$

Classification confidence influence score: the degree to which a word affects the classification result of a classifier. For text X, classifier F, the confidence score of the original text classified as Y is $F(X)$. The word x_i in X is deleted and the classifier F is used for the remaining text x_i. The confidence score of the original text classified as Y is $F(x_i)$. The classification confidence influence score of vocabulary is shown as formula (2).

$$P_i = F(X) - F(X_i) \tag{3}$$

The algorithm of word importance calculation is is shown as formula (4). w_s and w_p are the weight of the influence of word on semantic and classification respectively. We rank words from most important to least important. When carrying out mutation, the k words with the highest rank are preferentially selected for mutation. After variation, such words can influence the classification results to the greatest extent while minimizing the semantic changes of the text.

$$score(x_i) = w_s * S_i + w_p * P_i \tag{4}$$

4   Mutation Strategies

4.1   Single Mutation

This paper focuses on the generation of word-level adversarial samples. We adopt homophonic substitution, visual substitution and letter substitution. These mutations are shown in Fig. 2.

The core idea of homophonic substitution is to replace the original words with words that have the same pinyin as the original words, and we do not consider the tone of pinyin.

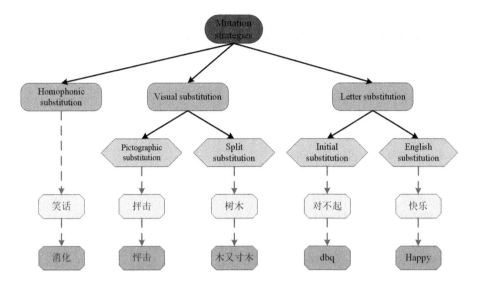

Fig. 2. Mutation strategies

In the visual substitution, the substituted words are highly similar to the original words visually, so they do not affect people's reading. There are two ways of visual substitution, split substitution and pictographic substitution. If a Chinese character has a left - right structure or a left - middle - right structure, and each structure can exist as a separate Chinese character, the Chinese character can be split. Such as "qing(晴)" can be divided into "ri qing(日青)", "shu(树)" can be divided into "mu you cun(木又寸)" and so on. But the split does not apply to all Chinese characters, such as "ren(人)", "wo(我)" and so on. Pictographic replacement refers to replacing words that are similar to the original words in appearance, such as "peng(抨)" and "peng(怦)".

In the letter substitution, the initial substitution extracts the pinyin of the words, and put all the pinyin initials in the order of the original word, such as "dui bu qi(对不起)" to "DBQ"; the English substitution uses the corresponding English word of the original word and replace the position of the word in the text, such as "快乐 " to "happy".

The specific algorithm for generating adversarial samples by mutating important words is given in Algorithm 1. The first k words sorted by important words will be mutated in three ways. Semantic extraction G is used to extract the semantics of the mutated sample, and cosine similarity of the semantic Q of the original sample is calculated. Compared with the set similarity threshold, if the similarity value exceeds the threshold, it is the generated effective adversarial sample; otherwise, the sample is discarded.

Algorithm 1. Mutation algorithm of important words

Input: Semantic extraction G, Original sample X, Sorted words $W = \{x_1, x_2, ..., x_n\}$

1: $Q = G(X)$
2: $Mutations = \{mutation_1, mutation_2, mutation_3\}$
3: **for** x_i in W **do**
4:    **for** b_j in $Mutations$ **do**
5:       $word = b_j(x_i)$
6:    **end for**
7: **end for**
8: $Sentence = X.\text{replace}(x_i, word)$
9: $Q' = G(Sentence)$
10: $Sim = 1 - \frac{QQ'}{\|Q\|\|Q'\|}$
11: **if** $Sim > \sigma$ **then**
12:    $Out.\text{append}(Sentence)$
13: **end if**
14: **return** Out

Output: Sample after mutations Out

4.2   Combination of Mutations

We can mutate several words in a text at the same time. This combination of mutations can greatly increase the number of samples generated. However, the semantic similarity will be reduced once there are too many mutated words. This means that the generated sample quality is will decrease, difference will increase with the original sample.

n words are selected from the k words to be mutated, and the selected words mutate in any way. The flow of multiple combinations of mutations as shown in Fig. 3.

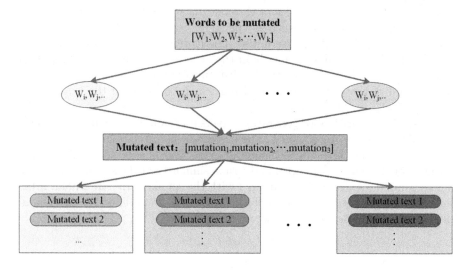

Fig. 3. The flow of multiple combinations of mutations

5   Model Retraining

In order to improve the performance of the filtering model from the data level of the training set, we combined the adversarial samples generated after mutation with the data in the original data set, and added enough normal text in the new data set to balance the positive and negative samples to form the new data set. We retrain the original filter model with the new data set. The trained model has the same structure and different parameter values as the original model, but has better filtering performance than the original model (Fig. 4).

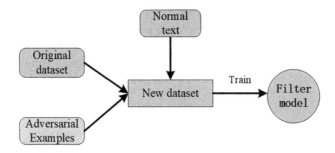

Fig. 4. The workflow of model retraining

6   Experiments

Data Set. We mainly used bad text data sets. Abusive, pornographic, violent and politically sensitive texts are collectively referred to as bad texts. Bad text in the network is complex and diverse, and there is no authoritative bad text data set. Therefore, we use crawler technology to collect nearly 2W texts from web texts. After text preprocessing, the text is divided into normal text and bad text according to the text content. There were 8,400 normal texts and 8,700 bad ones. We divided all texts into two categories according to normal and undesirable information, corresponding to 0 and 1 marks respectively, forming a complete undesirable text dataset, which was recorded as BTD dataset. Some data in the dataset are shown in Table 2. During the experiment, data in BTD were divided into training set and test set according to 7:3.

Table 3. Samples of BTD dataset

Category	Sample	Quantity		Label
		Training set	Testing set	
Normal text	jin tian tian qi hen hao.	5880	2520	0
	dian yin heng hao kan.			
Bad text	fa lun gong da fa hao.	6090	2610	1
	chu shou qiang zhi dan yao.			

Semantic Extractor. For semantic extractor, we use 12-layer GPT2 pre-training model as the basis. After training in a corpus of about 40GB, the model contains 117M parameters, and the semantic characteristics are better learned. The pre-training model is fine-tuned in the BTD dataset constructed by us to make it fully learn the semantic characteristics of bad texts.

Classifier. Classifier refers to the filtering model to be improved performance. In the experimental stage, LSTM model, which is often used for classification tasks, is adopted as the classifier. The input of classifier is the text to be classified, which can be either the original text or the generated adversarial sample. The output is the label of the text and the confidence of that label. The classifier is also trained in the BTD data set constructed by us. When no adversarial samples are added, the classification score of the classifier is shown in Table 3. Then, the model is retrained with the generated adversarial sample to test the effect of adversarial sample data set on improving model performance (Table 4).

Table 4. Classifier baseline scores

Index	Precision	Accuracy	Recall	Average confidence
Score	83.5	82.5	88.1	78.2

Experiment Process. The overall generation process of adversarial samples is shown in Fig. 5. First, word segmentation and words sorting are performed on the original samples. Second, we mutate the first k words (the mutation can be a single mutation or a combination). And the mutated words replace the corresponding words in the original text to generate antagonistic samples. All adversarial samples are generated from bad text. Because of the diversity of mutated words and mutated ways, each original text can generate multiple antagonistic samples. Finally, the generated adversarial samples are combined with the original samples into a new data set to retrain the classification model.

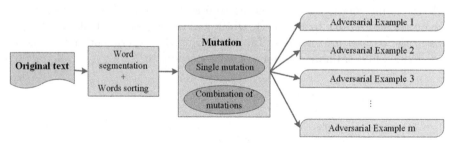

Fig. 5. Adversarial sample generation process

7 Result

7.1 Result of Single Mutation

Similarity threshold w has an important influence on the quantity and quality of adversarial samples. Single mutation means that only one word in the original sample is mutated during the generation of each mutated text. We then calculate the similarity between the mutated text and the original text. If the similarity of the variant text is greater than the similarity threshold w, the text is considered as the adversarial sample of the original sample; otherwise, the text is discarded. It can be seen that the similarity threshold has an important influence on the quantity and quality of adversarial samples. If the threshold value is relatively high, the quality of adversarial samples is high but the quantity is small; if the threshold value is relatively low, the quality of adversarial samples is poor but the quantity is large.

In the experiment, no threshold less than 0.6 is selected. Because when the threshold value is less than 0.6, the mutant statements have seriously affected normal reading, and such statements are of little significance. At the same time, when the threshold interval is too small, there is little difference in their experimental results, so we select a relatively moderate threshold interval of 0.1. In Sect. 7.2 is the same reason.

Table 5 shows the classification results of single mutation at multiple thresholds. The average number in Table 5 refers to the number of effective counter samples that can be generated by an average original sample. Average confidence refers to the average probability of all adversarial samples being classified as undesirable samples.

As can be seen from Table 5, with the similarity threshold from 0.6 to 0.8, the precision, accuracy and average confidence index all show a downward trend. The result shows that the higher the similarity threshold, the quality generated adversarial samples is better. More adversarial samples are wrongly classified as normal samples, and even if they are not classified as normal samples, the probability of being bad samples in classifier judgment is significantly reduced. According to the statistics of recall of normal texts, normal texts are not mutated during the experiment and are less affected by antagonistic samples, so the index not changed significantly. And with the increase of threshold, the number of adversarial samples that can be generated by each sample decreases significantly, which means that more and more mutated texts are discarded. With the threshold of similarity rising from 0.8 to 0.9, except for the average number, the values of other indexes all increased slightly. This result indi-cates that when the semantic similarity between the adversarial sample and the original sample is too high, the gap between some adversarial samples and the original sample is too small to fool the classifier. At the same time, if the threshold is too high, a large number of variation samples will be abandoned, and only 1 or 2 counter samples can be generated for each original sample.

Therefore, for a single mutation process, when the similarity threshold is set to 0.8 (compared to 0.6, 0.7 and 0.9), the effect of adversarial sample generation is the best. At this time, the classification efficiency and the number of generated samples can be better considered.

Table 5. The new classification result of single mutation at multiple thresholds

Threshold ω	Precision	Accuracy	Average number	Recall	Average confidence
0.6	62.2	62.5	4.1	87.8	72.2
0.7	60.1	63.3	3.8	88.3	68.7
0.8	57.7	58.0	3.1	89.0	60.5
0.9	63.7	67.4	1.4	88.9	69.2

7.2 Result of Combinatorial Mutations

Due to the diversity of vocabulary combinations, more samples of mutation can be generated after combinatorial mutations. However, too many mutations will have a greater impact on the semantics of the sample. Therefore, the semantic similarity between the generated variant text and the original text decreases with the increase of the number of words in the combination. Therefore, to take into account the quantity and quality of the resulting antagonistic samples, we tested the case when the variant combination contains two and three words. The results are shown in Table 6 and Table 7.

Table 6. Result of combinatorial mutations with two words

Threshold ∂	Precision	Accuracy	Recall	Average number	Average confidence
0.6	55.2	60.9	88.2	40.5	60.5
0.7	48.7	50.8	87.6	35.7	58.3
0.8	50.5	57.2	87.9	32.2	58.2
0.9	55.2	61.5	86.1	25.6	58.1

Table 7. Result of combinatorial mutations with three words

Threshold ∂	Precision	Accurate	Recall	Average number	Average confidence
0.6	65.1	58.9	87.3	36.3	65.2
0.7	49.4	56.4	87.3	30.8	64.2
0.8	57.8	56.8	88.0	24.2	61.5
0.9	60.4	57.2	87.1	10.1	60.7

The above results show that the recall rate of the classifier does not change significantly no matter how many words have been mutated. This means that the generated counter samples only increase the probability that the bad samples will not be filtered, but have no effect on the detection of normal text. When two vocabularies are combined and three vocabularies are combined to mutate, the resulting adversarial sample is the best at a threshold of 0.7(compared to 0.6, 0.8 and 0.9). When the threshold value is less than 0.7, the results of other indicators are poor except for the better average number. When the threshold value is greater than 0.7, not only does each index not increase significantly, but the average number and average confi-dence index are even worse than before.

8   Conclusion

We first propose a text adversarial samples generation method based on GPT2 model. By understanding the semantics of the GPT2 model, the semantic similarity between the adversarial samples and the original samples is guaranteed while generating adversarial samples. Two variant forms, single mutation and combination of mutations, are proposed. The resulting adversarial samples can successfully deceive the classifier while still conforming to the form of network text and have no impact on people's reading. Subsequently, the performance of classifier detection is significantly improved by using the generated adversarial samples to train the classifier again. Therefore, the performance of the classification model can be improved by generating a dataset with expanded bad text adversarial samples.

In addition, the effectiveness of adversarial samples demonstrates that there are many potential vulnerabilities in many practical applications of the network, which need further improvement. And as spelling checking becomes more stringent, the type of spelling errors becomes less effective adversarial samples of attack. But the ability to filter the variant form of abbreviation and Chinese and English interspersed remains to be improved.

Acknowledgements. This research is funded by National Key R&D Program of China (No.2018YFB0804102), Key Projects of NSFC Joint Fund of China (No. U1866209), National Natural Science Foundation of China (No. 61772162).

References

1. Devlin, J., Chang, M.W., Lee, K., Toutanova, K.: Bert: Pre-training of deep bidirectional transformers for language understanding. arXiv preprint arXiv:1810.04805 (2018)
2. DU Xiaohu, W.H., YI Zibo, L.S., MA Ju, N.Y.J.: Adversarial text attack and defense:a review. J. Chin. Inf. Process. **35**(08), 1–15 (2021)
3. Ebrahimi, J., Lowd, D., Dou, D.: On adversarial examples for character-level neural machine translation. arXiv preprint arXiv:1806.09030 (2018)
4. Ebrahimi, J., Rao, A., Lowd, D., Dou, D.: Hotflip: white-box adversarial examples for text classification. arXiv preprint arXiv:1712.06751 (2017)

5. Gao, J., Lanchantin, J., Soffa, M.L., Qi, Y.: Black-box generation of adversarial text sequences to evade deep learning classifiers. In: 2018 IEEE Security and Privacy Workshops (SPW), pp. 50–56. IEEE (2018)
6. Goodfellow, I., et al.: Generative adversarial nets. Adv. Neural Inf. Process. Syst. **27** (2014)
7. Goodfellow, I.J., Shlens, J., Szegedy, C.: Explaining and harnessing adversarial examples. arXiv preprint arXiv:1412.6572 (2014)
8. Jia, R., Liang, P.: Adversarial examples for evaluating reading comprehension systems. arXiv preprint arXiv:1707.07328 (2017)
9. Li, L., Shao, Y., Song, D., Qiu, X., Huang, X.: Generating adversarial examples in Chinese texts using sentence-pieces. arXiv preprint arXiv:2012.14769 (2020)
10. Liang, B., Li, H., Su, M., Bian, P., Li, X., Shi, W.: Deep text classification can be fooled. arXiv preprint arXiv:1704.08006 (2017)
11. Radford, A., Narasimhan, K., Salimans, T., Sutskever, I.: Improving language understanding by generative pre-training (2018)
12. Radford, A., Wu, J., Child, R., Luan, D., Amodei, D., Sutskever, I., et al.: Language models are unsupervised multitask learners. OpenAI Blog **1**(8), 9 (2019)
13. Szegedy, C., et al.: Intriguing properties of neural networks. arXiv preprint arXiv:1312.6199 (2013)
14. Tong, X., Wang, L., Wang, R., Wang, J.: A generation method of word-level adversarial samples for Chinese text classification. Netinfo Secur. **20**(9), 12–16 (2020)
15. Tsai, Y.T., Yang, M.C., Chen, H.Y.: Adversarial attack on sentiment classification. In: Proceedings of the 2019 ACL Workshop BlackboxNLP: Analyzing and Interpreting Neural Networks for NLP, pp. 233–240 (2019)
16. Wang, C.L., Yang, Y.H., Deng, F., Lai, H.Y.: A review of text similarity approaches. Inf. Sci. **37**(3), 158–168 (2019)
17. Wang, W., Wang, R., Wang, L., Tang, B.: Adversarial examples generation approach for tendency classification on Chinese texts. Ruan Jian Xue Bao/J. Softw. **30**, 1–14 (2019). in Chinese
18. Wu, Z., Tian, L., Li, P., Wu, T., Jiang, M., Wu, C.: Generating stable biometric keys for flexible cloud computing authentication using finger vein. Inf. Sci. **433**, 431–447 (2018)
19. Wu, Z., Kang, J., Jiang, Q.: Semantic key generation based on natural language. Int. J. Intell. Syst. **37**(7), 4041–4064 (2021)
20. Wu, Z., Lv, Z., Kang, J., Ding, W., Zhang, J.: Fingerprint bio-key generation based on a deep neural network. Int. J. Intell. Syst. (2021)

Research on Detection Method of Large-Scale Network Internal Attack Based on Machine Learning

Chang Liu[1]($\boxtimes$), Chaozhong Long[2], Yuchuan Yu[3], and Ziqi Lin[4]

[1] Jiangsu Fengren Information Technology Co., Ltd., Nanjing 241000, China
z002s0@163.com
[2] Kunshan Open University, Kunshan 215316, China
[3] Information Center of Public Security Bureau of Rongshui Miao Autonomous County, Liuzhou 545399, China
[4] Shandong Information Vocational and Technical College, Weifang 261044, China

Abstract. Aiming at the problem of inaccurate analysis of forged address attack behavior in current detection methods, this paper proposes a large-scale network attack detection method based on machine learning. A large-scale network internal attack detection model is constructed to analyze the degree of network internal attack. The model is trained by machine learning method to improve the convergence speed of model detection. After determining the attack target, analyzing the network vulnerability attribute, tracing the network internal attack source. Computes the hash of a function to ensure that the data set is complete and not tampered with. Alarm windows automatically check the point, set different alarm levels. The Euclidean distance is used as the distance measure of clustering process to distinguish the attack behavior. The detection formula of large-scale network internal attack is constructed, and the calculation result is divided into the level of large-scale network internal attack. Experimental results show that the method is consistent with the actual path, and the highest recall is 93%, the highest precision is 0.98, with good detection results.

Keywords: Machine learning · Large scale network · Internal attack · Testing

1 Introduction

With the rapid development of network attack technology, the network mode is becoming more and more diverse and the network attack means are becoming more and more complex. Highly developed network attackers can use fake IP address packets to attack the client, so that the attacked client cannot accurately locate the attacker's location. Hackers can also cross the gangplank host, attack the network, and hide the attacker's real IP information. There are many ways to hack, too. Sending just one message can cause a system to crash. Wireless network crimes, such as "network breaking", "wireless fishing" and so on, often occur the risk of personal information leakage, tampering, and even occasionally personal economic losses. With the continuous updating of the Internet,

Y. Xu et al. (Eds.): ML4CS 2022, LNCS 13656, pp. 75–88, 2023.
https://doi.org/10.1007/978-3-031-20099-1_7

network traffic data presents massive, high-dimensional characteristics, combining these characteristics, it is very difficult to discover wireless network attacks directly.

Some scholars have studied the above problems. Duran et al. [1] proposed a SAR target detection network method based on semi supervised learning. Based on the semi supervised learning method, a semi supervised learning model is established to realize the network monitoring of SAR targets, but the accuracy of this method is not high. Li Pengwei et al. [2] proposed a strong resistance Android malicious code detection method based on deep learning. Analysis of wireless network traffic data through deep learning method has strong learning ability, because the data obtained by wireless network attack behavior is not comprehensive, most of the work is detected by the existing dataset oriented communication network attack behavior, and the research on attack behavior detection under wireless network environment is limited.

Aiming at the existing problems, a large-scale network attack detection method based on machine learning is proposed. Through the establishment of a large-scale network internal attack model, the degree of attack within the network is analyzed. Machine learning method is used to determine the attack target, and network vulnerability attributes are analyzed to track the attack source. Using Euclidean distance method to calculate the level of large-scale network internal attack. This method can effectively improve recall and accuracy, and has good detection results.

2   Construction of Large-Scale Network Internal Attack Detection Model

For secondary users who need to use any frequency band, local spectrum detection is performed first, and then perceptual reports are sent to the billing records center. If the perceived result is idle, the adjacent secondary user is required to interact with the perceived information. When the number of interactions is small, the recommendation request needs to be sent to the neighborhood users with high reputation, and the recommender provides the recommendation value as the reputation value. Because the same level of secondary users do not know each other, one of the secondary users through information exchange can be another adjacent to the secondary user recommendations. So malicious secondary users is to use this channel, will be a number of malicious secondary users through a large number of false transactions together. If one of the sub-users engaged in fraudulent transactions becomes a referrer, the associated user, backed by a high reputation value, will cheat the sub-user, who trusts the referrer and accepts the request [3]. In this way, the number of spurious transactions is increasing, and the reputation of conspirators is also increasing. Therefore, the conspirators become the secondary users with the highest comprehensive credibility. Stealing the information of the attacker according to the weight of the internal attack target of the network to ensure that the data will not be lost [4]. Using this weight as a parameter, a judgment matrix is constructed, as follows:

For the comparison of two elements in the elements, the judgment matrix can be obtained. After the normalization of the matrix, the consistency index can be obtained. The formula is:

$$I = \frac{E_{\max} - N}{N - 1} \tag{1}$$

In formula (1), E_{max} represents the main characteristic root of the matrix; N represents the number of stages. The network entropy difference of the system before and after the attack can be calculated synthetically, so that the network attack effect can be evaluated synthetically, and the network attack effect can be described quantitatively, and the attack effect can also be described qualitatively by dividing the attack effect level (the attack effect level as the throughput level) [5].

The model of network attack detection before and after network attack is as follows:

$$\Delta f_i = \sum_{i=1}^{N} w_i \times \left(S' - S\right) \tag{2}$$

In formula (2), S and S' respectively represent the entropy before and after the network attack. The larger the calculation result of the formula, the greater the degree of attack within the large-scale network.

3 Large Scale Network Internal Attack Detection Based on Machine Learning

The basic structure of machine learning network is shown in Fig. 1.

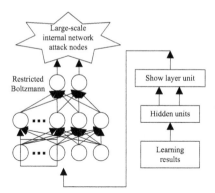

Fig. 1. Machine learning network architecture

As you can see in Fig. 1, multilayer Boltzmann sets form a machine learning network. Neural network divides neurons into dominant neurons and recessive neurons, and there are associative memory units between upper and lower neurons.

3.1 Training Based on Machine Learning Model

The detection method based on machine learning uses Bayesian algorithm, which uses maximum likelihood to estimate the mean and variance of data. Because of its simplicity and easy implementation, Bayes has been widely used in many complex problems and works well.

Based on Bayesian probabilistic model, machine learning network trains and adjusts the weight parameters between hidden layer and visible layer, so that the target data can be generated with maximum probability. [6].

Using the training and learning methods of machine learning networks to solve the model, the detailed steps are as follows:

Step 1: Unsupervised training.

The specific task is to train the constrained Boltzmann machine in layers, with the output of each layer as input to the upper layer. When the upper neurons are labeled, they need joint labeling [7].

Step 2: Tune.

There are two stages of optimization: cognitive stage and production stage. In the recognition stage, the machine learning network generates the outputs of each layer one by one according to the input feature information. The basic status information consists of top-level label annotation and downward weight information in the generation stage, and upward weight information is also modified in this stage.

In the process of feature extraction of machine learning network, the input signal needs to be represented and trained by vector. The highest-level associative memory unit divides tasks according to clues provided by the lower level. Using labeled data-based feedforward neural networks, machine learning networks can accurately adjust classification performance and perform recognition at the final training level [8]. Compared with the direct use of FNN, this method has higher efficiency, because machine learning network can be trained locally only by modifying weight parameters, so the training speed is fast and the convergence time is short.

3.2 Attack Injection Point Analysis

After determining the attack target, the network vulnerability attribute analysis, the attacker may use the different vulnerability to carry on the attack, and the different attack will change with time [9]. Using the evolutionary computation method, a particle swarm optimization algorithm with time-varying weights is obtained, as follows: Set in t time, for any particle n cluster calculation, each particle has m individual gene, set here for three kinds of attack difficulty, respectively, the degree of difficulty, exposure and recoverable degree. The starting position of the attacker's injection point is regarded as a three-dimensional coordinate system. In the iterative process, the q_i position of the i-th particle is taken as a problem for detailed analysis [10].

Let the particle's initial velocity be V_0, and find the best position Z_i. For each particle motion, its r dimension attribute can be calculated by the following formula:

$$V_{i+1,r} = \omega V_{0r} + \varepsilon(Z_{ir} - P_{ir}) \tag{3}$$

$$Z_{i+1,r} = Z_{ir} + V_{i+1,r} \tag{4}$$

In formulas (3) and (4), ε represents the learning coefficient; P_i is the probability of use. Since the fast convergence can be achieved only when the inertia coefficient ω is between 0–1, the value is determined according to the attack situation. In the case of this attack, there are a total of M vulnerabilities. When the network vulnerabilities are exposed to a large degree, the degree of repair will become larger, and the vulnerability will be more difficult to apply, and the use probability will decrease with time. Therefore, probability is used as the initial weight to meet the actual convergence criteria. The weight of the vulnerability is multiplied by the probability, and the result is regarded as the result of the attack, which completes the analysis of the attack injection point.

3.3 Network Internal Attack Detection Process

After all the unknown attack types are determined, the network internal attack behavior detection process is designed. Take the user access request as the input data, and realize the detection of network internal attack behavior through machine learning. The specific process is as follows:

Step 1: Network internal attack source tracking.

The consistency index is determined by evaluating network attack quantitatively, and the adaptive collaborative tracing mechanism based on network entropy is established. During the tracking process, the global tracking task is decomposed into several local tracking tasks to achieve fast tracking. The key of using network entropy to track network attack is to control cooperative granularity. Too fine granularity can increase the complexity of single tracking task and the false alarm rate. But the coarse granularity will reduce the use of tracking information and reduce the reliability of the system. The monitoring agents send query tracking packets to each other to achieve the purpose of gathering and sharing information tracking.

Step 2: Hash the function to ensure that the data set is complete and not tampered with. Function hash value calculation process: the input length is not fixed, given function $y = h(x)$. The hash value of the function ranges from 224 bits to 512 bits and is looped 80 times. The data in this restricted range is not tampered with, and has integrity and usage security.

Step 3: Automatic point-to-point acceptance based on machine learning alert windows.

Step 3.1: The scheduling structure of the alarm window action description and text color features to organize the formation of XML format alarm window configuration instructions. The signal behavior description in the alarm window is divided into 0 and 1 values, and the remote value 0 in the alert window configuration description file can be described as interrupt and reversal.

The remote value 1 can be described as closing and action. The signal alarm mainly has four levels, namely, rapid change alarm, over limit alarm, abnormal behavior alarm and accident alarm. The level setting is related to the color of the text in the alarm window. Therefore, in the alarm window configuration document, set the RGB color parameter to indicate different signal alarm levels.

Step 3.2: Preprocess the screenshot of the alarm window, extract the point signal of the screenshot of the alarm window, and refresh the lower half of the window image in real time.

Step 3.3: Identify the image in the bottom half of the alert window and the text information in each row of alert window.

Step 3.4: See if the image text recognition results in the bottom half of the alert window contain the same information as the signal description for matching: the signal is correct when the recognition results have the same information as the matched signal. When the recognition result is different from the signal to be matched, the signal cannot be matched, which completes the network internal attack signal recognition.

Step 4: Correct the identification of unknown attack types within the perceived frequency band of possible network attack behaviors. Take the user's request to access the wireless network data set as the input data, analyze and generate the unknown attack type, and the correction items are:

$$\lambda = A \times B \tag{5}$$

In formula (5), A represents the accuracy of classification of input data by block chain technology at the stage of recording account book; B represents the discrimination result of attack behavior in input data set by block chain technology at the stage of reasonableness verification, and if the judgment result is 1, it indicates that the attack type is unknown; otherwise, it is 0.

The generating process of the unknown attack behavior type discriminant mainly includes two processes, one is to record the clustering process of accounting stage as input data, the other is to get the discrimination process of accounting stage. In order to obtain the central data needed in the stage of recording account book and the judgment process, the data set of the judgment process is identified as the data set of the input attack behavior.

Step 4.1: Data clustering.

In this stage, all the data are divided into two parts, one is chosen randomly and the other is divided into two parts. Let $U = \{u_1, u_2, \cdots, u_j\}$ represent the unmarked data set in the set, and within this data set, it is divided into n subsets after classification, and the minimum average error is calculated according to the following formula:

$$e_{\min} = \underset{c}{\arg\min} \sum_{i=1}^{k} \sum_{u_j \in c} \left\| u_j - z_i^t \right\|^2 \tag{6}$$

In formula (6): c means cluster parameter; z_i^t means average vector of all samples in cluster. This process is repeated until the set number of clusters is satisfied. The data of the cluster is taken as the optimal data, and the center point of the cluster is recorded.

The specific process of clustering is as follows:

In the assignment stage, if the samples meet the clustering conditions, the data will be divided into the cluster set; In the update stage, each cluster center will be updated, and the distance from each center will be analyzed until the parameters no longer change.

Adopt the Schwarz information guidelines:

$$BI = P'_m - \frac{P_m}{2} \lg m \tag{7}$$

In formula (7): P'_m represents the corresponding log likelihood probability when the number of clusters is m; P_m is a posteriori probability. The larger the calculation result of the above formula, the more obvious the data clustering.

Step 4.2: Attack behavior discrimination.

Euclidean distance was used as the distance measure of clustering process, and the distance from the input data to the center of each cluster was calculated. If the minimum cluster distance is greater than the maximum distance between two points in the cluster, then the cluster contains a certain number of similar nodes, and the similar nodes are all unknown attacks.

According to the result, the understanding mapping elements related to situation element are extracted to evaluate and predict the risk of large-scale network internal attack detection.

The formula for detecting internal attacks on large-scale networks can be:

$$f_i = \frac{\omega_i \times d}{u_1} \tag{8}$$

In formula (8), ω_i represents the weight; d refers to information assets; u_1 denotes network attack threat respectively. Considering the weight of each index, the detection value of large-scale network internal attack is obtained, and then the detection of large-scale network internal attack is realized. Based on this, the internal attack level of large-scale network is calculated as follows:

Network security standard: $f_i < 0.01$; The criteria for minor attacks within the network are: $0.01 < f_i < 0.25$; The criteria for moderate attacks within the network are: $0.25 < f_i < 0.50$ the internal network is seriously attacked. The standard is $0.50 < f_i < 0.10$. At this time, the network is completely paralyzed.

4 Experiment

4.1 Examples of Experimental Vulnerabilities

In the application of broadband access, RADIUS server is used as the authentication server to improve the efficiency and performance of authentication service, because of the weak performance of handling a large number of complex authentication. Also, when the authentication point completes authentication via a remote authentication server, the authentication point also runs as a RADIUS client, as shown in Fig. 2.

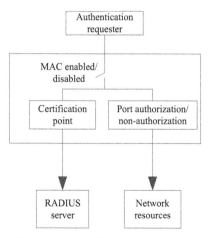

Fig. 2. Radius client running process

The authentication requester PAE submits the user's authentication information to the authentication point PAE, and they communicate with each other using EAPOL (EAP Over LANS). The authentication point PAE encapsulates the received authentication information in the EAP/RADIUS mode (namely, loading the EAP information on the RADIUS message and then encapsulating the actual RADIUS message in the UDP message for transmission through the P protocol), and sends it to the RADIUS server for authentication. The authentication point PAE controls the state of the port based on the authentication result of the RADIUS server to control whether the user connected to the port can access network resources.

During the above run, the resulting vulnerability description is shown in Table 1.

Table 1. Vulnerability description

Number	Name	Reason	Describe
1	Message integrity attack vulnerability	There are some integrity protections for messages without client management attributes, and attackers can destroy messages	Frequently, the transmitted protocol message or message cannot be processed normally
2	Server own memory overflow vulnerability	Vulnerability server own memory overflow vulnerability	Exception occurred in the server. There is a superuser rights manager
3	Billing error vulnerability	An attacker may steal an account	The attacker may steal the account
4	Negotiation defect	Hackers exploit negotiable opportunities in authentication mode to attack targets	You can only use the worst security method for authentication
5	One way authentication vulnerability	It only provides one-way authentication from the access authenticator to the access requestor, but does not provide an authentication mechanism from the access requestor to the access authenticator	The server often fails to give correct response information

In order to test whether the large-scale network attack detection method based on machine learning achieves the target, the semi-supervised learning and deep learning methods are used as the control.

4.2 Experimental Parameters and Environment

For the vulnerabilities described above, analyze the attacked path, as shown in Fig. 3.

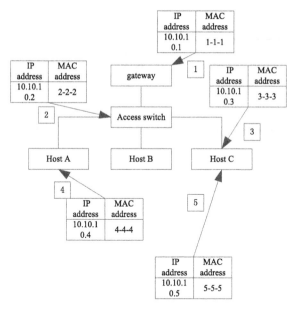

Fig. 3. Vulnerability attack path

In order to ensure the reliability of the experimental results, the experimental environment is set as follows:

(1) The node represents that the external network host enters into the intrusive subnet host.

(2) The network environment is mainly provided by the server, database server, administrator and intranet server. The database server mainly provides database services. The administrator is responsible for protecting the server, data server and management personnel, and storing important documents.

(3) When accessing internal network nodes, external network nodes need to go through firewalls. The firewall only allows external network nodes to access the Web server and does not allow other internal network servers.

(4) An external network node needs to go through a firewall when it accesses an internal network node, and the firewall only allows the external network node to access the Web server, while other internal network servers do not.

The test dataset comes from Kolias, which is the most comprehensive and real network attack dataset collected in wireless network environment. The dataset is divided into CLS dataset and ATK dataset. The AWID dataset in ATK dataset belongs to the masking attack type of CLS dataset. The AWID dataset contains the complete dataset and the condensed dataset. The distribution is shown in Table 2.

Table 2. Data set distribution

Types of attacks	Training data set	Test data set
Normal behavior	563129	59784
Camouflage attack behavior	38420	18230
Flooding attack	22556	22215
Injection attack behavior	43021	15850
Total	667126	116079

4.3 Experimental Index

The detection indicators are mainly recall and precision. The formula is as follows:

$$R = \frac{T}{T + N} \tag{9}$$

$$P = \frac{T}{T + F} \tag{10}$$

In formulas (9) and (10), T means that there is an attack on the identification result, and there is an attack on the actual situation; N means that there is no attack on the identification result, but there is an attack on the actual situation; F means that there is an attack on the identification result, but there is no attack on the actual situation.

An AUC curve is used to check each pair of features including all data sets, as shown in Fig. 4.

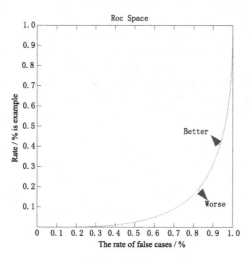

Fig. 4. AUC curve

It can be seen from Fig. 5 that the curve passes through (0,0) and (1,1). The AUC value is the area under the curve. The larger the AUC value, the more stable the data attribute is. According to the indicators in Fig. 5, the selected experimental data are stable.

4.4 Experimental Results and Analysis

Vulnerability Tracking
For the above five vulnerability points, semi supervised learning, deep learning detection and machine learning detection methods are used to compare and analyze whether the vulnerability tracking path is consistent with the actual path. The comparison results are shown in Fig. 5.

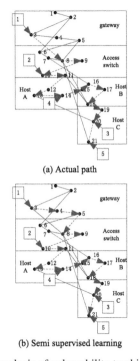

(a) Actual path

(b) Semi supervised learning

Fig. 5. Comparison and analysis of vulnerability tracking paths of three methods

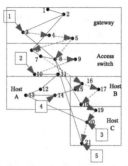

(c) Deep learning detection method

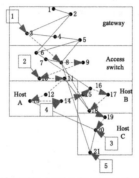

(d) Machine learning detection method

Fig. 5. (*continued*)

As shown in Fig. 6, the vulnerability tracking path using the semi-supervised learning approach is 3-4-5-8-9-10-11-12-13-14-15-16-17-18-19-20-21; the vulnerability tracking path using the deep learning approach is 3-4-5-6-6-16-17-18-20-21; and the vulnerability tracking path using the machine learning approach is 3-8-9-10-11-12-13-15-15-16-18-19-20. Only vulnerability tracking paths using machine learning detection methods are closer to actual paths 3-8-9-10-11-12-13-14-15-16-17-18-19-20-21.

According to the above analysis results, the vulnerability tracking results using machine learning detection method are more accurate.

Recall Rate

The recall comparison results of the three methods are shown in Fig. 6.

It can be seen from Fig. 6 that the highest recall rate using semi supervised learning is 79.8%; Using deep learning, the highest recall rate was 58%; The highest recall rate of machine learning method is 93%. Therefore, the recall rate of machine learning based method is high.

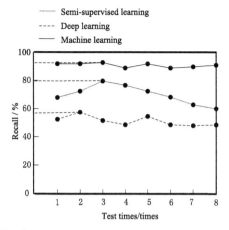

Fig. 6. Comparison of recall rate of three methods

Precision

The comparison results of the three methods are shown in Table 3.

Table 3. Comparative analysis of the accuracy of the three methods

Test times/times	Semi-supervised learning	Deep learning	Machine learning
1	0.59	0.72	0.94
2	0.58	0.77	0.95
3	0.55	0.73	0.95
4	0.57	0.74	0.93
5	0.56	0.73	0.96
6	0.58	0.71	0.95
7	0.59	0.70	0.96
8	0.54	0.75	0.98

As can be seen from Table 3, using semi-supervised learning, the precision rate is the lowest, followed by deep learning, and machine learning has the highest precision rate of 0.98. Thus, using machine-learning-based method is more accurate.

5   Conclusion

Research on large-scale network attack detection based on machine learning can detect network anomalies and known attacks, which has been studied at home and abroad. This method establishes a large-scale network internal attack detection model to analyze the internal attack degree. After determining the attack target, trace the attack source inside the network. Euclidean distance method is used to distinguish attacks, and the calculation results are divided into large-scale network internal attack levels. This method enhances the flexibility of network defense, can be deployed on virtual or physical hosts, can actively carry out network attacks, and record attacks. This "active" behavior makes up for the shortcomings of the traditional passive system, and combines its advantages, which can greatly improve the effectiveness of network security protection.

References

1. Du, R., Wei, D., Li, L., et al.: SAR target detection network via semi-supervised learning. J. Electron. Inf. Technol. **42**(01), 154–163 (2020)
2. Li, P.W., Jiang, Y.Q., Xue, F.Y., et al.: A robust approach for android malware detection based on deep learning. Acta Electronica Sinica **48**(08), 1502–1508 (2020)
3. Liu, L.M., Li, Q.Y., Hao, C., et al.: Intelligent tracking technology for communication network attack path based on abnormal traffic visualization. Sci. Technol. Eng. **19**(11), 230–235 (2019)
4. Yin, R.R., Zhang, W.Y., Yang, S., et al.: A selective forwarding attacks detection approach based on multi-hop acknowledgment and trust evaluation. Control Decis. **35**(04), 184–190 (2020)
5. Liu, S., Liu, D.Y., Muhammad, K., Weiping, D.: Effective template update mechanism in visual tracking with background clutter. Neurocomputing **458**, 615–625 (2021)
6. Ding, S.J., Xie, J.: Cross-network user dynamic bi-directional identity accurate authentication simulation. Comput. Simul. **36**(01), 300–303396 (2019)
7. Liu, S., Wang, S., Liu, X.Y., et al.: Human memory update strategy: a multi-layer template update mechanism for remote visual monitoring. IEEE Trans. Multimedia **23**, 2188–2198 (2021)
8. Liu, S., Wang, S., Liu, X.Y., et al.: Fuzzy detection aided real-time and robust visual tracking under complex environments. IEEE Trans. Fuzzy Syst. **29**(1), 90–102 (2021)
9. Wang, K.Y., Wei, L.N., Tian, E.G., et al.: Memory-event-triggered control of networked control systems subject to DoS attacks. Inf. Control **48**(05), 528–535 (2019)
10. Ding, S.H., Xie, J.C., Zhang, P., et al.: Dynamic migration method of key virtual network function based on risk awareness. J. Commun. **41**(04), 102–113 (2020)

Federated Community Detection in Social Networks

Zhiwei Zheng[1], Zekai Chen[1], Ximeng Liu[1(✉)], and Nan Jiang[2]

[1] College of Computer and Data Science, Fuzhou University, Fuzhou 350108, China
snbnix@gmail.com
[2] Department of Internet of Things, East China Jiao Tong University,
Jiangxi 334000, China

Abstract. Community detection is an effective approach to unveiling relationships among individuals in social networks. Detecting communities without privacy leakage remains an area of ongoing and indispensable focus. Therefore, anonymization and differential privacy based community detection methods are proposed to protect the privacy of social network information. However, the above methods cause inevitable accuracy loss in some way, resulting in the low utility in the final community division. In this paper, we propose a secure and efficient interaction protocol based on homomorphic encryption to find the index of the maximum value of encrypted floating-point numbers. Besides, we design a novel federated community detection framework, using user-server interactions to adjust and construct global optimal community division results, which could not only get an effective community division model but also guarantee strong privacy preservation. Through theoretical analysis and empirical experiments, the time cost of our proposed secure protocol is 4× faster than previous works. Meanwhile, our framework ensures modularity error in the range of 0.03 comparing with the plaintext framework, and modularity improves at least 0.3 with 3 other state-of-the-art privacy-preserving community detection schemes.

Keywords: Community detection · Federated learning · Homomorphic encryption · Privacy-preserving

1 Introduction

In the era of big data, graph data modeled as complex networks have been widely used in many fields, such as knowledge map [1], device management [2], social network [3,4]. The social network represents the social relationship between various individuals and organizations. With the fast advancements in internet technology, a great number of social apps can mine more valuable community information. Thus, the exploration of community information from social networks has attracted much attention in both academic and industrial fields. In the past few years, a large number of traditional algorithms [5–7] have been proposed in different community detection (CD) scenarios. These algorithms mainly work

© The Author(s), under exclusive license to Springer Nature Switzerland AG 2023
Y. Xu et al. (Eds.): ML4CS 2022, LNCS 13656, pp. 89–103, 2023.
https://doi.org/10.1007/978-3-031-20099-1_8

on some directed/undirected, weighted/unweighted, and uncertain graphs to dig potential community relationships [8]. CD algorithms usually require the collection of users' personal information and social links. However, traditional CD algorithms focus on network topologies only [9]. In practice, third-party agents collect social networks information from users for different purposes. The information may contain user sensitive characteristics and attributes. If user private data is directly sent to third parties, it may be leaked and suffer inference attack, which can result in significant privacy accidents. For example, Facebook was accused of leaking millions of users' community relationships information without their authorization in 2018. Therefore, how to realize the privacy-preserving has become one of the biggest problems in social networks for CD.

In order to alleviate the privacy concerns, some previous works have attempted to address it, which mainly is categorized as anonymization techniques and differential privacy (DP) based schemes. Generally speaking, three categories of privacy threats in the social network are recognized as disclosure of identity, disclosure of the attribute, and link disclosure [10]. Anonymization techniques protect users' privacy through graph modification techniques. However, as it can be vulnerable to de-anonymization techniques [11], the attribute and link information may still be inferred in some situations. DP technique for community detection is classified as input perturbation and algorithm perturbation [12]. The method of adding noise to protect user information in input perturbation will cause serious damage to the network topologys. This will eventually lead to the excessive loss of graphic structure information and seriously affect the utility of the community detection results [13,14]. Another DP scheme by the algorithm perturbation [15] only tries to protect the privacy of network topologies while ignoring the sensitive information of users, which brings users' private personal information safety risks. Homomorphic encryption (HE) [16] is a promising solution to avoid privacy leakage risks while protecting data integrity and confidentiality. Recently, HE tools are added to the Federated Learning (FL) framework [17] against these schemes becomes the research hotspot, but the scheme usually leads to incurring expensive calculations due to the great number of encryption and decryption operations. Therefore, how to keep high efficiency and less performance loss under this framework at the same time is still a challenging and open problem.

In this paper, we propose a community detection framework called Federated Community Detection in social networks (FedCD) framework. To ensure community detection with both security and accuracy, we design a federated community detection graph algorithm model over encrypted best model parameters to construct global best communities. In this framework, due to the good evaluation of modularity (Q) in the Louvain algorithm, we choose it as the basis of the CD method. When executing Louvain algorithm, the total number of queries on the Q and the times of community adjustment will increase sharply with the network scale. Therefore, we propose a more efficient secure argmax algorithm base on HE to address this problem. At the same time, appropriate refinements are also made to the existing Louvain algorithm to significantly reduce the total interaction times between data users and the centre server under FL. Our FedCD framework has the main contributions as follows:

- **Secure Floating Argmax Algorithm (SFAM):** We propose a more efficient SFAM, which finds the index of the maximum value of some encrypted floating-point numbers (FPNs). Besides, the protocol can be used not only in our proposed framework but also in other relevant application scenarios.
- **Federated Community Detection:** To the best of our knowledge, FedCD framework proposed in this paper is the first attempt to build a community detection network base on HE. Meanwhile, it can avoid privacy leakage risks while multi-user collaborative training obtains the best community partition without exposing their sensitive data.
- **Efficiency and Accuracy:** The performance analysis and experimental evaluation show our SFAM outperforms previous work in terms of the runtime and the communication overhead, which costs at least $4\times$ faster than previous work. Our FedCD ensures modularity error in range of 0.03 comparing with plaintext framework, and modularity improves at least 0.3 with 3 other state-of-the-art privacy-preserving CD schemes.

The rest of the paper is structured as follows. We introduce the related work in Sect. 2 and the necessary preliminaries in Sect. 3. Then we give the problem formulation in Sect. 4. Section 5 describes the framework of FedCD and its implementation details. Section 6 presents security analysis. Section 7 gives experimental analysis. Finally, Sect. 8 draws the conclusion.

2   Related Work

Early works focus on anonymization techniques such as k-anonymity [18] and l-diversity to construct privacy-preserving graph, but these methods have a limitations on protect all elements such as node information and link attribute [19]. Mohapatra et al. [20] presented another clustering-based privacy-preserving scheme to anonymize all of the node elements. However, the integrity of graph may be destroyed, this method is not appropriate for graph statistical metrics in local structures. Yuan et al. [21] presented the method based on edge add/delete or edge rotation in the original data to preserve against disclosure of graph information. However, above approaches are vulnerable to de-anonymization techniques [11]. Qian et al. [22] proposed a LSH based de-anonymization scheme and model attacker's knowledge to reveal the impact of user attributes on de-anonymization accuracy. Shao et al. [23] designed a novel low computation expense and effective seedless network de-anonymization scheme.

Recently, more and more DP based schemes have proposed to address the privacy issue in graph release. DK-Graph proposed in [24] can generate a set of structural statistics graph structure by original graph, then uses DK-series as input to produce a disturbance graph. More graph models under DP technique include Stochastic Kronecker Graph (SKG) model [25], Hierarchical Random Graph (HRG) [26], and L-opacity [27]. In principle, we can do any mining tasks on the graph after releasing it satisfying DP graph models. Nguyen et al. [28] proposed to use input perturbation on Louvain algorithm to deal with noisy super-graph called LouvainDP. Ye et al. [29] proposed the LFGDPR framework that can not only enable graph metric estimation of any subgraph but also ensure privacy-preserving data collection. Zhang et al. [30] proposed a local differential privacy community detection method (LDPCD). LDPCD refines the extremal optimization (EO) algorithm to adjust community partition between the sever and users.

3   Preliminary

In this section, we outline some important notation definitions and introduce some technologies. The notation definitions are shown in Table 1.

Table 1. Notation definitions in FedCD framework

Symbol	Definition
V	Set of nodes in graph G
E	Set of edges in graph G
c_i^v	The i-th node of the set of neighbor nodes of vertex v
Q	The estimated modularity of a community division
$Q_{c_i}^v$	Q of vertex v moving to neighbor community c_i^v
W_j	The total weight of the j-th Data users
pk, sk	A pair of public-private keys
sk_1, sk_2	Partial decrypted private keys
κ	The security parameter variable
p, q	p and q are two big primes, $\|p\| = \|q\| = \kappa$
N	N is a big integer satisfying $N = p \times q$
$[\![m]\!]$	Encrypted object of m with integer
$\langle m \rangle$	Encrypted object of m with FPN

3.1   Louvain Algorithm

The CD algorithm aims to divide groups with close internal associations and sparse external connections in social networks. Louvain is an algorithm based on Q optimization for CD. Therefore, each iteration of Louvain moves the node to the neighborhood community with the largest change in modularity, and through repeated iterations until the modularity converges.

Supporting a graph $G = \{V, E, W, C\}$, adjacency matrix of G as A, $k_i = \sum_{(i,j)\in E}(w_{i,j})$, and $\delta(c_i, c_j) = 1$ if $c_i = c_j$, otherwise $\delta(c_i, c_j) = 0$, where V is all vertices of G and E is the set of edges of G, we denote modularity as Q, which is given by:

$$Q = \frac{1}{2m} \sum_{i,j} (A_{i.j} - \frac{k_i \times k_j}{2m}) \delta(c_i, c_j) \qquad (1)$$

3.2 Two Trapdoors Public-Key Cryptosystem

Two trapdoors public-key cryptosystem contains five algorithms, which follows the idea in [31]. We briefly describe them as follows:

- $(pk, sk) \leftarrow KeyGen(k)$: Given a security parameter k and distinct odd prime numbers p, q, which satisfy $|p| = |q| = k$. Then we compute $N = p \times q$, $\lambda = lcm(p-1, q-1)$ and $g = -a^{2N}$, where $a \in \mathbb{Z}_{N^2}$ denotes a random number. We can represent key pair (pk, sk) by the tuple (N, g), where the public $pk = (N, g)$ and secret key $sk = \lambda$.
- $[\![m]\!]_{pk} \leftarrow Enc(m, pk)$: Given a message $m \in \mathbb{Z}_N$, the ciphertext is generated as $[\![m]\!]_{pk} = (1 + m \times N) \times r^N \mod N^2$, where $r \in \mathbb{Z}_N$ denotes a random number.
- $m \leftarrow Dec([\![m]\!]_{pk}, sk)$: Given a message $[\![m]\!]_{pk}$, we can use the secret key sk decrypt to obtain m, where $m = L\left([\![m]\!]^\lambda \mod N^2\right) \times \lambda^{-1} \mod N$ and $L(x) = \frac{x-1}{N}$.
- $(sk_1, sk_2) \leftarrow SkeyS(sk)$: The secret key sk is divided into two partial shares sk_1 and sk_2 satisfying $sk_1 + sk_2 \equiv 0 \mod \lambda$ and $sk_1 + sk_2 \equiv 1 \mod N^2$.
- $m \leftarrow SkeyDec([\![m]\!]_{pk}, sk_1, sk_2)$: Given a $[\![m]\!]_{pk}$, two parties that own partial secret key shares decrypt to obtain $[\![m]\!]^{(1)}$ and $[\![m]\!]^{(2)}$, respectively. Then, it outputs the decryption $[\![m]\!]$, where $m = L\left(([\![m]\!]^{(1)} + [\![m]\!]^{(2)}) \mod N^2\right)$.

4 Problem Formulation

In this section, we formalize the system model, define the threat model, and outline the design goals of FedCD, respectively.

4.1 System Model

FedCD framework comprises three kinds of entities, namely Key Generation Center ($\mathcal{KGC}$), Center Server ($\mathcal{CS}$) and Data User ($\mathcal{DU}$).

- $\mathcal{KGC}$: The fully trusted $\mathcal{KGC}$ is tasked with the distribution and management of both public and private keys in the system. $\mathcal{CS}$ and $\mathcal{DU}$s use distribution keys to construct optimal model.
- $\mathcal{CS}$: $\mathcal{CS}$ stores all the intermediate and final model parameters in encrypted form. $\mathcal{CS}$ receives the encrypted local optimal model from multiple $\mathcal{DU}$s to choose the encrypted global optimal model, then sends it to $\mathcal{DU}$s.
- $\mathcal{DU}$: $\mathcal{DU}$ provides limited community network graph data. $\mathcal{DU}$s participate in the calculation of local model and collaboratively construct a global model by submitting a local optimal model to $\mathcal{CS}$.

4.2 Attacker Model

In our attack model, we consider potential threats from internal entities and external adversary in multiple rounds of interaction between $\mathcal{CS}$ and $\mathcal{DU}$s.

- **Threats from internal entities:** The $\mathcal{KGC}$ is considered as a trusted entity to generate necessary public and private keys to $\mathcal{CS}$ and $\mathcal{DU}$s. On the other hand, $\mathcal{CS}$ and $\mathcal{DU}$s are curious-but-honest parties, which strictly follow the protocol but want to learn more data belonging to other parties. At the same time, we assume that there is no collusion between $\mathcal{CS}$ and $\mathcal{DU}$s.
- **Threats from external adversary:** We assume that the external adversary is able to eavesdrop all communications to obtain the encrypted data between $\mathcal{CS}$ and $\mathcal{DU}$s. The adversary can compromise $\mathcal{CS}$ or $\mathcal{DU}$s to obtain access to their decryption capabilities, but it is restricted from compromising both $\mathcal{CS}$ and $\mathcal{DU}$s concurrently.

4.3   Design Goals

Our FedCD framework mainly is designed with the following goals:

- **Security.** (a) Algorithm toolkit provides secure privacy assurance. (b) The intermediate computation results and local model parameters cannot be leaked during BuildGlobalLouvain.
- **Accuracy.** The proposed protocols in our framework strictly follow the greedy approach of Louvain algorithm, thus the result returning from $\mathcal{CS}$ is always correct.
- **Efficiency.** Our protocols maintain relatively low communication, computing and storage overhead, regardless of the $\mathcal{CS}$ or $\mathcal{DU}$.

5   FedCD Framework

In this section, we present the details of SFAM protocol and how to construct a basic FedCD framework. Other basis protocols contain such as SADD, SFADD, and SFDIV.

5.1   Secure FPN Argmax

We focus on describing our proposed SFAM protocol in this paper. First, we present FPN as $\mathcal{F} = (\mathcal{S}, \mathcal{B}, \mathcal{E})$. Among them, $\mathcal{S}$, $\mathcal{B}$, and $\mathcal{E}$ respectively represent mantissa of FPN, base of FPN, and exponent of FPN. In general, we set $\mathcal{B} = 16$. On this basis, we introduce a framework for computation toolkit on FPN, such as SADD, SFADD, and SFDIV can be found in the [31].

As presented in Algorithm 1, SFAM protocol is to realize that securely compute the result of the maximum index of two encrypted FPNs ($\langle u \rangle$ and $\langle v \rangle$) . For convenience, we denote SFADD as $\langle \cdot \rangle \times \langle \cdot \rangle$, SADD as $[\cdot] \times [\cdot]$. The overall steps of SFAM protocol are shown in Algorithm 1.

Step 1: To confuse the calculation result, $\mathcal{CS}$ generates coins to decide the operation performed (line 1). At the same time, the corresponding secure masked index difference is generated, which is $[I_v - I_u + r]_{pk}$ or $[I_u - I_v + r]_{pk}$. The above operations are executed that corresponds to line 2–8 in Algorithm 1.

Algorithm 1. Secure floating argmax protocol (SFAM)

Require: Encrypted $\langle u \rangle_{pk}$ and $\langle v \rangle_{pk}$, $[I_u]_{pk}$ and $[I_v]_{pk}$.

1: **In** $\mathcal{CS}$:   generates random coin $\in \{0, 1\}$.
2: **if** coin $== 1$ **then**
3:      $\langle l \rangle_{pk} \leftarrow (\langle u \rangle_{pk} \times \langle v \rangle_{pk}^{N-1})^r = \langle r(u - v) \rangle_{pk}$.
4:      $[I_t]_{pk} \leftarrow [I_v]_{pk} \times [I_u]_{pk}^{N-1} \times [r]_{pk} = [I_v - I_u + r]_{pk}$.
5: **else**
6:      $\langle l \rangle_{pk} \leftarrow (\langle v \rangle_{pk} \times \langle u \rangle_{pk}^{N-1})^r = \langle r(v - u) \rangle_{pk}$.
7:      $[I_t]_{pk} \leftarrow [I_u]_{pk} \times [I_v]_{pk}^{N-1} \times [r]_{pk} = [I_u - I_v + r]_{pk}$.
8: **end if**
9: **In** $\mathcal{DU}$: l greater than $\frac{N}{2}$ expressed negative number.
10: **if** compareTo$(l, \frac{N}{2}) == -1$ **then**
11:      $([U]_{pk}, [D]_{pk}) \leftarrow ([0]_{pk}, [0]_{pk})$.
12: **else**
13:      $([U]_{pk}, [D]_{pk}) \leftarrow ([1]_{pk}, [I_t]_{pk})$.
14: **end if**
15: **In** $\mathcal{CS}$:   use the same way to get max encrypted FPN.
16: **if** coin $== 1$ **then**
17:      $[I_{max}]_{pk} \leftarrow [I_u]_{pk} \times [D]_{pk} \times [U]_{pk}^{-r}$.
18: **else**
19:      $[I_{max}]_{pk} \leftarrow [I_v]_{pk} \times [D]_{pk} \times [U]_{pk}^{-r}$.
20: **end if**
21: **return** $\langle max \rangle_{pk}$ and $[I_{max}]_{pk}$.

Step 2: Firstly, $\mathcal{DU}$ receives $\langle l \rangle$ and $[I_t]$, and partial decrypts $\langle l \rangle$ by sk_2 to get revealed value. When $\langle l \rangle_{pk}$ is revealed in $\mathcal{DU}$, in [31] the properties will be followed: $l > \frac{N}{2}$, $l < \frac{N}{2}$, and $l = \frac{N}{2}$, which respectively indicates that revealed number is less than zero, equal to zero, and greater than zero, respectively (line 10). According to the comparison between l and $\frac{N}{2}$, $\mathcal{DU}$ produces the corresponding $[U]_{pk}$ and $[D]_{pk}$ (line 11–14), and sends them to $\mathcal{CS}$.

Step 3: Based on random coin tossed, $\mathcal{CS}$ chooses corresponding $[I]$ (line 16). And it does secure addition with $[D]$ and $[U]$ to get SFAM result that corresponds to line 17–20 in Algorithm 1.

5.2   Overall Framework Design

The overall framework of FedCD is shown in Fig. 1. Our setting is typically referred as vertical FL. As each $\mathcal{DU}$ possesses different network topologies, the process is mainly composed of two parts as follows:

- **Key generation and distribution:** $\mathcal{KGC}$ invokes *KeyGen* algorithm to generate (pk, sk). $\mathcal{KGC}$ distributes $\{sk_1, pk\}$ to $\mathcal{CS}$ and $\{sk_2, pk\}$ to $\mathcal{DU}s$.
- **Secure Community Construction:** With key generated and distributed, BuildLocalLouvain and BuildGlobalLouvain algorithms take an iterative process to construct a global optimal model. The process consists of three steps as

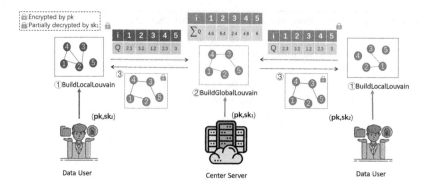

Fig. 1. FedCD framework.

follows: (**Step 1**) $\mathcal{DU}s$ train the local model to pick out the optimal community information for node consolidation and encrypt modularity (Q) of community partition information before sending them to $\mathcal{CS}$ by BuildLocalLouvain algorithm. (**Step 2**) $\mathcal{CS}$ invokes BuildGlobalLouvain algorithm to choose the optimal global community partition from the local optimal community information node. (**Step 3**) $\mathcal{CS}$ sends the optimal community partition to each $\mathcal{DU}$ and records the global model parameters. Each $\mathcal{DU}$ updates local model based on the optimal node information and proceeds to the next iteration.

5.3   Secure Community Construction

In order to accomplish secure community construction in real-world networks, we present FedCD that can not only accelerate to construct high quality communities in each $\mathcal{DU}$, but also find the best community partition according to Q of $\mathcal{DU}s$' all vertexes.

BuildLocalLouvain Suppose that threshold is represented as τ, the j-th ($j \in 1; N$) $\mathcal{DU}s$ sends encrypted locally optimal partition and the evaluation Q_j of each vertex to $\mathcal{CS}$, where $\Delta Q_j \geq 0$. For the j-th ($j \in [1; N]$) $\mathcal{DU}s$, the best community partition is selected by maximization of ΔQ. Modularity, is the gain in modularity obtained by moving an isolated vertex u into a community $c \in C$ [5]. Before introducing BuildLocalLouvain, we define ReBuildGraph graph rebuilt, by merging all vertices within the community into a single meta-vertex, and continuing the process until there is no significant change in Q between consecutive phases, and Modularity is calculated by Eq. 1. Briefly, the BuildLocalLouvain consists of the following:

Step 1: Each $\mathcal{DU}$ calculates the optimal community partition for each vertex by ReBuildGraph. Before this, we can define W_j is the total weight of the j-th $\mathcal{DU}s$, and $Q_{c_i}^v$ that it is Modularity of vertex v moving to neighbor community c_i^v multiplied by W_j. First, each vertex attempts to move to its neighbors' communities. In addtion, the j-th $\mathcal{DU}s$ can calculate $Q_{c_i}^v$ and W_j, and encrypts $Q_{c_i}^v$,

c_i^v, and W_j into $\langle Q_{c_i}^v \rangle^j$, $[I_{c_i}^v]$, and $[W_j]$. Finally, each $\mathcal{DU}$ sends them to $\mathcal{CS}$ to get the best partition.

Step 2: $\mathcal{CS}$ gets best partition by collaboratively all $\mathcal{DU}$s' encrypted data to construct the global best community partition. Afterward, $\mathcal{CS}$ calculates the best partition, and broadcasts partial decrypted the best partition $[I_m]$ and maximum $\langle Q_g \rangle$ by sk_1 to each $\mathcal{DU}$.

Step 3: In each $\mathcal{DU}$, it receives encrypted data broadcast from $\mathcal{CS}$, and decrypts them by sk_2. Afterward, each $\mathcal{DU}$ updates local community partition by global community partition, and it compares ΔQ_j and τ_j. If $\Delta Q_j \geq \tau_j$, the j-th $\mathcal{DU}$s update Q. Otherwise, each $\mathcal{DU}$ continues to find the best community partition. When all vertexes are partitioned once, the graph is reconstructed, and steps are repeated until the Q of the reconstructed graph remains unchanged.

BuildGlobalLouvain. Before introducing BuildGlobalLouvain, we have designed SFAM to compare encrypted data to find the maximum $\langle Q_g \rangle$ between $\{\langle Q_0^v \rangle \cdots \langle Q_i^v \rangle\}$ in vertex v of all $\mathcal{DU}$s to get $\langle Q_g \rangle$ for global optimization community partition. The specific process is shown as follows:

Algorithm 2. BuildGlobalLouvain

Require: Encrypted data from all $\mathcal{DU}$s.
1: //enumerate vertex v of all $\mathcal{DU}$s
2: //n is number of neighbor community of v
3: **for** $i = 0$ to n **do**
4:     $\langle Q_i^v \rangle = \sum_{j=1}^{k} \langle Q_{c_i}^v \rangle^j$, where k is number of $\mathcal{DU}$s.
5: **end for**
6: $[I_m] = [0]$.
7: $\langle Q_m^v \rangle = \langle Q_0^v \rangle$.
8: **for** $i = 1$ to n **do**
9:     $\langle Q_m^v \rangle, [I_m] = \mathsf{SFAM}(\langle Q_i^v \rangle, \langle Q_m^v \rangle, [I_i], [I_m])$.
10: **end for**
11: $\langle Q_g \rangle = \frac{\langle Q_m^v \rangle}{\sum_{j=1}^{k} \langle W_j \rangle}$, where k is number of $\mathcal{DU}$s.
12: Send $\langle Q_g \rangle$ and $[I_m]$ to all $\mathcal{DU}$s.

Computing with SFAM, $\mathcal{CS}$ can choose the globally optimal partition according to each $\mathcal{DU}$' partition (line 3–11). Then, global optimal results $\langle Q_g \rangle$ and $[I_m]$ will be sent to each $\mathcal{DU}$ as the best optimal partition (line 12). The specific process of global optimal CD is shown in Algorithm 2. Once receiving the global optimal CD $[I_m]$, each $\mathcal{DU}$ builds the j-th communities partition with the global optimal CD after decryption to obtain I_m and Q_g. Then, each $\mathcal{DU}$ will rebuilt graph, by merging all vertices within a community into a single meta-vertex, and until $\Delta Q < \tau$. After that, each $\mathcal{DU}$ will obtain locally optimal CD. This process is iterated until an optimal CD is reached.

6   Security Analysis

In this section, we will analyze the security of all protocols involved in FedCD. In particular, the theorem will describe the security of the FedCD against various potential adversaries.

Definition 1. *We manipulate the simulator Sim to interact with the adversary $\mathcal{A}$ to simulate the interaction of $\mathcal{A}$ with the real world, and use Sim to perform real-world operations. We assume that Π represents the executed protocol, $\langle x \rangle$ and $[y]$ are private inputs to Sim, and $\equiv_c$ represents computational indistinguishability. We assume that FedCD is secure, then we have $\{\text{IDEAL}_{\Pi,\text{sim}}(\langle x \rangle, [y])\} \equiv_c \{\text{REAL}_{\Pi,\text{A}}(\langle x \rangle, [y])\}$.*

Lemma 1. *If a protocol is fully simulatable, then all subprotocols it involves are also simulatable.*

Lemma 2. *The protocol of SFADD, SADD and two trapdoors public-key cryptosystem are semantically safe in a semi-honest model.*

Theorem 1. *Against semi-honest adversaries $\mathcal{A} = (\mathcal{A}_{CS}, \mathcal{A}_{DU})$, the protocol SFAM is secure.*

Proof. Phase 1: For Sim_{CS}, $\text{view}^1_{CS} = (\langle x \rangle, \langle y \rangle, \langle l \rangle, [I_x], [I_y], [I_t])$ will be executed in SFAM. According to Lemma 2, it is trivial to see that we can acquire $\langle l \rangle$ and $[I_t]$ by SFADD and SADD protocols. *Phase 2*: Then, Sim_{DU}' view $\text{view}_{DU} = (\langle l \rangle, [I_t])$ in SFAM will be executed. Due to l and I_t are hidden by random number, its maintain security while its are revealed. Besides, Sim_{DU} adpots revealed l to choose $[U]$ and $[D]$ by obfuscation. *Phase 3*: For Sim_{CS}, the executed view can be expressed as $\text{view}^2_{CS} = ([U], [D])$. According to Lemma 2, it is trivial to see that the process of $[I_{max}]$ and $[max]$ being acquired is secure.

Theorem 2. *Against semi-honest adversaries $\mathcal{A} = (\mathcal{A}_{CS}, \mathcal{A}_{DU})$, Our proposed FedCD is secure.*

Proof. Phase 1: From Sim_{DU}, in each iteration of BuildLocalLouvain, each DU calculates Q locally, and the j-th DU encrypts its local best $\langle Q^v_{c_i} \rangle^j$ and corresponding label $[I]^j$. Obviously, encrypted data has been proved. *Phase 2:* In BuildGlobalLouvain, view_{CS} of $\mathcal{A}_{CS}$ is defined as $\{(\langle Q^v_{c_i} \rangle, [I])\}^N_{j=1}$. The Sim_{CS} adopts SFADD to obtain secure aggregated result of $\langle Q^v_i \rangle$. Obviously, due to Lemma 2, it still owns semantic security. Besides, Sim_{CS} computes $\langle Q^v_m \rangle$ and $[I_m]$ by SFAM. Since the security of SFAM has been proven, this process is equally secure. Finally, global $\langle Q_g \rangle$ is obtained by CS. Due to Lemma 2, this procession will be performed safely in semi-honest model. *Phase 3:* $\mathcal{A}_{DU}$ will get intermediate results $\{\langle Q_g \rangle, I_m\}$ in each round of interaction with CS. Sim_{DU} receives $\mathcal{A}_{DU}$'s inputs $\{\langle Q_g \rangle, I_m\}$ and returns next iterator of encrypted data. Due to Lemma 2, we can consider the view to be indistinguishable in real and ideal execution.

7   Experiments Analysis

In this section, we present detailed experimental results and corresponding analysis of our framework with regard to HE based argmax protocol and FedCD framework.

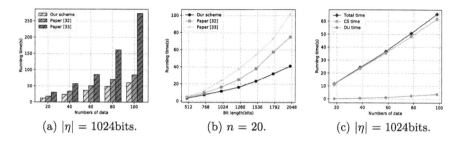

(a) $|\eta| = 1024$bits.   (b) $n = 20$.   (c) $|\eta| = 1024$bits.

Fig. 2. Performance of SFAM protocol.

7.1   Performance of SFAM Protocol

To validate the potency of SFAM, we implement [32,33] protocols to compare them to our SFAM. We can optimize the performance of secure argmax scheme. Without loss of generality, we estimate the computational costs, measured in terms of required secure addition with HE (sadd.), secure comparison with HE (scomp.) and comparison with plaintext (comp.) operations. Here n denotes the number of data, and T denotes the time of operation. The results are shown in Table 2. Having shown the performance of [32,33], the computation cost of secure argmax per iteration mainly depends on two parameters: (i) the number of data, (ii) the number of operations, (iii) the bit length of encrypted data.

Due to [32] comparison of each data, it can hardly avoid expensive security comparisons. Also, it applies a random permutation before the secure comparison, which makes secure argmax inefficient and risk of leaking privacy from each $\mathcal{DU}$ to negotiate a reasonable permutation. More specifically, [33] compares data and accumulates the comparison results. Once decrypted, the position of the only non-zero value is result of secure argmax. Thus, fewer operations and independence between $\mathcal{DU}$s make our protocol efficient computational perspective.

To show the effectiveness of SFAM, we first evaluate their computation cost using different sampled datasets of varying sizes. From Fig. 3(a), we observe that the computation time of [33] is around $4\times$ than our protocol due to T_{sscomp}. Also, the running time of [32] is in few milliseconds (since [32] doesn't involve in even more expensive operations), which makes its protocol more efficient computational perspective. However, the running time of our protocol grows linearly with n, and it costs $\frac{1}{4}\times$, $\frac{2}{3}\times$ less than [32,33], respectively.

In order to pursue higher precision calculation, we show the performance of three schemes in Fig. 3(b). The running time of our scheme increases with the growth of bit length $|\eta|$. The reason is that the cost of the HE operation will increase accordingly. Besides, the running time of [33] has an important influence with the vary of $|\eta|$.

This is due to the fact that almost more time is being spent in [33]' T_{scomp} than [32]' T_{sadd}, and more operations than [32]. T_{scomp} is a more time-consuming operation than T_{sadd}. One can notice that the performance of our SFAM is noticeably faster than [32,33], under different bit lengths.

Table 2. Comparison of the SFAM protocol complexities.

Protocol	Computational complexity
Our SFAM	$\mathcal{O}((n-1)T_{comp} + 5(n-1)T_{sadd})$
[32]	$\mathcal{O}((n-1)T_{scomp} + 5(n-1)T_{sadd})$
[33]	$\mathcal{O}((n^2-n)T_{sadd} + n^2 T_{scomp})$

With setting of $|\eta| = 1024$, Fig. 3(c) demonstrates the consumption of time between $\mathcal{CS}$ and each $\mathcal{DU}$ in our SFAM. With the numbers of data n growing, the running time in each $\mathcal{DU}$ keeps basically unchanged. The reason is that $\mathcal{CS}$ undertakes most of the ciphertext calculation process.

In summary, the above results show that the proposed SFAM, together with our optimizations, achieve reasonable efficiency given the stronger privacy guarantees.

7.2   Performance of FedCD Framework

Experiment Setup. The performance of FedCD framework experiments are performed on three laptops with an Intel(R) Core(TM) i7-9500 CPU @3.0 Ghz and 16 G RAM. Our system is implemented in Python. The Python program runs on three laptops to simulate the multi-users to compute secure community construction tasks. In order to guarantee data security and high efficient performance, we set bit length $|\eta| = 1024$ bits.

Datasets. Five graphs datasets Netscience, Facebook, Ca-AstroPh, Enron, Youtube[1] are used in our experiments.

Utility Metrics. We evaluate the scheme performance of different competitors by clustering quality. The Q [34] is a measure of clustering quality. We manipulate it as an evaluation indicator, and the value range is $[-\frac{1}{2}, 1]$.

Effectiveness of FedCD. To show the effectiveness of FedCD, we compare the Q achieved by FedCD with Louvain [5] algorithm without taking privacy into consideration and other 3 state-of-the-art DP CD algorithms LouvainDP [28], LF-GDPR [29] and LDPCD [30]. If the privacy budget/cost value is greater than 2.5 [29], the probability of each bit in the neighbor vector not being flipped will exceed 90%, which will lead to privacy leakage of the user's connected edges.

---

[1] http://www-personal.umich.edu/~mejn/netdata/.

Therefore, we set $(\varepsilon) = 2.5$ in [28–30] comparing with our FedCD. From the Table 3, we can see that our proposed FedCD can achieve the Q close to original Louvain [5] algorithm and greatly outperforms the other DP schemes. For five datasets, the error of Q is only 0.001, 0.018, 0.011, 0.012, 0.036 respectively comparing with [5]. The reason of the error is that we select the best Q in local optimal solution of all parties. However, the total times of recalculation of Q query will be reduced in this framework. Our FedCD dominates the other schemes by a large margin in Q comparing with [28,29], and [30]. Especially in small-scale graphs Netscinet dataset, the error of Q are 0.502, 0.362, 0.321 for [28,29], and [30] respectively comparing with our FedCD framework. The reason is that DP schemes perturbed graph data by adding noise, thus inevitably leading to the loss of some local information in the original social graph. In contrast, in our FedCD framework, we calculate the contribution of user to the total Q, and gradually restore the optimal community structure through multiple times of Q comparison. Moreover, with increasing total number of edges and nodes, there is still a big gap between DP schemes and our FedCD framework in two medium-sized graphs Ca-AstroPh and Enron and one large graph Youtube.

Table 3. Comparision of Q in different scheme

Datasets	Nodes	Edges	[5]	[28]	[29]	[30]	FedCD
Netscience	1,589	5,848	0.954	0.451	0.591	0.632	**0.953**
Facebook	4,039	88,234	0.813	0.437	0.575	0.665	**0.795**
Ca-AstroPh	18,772	198,110	0.624	0.211	0.382	0.401	**0.613**
Enron	36,692	183,831	0.801	0.381	0.638	0.574	**0.789**
Youtube	1,134,890	2,987,624	0.710	0.344	0.564	0.583	**0.674**

Efficiency of FedCD. The total computation cost for FedCD in BuildGlobal-Louvain occupies most of the time. That is, the time cost of ciphertext operation is high if it is not processed in parallel. Thus, our BuildGlobalLouvain makes use of a limited degree of parallelism. In particular, when a number of SFAM of the same type could be carried out in parallel, we can execute them in a single batch. Its computational time complexity can be reduced from $\mathcal{O}((n-1)T_{comp} + 5(n-1)T_{sadd})$ to $\mathcal{O}(T_{comp} + (n+5)T_{sadd})$. Because we can parallel the result by each number with the other numbers in SFAM and accumulating SFAM results with the other numbers. Once decrypted, the position of the only non-zero value is result of SFAM. For instance, in n independent SFAM can be carried out simultaneously, and then $(n^2 - n)$ secure addition operation that will be performed in order to parallelize also can be executed in a single batch. While this type of processing allows us to greatly reduce the computation time compared to the sequential execution of each operation in BuildGlobalLouvain, it by no means is optimal in terms of its running time and the performance can be improved. By the above result, it means that our framework is precise extension under the federated graph learning mode and keep no graph information loss.

8   Conclusion

In this paper, while preserving the privacy of $\mathcal{DU}s$' data with partial HE computation, we proposed FedCD, a federated community detection framework, in order to collaboratively get the best community partition. In addition, we proposed an efficient SFAM protocol to find the index of the maximum value of some encrypted several encrypted FPN, which was faster than previous works. Experimental results over real-world datasets verified the efficiency and security of our FedCD framework. In the future work, we will focus on the optimization of communication and the application of more large social networks.

Acknowledgements. This work is supported by the National Natural Science Foundation of China (No. 62072109, No. U1804263) and Natural Science Foundation of Fujian Province (No. 2021J06013).

References

1. Chan, K., Liebowitz, J.: The synergy of social network analysis and knowledge mapping: a case study. Int. J. Manage. Decis. Making **7**(1), 19–35 (2006)
2. Ji-Yeon, S., et al.: Resource-aware smart home management system by constructing resource relation graph. IEEE Trans. Consum. Electr. **57**(3), 1112–1119 (2011)
3. Dhand, A., et al.: Social network structure and composition in former NFL football players. Sci. Rep. **11**(1), 1–9 (2021)
4. Block, P., et al.: Social network-based distancing strategies to flatten the COVID-19 curve in a post-lockdown world. Nature Hum. Behav. **46**, 588–596 (2020)
5. Blondel, V.D., et al.: Fast unfolding of communities in large networks. J. Stat. Mech. Theor. Exp. **2008**(10), P10008 (2008)
6. Gregory, S.: Finding overlapping communities in networks by label propagation. New J. Phys. **12**(10), 103018 (2010)
7. Acharya, D.B., Zhang, H.: Community detection clustering via gumbel softmax. SN Comput. Sci. **1**(5), 1–11 (2020). https://doi.org/10.1007/s42979-020-00264-2
8. Wu, X., et al.: A survey of algorithms for privacy-preservation of graphs and social networks (2010)
9. Wang, Y., Wu, X., Wu, L.: Differential privacy preserving spectral graph analysis. In: Pei, J., Tseng, V.S., Cao, L., Motoda, H., Xu, G. (eds.) PAKDD 2013. LNCS (LNAI), vol. 7819, pp. 329–340. Springer, Heidelberg (2013). https://doi.org/10.1007/978-3-642-37456-2_28
10. Dimple, M.A., Smit, T.: A review paper on privacy preservation of data mining using randomization response technique
11. Xuan, D., et al.: De-anonymizing dynamic social networks. In: Proceedings of the Global Communications Conference, GLOBECOM 2011, 5–9 December 2011, Houston, Texas, USA (2011)
12. Mülle, Y., Clifton, C., Böhm, K.: Privacy-integrated graph clustering through differential privacy. In: EDBT/ICDT Workshops, vol. 157 (2015)
13. Qin, Z., et al.: Generating synthetic decentralized social graphs with local differential privacy. In: Proceedings of the 2017 ACM SIGSAC Conference on Computer and Communications Security, pp. 425–438 (2017)
14. Yang, M., et al.: Local differential privacy and its applications: a comprehensive survey. arXiv preprint arXiv:2008.03686 (2020)

15. Pinot, R., et al.: Graph-based clustering under differential privacy (2018)
16. Paillier, P.: Public-key cryptosystems based on composite degree residuosity classes. In: Proceedings of EUROCRYPT'99, Czech Republic, May 1999
17. Hardy, S., et al.: Private federated learning on vertically partitioned data via entity resolution and additively homomorphic encryption (2017)
18. ZhouJian, B., Pei, J.: The k-anonymity and l-diversity approaches for privacy preservation in social networks against neighborhood attacks. In: Knowledge Information Systems (2011). https://doi.org/10.1007/s10115-010-0311-2
19. Praveena, A., Smys, S.: Anonymization in social networks: a survey on the issues of data privacy in social network sites. J. Int. J. Eng. Comput. Sci. **5**(3), 15912–15918 (2016)
20. Mohapatra, D., Patra, M.R.: Anonymization of attributed social graph using anatomy based clustering. Multimedia Tools Appl. **78**(18), 25455–25486 (2019)
21. Yuan, W., et al.: Edge-dual graph preserving sign prediction for signed social networks. IEEE Access **5**, 19383–19392 (2017)
22. Qian, J., et al.: Social network de-anonymization and privacy inference with knowledge graph model. IEEE Trans. Dependable Secure Comput. **16**(4), 679–692 (2017)
23. Shao, Y., et al.: Fast de-anonymization of social networks with structural information. In: Data Sci. Eng. **4**, 76–92 (2019)
24. Sala, A., et al.: Sharing graphs using differentially private graph models. In: Proceedings of the 2011 ACM SIGCOMM Conference on Internet Measurement Conference, pp. 81–98 (2011)
25. Mir, D., Wright, R.N: A differentially private estimator for the stochastic kronecker graph model. In: Proceedings of the 2012 Joint EDBT/ICDT Workshops, pp. 167–176 (2012)
26. Xiao, Q., Chen, R., Tan, K.-L.: Differentially private network data release via structural inference. In: Proceedings of the 20th ACM SIGKDD International Conference on Knowledge Discovery and Data Mining, pp. 911–920 (2014)
27. Nobari, S., et al.: L-opacity: linkage-aware graph anonymization (2014)
28. Nguyen, H.H., Imine, A., Rusinowitch, M.: Detecting communities under differential privacy. In: Proceedings of the 2016 ACM on Workshop on Privacy in the Electronic Society, pp. 83–93 (2016)
29. Ye, Q., et al.: LF-GDPR: a framework for estimating graph metrics with local differential privacy. IEEE Trans. Knowl. Data Eng. **34**, 4905–4920 (2020)
30. Zhang, Z.: LDPCD: a novel method for locally differentially private community detection. Comput. Intell. Neurosci. **2022** (2022)
31. Chen, Z., Zheng, Z., Liu, X., Guo, W.: Privacy-preserving computation tookit on floating-point numbers. In: Xiong, J., Wu, S., Peng, C., Tian, Y. (eds.) MobiMedia 2021. LNICST, vol. 394, pp. 462–476. Springer, Cham (2021). https://doi.org/10.1007/978-3-030-89814-4_33
32. Bost, R., et al.: Machine learning classification over encrypted data. In: NDSS, Vol. 4324, p. 4325 (2015)
33. Grivet, S.A., et al.: SPEED: secure, PrivatE, and efficient deep learning. Mach. Learn. **110**(4), 675–694 (2021)
34. Newman, M.E.J., Girvan, M.: Finding and evaluating community structure in networks. Phys. Rev. **E 69**(2), 26113 (2004)

A Textual Adversarial Attack Scheme for Domain-Specific Models

Jialiang Dong[1], Shen Wang[1], Longfei Wu[2], Huoyuan Dong[1], and Zhitao Guan[1(✉)]

[1] North China Electric Power University, Beijing 102206, China
{jialiang_dong,donghy,guan}@ncepu.edu.cn
[2] Fayetteville State University, Fayetteville, NC 28301, USA
lwu@uncfsu.edu

Abstract. Most of the textual adversarial attack methods generate adversarial examples by searching solutions from a perturbation space, which is constructed based on universal corpus. These methods possess high performance when attacking models trained on universal corpus, whereas have a greatly reduced attack capability when attacking domain-specific models. In this paper, we inject domain-specific knowledge into the perturbation space and combine the new domain-specific space with the universal space to enlarge the candidate space for attacking. Specifically, for a domain-specific victim model, the corresponding corpus is used to construct a domain-specific word embedding space, which is utilized as the augmented perturbation space. Besides, we use beam search to augment the search range to further improve the attack ability. Experiment results, involving multiple victim models, datasets, and baselines, reflect that our attack method realized significant improvements on domain-specific model attack.

Keywords: Textual adversarial attack · Domain-specific model · Natural language processing · Deep learning security

1 Introduction

In natural language processing (NLP) fields, numerous attack methods have been proposed, that include some with excellent performance. Textual adversarial examples are textual examples generated by crafting original examples, which have high similarity with the original ones and can deceive the victim model. The similarity is mainly embodied in: (1) visual similarity with the original examples, such as similar sentence structure and lexical expression [1], (2) semantic similarity with the original examples [2]. To meet the above requirements, different granularity of modification is used to add appropriate perturbations to deceive the victim, such as modifying individual letters [3,4], replacing words [2,5] and rewriting whole sentences [6], in the examples.

Existing textual attack idea can be mainly summarized as searching optimal solutions (although in most cases [2,5,7,8] are suboptimal solutions) in a

Y. Xu et al. (Eds.): ML4CS 2022, LNCS 13656, pp. 104–117, 2023.
https://doi.org/10.1007/978-3-031-20099-1_9

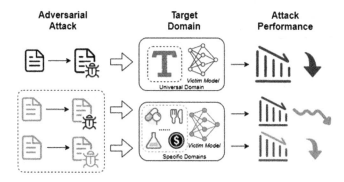

Fig. 1. Textual adversarial attack towards distinct domains. In the leftmost column of "Adversarial Attack", black text patterns represent universal domain text examples, orange text patterns represent domain-specific examples, and black and orange bugs represent adversarial examples generated based on universal perturbation space and domain-specific perturbation space, respectively. The middle column shows universal domain tasks and domain-specific tasks resepctively. The rightmost column "Attack Performance" shows the performance degradation of existing textual adversarial attack methods in domain-specific attacks. (Color figure online)

perturbation space, to generate adversarial examples. The searching process is usually a trade-off between two intentions: better deception effect on the victim model and smaller perturbation to the original example. The perturbation space determines the upper limit of adversarial attack performance, that is, given the victim model and one original example, under appropriate similarity constraints, a larger perturbation space tends to be more likely to contain a perturbed one that can deceive the model. Most of the existing methods construct perturbation space based on universal corpus, and these attack methods can have excellent attack effect against the models trained on universal corpus. But in contrast with theoretical scene, domain-specific data and applications occupy a large proportion in actual scenarios. Although it is also natural language data, the domain-specific textual data are quite distinct from the textual data in universal corpus, in narrative style, terminology use, and expression logic. The gap between universal corpus and domain-specific corpus results the deficiency of searching adversarial example in a universal-corpus based perturbation space to deceive a domain-specific mode. And as a result, as illustrated in Fig. 1, aiming domain-specific models and examples, most of the existing attack methods show significant performance degradation.

To alleviate the above problem, in this paper, we develop a textual attack method against domain-specific NLP models, that is **DO**main-specific corpus **A**ugmen**T**a**T**ion and be**A**m sear**C**h based attac**K** (**DoAttack**). Concretely, we use domain-specific corpora as the basis to optimize word embedding spaces which can reflect the language characteristics of specific domains, and the constructed domain-specific embedding space and the universal embedding space are used together as the candidate perturbation space of adversarial attack. The idea of substituting original words in original examples with synonyms is used to generate adversarial example. In order to expand the search scope and make effective use of the perturbation space, we use beam search to search for suitable substitution words. And to verify the effectiveness of DoAttack, we take experiments involving three domain-specific datasets, three victim models, and two baselines, to test the attack performance with domain-specific scenarios. Compared with baselines, our method achieves better performance on both attack success rate and perturbation rate. To the best of our knowledge, we are the first to explore the textual adversarial attack performance gap between on domain-universal models and on domain-specific models. The contributions of this paper are summarized as follows:

- We analyze the characteristics of domain-specific corpus and models trained on this type of corpus, and shortcomings of existing textual attack methods which are trained on general corpus. Based on the analyzation, we discuss the corresponding improvement ideas.
- We develop a textual adversarial attack method which is aiming to evaluate the robustness of domain-specific models. Compared with existing attack methods that are used in attacking universal domain models, our method possesses stronger pertinence to domain-specific models.
- We conduct extensive simulations to verify the effectiveness of the proposed attack method. We use three domain-specific datasets, three victim models including SOTA pretrained models, and compare with two baselines. Experiment results show that our method has obvious advantages over baselines in both after-attack accuracy and the perturbation rate.

In the following sectors, we subsequently introduce the research background of adversarial attack on NLP models in "Related Work", and describe our proposed attack methodology DoAttack detailedly in "Methodology". Then we develop experimental simulation by comparing with existing baselines to verify the effectiveness of our scheme and organize all the results in "Experiments". Finally, we summarize the contents of this paper.

2   Related Work

Existing works often adopt heuristic rules to change or replace tokens at different levels for textual adversarial attacks. Pruthi et al. [9] successfully fooled models by using character-level transformation including deleting, inserting, and swapping characters in the original input. To preserve the readability and fluency of the examples, Alzantot et al. [10] crafted adversarial text with semantically or syntactically relevant words and leverage a genetic algorithm to select appropriate candidates formed by close words in embedding space. Based on the synonyms substitution strategy, Ren et al. [7] optimized word replacement order by word saliency and the classification probability. Similarly, Zang et al. [11] constructed a search space to substitute clean words based on HowNet [12]. Candidates sets in these methods are built on non-contextualized static word embedding space such as Word2Vec [13] and GLoVe [14]. As a result, the meaning of examples is hard to maintain, although examples adhere to certain linguistic constraints [15].

To address the above issue of semantic loss, some work [8,16] leveraged pre-trained models to generate contextualized perturbations, while Wang et al. [17] explored the BERT embedding clusters to generate high-quality perturbations. In addition to black-box attacks that rely on querying the victim models, there are also some work on white-box attacks, where model parameters and architecture are accessible. For example, Ebrahimi et al. [3] swapped one token for another based on the gradients of the one-hot input vector. Guo et al. [18] studied gradient-based methods to search for a distribution of adversarial examples. And Cheng et al. [19] propose a projected gradient method that combines group lasso and gradient regularization.

These earlier works are mainly utilized for general purpose domains, whether they are black-box or white-box attacks. However, due to the gap between features of universal corpus and domain-specific corpus, generic attack methods are substantially less successful on specific domains. Here, unlike previous work, we add domain knowledge to construct a new perturbation space, which effectively strengthens the attack on domain-specific models. Furthermore, we use a beam search approach to take full advantage of the enlarged perturbation space and enhance the attack success rate and adversarial example quality. It should be noted that our approach can be easily transferred to various specific domains.

3   Methodology

On the whole, we use synonym-substitution based strategy to craft textual examples for adversarial attack. The perturbation space corresponds to the possible synonyms used for substituting, and the search strategy is reflected by the substitution order of the words in original examples $\{x_i| = 1, 2, ...\}$ and which candidate synonym w_{syn} is chosen for a given original word w_{ori}. Choosing candidate words from word embedding space Emb based on cosine similarity (SIM_{cos}) is a common method, that can be denoted as $\{w_{cand}|w_{cand} \in Emb$ and $SIM_{cos}(w_{cand}, w_{ori}) > \epsilon\}$, in which ϵ is a pre-set similarity threshold. However, most of existing researches use universal-corpus based word embedding Emb_{uni} as the candidate space (such as Word2Vec [13], Glove [14]), which leads to poor performance of textual attack methods when attacking domain-specific models. To alleviate the above deficiency, we use the domain-specific corpus to construct an additional domain-specific word embedding Emb_{dom}. We further use beam search to expand the search range, and further improve the attack ability against domain-specific NLP models.

3.1   Domain-Specific Perturbation Space Augmentation

Domain-Specific Word Embeddings Construction

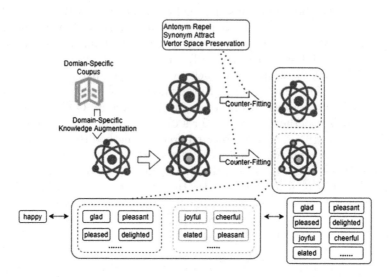

Fig. 2. The principle and an example of Domain-Specific Perturbation Augmentation. Aiming at the domain-specific models, we introduce the corpus knowledge into the universal word embedding space to enlarge the pertinence of the perturbation space to specific domain.

To enrich the domain-specific knowledge of a word embedding space, the critical point is to optimize the word embeddings for better fitting the domain-specific language contexts. In this paper, we use Attentive Mimicking (AM) [20] to calculate a new domain-specific word embedding space for one domain-specific task. The details are described in Fig. 2.

Specifically, word embeddings are trained by analyzing the word co-occurrence. Word semantics similarity quantified by SIM_{cos} is essentially reflected by words and the corresponding contexts. We use AM to improve the representational capability of word embeddings on domain-specific corpus, especially on the low-frequency words in universal corpus but normally used in domain-specific corpus, including terminologies and other domain-specific usages. As shown in Eq. (1), w is a word, C is a set of contexts which contain w, α is a weighting coefficient, and A is a matrix with the same size of dimensions with original word embeddings. The basic idea of AM is to calculate a high quality embedding representation for medium-frequency words and low-frequency words, that is realized by combining the surface-form word embedding $v_{(w,C)}^{form}$ and the contextual embedding obtained based on contextual information, as the whole calculation process represented by $Func_{AM}$. As described in Eq. (2), C_i is one context from C, vC_i is the average of the word embeddings in C_i, and ρ is used to measure the reliability of context. AM allocates distinct weights to different word contexts by calculating "reliability" of contexts, which can reasonably use the contexts and avoid the effects of invalid contexts. See [20] for more calculation details.

$$Func_{AM}(w, C) = \alpha \cdot Av_{(w,C)}^{context} + (1 - \alpha) \cdot v_{(w,C)}^{form} \tag{1}$$

$$v_{(w,C)}^{form} = \sum_{i=1}^{m} \rho(C_i, C) \cdot vC_i \tag{2}$$

We use Emb_{uni} which is a universal word embedding space (in this paper GloVe is used as Emb_{uni}) as the input of AM, and a new domain-specific word embedding space Emb_{dom} is obtained by incorporating domain-specific corpus.

Semantic Representation Capability Improvement

Word embeddings trained on word co-occurrence can express the similarity of contextual usage of words by cosine similarity. Nevertheless, the similarity of word context is not equal to the similarity of word semantics. In particular, a word and its antonyms often appear in the same context. For instance, as to sentences "I am happy" and "I am sad", "happy" and "sad" are among the totally same context but poss diametrically opposite semantics. Our aim is to use the word embedding space to get synonyms for an original word, which is seriously affected by the above shortage.

To solve this deficiency, we reference the strategy of Counter-Fitting (CF) proposed in [21], which is also used in other textual attack research [36], to further strengthen our domain-specific word embedding space. CF is also a post-processing method, which can add linguistic constraints to a given word embedding space. CF takes three additional restraints to enhance the semantic distinction between words with the corresponding synonyms and antonyms: (1) Antonym Repel (AR), (2) Synonym Attract (SA), and (3) Vector Space Preservation (VSP), which are used to expand the distance between vectors of words and antonyms, to narrow the distance between vectors of words and synonyms, and to keep the original relative position of word vectors unchanged as much as possible, respectively. As shown in Eq. (3) that is a description of CF calculating process $Func_{CF}$, Emb_{given} and Emb_{CF} are one given word embedding space (such as a universal word embedding space and a domain-specific word embedding space) and the aiming counter-fitted word embedding space, respectively. k_i is the weighting coefficient, AR, SA, VSP, are the three quantified functioins, Emb_{given} and Emb_{CF} are the original given word embedding space and the counter-fitted word embedding space, respectively. The objective function $Func_{CF}$ for counter-fitting is:

$$\begin{aligned} Func_{CF}(Emb_{given}, Emb_{CF}) = \\ k_1 AR(Emb_{CF}) + K_2 SA(Emb_{CF}) + K_3 VSP(Emb_{given}, Emb_{CF}) \end{aligned} \tag{3}$$

See [21] for more details of counter-fitting.

To improve the representational capacity on word semantics similarity of word embeddings, Emb_{uni} and Emb_{dom} are all processed by counter-fitting, and two candidate spaces, P_{uni} and P_{dom}, for generating synonyms, are obtained. As described in Eq. (4), these two candidate spaces are used as the candidate perturbation space together, to augment the adversarial perturbation space aiming to domain-specific NLP models. To be specific, given a word w in example X, the candidate synonyms can be obtained in both P_{uni} and P_{dom}, and the two sets of synonyms are merged with duplicated words eliminated. The combined synonym set is used as the candidate perturbation space for w, and the candidate perturbation spaces of all the words in X together constitute the perturbation space.

$$Synonyms(w) = \{w_i|SIM_{cos}(w, w_i) > \epsilon, w_i \in P_{uni} \text{ } or \text{ } w_i \in P_{dom}\} \quad (4)$$

3.2   Beam Search Based Synonym Substitution

For attacking, we first calculate the substitution order of each word, that we draw upon the idea used in [15], by calculating word important scores which considers the change of model prediction labels with masking words. In (5), $I(w_i)$ is the importance score of word w_i, $C_Y(X)$ is the prediction confidence score of a model on label Y with input X, X_{nw_i} is a variation of the input X whose i-th word is masked with <OOV>, and F is the prediction label of the model.

$$f(x) = \begin{cases} C_Y(X) - C_Y(X_{nw_i}), \text{ } if \text{ } F(X) = F(X_{nw_i}) = Y \\ (C_Y(X) - C_Y(X_{nw_i})) \text{ } + \text{ } (C_{\hat{Y}}(X_{nw_i}) - C_{\hat{Y}}(X)), \\ \quad\quad\quad if \text{ } F(X) \neq F(X_{nw_i}) \end{cases} \quad (5)$$

Furthermore, following the settings used in [8,15], we additionally add linguistic constraints on candidate synonyms, to improve the linguistic quality of generated textual adversarial examples, that include **Consistency of parts of speech (POS)**, **Semantic similarity**, and **Stop words filterring**.

Then we substitute the words in the example according to the descending order of word importance scores. In view of the fact that each word has multiple candidate words, and the search strategy of candidate words determines the actual attack effect, we use beam search to expand the search range. For each round of word substitution, for word w_i and its N_i candidate synonyms $\{s_1, s_2, ..., s_{N_i}\}$, K synonyms that cause the most declines in the confidence of the model prediction on the true label are added to the beam (K is the beam size, and in this paper, we set K as 3), to save more intermediate results and reduce the possibility of falling into local optimum.

$$Examples_i = \{(X_m, s_n)|X_m \in Beam_{i-1}, s_n \in \{s_1, s_2, ..., s_n\}\} \quad (6)$$

$$Beam_i = \{(X_m, s_n)|(X_m, s_n) \in Examples_i,$$
$$C_{label}((X_m, s_n)) \in Min_k(c_{label}(\{Examples_i\}))\} \quad (7)$$

As shown Eq. (6), $K \times N_i$ temp examples $Examples_i$ are generated each round that are constructed by substituting the K examples $\{X_m|m = 1, 2, ..., K\}$ in $Beam_{i-1}$ generated in the $(i-1)th$ round, that the beam is updated by K examples with the most declines of confidence on the true label among the

Algorithm 1: Textual Adversarial Example Generation of DoAttack

---

Input: an original text example, $X = \{w_i | i = 1, 2, 3, ...\}$

         the corresponding original label, Y_{true}

         Importance Score function, I

         Perturbation Space, P

         Candidate Words Filter function, $Filter$

         Confidence Score function, C

         Model Prediction Label Calculation, F

         Beam Size, k

Output: Textual adversarial example X^*

1   /*—Substitution Order Calculation—*/

2   for w_i in $X = \{w_i | i = 1, 2, 3, ...\}$

3     $I(w_i) calculation$

4   **end for**

5   $Order_{sub} = X(Desc(\{I(w_i)\}))$

6   /*—Word Substitution—*/

7   $Beam_0 = [X]$

8   **for** w_i **in** $Order_{sub}$

9   /*—Generate Candidate Words—*/

10    $Synonyms(w_i) = Filter(P(w_i))$

11   **for** X_{temp} **in** $Beam_i$:

12   **for** s_i **in** $Synonyms(w_i)$:

13      $\Delta Conf(s_j) = C_{Y_{true}}(X) - C_{Y_{true}}(X_{temp \backslash w_i / s_j})$

14   **if** $F(X_{temp \backslash w_i / s_j}) \neq F(X)$:

15       $X^* = X_{temp \backslash w_i / s_j}$

16   **return**

17   **end if**

18   **end for**

19   **end for**

20   $Beam_{i+1} = TopK_{MIN}(\{X_{temp \backslash w_i / s_j} | X_{temp} \in Beam_i, s_j \in Synonyms(w_i)\})$

21 **end for**

$K \times N_i$ temp examples. And until there is a perturbed example that can deceive the victim model to predict wrongly among the K examples, the attack on this original example ends and textual adversarial example is generated successfully. Distinctively, when there are multiple perturbed examples which can deceive the victim model, the one caused the most confidence decline is chosen as the textual adversarial example.

3.3   Complete Process of Adversarial Example Generation

To sum up, in our scheme, the complete process of textual adversarial example generation can be summarized as follows: (1) given an original example, we calculate the word substitution order which is quantified by importance scores; (2) according to the descending order of importance scores, for the current word to be substituted, candidate substitution words are generated, which are based on both the domain-specific perturbation space and the universal perturbation

Table 1. Detailed information of datasets used in simulation.

Dataset	Num.Labels	Sum.Size	Train.Size	Test.Size	Domain.Size
YELP	2	560,000	19,000	1,000	540,000
Bank	3	448,102	49,000	1,000	398,102

space; (3) based on beam search, we select appropriate words to perturb the current perturbed examples in the beam, and select the appropriate K (beam size) perturbed results to update the beam; (4) repeat the above process until a text adversarial example which can successfully make the victim model predict wrongly is generated. The complete process of Textual Adversarial Example Generation is described in Algorithm 1.

4   Experiments

4.1   Experimental Settings

Datasets

For simulation, we use domain-specific datasets to evaluate the attack performance. The specific information of datasets is as follows and shown in Table 1.

YELP [22]: A dataset of reviews of restaurants, which construct a classification task: predicting a polarity label including "Positive" and "Negative" that essentially a binary classification task. We follow the settings in [22].

Banks of Twitter[1]: A dataset of Twitter items of 4 South African Banks with sentiments. For each Twitter item, there is a corresponding sentiment label from "Neutral", "Positive", and "Negative". In experimental results we abbreviate "Bank of Twitter" as "Bank.".

Victim Models

WordCNN [23]: A convolutional neural network (CNN)-based text classification, which is take word as the input granularity of the model. Following the baseline settings used in [15], we use three window sizes, 3, 4, 5, and 100 filters for each window size. The dropout is set to 0.3.

BERT [24]: We use the 'bert-base-uncased' model from Huggingface transformers library[2], and we finetune the model on corresponding datasets, respectively.

RoBERTa [25]: We use the 'roberta-base' model from Huggingface transformers library, and we finetune the model as the use of BERT model.

Baselines

We use two strong baselines to compare and evaluate the performance of our proposed method.

PWWS [7][3]: A textual adversarial attack method, which calculates the perturbation order based on word saliency value, and constructs the perturbation

---

[1] https://www.kaggle.com/datasets/slythe/tweets-of-4-banks-in-south-africa-poc.

[2] https://huggingface.co.

[3] https://github.com/JHL-HUST/PWWS.

space using synonym dictionary. This method selects substitution words based on greedy search.

TextFooler [15][4]: This method proposes an approach to calculate word importance score which can be used to sort the word substitution, and use word embedding space to construct the perturbation. Greedy search idea is also used to choose substitution words for generating textual adversarial examples. In experiment results we summarize "TextFooler" as "TF.".

Evaluation Indexes

We use After-Attack Accuracy and Perturbation Rate to quantify the adversarial attack performance, which are all common used evaluation indexes.

After-Attack Accuracy: This index is the accuracy of victim model when dealing with the generated adversarial examples, which shows the performance degradation of the victim before and after the attack. The lower the value of this index, the better the attack performance of the attack method.

Perturbation Rate: This index is the average perturbation rate of generating adversarial examples. The lower the value of this index, the less the perturbations added on original examples.

4.2   Attack Performance Results and Analysis

In this section, we exhibit the attack performance results of DoAttack on both three datasets and corresponding victim models, and compare the results with baseline attack methods. The simulation results of attack performance are exhibited in Table 2 and Table 3.

First, it can be accessed that all the models can achieve excellent classification performances on both the three original test sets. Even WordCNN can achieve more than 90% (92.7%) classification accuracy on YELP dataset, and possess accuracy over 80% on another datasets, Bank. (85.4%). The After-Attack Accuracy results reveal that both these attack methods can make the victim drop

Table 2. Details of the after-Attack acuracy performance including both the baseline methods and our proposed method DoAttack.

Dataset	Victim Models	Original Accuracy (%)	After-attack accuracy (%)		
			PWWS	TF.	DoAttack
YELP	WordCNN	92.7	22.0	1.0	**0.1**
	BERT	93.7	39.4	17.2	**14.7**
	RoBERTa	95.1	46.7	34.2	**28.7**
Bank.	WordCNN	85.4	41.2	12.8	**9.0**
	BERT	96.7	44.5	13.4	**7.2**
	RoBERTa	97.0	48.4	18.2	**9.8**

---

[4] https://github.com/jind11/TextFooler.

Table 3. Details of the perturbation rate performance including both the baseline methods and our proposed method DoAttack.

Dataset	Victim Models	Perturbation Rate (%)		
		PWWS	TF.	DoAttack
YELP	WordCNN	12.179	7.788	**6.668**
	BERT	16.720	10.066	**9.040**
	RoBERTa	18.432	14.193	**11.769**
Bank.	WordCNN	27.691	24.940	**24.449**
	BERT	27.144	25.553	**23.742**
	RoBERTa	28.862	28.241	**25.807**

on classification performance. For instance, when the task is YELP classification task and the victim model is WordCNN, PWWS can make the accuracy drop from 92.7% to 22.0%, which reveals that an excellent textual classification model is easily attacked to be useless. However, it shows that for different domain-specific models, the attack performances of baselines vary hugely, and when the domain-specific model is a relatively robust model, such as BERT, the attack performances drop obviously (we also consider the situation that dataset is YELP, and when the victim model is RoBERTa and the attack method is PWWS, the After-Attack Accuracy is 46.7%, which is significantly higher than 22.0% that WordCNN is as victim model).

As shown in Table 2 and Table 3, the optimal values for each set of experimental results, that are the lowest After-Attack Accuracy and Perturbation Rate, are bolled in the two tables. Under all experimental settings with distinct tasks and victim models, DoAttack possesses the best performance on both After-Attack Accuracy and Perturbation Rate. Compared with TextFooler, DoAttack has a significant advantage in attack success rate, which exceeds the former by 0.9% (dataset is YELP, and victim model is WordCNN) to 8.4% (dataset is Bank., and victim model is RoBERTa) in different experimental settings. And at the same time, DoAttack also possesses lowest Perturbation Rates with all the datasets and victim models, which exceeds TextFooler by 0.491% (dataset is BANK., victim model is WordCNN) to 2.434% (dataset is BANK, victim model is RoBERTa). Comparing with PWWS, DoAttack has a more significant superiority, which can achieve 21.9% (dataset is YELP, victim model is WordCNN) to 38.6% (dataset is Bank., victim model is RoBERTa), and also exceeds PWWS on Perturbation Rate by 3.055% (dataset is Bank, and victim model is RoBERTa) to 7.680% (dataset is YELP., victim model is BERT).

5   Conclusion

In this paper, we expand the perturbation space of textual adversarial attack by introducing the specific-domain knowledge, to solve the problem that most of the existing attack methods generate adversarial examples based on universal perturbation space, which is difficult to effectively evaluate the robustness of domain-specific models. Concretely, we augment and adjust the universal word embedding space by incorporating the domain-specific corpus with universal corpus-based word embeddings, so that the word embeddings are more suitable for representing the language features of the specific domains. Combining the universal perturbation space and the domain-specific perturbation space which is constructed with domain-specific knowledge, the candidate perturbation space of textual adversarial attack is enlarged. In addition, we expand the search range of the attack through beam search that further improves the attack success of the method and reduces the perturbation rate. Extensive experiments are developed by comparing with existing attack methods. Simulation results show that the method proposed in this paper can effectively reduce the performances of existing text classification models used in domain-specific tasks, even SOTA models such as BERT and RoBERTa, which shows DoAttack is significantly superior to baselines and can be used to evaluate robustness of domain-specific NLP models.

Acknowledgements. The work is supported by the National Natural Science Foundation of China under Grant 61972148.

References

1. Ebrahimi, J., Lowd, D., Dou, D.: On adversarial examples for character-level neural machine translation. In: Proceedings of the 27th International Conference on Computational Linguistics, pp. 653–663, Association for Computational Linguistics, Santa Fe, New Mexico, USA, August 2018
2. Yang, P., Chen, J., Hsieh, C.J., Wang, J.L., Jordan, M.I.: Greedy attack and gumbel attack: generating adversarial examples for discrete data. J. Mach. Learn. Res. **21**(43), 1–36 (2020)
3. Ebrahimi, J., Rao, A., Lowd, D., Dou, D.: HotFlip: white-box adversarial examples for text classification. In: Proceedings of the 56th Annual Meeting of the Association for Computational Linguistics (Volume 2: Short Papers), Association for Computational Linguistics, pp. 31–36, Melbourne, Australia, July 2018
4. Gil, Y., Chai, Y., Gorodissky, O., Berant, J.: White-to-black: efficient distillation of black-box adversarial attacks. In: Proceedings of the 2019 Conference of the North American Chapter of the Association for Computational Linguistics: Human Language Technologies, Volume 1 (Long and Short Papers), Association for Computational Linguistics, pp. 1373–1379, Minneapolis, Minnesota, June 2019
5. Liu, S., Ning, L., Chen, C., Tang, K.: Efficient combinatorial optimization for word-level adversarial textual attack. IEEE/ACM Trans. Audio Speech Lang. Process. **30**, 98–111 (2021)

6. Wang, T., et al.: CAT-gen: improving robustness in NLP models via controlled adversarial text generation. In: Proceedings of the 2020 Conference on Empirical Methods in Natural Language Processing (EMNLP), Association for Computational Linguistics, pp. 5141–5146, Online, November 2020

7. Ren, S., Deng, Y., He, K., Che, W.: Generating natural language adversarial examples through probability weighted word saliency. In: Proceedings of the 57th Annual Meeting of the Association for Computational Linguistics, Association for Computational Linguistics, pp. 1085–1097, Florence, Italy, July 2019

8. Li, L., Ma, R., Guo, Q., Xue, X., Qiu, X.: BERT-ATTACK: adversarial attack against BERT using BERT. In: Proceedings of the 2020 Conference on Empirical Methods in Natural Language Processing (EMNLP), pp. 6193–6202. Association for Computational Linguistics, November 2020

9. Pruthi, D., Dhingra, B., Lipton, Z.C.: Combating adversarial misspellings with robust word recognition. In: Proceedings of the 57th Annual Meeting of the Association for Computational Linguistics, pp. 5582–5591. Association for Computational Linguistics, Florence, Italy, July 2019

10. Alzantot, M., Sharma, Y., Elgohary, A., Ho, B.J., Srivastava, M., Chang, K.W.: Generating natural language adversarial examples. In: Proceedings of the 2018 Conference on Empirical Methods in Natural Language Processing, pp. 2890–2896. Association for Computational Linguistics, Brussels, Belgium, October-November 2018

11. Zang, Y., et al.: Word-level textual adversarial attacking as combinatorial optimization. In: Proceedings of the 58th Annual Meeting of the Association for Computational Linguistics, pp. 6066–6080. Association for Computational Linguistics, July 2020

12. Dong, Z., Dong, Q., Hao, C.: HowNet and its computation of meaning. In: Coling 2010: Demonstrations, pp. 53–56. Coling 2010 Organizing Committee, Beijing, China, August 2010

13. Mikolov, T., Chen, K., Corrado, G., Dean, J.: Efficient estimation of word representations in vector space. arXiv preprint arXiv:1301.3781 (2013)

14. Pennington, J., Socher, R., Manning, CD.: Glove: global vectors for word representation. In: Proceedings of the 2014 Conference on Empirical Methods in Natural Language Processing (EMNLP), pp. 1532–1543 (2014)

15. Jin, D., Jin, Z., Zhou, J.T., Szolovits, P.: Is bert really robust? a strong baseline for natural language attack on text classification and entailment. In: Proceedings of the AAAI Conference on Artificial Intelligence, vol. 34, pp. 8018–8025 (2020)

16. Garg, S., Ramakrishnan, G.: BAE: BERT-based adversarial examples for text classification. In: Proceedings of the 2020 Conference on Empirical Methods in Natural Language Processing (EMNLP), pp. 6174–6181. Association for Computational Linguistics, November 2020

17. Wang, B., Xu, C., Liu, X., Cheng, Y., Li, B.: Semattack: natural textual attacks via different semantic spaces. arXiv preprint arXiv:2205.01287 (2022)

18. Guo, C., Sablayrolles, A., Jégou, H., Kiela, D.:. Gradient-based adversarial attacks against text transformers. In: Proceedings of the 2021 Conference on Empirical Methods in Natural Language Processing, pp. 5747–5757. Association for Computational Linguistics, Online and Punta Cana, Dominican Republic, November 2021

19. Cheng, M., Yi, J., Chen, P.-Y., Zhang, H., Hsieh, C.-J.: Seq2sick: evaluating the robustness of sequence-to-sequence models with adversarial examples. In: Proceedings of the AAAI Conference on Artificial Intelligence, vol. 34, pp. 3601–3608 (2020)

20. Schick, T., Schütze, H.: Attentive mimicking: better word embeddings by attending to informative contexts. In: Proceedings of the 2019 Conference of the North American Chapter of the Association for Computational Linguistics: Human Language Technologies, Volume 1 (Long and Short Papers), pp. 489–494. Association for Computational Linguistics, Minneapolis, Minnesota, June 2019

21. Mrkšić, N., et al.: Counter-fitting word vectors to linguistic constraints. In: Proceedings of the 2016 Conference of the North American Chapter of the Association for Computational Linguistics: Human Language Technologies, pp. 142–148. Association for Computational Linguistics, San Diego, California, June 2016

22. Zhang, X., Zhao, J., LeCun, Y.: Character-level convolutional networks for text classification. Adv. Neural Inf. Process. Syst. **28** (2015)

23. Kim, Y.: Convolutional neural networks for sentence classification. In: Proceedings of the 2014 Conference on Empirical Methods in Natural Language Processing (EMNLP), pp. 1746–1751. Association for Computational Linguistics, Doha, Qatar, October 2014

24. Devlin, J., Chang, M.-W., Lee, K., Toutanova, K.: BERT: pre-training of deep bidirectional transformers for language understanding. In: Proceedings of the 2019 Conference of the North American Chapter of the Association for Computational Linguistics: Human Language Technologies, Volume 1 (Long and Short Papers), pp. 4171–4186. Association for Computational Linguistics, Minneapolis, Minnesota, June 2019

25. Liu, Y., et al.: Roberta: a robustly optimized bert pretraining approach. arXiv preprint arXiv:1907.11692 (2019)

An Improved Conv-LSTM Method for Gear Fault Detection

Yang Zhang, Jianwu Zhang, Guanhong Zhang, and Hong Li[✉]

School of Artificial Intelligence and Big Data, Hefei University, Hefei, China
lihong@hfuu.edu.cn

Abstract. Reducing the occurrence of gear failures and extending their service life is a vital issue in industrial production. To solve the problem that the method of gear fault detection with Convolution Neural Network (CNN) is difficult to extract the temporal features of the vibration data, an improved Convolutional-LSTM (Conv-LSTM) gear fault detection method was proposed. First, the raw data was fed into the convolutional layer, followed by the pooling and LSTM layers. A batch normalisation layer (BN) was added after the convolutional layer to speed up convergence. Second, to reduce the complexity of the model, a Global Maximum Pooling layer (GMP) was used to replace the flattened layer, and the Hinge functions are used as loss functions. Finally, classification is carried out by the Softmax classifier. The overall accuracy of model architecture could reach 99.64% on the University of Connecticut gear fault dataset. The results show that the proposed method is effective and can meet gear fault diagnosis's accuracy and timeliness requirements.

Keywords: Gear · Fault diagnosis · Convolutional-LSTM · Global maximum pooling layer · Batch normalization

1 Introduction

Many countries have increased their investment in mechanical equipment with the continuous advancement of the concept of intelligent manufacturing. At the same time, the loss caused by the mechanical equipment's fault is getting more serious. Gears are a major component in the transmission of mechanical equipment. Due to the long-term heavy load condition, its faults account for a large proportion of mechanical faults. Moreover, the parts of the machinery are so closely related that only a small defect in the gears can make the whole machinery paralyzed. Reducing the occurrence of gear failures [1] and extending their service life is a vital issue in industrial production. Therefore, scientific and effective fault diagnosis of gears is of great significance.

Deep learning [2] can extract features with good abstraction and generalisation from fault data, which is especially suitable for processing complex fault diagnosis data. Convolutional neural network (CNN), one of the classical algorithms of deep learning, have been widely used in fault detection and have achieved good results. However, the following problems still exist: Since gear performance degradation is generally a continuous evolution dependent on service time, the original gear fault vibration signals are one-dimensional data based on time series. However, the long-term dependence relation hidden in time series data is not considered in CNN, which is the key to forming classifiable features. Ignoring temporal features may result in data loss, exceptions, and other problems. Therefore, it is necessary to extract the temporal characteristics of the data. LSTM is a time-loop neural network improved from a recurrent neural network with long-term memory function. For time-series data, LSTM can find the potential relationship between data and time.

In view of the above problems, this paper proposes an improved CNN-LSTM gear fault detection method. Firstly, the convolutional neural network is used to extract the complex local characteristics of the gear data, and then the output characteristic information is loaded into LSTM to obtain the whole local characteristics of the temporal sequence data. By improving the structure of the network model and loss function, the gear faults can be accurately classified.

2 Related Research

In recent years, deep learning techniques have been widely used in the field of fault detection [3, 4] with good results. Yang Wang et al. [5] proposed a novel convolutional neural network model with multi-dimensional signal inputs and task outputs, which effectively improves the bearing diagnosis capability of the deep learning model. Tong-tong Jin et al. [6] used CNN to extract features from the original vibration signal and identify fault types through global average pooling. The proposed method has better normal signals while maintaining good performance under different working loads. The MS-DCNN model proposed by Zhuang et al. [7] can expand and deepen the neural network to learn better and more powerful feature representations due to the use of multi-scale convolutional layers to effectively identify faults in bearings. Pei Cao et al. [8] proposed a transfer learning method based on deep convolutional neural networks for diagnosing gear faults.

In general, CNN can deeply mine the inherent feature information of data through multiple convolutional layers and provide rich feature samples for subsequent neural network training. However, CNN is not as efficient as a recurrent neural network (RNN) in dealing with sequential problems. As a variant of RNN, LSTM solves the problems of remote information context dependence, gradient disappearance, or gradient explosion that are difficult to process by RNN through forgetting gate, input gate, and output gate. Therefore, it is widely used in fault diagnosis to extract the features of fault signal time series. R. Sabir et al. [9] proposed a fault diagnosis method based on LSTM, and the diagnosis result is better than most current algorithms using stator current for bearing fault diagnosis. ZK Abdul et al. [10] proposed a new LSTM gear fault diagnosis method based on cheap mixed manual feature sets such as source code coefficient (GTCC) of gamma-sound signals temporarily extracted from vibration signals and Meir frequency cephalosporin coefficient (MFCC), which can effectively identify gear faults. H.Zhao et al. [11] designed an end-to-end online fault diagnosis method based on the LSTM network and successfully applied it to bearings.

In view of the above analysis, an improved Convolutional-LSTM model with a global pooling layer and a batch normalisation layer is proposed in this paper. Firstly, a one-dimensional convolutional neural network (1D-CNN) is used for feature extraction. A batch normalisation layer is added after the convolutional layer to accelerate the convergence speed; the special information is added to the LSTM to mine the temporal characteristics of the data. Secondly, the Flatten layer in the traditional CNN network structure is replaced by the global maximum pooling layer to avoid splitting parameter features caused by the Flatten operation to adapt to the temporal problem and improve the fault diagnosis accuracy. Hinge loss functions are used as loss functions. Finally, the Softmax classifier is used for classification. The experiment results indicate that this method performs well on fault diagnosis based on the University of Connecticut Gear datasets.

3   Methodology

3.1   Convolutional Neural Networks

A convolutional neural network (CNN) is a feed-forward neural network that includes convolutional computation. It consists of an input layer, a convolutional layer, a pooling layer, a fully connected layer, and an output layer. The architecture of a convolutional neural network is shown in Fig. 1.

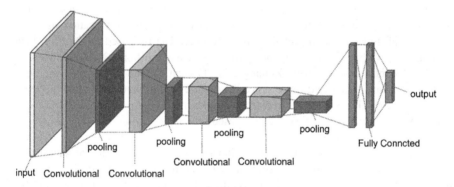

Fig. 1. CNN architecture

Convolutional Operation: The convolution layer performs a convolution operation on the input data to extract features. The convolution layer can be defined as:

$$x_j^l = f\left(\sum x_i^{l-1} * k_{ij}^l + b_j^l\right) \tag{1}$$

where l is the lth layer of the network. k is the convolution kernel, and f denotes a two-dimensional matrix. f is the non-linear activation function and b represents the bias.

Pooling Layer: After pooling layers, we can reduce the size of the feature map while retaining the most critical information. Examples of Max Pooling and Average Pooling are as follows:

$$x_j^l = f\left(\beta_j^l \text{down}\left(x_j^{l-1} + b_j^l\right)\right) \tag{2}$$

where the *down* denotes the subsampling function.

Fully Connected Layer: Each neuron in the fully connected layer is connected to every other neuron in the upper layer. Its output is used as input to the SoftMax classification, which is able to map multiple inputs to the (0, 1) interval to complete multiple classifications. The Softmax function is defined as:

$$S_i = \frac{e^{z_i}}{\sum\limits_{1}^{N} e^{z_N}}, i = 1, \dots, N \tag{3}$$

where Z_i denotes the output value of the ith node and N indicates the number of categories classified.

3.2 Long Short-Term Memory Neural Networks

The Long Short Term Memory (LSTM) [12] network is an extension of the artificial recurrent neural network (RNN) that aims to learn sequence data and its long-term dependencies more accurately than the traditional RNN. In addition to hidden memory gates, input/output gate and forget gate is also implemented in this network. The input gate sets the rate at which information is held from the last layer in the cell. The output gate determines the rate at which information is passed from the cell. The forgetting gate is concerned with ignoring the information and cancelling the dependencies between the layers. A schematic of the LSTM structure can be seen in Fig. 2.

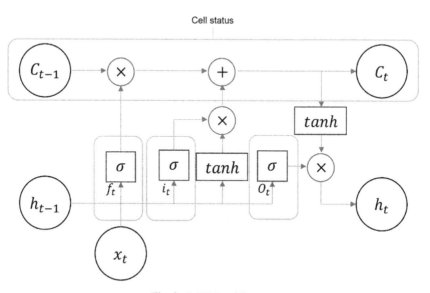

Fig. 2. LSTM architecture

where f_t denotes the forgetting gate. The information from the current input and the previous hidden state is passed through the sigmoid activation function. If the output value is closer to 0, it means to forget, and closer to 1, it means to retain.

$$f_t = \sigma\left(W_f[h_t - 1, x_t] + b_f\right) \tag{4}$$

where σ denotes the sigmoid function, W_f is the weight, and b is the bias. it represents the input gate, which controls the input of new information together with the tanh function, and can be defined as:

$$i_t = \sigma(W_i[[h_t - 1, x_t] + b_i]) \tag{5}$$

$$\tilde{C}_t = \tanh(W_c[h_t - 1, x_t] + b_c) \tag{6}$$

$$C_t = f_t * C_t - 1 + i_t * \tilde{C}_t \tag{7}$$

where $\tilde{C}_t$ is the cell's temporary state, and C_t is the cell status. O_t represents the output gate, which is used to control the current unit state filtering and is expressed as:

$$O_t = \sigma\left(W_o * \left[h_{t-1}, x_t\right] + b_o\right) \tag{8}$$

$$h_t = O_t * \tanh(C_t) \tag{9}$$

where h_{t-1} denotes the hidden state of the previous iteration, and h_t denotes the hidden state layer of the next layer.

3.3   Improved Conv-LSTM Fault Diagnosis Model

Traditional CNN usually uses flattening dimension reduction. The flatten operation achieves data dimension reduction by flattening 2D matrices into rows or columns, which changes the spatial position of each data when splitting graph matrices, thus losing some valuable features. In this paper, the global maximum pooling layer replaces the Flatten layer to avoid the loss of these features.

The Hinge loss function [13] commonly used in support vector machines, has better small sample data with lower losses than Cross-entropy [14] loss function. The Hinge loss function has no loss when the sample classification satisfies the confidence interval. In contrast, for the Cross-entropy loss function, the loss is unsatisfiable. There will always be a loss value, while the Hinge loss function is relatively robust and insensitive to outliers and noise. Based on this, the Hinge loss function replaces the Cross-entropy loss function in the model. The Hinge loss function is defined as follows:

$$L(y) = \max(0, 1 - \hat{y}y) \tag{10}$$

$\hat{y}$ is the predicted output value, usually, a soft result, and y is the correct category, with a loss of $1 - \hat{y}y$ if $\hat{y} < 1$ or 0 if $\hat{y} \geq 1$. Data features are extracted by constructing a feature extraction layer consisting of a 1D convolutional layer, a batch layer, an activation function layer, and a max-pooling layer. To unify the scattered feature data and improve the performance of the network, the features extracted from the convolution are fed into the Batch Normalization layer for normalization. The Relu function [15] is used as the activation function to prevent the gradient from disappearing and speed up the model's convergence. The complexity of the data input to the LSTM is reduced by using max-pooling to reduce the number of parameters, and the LSTM can further extract time-series features that the CNN partially ignores through selective filtering operations of input gates, output gates, and forgetting gates to improve the accuracy of the fault diagnosis model.

To prevent overfitting and enhance the robustness of the model, a random drop mechanism is added to the fully connected layer to randomly drop the weights of neurons with a certain probability to reduce the dependence of the network model on specific neurons. An adaptive moment estimation (Adam) [16] optimizer is used for gradient descent to improve the convergence speed. Lastly, the Softmax layer is used to classify the output gear fault classes and prediction accuracy, and the model is validated by testing the accuracy. The architecture of this network can be seen in Fig. 3.

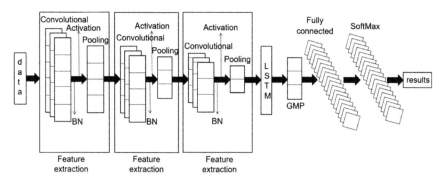

Fig. 3. Conv-LSTM architecture

4 Experimental Results and Analysis

4.1 Experimental Setup

In this study, an experimental setup of a gearbox system located at the University of Connecticut, USA has been considered as a case study. It includes a motor, a tachometer, and a two-stage gearbox. The gearbox contains two input shafts and four gears. Multiple test gears with various health conditions are considered in the experiments. A 32-tooth pinion and an 80-tooth gear are installed on the first stage input shaft. The second stage consists of a 48-tooth pinion and a 64-tooth gear. The input shaft speed is measured by a tachometer, and gear vibration signals are measured by an accelerometer. The sampling frequency was 20 kHz. Nine different gear conditions are introduced to the pinion on the input shaft, including healthy condition, missing tooth, root crack, spalling, and chipping tip with five different levels of severity. The experimental Gearbox system can be seen in Fig. 4.

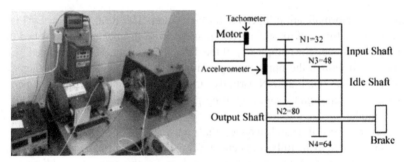

Fig. 4. Gearbox system experimental setup

4.2 Experiments Based on the Test Rig

1) Data Labeling

The dataset is one-dimensional time-domain data of vibration responses related to gear fault patterns. 104 signals are collected for each gear condition using the experimental gearbox system. For each signal, 3,600 samples were recorded during four gear revolutions, and the sample data was labelled with the unique thermal coding technology. A random ordering of the data makes the data distribution more random and the results more convincing. The data conditions are shown in Table 1.

2) Divide the dataset

A randomly select 70% of the dataset is used as the training set and the rest as the test set.

3) Training models

If the model fails to converge or converges abnormally, the model parameters must be modified. If convergence occurs as expected, the trained network model is saved and used to verify the model's impact on the classification accuracy and classification result output. The structure of the experiment is shown in Fig. 5.

The initial feature extraction layer has three one-dimensional convolutional layers with a convolution kernel length of 4 and a step size of 1. There are several 32, which are normalised after the feature extraction layer is constructed. The activation function uses Relu, pooling pool size to 2 and the step size to 1. The boundaries are filled with zeros so that the size of the output does not change. The settings of the second feature extraction layer are kept the same as the first one. Three convolutional layers are used in the third feature extraction layer, again with 64 convolutional kernels, four convolutional layers, one step size, and the rest of the settings are the same. We add a 64-cell LSTM network to mine the temporal information in the feature sequence with a dropout parameter of 0.5, L2 regularisation to prevent overfitting, and a parameter of 0.0002. In order to improve the efficiency of the model calculation, the hinge loss function is selected as a loss function, and Adam is selected as the model optimizer.

Since the choice of learning rate and batch size affects the accuracy of the network, different learning rates [17] and batch sizes [18] are used as the initial parameters of the

Table 1. Data conditions

Fault type	Length	Number	Fault type label
Health	**3600**	**104**	1
Missing Teeth	**3600**	**104**	2
Cracked Tooth Roots	**3600**	**104**	3
Spalling	**3600**	**104**	4
chip-5a (Least)	**3600**	**104**	5
chip4a	**3600**	**104**	6
chip3a	**3600**	**104**	7
chip2a	**3600**	**104**	8
chip1a (Severe)	**3600**	**104**	9

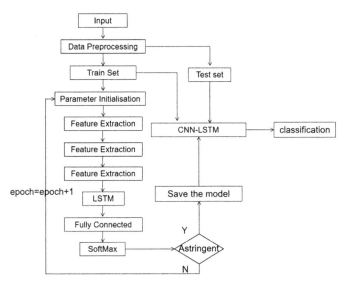

Fig. 5. The structure of Conv-LSTM model

network, with learning rates of 1e-3, 1e-4, and 1e-5, respectively, and batch sizes of 12, 24 and 32 respectively. The optimal combination of parameters is chosen according to the accuracy results of the network run. The accuracy of the network run with different learning rates and batch sizes is shown in Fig. 6. As shown in Fig. 6, the model's accuracy is closest to 99.5% at a learning rate of 1e-5 and a batch size of 12. The batch size affects the degree of optimization and speed of the model. The smaller the value taken, the longer the training and computation time of the model and the corresponding increase accordingly. While the learning rate controls the speed of updating the model parameters, if the learning rate is too low, it will reduce the training speed of the model. If it is too large, it may lead to parameter oscillations and loss of accuracy. Therefore, it is necessary to choose the correct learning rate and batch size for the model.

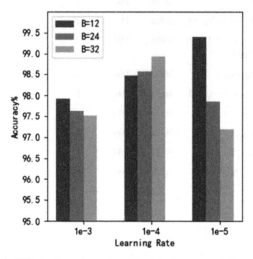

Fig. 6. Effect of learning rate and batch size on model accuracy

In this paper, we use the above model to conduct experiments with 500 iterations. The relationship between accuracy and the number of iterations is shown in Fig. 7(left), and the relationship between loss value and the number of iterations is shown in Fig. 7(right).

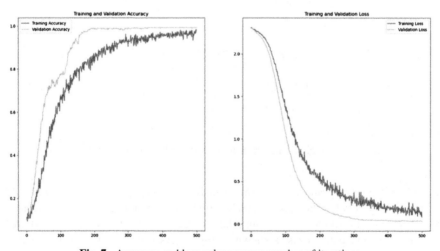

Fig. 7. Accuracy and loss values versus number of iterations

From Fig. 7, it can be seen that the model recognition accuracy rises rapidly in the first 200 iterations, and the loss value decreases rapidly, then gradually levels off and converges gradually in the range of 400–500 iterations, with the loss value curve approaching the level and the classification accuracy reaching 99.64%.

The improved Conv-LSTM fault detection method is compared with CNN, CNN-SVM, and CNN-LSTM. A total of five repeated experiments are implemented to avoid accidental errors. The evaluation indicators are fault detection accuracy rate, precision rate, recall rate, and f1 score. The experimental results are shown in Table 2. The detailed accuracy rates of the first run results of the four different models are shown in Table 3.

Table 2. Evaluation results of 4 different models

Diagnostic methods	Average accuracy	Average Precision	Average Recall rate	Average F1 score
CNN	0.9537	0.9586	0.9525	0.9555
CNN - SVM	0.9715	0.9715	0.9734	0.9724
CNN - LSTM	0.9893	0.9887	0.9891	0.9889
Improved CNN - LSTM	0.9964	0.9967	0.9969	0.9968

Table 3. Detailed accuracy of 4 different models

Fault category	CNN	CNN - SVM	CNN - LSTM	Improved CNN - LSTM
1	0.97	0.98	0.98	1.00
2	0.94	1.00	1.00	1.00
3	0.92	1.00	1.00	1.00
4	0.87	0.90	0.92	0.98
5	1.00	1.00	0.98	0.92
6	1.00	0.97	1.00	1.00
7	1.00	0.90	1.00	1.00
8	0.97	1.00	0.99	1.00
9	0.93	0.98	0.96	1.00

As can be seen from Table 2 and 3 the improved CNN - LSTM fault detection method performs best, with a detection accuracy rate of over 99.0%, and is able to identify various faults and accurately. Compared with CNN and CNN - SVM, CNN - LSTM and improved CNN - LSTM have higher accuracy rates, indicating that the addition of LSTM can indeed improve the fault detection performance of network models.

In order to evaluate the performance of the trained network, confusion analysis is performed and is shown in Fig. 8. The horizontal axis represents the predicted failure category, and the vertical axis represents the correct failure category. As can be seen from Fig. 8, the improved Conv-LSTM network can classify gear faults accurately. In the confusion matrix, except for one class 4 fault identified as a class 3 fault, the rest of the fault classes are predicted correctly, which is better than the other three models, indicating that the model has obvious superiority in gear fault detection classification.

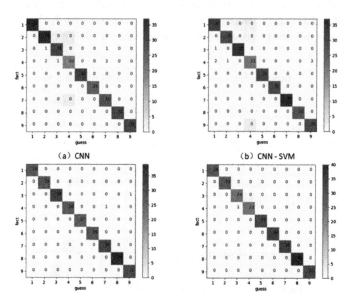

Fig. 8. Confusion matrix of four methods

5   Conclusion

Convolutional neural networks have received a lot of attention in the classification of mechanical system faults. However, the temporal feature information is often ignored. An improved Conv-LSTM network has been trained based on a dataset from the University of Connecticut, USA. In this network, the ability of CNN to extract robust and informative features has been combined with LSTM in time series modeling. This network has been used for multi-class fault classification. The accuracy of this network could reach 99.64%. The results show that the proposed method has certain advantages in terms of accuracy, compared with the CNN network, CNN-SVM network, and CNN-LSTM network. And it has better feature extraction and fault classification capabilities through confusion matrix experiments.

Acknowledgment. This work was supported by the Major Science and Technology Projects of Anhui Province under Grant 201903a05020011.

References

1. Errichello, R.: How to analyze gear failures. Pract. Fail. Anal. **2**(6), 8–16 (2002)

2. Hinton, G.E., Salakhutdinov, R.R.: Reducing the dimensionality of data with neural networks. Science **313**(5786), 504–517 (2006)
3. Li, S., Huang, S., Zhang, Y.: Deep learning in fault diagnosis of complex mechanical equipment. Int. J. Performability Eng. **16**(10), 1548 (2020)
4. Li, C., Zhang, S., Qin, Y.: A systematic review of deep transfer learning for machinery fault diagnosis. Neurocomputing **407**, 121–135 (2020)
5. Wang, Y., Yang, M., Li, Y.: A multi-input and multi-task convolutional neural network for fault diagnosis based on bearing vibration signal. IEEE Sens. J. **99**, 1–11 (2021)
6. Jin, T., Yan, C., Chen, C.: Light neural network with fewer parameters based on CNN for fault diagnosis of rotating machinery. Measurement **181**(3), 109639–109649 (2021)
7. Zhuang, Z., Qin, W.: Intelligent fault diagnosis of rolling bearing using one-dimensional multi-scale deep convolutional neural network based health state classification. In: 15th IEEE International Conference on Networking, Sensing and Control, pp. 1–8. ICNSC Proceedings, Zhuhai (2018)
8. Cao, P., Zhang, S., Tang, J.: Pre-processing-free gear fault diagnosis using small datasets with deep convolutional neural network-based transfer learning. IEEE Access **6**, 26241–26253 (2017)
9. Sabir, R., Rosato, D., Hartmann S., Guehmann, C.: LSTM based bearing fault diagnosis of electrical machines using motor current signal. In: 18th IEEE International Conference on Machine Learning and Applications (ICMLA), pp. 613–618. Boca Raton, FL, USA (2019)
10. Abdul, Z.K., Al-Talabani, A.K., Ramadan, D.O.: A hybrid temporal feature for gear fault diagnosis using the long short term memory. IEEE Sens. J. **23**(20), 14444–14452 (2020)
11. Zhao, H., Sun, S., Jin, B.: Sequential fault diagnosis based on LSTM neural network. IEEE Access **6**, 12929–12939 (2018)
12. Hochreiter, S., Schmidhuber, J.: Long short-term memory. Neural Comput. **9**(8), 1735–1780 (1997)
13. Bartlett, P.L., Wegkamp, M.H.: Classification with a reject option using a hinge loss. J. Mach. Learn. Res. **9**, 1823–1840 (2008)
14. Andreieva, V., Shvai, N.: Generalization of cross-entropy loss function for image classification. Mohyla Math. J. **3**, 3–9 (2020)
15. Han, J.S., Kwak K.C.: Image classification using convolutional neural network and extreme learning machine classifier based on ReLU function. J. Korean Inst. Inf. Technol. **15**(2), 15–23 (2017)
16. Fletcher, R.: Practical methods of optimization. SIAM Rev. **26**(1), 143–144 (1984)
17. Yu, X.H., Chen, G.A., Cheng, S.X.: dynamic learning rate optimization of the backpropagation algorithm. IEEE Trans. Neural Netw. **6**(3), 669–677 (1995)
18. Mostowy, W.M., Foster, W.A.: Antagonistic effects of energy status on meal size and egg-batch size of aedes aegypti (diptera: culicidae). J. Vector Ecol. **29**(1), 84–96 (2004)

Extracting Random Secret Key Scheme for One-Time Pad Under Intelligent Connected Vehicle

Junjie Chu[1], Mu Han[1(✉)], and Shidian Ma[2]

[1] School of Computer Science and Communication Engineering, Jiangsu University,
Zhenjiang 212013, China
`hanmu@ujs.edu.cn`
[2] Automotive Engineering Research Institute Jiangsu University,
Zhenjiang 212013, China

Abstract. With the rapid development of vehicle intelligence, the in-vehicle network is no longer a traditional closed network. External devices can be connected through Bluetooth, WiFi or OBD interfaces, so that attackers can remotely attack vehicles through these channels. Hence we create one-time pads to protect the in-vehicle network. Intelligent connected vehicle (ICV) is an information physical system, thus finding a suitable entropy source from its physical properties to extract true random numbers as a one-time pad can well ensure the security of ICV. During the driving process of ICV, the driving decision will change in real time, and these changes will directly act on the generator of the vehicle's power system, causing the voltage to change in real time. Therefore, we observe that the on-board power voltage of ICV is a very useful source of entropy. We propose a scheme to extract random numbers from the voltage entropy source. First, we filter the weak periodicity in the voltage signal using wavelet variations. After obtaining the non-periodic voltage signal, we fuse the high voltage time interval with it as a second entropy source to improve the extraction efficiency of the random numbers. Secondly, we build Markov chains by analysing the partial autocorrelation coefficient of the quantized bits of one trace. Finally, we extract perfect random numbers from the Markov chain by using cascaded XOR and hash function. Extensive realistic experiments are conducted to validate our scheme.

Keywords: Intelligent Connected Vehicle · On-board power voltage · Secret key extraction · One-time pad · Markov chain

1 Introduction

Intelligent connected vehicle face many security threats posed by network technologies and smart devices, making it possible for adversaries to attack the in-vehicle electronic control unit (ECU) [1]. Communication between in-vehicle ECU is broadcast in plaintext and all communication content is directly available on the in-vehicle bus, enabling an attacker to easily impersonate the ECU

Y. Xu et al. (Eds.): ML4CS 2022, LNCS 13656, pp. 130–143, 2023.
https://doi.org/10.1007/978-3-031-20099-1_11

to achieve an attack on the in-vehicle network [2]. Since the in-vehicle network is a critical part of the attack protection and the existing protection methods are weak, encrypting the information transmitted in the network is an effective security protection method to address the characteristics of in-vehicle network communication broadcast in plaintext [3].

According to the Kerckhoff's principle, the security of a system should be only depended on the security of its secret key. Pseudo-random numbers are generated quickly using deterministic mathematical algorithms, however such pseudo-random numbers have been proven to be periodic, making it difficult to guarantee the security of keys [4]. Hence, a truly random key is significant for the security of cryptographic schemes. Obtaining random numbers from an entropy source with unpredictability and uncertainty is a well-established method for generating random keys [5]. It can be various entropy sources in nature, such as quantum noise [6], thermal noise [7], etc., or chaos-based entropy sources [8], and the random numbers extracted through these entropy sources are true random numbers.

Sunar et al. proposed that the performance of random numbers is influenced by three dimensions: the selection of the entropy source, the collection of the entropy source and the post-processing method of the random sequence [9]. We propose our solution in these three dimensions and address the following challenges from in-vehicle networks.

The main contributions of this paper are summarized as follows:

- We evaluate against the vehicle generator system and show that voltage is suitable as a source of entropy for extracting random numbers.
- We propose an entropy source optimization method. We find that there is a fixed periodic signal in the voltage signal, so we use the decomposition and reconstruction of wavelets to obtain a non-periodic voltage signal. In order to further increase the quality of the entropy source and improve the efficiency of the extraction of true random numbers, we introduce a second entropy source to achieve this target.
- We propose a systematic way to ensure the randomness of the resulting key. We discover that a Markov model is appropriate to capture the dependency among random bits, based on which we select a randomness extractor to produce perfect random bits. The extracted bits pass the NIST test [10].

2   On-Board Power Supply

Finding a suitable entropy source from the physical characteristics of the on-board power supply to extract a true random number as a key guarantees the security of the cryptographic algorithm [11]. The variation of the voltage depends mainly on the generator, so an analysis for the generator system provides a good demonstration of the principle of voltage variation [12].

We have a clear view of the composition of the generator system from Fig. 1. In the figure i_A, i_B and i_C are the phase currents of stators A, B and C respectively, i_f is the excitation current, EB is the battery voltage and ω is the speed.

When the vehicle is started, the battery acts on the current control system to generate the excitation current i_f, while the step signal affects the engine, and the combined effect of the speed ω and excitation current i_f forms a rotary magnetic field that causes the flux in the stators A, B and C to change. The speed of the vehicle changes in real time during travel due to a variety of factors, resulting in unpredictable and random changes in speed.

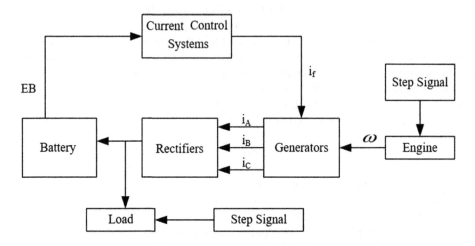

Fig. 1. Generator model systems

To specify the process of voltage change, the input speed ω_1 and the input speed ω_2 are calculated to obtain the electrical angle, which is shown in Eq. 1.

$$\frac{d\theta_e}{dt} = p \cdot (w1 + w2) \tag{1}$$

When the generator starts, the rotor magnetic chain equation is changed by the combined effect of the stators, current and electrical angle, which is shown in Eq. 2. Where M_{sf} is mutual inductance between stators and rotors, θ_e is electrical angle, I_{fl} is input current, I_{sA}, I_{sB}, I_{sC} are the currents in stators A, B and C, L_f is self-sensing factor.

$$\psi_{fl} = \left(M_{sf} \cdot \cos\left(\theta_e\right), M_{sf} \cdot \cos\left(\theta_e - \frac{2\pi}{3}\right), M_{sf} \cdot \cos\left(\theta_e + \frac{2\pi}{3}\right) \right) \begin{bmatrix} I_{sA} \\ I_{sB} \\ I_{sC} \end{bmatrix} + L_f \cdot I_{fl} \tag{2}$$

As can be seen from Eq. 3, the change in voltage U_{fl} is determined by the influence of the rotor magnetic chain Ψ_{fl}, which in turn is influenced by the change in speed. Therefore, under the influence of factors such as the traffic environment and weather factors, the rotational speed is in an unpredictable variation during vehicle driving, leading to an unpredictable variation in voltage noise as well. R_f is rotor resistance.

$$U_{fl} = R_f \cdot I_{fl} + \frac{d_{\psi_f}}{d_t} \tag{3}$$

3   Overview of Our Approach

We organize our solution into the framework in Fig. 2. To improve the efficiency of the acquisition, we use two oscilloscopes to capture the voltage and high voltage interval time simultaneously. The bandwidth of the oscilloscopes is set to 400 MHz and the sampling frequency is set to 3 GS/s. The time is recorded when the captured voltage value reaches the high voltage range and when the voltage reaches the high voltage range a second time, the timer is reset and the interval between the two high voltage values is recorded. Figure 3(a) and Fig. 3(b) show the voltage time domain and frequency domain plots respectively.

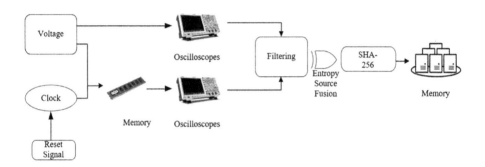

Fig. 2. Flowchart of the system

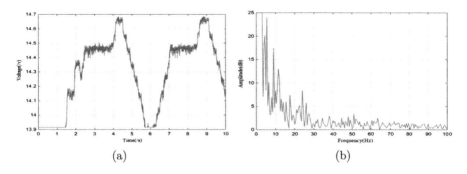

(a)   (b)

Fig. 3. Voltage time and frequency domain plots

The captured voltage needs to be filtered. We observe that there is weak periodicity in the voltage signal, so we need to filter the periodic voltage signal and also introduce the high voltage interval time as a second source of entropy to enhance the robustness and robustness of the random sequence, the exact scheme of which we will describe carefully in Sect. 4.

By analysing the dependencies between bits, a Markov chain is established to set the stage for our work on extracting random numbers. We split the obtained dependent quantized bits into independent subsequence, and simultaneously process the subsequence using cascaded XOR and hash function to extract unbiased random bits for our purpose of extracting perfect random numbers.

4   Filtering

During the acquisition process we found a subtle periodicity in the supply voltage fluctuations. In Fig. 3(b) we can observe a number of spikes in the spectrum that exceed 10 dB, for example four peaks between frequencies 0 to 15 Hz that exceed 10 dB. This indicates that there is a weak periodicity in the supply voltage signal, which will affect the quality of the entropy source.

Therefore, we design a filtering method based on the decomposition and reconstruction of the wavelet transform to filter weak periodic signal in the voltage signal [13]. In practical acquisitions, the voltage signal we need is usually high-frequency signal and periodic signal is usually low-frequency signal. To obtain non-periodic voltage signal, voltage signal needs to be processed using wavelet decomposition and reconstruction, and the signal decomposition is shown in Fig. 4.

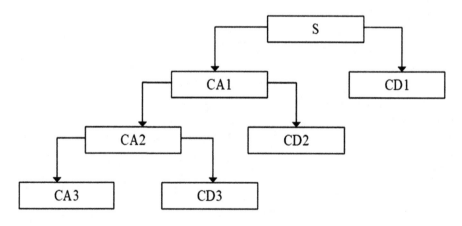

Fig. 4. Signal decomposition

After a three-level decomposition of the signal S, we get the high-frequency signals CD1, CD2 and CD3. The decomposed low-frequency signals are all reset to zero, and then the voltage signals are reconstructed to filter the periodic signal to give us the non-periodic voltage signal. We perform wavelet decomposition and reconstruction on 2000 sets of voltage signal. Figure 5 shows a comparison of the voltage signal before and after the reconfiguration

To enhance the robustness and robustness of the random sequence, we use entropy source fusion. We convert the high voltage interval and reconstructed voltage into binary sequence and then heterogeneously couple them to obtain dependent quantized bits.

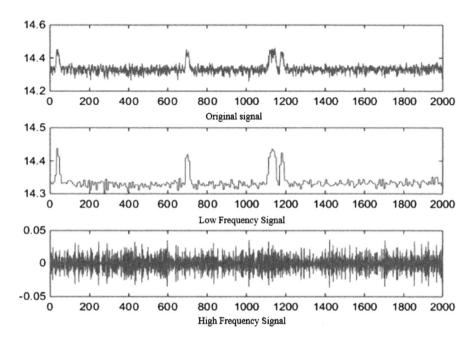

Fig. 5. Comparison of the voltage signal before and after the reconfiguration

5   Extracting a Perfect Random Key

In this section, we describe a method to extract a perfect random key from quantized bits. Here perfect random means that the bits of the key should be independent from each other and the probability of a bit being 1 should be 1/2.

5.1   Markov Modeling

We first show that quantized bits have limited dependency (each bit depends on finitely many previous bits), then we use a Markov chain to model the dependency.

To show the limited dependency property, we plot in Fig. 6 the partial auto-correlation coefficient (pacf) of the quantized bits of one trace [14]. Briefly, pacf describes the correlation between two bits after eliminating the influence of bits in-between, which does not eliminate the influence of bits in-between. We can see from the figure that for $lag \geq 5$, the absolute value of pacf is very small, meaning each bit only depends on the previous 4 bits. This observation suggests that it is appropriate to use Markov chains to model the dependencies.

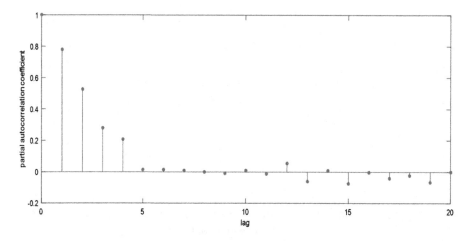

Fig. 6. The partial autocorrelation coefficient

We require a method to determine the order of the chain. For instance, if each bit depends on two previous bits, then we need to use a 2nd order Markov model with sate space $S^{(2)} = \{00, 01, 10, 11\}$. In general, we label the state space bits of a Markov model of order K with $S^{(k)}$.

We use the prevalent Bayesian Information Criterion (BIC) Markov order estimator to estimate the order [15]. Let there be n bits in the sequence, presence of subsequences in sequence $s_1^j = (s_1, s_2, \cdots, s_j)$, $N\left(s_1^j\right)$ is number of occurrences of the subsequences in the sequence. The order of a Markov chain is the minimum value of the function:

$$L(k) = -\log P_{ML(K)} + 2^{K-1} \log n \qquad (4)$$

It has been shown experimentally that Markov chains are always of order between 1 and 10. Therefore, the best order k can be determined by enumerating the $L(k)$. From Fig. 7, it can be seen that for the same number of bits in the sequence, the minimum value $L(k)$ is reached for k = 4. Thus, the sequence is suitable for building a Markov chain of order 4.

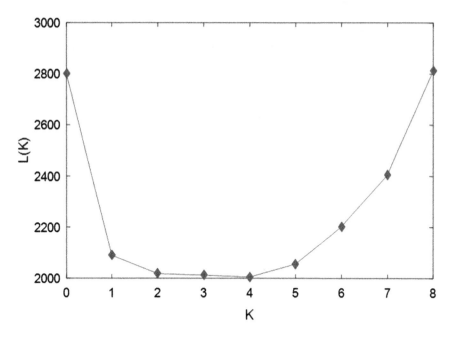

Fig. 7. Likelihood for quantized bits

After the prediction of the order is completed, a corresponding Markov chain model is built, and the entropy of the sequence can be calculated by the model [16]. By definition, the entropy of a Markov chain of order K is:

$$H = - \sum_{i \in S^{(k)}} \pi(i) \sum_{j \in S^{(k)}} p(i,j). \log p(i,j) \tag{5}$$

where $\pi(i)$ is the stationary distribution and $p(i,j)$ is the transition probability from state i to j. The entropy values for Markov chains of different orders are shown in Fig. 8.

In order to prove that the result of the Bayesian information quantity criterion Markov order determiner is accurate. We combine the partial autocorrelation coefficient and the entropy value to verify the order of the Markov chain model.

The method of determining the order of Markov chain by entropy value is to increase the order of Markov chain sequentially and calculate the entropy value of the sequence at different orders. As can be seen from Fig. 8, the entropy values are approximately the same when k = 2, 3, 4, so the order of Markov chain determined by this method is also 4, which is the same as the above two methods.

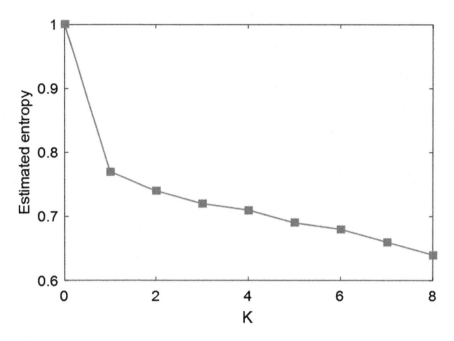

Fig. 8. Estimated entropy

The reason for not using the two methods of partial autocorrelation coefficient and entropy to calculate the order of a Markov chain is that it is not possible to quantify "very small" and "convergence", but it is possible to verify the results of the Bayesian information criterion for determining the order of a Markov chain by these two methods.

5.2   Randomness Extractor

We extract the perfect random bits from the dependent quantized bits. The randomness extractor consists of two steps. First, the sequence of bits is divided into a number of subsequences and each subsequence of the division contains independent bits. A bit belongs to a subsequence corresponding to the state determined by the previous k bits of that bit, where k is the estimated order of the Markov chain. Thus, each subsequence corresponds to a different Markov state yielding a total of 2^k subsequences. The splitting process can be done efficiently by scanning the bits from left to right. Figure 9 gives an example of splitting the bits in a second order Markov chain into four subsequences $S_{00}, S_{01}, S_{10}, S_{11}$. The dashed box starts with the two leftmost bits and slides one bit to the right at each step. At each step, the two bits inside the dashed box are represented as one of the four subsequences, and the right-hand bits outside the dashed box belong to that subsequence. This process is repeated until the dotted box reaches the end of the sequence. By dividing the sequence in this way, it is ensured that each subsequence has a separate bit in it.

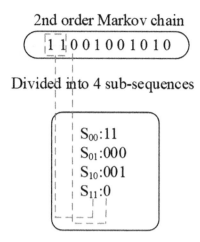

Fig. 9. Sub-sequence division diagram

Secondly, we extract unbiased bits from each subsequence. A bit is unbiased if the probability of it being 1 is equal to one half, otherwise it is biased. Ideally, the extracted true random number 0 and 1 probabilities should be equal, but in practice, the presence of other non-Gaussian type noise inside the circuit [17] and the influence of the external environment of the car on voltage fluctuations make it impossible for the resulting 0 and 1 probabilities to be absolutely equal. This affects the uniformity, bias and statistical properties of the random sequence, for which a digital post-processing method must be adopted to improve the subsequences [18] in order to achieve unbiased bits. We choose to post-process the subsequences with cascaded XOR and hash function, and the process is shown in Fig. 10. Cascaded XOR corresponds to a parity check that solves the problem of uniform distribution and deviation of the sequence. At the beat of the clock, we input the voltage-time signal sequence a(i) one by one into the six D flip-flops. After storing the shifts, we use the cascaded XOR to XOR them two by two to obtain a digital sequence b(i) to achieve a compression rate of 6 for the signal sequence. The resulting sequence is then processed by a hash function to improve the statistical properties of the numerical sequence. We use the SHA-256 algorithm, which is very fast in hardware and ensures the efficiency of the entire random number generator. SHA-256 can be easily implemented to compress the data. In order to minimize the speed of the data output, we use a data input to output ratio of 1:1. We set the input to 256 bits and set the output to 256 bits as well.

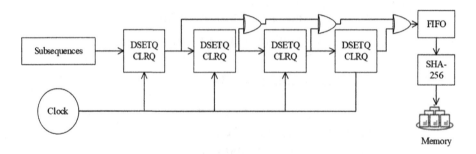

Fig. 10. Cascaded XOR and hash

5.3   Randomness Testing

The stability of the linear complexity LC(S) of a sequence is an important measure of its randomness [19]. The B-M algorithm states that as long as any two consecutive LC(S) elements of the sequence are known to determine the whole sequence, the linear complexity of the random sequence should be large enough in order to resist plaintext attacks. In this paper, we use the BM10 function to calculate the linear complexity of the resulting sequence, and finally arrive at a stable order 7 linear complexity of the sequence of about 49, while the order 7 linear complexity of the commonly used sequences Gold and Kasami are 14 and 17. Therefore, the performance of the random sequence in this paper is better than that of the commonly used sequences.

There are two widely used testing standards for random number performance, namely the Random Number Testing Requirements for Cryptographic Products published by the Chinese State Secrets Bureau and the NIST Random Number Test Standard published by the American Institute of Technology [20]. We use the NIST SP 800–22 test package to test the randomness of the extracted sequence to determine whether the sequence meet the requirement to be used as keys in the one-time pad.

A total number of 1000 random sequences of 92 Mbit are extracted and tested for randomness using the NIST test package. The test results are shown in Table 1. The tests show that the p-values of the 15 sets of test criteria are not less than the significant level of 0.01. We simultaneously compare it with Zhonghui's scheme [21], as shown in Fig. 11. We demonstrate that the sequences extracted based on the selected voltage variations in the supply voltage as the entropy source pass the NIST random number test criteria and can be used as true random numbers for one-time pad.

Table 1. Randomness test results

Test items	P-value
Frequency	0.419132
Frequency in a Block	0.810355
Runs	0.418424
Longest run of ones in a Block	0.181860
Binary matrix rank	0.379667
Discrete fourier transform	0.460588
Non-overlapping template Matching	0.411480
Overlapping template matching	0.412990
Universal statistical	0.820199
Linear complexity	0.156228
Serial	0.131349
Approximate entropy	0.975277
Cumulative sums1	0.166738
Cumulative sums2	0.422964
Random excursions	0.266250
Random excursions variant	0.244884

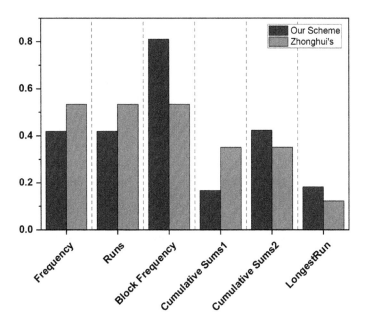

Fig. 11. Randomness testing comparison

5.4   Section Summary

In this section, we first determine the dependencies between quantized bits by using the partial autocorrelation coefficient to show that they are consistent with Markov modelling. Secondly, we use the BIC to initially determine the order of the Markov chain. Simultaneously, we combine the partial autocorrelation coefficient and entropy to further corroborate that the order determined by the BIC is correct. Finally, we extract unbiased bits from the Markov chain to reach the extraction of perfect random numbers. Our extracted random numbers pass the NIST test very successfully. This means that the random numbers we extracted are perfect for a one-time pad.

6   Conclusion

We start with the physical properties of the ICV and hope to find a suitable source of entropy. We demonstrate that voltage is a suitable source of entropy by analysing the generator model. We considered the possibility of extracting the random numbers from the on-board power voltage. We use wavelet variations to filter the weak periodicity of the voltage. To improve the efficiency of the random numbers extraction, we use the time interval of the high voltage as a second entropy source fused with the voltage. After obtaining the sequence of bits we firstly state the dependencies between the bits and find that the sequence fits the requirements of Markov model. Secondly we determine the order of the Markov chain by using BIC and entropy. Finally we generate subsequences from the resulting Markov chain to help us extract the perfect random key. Our solution extends the source of random key extraction. Measurements from real-world on-board power voltage show that in most cases we can help tolerate noise in different environments and provide stable performance through filtering.

References

1. Li, Y., Luo, Q., Liu, J., Guo, H., Kato, N.: TSP security in intelligent and connected vehicles: challenges and solutions. IEEE Wirel. Commun. **26**(3), 125–131 (2019). https://doi.org/10.1109/MWC.2019.1800289
2. Aliwa, E., Rana, O., Perera, C., et al.: Cyberattacks and countermeasures for in-vehicle networks. ACM Comput. Surv. (CSUR) **54**(1), 1–37 (2021)
3. Hu, Q., Luo, F.: Review of secure communication approaches for in-vehicle network. Int. J. Autom. Technol. **19**(5), 879–894 (2018)
4. Liming, K., Haifeng, Y., Chunyi, C., et al.: Extraction of true random number based on atmospheric turbulence light flicker. Appl. Opt. **40**(03), 165–172 (2019)
5. Herrero-Collantes, M., Garcia-Escartin, J.C.: Quantum random number generators. Rev. Mod. Phys. **89**(1), 015004 (2017)
6. Clerk, A.A., Devoret, M.H., Girvin, S.M., et al.: Introduction to quantum noise, measurement, and amplification. Rev. Mod. Phys. **82**(2), 1155 (2010)
7. Vizioli, L., Moeller, S., Dowdle, L., et al.: Lowering the thermal noise barrier in functional brain mapping with magnetic resonance imaging. Nat. Commun. **12**(1), 1–15 (2021)

8. Avaroğlu, E., Tuncer, T., Özer, A.B., et al.: A novel chaos-based post-processing for TRNG. Nonlinear Dyn. **81**(1), 189–199 (2015)
9. Sunar, B., Martin, W.J., Stinson, D.R.: A provably secure true random number generator with built - in tolerance to active attacks. IEEE Trans. Comput. **56**(1), 109–119 (2007)
10. Rukhin, A., et al.: A statistical test suite for random and pseudorandom number generators for cryptographic applications. NIST Special Publication 800–22 Revision 1a, April 2010. https://doi.org/10.6028/NIST.SP.800-22r1a
11. Wu, H., Yin, Z., Xie, J., et al.: Design and implementation of true random number generators based on semiconductor superlattice chaos. Microelectron. J. **114**, 105119 (2021)
12. Baran, M.E., El-Markabi, I.M.: A multiagent-based dispatching scheme for distributed generators for voltage support on distribution feeders. IEEE Trans. Power Syst. **22**(1), 52–59 (2007)
13. Zhang, D.: Wavelet transform. In: Fundamentals of Image Data Mining. TCS, pp. 35–44. Springer, Cham (2019). https://doi.org/10.1007/978-3-030-17989-2_3
14. Liang, F., Song, Q., Qiu, P.: An equivalent measure of partial correlation coefficients for high-dimensional gaussian graphical models. J. Am. Stat. Assoc. **110**(511), 1248–1265 (2015)
15. Csiszár, I., Shields, P.C.: The consistency of the BIC Markov order estimator. Ann. Stat. **28**(6), 1601–1619 (2000)
16. Su, F., Wu, J., He, S.: Set pair analysis-Markov chain model for groundwater quality assessment and prediction: a case study of Xi'an city, China. Hum. Ecol. Risk Assess. Int. J. **25**(1–2), 158–175 (2019)
17. Zhang, Y., Srivastava, A.: Accurate temperature estimation using noisy thermal sensors for Gaussian and non-Gaussian cases. IEEE Trans. Very Large Scale Integr. (VLSI) Syst. **19**(9), 1617–1626 (2010)
18. Guo, X., Shu, Y., Kim, G.H., et al.: Pseudorandom orbiting stroke for freeform optics postprocessing. Opt. Eng. **58**, 092608 (2019)
19. Li, Z., Cai, J., Chang, Y.: Determining the complexity of FH/SS sequence by approximate entropy. IEEE Trans. Commun. **57**(3), 812–820 (2009)
20. Sýs, M., Říha, Z.: Faster randomness testing with the NIST statistical test suite. In: Chakraborty, R.S., Matyas, V., Schaumont, P. (eds.) SPACE 2014. LNCS, vol. 8804, pp. 272–284. Springer, Cham (2014). https://doi.org/10.1007/978-3-319-12060-7_18
21. Zhonghui, L., Chunyi, C., Haifeng, Y., et al.: Study on extraction of true random numbers based on propagated laser speckle in atmospheric turbulence. Infrared Laser Eng. **48**(12), 1205005–1205005 (2019)

Semi-supervised Learning with Nearest-Neighbor Label and Consistency Regularization

Guolin Zheng[1], Zuoyong Li[2], Wenkai Hu[3], Haoyi Fan[3], Fum Yew Ching[4], Zhaochai Yu[5(✉)], and Kaizhi Chen[1(✉)]

[1] College of Computer and Data Science, Fuzhou University, Fuzhou 350108, China
ckz@fzu.edu.cn
[2] Fujian Provincial Key Laboratory of Information Processing and Intelligent Control, College of Computer and Control Engineering, Minjiang University, Fuzhou 350121, China
[3] School of Computer and Artificial Intelligence, Zhengzhou University, Zhengzhou 450001, China
[4] School of Computer Sciences, Universiti Sains Malaysia, Penang 11800, Malaysia
[5] College of Mathematics and Data Science (Software College), Minjiang University, Fuzhou 350121, China
yzchair@126.com

Abstract. Semi-supervised learning, a system dedicated to making networks less dependent on labeled data, has become a popular paradigm due to its strong performance. A common approach is to use pseudo-labels with unlabeled data for training, however, pseudo-labels cannot correct their own errors. In this paper, we propose a semi-supervised method that uses nearest neighbor samples to obtain pseudo-labels and combines consistency regularization for image classification. Our method obtains pseudo-labels by computing the similarity of the data distribution between the weakly-augmented version of the unlabeled data and the labeled data stored in the support set and combines the consistency of the strongly-augmented version and the weakly-augmented version of the unlabeled data. We compared with several standard semi-supervised learning benchmarks and achieved a competitive performance. For example, we achieved an accuracy of 94.02% on CIFAR-10 with 250 labels and 97.50% on SVNH with 250 labels. It even achieved 91.59% accuracy with only 40 labels data in the CIFAR-10.

Keywords: Semi-supervised learning · Consistency regularization · Pseudo-label · Nearest-neighbor

1 Introduction

For many learning tasks, collecting a large annotated dataset is labor-intensive. And for a medical task, producing a complete medical dataset is even more

Y. Xu et al. (Eds.): ML4CS 2022, LNCS 13656, pp. 144–154, 2023.
https://doi.org/10.1007/978-3-031-20099-1_12

complex because the analysis of medical data requires expensive instruments and specialized domain knowledge. Therefore, there are labeled data that are particularly scarce. Semi-supervised learning [4,10] (SSL) attempts to reduce the reliance on labeled data by allowing the model to utilize unlabeled data. Semi-supervised learning (SSL) trains the network with only a limited amount of labeled data and back propagates in the direction of the pre-defined task.

Recently, research on SSL methods has produced a diverse collection of approaches, such as consistency regularization [15,26], self-training[18,34]. Consistency regularization encourages that even after unlabeled samples are injected with noise, the classifier should output the same probability of class distribution for them. Many works [2,3,15,26,32] use data augmentation as a perturbation so that the same input has exactly different values at the output, but remains consistent. Self-training encourages the model to find out the information related to unlabeled data for training by itself. The idea of self-training has been applied for many years in various fields, such as NLP [18], object detection [25], image classification [16,33], domain adaptation [38]. The most classical pseudo-labeling [16] approach is to use predictions generated from unlabeled data, which fall into this class if the probability assigned to the most likely class is higher than a predetermined threshold τ.

Pseudo-labeling cannot correct its own errors, which can lead to model errors being magnified. There are some works [1,22] that add pseudo-labeling to their pipeline to improve their results. However, many SSL methods that use pseudo-labeling are also becoming increasingly complex. In this work, we sample the labels of the most similar samples as pseudo-labels by using the nearest neighbor method and construct paired strongly-augmented and weakly-augmented versions of the unlabeled data to perform consistency regularization. We obtain pseudo-label by encouraging proximity between the unlabeled data and their nearest neighbors' data distribution. We consider using weakly-augmented versions of the unlabeled images to obtain artificial labels by finding the most similar samples in the support set. Combining the consistency between weakly and strongly augmented versions of the same image, the artificial labels obtained from the weakly-augmented version of the image are used as targets for the strongly-augmented version of the same image. We demonstrate in our experiments that this is a simple but effective semi-supervised method and still performs well with a small number of labeled data.

We make the following contributions:

- We propose a new semi-supervised method that trains by obtaining artificial labels for unlabeled data and combining it with consistent regularization.
- We obtain more reliable sample labels by setting a high confidence threshold on the pseudo-labels obtained by the nearest neighbor method and greatly improve the performance of the model by setting a strongly-augmented version and a weakly-augmented version of the unlabeled data pairs.
- We investigate the performance of our method with a small amount of labeled data (40 labels) and still achieve competitive results compared to several standard semi-supervised benchmarks.

2   Related Work

2.1   Self-training

Self-training [18,31,34] uses the model's own predictions on unlabeled data to obtain additional information that can be used in training. Self-training, also known as pseudo-labeling, typically converts the model's output data distribution to hard labels, using the highest confidence. Obtaining pseudo-labels by encouraging the model to output low entropy (i.e., to make "high-confidence" predictions [16]) on unlabeled data, which is often accompanied by a confidence-based threshold that retains unlabeled samples only if the highest value of the classifier output is greater than a predetermined value. Incorrect pseudo-labeling affects model learning and the model does not self-correct, which makes learning more difficult. UPS [24] is an uncertainty-aware pseudo-label selection framework that improves the accuracy of pseudo-label by significantly reducing the amount of noise encountered during training.

2.2   Consistency Regularization

Consistency regularization [2,3,9,15,19,26,28,32,36] utilizes the unlabeled data based on the assumption that the predicted distribution will remain consistent for different versions of the same image using different perturbations as input.Π-Model [15] use dropout as a perturbation to generate different distribution, and use l_2 loss to minimize the difference between them. There exists some work [19] using the concept of adversarial attack for consistency regularization. The most common way of perturbation remains the domain-specific data augmentation [2,3,15,26,32]. MixMatch [2] has made great progress using the powerful MixUp regularization [37], a linear interpolation approach that mixes unlabeled and labeled data. ReMixmatch [2] proposes two more techniques based on MixMatch [2]: distribution alignment and augmentation anchoring, which maintain the use of a weakly-augmented version image as the input to the "guess label" component, and a strongly-augmented version of the same input for consistency regularization. UDA [32] applied AutoAugment [5] on unlabeled data and found that stronger data augmentation could improve the performance of consistency regularization.

2.3   Nearest Neighbors Search in Computer Vision

There are many applications in computer vision that use nearest neighbor search [7,12,13]. [29] learns the landmarks on the object using nearest-neighbor in the unsupervised case. NNCLR [8] samples the nearest neighbors from the latent space and treats them as positives to achieve contrastive learning. [11] uses nearest neighbor retrieval to help unify videos of different modalities. Neighbor Matching [30] defines a mapping function implemented based on an attention mechanism to predict pseudo labels. In contrast, in this work we use nearest neighbor retrieval combined with consistency regularization, and we maintain an explicit support set to store the data distribution to increase diversity.

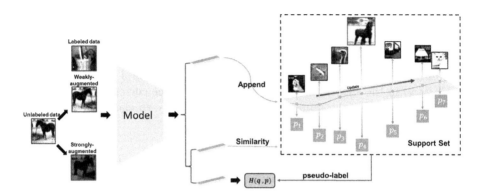

Fig. 1. Overview of our method. Our method uses the weakly-augmented version of the image to find the label of the most similar sample in the support set as a pseudo-label for the strongly-augmented version of the same image.

3   Method

In this section, we introduce our proposed semi-supervised method. Our method consists of two approaches: consistent regularization and pseudo-labels obtained from the nearest neighbors. We generate pseudo-labels for unlabeled data by finding the nearest neighbor samples in the support set (see Fig. 1).

3.1   Overview

For a semi-supervised learning task, given a batch of B labeled samples $\mathcal{X} = \{(x_b, p_b) : b \in (1, \ldots, B)\}$, where x_b are the training samples and p_b are one-hot labels. Let $\mathcal{U} = \{u_b : b \in (1, \ldots, \mu B)\}$ be a batch of μB unlabeled samples where μ is the hyperparameter that determines the relative size between $\mathcal{X}$ and $\mathcal{U}$. The goal of semi-supervised learning is to learn a model that can correctly output the class distribution of labeled and unlabeled data given a valid number of labels. We initialize a model $f_\theta(\cdot)$ with parameters consisting of a learnable weight θ. Two types of data augmentations $\alpha(\cdot)$ and $\mathcal{A}(\cdot)$ are used in our approach, where $\mathcal{A}(\cdot)$ is a stronger data augmentation than $\alpha(\cdot)$. Let $p_m(y|x)$ is the prediction class distribution of the data x input to the model. For each given labeled data, we use the weaker data augmentation $\alpha(\cdot)$ to generate the data distribution, and then use a standard cross-entropy loss term for the labels. At the same time, we add data distributions from labeled data and their corresponding labels to a support set for labeled search of unlabeled data.

Cosine similarity measures the similarity between two vectors by measuring the cosine of the angle between them. For the more similar samples, the value of cosine similarity will get closer. The formula for calculating the similarity in our work is as follows:

$$sim(u, v) = \frac{u^{\mathrm{T}} v}{\|u\|\|v\|} \tag{1}$$

To obtain an artificial label, we first compute the similarity between the data distribution of a given weakly augmented version of the unlabeled data and the distribution of all data stored in the support set to obtain a similarity vector v. $p_m(y_i|x_i)$ in the support set is the most similar to the current distribution of unlabeled data, where y_i represents x_i belongs to the c-th class. Therefore, we have

$$\delta[v] = c \tag{2}$$

Then, we use $\hat{p}_b = \delta[v]$ as a pseudo-label, where $\delta[v]$ denotes the class when the vector v reaches the index of the largest element.

3.2 Augmentation

In ReMixMatch [2], "Augmentation Anchoring" is derived, the idea is to use the weakly-augmented version of the unlabeled image to provide labels for the strongly-augmented version of the image. For image classification tasks, AutoAugment [5] provides a powerful boost. RandAugment [6] is a variant of AutoAugment, which is used as a strong data augmentation for our work. Our method use two type of data augmentation: $\alpha(\cdot)$ and $\mathcal{A}(\cdot)$, where $\alpha(\cdot)$ denote to the weaker data augmentation (e.g. using only a flip and a crop) and $\mathcal{A}(\cdot)$ denote to the stronger data augmentation (e.g. RandAugment).

3.3 Support Set

Our support set Q uses two queues for storing historical data distributions with labels and their corresponding labels, where the size of the queue for storing data distributions is $[num\_classes, L]$ and the size of the queue for storing labels is $[1, L]$. The size L of the support set is kept large enough so as to store the full class distribution. We update the support set when the labeled data are distributed by the model output by taking the n (batch size) of distribution and their corresponding labels into the support set. When the support set is full, we replace the oldest n distributions with the new ones.

3.4 Loss Functions

Our method contains two cross-entropy loss functions: (1) supervised loss l_s for labeled data and (2) unsupervised loss l_u for unlabeled data.

For labeled data, we use weaker data augmentation $\alpha(\cdot)$ acting on it and the standard cross-entropy l_s as a loss term:

$$l_s = \frac{1}{B} \sum_{b=0}^{B} H(p_b, p_m(y|\alpha(x_b))) \tag{3}$$

To obtain an artificial label, we render the unlabeled data using the same weaker data augmentation $\alpha(\cdot)$ as the labeled data. Our method uses the weakly augmented sample which is the same version of the strongly augmented sample to search for the most similar sample in the support set whose corresponding labels are used as pseudo labels. We provide an artificial label for each unlabeled sample and apply it to a cross-entropy loss function:

$$l_u = \frac{1}{\mu B} \sum_{b=0}^{\mu B} \mathbb{1}(NN(p_m(y|\alpha(u_b)), Q) \geq \tau) H(\hat{p}_b, p_m(y|\mathcal{A}(x_b))) \tag{4}$$

where $NN(p_m(y|\alpha(u_b)), Q)$ is the nearest neighbor operator as defined below:

$$NN(p_m(y|\alpha(u_b)), Q) = \underset{q \in Q}{argmax}\, sim(p_m(y|\alpha(u_b)), q) \tag{5}$$

In total, our method loss is

$$l_{total} = l_s + \lambda \cdot l_u \tag{6}$$

Table 1. Error rates on CIFAR-10 and SVHN dataset.

Method	CIFAR-10			SVHN		
	40 labels	250 labels	4000 labels	40 labels	250 labels	1000 labels
Fully-supervised	4.62	4.68	4.62	2.13	2.13	2.14
Pseudo-Label [16]	74.61	46.49	15.08	64.61	15.59	9.40
MixMatch [3]	36.19	12.67	6.66	30.60	4.56	3.69
ReMixMatch [2]	9.88	6.25	4.84	3.10	2.92	2.65
Ours	8.41	5.98	4.44	2.96	2.50	2.20

4   Experiment

In this section, we evaluate the efficacy of our method on several standard semi-supervised learning benchmarks (see Table 1). Specifically, we tested the performance of each benchmarks on the CIFAR-10 [14] and SVHN [20] using varying amounts of labeled data, following standard SSL evaluation protocols [2,3,21]. We also show the ablation experiments of our method under different confidence-based thresholds.

4.1 Implement Details

Architecture. We use a Wide ResNet (WRN) [35] as our model. Noted that all experiments in this paper were conducted under the same architecture to produce the results.

Training. Our approach involves a number of hyperparameters, and we use the same set of hyperparameters in our experiments and datasets, where $B = 64, \tau = 0.98, \mu = 7, L = 65536 * 2, \lambda = 1, K = 2^{20}$. Concretely, we train all benchmarks to use a uniform batch size of data is 64. In Pseudo-Label, MixMatch and ReMixMatch, μ is set to 1, and our method is set to 7. τ is a confidence-based threshold, set to 0.95 in Pseudo-Label and 0.98 in our method. These setups follow the original papers. L represents the length of the support set. λ is used to balance supervised and semi-supervised losses and is set to 1. All the experiments use standard stochastic gradient descent (SGD) with a momentum of 0.9 [23,27] as optimizer. The schedule [17] of the cosine learning rate decay $\eta = \eta_0 \cos(\frac{7\pi k}{16K})$ was used in all experiments, where η_0 is a learning rate that is initialized to 0.03, k represents the current training steps and K is the total training step that is set to $K = 2^{20}$. For all experiments, we use one evaluation matrix, which is the best error rate in all checkpoints.

Evaluation Metrics. We adopt an evaluation metric: the best error rate in all checkpoints.

4.2 Main Results

Fully-Supervised Baseline. To begin, we trained fully-supervised baseline on CIFAR-10 [14] and SVHN [20]. The fully supervised experiment was added to enable a better understanding of the effectiveness of the SSL algorithm. This can be used to measure the highest accuracy we hope to obtain on our training pipeline. Many semi-supervised algorithms have shown competitive performance, even better with the addition of consistency regularization. Therefore, our fully supervised comparison uses all labeled data that use weakly-augmented $\alpha(\cdot)$ (e.g. using only a flip and a crop) and follows Eq. 3 for training. As can be seen from Table 1, the lowest error rate is 4.60% on CIFAR-10 and 2.13% on SVHN.

Result on CIFAR-10. We can see the results of CIFAR-10 in Table 1, left. We evaluate our method on CIFAR-10 with 40, 250 and 4000 labeled data. Compared with other semi-supervised methods, our method achieves the lowest error rates of 5.98% and 4.44% on 250 label and 4000 label, respectively. More importantly, our method still works with 40 label, achieving the error rate of 8.41%.

Result on SVHN. The experimental results of SVHN can be viewed in Table 1, right. Similarly, with only 40, 250, and 1000 labeled data, our method also performs well. Our method achieves an error rate of 2.96% on 40 labels of SVHN and the lowest error rate of 2.20% on 1000 labels.

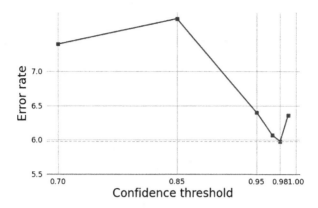

Fig. 2. Ablation study on confidence-based threshold. Effect of changing confidence-based thresholds on the results of semi-supervised experiments under our framework.

4.3   Ablation Study

Here we performed an ablation experiment on a confidence-based threshold. Figure 2 shows the error rate for varying thresholds in our semi-supervised framework. We focused on the effect of changing thresholds on the experimental results in the case of a single 250 labels split from CIFAR-10. Calculating the similarity of distributions to obtain pseudo-labels has proven to be effective in our experimental results. Using similarity to obtain artificial labels for unlabeled data can be faulty and fraudulent between samples, setting a higher confidence-based threshold can help us better filter some noisy samples. From Fig. 2, it can be seen that the lowest error rate 5.98% was obtained using 0.98 as the threshold, while the highest occurred at 0.85 is 7.77%.

4.4   Visualization

We also show the t-SNE [35] visualizations of the representations learned by FullySupervised, MixMatch, and our proposed method on the test set of CIFAR-10 with 4 labels per class (see Fig. 3). Compared to MixMatch, our proposed method shows better class separation and is closer to the FullySupervised benchmark.

(a) Fully-supervised(All labels)　　(b) MixMatch(40 labels)　　(c) Ours (40 labels)

Fig. 3. Fully-supervised, MixMatch and our method visualization for t-SNE on CIFAR-10. Fully-supervised uses all labeled data, while MixMatch and our method use 40 labeled data. Classes are indicated by colors (Color figure online).

5　Conclusion

In this paper, we propose a new semi-supervised method that combines consistency regularization and pseudo-labeling. Our method finds the most similar samples by matching images using a weakly-augmented version of the image with labeled data, using the labels of the found labeled data as targets for the strongly-augmented version of the same image. A simple and effective method that uses nearest neighbor matching to obtain artificial labels for unlabeled data, combined with consistency regularization achieves competitive performance. In future work, we are more committed to exploring the similarity between samples at the feature level, which will be more reliable.

Acknowledgements. This work is partially supported by National Natural Science Foundation of China (61972187), Natural Science Foundation of Fujian Province (2020J02024).

References

1. Arazo, E., Ortego, D., Albert, P., O'Connor, N.E., McGuinness, K.: Pseudo-labeling and confirmation bias in deep semi-supervised learning. In: 2020 International Joint Conference on Neural Networks (IJCNN), pp. 1–8. IEEE (2020)
2. Berthelot, D., et al.: Remixmatch: Semi-supervised learning with distribution alignment and augmentation anchoring. arXiv preprint arXiv:1911.09785 (2019)
3. Berthelot, D., Carlini, N., Goodfellow, I., Papernot, N., Oliver, A., Raffel, C.A.: Mixmatch: A holistic approach to semi-supervised learning. In: Advances in Neural Information Processing Systems 32 (2019)
4. Chapelle, O., Scholkopf, B., Zien, A.: Semi-supervised learning (chapelle, o. et al., eds.; 2006)[book reviews]. IEEE Transactions on Neural Networks **20**(3), 542–542 (2009)
5. Cubuk, E.D., Zoph, B., Mane, D., Vasudevan, V., Le, Q.V.: Autoaugment: Learning augmentation policies from data. arXiv preprint arXiv:1805.09501 (2018)

6. Cubuk, E.D., Zoph, B., Shlens, J., Le, Q.V.: Randaugment: Practical automated data augmentation with a reduced search space. In: Proceedings of the IEEE/CVF Conference on Computer Vision and Pattern Recognition Workshops, pp. 702–703 (2020)
7. Doersch, C., Singh, S., Gupta, A., Sivic, J., Efros, A.: What makes paris look like paris? ACM Trans. Graph. 31(4) (2012)
8. Dwibedi, D., Aytar, Y., Tompson, J., Sermanet, P., Zisserman, A.: With a little help from my friends: Nearest-neighbor contrastive learning of visual representations. In: Proceedings of the IEEE/CVF International Conference on Computer Vision, pp. 9588–9597 (2021)
9. Fan, H., Zhang, F., Gao, Y.: Self-supervised time series representation learning by inter-intra relational reasoning. arXiv preprint arXiv:2011.13548 (2020)
10. Fan, H., Zhang, F., Wang, R., Huang, X., Li, Z.: Semi-supervised time series classification by temporal relation prediction. In: ICASSP 2021–2021 IEEE International Conference on Acoustics, Speech and Signal Processing (ICASSP), pp. 3545–3549. IEEE (2021)
11. Han, T., Xie, W., Zisserman, A.: Self-supervised co-training for video representation learning (2020)
12. Hays, J., Efros, A.A.: Scene completion using millions of photographs. ACM Trans. Graph. (ToG) **26**(3), 4-es (2007)
13. Hays, J., Efros, A.A.: Im2gps: estimating geographic information from a single image. In: 2008 IEEE Conference On Computer Vision And Pattern Recognition, pp. 1–8. IEEE (2008)
14. Krizhevsky, A., Hinton, G., et al.: Learning multiple layers of features from tiny images (2009)
15. Laine, S., Aila, T.: Temporal ensembling for semi-supervised learning. arXiv preprint arXiv:1610.02242 (2016)
16. Lee, D.H., et al.: Pseudo-label: The simple and efficient semi-supervised learning method for deep neural networks. In: Workshop on Challenges In Representation Learning, ICML, vol. 3, p. 896 (2013)
17. Loshchilov, I., Hutter, F.: Sgdr: Stochastic gradient descent with warm restarts. arXiv preprint arXiv:1608.03983 (2016)
18. McClosky, D., Charniak, E., Johnson, M.: Effective self-training for parsing. In: Proceedings of the main conference on human language technology conference of the North American Chapter of the Association of Computational Linguistics, pp. 152–159. Citeseer (2006)
19. Miyato, T., Maeda, S.I., Koyama, M., Ishii, S.: Virtual adversarial training: a regularization method for supervised and semi-supervised learning. IEEE Trans. Pattern Anal. Mach. Intell. **41**(8), 1979–1993 (2018)
20. Netzer, Y., Wang, T., Coates, A., Bissacco, A., Wu, B., Ng, A.Y.: Reading digits in natural images with unsupervised feature learning (2011)
21. Oliver, A., Odena, A., Raffel, C.A., Cubuk, E.D., Goodfellow, I.: Realistic evaluation of deep semi-supervised learning algorithms. In: Advances in Neural Information Processing Systems 31 (2018)
22. Pham, H., Le, Q.V.: Semi-supervised learning by coaching (2020). https://openreview.net/forum?id=rJe04p4YDB
23. Polyak, B.T.: Some methods of speeding up the convergence of iteration methods. USSR Comput. Math. Math. Phys. **4**(5), 1–17 (1964)
24. Rizve, M.N., Duarte, K., Rawat, Y.S., Shah, M.: In defense of pseudo-labeling: An uncertainty-aware pseudo-label selection framework for semi-supervised learning. arXiv preprint arXiv:2101.06329 (2021)

25. Rosenberg, C., Hebert, M., Schneiderman, H.: Semi-supervised self-training of object detection models (2005)
26. Sajjadi, M., Javanmardi, M., Tasdizen, T.: Regularization with stochastic transformations and perturbations for deep semi-supervised learning. In: Advances in Neural Information Processing Systems 29 (2016)
27. Sutskever, I., Martens, J., Dahl, G., Hinton, G.: On the importance of initialization and momentum in deep learning. In: International Conference on Machine Learning, pp. 1139–1147. PMLR (2013)
28. Tarvainen, A., Valpola, H.: Mean teachers are better role models: Weight-averaged consistency targets improve semi-supervised deep learning results. In: Advances in Neural Information Processing Systems 30 (2017)
29. Thewlis, J., Albanie, S., Bilen, H., Vedaldi, A.: Unsupervised learning of landmarks by descriptor vector exchange. In: Proceedings of the IEEE/CVF International Conference on Computer Vision, pp. 6361–6371 (2019)
30. Wang, R., Wu, Y., Chen, H., Wang, L., Meng, D.: Neighbor matching for semi-supervised learning. In: de Bruijne, M., et al. (eds.) MICCAI 2021. LNCS, vol. 12902, pp. 439–449. Springer, Cham (2021). https://doi.org/10.1007/978-3-030-87196-3_41
31. Wu, J., Fan, H., Zhang, X., Lin, S., Li, Z.: Semi-supervised semantic segmentation via entropy minimization. In: 2021 IEEE International Conference on Multimedia and Expo (ICME), pp. 1–6. IEEE (2021)
32. Xie, Q., Dai, Z., Hovy, E., Luong, T., Le, Q.: Unsupervised data augmentation for consistency training. Adv. Neural. Inf. Process. Syst. **33**, 6256–6268 (2020)
33. Xie, Q., Luong, M.T., Hovy, E., Le, Q.V.: Self-training with noisy student improves imagenet classification. In: Proceedings of the IEEE/CVF Conference On Computer Vision And Pattern Recognition, pp. 10687–10698 (2020)
34. Yarowsky, D.: Unsupervised word sense disambiguation rivaling supervised methods. In: 33rd Annual Meeting of the Association For Computational Linguistics, pp. 189–196 (1995)
35. Zagoruyko, S., Komodakis, N.: Wide residual networks. arXiv preprint arXiv:1605.07146 (2016)
36. Zhang, B., et al.: Flexmatch: Boosting semi-supervised learning with curriculum pseudo labeling. In: Advances in Neural Information Processing Systems 34 (2021)
37. Zhang, H., Cisse, M., Dauphin, Y.N., Lopez-Paz, D.: mixup: Beyond empirical risk minimization. arXiv preprint arXiv:1710.09412 (2017)
38. Zou, Y., Yu, Z., Vijaya Kumar, B.V.K., Wang, J.: Unsupervised domain adaptation for semantic segmentation via class-balanced self-training. In: Ferrari, V., Hebert, M., Sminchisescu, C., Weiss, Y. (eds.) ECCV 2018. LNCS, vol. 11207, pp. 297–313. Springer, Cham (2018). https://doi.org/10.1007/978-3-030-01219-9_18

Bipolar Picture Fuzzy Graph Based Multiple Attribute Decision Making Approach–Part I

Shu Gong[1,2(✉)] and Gang Hua[2]

[1] Department of Computer Science, Guangdong University of Science and Technology, Dongguan 523083, China
gongshu_gk@126.com
[2] School of Information and Control Engineering, China University of Mining and Technology, Xuzhou 221116, China

Abstract. The multiple attribute decision making (MADM) is a one of most crucial topic in decision making and computer science. The key technology for MADM is to learn the correlation between different attributes, and the graph model is an appropriate tool to analyze it. In this work, the MADM problem is formulated in the bipolar picture fuzzy graph framework, and decision making algorithms are designed to characterize the relationships among attributes. The numerical example is introduced in this paper to show how to handle the MADM problem in terms of bipolar picture graph model.

Keywords: Bipolar fuzzy set · Bipolar picture fuzzy set · Bipolar picture fuzzy graph · Multiple attribute decision making

1 Introduction

In the design of decision making system, to evaluate objectives comprehensively and objectively, we need to evaluate and assess each attribute of the objective. When making decisions between different objectives, it is necessary to compare the similar attributes, and to clarify the correlation between multiple attributes. The decision-making problem that considers multiple attributes at the same time is called the multiple attribute decision making (MADM) problem, which is a hot issue in the current decision support system research.

When the target thing has uncertain properties, fuzzy mathematics is used as a tool to describe the uncertainty of things, where any attribute has positive and negative effects on things. In fuzzy set theory, positive and negative membership functions are used to characterize positive and negative uncertainties, respectively. When it is necessary to describe the uncertain relationship between things, then the bipolar fuzzy graphs are introduced into fuzzy theory to deal with structured data with double-sided uncertainty information. The so-called structured data means that there is a certain connection between the data, and the graph model just describes this interrelated nature (see [1–8]).

The main contribution of this paper is to propose the bipolar picture fuzzy graph based multiple attribute decision making algorithm. The organization of the reminder paper is listed as follows. We first give some basic concepts and notations, then we present the main algorithm and an example is obtained to explain how to deal with a specific MADM problem using bipolar picture fuzzy graph model.

2 Preliminary

ThE main purpose of this section is to present the terminologies and notations in bipolar picture fuzzy graph setting.

Let V be a universal set. The set

$$A = \{(v, \mu_A^P(v), v_A^P(v), \iota_A^P(v), \mu_A^N(v), v_A^N(v), \iota_A^N(v)) : v \in V\}$$

is a bipolar picture fuzzy set on V if maps $\mu_A^P : V \to [0, 1]$, $v_A^P : V \to [0, 1]$, $\iota_A^P : V \to [0, 1]$, $\mu_A^N : V \to [-1, 0]$, $v_A^N : V \to [-1, 0]$ and $\iota_A^N : V \to [-1, 0]$ satisfy that $\mu_A^P(v) + v_A^P(v) + \iota_A^P(v) \leq 1$ and $\mu_A^N(v) + v_A^N(v) + \iota_A^N(v) \geq -1$ for any $v \in V$.

Let $A_1 = \{(v, \mu_{A_1}^P(v), v_{A_1}^P(v), \iota_{A_1}^P(v), \mu_{A_1}^N(v), v_{A_1}^N(v), \iota_{A_1}^N(v)) : v \in V\}$ and $A_2 = \{(v, \mu_{A_2}^P(v), v_{A_2}^P(v), \iota_{A_2}^P(v), \mu_{A_2}^N(v), v_{A_2}^N(v), \iota_{A_2}^N(v)) : v \in V\}$ be two bipolar picture fuzzy sets on V. Then, the union and intersection of A_1 and A_2 are denoted by

$$A_1 \cup A_2 = \{(v, \mu_{A_1}^P(v) \vee \mu_{A_2}^P(v), v_{A_1}^P(v) \vee v_{A_2}^P(v), \iota_{A_1}^P(v) \vee \iota_{A_2}^P(v),$$
$$\mu_{A_1}^N(v) \wedge \mu_{A_2}^N(v), v_{A_1}^N(v) \wedge v_{A_2}^N(v), \iota_{A_1}^N(v) \wedge \iota_{A_2}^N(v)) : v \in V\},$$

$$A_1 \cap A_2 = \{(v, \mu_{A_1}^P(v) \wedge \mu_{A_2}^P(v), v_{A_1}^P(v) \wedge v_{A_2}^P(v), \iota_{A_1}^P(v) \wedge \iota_{A_2}^P(v),$$
$$\mu_{A_1}^N(v) \vee \mu_{A_2}^N(v), v_{A_1}^N(v) \vee v_{A_2}^N(v), \iota_{A_1}^N(v) \vee \iota_{A_2}^N(v)) : v \in V\}.$$

A mapping $B = (\mu_B^P(v, v'), v_B^P(v, v'), \iota_B^P(v, v'), \mu_B^N(v, v'), v_B^N(v, v'), \iota_B^N(v, v'))$ is a bipolar picture fuzzy relation on $V \times V$ if $v_B^P(v, v') \in [0, 1], \mu_B^P(v, v') \in [0, 1]$, $\iota_B^P(v, v') \in [0, 1], \mu_B^N(v, v') \in [-1, 0], v_B^N(v, v') \in [-1, 0], \iota_B^N(v, v') \in [-1, 0]$, and $\mu_B^P(v, v') + v_B^P(v, v') + \iota_B^P(v, v') \leq 1, \mu_B^N(v, v') + v_B^N(v, v') + \iota_B^N(v, v') \geq -1$ for any $(v, v') \in V \times V$.

The bipolar picture fuzzy graphs are defined as follows. If $A = \{(v, \mu_A^P(v), v_A^P(v), \iota_A^P(v), \mu_A^N(v), v_A^N(v), \iota_A^N(v)) : v \in V\}$ is a bipolar picture fuzzy set on an underlying set V and $B = (\mu_B^P(v, v'), v_B^P(v, v'), \iota_B^P(v, v'), \mu_B^N(v, v'), v_B^N(v, v'), \iota_B^N(v, v'))$ is a bipolar picture fuzzy set on $\tilde{V}^2$ where

$$\mu_B^P(v, v') \leq min\{\mu_A^P(v), \mu_A^P(v')\},$$

$$v_B^P(v, v') \geq max\{v_A^P(v), v_A^P(v')\},$$

$$\iota_B^P(v, v') \geq max\{\iota_A^P(v), \iota_A^P(v')\},$$

$$\mu_B^N(v, v') \geq max\{\mu_A^N(v), \mu_A^N(v')\},$$

$$v_B^N(v, v') \leq min\{v_A^N(v), v_A^N(v')\},$$

$$\iota_B^N(v, v') \leq min\{\iota_A^N(v), \iota_A^N(v')\},$$

for any $(v, v') \in \tilde{V}^2$, and $\mu_B^P(v, v') = v_B^P(v, v') = \iota_B^P(v, v') = \mu_B^N(v, v') = v_B^N(v, v')$
$= \iota_B^N(v, v') = 0$ for any $(v, v') \in \tilde{V}^2 - E$, then $G = (V, A, B)$ is a bipolar picture fuzzy graph (in short, is called BPFG) of the graph $G* = (V, E)$.

3 Bipolar Picture Fuzzy Graph-Based MADM Algorithm

The main purpose of this section is to present the bipolar picture fuzzy graph-based multiple attribute decision making algorithm.

Let $A = \{A_1, \cdots, A_m\}$ be the set of alternatives, $C = \{C_1, \cdots, C_n\}$ be the set of attributes, and $w^P = \{w_1^P, \cdots, w_n^P\}$ and $w^N = \{w_1^N, \cdots, w_n^N\}$ be the set of positive weight vector and negative weight vector for the attributes C_i $(i \in \{1, \cdots, n\})$ respectively, where $w_i^P \geq 0$, $w_i^N \leq 0$, $\sum_{i=1}^{n} w_i^P = 1$ and $\sum_{i=1}^{n} w_i^N = -1$. Let $M = [b_{ij}]_{m \times n} = [\mu_{ij}^P, v_{ij}^P, \iota_{ij}^P, \mu_{ij}^N, v_{ij}^N, \iota_{ij}^N]_{m \times n}$ be a bipolar picture fuzzy decision matrix, where $\mu_{ij}^P \in [0, 1]$, $v_{ij}^P \in [0, 1]$, $\iota_{ij}^P \in [0, 1]$, $\mu_{ij}^N \in [-1, 0]$, $v_{ij}^N \in [-1, 0]$, $\iota_{ij}^N \in [-1, 0]$ are for alternative A_i and attribute C_j, and $0 \leq \mu_{ij}^P + v_{ij}^P + \iota_{ij}^P \leq 1$, $-1 \leq \mu_{ij}^N + v_{ij}^N + \iota_{ij}^N \leq 0$ for $i \in \{1, \cdots, m\}$. The bipolar picture fuzzy relation between two attributes $C_i = (\mu_i^P, v_i^P, \iota_i^P, \mu_i^N, v_i^N, \iota_i^N)$ and $C_j = (\mu_j^P, v_j^P, \iota_j^P, \mu_j^N, v_j^N, \iota_j^N)$ is defined by $f_{ij} = (\mu_{ij}^P, v_{ij}^P, \iota_{ij}^P, \mu_{ij}^N, v_{ij}^N, \iota_{ij}^N)$, where $\mu_{ij}^P \leq \mu_j^P \wedge \mu_j^P$, $v_{ij}^P \geq v_j^P \vee v_j^P$, $\iota_{ij}^P \geq \iota_j^P \vee \iota_j^P$, $\mu_{ij}^N \geq \mu_j^N \vee \mu_j^N$, $v_{ij}^N \leq v_j^N \wedge v_j^N$ and $\iota_{ij}^N \leq \iota_j^N \wedge \iota_j^N$ for $i, j \in \{1, \cdots, n\}$. Otherwise, $f_{ij} = (0, 0, 1, 0, 0, -1)$.

We raise two bipolar picture fuzzy graph based algorithm for multiple attribute decision making problem below.

Algorithm A. Calculate the optimal alternative

A1: Determine the bipolar impact coefficient between attributes $C_i = (\mu_i^P, v_i^P, \iota_i^P, \mu_i^N, v_i^N, \iota_i^N)$ and $C_j = (\mu_j^P, v_j^P, \iota_j^P, \mu_j^N, v_j^N, \iota_j^N)$ by

$$\eta_{ij}^P = \frac{\mu_{ij}^P + (1 - v_{ij}^P)(1 - \iota_{ij}^P)}{3},$$

$$\eta_{ij}^N = \frac{\mu_{ij}^N - (-1 - v_{ij}^N)(-1 - \iota_{ij}^N)}{3},$$

for $i, j \in \{1, \cdots, n\}$, where $\eta_{ij} = (\mu_{ij}^P, v_{ij}^P, \iota_{ij}^P, \mu_{ij}^N, v_{ij}^N, \iota_{ij}^N)$ is the bipolar picture fuzzy edge between vertices C_i and C_i for $i, j \in \{1, \cdots, n\}$. We have $\eta_{ij}^P = \eta_{ji}^P = 1$ and $\eta_{ij}^N = \eta_{ji}^N = -1$ if $i = j$.

A2: Determine the attribute of alternative A_k by

$$\tilde{A}_k = (\tilde{\mu}_k^P, \tilde{v}_k^P, \tilde{\iota}_k^P, \tilde{\mu}_k^N, \tilde{v}_k^N, \tilde{\iota}_k^N) = \left(\frac{\sum_{j=1}^{n} w_j^P (\sum_{t=1}^{n} \eta_{tj}^P b_{kt}^P)}{3}, \frac{\sum_{j=1}^{n} w_j^N (\sum_{t=1}^{n} \eta_{tj}^N b_{kt}^N)}{3}, \right.$$

where b_{kt}^P and b_{kt}^N denote the positive and negative parts of element b_{kt}, and $f_{tj} = (\mu_{tj}^P, v_{tj}^P, \iota_{tj}^P, \mu_{tj}^N, v_{tj}^N, \iota_{tj}^N)$.

A3: Compute the score function of alternative $\tilde{A}_k$ by

$$S(\tilde{A}_k) = \frac{\tilde{\mu}_k^P - 2\tilde{v}_k^P - \tilde{\iota}_k^P + \tilde{\mu}_k^N - 2\tilde{v}_k^N - \tilde{\iota}_k^N}{2}.$$

A4: Rank all the alternative A_k by means of $S(\tilde{A}_k)$ and select the optimal alternative.
A5: Output
The next algorithm is another strategy to get the best alternative.

Algorithm B. Calculate the optimal alternative based on similarity computation.

B1: Determine the bipolar impact coefficient between attributes $C_i = (\mu_i^P, v_i^P, \iota_i^P, \mu_i^N, v_i^N, \iota_i^N)$ and $C_j = (\mu_j^P, v_j^P, \iota_j^P, \mu_j^N, v_j^N, \iota_j^N)$ by

$$\eta_{ij}^P = \frac{\mu_{ij}^P + (1 - v_{ij}^P)(1 - \iota_{ij}^P)}{3},$$

$$\eta_{ij}^N = \frac{\mu_{ij}^N - (-1 - v_{ij}^N)(-1 - \iota_{ij}^N)}{3},$$

for $i, j \in \{1, \cdots, n\}$, where $\eta_{ij} = (\mu_{ij}^P, v_{ij}^P, \iota_{ij}^P, \mu_{ij}^N, v_{ij}^N, \iota_{ij}^N)$ is the bipolar picture fuzzy edge between vertices C_i and C_i for $i, j \in \{1, \cdots, n\}$. We have $\eta_{ij}^P = \eta_{ji}^P = 1$ and $\eta_{ij}^N = \eta_{ji}^N = -1$ if $i = j$.
B2: Determine the associated weighted value of attribute C_j ($j \in \{1, \cdots, n\}$) over the other criteria by

$$\tilde{b}_{kj} = (\tilde{\mu}_{kj}^P, \tilde{v}_{kj}^P, \tilde{\iota}_{kj}^P, \tilde{\mu}_{kj}^N, \tilde{v}_{kj}^N, \tilde{\iota}_{kj}^N) = \left(\frac{w_j^P \sum_{t=1}^n \eta_{tj}^P b_{kt}^P}{3}, \frac{w_j^N \sum_{t=1}^n \eta_{tj}^N b_{kt}^N}{3} \right),$$

where b_{kt}^P and b_{kt}^N denote the positive and negative parts of element b_{kt}.
B3: Compute the similarity measure between the decision solution $A = (\mu_j^P, v_j^P, \iota_j^P, \mu_j^N, v_j^N, \iota_j^N), j \in \{1, \cdots, n\}$, and each alternative $A_k, k \in \{1, \cdots, m\}$, by

$$S(A, A_k) = 1 - \frac{1}{6n} \sum_{j=1}^n \left(\left| \mu_j^P - \tilde{\mu}_{kj}^P \right| + \left| v_j^P - \tilde{v}_{kj}^P \right| + \left| \iota_j^P - \tilde{\iota}_{kj}^P \right| \right.$$

$$\left. + \left| \mu_j^N - \tilde{\mu}_{kj}^N \right| + \left| v_j^N - \tilde{v}_{kj}^N \right| + \left| \iota_j^P - \tilde{\iota}_{kj}^N \right| \right).$$

B4: Rank all the alternative A_k by means of $S(A, A_k)$ for $k \in \{1, \cdots, m\}$ and select the optimal alternative.
B5: Output.

4 Numerical Example for Algorithm A

IN this section, we explain how to implement the Algorithm A by showing the following instance. It is noted that the implement of Algorithm B will be explained in "Bipolar Picture Fuzzy Graph Based Multiple Attribute Decision Making Approach-Part II". The data of the simulation experiments in this paper are mainly adapted from Ashraf et al. [9] and Amanathulla et al. [10].

The investment company has to make decisions on several alternative companies and choose the best investment object. There are four alternatives:

A_1: a car company;
A_2: a food company;
A_3: a computer company;
A_4: an energy company.

There are three attributes for these four companies with positive weight vector $w^P = \{0.3, 0.2, 0.5\}$ and negative weight vector $w^N = \{-0.2, -0.2, -0.6\}$:

C_1: risk analysis;
C_2: growth analysis;
C_3: environmental impact analysis.

The four candidate alternatives are to be considered under the three attributes and are shown by means of bipolar picture fuzzy information by decision-making according to three attributes C_1, C_2 and C_3 and the evaluation information on the alternative A_1, A_2, A_3 and A_4 under the factors C_1, C_2 and C_3 can be shown in the following 4×3 bipolar picture fuzzy decision matrix M:

$$
M = \begin{bmatrix}
(0.5, 0.2, 0.3, & (0.8, 0.1, 0.1, & (0.6, 0.2, 0.2, \\
-0.4, -0.3, -0.3) & -0.2, -0.4, -0.4) & -0.5, -0.2, -0.3) \\
(0.6, 0.2, 0.2, & (0.5, 0.3, 0.2, & (0.8, 0.1, 0.1, \\
-0.5, -0.2, -0.3) & -0.5, -0.2, -0.3) & -0.1, -0.4, -0.5) \\
(0.4, 0.3, 0.3, & (0.7, 0.1, 0.2, & (0.4, 0.4, 0.2, \\
-0.5, -0.3, -0.2) & -0.4, -0.3, -0.3) & -0.5, -0.2, -0.3) \\
(0.3, 0.2, 0.5, & (0.7, 0.2, 0.1, & (0.4, 0.2, 0.4, \\
-0.2, -0.3, -0.5) & -0.1, -0.3, -0.6) & -0.1, -0.8, -0.1)
\end{bmatrix}.
$$

The relationship among the attributes C_1, C_2 and C_3 is assumed to be a complete graph $G = (V, E)$ with vertex set $V = \{C_1, C_2, C_3\}$ and edge set $E = \{C_1C_2, C_2C_3, C_1C_3\}$, see Fig. 1. This graph is a bipolar fuzzy graph corresponding to the relationship between attribute for all alternatives.

The bipolar membership functions on the edge set of G which feature the relative among the attributes are defined as follows:

$$
f_{12} = (\mu_{12}^P, v_{12}^P, \iota_{12}^P, \mu_{12}^N, v_{12}^N, \iota_{12}^N) = (0.3, 0.3, 0.6, -0.1, -0.4, -0.7),
$$

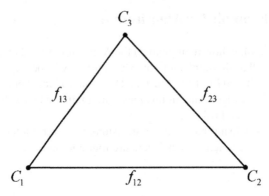

Fig. 1. A graph of relationship between attributes.

$$f_{13} = (\mu_{13}^P, v_{13}^P, \iota_{13}^P, \mu_{13}^N, v_{13}^N, \iota_{13}^N) = (0.1, 0.4, 0.6, -0.1, -0.8, -0.5),$$

$$f_{23} = (\mu_{23}^P, v_{23}^P, \iota_{23}^P, \mu_{23}^N, v_{23}^N, \iota_{23}^N) = (0.4, 0.4, 0.4, -0.4, -0.5, -0.2).$$

To search for the optimal alternative, the following steps are implemented.
Step 1: Compute the bipolar impact coefficient between attributes C_1, C_2 and C_3.

$$\eta_{12}^P = \frac{\mu_{12}^P + (1 - v_{12}^P)(1 - \iota_{12}^P)}{3} = \frac{0.3 + (1 - 0.3)(1 - 0.6)}{3} = \frac{19}{150},$$

$$\eta_{12}^N = \frac{\mu_{12}^N + (-1 - v_{12}^N)(-1 - \iota_{12}^N)}{3} = \frac{-0.1 - (-1 + 0.4)(-1 + 0.7)}{3} = -\frac{7}{75},$$

$$\eta_{13}^P = \frac{\mu_{13}^P + (1 - v_{13}^P)(1 - \iota_{13}^P)}{3} = \frac{0.1 + (1 - 0.4)(1 - 0.6)}{3} = \frac{17}{150},$$

$$\eta_{13}^N = \frac{\mu_{13}^N + (-1 - v_{13}^N)(-1 - \iota_{13}^N)}{3} = \frac{-0.1 - (-1 + 0.8)(-1 + 0.5)}{3} = -\frac{1}{15},$$

$$\eta_{23}^P = \frac{\mu_{23}^P + (1 - v_{23}^P)(1 - \iota_{23}^P)}{3} = \frac{0.4 + (1 - 0.4)(1 - 0.4)}{3} = \frac{19}{75},$$

$$\eta_{23}^N = \frac{\mu_{23}^N + (-1 - v_{23}^N)(-1 - \iota_{23}^N)}{3} = \frac{-0.4 - (-1 + 0.5)(-1 + 0.2)}{3} = -\frac{4}{15}.$$

Step 2: determine the alternatives A_k as follows:

$$\tilde{A}_1 = \frac{1}{3}[w_1^P(\eta_{11}^P b_{11}^P + \eta_{21}^P b_{12}^P + \eta_{31}^P b_{13}^P) + w_2^P(\eta_{12}^P b_{11}^P + \eta_{22}^P b_{12}^P + \eta_{32}^P b_{13}^P)$$
$$+ |\mu_j^N - \tilde{\mu}_{kj}^N| + |v_j^N - \tilde{v}_{kj}^N| + |\iota_j^P - \tilde{\iota}_{kj}^N|)$$
$$+ w_2^N(\eta_{12}^N b_{11}^N + \eta_{22}^N b_{12}^N + \eta_{32}^N b_{13}^N) + w_3^N(\eta_{13}^N b_{11}^N + \eta_{23}^N b_{12}^N + \eta_{33}^N b_{13}^N)]$$

$$= \frac{1}{3}[0.3\{1 \times (0.5, 0.2, 0.3) + \frac{19}{150} \times (0.8, 0.1, 0.1) + \frac{17}{150} \times (0.6, 0.2, 0.2)\}$$

$$+ 0.2\{\frac{19}{150} \times (0.5, 0.2, 0.3) + 1 \times (0.8, 0.1, 0.1) + \frac{19}{75} \times (0.6, 0.2, 0.2)\}$$

$$+ 0.5\{\frac{17}{150} \times (0.5, 0.2, 0.3) + \frac{19}{75} \times (0.8, 0.1, 0.1) + 1 \times (0.6, 0.2, 0.2)\}],$$

$$\frac{1}{3}[-0.2\{-1 \times (-0.4, -0.3, -0.3) - \frac{7}{75} \times (-0.2, -0.4, -0.4) - \frac{1}{15}$$
$$\times (-0.5, -0.2, -0.3)\}$$

$$-0.2\{-\frac{7}{75} \times (-0.4, -0.3, -0.3) - 1 \times (-0.2, -0.4, -0.4) - \frac{4}{15}$$
$$\times (-0.5, -0.2, -0.3)\}$$

$$-0.6\{-\frac{1}{15} \times (-0.4, -0.3, -0.3) - \frac{4}{15} \times (-0.2, -0.4, -0.4) - 1$$
$$\times (-0.5, -0.2, -0.3)\}]]$$

$$= (0.28, 0.11, 0.09, -0.171, -0.121, -0.143),$$

$$\tilde{A}_2 = \frac{1}{3}[w_1^P(\eta_{11}^P b_{21}^P + \eta_{21}^P b_{22}^P + \eta_{31}^P b_{23}^P) + w_2^P(\eta_{12}^P b_{21}^P + \eta_{22}^P b_{22}^P + \eta_{32}^P b_{23}^P)$$

$$+ w_3^P(\eta_{13}^P b_{21}^P + \eta_{23}^P b_{22}^P + \eta_{33}^P b_{23}^P)], \frac{1}{3}[w_1^N(\eta_{11}^N b_{21}^N + \eta_{21}^N b_{22}^N + \eta_{31}^N b_{23}^N)$$

$$+ w_2^N(\eta_{12}^N b_{21}^N + \eta_{22}^N b_{22}^N + \eta_{32}^N b_{23}^N) + w_3^N(\eta_{13}^N b_{21}^N + \eta_{23}^N b_{22}^N + \eta_{33}^N b_{23}^N)]$$

$$= \frac{1}{3}[0.3\{1 \times (0.6, 0.2, 0.2) + \frac{19}{150} \times (0.5, 0.3, 0.2) + \frac{17}{150} \times (0.8, 0.1, 0.1)\}$$

$$+ 0.2\{\frac{19}{150} \times (0.6, 0.2, 0.2) + 1 \times (0.5, 0.3, 0.2) + \frac{19}{75} \times (0.8, 0.1, 0.1)\}$$

$$+ 0.5\{\frac{17}{150} \times (0.6, 0.2, 0.2) + \frac{19}{75} \times (0.5, 0.3, 0.2) + 1 \times (0.8, 0.1, 0.1)\}],$$

$$\frac{1}{3}[-0.2\{-1 \times (-0.5, -0.2, -0.3) - \frac{7}{75} \times (-0.5, -0.2, -0.3) - \frac{1}{15}$$
$$\times (-0.1, -0.4, -0.5)\}$$

$$-0.2\{-\frac{7}{75} \times (-0.5, -0.2, -0.3) - 1 \times (-0.5, -0.2, -0.3) - \frac{4}{15}$$
$$\times (-0.1, -0.4, -0.5)\}$$

$$-0.2\{-\frac{7}{75} \times (-0.5, -0.2, -0.3) - 1 \times (-0.5, -0.2, -0.3) - \frac{4}{15}$$
$$\times (-0.1, -0.4, -0.5)\}$$

$$= (0.293, 0.081, 0.069, -0.068, -0.059, -0.085),$$

$$\tilde{A}_3 = \frac{1}{3}[w_1^P(\eta_{11}^P b_{31}^P + \eta_{21}^P b_{32}^P + \eta_{31}^P b_{33}^P) + w_2^P(\eta_{12}^P b_{31}^P + \eta_{22}^P b_{32}^P + \eta_{32}^P b_{33}^P)$$

$$+ w_3^P(\eta_{13}^P b_{31}^P + \eta_{23}^P b_{32}^P + \eta_{33}^P b_{33}^P)], \frac{1}{3}[w_1^N(\eta_{11}^N b_{31}^N + \eta_{21}^N b_{32}^N + \eta_{31}^N b_{33}^N)$$

$$+ w_2^N(\eta_{12}^N b_{31}^N + \eta_{22}^N b_{32}^N + \eta_{32}^N b_{33}^N) + w_3^N(\eta_{13}^N b_{31}^N + \eta_{23}^N b_{32}^N + \eta_{33}^N b_{33}^N)]$$

$$=\frac{1}{3}[0.3\{1 \times (0.4, 0.3, 0.3) + \frac{19}{150} \times (0.7, 0.1, 0.2) + \frac{17}{150} \times (0.4, 0.4, 0.2)\}$$

$$+ 0.2\{\frac{19}{150} \times (0.4, 0.3, 0.3) + 1 \times (0.7, 0.1, 0.2) + \frac{19}{75} \times (0.4, 0.4, 0.2)\}$$

$$+ 0.5\{\frac{17}{150} \times (0.4, 0.3, 0.3) + \frac{19}{75} \times (0.7, 0.1, 0.2) + 1 \times (0.4, 0.4, 0.2)\}],$$

$$\frac{1}{3}[-0.2\{-1 \times (-0.5, -0.3, -0.2) - \frac{7}{75} \times (-0.4, -0.3, -0.3) - \frac{1}{15}$$

$$\times(-0.5, -0.2, -0.3)\}$$

$$-0.2\{-\frac{7}{75} \times (-0.5, -0.3, -0.2) - 1 \times (-0.4, -0.3, -0.3) - \frac{4}{15}$$

$$\times(-0.5, -0.2, -0.3)\}$$

$$-0.6\{-\frac{1}{15} \times (-0.5, -0.3, -0.2) - \frac{4}{15} \times (-0.4, -0.3, -0.3) - 1$$

$$\times(-0.5, -0.2, -0.3)\}]$$

$$= (0.275, 0.128, 0.101, -0.205, -0.108, -0.068),$$

$$\tilde{A}_4 = \frac{1}{3}[w_1^P(\eta_{11}^P b_{41}^P + \eta_{21}^P b_{42}^P + \eta_{31}^P b_{43}^P) + w_2^P(\eta_{12}^P b_{41}^P + \eta_{22}^P b_{42}^P + \eta_{32}^P b_{43}^P)$$

$$+ w_3^P(\eta_{13}^P b_{41}^P + \eta_{23}^P b_{42}^P + \eta_{33}^P b_{43}^P)], \frac{1}{3}[w_1^N(\eta_{11}^N b_{41}^N + \eta_{21}^N b_{42}^N + \eta_{31}^N b_{43}^N)$$

$$+ w_2^N(\eta_{12}^N b_{41}^N + \eta_{22}^N b_{42}^N + \eta_{32}^N b_{43}^N) + w_3^N(\eta_{13}^N b_{41}^N + \eta_{23}^N b_{42}^N + \eta_{33}^N b_{43}^N)]$$

$$=\frac{1}{3}[0.3\{1 \times (0.3, 0.2, 0.5) + \frac{19}{150} \times (0.7, 0.2, 0.1) + \frac{17}{150} \times (0.4, 0.2, 0.4)\}$$

$$+0.2\{\frac{19}{150} \times (0.3, 0.2, 0.5) + 1 \times (0.7, 0.2, 0.1) + \frac{19}{75} \times (0.4, 0.2, 0.4)\}$$

$$+0.5\{\frac{17}{150} \times (0.3, 0.2, 0.5) + \frac{19}{75} \times (0.7, 0.2, 0.1) + 1 \times (0.4, 0.2, 0.4)\}],$$

$$\frac{1}{3}[-0.2\{-1 \times (-0.2, -0.3, -0.5) - \frac{7}{75} \times (-0.1, -0.3, -0.6) - \frac{1}{15}$$

$$\times(-0.1, -0.8, -0.1)\}$$

$$-0.2\{-\frac{7}{75} \times (-0.2, -0.3, -0.5) - 1 \times (-0.1, -0.3, -0.6) - \frac{4}{15}$$

$$\times(-0.1, -0.8, -0.1)\}$$

$$-0.6\{-\frac{1}{15} \times (-0.2, -0.3, -0.5) - \frac{4}{15} \times (-0.1, -0.3, -0.6) - 1$$

$$\times(-0.1, -0.8, -0.1)\}]$$

$$= (0.262, 0.119, 0.219, -0.052, -0.242, -0.141).$$

Step 3. Calculate the score function for each alternative.

$$S(\tilde{A}_1) = \frac{\tilde{\mu}_1^P - 2\tilde{v}_1^P - \tilde{\iota}_1^P + \tilde{\mu}_1^N - 2\tilde{v}_1^N - \tilde{\iota}_1^N}{2}$$
$$= \frac{0.28 - 2 \times 0.11 - 0.09 - 0.171 + 2 \times 0.121 + 0.143}{2} = 0.092,$$

$$S(\tilde{A}_2) = \frac{\tilde{\mu}_2^P - 2\tilde{v}_2^P - \tilde{\iota}_2^P + \tilde{\mu}_2^N - 2\tilde{v}_2^N - \tilde{\iota}_2^N}{2}$$
$$= \frac{0.293 - 2 \times 0.081 - 0.069 - 0.068 + 2 \times 0.059 + 0.085}{2} = 0.0985,$$

$$S(\tilde{A}_3) = \frac{\tilde{\mu}_3^P - 2\tilde{v}_3^P - \tilde{\iota}_3^P + \tilde{\mu}_3^N - 2\tilde{v}_3^N - \tilde{\iota}_3^N}{2}$$
$$= \frac{0.275 - 2 \times 0.128 - 0.101 - 0.205 + 2 \times 0.108 + 0.068}{2} = -0.0015,$$

$$S(\tilde{A}_4) = \frac{\tilde{\mu}_4^P - 2\tilde{v}_4^P - \tilde{\iota}_4^P + \tilde{\mu}_4^N - 2\tilde{v}_4^N - \tilde{\iota}_4^N}{2}$$
$$= \frac{0.262 - 2 \times 0.119 - 0.219 - 0.052 + 2 \times 0.242 + 0.141}{2} = 0.1895.$$

Step 4. We rank the alternatives as $A_4 > A_2 > A_1 > A_3$. Hence, A_4 is the optimal choice in the decision making problem.

5 Conclusion

In this paper, we discuss the multiple attribute decision making problem in term of the bipolar picture fuzzy graph framework. Two decision making algorithms are raised and an example is presented to show how to implement the algorithm for a specific decision making problem. More about the algorithm and specific application of the decision support system graph model need to be further studied in the future.

Acknowledgements. This work is supported by 2021 Guangdong Basic and Applied Basic Youth Fund Project (No. 2021A1515110834), Guangdong University of Science and Technology University Major Scientific Research Achievement Cultivation Program Project 2020 (No. GKY-2020CQPY-2), Characteristic Innovation Project of Universities in Guangdong Province in 2022, and Guangdong Provincial Department of Education Project (No. 2020KTSCX166).

References

1. Sitara, M., Akram, M., Riaz, M.: Decision-making analysis based on q-rung picture fuzzy graph structures. J. Appl. Math. Comput. **67**, 541–577 (2021)
2. Jia, J., Rehman, A.U., Hussain, M., Mu, D., Siddiqui, M.K., Cheema, I.: Consensus-based multi-person decisionmaking using consistency fuzzy preference graphs. IEEE Access **7**, 178870–178878 (2019)
3. Karaaslan, F.: Hesitant fuzzy graphs and their applications in decision making. J. Intell. Fuzzy Syst. **36**(3), 2729–2741 (2019)
4. Akram, M., Habib, A., Davvaz, B.: Direct sum of n pythagorean fuzzy graphs with application to group decision-making. J. Multiple-Valued Logic Soft Comput. **33**(1–2), 75–115 (2019)
5. Akram, M., Feng, F., Saeid, A.B., Leoreanu-Fotea, V.: A new multiple criteria decision-making method based on bipolar fuzzy soft graphs. Iran. J. Fuzzy Syst. **15**(4), 73–92 (2018)

6. Akram, M., Waseem, N.: Novel applications of bipolar fuzzy graphs to decision making problems. J. Appl. Math. Comput. **56**(1–2), 73–91 (2016). https://doi.org/10.1007/s12190-016-1062-3

7. Gao, W., Wang, W., Chen, Y.: Tight bounds for the existence of path factors in network vulnerability parameter settings. Int. J. Intell. Syst. **36**(3), 1133–1158 (2021)

8. Gao, W., Chen, Y., Wang, Y.: Network vulnerability parameter and results on two surfaces. Int. J. Intell. Syst. **36**(8), 4392–4414 (2021)

9. Ashraf, S., Mahmood, T., Abdullah, S., Khan, Q.: Picture fuzzy linguistic sets and their applications for multi-attribute group decision making problems. Nucleus **55**(2), 66–73 (2018)

10. Amanathulla, S.K., Muhiuddin, G., Al-Kadi, D., Pal, M.: Multiple attribute decision-making problem using picture fuzzy graph. Math. Prob. Eng., 9937828 (2021). https://doi.org/10.1155/2021/9937828

Priv-IDS: A Privacy Protection and Intrusion Detection Framework for In-Vehicle Network

Simin Li and Mu Han[✉]

School of Computer Science and Communication Engineering, Jiangsu University,
Zhenjiang 212013, China
hanmu@ujs.edu.cn

Abstract. Intelligent connected vehicle (ICV) is equipped with advanced on-board sensors, controllers, actuators and other equipment of the new generation of vehicles, integrated with modern communication and network technology, to achieve intelligent information exchange and sharing. As an international standardized communication protocol, controller area network (CAN) plays an important role in vehicle communication. However, due to the CAN is plaintext broadcast communication, lack of encryption technology, CAN faces the challenge of malicious attack and privacy disclosure. In this paper, a machine learning method Priv-IDS based on local differential privacy (LDP) is proposed to protect the privacy of CAN data and detect malicious intrusion. The method performs random perturbation on CAN data and detects malicious attacks through temporal convolutional network (TCN). We propose a $\alpha\beta$-LDP method, which ensures data availability as much as possible while protecting data privacy. This method provides a way to solve the problem of privacy disclosure caused by CAN data in machine learning intrusion detection. Based on the standard data set, this scheme is compared with other vehicle intrusion detection methods. The experimental results show that the proposed intrusion detection method is not different from other intrusion detection methods in terms of accuracy and time efficiency, but it is the first intrusion detection method to better protect CAN data based on LDP.

Keywords: Intelligent connected vehicle (ICV) security · Controller area network (CAN) · Local differential privacy (LDP) · Temporal convolutional network (TCN)

1 Introduction

1.1 Background

With the development of computer technology and communication technology, Intelligent connected vehicle (ICV) realizes the information interaction between vehicle and human, vehicle and vehicle, vehicle and platform through the vehicle equipment and intelligent control system [1]. As an international standardized

Y. Xu et al. (Eds.): ML4CS 2022, LNCS 13656, pp. 165–179, 2023.
https://doi.org/10.1007/978-3-031-20099-1_14

communication protocol, controller area network (CAN) greatly improves the reliability of vehicle information transmission and plays an important role in vehicle communication [2].

There are a large number of controllers and sensors in CAN, which are used to realize information transmission and data sharing of the whole vehicle. At the same time, CAN is a reliable and lightweight protocol that has few security features, such as no encryption or authentication, and has been shown to be able to be exploited by direct or even remote access [3]. With more frequent interactions between vehicles and the outside world, such as the emergence of communication with infrastructure networks via USB, mobile networks and Bluetooth, there are more and more attack methods against CAN, which brings security risks that cannot be underestimated [4]. For example, attackers can forge CAN messages to control vehicles, which will bring great personal safety risks to the owners [5]. On the other hand, electronic control units (ECU) store a variety of sensitive data of vehicles, which are extremely easy to be collected by illegal invaders and malicious third parties, resulting in the disclosure of vehicle privacy [6].

In order to accurately detect abnormal information in CAN and analyze whether they are maliciously attacked, many scholars pay more and more attention to intrusion detection technology. In recent years, well-known deep learning (DP) methods such as convolutional neural networks (CNN) and long-short term memory (LSTM) have been applied to intrusion detection. Seo et al. proposed a new approach to train an anomaly detection model using generative adversarial networks (GAN). They use normal CAN flow data to train the detection model and generate flow data with noise [7]. Qin et al. proposed two detection models, which input the contents of CAN data field into the LSTM model in hexadecimal and binary forms, respectively [8]. Temporal convolutional network (TCN) was proposed in 2018. It is a structural innovation of one-dimensional CNN and has been proven to have better performance than CNN on timing models. However, in the process of DL, training set data still faces the risk of data leakage, and attackers can also obtain vehicle data related information through the model's response to data [9].

Some studies improve the security of CAN by adding digital signatures based on symmetric key cryptography [10]. However, digital signature communication costs a lot and CAN bandwidth is limited to 500 kbps. There are also studies that offer physical hardware-based approaches to feature protection, which, in addition to being expensive, is difficult to replace all of the equipment in existing vehicles [11]. It is necessary to research an intrusion detection system (IDS) that can be added to the existing system with low computation cost and deployment cost. Differential privacy (DP) has been an important method for data privacy protection in recent years. Compared with other private computing, DP has higher computing efficiency. And DP does not need to make assumptions about the prior knowledge of the opponent, so it has a stronger effect of privacy protection [12]. More importantly, local differential privacy (LDP) has the characteristics of distribution, so it has led to innovation in the development of distributed privacy protection algorithms in many modern distributed scenarios, such as scenarios based on the Internet of vehicles (IoV) [13].

In view of the above challenges of intrusion detection technology in vehicle network, this paper designs a DL intrusion detection Priv-IDS model based on LDP in vehicle network taking into account the computing capacity, intrusion detection accuracy and privacy protection requirements of vehicle terminal.

The main contributions of this paper are as follows:

- An improved LDP algorithm, α-LDP, is proposed to protect data through different random response perturbation algorithms. It provides more flexibility for randomization probability.
- By introducing an additional privacy budget coefficient β, into the α-LDP algorithm, namely $\alpha\beta$-LDP, the improved flexibility is achieved and the impact of privacy budget (ϵ) on accuracy is reduced.
- The intrusion detection model is trained by TCN, and simulation experiments are carried out using standard data sets. Compared with traditional intrusion detection algorithms, the Priv-IDS model has relatively stable performance in detecting malicious attacks in CAN on the premise of protecting the data privacy of CAN.

The remainder of this paper is organized as follows. Section 2 introduces the preliminary knowledge. In Sect. 3, we present the Priv-IDS design in detail. We analyze the experimental results in Sect. 4. In Sect. 5, we conclude this paper and put forward the future work.

2 Preliminaries

2.1 DP

DP can guarantee that the change of a single individual in a data set hardly affects the statistical results of the whole data set, thus providing strong privacy protection for sensitive personal information. We introduce some concepts related to DP.

Definition 1. *Adjacent Databases*
If two databases D *and* D$^{'}$ *are adjacent,* D$^{'}$ *can be obtained if and only if the label value of a piece of data* D *is changed, this is,* $D\Delta D^{'} = 1$.

Definition 2. *L1-Global Sensitivity*
For the algorithm $f : D \rightarrow R^n$, *the L1-Global sensitivity of* f *acting on databases* D *is expressed as*

$$S(f) = \max_{D\Delta D^{'}} \| f(D) - f(D^{'}) \|_1 \tag{1}$$

In Formula (1), $\| f(D) - f(D^{'}) \|_1$ is L1 norm distance. The noise size of DP depends on the global sensitivity of the query function f. Sensitivity is mainly determined by the specific algorithm and the domain of the data sets.

Definition 3. *DP*
Given D_1 *and* D_2 *of two adjacent databases and any output result* $O(O \in$ *Range(A)) of* A *satisfies the formula (2).*

$$\Pr[A(D_1) = O] \leq e^\epsilon \leq \Pr[A(D_2) = O] \tag{2}$$

When Formula (2) is established, privacy protection algorithm A satisfies the ϵ-DP. Where, ϵ is the privacy budget, and the value of probability is determined by the randomness of privacy protection algorithm A. For any $\epsilon \geq 0$, function A satisfies ϵ-DP. When ϵ is close to 0, the two probabilities of the output of function A are almost equal, which means that the higher the degree of privacy protection is, the more noise needs to be added.

Definition 4. *Combination theorem let* A_1, A_2... A_n *is n random algorithms, where algorithm* A_i *satisfies* ϵ_i *DP (i* $\in [1, k]$), *then sequence combination* A_1, A_2... A_n *satisfies* $\sum_{i=1}^{n} \epsilon_i = \epsilon$.

The existence of combination theorem makes it easy to deduce the global privacy loss in modular design.

2.2 LDP

The basic idea of LDP technology is to transfer the data privacy processing to each user, so that the user can deal with the privacy information locally and avoid the privacy leakage caused by uploading the original data to the third party server.

Definition 5. *LDP*
If an algorithm A *satisfies* ϵ-LDP, *then for any two local databases* $\widetilde{D}_1$ *and* $\widetilde{D}_2$, *any output* $O(O \in$ *Range(A)) of* A *satisfies the inequality (3).*

$$\Pr[A(\widetilde{D}_1) = O] \leq e^\epsilon \leq \Pr[A(\widetilde{D}_2) = O] \tag{3}$$

Where $\Pr[\ ]$ represents the probability of an event occurring. Intuitively, LDP guarantees that no matter what the value of a user's real data $\widetilde{D}_1$ is, the output view $O(O \in$ Range(A)) of A after privacy protection is almost indistinguishable. Therefore, similar to DP, LDP is able to defend against identity attack attribute attack probability knowledge attack.

2.3 Binary Random Response (BRR) Mechanism

Now consider the multiple input domain $\chi = \{X_1, ..., X_m\}$, that is, the Categorical Data with the number of categories m, which is similar to binary category Data. The real category x is published with a finite probability q, and a category is selected uniformly and randomly from $\chi - x$ with a probability $1.0 - q$.

Definition 6. *BRR*
For category data $x = X_i \in \chi$, where $\chi = \{X_1, ..., X_m\}$, the bit map of x is represented as $bx \in \{0,1\}^m$, the output of the binary random response mechanism is $z \in \{0,1\}^m$, and for any $j \in [1, m]$, the j_{th} bit z^j of z is equal to bx^j with probability $q(0 \leq q \leq 1.0)$ and equal to $1 - bx^j$ with probability $(1 - q)$.

3   Priv-IDS Model

In this section, we introduce the $\alpha\beta$-LDP method and Priv-IDS model. $\alpha\beta$-LDP disturbs CAN data to protect the privacy of CAN data. In Priv-IDS, we deployed the $\alpha\beta$-LDP scheme and trained the intrusion detection model using TCN.

3.1 $\alpha\beta$-LDP Method

In RAPPOR [14], the string is processed through h hash functions to produce a binary encoding with h 1s. Then the mechanism of random response is adopted, with a probability of $\frac{1}{2}f$ being set to 1, a probability of $\frac{1}{2}f$ being set to 0, and a probability of 1-f remaining constant.

We note that the RAPPOR method has some limitations in the case of large data, and the new algorithm is necessary to increase the probability of randomization and improve the unreliable random perturbation. Therefore, we propose $\alpha\beta$-LDP, which follows the BRR mechanism. $\alpha\beta$-LDP can greatly improve data availability after DP while protecting data privacy.

First, an instance V_i in the database is encoded as binary version B of length d bits. According to unary encoding [15], each bit of $B[i]$ in B is perturbed according to $\Pr[B'[i] = 1] = \begin{cases} p & \text{if } B[i] = 1 \\ q & \text{if } B[i] = 0 \end{cases}$ to get $B'[i]$.

Fixed length codes result in redundant bits. To ensure data consistency, we fill the redundant locations with 0s. Therefore, there are more 0s than 1s in a long binary string. In order to reduce the error caused by the conversion of 0 to 1, the probability of 0 to 1 ($\mathbf{P}_{0\rightarrow1}$) needs to be reduced. This means that the definition of DP can be satisfied only by increasing the probability of 1 to 0 ($\mathbf{P}_{1\rightarrow0}$). So the value of (1-$p$) is greater than the value of q. However, long binary strings increase sensitivity between adjacent data sets. To correct the values of p and q, MOUE [15] proposes to add a coefficient, α. α provides greater flexibility for the selection of disturbance probability.

We extended the coefficient α ($\alpha > 1$) to correct the values of p and q in random perturbation. We find that the encoded fixed-point binary number consists of three parts: sign bits, whole number bits, and fraction bits. The first part includes sign bits and whole number bits. The first part is called P1 and call the fraction part P2. As seen in Fig. 1. In order to balance data availability and data privacy protection, we designed different disturbance probabilities for P1 and P2. Suppose P1 has m bits and P2 has n bits, such that $l = m + n$. In general, the fraction place contains more data bits than the whole number, namely $n > m$.

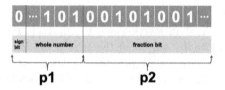

Fig. 1. Binary is divided into decimal P1 and P2 after the combination of sign bit and integer bit.

Theorem 1. $(\alpha - LDP)$ *Let* $\Pr(B[i])$ *be the probability of randomizing the* i_th *bit of the binary-encoded string of* V. *For any input* v_1, v_2 *with sensitivity of* l, *the probability* $p(B[i])$ *is defined as*

$$
p(B[i]|v) = \begin{cases} \Pr[B[v_1] = 1|v_1] = \frac{e^{\frac{\epsilon}{l}}}{\alpha + e^{\frac{\epsilon}{l}}} & \text{if } i \in \text{P1} \\ \Pr[B[v_2] = 0|v_1] = \frac{\alpha}{1+\alpha} & " \\ \Pr[B[v_1] = 1|v_1] = \frac{1}{1+\alpha} & \text{if } i \in \text{P2} \\ \Pr[B[v_2] = 0|v_1] = \frac{\alpha e^{\frac{\epsilon}{l}}}{1+\alpha e^{\frac{\epsilon}{l}}} & " \end{cases} \tag{4}
$$

Proof.

$$
\begin{aligned}
\frac{\Pr[B|v_1]}{\Pr[B|v_2]} &= \frac{\prod_{i \in [d]} \Pr[B[i]|v_1]}{\prod_{i \in [d]} \Pr[B[i]|v_2]} \\
&= \frac{\prod_{i \in [\text{P1}]} \Pr[B[i]|v_1]}{\prod_{i \in [\text{P1}]} \Pr[B[i]|v_2]} \times \frac{\prod_{i \in [\text{P2}]} \Pr[B[i]|v_1]}{\prod_{i \in [\text{P2}]} \Pr[B[i]|v_2]} \\
&\leqslant \left(\frac{\Pr[B[v_1] = 1|v_1]\Pr[B[v_2] = 0|v_1]}{\Pr[B[v_1] = 1|v_2]\Pr[B[v_2] = 0|v_2]} \right)^{m}_{i \in \text{P1}} \\
&\quad \times \left(\frac{\Pr[B[v_1] = 1|v_1]\Pr[B[v_2] = 0|v_1]}{\Pr[B[v_1] = 1|v_2]\Pr[B[v_2] = 0|v_2]} \right)^{n}_{i \in \text{P2}} \\
&= \left[\frac{\left(\frac{e^{\frac{\epsilon}{l}}}{\alpha + e^{\frac{\epsilon}{l}}}\right) \left(\frac{\alpha}{1+\alpha}\right)}{\left(\frac{\alpha}{\alpha + e^{\frac{\epsilon}{l}}}\right) \left(\frac{1}{1+\alpha}\right)} \right]^{m} \left[\frac{\left(\frac{1}{1+\alpha}\right) \left(\frac{\alpha e^{\frac{\epsilon}{l}}}{1+\alpha e^{\frac{\epsilon}{l}}}\right)}{\left(\frac{\alpha}{1+\alpha}\right) \left(\frac{1}{1+\alpha e^{\frac{\epsilon}{l}}}\right)} \right]^{n} \\
&= e^{\frac{m\epsilon}{l}} \cdot e^{\frac{n\epsilon}{l}} \\
&= e^{\epsilon}
\end{aligned}
$$

In $\alpha - LDP$, each bit in the long binary is assigned a privacy budget of $\frac{\epsilon}{l}$. To further improve the data availability of part P1, we want a larger privacy budget allocated to each bit in P1. To this end, we added a privacy budget coefficient of β $(0 < \beta < 1)$. Assuming that the privacy budget for the entire binary string is ϵ, the privacy budget allocated to part P1 is $\beta\epsilon$, and the privacy budget allocated to part P2 is $(1 - \beta)\epsilon$. Based on this, we designed a binary random response scheme $\alpha\beta - LDP$.

Theorem 2. *($\alpha\beta - LDP$) Let* $\Pr(B[i])$ *be the probability of randomizing the* i_th *bit of the binary-encoded string of* V. *For any input* v_1, v_2 *with sensitivity of* l, *the probability* $p(B[i])$ *is defined as*

$$
p(B[i]|v) =
\begin{cases}
\Pr[B[v_1] = 1|v_1] = \dfrac{e^{\frac{\beta\epsilon}{m}}}{1+e^{\frac{\beta\epsilon}{m}}} & \text{if } i \in \text{P1} \\[2ex]
\Pr[B[v_2] = 0|v_1] = \dfrac{\alpha}{1+\alpha} & \text{''} \\[2ex]
\Pr[B[v_1] = 1|v_1] = \dfrac{1}{1+\alpha^{1+\frac{m}{n}}} & \text{if } i \in \text{P2} \\[2ex]
\Pr[B[v_2] = 0|v_1] = \dfrac{\alpha e^{\frac{(1-\beta)\epsilon}{n}}}{1+\alpha e^{\frac{(1-\beta)\epsilon}{n}}} & \text{''}
\end{cases}
\tag{5}
$$

Proof.

$$
\frac{\Pr[B|v_1]}{\Pr[B|v_2]} = \frac{\prod_{i\in[d]} \Pr[B[i]|v_1]}{\prod_{i\in[d]} \Pr[B[i]|v_2]}
$$

$$
= \frac{\prod_{i\in[P1]} \Pr[B[i]|v_1]}{\prod_{i\in[P1]} \Pr[B[i]|v_2]} \times \frac{\prod_{i\in[P2]} \Pr[B[i]|v_1]}{\prod_{i\in[P2]} \Pr[B[i]|v_2]}
$$

$$
\leqslant \left(\frac{\Pr[B[v_1] = 1|v_1]\Pr[B[v_2] = 0|v_1]}{\Pr[B[v_1] = 1|v_2]\Pr[B[v_2] = 0|v_2]} \right)^m_{i\in P1}
$$

$$
\times \left(\frac{\Pr[B[v_1] = 1|v_1]\Pr[B[v_2] = 0|v_1]}{\Pr[B[v_1] = 1|v_2]\Pr[B[v_2] = 0|v_2]} \right)^n_{i\in P2}
$$

$$
= \left[\left(\frac{e^{\frac{\beta\epsilon}{m}}}{1+e^{\frac{\beta\epsilon}{m}}} \right) \cdot \left(\frac{\alpha}{1+\alpha} \right) \middle/ \left(\frac{1}{1+e^{\frac{\beta\epsilon}{m}}} \right) \left(\frac{1}{1+\alpha} \right) \right]^m
$$

$$
\cdot \left[\left(\frac{1}{1+\alpha^{1+\frac{m}{n}}} \right) \cdot \left(\frac{\alpha e^{\frac{(1-\beta)\epsilon}{n}}}{1+\alpha e^{\frac{(1-\beta)\epsilon}{n}}} \right) \middle/ \left(\frac{\alpha^{1+\frac{m}{n}}}{1+\alpha^{1+\frac{m}{n}}} \right) \left(\frac{1}{1+\alpha e^{\frac{(1-\beta)\epsilon}{n}}} \right) \right]^n
$$

$$
= \alpha^m e^{\beta\epsilon} \cdot \frac{e^{(1-\beta)\epsilon}}{\alpha^m}
$$

$$
= e^\epsilon
$$

The β coefficient in the $\alpha\beta - LDP$ scheme can adjust the privacy budget of P1 and P2 to make the long binary string meet the DP budget of ϵ. In P1, the privacy budget controls the disturbance of bit 1. The higher the privacy budget allocated, the smaller the $\mathbf{P}_{1\rightarrow0}$ value, resulting in higher data availability. In P2, the privacy budget controls the perturbation of bits 0. The smaller the β value assigned, the larger the q value, which brings a higher degree of privacy protection. In conclusion, $\alpha\beta - LDP$ scheme meets the nature that the smaller ϵ is in DP, the better the degree of privacy protection is.

The $\alpha\beta - LDP$ scheme has high scalability, and different lengths of bits can be selected according to the hardware capability and tolerance of communica-

Fig. 2. Merged binary.

tion delay. When the binary string length is constant, $\frac{m}{n}$ becomes smaller by increasing the number of fraction bits, thus increasing the p value in P2 and improving the availability of data in P2.

3.2 Priv-IDS Model

Priv-IDS deploy $\alpha\beta - LDP$ scheme on CAN data to protect the privacy of vehicle CAN data. Since CAN data is time-dependent sequence data, and vehicles have strict time requirements for intrusion detection, this paper uses TCN to model CAN data on vehicles. Finally, $\alpha\beta - LDP$ can guarantee the accuracy of intrusion detection while protecting CAN data privacy.

Standard binary numbers are a prerequisite for deploying $\alpha\beta - LDP$. Z-score standardizes CAN data and makes it easy to make a preliminary estimate of the number of bits needed for signed binary numbers. As shown Fig. 2, we combine all 16-bit binary strings into one long binary string to avoid a higher ϵ due to the combination of different privacy budgets, since a higher ϵ value implies weaker privacy protection. We respond randomly to the merged binary, and the privacy budget will be preserved.

After r binary combinations of length l, there are rl bits. According to A of Sect. 3, after the input of two instance databases, the sensitivity is rl, which satisfies the $\alpha\beta - LDP$ scheme. For P1, there are rm bits, and the privacy budget is $\beta\epsilon$. For P2, there are rn bits and the privacy budget is $(1 - \beta)\epsilon$. The combined binary string is substituted into formula (5) to obtain the disturbed data priv-data.

Priv-data is composed of multiple binary strings. If you encode binary strings directly, you tend not to get very good results because binary provides limited characteristics. Therefore, we convert every 16-bit binary string in the long binary string to 4-bit hexadecimal data, as shown in Fig. 3. After thermal imaging processing, a $4 * 16$ CAN image can be obtained.

In the single input channel case, a single convolution layer receives an input tensor of shape $(batch\_size, input\_length, input\_Channels = 1)$ and outputs a tensor of shape $(batch\_size, input\_length, input\_Channels = 1)$. To evaluate an element of the output, you need to move a kernel_size window by one element. The input of the model in this paper is $16 * 64$ CAN image. As the kernel window moved, a Conv2D was generated at each step. Following this, the process is repeated for each input channel, but a different kernel can be used each time. Then add all the intermediate output vectors to get the final output vector.

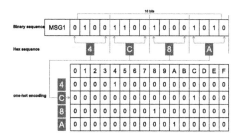

Fig. 3. Hexadecimal one-HOT encoding process.

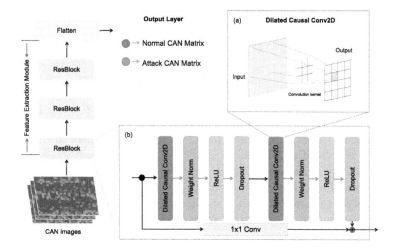

Fig. 4. TCN-IDS model based on TCN for CAN image. (a) A dilated causal convolution with dilation factors d = 1 and filter size k = 3 * 3. (b)TCN residual block. An 1×1 convolution is added when residual input and output have different dimensions.

When kernel_size = k and the receptive field size with n-layer structure is $r(r = 1 + N * (k - 1))$. This means that, given a fixed kernel_size, the number of layers required for complete coverage is linear to the length of the input tensor. In addition, a large number of layers will cause degradation problems associated with loss function gradients. Dilated Causal Convolutions are used to increase the size of experiencing fields while maintaining a relatively small number of layers. Where the dilation factor is **d**. Dilation is equivalent to introducing a fixed step size between every two adjacent filters. Figure 4 shows the final IDS model based on TCN for CAN images. Where k is kernel_size, d is dilation_base, and the minimum number of residual blocks n for complete history coverage. As shown in Fig. 4 (a), when **d** = 1, a dilated convolution becomes a regular convolution. The convolutional neural network in the receiving field is effectively expanded by using a larger expansion to make the top-level output represent a wider input range.

To add some improvements to the TCN architecture to improve performance, we changed the basic building blocks of the model from a simple causal convolution layer to a 2-level residual block with the same dilation factor and residual connection. As shown in Fig. 4 (b), the output of the two convolution layers are added to the input of the residual block to produce the input of the next block. Since the first convolution layer of the first residual block and the second convolution layer of the last residual block may have different input and output channel widths, $1*1$Conv may be required to adjust the width of the residual tensor.

ReLU activation is added between the two convolutional layers. The normalization of weights applied to each convolution layer can counteract the gradient explosion problem. At the same time, regularization is introduced after each convolution layer in each residual block to prevent overfitting.

4   Experiments and Evaluation

4.1   Dataset

The experimental dataset is from the public dataset http://ocslab.hksecurity. net/Datasets/CAN-intrusion-dataset provided by Eunbi Seo et al. [7]. Table 1 shows the specific components of this data set. The data set flags the captured attack-free state traffic and attack traffic data of which there are four types. Each attack is defined as follows.

♯CAN message in Table 1 represents the total number of normal and abnormal CAN messages during the attack. ♯Attack image refers to the total number of CAN images that contain at least one abnormal CAN message. Each dataset in Table 1 is independent of each other rather than a multi-class dataset.

Table 1. Data size and type

Data type	♯Can message	♯Attack image
Normal data	1171637	N/A
DoS attack data	3665771	17128
Fuzzy attack data	3838860	20317
Gear attack data	4621702	32501
RPM spoofing data	4443143	29751

4.2   Evaluation Metrics

An accurate IDS should be able to detect as many intrusions as possible and reduce false positives, so the optimal parameter values are selected for intrusion detection experiment.

Meanwhile, four statistical indicators, TP, FP, TN and FN, were constructed. TP (true positive) and TN(true negative) were correctly classified as attack frames and normal frames, FP(false positive) and FN(false negative) were incorrectly classified as attack frames and normal frames, respectively. The above four indexes are used to measure the classification performance of intrusion detection system, namely accuracy, precision, and recall rate. The calculation formula is:

$$Accuracy = (TP + TN)/(TP + FN + TN + FP) \qquad (6)$$
$$Precision = TP/(TP + FP) \qquad (7)$$
$$Recall = TP/(TP + FN) \qquad (8)$$
$$F1 = 2 \times Precision \times Recall/(Precision + Recall) \qquad (9)$$

Formula (9) represents the accuracy of correctly classifying sample proportion. Formula (7) represents the proportion of samples that really belong to this category. The recall rate of Eq. (8) represents the attack detection capability of IDS, that is, the ratio of detected abnormal packets to total abnormal packets. The value of F1 represents the balance between accuracy and recall, which is often used to measure classification performance.

4.3   The Parameters of $\alpha\beta - LDP$

For $\alpha\beta - LDP$, the effect of ϵ on the change of value is obtained by adjusting the value of the ϵ while α remains unchanged. Under the condition of keeping the ϵ and the value of α unchanged, the value of β is adjusted between 0 and 1. In the case that ϵ and β are determined, the influence of different α on intrusion detection accuracy can be obtained.

when the sensitivity is 256, $p = (e^{\frac{\epsilon}{256}})/(\alpha + e^{\frac{\epsilon}{256}})$. As shown in Fig. 5 (a), when α remains at 1, the randomization probability (p) of the acceptable value of ϵ (less than 10) is greater than 0.5. Therefore, we adjust the value of ϵ in the experiment to produce the result of the total data change after randomization, while keeping α unchanged.

We find that when ϵ is near 1, the total data change decreases greatly. When $\epsilon \geq 2$, the total amount of data change does not change significantly. Therefore, we chose to conduct the experiment for $\epsilon = 2$. To ensure the accuracy of the model while protecting the maximum degree of privacy. Similarly, when $\epsilon = 2$, $\alpha = 1$, we test the influence of different β values on the perturbation probability

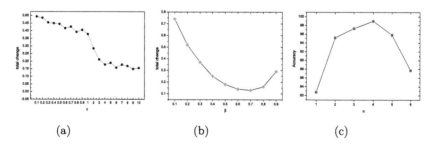

(a)   (b)   (c)

Fig. 5. the parameters of $\alpha\beta - LDP$. (a) The influence of different ϵ values on the total data change. (b) The influence of different β values on the total data change. (c) The influence of different α values on the accuracy of IDS for normal data.

176   S. Li and M. Han

Table 2. Hyperparameter settings.

Hyperparameter	Hyperparameter settings
Batch_size	32, **64**, 128, 256
Learing rate	10^{-3}, 10^{-4}, $\mathbf{10^{-5}}$, 10^{-6}
Number of epochs	50, **100**, 150, 200
Optimizer	SGD, Adam, **RMSProp**

according to formula (5). As shown in Fig. 5 (b), when β remains at 0.7, this is the minimum of the probability of disturbance.

In order to observe the influence of α on the accuracy of intrusion detection, we tested the influence of different α values on the accuracy of intrusion detection for normal data when $\epsilon = 2$ and $\beta = 0.7$. See Fig. 5(c). It can be seen that when $\alpha = 4$, the accuracy rate reaches the optimal 99.03%. Therefore, we select $\epsilon = 2$, $\beta = 0.7$, $\alpha = 4$ to perform DP perturbation for data.

4.4   Priv-IDS Performance

In this paper, we debug the model from three aspects of batch size, learning rate and optimization function, and finally achieve the best performance of the model. Therefore, the final learning rate is 10^{-5}, the Batch_size is 64, and RMSProp is used as the final optimization function for model learning. The comparison of hyperparameters is shown in Table 2.

It is well known that the detection performance of an IDS is of the utmost importance because it is the vehicle's communication security. In Fig. 6, we show the accuracy of Priv-IDS in detecting attack data. As shown in Fig. 6, the detection performance of this model on DoS, Gear and RPM attack data sets is relatively stable, with an average detection accuracy of more than 98%, while the detection performance on fuzzy attack data sets is relatively low. Therefore, the complexity of fuzzy attack data is much higher than other attack data, and more training iterations are needed to establish a stable model. Compared with other traditional algorithms, the Priv-IDS model also shows good detection performance against DoS, gear, and RPM attacks. Detailed inspection results,

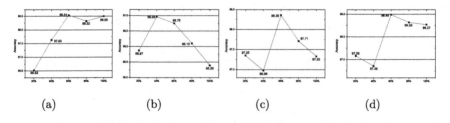

Fig. 6. The accuracy of Priv-IDS in detecting attack data. (a) DoS attack. (b) Fuzzy attack. (c) RPM attack. (d) Gear attack.

Table 3. performance of Priv-IDS.

Data Type	Precise	Recall	F1
Normal data	0.988	0.985	0.986
DoS attack data	0.981	0.976	0.978
Fuzzy attack data	0.936	0.942	0.939
Gear attack data	0.978	0.957	0.967
RPM spoofing data	0.976	0.964	0.970

including Precise and Recall, are summarized in Table 3. In the best case, the proposed PRIV-IDS display precision and Recall greater than 95% in DoS, Gear and RPM attack data sets, and 93% and 94% in fuzzy data sets. Nevertheless, the PRIV-IDS model performed well in terms of overall performance.

4.5 Comparison

In this research, two 3.60 GHz Intel Core CPUs and an Nvidia GeForce GTX 1650 GPU were used to test the performance of the proposed model. In addition, the time cost is proportional to the batch size.

We conducted a comparative experiment on time and accuracy of Priv-IDS in the research of vehicle-mounted intrusion detection. The comparative experimental results are shown in Fig. 7. It can be seen that compared with previous algorithms [16], our anomaly detection time is less than that based on autoencoder, because encoder affects efficiency. In addition, in terms of accuracy, the accuracy of our model is slightly reduced compared with most intrusion detection models without privacy protection due to the use of $\alpha\beta$-LDP disturbance data. However, because we use TCN time neural network which is more suitable for time series and adjust the model to the optimal hyperparameter, the accuracy is still higher than the ordinary neural network model.

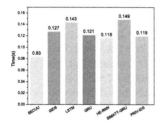

(a) Efficiency comparison.

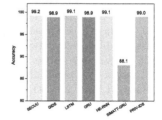

(b) Accuracy comparison.

Fig. 7. Illustration of the IDS compares with previous work in the efficiency and accuracy aspects.

5 Conclusion

Priv-IDS designs a vehicle-mounted intrusion detection framework based on LDP and TCN. $\alpha\beta - LDP$ is used to protect CAN data, and TCN is used in intrusion detection model training, which reduces the computation and memory cost of vehicles, protects data privacy and enables fast detection results. The hardware and performance of different vehicles vary greatly. As a random disturbance framework, $\alpha\beta - LDP$ is designed to meet the privacy requirements of different vehicles. As mentioned above, Priv-IDS offers excellent performance, including stable accuracy, high security, and scalability. We have done a good job with accuracy, but we still have room for improvement. In the future, we will explore a more suitable detection model for intrusion detection to achieve higher accuracy.

Acknowledgements. This research is supported by the Key Research and Development Plan of Jiangsu province in 2007(Industry Foresight and Generic Key Technology) and the Project of Jiangsu University Senior Talents Fund(1281170019).

References

1. Sharma, P., Liu, H.: A Machine-learning-based data-centric misbehavior detection model for internet of vehicles. IEEE Internet Things J. 4991–4999 (2021)
2. Han, M., Wan, A., Zhang, F., Ma, S.: An attribute-isolated secure communication architecture for intelligent connected vehicles. IEEE Trans. Intell. Veh. pp. 545–555 (2020)
3. Whelan, J., Almehmadi, A., El-Khatib, K.: Artificial intelligence for intrusion detection systems in Unmanned Aerial Vehicles. Comput. Electr. Eng. **99**, 107784 (2022)
4. Vijayasarathy, R., Raghavan, S.V., Ravindran, B.: A system approach to network modeling for DDoS detection using a Naíve Bayesian classifier. In: Proceedings of 2011 Third International Conference on Communication Systems and Networks, Bangalore, India, pp. 4–8 (2011). https://doi.org/10.1109/COMSNETS.2011.5716474
5. Javed, A. R., Rehman, S. u., Khan, M. U., Alazab, M.: CANintelliIDS: Detecting In-Vehicle Intrusion Attacks on a Controller Area Network Using CNN and Attention-Based GRU. IEEE Trans. Netwl Sci. Eng. pp. 1456–1466 (2021)
6. Fassak, S., El Hajjaji El Idrissi, Y., Zahid, N., Jedra, M.: A secure protocol for session keys establishment between ECUs in the CAN bus. In: 2017 International Conference on Wireless Networks and Mobile Communications (WINCOM), pp. 1–6 (2017). https://doi.org/10.1109/WINCOM.2017.8238149
7. Seo, E., Song, H.M., Kim, H.K.: GIDS: GAN based intrusion detection system for in-vehicle network. In: 2018 16th Annual Conference on Privacy, Security and Trust (PST), pp. 1–6 (2018), https://doi.org/10.1109/PST.2018.8514157
8. Tan, X., Zhang, C., Li, B., Ge, B., Liu, C.: Anomaly detection system of controller area network (can) bus based on time series prediction. In: SmartCom, pp. 318–328 (2021)
9. Shokri, R., Stronati, M., Song, C., Shmatikov, V.: Membership inference attacks against machine learning models. In: 2017 IEEE Symposium on Security and Privacy, SP 2017, San Jose, CA, USA, 22–26 May 2017, pp. 3–18 (2017)

10. Marchetti, M., Stabili, D.: Anomaly detection of CAN bus messages through analysis of ID sequences. In: 2017 IEEE Intelligent Vehicles Symposium (IV), pp. 1577–1583 (2017). https://doi.org/10.1109/IVS.2017.7995934
11. Cai, S., Bakhouya, M., Becherif, M., Gaber, J., Wack, M.: An In-Vehicle Embedded System for CAN-bus Events Monitoring. J. Mobile Multimedia 10(1&2), 128–140 (2014)
12. Dwork, C., McSherry, F., Nissim, K., Smith, A.: Calibrating noise to sensitivity in private data analysis. In: Halevi, S., Rabin, T. (eds.) TCC 2006. LNCS, vol. 3876, pp. 265–284. Springer, Heidelberg (2006). https://doi.org/10.1007/1168187814
13. Abadi, M., et al.: Deep learning with differential privacy. In: Proceedings of the 2016 ACM SIGSAC Conference on Computer and Communications Security, Vienna, Austria, 24–28 October 2016, pp. 308–318 (2016)
14. Erlingsson, U., Pihur, V., Korolova, A.: RAPPOR: randomized aggregatable privacy-preserving ordinal response. In: CCS 2014, pp. 1054–1067 (2014)
15. Chamikara, M., Bertok, P., Khalil, I., Liu, D., Camtepe, S., Atiquzzaman, M.: Local Differential Privacy for Deep Learning. IEEE Internet Things J. 7(7), 5827–5842 (2020)
16. Han, M., Cheng, P., Ma, S.: PPM-InVIDS: Privacy protection model for in-vehicle intrusion detection system based complex-valued neural network. Veh. Commun. 31, 100374 (2021)

Dynamic Momentum for Deep Learning with Differential Privacy

Guanbiao Lin[1,2], Hu Li[1,2], Yingying Zhang[1,2], Shiyu Peng[1], Yufeng Wang[1], Zhenxin Zhang[1], and Jin Li[1(✉)]

[1] Institute of Artificial Intelligence and Blockchain, Guangzhou University, Guangdong 510006, China
linguanbiao@e.gzhu.edu.cn
[2] Pazhou Lab, Guangzhou 510330, China

Abstract. Deep learning models are often incompetent to privacy attacks, resulting in the leakage of private data. Recently, Differentially-Private Stochastic Gradient Descent (DP-SGD) has emerged as a prime method for training deep learning models with rigorous privacy guarantee, and has been widely adopted in both academic and industrial research. However, using the DP-SGD optimizer will make the model converge slower and worse, so improving the utility of the model while maintaining privacy becomes a challenge. In non-private training, setting momentum to the SGD optimizer is a common method to improve the utility of the model, but the performance of this method in DP-SGD optimizer is not yet known. In this paper, we empirically study the impact of momentum setting on the optimization of DP-SGD models. With extensive experiments, we were able to gain some fresh insights and proposed a method to dynamically set the momentum for DP-SGD to achieve better utility. The results showd that we achieved the new state-of-the-art on MNIST, Fashion-MNIST, CIFAR-10 and Imagenette datasets without any modification of differential-privacy analysis.

Keywords: Differentially-Private Stochastic Gradient Descent (DP-SGD) · Dynamic momentum · Deep learning

1 Introduction

Over the past several decades, Deep Neural Networks (DNNs) have been widely applied in various fields such as image classification [1,2], natural language processing [3] and speech recognition [4], which have brought great convenience to our daily life, but at the same time, there are also some hidden risks. Recently, a series of researchs have shown that deep learning models may remember or leak their sensitive information, such as membership information [5,6] and gradient information [7], which has raised great concerns. This worrying situation was greatly alleviated by the seminal work DP-SGD, provided by Abdai et al. [8]. At present, DP-SGD has become a prime method to provide data privacy protection for deep learning models.

Y. Xu et al. (Eds.): ML4CS 2022, LNCS 13656, pp. 180–190, 2023.
https://doi.org/10.1007/978-3-031-20099-1_15

However, there is a cost to the model when using DP-SGD to provide privacy guarantees. That is, the utility of the deep learning model will be reduced, and due to the unique algorithm design of DP-SGD, such damage is inevitable in most cases. At a high level, DP-SGD extends two additional steps on the basis of SGD: gradient clipping and adding noise. Obviously, these two steps both will destroy the utility of the model, gradient clipping will discard some useful gradient information, and noise addition will disrupt the learned gradient distribution and change the direction of gradient update.

Improving utility while also maintaining privacy guarantees in DP-SGD has attracted much interest, and various approaches have been proposed, such as gradient dimensionality reduction [9,10], adaptive gradient clipping [11,12], and adaptive noise addition [13,14]. All these works focus on the algorithm of DP-SGD to make improvements, but in fact, some of these improvements are not completely correct. For example, the method of [13] actually violates the definition of differential privacy. Therefore, a simple and effective strategy that does not require any changes to the algorithm may be a better choice. As we all know, in the non-private training, we usually set a momentum for the SGD optimizer to accelerate the convergence of the model, and rush out of the local optimum point of convergence to achieve better model utility. Recalling what we mentioned above, DP-SGD is actually an extension of SGD, so a question arises, *Can DP-SGD also improve the utility of the model by setting momentum and how to do it?*

In this paper, we report interesting insights gained from experience regarding the momentum settings in DP-SGD. We showed the performance of model convergence and utility with different momentum values in DP-SGD, and compared the performance in non-private training, drawing some constructive and unique conclusions. Then based on these experimental phenomena and conclusions, we designed a method to dynamically set the momentum for DP-SGD. We conducted experiments on four datasets, MNIST, Fashion-MNIST, CIFAR-10 and Imagnette, under different privacy budgets, and the results all show that our method improves the model utility significantly, especially on complex datasets. As far as we know, Papernot et al. [15] achieved state-of-the-art in the first three datasets, while our experimental results show that we achieved better results than theirs. The main contributions of this paper are summarized as follows:

1. We investigated the impact of the momentum value in DP-SGD on model convergence and utility, and gained some interesting insights. Meanwhile, by compared with its performance in non-private training, we verified the folklore that the setting of momentum on DP-SGD should be different from SGD.
2. We proposed a method to dynamically set the momentum value for DP-SGD, and our method achieved new state-of-the-art accuracy on four datasets: MNIST, Fashion-MNIST, CIFAR-10 and Imagenette.

2   Releted Work

Since DP-SGD was proposed, it has become a *de facto* training method for differentially private machine learning models. However, as pointed out by many papers [16,17], DP-SGD will compromise the utility of models when providing privacy protection, and this compromise is unavoidable. To this end, many works [9–15] have been proposed to improve model utility with meaningful privacy guarantees. Similarly, in non-private training scenarios, many researchs [22,23] on the momentum setting of SGD are also aimed at improving the utility of the model. We summarize the above in detail as follows.

2.1   Optimize the DP-SGD Algorithm

The improvement of DP-SGD algorithm includes adaptive gradient clipping and adaptive noise addition. Van et al. [18] proposed to set the gradient clipping threshold based on the differentially private mean ℓ_2-norm of the previous batch. Then, Yu et al. [19] proposed to set this value adaptively using a linearly decreasing function $C_t = \frac{C}{\min\left(2,1+\frac{t}{T}\right)}$. A recent work on adaptive gradient clipping was proposed by Du et al. [20]. They used a near-linear decreasing function $C_t = (\rho_c)^{-\frac{t}{T}}$ to set the gradient clipping threshold. As for adaptive gradient addition noise, Zhang et al. [21] proposed to set the noise variance varies with a linear decay model as $\sigma_{t+1}^2 = R\sigma_t^2$, where $R \in (0,1)$, and similar work was done in the ADADP proposed by Xu et al. [14]. It is worth noting that these works are very different from ours, so we do not compare with them in this paper, but we should mention that our work can be combined with these works, as there is no conflict between us.

2.2   Optimize Training Parameters

Recently, Papernot et al. [15] showed that using bounded activation functions (the tempered sigmoids) can lead to better utility than using unbounded ones in DP-SGD training. They achieved new state-of-the-art accuracy on MNIST, Fashion-MNIST, and CIFAR-10 datasets using the tempered activation function, respectively 98.1%, 86.1% and 66.2% at privacy budgets of 2.93, 2.7 and 7.56. Our paper mainly compared with this work, because we both do not need any modification to the DP-SGD algorithm.

2.3   Adaptive Setting Momentum

In non-private training, adaptively setting the momentum value of the SGD optimizer is a major approach to improve the model utility. Chen et al. [22] dynamically update the momentum β_t at epoch t-th according to $\beta_t = \beta_{\text{init}} \cdot \frac{\left(1-\frac{t}{T}\right)}{(1-\beta_{\text{init}})+\beta_{\text{init}}\left(1-\frac{t}{T}\right)}$, while in the work of Bai et al. [23], they adopt a more sophisticated method to update the momentum. However, none of them extended their strategy into DP-SGD.

3 Preliminaries

3.1 Differential Privacy

Differential privacy [8] provides a formal privacy definition, with the intuition that a randomized algorithm behaves similarly on "similar" input datasets.

Definition 1 (Differential Privacy). *A randomized mechanism* $\mathcal{M} : \mathcal{X}^n \to \mathbb{R}^d$ *satisfies* (ϵ, δ)*-differential privacy if for any two datasets* $\mathcal{D}, \mathcal{D}' \in \mathcal{X}^n$ *differing by a single element and for any set of possible output* $\mathcal{O} \subseteq \text{Range}(\mathcal{M})$:

$$\Pr[\mathcal{M}(\mathcal{D}) \in \mathcal{O}] \le e^\epsilon \Pr[\mathcal{M}(\mathcal{D}') \in \mathcal{O}] + \delta \tag{1}$$

In the above, ϵ is the privacy budget, a parameter that controls the trade-off between the utility and privacy protection of the differential privacy algorithm. Smaller ϵ usually means better privacy but also worse utility. The additive term δ, is a small probability that the output distributions differs more than the ϵ bound, and the value of δ is typically chosen to be smaller than $1/|\mathcal{D}|$.

Definition 2 (Global Sensitivity). *Given a query* $f : \mathcal{X}^n \to \mathbb{R}^d$*, the global sensitivity* Δ_f *is defined as:*

$$\Delta_f = \max_{\mathcal{D}, \mathcal{D}'} |f(\mathcal{D}) - f(\mathcal{D}')| \tag{2}$$

The global sensitivity measures the maximum possible change in $f(\mathcal{D})$ when one record in the dataset changes.

Theorem 1 (Gaussian Mechanism). *For a query function* $f : \mathcal{X}^n \to \mathbb{R}^d$ *with sensitivity* Δ_f*, the Gaussian Mechanism that adds noise generated from the Gaussian distribution* $\mathcal{N}(0, \sigma^2 \mathbb{I})$ *to the output of f satisfies* (ϵ, δ)*-differential privacy, where* $\epsilon, \delta \in (0, 1)$ *and* $\sigma \ge \frac{\sqrt{2 \ln(1.25/\delta)} \Delta_f}{\epsilon}$.

3.2 Differentially Private Stochastic Gradient Descent

DP-SGD [8] is a useful optimization technique for learning a model f under differential privacy constraints, the detailed procedure can be found in Appendix A. DP-SGD randomly draws a mini-batch of training examples, computes the gradients, clip them, then applies the Gaussian mechanism to the gradients. To bound the ℓ_2-sensitivity, a fixed threshold $\mathcal{C}$ is used to clip the per-example gradient. More formally, given the gradient g on an example and a threshold $\mathcal{C}$, gradient clipping does the following:

$$\text{clip}(g) = g \cdot \min\left(1, \frac{\mathcal{C}}{\|g\|_2}\right) \tag{3}$$

Based on the clipped gradients, DP-SGD crafts a randomized gradient $\tilde{g}$ through computing the average over the clipped gradients and adding noise whose scale is defined by $\mathcal{C}$ and σ_ε, where σ_ε is noise scaler to satisfy (ϵ, δ)-DP.

$$\tilde{g} = \frac{1}{B} \left(\sum_{i \in [B]} \text{clip} \, (g_i) + \mathcal{N} \left(0, (\sigma_\varepsilon \mathcal{C})^2 \mathcal{I} \right) \right) \tag{4}$$

3.3 Momentum SGD

SGD with Momentum is a stochastic optimization method that adds a momentum term to regular stochastic gradient descent. Let $\theta_t \in \mathbb{R}^p$ be the parameters of the network at time step t , where $\eta \in \mathbb{R}$ is the learning rate, and g_t is the stochastic gradient w.r.t. θ_t for empirical loss $\mathcal{L}(\cdot)$. SGDM is parameterized by $\beta \in \mathbb{R}$, the momentum coefficient, and follows the recursion:

$$\theta_{t+1} = \theta_t + \eta v_t, \quad v_t = \beta v_{t-1} - g_t \tag{5}$$

where $v_t \in \mathbb{R}^p$ accumulates momentum. Observe that for $\beta = 0$, the above recursion is equivalent to SGD. Common values for β are closer to one, with $\beta = 0.9$ the most used value, which is supported by recent works [24,25]. However, there is no indication that this choice is universally well-behaved.

4 Approach

4.1 DP-SGD with Momentum[1]

The training of DP-SGD is a more complex and variable situation where each gradient clipping and noise addition has an unpredictable impact on the convergence of the model. Therefore, some work and conclusions of setting momentum on SGD in non-private training may not be applicable to DP-SGD. To prove our intuition, we set different values of momentum for SGD and DP-SGD during model training, and conducted experiments on four datasets to observe the influence of momentum on model convergence and final utility. The results are shown in Fig. 1 and Fig. 2. Some interesting insights can be gained from this comparison of the two figures.

   In non-private training, all momentum settings can make the model continue to converge, and the utility of the model shows a certain robustness to the momentum setting, but a larger momentum allows the model to achieve a good model accuracy in the first few epochs. This performance validated why many papers recommend setting the momentum of SGD to 0.9. However, in DP-SGD, the phenomenon is different, as DP-SGD appears to be less robust to the momentum setting. A larger momentum value allows the DP-SGD model to converge to a good value at early stage, but as training continues, the utility of the model drops dramatically to a very low value. While a smaller momentum value can indeed make the model continue to converge, but the convergence speed in the early stage of training is not as fast as a larger momentum. In addition, on more complex dataset, such as the Imagenette dataset, the impact of different momentum settings on the model convergence is significantly greater than that of simple datasets, and this phenomenon holds for both non-private training and differential privacy training.

---

[1] Settings for the Experiments in This Section Can Be Found in Section 5.

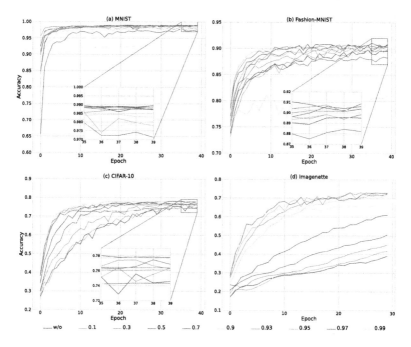

Fig. 1. Performance of setting different momentums for SGD in non-private training

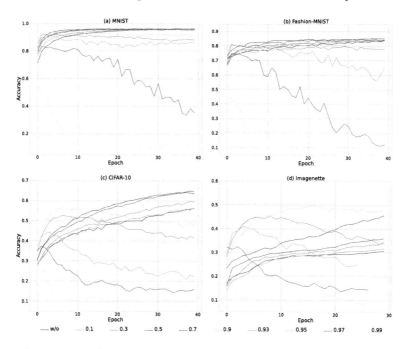

Fig. 2. Performance of setting different momentums for DP-SGD, the privacy budget is 3.0, 2.7, 7.56 and 11.0 respectively

4.2 Dynamic Momentum of DP-SGD

In the last section, we can see that a larger momentum can make DP-SGD converge quickly at the beginning of training, while a smaller momentum can make DP-SGD continue to converge. This inspired us to design a decreasing strategy for dynamically setting the momentum of DP-SGD. In our method, we set an initial momentum β_{init} for DP-SGD, and according to the above experimental phenomenon, β_{init} can be a large value. Then, we decrease β_{init} with the increase of the number of training rounds. At the t-th epoch, its momentum β_t should be:

$$\beta_t = \begin{cases} \beta_{\text{init}} - \alpha \cdot t & \text{where } 0 < t \leqslant 35 \text{ and } \alpha = 0.01 \\ 0.3 & \text{where } t > 35 \end{cases} \tag{6}$$

In the above, α is the decreasing factor, we recommend setting α to 0.01, the reason is that this will not make the momentum change too much in each epoch of model training. When the number of training epochs is greater than 35, we fix the momentum of the subsequent epochs to 0.3, which prevents the momentum from decreasing to an extremely small value.

5 Experiment

5.1 Datasets

The performance evaluation was performed on 4 widely used datasets: MNIST (handwritten digits), Fashion- MNIST (fashion products images), CIFAR-10 (tiny colored images) and Imagenette (a subset of 10 classes from ImageNet). The default training/testing split was used. More details of the datasets can be found below.

Table 1. Summary of datasets.

Dataset	#Sample	#Classes	#Dimension
MNIST	70000	10	784
Fashion-MNIST	70000	10	784
CIFAR-10	60000	10	3072
Imagenette	13394	10	150528

5.2 Network and Hyperparameters

For each of MNIST, Fashion-MNIST and CIFAR-10 datasets, we used the same CNNs as in Papernot et al. [15]. For Imagenette, we used Alexnet. In all our experiments, we set the batch size to 1024 for the first three datasets, and for the imagenette dataset, we set the batch size to 64. And for the learning rate, we set it to 0.1 for non-private training and 1.0 for differential privacy training.

5.3 Hardware and Software

All experiments were conducted on a personal workstation with an Intel Xeon Gold 6248R 3.00 GHz CPU, an NVIDIA Tesla V100S-PCIE-32 GB GPU and 128 GB memory. We implemented all algorithms on top of Opacus[2].

5.4 Experimental Results

In our experiments, we take the experimental results of the original DP-SGD proposed by Abadi et al. [8] as the baseline. Then we mainly compare the methods of Papernot et al. [15], as we mentioned above, becauser we both do not need any modification to the DP-SGD algorithm. We set the privacy budgets ϵ to 3.0, 2.7 and 7.56 for MNIST , Fashion-MNIST , and CIFAR-10, respectively, which are consistent with the experimental settings of Papernot et al. [15]. While for the Imagenette dataset, which is more complex and requires a larger privacy budget, we set ϵ to 11.0, a value that makes the privacy guarantee still meaningful. For the methods we compared, we report their best performance for the same privacy budget. Our experimental results are shown in Fig. 3 and Table 2.

From Table 2 we can see that our method achieves the best performance on all four datasets, we achieve classification accuracies of 97.94%, 87.57%, 68.69% and 56.47%, respectively, at ϵ set to 3.0 , 2.7 , 7.56 and 11.0. In Fig. 3, it can be seen that our method consistently outperforms other methods, our method can achieve fast convergence to a good classification accuracy in the training early stage, and continue to converge to a better result as training continues. Especially on more complex dataset, the advantages of our method are more obvious. Furthermore, the ability to quickly converge the model allows our method to incorporate early stopping strategies, which can cost a smaller privacy budget.

---

[2] Opacus is an open source library provided by Facebook that implements DP-SGD in the Pytorch framework.

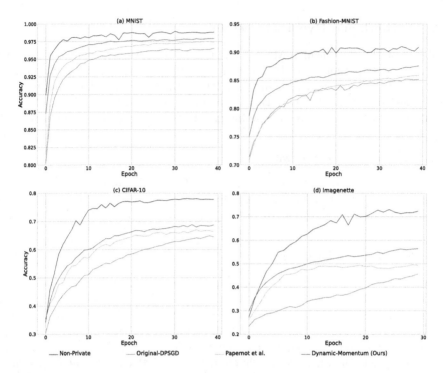

Fig. 3. Performance comparison of different methods, the privacy budget is 3.0, 2.7, 7.56 and 11.0 respectively

Table 2. Accuracy performance comparison of different methods, the privacy budget is 3.0, 2.7, 7.56 and 11.0 respectively.

Methods	Datasets			
	MNIST	Fashion-MNIST	CIFAR-10	Imagenette
Non-private	98.84%	90.89%	77.75%	72.28%
Original-DPSGD	96.57%	85.16%	64.55%	45.65%
Papernot et al.	97.44%	85.84%	66.36%	49.37%
Dynamic-Monentum (Ours)	**97.94%**	**87.57%**	**68.69%**	**56.47%**

6   Conclusion

In this paper, we investigated the effect of setting different momentums in the DP-SGD optimizer on model convergence, and we did extensive experiments and get some interesting insights. We further proposed our method based on the observed experimental phenomenon, our method can make the DP-SGD model converge quickly and achieve a better utility. Experimental results show that our method consistently outperforms other methods. We hope our research can provide some help for future theoretical analysis of the impact of momentum on DP-SGD models.

A DP-SGD

The DP-SGD algorithm [8] is shown in Algorithm 1.

Algorithm 1. Differentially private SGD

Input: Examples D, loss function L, parameters θ, batch size m, learing rate η_t, noise scale σ, gradient norm bound C

Output: θ_T and the overall privacy cost (ϵ,δ) using a privacy accounting methond.

1: **Initial** θ_0 randomly
2: **for** $t \in [T]$ **do**
3:     Take a random batch B_t with the size m
4:     **Compute Gradients**
5:     for each $i \in B_t$, compute $\mathbf{g_t}(x_i) \leftarrow \nabla_{\theta_t} L(\boldsymbol{\theta}_t, \mathbf{x}_i)$
6:     **Clip Gradients**
7:     $\overline{\mathbf{g}}_t(x_i) \leftarrow \mathbf{g}_t(x_i) / \max\left(1, \frac{\|\mathbf{g}_t(x_i)\|_2}{C}\right)$
8:     **Add Noise**
9:     $\widetilde{g}_t \leftarrow \frac{1}{m}\left(\sum_i \overline{\mathbf{g}}_t(x_i) + \mathcal{N}\left(0, \sigma^2 C^2 \mathbf{I}\right)\right)$
10:    **Descent**
11:    $\boldsymbol{\theta}_{t+1} \leftarrow \boldsymbol{\theta}_t - \eta_t \widetilde{g}_t$
12: **end for**

References

1. He, K., Zhang, X., Ren, S., Sun, J.: Delving deep into rectifiers: surpassing human-level performance on imagenet classification. In: Proceedings of the IEEE International Conference on Computer Vision, pp. 1026–1034 (2015)
2. Zheng, W., Yan, L., Gou, C., Wang, F.-Y.: Fighting fire with fire: a spatial-frequency ensemble relation network with generative adversarial learning for adversarial image classification. In: Int. J. Intell. Syst. **36**(5), 2081–2121 (2021)
3. Mikolov, T., Karafiát, M., Burget, L., Černocký, J., Khudanpur, S.: Recurrent neural network based language model. In: Proceedings of Interspeech (2010)
4. Deng, L., Hinton, G., Kingsbury, B.: New types of deep neural network learning for speech recognition and related applications: an overview. In: Proceedings of ICASSP'13 (2013)
5. Shokri, R., Stronati, M., Song, C., Shmatikov, V.: Membership inference attacks against machine learning models. In: Security and Privacy (SP), 2017 IEEE Symposium on IEEE, pp. 3–18 (2017)
6. Salem, A., Zhang, Y., Humbert, M., Berrang, P., Fritz, M., Backes, M.: Ml-leaks: model and data independent membership inference attacks and defenses on machine learning models. In: arXiv preprint arXiv:1806.01246, 2018
7. Zhu, L., Liu, Z., Han, S. : Deep leakage from gradients. In: Advances in Neural Information Processing Systems, pp. 14 747–14 756 (2019)
8. Abadi, M., Chu, A., Goodfellow, I., McMahan, H. B., Mironov, I., Talwar, K., Zhang, L.: Deep learning with differential privacy. In: Conference on Computer and Communications Security (2016)

9. Bertino, E., Shulman, H., Waidner, M. (eds.): ESORICS 2021. LNCS, vol. 12973. Springer, Cham (2021). https://doi.org/10.1007/978-3-030-88428-4

10. Tramer, F., Boneh, D.: Differentially private learning needs better features (or much more data). In: International Conference on Learning Representations (2021)

11. Pichapati, V., Suresh, A. T., Yu, F. X., Reddi, S. J., Kumar, S.: Adaclip: adaptive clipping for private SGD. arXiv preprint arXiv:1908.07643 (2019)

12. Andrew, G., Thakkar, O., McMahan, H. B., Ramaswamy, S.: Differentially private learning with adaptive clipping. In: NeurIPS (2021)

13. Gong, M., Pan, K., Xie, Y., Qin, A. K., Tang, Z.: Preserving differential privacy in deep neural networks with relevance-based adaptive noise imposition. Neural Netw. **125**, 131–141 (2020)

14. Xu, Z., Shi, S., Liu, A. X., Zhao, J., Chen, L.: An adaptive and fast convergent approach to differentially private deep learning. In: IEEE INFOCOM 2020-IEEE Conference on Computer Communications, pp. 1867–1876 IEEE (2020)

15. Papernot, N., Thakurta, A., Song, S., Chien, S., Erlingsson, U.: Tempered sigmoid activations for deep learning with differential privacy. arXiv preprint arXiv:2007.14191 (2020)

16. Leino, K., Fredrikson, M.: Stolen memories: leveraging model memorization for calibrated white-box membership inference. In: 29th USENIX Security Symposium (USENIX Security 20), pp. 1605–1622 (2020)

17. Jayaraman, B., Evans, D.: Evaluating differentially private machine learning in practice. In: 28th USENIX Security Symposium (USENIX Security 19), pp. 1895–1912 (2019)

18. van der Veen, K. L., Seggers, R., Bloem, P., Patrini, G.: Three tools for practical differential privacy. In: NeurIPS 2018 Workshop (2018)

19. Yu, D., Zhang, H., Chen, W.: Improve the gradient perturbation approach for differentially private optimization. In: NeurIPS 2018 Workshop (2018)

20. Du, J., Li, S., Feng, M., Chen, S.: Dynamic differential-privacy preserving SGD. arXiv preprint arXiv:2111.00173 (2021)

21. Zhang, X., Ding, J., Wu, M., Wong, STC.: Adaptive privacy preserving deep learning algorithms for medical data. In: Proceedings of the IEEE/CVF Winter Conference on Applications of Computer Vision (2021)

22. Chen, J., Wolfe, C., Li, Z., Kyrillidis, A.: Demon: improved neural network training with momentum decay. In: ICASSP 2022-2022 IEEE International Conference on Acoustics, Speech and Signal Processing (ICASSP), IEEE, pp. 3958–3962 (2022)

23. Bai, J., Ren, Y., Zhang, J.: Adaptive momentum with discriminative weight for neural network stochastic optimization. Int. J. Intell. Syst. **37**, 6531-6554 (2022)

24. Keskar, N. S., Socher, R.: Improving generalization performance by switching from Adam to SGD. arXiv preprint arXiv:1712.07628 (2017)

25. Liu, Y., Gao Y., Yin, W.: An improved analysis of stochastic gradient descent with momentum. arXiv preprint arXiv:2007.07989

An Unsupervised Surface Anomaly Detection Method Based on Attention and ASPP

Yuhui Huang[1]([⊠]) (ID), Xin Xie[1] (ID), Weiye Ning[1] (ID), Dengquan Wu[1] (ID), Zixi Li[1] (ID),
and Hao Yang[2] (ID)

[1] School of Information Engineering, East China Jiaotong University, Nanchang 330013, China
huiyuhyh@163.com
[2] State Grid Jiangxi Electric Power Co. Ltd. Electric Power Research Institute, Nanchang, China

Abstract. It is the main task of visual anomaly detection to find local regions whose saliency is inconsistent with normal appearance. However, existing mainstream anomaly detection models suffer from low detection accuracy and poor generalization performance. Therefore, this paper designs an unsupervised surface anomaly detection model based on attention and atrous spatial pyramid pooling. The proposed model learns anomaly images and their normal reconstruction and simultaneously learns the decision boundaries of normal and anomaly images. The method utilizes a squeeze-and-excitation block to assign attention to feature channels to improve the sensitivity of related favorable features, thus enhancing the model's ability to learn normal and anomaly boundaries. In addition, atrous spatial pyramid pooling is introduced in the discriminative sub-network to obtain the multi-scale semantic information of the training image, which improves the detection ability of defects of different sizes and enhances the universality of the model. The superiority of our method is demonstrated in the anomaly detection benchmark MVTec dataset.

Keywords: Surface anomaly detection · Atrous spatial pyramid pooling · Attention · Squeeze-and-Excitation blocks

1 Introduction

Finding features in a set of homogeneous images that do not match the images is an inherent human cognitive ability, which is also known as anomaly detection. Anomaly detection includes downstream tasks such as visual anomaly detection [1] and network traffic anomaly [2]. Visual anomaly detection includes applications such as video surveillance [3], medical image analysis [4], and industrial defect detection [5]. In visual anomaly detection, anomaly detection provides anomaly scores for images, and anomaly localization outputs anomaly scores for each pixel in the image to provide anomaly localization maps. In the industrial manufacturing process, anomaly regions generally only occupy a very small part of the whole image, so anomaly localization is a very challenging task. Figure 1 shows normal as well as anomaly examples of the MVTec dataset [6].

Y. Xu et al. (Eds.): ML4CS 2022, LNCS 13656, pp. 191–201, 2023.
https://doi.org/10.1007/978-3-031-20099-1_16

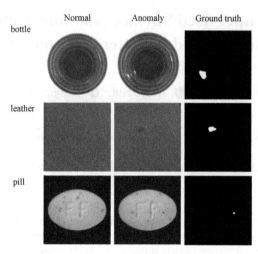

Fig. 1. Sample image of MVTec dataset.

Existing surface unsupervised anomaly detection methods contain those reconstruction-based [7–9] or pre-trained networks [10–12]. The former is based on a hypothesis that only normal images are used in the training stage, and the unknown anomaly region in the test stage has poor reconstruction ability. Due to the powerful reconstruction ability of the convolutional neural network (CNN), the anomaly samples are reconstructed like normal samples when anomaly regions are similar to normal regions. Therefore, reconstruction-based methods rely on defect detection scenarios and have certain limitations. The latter uses the pre-trained network to extract the features of the image to obtain its embedded vector and usually calculates the anomaly score based on the distance between the reference vector of the normal sample in the training image and the embedding vector of the test samples. The statistical methods used by existing pre-trained methods are limited to the normal distribution, which is not applicable in many cases.

Both the above reconstruction-based and pre-trained network-based methods have shortcomings. Therefore, this paper designs an unsupervised surface anomaly detection model based on attention and atrous spatial pyramid pooling (ASPP). The model consists of a reconstructive sub-network and a discriminative sub-network. The former learns anomaly images and the reconstruction of their normal images, and the latter learns the decision boundaries of normal and anomaly images. The innovative nature of our approach is summarized in three points.

1. Squeeze-and-Excitation blocks are added to the encoder layer of the discriminative sub-network to enhance its sensitivity to related features and suppress unnecessary features. Therefore, the ability to learn boundaries of normal and anomaly for discriminative sub-network is improved.
2. The ASPP is introduced into the discriminative sub-network to capture multi-scale information of the image, which enhances the detection ability of the model for anomaly regions of different sizes and the universality of the model.

3. We performed experiments on the MVTec dataset, which proves that method is better than previous advanced methods.

The rest of this paper is organized as follows. Section 2 presents related work. Section 3 presents our model. Section 4 is the experimental part, which verifies the effectiveness of the model. Section 5 is the summary and prospective research directions.

2 Related Work

2.1 Reconstruction-Based Methods

Reconstruction-based methods are widely used in image anomaly detection. Xia [7] et al. proposed a generation discriminant method, in which the generator learns under the guidance of the discriminator. Perera [8] et al. proposed a model OCGAN, which is mainly composed of convolutional denoising autoencoder (CDAE), latent discriminator, image discriminator, and classifier. Hou [9] et al. proposed a generative memory augmentation model, adding a multi-scale memory module to the autoencoder (AE) network to prevent the AE from over-generalizing so that normal and anomaly reconstructions can be distinguished.

2.2 Pre-trained Network-Based Methods

There has also been a lot of recent work not directly processing images, but using the features of pre-trained networks for defect detection. Rippel et al. [10] used the feature representation of the classification network trained on ImageNet to simulate the normal distribution and the anomaly score was obtained by the Mahalanobis distance. Defard et al. [11] adopted a pre-trained CNN to generate patch embedding vectors, exploited a multivariate gaussian distribution to obtain probabilistic representations of normal classes, and exploited the correlation between different semantic levels of CNN to obtain more accurate locating anomalies. Rudolph et al. [12] used a pre-trained feature extraction network to extract features from anomaly-free images at multiple scales, performed maximum likelihood training on the extracted features using a normalizing flow to obtain the normal distribution of anomaly-free images, and calculated log-likelihood to determine whether it is abnormal.

3 Proposed Approach

3.1 Network Architecture

We design an unsupervised surface anomaly detection model based on attention and ASPP, as shown in Fig. 2. We refer to the anomaly image generation process of reference [13]. The anomaly images generated by Perlin noise and the anomaly source images are mixed with the normal images in the training stage to produce anomaly images that are just beyond the normal distribution. The model in this paper mainly consists of two components: reconstructive sub-network and discriminative sub-network. During training, anomaly images are generated from normal images through the anomaly image generation process. The anomaly image is reconstructed without anomalies by the reconstructive sub-network. Anomaly images and their reconstructed images are cascaded to the discriminative sub-network. In this model, four squeeze-and-excitation (SE) blocks are added to the discriminative sub-network to make it redistribute the weight of the feature map, improve the attention of the region of interest and suppress other invalid region information. Thus, the ability to learn boundaries of normal and anomaly for discriminative sub-network is improved. In addition, ASPP is introduced to capture multi-scale information of the image, which enhances the detection ability of the model for defects of various sizes, and enhances the generality of the model.

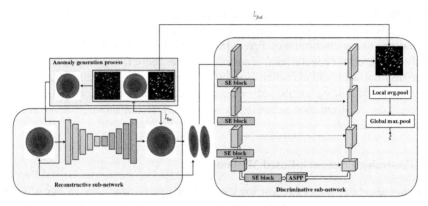

Fig. 2. The proposed model architecture.

3.2 SE Block

SE [14] has the advantage of focusing on the relationship between feature channels, which helps our discriminative sub-network to obtain important feature channels. Its structure is shown in Fig. 3.

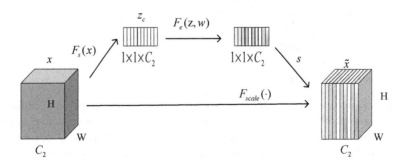

Fig. 3. SE block.

SE block mainly consists of Squeeze ($F_s(\cdot)$) and Excitation ($F_e(\cdot, w)$). Squeeze obtains a global compressed feature z of size $1 \times 1 \times C_1$ by performing global average pooling on the feature map of size $H \times W \times C_1$, as shown in Eq. (1).

$$z_c = F_s(x_c) = \frac{1}{W \times H} \sum_{i=1}^{W} \sum_{j=1}^{H} x_c(i,j) \tag{1}$$

where x_c represents the feature matrix of the c-th feature channel of the feature map. The global compressed feature z is passed through Excitation, which consists of two fully connected layers. Then use the sigmoid function to limit the value to [0, 1], taking this value as s, as shown in Eq. (2).

$$s = F_e(z, W) = \sigma(W_2\delta(W_1 z)) \tag{2}$$

where δ represents the ReLU activation function, W_1 and W_2 are the weights of the above fully connected layers, and σ represents the sigmoid function. The final output of the SE block is weighted by the feature maps x and s.

3.3 Atrous Spatial Pyramid Pooling

The advantage of ASPP [15] is that it can capture multi-scale feature information, which increases the detection ability of our model for anomaly regions of different sizes. Based on spatial pyramid pooling, ASPP uses multiple atrous convolutions with different dilation rates to carry out multi-scale sampling of a given feature map. Figure 4 is the structure of the ASPP.

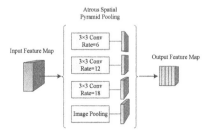

Fig. 4. The structure of Atrous Spatial Pyramid Pooling.

3.4 Training Objective

The reconstructive sub-network takes the reconstruction loss as the optimization goal. The definition of the reconstruction loss is as follows.

$$L_{\text{rec}}(X, X_r) = \gamma L_{SSIM}(X, X_r) + L_2(X, X_r)_{(i,j)} \tag{3}$$

where γ is the parameter that balances the two losses. $L_2(X, X_r)_{(i,j)}$ is the L_2 loss value of image block centered on coordinates (i, j) of the image X and its reconstructed image X_r, $L_{SSIM}(X, X_r)$ represents the SSIM loss, and its definition is shown in Eq. (4).

$$L_{SSIM}(X, X_r) = \frac{1}{N} \sum_{i=1}^{H} \sum_{j=1}^{W} 1 - SSIM(X, X_r)_{(i,j)} \tag{4}$$

where N represents the number of pixels in the image X. H and W are the height and width of the image. SSIM represents the SSIM value of the image X and its reconstructed image X_r with coordinates (i, j) as the center image patch.

Focal loss [16] is adopted as the optimization objective of the discriminative subnetwork. Equation (5) is the overall loss of the proposed model.

$$L(X, X_r, M_t, M_s) = L_{rec}(X, X_r) + L_{focal}(M_t, M_s) \tag{5}$$

where $L_{rec}(X, X_r)$ is reconstruction loss, $L_{focal}(M_t, M_s)$ is focal Loss. M_t is ground truth, and M_s is an anomaly segmentation mask.

The anomaly localization of the image is obtained by the anomaly segmentation mask M_s. The image-level anomaly score ξ is shown in Eq. (6).

$$\xi = \max(M_s * f_{s \times s}) \tag{6}$$

where $*$ represents convolution operator, $f_{s \times s}$ is the mean filter of size $s \times s$.

4 Experiments

4.1 Dataset

To verify the effectiveness of the surface anomaly detection model, we conduct experiments using the MVTec dataset [6]. The dataset contains ten objects and five textures and provides fine annotations of anomaly samples. Each class has many different types of anomaly images, which is a very challenging task for anomaly detection models.

4.2 Evaluation Metrics

The performance of anomaly detection uses image-level AUROC. The performance of anomaly localization uses pixel-level AUROC and pixel-level Average Precision (AP).

4.3 Implementation Details

The anomaly source dataset used the Describable Textures Dataset [17]. We trained the model on NVIDIA Tesla V100, adjusted the image size to 256×256 pixels, trained 700 epochs with a batch size of 4, and used Adam optimizer for training. The initial learning rate was 0.0001.

Table 1. Surface anomaly detection results.

Class	GANomaly [18]	DAAD [9]	Padim [11]	DRAEM [13]	Ours
Bottle	79.4	97.6	**99.9**	99.2	98.7
Capsule	72.1	76.7	91.3	**98.5**	93.1
Grid	74.3	95.7	96.7	99.9	**100**
Leather	80.8	86.2	**100**	**100**	99.9
Pill	67.1	90	93.3	98.9	98.5
Tile	72	88.2	98.1	99.6	**100**
Transistor	80.8	87.6	**97.4**	93.1	93.6
Zipper	74.4	85.9	90.3	100	**100**
Cable	71.1	84.4	92.7	91.8	**93.8**
Carpet	82.1	86.6	**99.8**	97	97.4
Hazelnut	87.4	92.1	92	**100**	**100**
metal_nut	69.4	75.8	98.7	98.7	**99.8**
Screw	**100**	98.7	85.8	93.9	99
Toothbrush	70	99.2	96.1	**100**	**100**
Wood	92	98.2	99.2	**99.1**	98.4
Avg	78.2	89.5	95.5	98.0	**98.1**

4.4 Comparison with Other Methods

Anomaly Detection. Our model achieves the most excellent results in 7 out of 15 classes. In five of these classes, our method achieves 100% AUROC, and the average result for 15 classes is 0.1 percentage points higher than the previous state-of-the-art methods, which is a breakthrough. Our methods are comparable to other state-of-the-art methods in other classes, and the results are shown in Table 1.

Table 2. Anomaly localization results.

Class	US [19]	Padim [11]	DRAEM [13]	Ours
Bottle	97.8/74.2	98.2/77.3	99.1/86.5	**99.3/90.5**
Capsule	96.8/25.9	**98.6**/46.7	94.3/**49.4**	88.6/43.0
Grid	89.9/10.1	97.1/35.7	**99.7/65.7**	99.5/57.9
Leather	97.8/40.9	**99.0**/53.5	98.6/**75.3**	98.6/68.8
Pill	96.5/**62.0**	95.7/61.2	97.6/48.5	**97.4**/36.0
Tile	92.5/65.3	94.1/52.4	99.2/92.3	**99.2/95.5**
Transistor	73.7/27.1	**97.6/72.0**	90.9/50.7	90.2/51.2

(continued)

Table 2. (*continued*)

Class	US [19]	Padim [11]	DRAEM [13]	Ours
Zipper	95.6/36.1	98.4/58.2	98.8/81.5	**99.2/82.8**
Cable	91.9/48.2	96.7/45.4	94.7/52.4	**96.0/60.2**
Carpet	93.5/52.2	**99.0**/60.7	95.5/53.5	97.7/**75.2**
Hazelnut	98.2/57.8	98.1/61.1	**99.7/92.9**	99.6/87.6
metal_nut	97.2/83.5	97.3/77.4	**99.5**/96.3	99.4/**96.4**
Screw	97.4/7.8	98.4/21.7	97.6/58.2	**99.5/72.7**
Toothbrush	97.9/37.7	**98.8/54.7**	98.1/44.7	96.4/45.0
Wood	92.1/53.3	94.1/46.3	**96.4/77.7**	95.9/75.3
Avg	93.9/45.5	**97.4**/55.0	97.3/68.4	97.1/**69.2**

Anomaly Localization. Table 2 reports the results of anomaly localization of the challenging MVTec dataset. Average results for both measures yielded the best results, where the AP metric outperforms the previous most advanced method by 0.8 percentage points. In 9 out of 15 classes, our method achieves the best AUROC or AP. Figure 5 shows a segmented comparison of anomaly locations. Our method significantly outperforms other methods, and the segmentation results are more detailed.

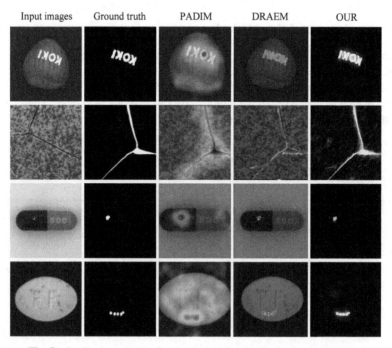

Fig. 5. Qualitative results of anomaly localization in the MVTec dataset.

4.5 Ablation Studies

The proposed model performs ablation experiments on the added modules on the MVTec dataset. Specifically, experiments are carried out under the parameters described in Sect. 4.3. The quantified modules include SE and ASPP. The experimental results are shown in Table 3.

Table 3. Ablation study.

Method	Detection	Location
Original	98.0	97.3/68.4
Original (with SE)	**98.1**	**97.4**/68.8
Original (with ASPP)	98.0	97.0/**69.8**
Ours	**98.1**	97.1/**69.2**

The experimental results show that the introduction of SE block can improve the accuracy of anomaly detection. The SE block effectively suppresses unnecessary features in the encoding stage, thereby enhancing the identification of anomaly regions by the discriminative sub-network. ASPP can improve the accuracy of localization, and it can capture information at multiple scales to improve localization performance. Our proposed method combines SE block and ASPP, and the anomaly detection effect is further improved compared to the original method.

5 Conclusion

In view of the existing methods of low accuracy and poor generalization performance problem, we propose an unsupervised surface anomaly detection model based on attention and ASPP, which compose of a reconstructive sub-network and a discriminative sub-network. We add the SE block to the discriminative sub-network, which is conducive to the discriminative sub-network learning the boundaries of normal and anomaly. In addition, ASPP is added to the discriminative sub-network to enhance the model's ability to detect anomalies of different sizes. Our method performs excellently on the MVTec dataset, there is still room for improvement in anomaly localization, and improving the accuracy of localization has become the direction of future work.

Acknowledgments. This paper is supported by the National Natural Science Foundation of China, under Grant No. 62162026, the Science and Technology Key Research and Development Program of Jiangxi Province, under Grant No. 20202BBEL53004 and Science and Technology Project supported by Education Department of Jiangxi Province, under Grant No. GJJ210611.

References

1. Li, S.B., Yang, J., Wang, Z.: Review of development and application of defect detection technology. Acta Automatica Sinica **46**(11), 2319–2336 (2020)
2. Wu, C., Li, W.: Enhancing intrusion detection with feature selection and neural network. Int. J. Intell. Syst. **36**(7), 3087–3105 (2021)
3. Yan, H., Chen, M., Hu, L., Jia, C.: Secure video retrieval using image query on an untrusted cloud. Appl. Soft Comput. **97**, 106782 (2020)
4. Fang, M., Jin, Z., Qin, F., Peng, Y., Jiang, C., Pan, Z.: Re-transfer learning and multi-modal learning assisted early diagnosis of Alzheimer's disease. Multimedia Tools Appl. **81**, 29159–29175 (2022). https://doi.org/10.1007/s11042-022-11911-6
5. Mei, S., Yang, H., Yin, Z.: An unsupervised-learning-based approach for automated defect inspection on textured surfaces. IEEE Trans. Instrum. Meas. **67**(6), 1266–1277 (2018)
6. Bergmann, P., Fauser, M., Sattlegger, D., et al.: MVTec AD–a comprehensive real-world dataset for unsupervised anomaly detection. In: Proceedings of the IEEE/CVF Conference on Computer Vision and Pattern Recognition, pp. 9592–9600 (2019)
7. Xia, X., Pan, X., He, X.: Discriminative-generative representation learning for one-class anomaly detection (2021)
8. Perera, P., Nallapati, R., Bing, X.: OCGAN: one-class novelty detection using GANs with constrained latent representations. In: 2019 IEEE/CVF Conference on Computer Vision and Pattern Recognition, pp. 2898–2906 (2019)
9. Hou, J., Zhang, Y., Zhong, Q., et al.: Divide-and-assemble: learning block-wise memory for unsupervised anomaly detection. In: Proceedings of the IEEE/CVF International Conference on Computer Vision, pp. 8791–8800 (2021)
10. Rippel, O., Mertens, P., Merhof, D.: Modeling the distribution of normal data in pre-trained deep features for anomaly detection. In: 2020 25th International Conference on Pattern Recognition, pp. 6726–6733 (2021)
11. Defard, T., Setkov, A., Loesch, A., Audigier, R.: PaDiM: a patch distribution modeling framework for anomaly detection and localization. In: Del Bimbo, A., Cucchiara, R., Sclaroff, S., Farinella, G.M., Mei, T., Bertini, M., Escalante, H.J., Vezzani, R. (eds.) ICPR 2021. LNCS, vol. 12664, pp. 475–489. Springer, Cham (2021). https://doi.org/10.1007/978-3-030-68799-1_35
12. Rudolph, M., Wandt, B., Rosenhahn, B.: Same same but DifferNet: semi-supervised defect detection with normalizing flows. In: Proceedings of the IEEE/CVF Winter Conference on Applications of Computer Vision, pp. 1907–1916. (2021)
13. Zavrtanik, V., Kristan, M., Skočaj, D.: DRAEM-a discriminatively trained reconstruction embedding for surface anomaly detection. In: Proceedings of the IEEE/CVF International Conference on Computer Vision, pp. 8330–8339 (2021)
14. Hu, J., Shen, L., Sun, G.: Squeeze-and-excitation networks. In: Proceedings of the IEEE Conference on Computer Vision and Pattern Recognition, pp. 7132–7141 (2018)
15. Chen, LC., Papandreou, G., Kokkinos, I.: Semantic image segmentation with deep convolutional nets and fully connected CRFs. In: International Conference on Learning Representations, pp. 357–361 (2014)
16. Lin, T.Y., Goyal, P., Girshick, R., et al.: Focal loss for dense object detection. In: Proceedings of the IEEE International Conference on Computer Vision, pp. 2980–2988 (2017)
17. Cimpoi, M., Maji, S., Kokkinos, I.: Describing textures in the wild. In: Proceedings of the IEEE Conference on Computer Vision and Pattern Recognition, pp. 3606–3613 (2014)

18. Akcay, S., Atapour-Abarghouei, A., Breckon, T.P.: GANomaly: semi-supervised anomaly detection via adversarial training. In: Jawahar, C.V., Li, H., Mori, G., Schindler, K. (eds.) ACCV 2018. LNCS, vol. 11363, pp. 622–637. Springer, Cham (2019). https://doi.org/10. 1007/978-3-030-20893-6_39
19. Bergmann, P., Fauser, M., Sattlegger, D., Steger C.: Uninformed students: student-teacher anomaly detection with discriminative latent embeddings. In: Proceedings of the IEEE/CVF Conference on Computer Vision and Pattern Recognition, pp. 4183–4192 (2020)

PCB Defect Detection Method Based on Improved RetinaNet

Yusheng Xu[1], Xinrong Cao[2], Rong Hu[1(✉)], Pantea Keikhosrokiani[3],
and Zuoyong Li[2(✉)]

[1] College of Computer Science and Mathematics, Fujian University of Technology,
Fuzhou 350118, China
hurong@fjut.edu.cn

[2] Fujian Provincial Key Laboratory of Information Processing and Intelligent Control, College
of Computer and Control Engineering, Minjiang University, Fuzhou 350121, China
fzulzytdq@126.com

[3] School of Computer Sciences, Universiti Sains Malaysia, 11800 Penang, Malaysia

Abstract. In the electronic industry product quality control, PCB defect detection is a crucial part, which has the characteristics of small defect size and high similarity. The existing defect detection methods are still not good enough for detecting small target defects; therefore, the algorithm in this paper proposes an improved algorithm for PCB defect detection based on the RetinaNet model. The ResNet-D residual structure and efficient channel focus module are introduced in the model backbone network to enhance its feature extraction capability and achieve the purpose of improving the detection accuracy. At the same time, the method replaces the original multi-step learning decay strategy with a cosine annealing scheduling learning strategy, which optimizes the training process of the model. Finally, the performance of the method is verified on the publicly available PCB defect dataset from the Open Laboratory of Intelligent Robotics, Peking University. The experimental results show that the algorithm improves the mAP value by 3.2% compared with the original algorithm, while the fastest detection speed reaches 36.9 FPS, which can effectively improve the defect detection performance of PCB.

Keywords: Defect detection · RetinaNet · Channel attention

1 Introduction

Into the 21st century, With the rapid development of the electronics industry and electronic products industry, the application of PCB is becoming more and more widespread. But in the actual production process, the surface of the circuit board will inevitably produce many defects, which will affect the quality of electronic products, the use of serious problems with the circuit board products, may cause harm to users. In the PCB industry, defect detection is an important part of product quality control, the purpose is to detect defective PCBs in a timely manner, to avoid additional economic losses. However, in the traditional method [1], mainly by manual visual inspection, not only requires a lot of manpower, and limited by the experience of workers and physiological and other factors, easy to cause problems such as false detection, and even cause accidents, it is necessary to develop a computer vision-based PCB board defects automatic detection method.

With the development of Convolutional Neural Network (CNN) and computational power, deep learning-based defect detection methods have received increasing attention from researchers. Unlike traditional methods, deep learning methods mainly use CNNs for feature extraction. A series of convolution, activation function, pooling and other operations are used to generate the hierarchical feature maps of the input image. CNN-based deep learning models have powerful feature learning capability and have been widely used in various subfields of defect detection, such as PCB board defect detection, lithium battery defect detection, etc. As a branch of deep learning, defect detection algorithms can be divided into two main categories:

Two-stage approach: similar to Faster -RCNN [2] and RFCN [3], region proposal network (RPN) detection algorithms are required, which can achieve high accuracy but are slower. For example, Hu et al. constructed an optimized network based on the Faster RCNN with a feature pyramid network as the backbone network and added the residual module of ShuffleNetV2 to the region generation network, which can generate more accurate anchor points and truly achieve end-to-end detection, but further improvement in detection time is needed [4]. Yiting Li et al. combined sparse filtering with convolutional neural networks to propose a SF-VGG feature extraction network, which improves the accuracy of defect location detection and identification of the Faster RCNN algorithm [5].

One-stage methods: refers to algorithms like YOLO [6], SSD [7], RetinaNet [8], etc., which do not need to extract candidate target regions and perform target target classification and position extraction directly from the feature map, which are fast but usually less accurate than two-stage methods. Liu et al. first used the SSD algorithm in defect detection, and in the feature pyramid Liu et al. first used the SSD algorithm in defect detection and added a new level 1 feature as conv3_3, which has improved the detection effect of small targets [9]. Liu Yajiao et al. proposed a steel surface defect detection algorithm Steel-YOLOv3 based on deformable convolution and multiscale -dense pyramid, which solves the problem of low detection efficiency and poor detection accuracy due to the diverse morphology of steel surface defects and numerous micro-defects [10].

The above methods can solve some problems in the field of defect detection, but the defect size in PCB images is small, and after multiple convolution and pooling operations, the information loss of defect targets is more serious, which affects the accuracy of defect detection.

Based on the above problems, this paper proposes an improved RetinaNet method for PCB defect detection, which mainly consists of two parts: to improve the feature extraction capability of the model, the final backbone network is built on the basis of ResNet50 by adding the ResNet50-D [11] residual structure and ECA attention module to improve the backbone structure; meanwhile, cosine annealing is used to learning rate to optimize the model training process. These methods can improve the performance of PCB defect detection without introducing too much additional computational overhead in the inference process. The mAP and F1 scores of this method exceed 92% and 85%, respectively, on the publicly available PCB defect dataset from the Open Laboratory of Intelligent Robotics at Peking University.

The main contributions of this work are as follows. (1) the ResNet-D residual block is used as the basic structure of the network, and the ECA attention module is introduced into the residual block in order to improve the focus on small target defects, which is used to construct the backbone of the method in this paper; (2) the impact of cosine annealing scheduling strategy in the field of PCB defect detection is verified and successfully applied to the method in this paper.

2 Related Work

The algorithms for target detection can be divided into two main categories: one-stage and two-stage, usually the one-stage detection is faster than the two-stage algorithm, and the detection accuracy is inferior to the two-stage algorithm. The reason why the accuracy of one-stage is inferior to that of two-stage detectors is that the categories of samples are unbalanced, the number of negative samples is too large, accounting for most of the total loss, and most of them are easy to classify, which makes the optimization direction of the model unsatisfactory. Therefore, to solve the problem of category imbalance, researchers proposed a new loss function, Focal loss, which can make the model focus more on the hard-to-classify samples during training by reducing the weight of the easy-to-classify samples, and RetinaNet is the algorithm RetinaNet proposed to verify the effectiveness of Focal loss. The model's structure is the same as other single-stage detectors, using ResNet50 or ResNet101 as the backbone for feature extraction, the classical FPN network as the neck structure, and finally the feature map output from FPN is passed into the head structure to predict the defect type and regress the bounding box information. It is proved that RetinaNet, as a one-stage detector, can not only achieve the speed of one-stage but also have the accuracy of two-stages.

2.1 Attentional Mechanism

Attention mechanisms have been proven to be effective in image classification and target detection tasks in computer vision, and inserting attention modules into convolutional neural networks (CNNs) can effectively enhance CNN feature extraction.SE-Net [12] was the first successful application of channel attention mechanisms in neural networks. Since then, attention mechanisms began to develop rapidly and are broadly divided into two research directions: (1) feature enhancement aggregation; (2) the combination of channel and spatial attention; For example, CBAM [13] further advanced this idea by introducing spatial information coding with large kernel convolution. Later proposed models, such as GENet [14], GALA [15], AA [16], and TA [17], extend this idea by employing different spatial attention mechanisms or designing advanced attention blocks. In addition, non-local (Non-local)/self attention networks (self attention) have become very popular in recent years due to their ability to construct spatial or channel attention, typical examples include NLNet [18], GCNet [19], SCNet [20], and CcNet [21], all of which use non-local mechanisms to capture different types of spatial information. However, due to the computationally intensive nature of the self-attentive module, it is often used in large models and is not applicable to lightweight networks. Therefore, later researchers have proposed some lightweight attention models, such as ECA-Net and Coordinate Attention [22], which have achieved better performance improvement with reduced model complexity.

3 Method

Inspired by the mechanism, we propose a modified version of the RessNet50 feature extraction network. Firstly, an average pooling such operation is added to the branches of the residual block of the network to avoid the neglect of the input feature map information by the convolution on the branch structure. Afterwards, the ECA attention module is introduced into the residual block to enhance the feature learning ability for specific targets. Specifically, the new feature extraction network can better ensure that the input feature information is not ignored, while focusing more on learning feature information of defective targets. Finally, the extracted feature maps are passed into the feature pyramid structure for feature information fusion to classify and localise the defective targets, Fig. 1 illustrates the architecture of the proposed method.

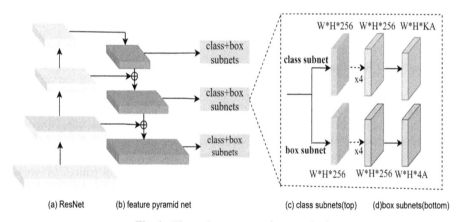

Fig. 1. The main structure of our method

3.1 Improved Backbone

RetinaNet uses ResNet50 as the backbone network. To further enhance its feature extraction capability, this paper upgrades the original ResNet residual structure to ResNet-D residual structure to ensure that the feature map information is not ignored; secondly, the channel attention mechanism (ECA) is introduced to enhance the extraction of target feature information, and the final structure adjustment is shown in Fig. 2.

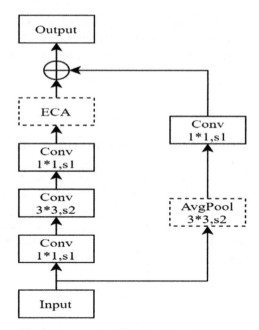

Fig. 2. Improved residual structure of ResNet50

3.2 ResNet-D Residual Structure

The residual structure of ResNet greatly alleviates the problem of gradient explosion in neural networks, which enables deep neural networks to be constructed and greatly enhances the feature extraction capability of convolutional neural networks. However, the residual structure of the initial ResNet suffers from the problem of ignoring the feature map information. As shown in Fig. 3a, path A uses a convolution of 1×1 with stride 2 to downsample the input feature map, however, this causes path A to ignore three-quarters of the information of the input feature map, and similarly the convolution of 1×1 in the downsampled block in path B also ignores 3/4 of the information of the input feature map, thus affecting the feature extraction ability of the backbone network.

Therefore, this paper adopts an adjusted residual structure ResNet-D to construct the backbone network, and ResNet-D firstly displace the stride of the first two convolutions in path A, as shown in Fig. 3b, so that the input feature map information is not ignored. Next, an average pooling layer of size 2×2 with stride 2 is added before the 1×1 convolution in path B, and the 1×1 convolution stride is changed to 1, again so that the feature map information in path B is not ignored. Figure 3(b) shows the final restructuring.

3.3 Channel Attention-ECA Module

PCB image defects are mostly small targets, and the defect size accounts for a small proportion of the overall image, after the ResNet50 network layer by layer convolution

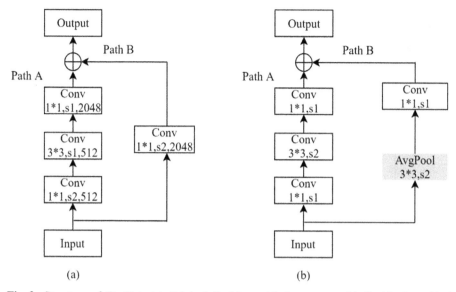

Fig. 3. Structure of ResNet; (a) Original ResNet residual structure; (b) ResNet-D residual structure

operation, the feature map contains less and less target information, thus affecting the effect of defect detection.

The ECA module is an extremely lightweight channel attention module, which is improved from the SE module. As shown in Fig. 4, The ECA module removes the fully connected layer from the original SE module, after which the features are learned directly by one-dimensional convolution of shared weights after global average pooling, which avoids the side effects of the dimensionality reduction operation in the SE module on the prediction of the channel attention mechanism. The weight parameter is multiplied by the corresponding feature channel to update the feature map. The 1D convolution involves the hyperparameter k, which is the size of the convolution kernel and represents the coverage of the local cross-channel interaction. For different number of channels C, the size of the 1D convolutional kernel should be varied as follows:

$$K = \varphi(c) = \left| \frac{\log_2 c}{\gamma} + \frac{b}{y} \right| \tag{1}$$

where, $|t|$ is taken as the odd number closest to t; C is the number of channels being specified; α and γ are specified as 1 and 2, respectively.

The ECA module is a plug-and-play module that can be simply fused into common convolutional neural networks, so this paper finally decided to add the ECA module to each residual block of ResNet50-D to improve its feature extraction capability, while the ECA module brings almost no additional number of parameters.

3.4 Cosine Annealing Scheduling Method

The original RetinaNet algorithm uses a multi-step decay learning rate strategy (i.e., decreasing the learning rate according to a set time interval), and the method in this

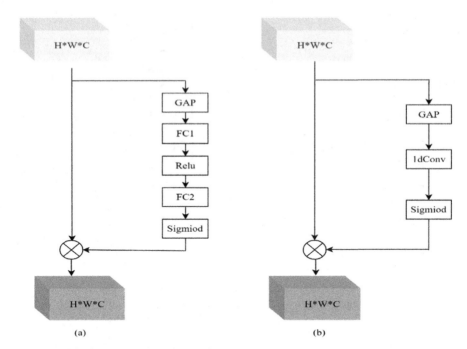

Fig. 4. Channel Attention Mechanism; (a) SE Module; (b) ECA Module

paper uses a cosine annealing scheduling learning strategy to optimize the learning rate decay process to help train the model better. The cosine annealing scheduler adjusts the learning rate in the intermediate iteration or δ_t phase, which is calculated as:

$$\delta_t = \delta_{min} + \frac{(\delta_{max} - \delta_{min})(1 + \cos(\frac{T_{cur}}{T_{max}}\pi))}{2} \quad (2)$$

where, δ_{min} is the valley of the cosine function, δ_{min} is set to 0 in the experiment. β_{max} is the peak of the cosine function (Initial learning rate). δ_{max} is set to 10^{-4}. T_{max} is the half of the period of the cosine function, T_{max} is set to 100 epochs. T_{cur} is the number of epochs or iterations recorded from the last time.

As shown in Fig. 5, the cosine annealing scheduler resets the learning rate to the maximum of each cycle with the cosine function as the period. The initial learning rate is the maximum learning rate, and the period is $2 \times$ T_max, which decreases and then increases in one cycle. Total epochs is 100 epochs.

4   Experimental Results

4.1   Data and Parameter Settings

The dataset used in this paper is from the publicly available PCB defect dataset from the Open Laboratory of Intelligent Robotics, Peking University [23], which was obtained by photographing PCB boards. It contains 693 images with the image size of 3034

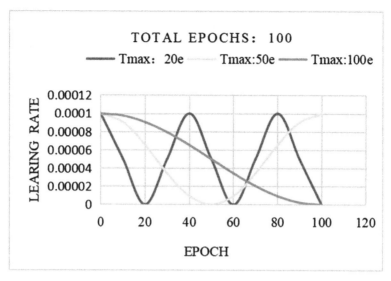

Fig. 5. Cosine annealing scheduling method at different T_{max}

× 1586, and there are 6 types of defects: mouse bite, open circuit, short circuit, burr, and residual copper, each of which covers a variety of different shapes, orientations, and scales. However, due to the large image size and small amount of data in this dataset, it is not suitable for direct training. In order to balance the distribution of defect types and proportions in the training data and test data, data enhancement operations such as cropping and data expansion are required. After data enhancement, the new dataset has 4800 images with the image size of 600 × 600, and 800 images for each defect category. The final dataset was randomly divided in the ratio of 9:1 between the training validation set and the test set, with 4320 images in the training validation set and 480 images in the test set. On the PCB dataset, 100 epochs were trained with a batch size of 8; the optimizer was Adam, and the cosine annealing learning rate method was used with an initial learning rate size of 0.0001.Combining the basic models of existing object detection-based PCB board defect detection methods, Faster RCNN (2015, NIPS), SSD (2016, ECCV), YOLOV3 (2018, CVPR) and many other commonly used object detection models as a comparison method to demonstrate the advantages of the method in this paper.

4.2 Comparative Experiments and Analysis of Results

In this paper, six commonly used metrics are used to evaluate the performance of the algorithm in this paper, namely Precision, Recall, F1 score, mAP, Param. And FPS. Where P, R, F1 score, and mAP are calculated as shown in Eqs. (3)–(9).

$$P = \sum_{k=1}^{c} P_k \tag{3}$$

$$R = \sum_{k=1}^{c} R_k \tag{4}$$

$$mAP = \sum_{k=1}^{c} AP_k \tag{5}$$

$$F1 - Score = \frac{2 \times P \times R}{P + R} \tag{6}$$

where,

$$P_k = \frac{TP_k}{TP_k + FP_k} \tag{7}$$

$$P_k = \frac{TP_k}{TP_k + FN_k} \tag{8}$$

$$AP_k \int_0^1 P_k(R_k)dR_k \tag{9}$$

C is the number of defect classes on the PCB dataset. TP_k is the number of true defect classes K, which are correctly detected as defect classes. FN_k is the number of true defect classes K, which are incorrectly detected as non-defective or other classes of defects. And FP_k refers to the number of non-defective class K that are incorrectly detected as defective class K.

The mAP is the area enclosed by the P-R curve and the R-axis. The F1-Score metric is a combined assessment, calculated from the R and P metrics. In addition, metrics such as Param. And detection time (FPS) are used to show quantitatively the spatial and temporal complexity of the model.

On PCB dataset, after 100 epoch iterations, the loss function of this paper's method decreases continuously in the training phase until convergence completes the training of the model parameters. In order to demonstrate the superiority of this paper's method in PCB board defect detection, the same dataset was first used on the base RetinaNet model, then on the commonly used detection models such as Faster RCNN, SSD and YOLOV3, and finally tested on the proposed method in this paper. From Table 1, we can see that the method in this paper has the optimal effect on the defect detection of PCB boards, with the highest mAP value of 92.8%, F1 score of 85.2%, and detection speed of 36.9 FPS, which can meet the requirement of real-time. In comparison with other commonly used methods, the target detection benchmark metric mAP is 41.5%, 5.8%, 46.1% and 13.6% better than Faster- RCNN, SSD and YOLOv3, respectively. In terms of the composite metric F1 score, this method outperforms Faster RCNN, SSD, and YOLOV3 by 36.2%, 66.6%, and 9.7%, respectively. In terms of detection speed, compared with the original RetinaNet, this method only increases a small amount of time cost. The detection time reaches 36.9 frames per second (FPS), which can meet the demand of real-time detection. The above experimental results show that the method achieves a balance between detection time and localization accuracy, and is able to detect various defects on PCB images efficiently and quickly (Fig. 6).

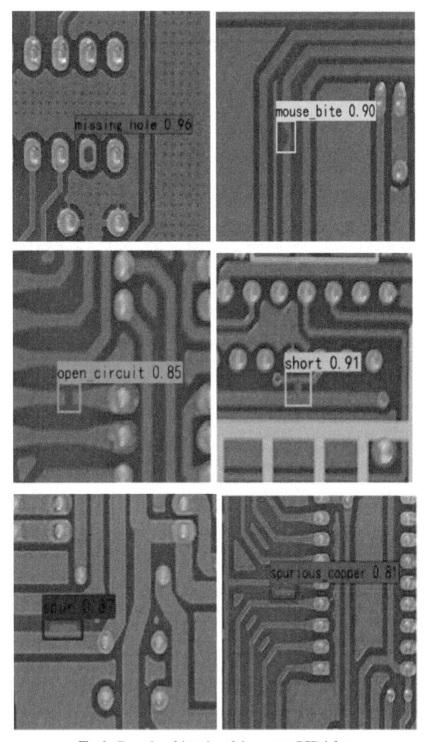

Fig. 6. Examples of detection of six common PCB defects

Table 1. Performance of different methods on PCB dataset

Model	mAP (%)	F1-Score (%)	Parm	Detection time (FPS)
Faster RCNN	51.3	49.0	41.1M	27.9
SSD	86.9	19.6	24.2M	174.3
YOLOV3	79.3	75.4	63.0M	47.6
RetinaNet	89.6	83.6	37.9M	40.6
Ours	92.8	85.2	37.9M	36.9

5 Conclusion

In this paper, a deep neural network model based on RetinaNet is proposed and applied to PCB defect detection. The ResNet-D residual structure and ECA attention module are introduced in the model backbone network, while the cosine annealing scheduling learning strategy is used to replace the learning rate scheduling strategy of the original method, both of which can effectively improve the detection accuracy of small target defects with almost no increase in the number of parameters. The experimental results show that the algorithm improves the average accuracy mAP of defect detection from 89.6% to 92.8% of the original algorithm, and the fastest detection speed reaches 36.9 fps, which can meet the real-time requirements of defect detection and can be well applied to practical scenarios.

Acknowledgments. This work was supported in part by National Natural Science Foundation of China (61972187), Natural Science Foundation of Fujian Province (2021J011016, 2020J02024, 2020Y4018, and 2019J01756), Fujian Provincial Leading Project (2019H0025), Government Guiding Regional Science and Technology Development (2019L3009), Open Fund Project of Fujian Provincial Key Laboratory of Information Processing and Intelligent Control (Minjiang University) (MJUKF-IPIC202106), Guangdong Provincial Key Laboratory of Cyber-Physical Systems (2020B1212060069), and National&Local Joint Engineering Research Center of Intelligent Manufacturing Cyber-Physical Systems.

References

1. Zhu, X.Y., Xiong, J., Wang, L.S., et al.: Research on YOLOv4 based on PCB bare board defect detection method. Ind. Control Comput. **34**(09), 39–40+45 (2021)
2. Ren, S., He, K., Girshick, R., et al.: Faster R-CNN: towards real-time object detection with region proposal networks. In: Advances in Neural Information Processing Systems, vol. 28 (2015)
3. Dai, J.F., Li, Y., He, K.M., et al.: R-FCN: object detection via region-based fully convolutional networks. In: Advances in Neural Information Processing Systems, vol. 29, pp. 379–387. MIT Press, Cambridge (2016)
4. Hu, B., Wang, J.: Detection of PCB surface defects with improved faster-RCNN and feature pyramid network. IEEE Access **8**, 108335–108345 (2020)

5. Li, Y.T., Xie, Q.S., Huang, H.S., et al.: Fast area calibration based convolutional neural network for surface defect detection. Comput. Integr. Manuf. Syst. **25**(8), 1897–1907 (2019)
6. Redmon, J., Divvala, S., Girshick, R., et al.: You only look once: unified, real-time object detection. In: IEEE Conference on Computer Vision and Pattern Recognition, pp.779–788 (2016)
7. Liu, W., et al.: SSD: single shot multibox detector. In: Leibe, B., Matas, J., Sebe, N., Welling, M. (eds.) ECCV 2016. LNCS, vol. 9905, pp. 21–37. Springer, Cham (2016). https://doi.org/10.1007/978-3-319-46448-0_2
8. Lin, T.Y., Goyal, P., Girshick, R., et al.: Focal loss for dense object detection. In: IEEE International Conference on Computer Vision, pp. 2980–2988 (2017)
9. Liu, Z., Liu, S., Li, C., et al.: Fabric defects detection based on SSD. In: 2nd International Conference on Graphics and Signal Processing, pp. 74–78 (2018)
10. Liu, Y.J., Yu, H.T., Wang, J., et al.: Deep learning-based algorithm for detecting polymorphic micro defects on steel surface. Comput. Appl. **42**(8), 2601 (2021)
11. He, T., Zhang, Z., Zhang, H., et al.: Bag of tricks for image classification with convolutional neural networks. In: IEEE/CVF Conference on Computer Vision and Pattern Recognition, pp. 558–567 (2019)
12. Hu, J., Shen, L., Sun, G.: Squeeze-and-excitation networks. In: IEEE Conference on Computer Vision and Pattern Recognition, pp. 7132–7141 (2018)
13. Woo, S., Park, J., Lee, J.-Y., Kweon, I.S.: CBAM: convolutional block attention module. In: Ferrari, V., Hebert, M., Sminchisescu, C., Weiss, Y. (eds.) ECCV 2018. LNCS, vol. 11211, pp. 3–19. Springer, Cham (2018). https://doi.org/10.1007/978-3-030-01234-2_1
14. Hu, J., Shen, L., Albanie, S., et al.: Gather-excite: exploiting feature context in convolutional neural networks. In: Advances in Neural Information Processing Systems, vol. 31 (2018)
15. Linsley, D., Shiebler, D., Eberhardt, S., et al.: Learning what and where to attend. arXiv preprint arXiv, 1805-08819 (2018)
16. Bello, I., Zoph, B., Vaswani, A., et al.: Attention augmented convolutional networks. In: IEEE/CVF International Conference on Computer Vision, pp. 3286–3295 (2019)
17. Misra, D., Nalamada, T., Arasanipalai, A.U., et al.: Rotate to attend: convolutional triplet attention module. In: IEEE/CVF Winter Conference on Applications of Computer Vision, pp. 3139–3148 (2021)
18. Wang, X., Girshick, R., Gupta, A., et al.: Non-local neural net-works. In: IEEE Conference on Computer Vision and Pattern Recognition, pp. 7794–7803 (2018)
19. Cao, Y., Xu, J., Lin, S., et al.: GCNet: non-local networks meet squeeze-excitation networks and beyond. In: IEEE/CVF International Conference on Computer Vision Workshops (2019)
20. Liu, J.J., Hou, Q., Cheng, M.M., et al.: Improving convolutional net-works with self-calibrated convolutions. In: IEEE/CVF Conference on Computer Vision and Pattern Recognition, pp. 10096–10105 (2020)
21. Huang, Z., Wang, X., Huang, L., et al.: CCNet: criss-cross attention for semantic segmentation. In: IEEE/CVF International Conference on Computer Vision, pp. 603–612 (2019)
22. Hou, Q., Zhou, D., Feng, J.: Coordinate attention for efficient mobile network design. In: IEEE/CVF Conference on Computer Vision and Pattern Recognition, pp. 13713–13722 (2021)
23. Ding, R., Dai, L., Li, G., et al.: TDD-Net: a tiny defect detection network for printed circuit boards. CAAI Trans. Intell. Technol. **4**(2), 110–116 (2019)

A Method of Protecting Sensitive Information in Intangible Cultural Heritage Communication Network Based on Machine Learning

Xiaoyu Zhang[✉] and Ye Jin

Wuxi Vocational Institute of Commerce, Wuxi 214153, China
zxy52640@163.com

Abstract. In order to accurately identify the sensitive information in the intangible cultural heritage communication network and realize the reasonable protection of intangible cultural heritage data, a method for protecting the sensitive information in the intangible cultural heritage communication network based on machine learning is proposed. With the support of machine learning algorithm, the distance measurement results are solved, and then the specific values of compressed characteristic indexes are calculated by establishing a random measurement matrix to complete the tracking and processing of the target parameters of intangible cultural heritage. On this basis, according to the encryption processing results of sensitive information, the implementation standard of OSBE protocol is established, and then with the help of the formed sensitive information processing process, the effective protection of sensitive information of intangible cultural heritage communication network is realized. The results of comparative experiments show that under the effect of machine learning algorithm, the recognition accuracy of the network host for the sensitive information of intangible cultural heritage has significantly improved, and it really has strong practical value in the reasonable protection of intangible cultural heritage data parameters.

Keywords: Machine learning · Intangible cultural heritage · Communication network · Sensitive information · Target tracking

1 Introduction

Machine learning is an algorithm that continuously learns from past experience to continuously optimize its own performance. Specifically, machine learning can automatically extract some features or analyze a group of rules from the input data according to the specific objectives, use these features and rules to predict and analyze the unknown data, and optimize the extracted features and rules according to the new results.

Machine learning theory is the core of artificial intelligence and the fundamental way to make computers intelligent. Machine learning consists of four elements: data, model, criterion and algorithm [1].

(1) Data is divided into training data and test data, which represents intrusion data or simulated intrusion data in intrusion detection.

© The Author(s), under exclusive license to Springer Nature Switzerland AG 2023
Y. Xu et al. (Eds.): ML4CS 2022, LNCS 13656, pp. 214–227, 2023.
https://doi.org/10.1007/978-3-031-20099-1_18

(2) The model determines the specific form of machine learning. All possible model sets constitute a hypothesis space. Before the training task is completed, the hypothesis space contains all possible conditional probability distributions or decision functions.

(3) The criterion is to select the evaluation index of the optimal model from the hypothesis space. The error between the prediction result and the actual situation of the model is expressed by the cost function. The smaller the value of the loss function is, the better the model is.

(4) The algorithm is a method to select the optimal model from the hypothesis space with criteria as the objective.

Machine learning is a common research hotspot in the field of artificial intelligence and pattern recognition. Its theories and methods have been widely used to solve complex problems in engineering applications and scientific fields. Data analysis and mining technology is the combination of machine learning algorithm and data access technology. It uses statistical analysis, knowledge discovery and other means provided by machine learning to analyze massive data, and uses data access mechanism to achieve efficient data reading and writing [2]. Machine learning is not only applied in knowledge-based systems, but also widely used in many fields, such as natural language understanding, non monotonic reasoning, machine vision, pattern recognition and so on. Whether a system has the ability to learn has become a sign of whether it has "intelligence". The research of machine learning is mainly divided into two types: the first is the research of traditional machine learning, which mainly studies the learning mechanism and pays attention to exploring the learning mechanism of simulated human; The second category is the research on machine learning in the big data environment, which mainly focuses on how to effectively use information and focus on obtaining hidden, effective and understandable knowledge from huge amounts of data.

Intangible cultural heritage refers to various forms of traditional cultural expressions handed down from generation to generation by people of all ethnic groups and regarded as an integral part of their cultural heritage, as well as physical objects and places related to traditional cultural expressions. Intangible cultural heritage is an important symbol of the historical and cultural achievements of a country and nation, and an important part of excellent traditional culture. "Intangible cultural heritage" is opposite to "material cultural heritage" and is collectively referred to as "cultural heritage". "Intangible cultural heritage" has the function of etiquette and music to humanize people. Most of it is the expression of ancestors' awe and attitude towards happiness, life and death, marriage, ancetors, nature and heaven and earth in their work and life. It is a living culture that meets people's natural, social and spiritual needs. Its practicality is based on people-oriented [3, 4]. However, in the actual protection, the cultural quality of the heritage is continuously digested, and the utilitarian purpose is becoming more and more prominent. Even the preservation, declaration and protection of "intangible cultural heritage" have a strong interest drive. Not only personal needs, but also the boost of the local government, make the application for the world heritage a way of local advertising, tourism publicity and value-added. "Intangible cultural heritage" is the cultural wealth that our ancestors retained to modern times through the use of daily life. In the long river of history, natural generation and continuous development and change. Although the intangible cultural heritage handed down from generation to generation has been inno- vated with the changes of the ethnic group's environment, the relationship with nature and historical conditions, the cultural identity and historical sense of the heritage remain unchanged from beginning to end. In modern "intangible cultural heritage", how to pre- serve the natural state and authenticity of the relics and reduce the artificial elements, how to continue to maintain the daily nature and reduce the festival nature, how to enhance the practicality and reduce the performance nature, and how to reflect the folk nature and reduce the official nature are the ways to restore the role of the predecessors' Heritage on future generations. If this role is lost, the heritage will become a burden. Therefore, a sensitive information protection method based on machine learning for intangible cul- tural heritage communication network is proposed. With the support of machine learning algorithm, the target parameters of intangible cultural heritage can be tracked and pro- cessed according to the processing flow of distance measurement solution, the setting of random measurement matrix and the calculation of compression characteristics. The extracted low dimensional features can be used to restore high-dimensional features, and the target can be separated from the background in target classification. Establish OSBE agreement documents to encrypt sensitive information of intangible cultural heritage communication network.

2 Intangible Cultural Heritage Target Tracking Based on Machine Learning

With the support of machine learning algorithm, the target parameters of intangible cul- tural heritage can be tracked and processed according to the processing flow of distance measurement solution, random measurement matrix setting and compression feature calculation.

2.1 Distance Value Measurement

In order to classify patterns, that is, to enable the tracker to track the correct target, we must first define the similarity measure of patterns, that is, to find the sample most similar to the real target. The sample selection method is measured by the similarity between the sample and the target [5]. Common similarity measures include distance measure, similarity measure, matching measure and tangent distance. Here, the most commonly used distance measure is used to measure the similarity of samples. However, since the negotiating party submits all certificates to the other party at one time, it is likely to lead to the exposure of irrelevant certificates. It can be seen that in the authentication method of identity based encryption system, the user does not need to establish a key channel to obtain the public key and verify the legitimacy of the public key, because the user's identity is his public key, and the public key is not random and easy to obtain. In the process of signature verification, the legitimacy of the public key and the relationship between the user's identity and the public key are verified at the same time.

In the intangible cultural heritage communication network, the features of sensitive information targets and samples are both feature vectors, and each feature vector can be considered to correspond to a point in the feature space. Distance measurement is based on the distance between the endpoints of two vectors. Therefore, distance measurement is a function of the difference between the corresponding components of two vectors [6]. There are many methods to measure the distance between two vectors. Generally speaking, the definition of two-point distance should meet the following axioms, Let the distance between vectors x and y be $d(x, y)$, then $d(x, y)$ shall meet the following conditions:

(1) $d(x, y) \geq 0$, if and only if $x = y$, the equal sign holds, i.e. $d(x, y) = 0 \Rightarrow x = y$.
(2) $d(x, y) = d(y, x)$.
(3) $d(x, y) \leq d(x, z) + d(z, y)$.

It should be pointed out that some distance measures defined in pattern recognition do not satisfy condition (3) and can only be called generalized distance. Here we briefly introduce the definitions of the seven commonly used distance measures. First, let's set the vectors $x = (x_1, x_2, \cdots, x_n)^T$ and $y = (y_1, y_2, \cdots, y_n)^T$. the definitions of several distance measures are:

(1) Euclidean distance of intangible cultural heritage sensitive information:

$$d(x, y) = \left[\sum_{i=1}^{n} (x_i - y_i)^2 \right]^{\frac{1}{2}} \tag{1}$$

where, i represents a randomly selected marking coefficient of intangible cultural heritage sensitive information;
(2) Absolute value distance of intangible cultural heritage sensitive information:

$$d(x, y) = \sum_{i=1}^{n} (x_i - y_i) \tag{2}$$

(3) Chebyshev distance of intangible cultural heritage sensitive information:

$$d(x, y) = \max_{i=1} (x_i - y_i) \tag{3}$$

(4) Mins distance of intangible cultural heritage sensitive information:

$$d(x, y) = \left[\sum_{i=1}^{n} (x_i - y_i)^m \right]^{\frac{1}{m}} \tag{4}$$

where, m represents the value parameter of Mings coefficient based on machine learning theory;
(5) Mahalanobis distance of intangible cultural heritage sensitive information:

$$d^2(x, y) = (x - y)^T V^{-1} (x - y) \tag{5}$$

where, T represents the marking time of intangible cultural heritage sensitive information, and V represents the definition item of distance index;

(6) Camberra distance of intangible cultural heritage sensitive information:

$$\begin{cases} d(x, y) = \sum_{i=1}^{m} \frac{|x_i - y_i|}{x_i + y_i}, \\ x_i, y_i \geq 0 \\ x_i + y_i \neq 0 \end{cases} \tag{6}$$

(7) Normalized distance of intangible cultural heritage sensitive information:

$$d(x, y) = \frac{||x - y||}{||x|| + ||y||} \tag{7}$$

Due to the different selection of the dimension of intangible cultural heritage sensitive information, the judgment basis of a feature may change, which may change the contribution of the feature to the judgment results, and even lead to wrong classification results. This is because changing the dimension of a component of the feature vector, the value of the corresponding component of the two vectors to be compared will also change [7]. If the component value becomes larger, Then its corresponding features will play a greater role in distance measurement, that is, the weight of classification based on its judgment will become larger, otherwise it will decrease, so it can not correctly reflect the facts.

Sensitive information protection method can be regarded as a sub problem of trust management. Its basic idea is that the establishment of trust is a gradual process, and the information exchange between the two sides in this process is cautious. The research on this problem is conducive to the security protection of trust certificates in the process of transmission and use in the trust management system, so as to prevent the leakage of sensitive information. During the establishment of trust relationship between strangers, the protection of sensitive trust certificates and access control policies poses an important challenge to the research of automatic trust negotiation.

2.2 Random Measurement Matrix

In the research of random measurement matrix, a problem that is often ignored is how to select positive and negative samples when updating the classifier to determine the target model. The most commonly used method is to take the target in the current frame as a positive sample, while all other samples are taken as negative samples. One drawback of this method is that there is only one positive sample [8]. If the position of the target is inaccurate in the tracking process, the accumulation of tracking errors will become larger and larger as the target template is updated in the tracking process, resulting in tracking failure.Under the influence of machine learning algorithm, the typical measurement matrix of sensitive information parameters in intangible cultural heritage communication network is a random Gaussian matrix $R \in \mathbb{R}^{c \times m}$ satisfying the restricted isometry property condition, where the vector $r_{ij} \sim N(0, 1)$ of R. When the value of m is very large, if the vector R is a dense matrix, the calculation amount of projection vector calculated according to formula $v = mR$ will be very large, which will occupy a lot of computer memory and computing resources in the calculation process.

Here, a very sparse random measurement matrix is used, and the definition is shown in formula (8):

$$r_{ij} = \sqrt{R} \begin{cases} 1, \text{ with probability, } \frac{1}{2R} \\ 0, \text{ with probability, } 1 - \frac{1}{R} \\ -1, \text{ with probability, } \frac{1}{2R} \end{cases} \quad (8)$$

When $R = 2$ or $R = 3$, the matrix r_{ij} satisfies the machine learning algorithm lemma, and when $R = 3$, r_{ij} is a very sparse matrix, and the amount of computation can be reduced by two thirds. And this kind of matrix is easy to generate in the process of calculation. When $R = 0$, the matrix is asymptotically normal.

For the sensitive information parameters in the intangible cultural heritage communication network, the basic method of machine learning algorithm is that in the training process, the marking of samples is not to mark a single sample, but to treat multiple samples of the same category as a sample set and mark multiple entire sample sets [9]. If a sample set is marked as a positive sample set, it means that at least one sample in the sample set is a positive sample, otherwise, At least one of the samples is negative. Generally, in the tracking process, after the position of the positive sample is determined, the samples in a certain neighborhood around the sample are considered as positive samples, that is, there must be certain positive and negative samples in the positive and negative sample set. Therefore, the problem of marking the target category in the sample set is transferred from manual marking to algorithm marking, that is, the algorithm is used to calculate which sample in the sample set is the best positive sample, that is, which sample is the most likely target sample to be tracked.

In the process of searching for intangible cultural heritage to spread network sensitive information, it is generally necessary to express and describe the target in a certain form, and the commonly used representation is feature representation. Feature is the key factor to determine the target similarity and tracking effect. A good feature can make the target tracking problem get twice the result with half the effort. The complexity of the feature affects the complexity of the whole algorithm to a certain extent. The more complex the feature is, the higher the complexity of the algorithm is. When the purpose of classification is decided, how to find the appropriate features becomes one of the core issues of target tracking.

2.3 Compression Characteristics

The compressed feature of sensitive information in intangible cultural heritage communication network is a feature that is easy to calculate and fast to calculate. It is widely used in target detection of machine learning algorithms. Here, the compressed feature is used to represent the data information samples. Usually, when the compressed feature is used as the sensitive information discrimination feature, the dimension of the processing feature of each original data sample will be very high, which undoubtedly makes the amount of calculation very large. According to the theory of machine learning algorithm, the extracted low dimensional features contain almost all the features of the sample [10]. Therefore, the extracted low dimensional features can be used to recover the high dimensional features, and the target can be separated from the background in the target classification.

Here, the tracking window is set to have been determined in the first frame of the video. Positive samples are selected from the periphery of the target in the current frame, and negative samples are selected from the position far from the target to update the classifier. The selection position of the compressed feature in the new frame is the same as that in the initialization frame, so that the feature selection of the target in each frame is consistent and will not affect the calculation of the target.

Machine learning algorithm is a kind of learning algorithm without label information, which lacks sufficient prior knowledge. Since there is no label information, it is necessary to find and summarize the rules and structures from the data set. Clustering is a typical application of unsupervised learning. It gathers similar samples through the relationship between variables in data, without knowing what each category is.

When solving the compression characteristics of sensitive information on the intangible cultural heritage communication network, the principles shown in Table 1 must be followed.

Table 1. Compression feature selection of intangible cultural heritage sensitive information

Data subset	Category	Total number of features	Number of samples	Total samples
KDD1	Training set	41	1000	1311
			100	
			100	
			11	
			100	
	Test set	41	500	750
			75	
			75	
			50	
			50	

The stage of sensitive information classification of intangible cultural heritage communication network is the stage of specific machine learning algorithm work, and it is also the focus of this paper. This paper will study intrusion detection technology based on supervised learning, unsupervised learning, in-depth learning and integrated learning in the following paper. We take the training set data in the data extraction stage as the training data of the machine learning algorithm, generate the classification results after the algorithm runs, and then use the test data set to predict the new intrusion types, analyze the final results, and enter the performance test stage.

In the performance test stage, various performance indicators are calculated from the results generated after the classification stage. The classification results generated by supervised learning algorithm mainly include the values of false positive (FP), true negative (TN), false negative (FN) and true positive (TP). From the weighted average of these values, the following common performance indicators can be calculated: accuracy, recall, measurement, false positive rate, etc. In addition, we also need to consider the complexity and running time of the algorithm. By calculating these performance indicators, we can comprehensively compare and evaluate different machine learning algorithms, so as to select the best algorithm.

3   Protection of Sensitive Information of Intangible Cultural Heritage Communication Network (Based on Data)

According to the application standard of machine learning algorithm, the sensitive information in the intangible cultural heritage communication network is encrypted, and then the specific implementation process of the protection algorithm is improved with the help of OSBE protocol file. This chapter will study the above contents.

3.1   Encryption of Sensitive Information

In the cognition of machine learning algorithm, the emergence and development of the public key cryptosystem for encrypting sensitive information in intangible cultural heritage communication network provides a more secure and convenient method for many security requirements that cannot be easily solved by symmetric cryptosystems. Public key infrastructure (PKI) is developed on the basis of public key cryptosystem. The Internet security term in RFC defines PKI as the hardware, software, personnel, policies and processes used to generate, manage, store, allocate and revoke digital certificates based on public key cryptosystem. The main goal of developing a PKI is to make it possible to obtain the public key safely and efficiently.

Figure 1 shows a simplified processing model for sensitive information encryption.

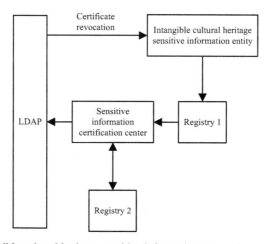

Fig. 1. Intangible cultural heritage sensitive information encryption processing model

The main factors in the figure include:

Intangible cultural heritage sensitive information entity: used to represent entities such as end users or devices.

Certification authority: the issuer of a certificate, usually the issuer of the certificate revocation list.

Registry: an optional part that takes on many administrative functions inherited from the CA.

LDAP: represents the lightweight directory access protocol, which runs over tcp/ip.

Database: a database used to store certificates and CRLs (certificate revocation list) so that certificates and CRLs can be retrieved by client entities through LDAP.

For the sensitive information of intangible cultural heritage communication network, CA is a special subject. All subjects in its service domain trust it, and can be trusted by subjects in a larger domain through indirect means (such as cross certification). Generally speaking, public key certificates include the unique and identifiable identity of the holder, the public key and the signature of the CA, that is, the signature of the CA to the certificate provides the binding of the holder's identity and its public key. If an entity trusts the Ca, after verifying the validity of another entity's certificate, it should believe that the public key is the public key of the entity with the identity information declared in the certificate, because the CA will issue a certificate to the public key he requested only after correctly identifying the holder.

Under this authentication framework, the communication parties need to establish a channel to obtain each other's certificates in order to verify their legitimacy before exchanging information. The service provided by this process is message authentication, which does not need to handle any secrets (because only the CA's public key is required to verify the CA's signature). Because the authentication service can be offline, the large-scale system can be handled by increasing the scale, that is, the certificate issued by the CA can be verified by its public key. Certificate and encryption can be used together to provide a more complete scheme to handle the authentication of the identities of all parties in the communication process.

3.2 OSBE Protocol

Under the action of machine learning algorithm, in order to effectively protect the sensitive information of intangible cultural heritage communication network, OSBE protocol document can be established. The so-called OSBE protocol file is also called the signature based memoryless envelope (OSBE) protocol, which enables the sender to send encrypted messages without determining the corresponding authority of the receiver, and the receiver must hold the signature of a trusted third party before decrypting the message plaintext. Starting from data integrity, OSBE protocol uses the uniqueness of digital signature to ensure that unauthorized users cannot obtain the transmitted plaintext.

In the OSBE protocol, when the network sender sends an encrypted message to the receiver, the receiver can decrypt the message only if he has a third-party signature negotiated about the previous message. Other entities cannot know the plaintext of the sent message and whether the recipient has the corresponding certificate. Therefore, the recipient can prove that he has the relevant certificate without exposing it. OSBE scheme is suitable for anonymous communication. It allows the receiver to obtain information from the sender without being concerned about the exposure of his own certificate.

The OSBE protocol consists of three phases: setup, interaction, and open. Assuming that the sensitive information of the intangible cultural heritage transmission network to be protected is a trusted third party, S is the message sender, a_1 and a_2 are two different message receivers (a_1 has a digital signature, while a_2 does not), and Sig is a digital signature, the OSBE protocol can be described as:

$$D = \frac{Sig \cdot r_{ij}}{(a_1 + a_2)S} \tag{9}$$

(1) Setup - establishment stage: the sensitive information of the intangible cultural heritage to be protected is transmitted through the network to generate system parameters according to the randomly selected security parameters. The first type of information is the message transmitted with, the second type of information is the message without digital signature, and the third type of information is the complete message. Then, the key generation algorithm is run to create the signature key and the corresponding public key text. The secret signature key can send the message to the private key host. Finally, the signature message can be sent to the receiving host along with the signature result.

(2) Interaction - interaction stage: in this stage, the sender of sensitive information in the intangible cultural heritage communication network establishes communication relations with different machine hosts, and the key text can generate a new OSBE protocol executive body with the change of the storage form of the data to be transmitted.

(3) Open - start phase: when the host element receives the sensitive information of intangible cultural heritage communication network, it will judge whether the stored data parameters meet the actual application requirements according to the running state of the machine learning algorithm.

3.3 Sensitive Information Processing Flow

The protection of sensitive information on the intangible cultural heritage communication network is generally divided into the following implementation processes:

Determine the ciphertext only attack strength: the attacker has one or more ciphertexts encrypted with the same key. This attack is an exhaustive attack when only the encrypted message is known. This scheme is used to attack both symmetric and asymmetric cryptosystems.

Select plaintext translation text: during this implementation, the sensor network host can get all the ciphertext information. For example, the enemy can be a black box that can only be encrypted but not decrypted. Choosing plaintext attack in asymmetric encryption system simulates a very weak attack model, and anyone can use any encryption (symmetric/asymmetric) algorithm to encrypt plaintext messages.

Define the execution form of adaptive protection instructions: a very strong attack model. The adversary can poll the decryption box for any ciphertext except the target ciphertext.

The specific sensitive information processing flow of intangible cultural heritage sensor network is shown in Fig. 2.

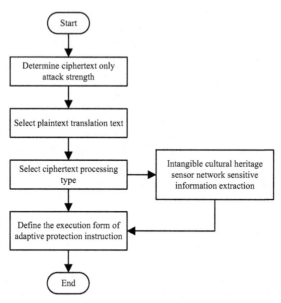

Fig. 2. Sensitive information processing flow of intangible cultural heritage sensor network

The improvement of processing flow is a crucial step in the informatization process. As the basis of information processing is data, with the further deepening of machine learning division of labor and cooperation, data sharing has become an effective way of cooperation and exchange. In short, data sharing means that different systems and users share non owned data with each other for data users to perform various operations and analysis. This is the definition of science and technology. Generally speaking, the so-called data sharing refers to the sharing of data for the use of cooperative units and individuals, or as public data to realize public welfare value. Therefore, data sharing has far-reaching and great significance for social development. Effective data sharing can enable more people to make full use of existing data resources.

4   Case Analysis

Taking the machine learning based intangible cultural heritage communication network sensitive information protection method as the implementation technology of the experimental group and the traditional sensitive information protection processing method as the implementation technology of the control group, the following comparative experiments are designed.

Two equal sensitive information parameters are intercepted in the intangible cultural heritage communication network, one of which is used as the data of the experimental group and the other as the variable of the control group. The selected host components are controlled by the implementation methods of the experimental group and the control group respectively, and the numerical changes of the identification accuracy indicators of the experimental group and the control group are recorded in the same experimental time.

The expression for the identification accuracy ξ of sensitive information of intangible cultural heritage communication network is as follows:

$$\xi = \frac{\phi}{\beta} \times 100\% \tag{10}$$

In the above formula, ϕ represents the sensitivity identification index, and β represents the data information discrimination coefficient.

Table 2. Record of experimental values

(1) ϕ Indicators			
Experimental group	Experiment time/(min)	Index value	
		Experimental group	Control group
1	5	0.15	0.14
	10	0.15	0.14
	15	0.15	0.14
2	20	0.17	0.14
	25	0.17	0.14
	30	0.17	0.16
3	35	0.19	0.16
	40	0.19	0.16
	45	0.19	0.16
(2) β Indicators			
Experimental group	Experiment time/(min)	Index value	
		Experimental group	Control group
1	5	0.45	0.89
	10	0.43	0.85
	15	0.42	0.84
2	20	0.41	0.83
	25	0.40	0.82
	30	0.38	0.84
3	35	0.36	0.86
	40	0.35	0.87
	45	0.33	0.90

The following table records the experimental values of ϕ Index and β index of the experimental group and the control group.

It can be seen from Table 2 (1) that the ϕ Index of the experimental group maintained the numerical change state of periodic rise, and the global maximum value of 0.19 increased by 0.04 compared with the global minimum value of 0.15; The ϕ Index of the control group also maintained the numerical change state of gradual increase, and the global maximum value was 0.16, which increased by 0.02 compared with the global minimum value of 0.14.

It can be seen from Table 2 (2) that the index β of the experimental group maintained a state of continuous decline, and the global maximum value of 0.45 increased by 0.12 compared with the global minimum value of 0.33; In the control group, the value of index β decreased first and then increased. Compared with the global minimum value of 0.82, the global maximum value of 0.90 increased by 0.08.

The accuracy index ξ is calculated by combining the numerical records in Table 2. The specific experimental results are shown in Table 3.

Table 3. Recognition accuracy

Experimental group	Experiment time /(min)	Index value /(%)	
		Experimental group	Control group
1	5	33.3	15.7
	10	34.9	16.5
	15	35.7	16.7
2	20	41.5	16.9
	25	42.5	17.1
	30	44.7	19.0
3	35	52.8	18.6
	40	54.3	18.4
	45	57.6	17.8

It can be seen from Table 3 that with the extension of the experimental time, the accuracy index ξ of the experimental group showed a trend of continuous increase, with the global maximum value of 57.6% increased by 24.3% compared with the global minimum value of 33.3%; The accuracy index ξ of the control group showed a trend of increasing first and then decreasing. The global maximum value of 19.0% increased by 3.3% compared with the global minimum value of 15.7%. However, the average value of the accuracy index ξ of the control group was always lower than that of the experimental group throughout the experiment.

5   Conclusion

The named data network represented by the content center network has become one of the future Internet architectures in the research field of academia and industry. Although many security mechanisms have been added to the NDN architecture, there are still some new privacy challenges, such as the privacy of sensitive information such as content privacy and name privacy, which exist in both the controller and the signer. In addition, the signer also has signature privacy.

In the machine learning algorithm model, the sensitive information of the intangible cultural heritage communication network is decrypted layer by layer, and the receiver should decrypt it with certificates in a certain order. Whether the idea of exchangeable encryption can be used for reference to realize the sequence independence of the decryption process and increase the efficiency of the decryption process on the premise of ensuring security is a problem worth considering in the next step. The use of data protection execution scheme can bring a lot of security features, but the amount of calculation is relatively large, which affects the performance of the system. Research and propose a more secure and efficient threshold scheme will be the focus of future work.

References

1. Gleim, L., Bergs, T., Brecher, C., et al.: FactDAG: formalizing data interoperability in an internet of production. IEEE Internet Things J. **7**(4), 3243–3253 (2020)
2. Kalyakulin, S.Y., Kuz'Min, V.V., Mitin, E.V., et al.: Automated design of information processing in preproduction. Russ. Eng. Res. **40**(5), 413–415 (2020)
3. Wang, L., Xu, Y., Kang, Y.: Simulation of node-level data privacy protection mining method in cloud computing. Comput. Simul. **37**(10), 433–436+460 (2020)
4. Denkena, B., Behrens, B.A., Bergmann, B., et al.: Potential of process information transfer along the process chain of hybrid components for process monitoring of the cutting process. Prod. Eng. Res. Dev. **15**(2), 199–209 (2021)
5. Shuai, L., Shuai, W., Xinyu, L., et al.: Fuzzy detection aided real-time and robust visual tracking under complex environments. IEEE Trans. Fuzzy Syst. **29**(1), 90–102 (2021)
6. Liu, S., et al.: Human memory update strategy: a multi-layer template update mechanism for remote visual monitoring. IEEE Trans. Multimedia **23**, 2188–2198 (2021)
7. Yang, J., Palazzolo, A.: Tilt pad bearing distributed pad inlet temperature with machine learning—Part I: static and dynamic characteristics. J. Tribol. **144**(6), 1–45 (2021)
8. Ostasevicius, V., Karpavicius, P., Paulauskaite-Taraseviciene, A., et al.: A machine learning approach for wear monitoring of end mill by self-powering wireless sensor nodes. Sensors **21**(3137), 1–26 (2021)
9. Liu, S., Liu, D., Muhammad, K., Ding, W.: Effective template update mechanism in visual tracking with background clutter. Neurocomputing **458**, 615–625 (2021)
10. Okumu, F., Ekmekiolu, A., Kara, S.S.: Modelling ships main and auxiliary engine powers with regression-based machine learning algorithms. Pol. Marit. Res. **28**(1), 83–96 (2021)

Decision Making Analysis of Traffic Accidents on Mountain Roads in Yunnan Province

Shu Gong[1,2(✉)] and Gang Hua[2]

[1] Department of Computer Science, Guangdong University Science and Technology,
Dongguan 523083, China
gongshu_gk@126.com
[2] School of Information and Control Engineering, China University of Mining and Technology,
Xuzhou 221116, China

Abstract. Bipolar objects are widespread in nature, and they describe the opposition and unity of the things. Inspired by decision making characterizing in terms of fuzzy graph structures, we propose a bipolar fuzzy graph-based case study on mountain road traffic accident analysis in Yunnan province. The bipolar membership functions on corresponding bipolar graph are proposed and a novel algorithm for mountain road traffic accident in specific area is given. We analyze the result and give a reasonable explanation for this phenomenon. Some suggestions for reducing the number of mountain traffic accident are proposed.

Keywords: Bipolar fuzzy set · Decision making · Traffic accident · Mountain road

1 Introduction

The fuzzy set is an important tool to deal with uncertainty information, and the positive membership cannot characterize the measure of negative side, so extra membership function is needed to describe the negative uncertainty. From this point of view, a bipolar fuzzy set is defined, in which the negative membership function is used to characterize the negative uncertainty. Due to the validity of bipolar fuzzy sets, it is known as one of the key areas of fuzzy field research in recent years (see [1–8]).

Bipolar fuzzy sets are widely used in decision making systems with negative uncertainty information to make optimal decisions based on the uncertain characteristics of both positive and negative aspects of existing things. The membership function is used to quantify the uncertainty, and the fusion of the data depends on the aggregation operator.

In order to represent fuzzy data in a structured way, we use fuzzy graphs to describe the fuzzy relationships between set elements. Correspondingly, the bipolar fuzzy graph can describe the positive and negative structural uncertainties by setting the positive edge membership function and the negative edge membership function.

Y. Xu et al. (Eds.): ML4CS 2022, LNCS 13656, pp. 228–237, 2023.
https://doi.org/10.1007/978-3-031-20099-1_19

In this paper, a bipolar fuzzy graph based case study on mountain road traffic analysis is analyzed. Subsequent parts of article are organized as follows. Firstly, the definition of bipolar fuzzy graph and its basic operations are given; then, we present the decision making analysis of traffic accidents on mountain roads in Yunnan province, where the data are from the recent 10 years.

2 Preliminary

2.1 Bipolar Fuzzy Graph

Let V be a set with at least one element. The set $A = \{(v, \mu_A^P(v), \mu_A^N(v)) : v \in V\}$ is a bipolar fuzzy set in V if two maps satisfy $\mu_A^P : V \rightarrow [0, 1]$ and $\mu_A^N : V \rightarrow [-1, 0]$. A mapping $B = (\mu_B^P, \mu_B^N) : V \times V \rightarrow [0, 1] \times [-1, 0]$ is a bipolar fuzzy relation on $V \times V$ if $\mu_B^P(v, v') \in [0, 1]$, $\mu_B^N(v, v') \in [-1, 0]$, $\mu_B^P(v, v') \leq min\{\mu_A^P(v), \mu_A^P(v')\}$, and $\mu_B^N(v, v') \geq max\{\mu_A^N(v), \mu_A^N(v')\}$ for any $(v, v') \in V \times V$.

If $\mu_A^P(v) = \mu_A^N(v) = 0$ hold for any $v \in V$, then V is a null bipolar fuzzy set which is denoted by $\varnothing_V$. If $\mu_A^P(v) = 1$ and $\mu_A^N(v) = -1$ hold for any $v \in V$, then V is an absolute bipolar fuzzy set. The compliment of V is denoted by

$$V^c = \{(v, 1 - \mu_A^P(v), -1 - \mu_A^N(v))\}.$$

Let $V_1 = \{(v, \mu_{A_1}^P(v), \mu_{A_1}^N(v))\}$ and $V_2 = \{(v, \mu_{A_2}^P(v), \mu_{A_2}^N(v))\}$ be two bipolar fuzzy sets on V. If for any $v \in V$, we have $\mu_{V_1}^P(v) \leq \mu_{V_2}^P(v)$ and $\mu_{V_1}^N(v) \geq \mu_{V_2}^N(v)$, then we say V_2 inclusion V_1, or V_1 is a subset of V_2, denoted by $V_1 \subseteq V_2$. The intersection of V_1 and V_2 is denoted by

$$V_3 = V_1 \cap V_2 = \{(v, min\{\mu_{V_1}^P(v), \mu_{V_2}^P(v)\}, max\{\mu_{V_1}^N(v), \mu_{V_2}^N(v)\})\}.$$

The union of V_1 and V_2 is denoted by

$$V_4 = V_1 \cup V_2 = \{(v, max\{\mu_{V_1}^P(v), \mu_{V_2}^P(v)\}, min\{\mu_{V_1}^N(v), \mu_{V_2}^N(v)\})\}.$$

The bipolar fuzzy graphs are defined as follows. If $A = \{(v, \mu_A^P(v), \mu_A^N(v)) : v \in V\}$ is a bipolar fuzzy set on an underlying set V and $B = (\mu_B^P, \mu_B^N)$ is a bipolar fuzzy set in $\tilde{V}^2$ where $\mu_B^P(v, v') \leq min\{\mu_A^P(v), \mu_A^P(v')\}$, $\mu_B^N(v, v') \geq max\{\mu_A^N(v), \mu_A^N(v')\}$ for any $(v, v') \in \tilde{V}^2$, and $\mu_B^P(v, v') = \mu_B^N(v, v') = 0$ for any $(v, v') \in \tilde{V}^2 - E$, then $G = (V, A, B)$ is a bipolar fuzzy graph (in short, is called BFG) of the graph $G* = (V, E)$.

2.2 Road Structure in Yunnan Province

Yunnan Province is located in the mountainous areas of China. Although the Chinese government has invested a lot of money in the infrastructure construction in Yunnan province in the past 10 years, building railways and highways between major cities, due to the complex terrain of Yunnan province (mountainous and no plain), the strategy of digging mountains and building roads consumes a lot of manpower and material resources. The traffic between county-level cities in Yunnan province is still underde-veloped. In addition, Yunnan is a province of many ethnic groups, and many ethnic minorities have maintained the original ecological environment and living habits, so that the only possible transportation in the areas related to ethnic minorities is cars. On the other hand, in order to protect ethnic minorities, the local government regards them as China's cultural heritage and prohibits the transitional tourism development in prim-itive tribes and ethnic minority areas. All these have led to the traffic in most areas of Yunnan province being dominated by mountain roads. The complexity of the mountain road and the poor road conditions have led to the frequent accidents. The simulation experiments in this paper use bipolar fuzzy graphs to model Yunnan province, and use decision support algorithms to obtain relevant evaluation reports. The distribution of various cities in Yunnan province is shown in Fig. 1.

Fig. 1. City Distribution Map of Yunnan Province (copy from the internet).

According to Fig. 1, we get the following structure in Fig. 2, where each vertex represents a prefecture-level city, and there is an edge between two cities if and only if they are adjacent.

The correspondence between cities and vertices is presented in Table 1.

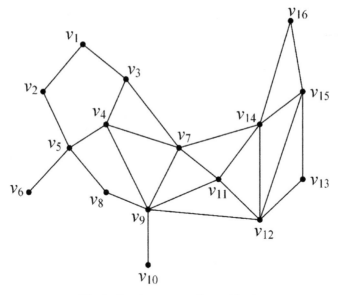

Fig. 2. Graph corresponding to Fig. 1.

Table 1. Vertex and city comparison

Vertex	City
v_1	Diqing
v_2	Nujiang
v_3	Lijiang
v_4	Dali
v_5	Baoshan
v_6	Dehong
v_7	Chuxong
v_8	Lincang
v_9	Pu'er
v_{10}	Xshuangbanna
v_{11}	Yuxi
v_{12}	Honghe
v_{13}	Wenshan
v_{14}	Kunming
v_{15}	Qujing
v_{16}	Zhaotong

3 A Case Study on Traffic Accident on Mountain Roads in Yunnan Province

In this section, we fuzzify the above graph, carry out decision support analysis of mountain road accidents according to the data of recent 10 years, and draw a conclusion from the analysis results.

3.1 Setting of Bipolar Fuzzy Graph

First, we need to give the bipolar membership function value of the vertex, based on the following three aspects:

- Political status of the city. For example, whether it is a provincial capital, a deputy provincial capital, or a regional center;
- Economic status of the city: degree of economic development, infrastructure development and local financial strength;
- The cultural and educational level of the city: the accumulation of history and culture, the level of school development, and the general education level of the local public.

The above three aspects are considered according to the weights 0.3, 0.4 and 0.3, and the bipolar membership function value of each vertex is obtained as follows (see Table 2).

Table 2. Bipolar Membership values of each city

Vertex	(μ_A^P, μ_A^N)
v_1	$(0.19, -0.86)$
v_2	$(0.2, -0.86)$
v_3	$(0.67, -0.29)$
v_4	$(0.63, -0.42)$
v_5	$(0.51, -0.46)$
v_6	$(0.28, -0.75)$
v_7	$(0.27, -0.84)$
v_8	$(0.13, -0.89)$
v_9	$(0.29, -0.79)$
v_{10}	$(0.72, -0.26)$
v_{11}	$(0.46, -0.46)$
v_{12}	$(0.41, -0.62)$
v_{13}	$(0.18, -0.86)$
v_{14}	$(0.87, -0.11)$
v_{15}	$(0.85, -0.15)$
v_{16}	$(0.28, -0.84)$

Below we summarize the causes of mountain road accidents into the following two categories:

- The driver or the vehicle itself. This type of accident is mainly caused by the driver's fatigue driving or inattention due to reasons such as making a phone call, the driver's operation error, or the failure of key parts of the vehicle at a critical moment.
- Accidents caused by rough roads. For example, accidents caused by slippery mountain roads due to rain or other weather reasons; or two vehicles collided at large-angle turns.

Table 3. Calculation of edge membership function of bipolar fuzzy graph in Fig. 2.

edge	(e_1^P, e_1^N)	(e_2^P, e_2^N)
$v_1 v_2$	$(0.19, -0.6)$	$(0.15, -0.7)$
$v_1 v_3$	$(0.19, -0.29)$	$(0.05, -0.25)$
$v_2 v_5$	$(0.2, -0.4)$	$(0.1, -0.45)$
$v_3 v_4$	$(0.62, -0.15)$	$(0.58, -0.24)$
$v_4 v_5$	$(0.5, -0.40)$	$(0.43, -0.38)$
$v_5 v_6$	$(0.28, -0.25)$	$(0.26, -0.44)$
$v_5 v_8$	$(0.11, -0.45)$	$(0.10, -0.41)$
$v_4 v_9$	$(0.28, -0.42)$	$(0.21, -0.41)$
$v_4 v_7$	$(0.25, -0.42)$	$(0.23, -0.38)$
$v_3 v_7$	$(0.23, -0.2)$	$(0.23, -0.25)$
$v_8 v_9$	$(0.12, -0.75)$	$(0.09, -0.78)$
$v_9 v_{10}$	$(0.29, -0.2)$	$(0.25, -0.15)$
$v_9 v_7$	$(0.24, -0.74)$	$(0.25, -0.75)$
$v_9 v_{11}$	$(0.25, -0.45)$	$(0.23, -0.3)$
$v_7 v_{11}$	$(0.25, -0.45)$	$(0.23, -0.44)$
$v_9 v_{12}$	$(0.25, -0.45)$	$(0.25, -0.6)$
$v_7 v_{14}$	$(0.20, -0.05)$	$(0.18, -0.10)$
$v_{11} v_{12}$	$(0.35, -0.45)$	$(0.37, -0.39)$
$v_{12} v_{14}$	$(0.28, -0.1)$	$(0.40, -0.05)$
$v_{11} v_{14}$	$(0.38, -0.07)$	$(0.42, -0.1)$
$v_{12} v_{13}$	$(0.16, -0.6)$	$(0.15, -0.6)$
$v_{12} v_{15}$	$(0.40, -0.15)$	$(0.3, -0.1)$
$v_{13} v_{15}$	$(0.15, -0.15)$	$(0.14, -0.15)$
$v_{14} v_{15}$	$(0.81, -0.11)$	$(0.74, -0.04)$
$v_{14} v_{16}$	$(0.25, -0.11)$	$(0.26, -0.11)$
$v_{15} v_{16}$	$(0.23, -0.15)$	$(0.21, -0.14)$

Based on the statistics of mountain road accidents in Yunnan Province in the past 10 years (highway, railway and other traffic data are not within the scope of data collection, here we only focus on traffic accidents on mountain roads), experts give the membership for each edge as follows (see Table 3).

3.2 Algorithm Description

Our bipolar fuzzy graph based decision making algorithm for traffic accident analysis of mountain roads in Yunnan province is designed as follows (let n be the number of vertices).

Algorithm 1. Bipolar fuzzy graph based decision making algorithm.

Input: The structure of fuzzy graph, including the vertex set, edge set which can be represented as association matrix.

Initialization: Determine the bipolar membership function on vertex set and edge set (there are two kinds of bipolar membership functions on edge set) with the help of experts.

> For $i=1$ to n
> > For $j=i+1$ to n
> > > If $v_j \in N(v_i)$ (or $a_{ij} =1$ in its association matrix)
> > > > If $e_1^P(v_i v_j) > e_2^P(v_i v_j)$ and $e_1^N(v_i v_j) < e_2^N(v_i v_j)$
> > > > > Label $v_i v_j$ as R_1
> > > >
> > > > End if
> > > > If $e_1^P(v_i v_j) < e_2^P(v_i v_j)$ and $e_1^N(v_i v_j) > e_2^N(v_i v_j)$
> > > > > Label $v_i v_j$ as R_2
> > > >
> > > > End if
> > > End If
> > End For
> End For
> Output: Return the label of each edge (if marked).

It is easy to know that the edge marked R_1 indicates that the main cause of mountain road accidents between the two cities is human factors; while the edge marked R_2 corresponds to the main cause of mountain road accidents between the two cities is indeed caused by road conditions. It should be noted that not every entry is marked, in fact there are many edges that cannot satisfy any of the conditions in the algorithm.

3.3 Aggregation Operator

The role of aggregation operator is used to combine the mountain road accident data in Yunnan province in recent 10 years. Suppose there are collected related data with denoted by $\{D_1, \cdots, D_m\}$, where m is the total number of data. If data are weight, set $\{\varepsilon_1, \cdots, \varepsilon_m\}$ as the weights of corresponding data. Then the weighted averaging aggregation operator is a mapping $\Theta : D^m \to D$ which is formulated by

$$\Theta(D_1, \cdots, D_m) = \overset{m}{\underset{i=1}{\oplus}} \{\varepsilon_i D_i\}.$$

In bipolar fuzzy graph setting, the information is collected on its edge set, and can be denoted by $D_i = (\mu_{B_i}^P, \mu_{B_i}^N)$, here label i is not for edge number but for the number of collect data on a specific edge. We use the following two bipolar fuzz geometric aggregation operators (called P-operator and R-operator respectively) for our application:

$$\Theta_P(D_1, \cdots, D_m) = \{\overset{m}{\underset{i=1}{\oplus_P}}\}(\varepsilon_i D_i) = (\prod_{i=1}^{m}(\mu_{B_i}^P)^{\varepsilon_i}, -(1 - \prod_{i=1}^{m}(1 - (-\mu_{B_i}^N))^{\varepsilon_i})),$$

$$\Theta_R(D_1, \cdots, D_m) = \{\overset{m}{\underset{i=1}{\oplus_R}}\}(\varepsilon_i D_i) = (1 - \prod_{i=1}^{m}(1 - \mu_{B_i}^P)^{\varepsilon_i}, -(\prod_{i=1}^{m}(-\mu_{B_i}^N)^{\varepsilon_i})).$$

In the non-weighted bipolar setting (i.e., each data record is equally important), then the above aggregation operators can be re-written by

$$\Theta_P(D_1, \cdots, D_m) = \{\overset{m}{\underset{i=1}{\oplus_P}}\}(D_i) = (\prod_{i=1}^{m}\mu_{B_i}^P, -(1 - \prod_{i=1}^{m}(1 - (-\mu_{B_i}^N)))),$$

$$\Theta_R(D_1, \cdots, D_m) = \{\overset{m}{\underset{i=1}{\oplus_R}}\}(D_i) = (1 - \prod_{i=1}^{m}(1 - \mu_{B_i}^P), -(\prod_{i=1}^{m}(-\mu_{B_i}^N))).$$

3.4   Result and Analysis

From the results of the above algorithm, most of the marked edges are marked R_1, that is, the main cause of mountain road accidents is human factors. As long as there is no problem with the car and the driver drives carefully, the accident can be fully avoided. We believe that the cause of most mountain road accidents is man-made, and the main reasons are analyzed from the following perspectives:

- Yunnan is a mountainous province, with rugged mountain roads and frequent accidents on dangerous roads. Through the analysis of the specific location of the accident, it can be seen that on the mountain road with frequent accidents in the early stage, there are obvious prompts on both sides of the road, requiring drivers to drive carefully, which has attracted enough attention from drivers. Therefore, the distribution of accident locations is almost uniform, and no road section is the concentrated outbreak section of the accident. We believe it is human causes that play a leading role, and that accidents can be avoided even in dangerous areas where accidents have occurred before, as long as the driver drives carefully.

- Generally speaking, it is generally believed that the more difficult the road conditions are, the higher the probability of an accident. However, through our data analysis, we found that there is a serious deviation between this intuitive understanding and the fact. This can be explained from the following aspects. First of all, in the ethnic minority or native tribal areas in Yunnan with really poor road conditions, cars cannot pass through, and they can only use other means of transportation. The number of mountain road accidents in these areas is almost zero. Secondly, The poor road conditions (mainly gravel or muddy mountain roads) are also one of the main reasons. Due to the underdeveloped transportation, it's impossible for drivers to pass quickly, slowing down the situation, which in turn reduces the probability of an accident.

In this regard, we believe that the key to further reduce accidents on mountain roads is to strengthen the ideological education of drivers, to strengthen their awareness to drive without fatigue, even on flat mountain roads.

For the few edges marked as R_2, we believe that the road conditions between adjacent cities really need to be improved. In this regard, we suggest that the local government should increase investment in highway infrastructure construction, improve road conditions, or directly dig tunnels to build expressways. Only the investment is increased, can we make a difference to reduce the accidents in mountain roads.

4 Conclusion

In this paper, bipolar fuzzy graph modeling is carried out in Yunnan province to evaluate the causes of mountain road accidents between regions, and a specific decision-making algorithm is proposed. Although Yunnan is a relatively backward area with underdeveloped transportation in China., human factors still play a decisive role in the occurrence of mountain road accidents. As long as the driver's driving skills and awareness of prevention are strengthened, accidents can be largely avoided.

Acknowledgements. This work is supported by 2021 Guangdong Basic and Applied Basic Youth Fund Project (No. 2021A1515110834), 2023 Natural Science Fund Project of Guangdong basic and applied basic research foundation, Guangdong University of Science and Technology University Major Scientific Research Achievement Cultivation Program Project 2020 (No. GKY-2020CQPY-2), Characteristic Innovation Project of Universities in Guangdong Province in 2022, and Guangdong Provincial Department of Education Project (No. 2020KTSCX166).

References

1. Sitara, M., Akram, M., Riaz, M.: Decision-making analysis based on q-rung picture fuzzy graph structures. J. Appl. Math. Comput. **67**, 541–577 (2021)
2. Jia, J., Rehman, A.U., Hussain, M., Mu, D., Siddiqui, M.K., Cheema, I.: Consensus-based multi-person decisionmaking using consistency fuzzy preference graphs. IEEE Access **7**, 178870–178878 (2019)
3. Karaaslan, F.: Hesitant fuzzy graphs and their applications in decision making. J. Intell. Fuzzy Syst. **36**(3), 2729–2741 (2019)

4. Akram, M., Habib, A., Davvaz, B.: Direct sum of n pythagorean fuzzy graphs with application to group decision-making. J. Mult. Valued Log. Soft Comput. **33**(1–2), 75–115 (2019)
5. Akram, M., Feng, F., Saeid, A.B., Leoreanu-Fotea, V.: A new multiple criteria decision-making method based on bipolar fuzzy soft graphs. Iranian J. Fuzzy Syst. **15**(4), 73–92 (2018)
6. Akram, M., Waseem, N.: Novel applications of bipolar fuzzy graphs to decision making problems. J. Appl. Math. Comput. **56**(1–2), 73–91 (2016). https://doi.org/10.1007/s12190-016-1062-3
7. Gao, W., Wang, W., Chen, Y.: Tight bounds for the existence of path factors in network vulnerability parameter settings. Int. J. Intell. Syst. **36**(3), 1133–1158 (2021)
8. Gao, W., Chen, Y., Wang, Y.: Network vulnerability parameter and results on two surfaces. Int. J. Intell. Syst. **36**(8), 4392–4414 (2021)

Deep Adaptively Feature Extracting Network for Cervical Squamous Lesion Cell Detection

Zhonghua Peng[1], Rong Hu[1], Fuen Wang[2], Haoyi Fan[2], Yee Wei Eng[3], Zuoyong Li[4], and Liwei Zhou[5](✉)

[1] Fujian Provincial Key Laboratory of Big Data Mining and Applications, School of Computer Science and Mathematics, Fujian University of Technology, Fuzhou 350118, Fujian, China
[2] School of Computer and Artificial Intelligence, Zhengzhou University, Zhengzhou 450001, Henan, China
[3] School of Computer Sciences, Universiti Sains Malaysia, Penang 11800, Malaysia
[4] Fujian Provincial Key Laboratory of Information Processing and Intelligent Control, College of Computer and Control Engineering, Minjiang University, Fuzhou 350121, Fujian, China
[5] Department of Nutrition, The First Affiliated Hospital of Zhengzhou University, Zhengzhou 450052, Henan, China
zzuliweizhou@163.com

Abstract. Cervical cancer is one of the most widespread malignancies affecting women's health worldwide today. However, the task of detection is particularly difficult due to the complex background of the cervical smear, where cells are previously stacked in clusters. To address this problem, we utilize the YOLOv5 as the baseline and build on YOLOv5 by using the simple Transformer Block which only combines with multi-head self attention layers and MLP to better extract cell features as well as to obtain global information. In addition, we allow the model to refine features adaptively to assist with detection by using Convolutional Block Attention Module (CBAM), an attention module being simple and effective for feed-forward convolutional neural networks, in the complex background information. Finally, we compare the model with YOLOv5 as baseline. In CDetector dataset, our model obtains 52.5% mAP@.5, which is 6% better than baseline. In transfer learning, it is 62.2%, which outperforms baseline by 3.2%.

Keywords: Cervical squamous lesion cells · YOLOv5 · Transformer · Deep learning

1 Introduction

Currently, cancer is the one of leading cause of death among people aged less than 70 years worldwide [2]. In terms of prevention and early cure rates, compared to other cancers, for cervical cancer, very significant prevention can be achieved by

Y. Xu et al. (Eds.): ML4CS 2022, LNCS 13656, pp. 238–253, 2023.
https://doi.org/10.1007/978-3-031-20099-1_20

HPV vaccination and early screening. According to the WTO, if women in developing countries were screened for pre-cervical cancer every 5 years, the overall prevalence could be reduced by 60% or more [9]. Therefore, pre-cervical screening is very important and urgent for women to have a healthy and happy life. At present, the most effective screening method for cervical cancer according to clinical medical evidence still relies on doctors to analyze the morphological structure of the cell images by observing the cervical smear through a light microscope, and finally to make a diagnosis based on cytopathological principles [11,34]. However, this method undoubtedly requires a large number of experienced medical staffs, and the review of smears is lengthy, tedious and laborious.

Therefore, it has become important to use computer-assisted systems to assist medical staffs in cervical smear screening. The current assisted diagnostic system in cervical cell smear assists in three main aspects: cervical cell classification, detection and segmentation. Classification could be divided into cell classification and smear classification. Unlike cell classification, the purpose of smear classification is still mainly to predict the category of the whole smear. Moreover, segmentation is also divided into detect-then-segment method and segment-then-refine method, as well. Meanwhile, the cervical cell detection is mainly divided into two categories. One is the one-stage object detection, in which models of YOLO [18], RetinaNet [15] and EfficientDet [25] are introduced to many studies on this category because of faster inference speed and higher efficiency, the conspicuous features of these model due to there is no ROI recommendation and classification part like the two-stage. However, the accuracy of one-stage model is relatively lower than that of the two-stage detection model. The other is the two-stage detection, mainly based on the Fast R-CNN [7] and Faster R-CNN [20] variants, which has higher detection accuracy than the one-stage model, as mentioned above. However, the model has been iteratively updated, and the accuracy of some of the current one-stage detection models is now comparable to the current two-stage models. Moreover, the volume of screening smears is now particularly huge, and the smears are time-sensitive, so a fast and accurate detection model is urgently needed at present.

In previous works, there are a number of object detection models based on the first stage, and most of these object detection models are modified and supplemented by YOLOv3 [19]. They used their own datasets to train and fine-tune the models adequately, but in the final results, these are not particularly satisfactory in the distinction of squamous cells. Since the characteristics of squamous cells are so similar to each other that they are difficult to identify, current models as well as clinical medicine are keen to solve this problem. Therefore, in this paper, we introduce a cervical lesion cell detection model combining CNN and Transformer [28], which is based on YOLOv5. Transformer block has shown its great capability of extracting images feature in ViT [6]. Meanwhile, CBAM [31] is also suitable for adaptively extracting cervical cell features in complex backgrounds from both channel and spatial perspectives. Likewise, BiFPN [25] extracts features by using an adaptive weight from different levels of feature mapping. Thus, we replaced the last two original C3 block with Transformer block, replaced PAN neck modules with BiFPN and deployed CBAM block to prediction head modules. In addition, to further improve the efficiency of our model, we utilized the data augmentation in ramdon affine, which makes a significant improvement. Finally, we achieved better detection results than Baseline for four types of squamous lesion cells (ASCH, ASCUS, HSIL, LSIL) in the CDetector [14] dataset with the CDetector model and the default model of YOLOv5s 6.0 as Baseline. Moreover, to be able to demonstrate the transfer learning ability of our model in small datasets, we also performed transfer learning in a very small private data and the results were superior to the default YOLOv5s model.

Our contributions are as follows:

- We propose a model that can effectively improve the detection accuracy of 4 types (ASCUS, ASCH, HSIL, LISL) of cervical squamous lesion cells by using the Transformer Block, which can obtain global information for better cell characterization, based on YOLOv5.
- We employ Bidirectional Feature Network (BiFPN) instead of Path Aggregation Network (PAN) to better handle the different levels of image characteristics, since the complex background of cell detection affects cell screening. In addition, most of the cervical smears in clinical medicine have the problem of cell stacking and stray cells, so we added the Convolutional Block Attention Module (CBAM) to the prediction head in order to allow the model to detect cells adaptively.
- We confirm that the model has great potential in detecting squamous cells with high similarity, after conducting a large number of comparison experiments with other state-of-the-art models and ablation experiments. We also verify that the model also has a strong transfer learning capability in a small dataset.

2   Related Work

In this section, we will introduce traditional medical image processing methods as well as deep learning-based processing methods in cervical squamous lesion cells detection.

2.1   Medical Image Analysis

Early work related to the analysis of pathological images dates back to 1966, when the first attempts to use mechanical perception to complement for human perception in pathological image analysis were made in the 1960 s s [17]. Since deep learning methods have particularly good flexibility and the ability to distinguish features of different classes of samples, a number of researchers applied deep learning to cytological morphological analysis in the early 21st century [10], and some researchers [5,21,26] classified cells by analyzing their morphology. With the TOP1 result of AlexNet on the ImageNet in 2012, this made CNN attract the attention of a large number of researchers. Various state-of-the-art neural network models like VGG [23], GoogleNet [24], ResNet [8], etc. started to emerge, which at the same time pushed the advancement of cytological image analysis in lung, breast, and cervical. For example, in 2016, [4] introduced a cascaded neural network capable of efficiently detecting mitosis in breast cancer cells, which achieved more dazzling results than the 2014 TOP1 model on the ICPR MITOSATYPIA dataset. EMS-net [33] is a multi-scale model for classifying breast cancer cell images introduced by Xue, which obtained the best classification result in 2018 ICIAR BACH challenge. Similarly, on the lung pathology picture classification task, [27] and [22] introduced a VGG-based model and an AlexNet-based model, respectively, both of which achieved very good performance in the task of classifying benign and diseased cells in the lung.

2.2 Deep Learning Based Cervical Cell Recognition

The development of cell-assisted detection models for cervical lesions has also been a very long process. Specifically, it can be divided into classification, object detection, and segmentation tasks. Early classification tasks and segmentation tasks were based on some already cropped single-cell datasets for classification and segmentation. The classification task was usually to analyze the distribution state of nucleus and cytoplasm of a cell. In addition, the analysis method was to feed the segmented nucleus and cytoplasm information to a specific classifier for training to derive a classification model, while the segmentation methods used were threshold segmentation, watershed segmentation and c-means algorithms. For example, Thanatip [3] utilized a fuzzy C-means clustering approach to segment cell images and finally trained his own classifier. William [30], by training a Weka segmentation classifier and then combining it with a fuzzy c-means algorithm to perform classification. All the above conventional algorithms are based on pre-extraction of cellular tissue features using segmentation algorithms. In other words, a segmentation algorithm that can segment the nucleus and cytoplasm well is needed here as a guarantee of overall classification accuracy. Since CNNs have shown excellent capabilities in object feature extraction and the use of CNNs to extract cell features eliminates the need to use segmentation algorithms to obtain cell tissue information in advance, many CNN-based classifications [16,21,38] have emerged in recent studies. These models have achieved better results than earlier studies in the classification datasets of Herlev [10] and HEMLBC (H&E stained manual LBC) [37], but are still difficult to apply in clinical medicine to assist medical stuffs in analyzing and classifying smears, as the datasets they use are still relatively simple. In most cervical smears, most of the cells are overlapped, thus, before the classification cutting the smear into individual cells or cell clusters for classification are still required. Then the overall inference time is proportional to the number of cells, and cutting the smear is a very tedious task, so the classification task is still extremely limited for the actual clinical medicine.

2.3   Cervical Cell Detection Model

Cervical cell detection studies can be divided into two parts: one-stage method and two-stage method. A number of studies in the one-stage are based on the state-of-the-art models in one-stage method such as YOLO series, RetinaNet and EfficientNet. [32] used YOLOv3 as the basis for the overall network structure, but since YOLOv3 has poor classification ability for four classes of squamous cells, they added a cascade classifier to YOLOv3 to enhance the classification ability for four classes of squamous cells. [13] enhanced the ability to perceive global contextual information to YOLOv3 and proposed the image level classification branch ILCB, which can reduce and suppress the false positive (FPs) results. [29] is also based on YOLOv3, which uses Transformer to classify multi-task features at different scales. In [36], an improved object detection network on RetinaNet was attempted. In [1], it is based on the improved EfficientNet network model. And in the second stage task, [12] utilized Faster R-CNN and used a transfer learning approach in the LBC dataset with 680 cervical exfoliated cell samples for detection. [36] also improved and achieved good results in Faster R-CNN for the object detection task of cervical lesion cells. [14] proposed a scheme to learn background reference images in the data, resulting in a 19.7 mAP improvement in the Faster R-CNN for small datasets and a 3.6 mAP improvement for large datasets. Although the previously proposed work based on object detection achieved good results in cervical lesion cell detection, only [32] among them also noticed that the four classes of squamous cells were too similar to be distinguished, so measures were taken accordingly. However, due to the addition of new cascade classifiers, this made YOLOv3 lose the efficiency of the first stage. Therefore, we introduced a model based on YOLOv5 and modified only in the modes, without while the addition of external components, which ensured that the number of parameters and computation would not change too much, as well as not turning the first stage task into a second stage task.

3   Method

In order to cope with the task of squamous cell detection, we modified the backbone, neck and prediction head of the original YOLOv5 model, and the structure of the optimized YOLOv5 model is shown in Fig. 1.

Transformer Block. In clinical medicine, it is difficult to obtain correct results when screening for squamous lesions by directly analyzing the nucleoplasm ratio and nucleus size and shape of individual cells, and it is often necessary to identify the cell type based on the surrounding environment. Therefore, we modified layers 9 and 11 in the original YOLOv5 backbone, replacing the previous C3 Block with a Transformer Block that has better access to global information. The reason for the replacement at the end of the backbone is that, as shown at [35], deep neural networks usually extract high-dimensional features, which are more representative of the global information than low-dimensional features,

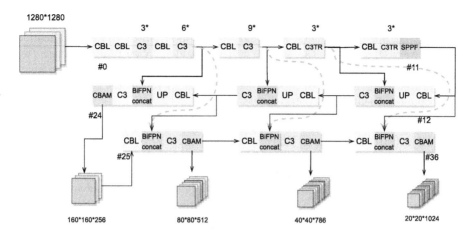

Fig. 1. The architecture of YOLOv5 optimized. C3TR is the model name of Transformer block. UP is the abbreviations of upsampling. CBL is the model consist with Conv2d, Batch Normalization and SiLU activation. C3 is formed from CBL and residual block in CSP structure.

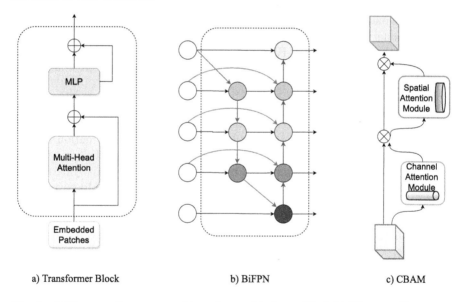

a) Transformer Block   b) BiFPN   c) CBAM

Fig. 2. a) The overall structure of transformer block modified. b) The overall structure of BiFPN. c) The overall structure of CBAM

and the computational effort does not increase too much after the replacement. Moreover, [6] applies Transformer to computer vision image classification tasks and demonstrates the powerful feature extraction capability of Transformer, so we want to employed Transformer to prompt the model to distinguish features between different classes of squamous lesion cells.

However, there are kind of difference between our Transformer Block to the ViT. During our experiments, we found that Dropout and Layer Normalization are not very effective for the accuracy of the model, so we removed these two parts, and the specific model structure is shown in Fig. 2. After the experiment, it is proved that Transformer Block can really help the model to improve the performance of feature extraction.

Bi-FPN. [25] According to EfficientDet, although FPN and PAN are widely used in various object detection models for multi-scale feature fusion of targets. However, the importance of features at different scales is not carefully analyzed, and almost all treat this information without any difference. To solve this problem, the authors designed Bi-FPN by a weighting approach, the structure of which is shown in Fig. 2. Bi-FPN introduces an additional weight for each input to the network, removes nodes with only one input edge and adds a jump connection between same scale input and output nodes. In general, Bi-FPN is equivalent to assigning different weights to each layer for fusion, allowing the network to focus more on the important layers and also reducing some unnecessary nodal connections of the layers. Consequently, we designed the model for detecting cervical squamous lesion cells by replacing the original PAN with Bi-FPN, so that the model can better handle different scale features. After experiments, it was shown that the use of Bi-FPN can increase the accuracy of the model for different categories while increasing the computation as little as possible.

CBAM. [31] This is an attention mechanism module that represents a convolutional module. It is an attention mechanism module that combines spatial and channel. It can achieve better results than SENet whose attention mechanism that only focuses on channels. This module is simple and efficient, and it is capable of adaptively refining the features of the input feature map by extracting attention from different angles for the intermediate feature map. Moreover, since CBAM is an end-to-end model structure, it can be flexibly applied to different models. The details of the model are presented in Fig. 2. Since most of the images we detect have a complex background, such as free nuclei, cytoplasm and mucus filaments or other impurities, and there is a large number of cells stacked, we use the CBAM module to assist YOLO in capturing the target objects to be detected.

Data Augmentation in Random Affine. When we trained the model, we considered that the deformation of the samples might cause the cells to change from positive to negative samples and thus the network would misidentify the cells. Therefore, we did not use random affine transform data augmentation that would cause cell deformation, such as translation, scale, flip, rotation, and shear, but the overall result was very poor. In a chance encounter, we mistakenly used data that could cause deformation, but the final result was exceptional. So we started to explore the most suitable data augmentation for this task, and finally apply the method as shown in Sect. 4, which can make 2.5% mAP higher than using the default data augmentation.

4   Experiments and Results

In this section, in order to perform the efficiency of our model, we conducted ablation experiments and comparison experiments with other baseline models. In addition, to verify the transfer learning capability of the model, we also did transfer learning experiments on a small sample dataset.

4.1   Dataset

In this experiment, we follow the same dataset of baseline Comparison Detector [14], which contains 7410 cervical microscopic image slices in 11 categories totally, i.e., atypical squamous cells cannot exclude HSIL (ASCH), atypical squamous cells of undetermined significance (ASCUS), high-grade squamous intraepithelial lesion(HSIL), low-grade squamous intraepithelial lesion (LSIL), flora, trichomonas (TRICH), atypical glandular cells (AGC), actinomyces (ACTIN), candida (CAND), herps, squamous-cell carcinoma (SCC). These are all cropped from slide microscopic images, including 6666 in the training set and 744 in the test set. The slide micrographs in the dataset were taken using the Pannoramic MIDI II digital slide scanner, while the corresponding specimens were prepared using the Thinprep method and stained with Papanicolaou. All the crops of the cervical microscopic images are labeled by experts according to the TBS categories and provided the corresponding ground truth bounding box and categories respectively. Since the appearance of the prior four categories of squamous lesion cells (ASCUS, ASCH, HSIL, LSIL) is an important symptom of HPV invasion and cervical pre-cancer or higher risk cancer type, which are very significant criteria for disease differentiation in clinical medicine. However, it is difficult to distinguish these four categories of cells either in clinical medicine or in existing neural network computer-aided recognition systems. Accordingly, we only select these four categories in CDetector for training and analysis. These images consist a total of 3502 in the training set and 505 in the test set, and we divide the training set into a training set and a validation set according to the ratio of 9:1, where there are 3151 in the training set and 351 in the validation set. Figure 3 shows some instance examples of each category of selected one and the number of instances is shown in Fig. 4

4.2   Baseline Methods

The following state-of-the-art methods are selected to compare with our model:

- **Faster R-CNN with FPN** [20] is a deep end-to-end model for object detection improved from Faster R-CNN, which consisting ResNet101 [8] and FPN [8] as backbone.

246   Z. Peng et al.

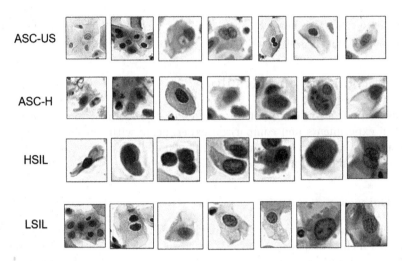

Fig. 3. Samples of each category in selected dataset, whose features are too similar to distinguish from subsets of different categories.

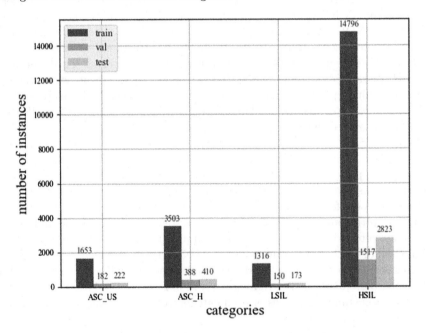

Fig. 4. Instance distribution of different categories on train,val and test set.

– **RetinaNet with FPN** [15] is a deep end-to-end model for object detection improved from RetinaNet [8], which consisting ResNet101 [8] and FPN [8] as backbone.

- **YOLOv5** is a one-stage object detection model, which consisting CSPDark-net53 as backbone and PAN as the neck.
- **Comparison Detector** [14] is a proposal-based model improved from Faster R-CNN by replacing certain classification layers and learning the representation of background category.

4.3 Evaluation Metrics

In this work, mAP@.5 score is employed as the model accuracy criterion. In particular, the mean Average Precision (mAP) score mentioned in the baseline paper is the PASCAL VOC mAP, which is quite different from the COCO mAP score. The previous uses an Intersection over Union (IoU) threshold of 0.5, while in order to better reflect the accuracy of the model for object detection, COCO mAP employs two criteria. mAP@.5 is consistent with PASCAL VOC's mAP in terms of definition. The other one is mAP@.5:0.95, which is the average of the model's accuracy when the IoU threshold is between 0.5 and 0.95 as the mAP score. Since our model is more of an adjunct to clinical medicine, and it does not require a particularly precise range of bounding box, therefore, mAP@.5 is introduced as the rubrics.

4.4 Implementation Details

In this paper, our framework is implemented at Ubuntu 20.04.3 LTS operating system, with NVIDIA GEFORCE RTX 3080Ti GPU for computing with 12GB memory, 128GB RAM, and Intel(R) Xeon(R) Silver 4210 CPU @ 2.20GHz CPU processor and all our models are Based on Python 3.8 runtime environment, Pytorch 1.11.0 deep learning framework, CUDA 11.6 and CuDNN 8.3 acceleration library.

We replaced the last two original blocks of the backbone of YOLOv5s 6.0 with Transformer Block as the backbone of our model, and replaced the PAN with BiFPN in the neck, and added CBAM to the last block at each branch in the projection head. Since our model has some weights to share with the backbone of YOLOv5s 6.0, and also some weights to share in the head. Hence, we used the pre-trained weights they provided which trained on the COCO dataset for the model initialization weights, which helps us to save a lot of training time. We used Adam optimizer with a learning rate of 0.01 following the cosine learning rate schedule. The model is trained on CDetector dataset for only 200 epochs, the first 3 epochs are used for warm-up, and an early stopping method is utilized to prevent overfitting of the model. The longest side of the input image is 1024 pixels and a batch size is 16. The weights with the highest mAP scores in the validation set are kept after training, and the mAP scores are recorded as result when the model is used for test set detection with best weight.

4.5 Ablation Studies

In this part of the experiment, the model following the CDetector paper is used as the baseline for comparison experiments, and we also compared it with the

YOLOv5s 6.0 model in order to better reflect the performance of our model. Moreover, we conduct a large number of ablation experiments for analyzing and verifying the role of each of the blocks we used, and the final overall result achieved a good mAP@.5 score of 52.5, whose detail is summarized in Table 1. And the loss value of during validation shown in Fig. 6, illustrates that the lowest values of the loss for obj, cls and box are only 0.0365, 0.0453 and 0.0105, respectively, which are higher than our model and are more likely to be overfitted than the proposed in the training process after 50–75 epochs.

Table 1. Ablation study on of squamous cells detection (%), averaged over all cross-validation.

Model	ASCUS	ASCH	HSIL	LSIL	mAP@.5	mAP@.5:0.95
Comparison detector [4]	27.4	6.7	41.7	40.1	28.4	–
Yolov5s6	52.5	28.3	52.3	53.4	46.6	24.4
+ Transformer Block	56	33.5	54	53.3	49.2($+2.6$)	25.6
+ CBAM	56.8	31.6	57.7	51.8	49.5($+0.3$)	25.1
+ BiFPN	57.2	30.9	57.5	54.4	50($+0.5$)	25.3
+ Augmentation	**62.5**	**34.5**	**57.9**	**55.2**	**52.5($+2.5$)**	**27.4**

Table 2. Hyper-paramaters of our data augmentation.

Rotation (degree)	Translation (fraction)	Scale (gain)	Shear (degree)	Perspective (fraction)	Up-down (probability)	Left-right (probability)
0.0	0.1	0.9	0.0	0.0	0.5	0.5

Effect of Transformer Block. Using Transformer replaced C3 and Conv block in backbone remains overall parameters of the model almost unchanged, still 12.6M, increases the number of layers from 355 to 357, only 2 layers. Meanwhile, the GFLOPS decreased from 16.9 to 16.7. Although the number of layers increased slightly, it is manifest that the overall performance of the model has been significantly improved in terms of model parameters, floating point computation and accuracy.

Effect of Data Augmentation in Random Affine. With our data augmentation strategy in random affine, while leaving the other network models unchanged, the mAP@.5 significantly rises from 50 to 52.5. The details of hyper-parameters of our data augmentation are shown in Table. 2

Effect of Model Ensemble. After adding the structure of Transformer, BiFPN and CBAM, the overall model parameters and number of network layers increased from 12.6M to 13.8M and 355 to 431, respectively. Furthermore, the GFLOPs rise from 16.9 to 17.9 as well. Although the overall computational cost increased slightly, the overall mAP increased promisingly from 46.6 to 52.5, nearly 6% points.

4.6   Comparison Studies

Comparison with Baseline Models. In order to reflect the performance of our model, we make comparison experiments with baseline. What is more, we compare it with other excellent object detection models and various series of YOLO models, as well as YOLOv5 models with different weights. The results are shown in Table 3. The confusion matrices of YOLOv5 and Our model are shown in Fig. 5

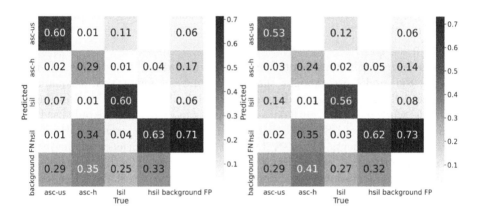

Fig. 5. Illustration of the confusion matrices of Our model and YOLOv5 are shown in figure from left to right.

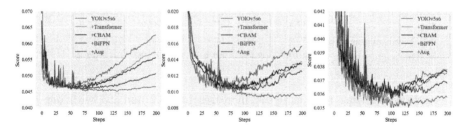

Fig. 6. Illustration of the object, class and bounding box loss is shown in figure from left to right.

Table 3. Comparison study of the contribution for each module in terms of squamous cells detection(%).

Model	mAP@.5	mAP@.5:0.95	Params	GFLOPs
Comparison detector [4]	28.4	–	42.0M	–
Faster R-CNN ResNet101 with FPN [5]	33.7	15.8	52.8M	850
RetinaNet ResNet101 with FPN [6]	39.1	19.1	53.0M	326
Yolov3-tiny	33.4	14.6	**8.8M**	**13.2**
Yolov3 [7]	40.6	19.1	61.5M	156.3
Yolov3-SPP	41.5	19.3	63.0M	157.1
Yolov5s6	46.6	24.4	12.6M	16.9
Yolov5l6	47.5	24.6	76.2M	111.5
Yolov5s6-C3TR-BiFPN-CBAM (Ours)	50	25.3	13.8M	17.9
Yolov5s6-C3TR-BiFPN-CBAM-with-Aug (Ours)	**52.5**	**27.4**	13.8M	17.9

Compared to these models mentioned in Table.3, our proposed model is more scalable, higher accurate and greater computational efficiency for four types of squamous cells.

Comparison with Different Data Augmentation Strategies. Before training the model, we thought that the features of four types of squamous epithelial cells is too similar to distinguish which leads to mislead the learning of the model while using too much data augmentations. Therefore, we only used the data augmentation of HSV (Hue, Saturation, Value) at the beginning. However, subsequent experiments demonstrated that the overall efficiency of the model was significantly improved after adding the appropriate data augmentations for the deformation (rotation, translation, scale, shear, perspective, flip). The results are shown in Table 4.

Table 4. Comparison study of the contribution for each strategies of augmentation in terms of squamous cells detection(%)

Augmentation	ASCUS	ASCH	HSIL	LSIL	mAP@.5	mAP@.5:0.95
w/o	32.4	21.4	47	48.4	37.3	17.9
w/ Default augmentation	57.2	30.9	57.5	54.4	50(+12.7)	25.3
w/ Our augmentation	**62.5**	**34.5**	**57.9**	**55.2**	**52.5**(+2.5)	**27.4**

As table showing that mAP@.5 increases by 15.2 and 2.5 with our data augmentation compared to data augmentation without deformation and with YOLOv5's default data augmentation, respectively.

4.7   Transfer Learning Studies

In addition to the CDetector dataset, we have a particularly small dataset of 456 cervical microscopic image slices, of which 367 are in the training set and 89 in the test set. This is cropped from a WSI at 1024*1024 size after 40 times magnification, after which the squamous cells are labeled by a professional physician. This sample includes 3 types of squamous cells (ASCUS, HSIL, LSIL). Initially, we intended to test this sample directly with the model trained in the CDetector dataset, and found that it did not work well. Thus, we used the weights trained in the large dataset as pre-training weights and the small dataset as training set for transfer learning, and the model performance significantly outperformed YOLOv5, as shown in Table 5.

Table 5. Comparison study of the contribution for each strategies of transfer learning Squamous cells detection coefficient (%).

Model	Pretrain dataset	Train dataset	Test dataset	ASCUS	LISL	HSIL	mAP@.5
YOLOv5s6	CDetector	Ours	Ours	62.2	66.8	38.9	59.0
Ours	CDetector			**67.5**	**68.9**	**50.4**	**62.2**

There is a significant improvement in the effectiveness of the model after transfer learning with a training set that is more closely matched to the actual distribution than with a dataset does not or with a smaller dataset.

5   Conclusion

In this paper, we employ some techniques such as Transformer Block and CBAM to YOLOv5 in order to solve the problem of too similar cervical squamous lesion cell characteristics to distinguish and complex detection background, so as to construct an object detection model that can effectively address the above problems. In addition, we optimize it while keeping the number of parameters and computation as constant as possible. We hope that this model will be able to assist health care professionals in screening cervical lesion cells.

References

1. Bhatt, A.R., Ganatra, A., Kotecha, K.: Cervical cancer detection in pap smear whole slide images using convnet with transfer learning and progressive resizing. PeerJ Comput. Sci. **7**, e348 (2021)
2. Cao, M., Chen, W.: Interpretation on the global cancer statistics of globocan 2020. Zhongguo Yi Xue Qian Yan Za Zhi (Dian Zi Ban) **13**(3), 63–69 (2021)
3. Chankong, T., Theera-Umpon, N., Auephanwiriyakul, S.: Automatic cervical cell segmentation and classification in pap smears. Comput. Methods Program. Biomed. **113**(2), 539–556 (2014)
4. Chen, H., Dou, Q., Wang, X., Qin, J., Heng, P.A.: Mitosis detection in breast cancer histology images via deep cascaded networks. In: Thirtieth AAAI Conference on Artificial Intelligence (2016)
5. Dimauro, G.: Nasal cytology with deep learning techniques. Int. J. Med. Inform. **122**, 13–19 (2019)

6. Dosovitskiy, A., et al.: An image is worth 16x16 words: Transformers for image recognition at scale. arXiv preprint arXiv:2010.11929 (2020)
7. Girshick, R.: Fast r-cnn. In: Proceedings of the IEEE international conference on computer vision, pp. 1440–1448 (2015)
8. He, K., Zhang, X., Ren, S., Sun, J.: Deep residual learning for image recognition. In: Proceedings of the IEEE Conference on Computer Vision and Pattern Recognition, pp. 770–778 (2016)
9. Health, W.H.O.R., Organization, W.H., Diseases, W.H.O.C., Promotion, H.: Comprehensive cervical cancer control: a guide to essential practice. World Health Organization (2006)
10. Jantzen, J., Norup, J., Dounias, G., Bjerregaard, B.: Pap-smear benchmark data for pattern classification. Nature inspired Smart Information Systems (NiSIS 2005), pp. 1–9 (2005)
11. Jusman, Y., Isa, N.A.M., Ng, S.C., Kanafiah, S.N.A.M., Osman, N.A.A.: Quadratic of half ellipse smoothing technique for cervical cells ftir spectra in a screening system. Proc. Comput. Sci. **59**, 133–141 (2015)
12. Li, X., Li, Q., et al.: Detection and classification of cervical exfoliated cells based on faster r-cnn. In: 2019 IEEE 11th International Conference on Advanced Infocomm Technology (ICAIT), pp. 52–57. IEEE (2019)
13. Liang, Y., Pan, C., Sun, W., Liu, Q., Du, Y.: Global context-aware cervical cell detection with soft scale anchor matching. Comput. Methods Program. Biomed. **204**, 106061 (2021)
14. Liang, Y., Tang, Z., Yan, M., Chen, J., Liu, Q., Xiang, Y.: Comparison detector for cervical cell/clumps detection in the limited data scenario. Neurocomputing **437**, 195–205 (2021)
15. Lin, T.Y., Goyal, P., Girshick, R., He, K., Dollár, P.: Focal loss for dense object detection. In: Proceedings of the IEEE International Conference on Computer Vision, pp. 2980–2988 (2017)
16. Liu, L., Wang, Y., Ma, Q., Tan, L., Wu, Y., Xiao, J.: Artificial classification of cervical squamous lesions in thinprep cytologic tests using a deep convolutional neural network. Oncol. Lett. **20**(4), 1–1 (2020)
17. Prewitt, J.M., Mendelsohn, M.L.: The analysis of cell images. Annals New York Acad. Sci. **128**(3), 1035–1053 (1966)
18. Redmon, J., Divvala, S., Girshick, R., Farhadi, A.: You only look once: Unified, real-time object detection. In: Proceedings of the IEEE conference on computer vision and pattern recognition, pp. 779–788 (2016)
19. Redmon, J., Farhadi, A.: Yolov3: An incremental improvement. arXiv preprint arXiv:1804.02767 (2018)
20. Ren, S., He, K., Girshick, R., Sun, J.: Faster r-cnn: Towards real-time object detection with region proposal networks. In: Advances in Neural Information Processing Systems, vol. 28 (2015)
21. Shanthi, P., Faruqi, F., Hareesha, K., Kudva, R.: Deep convolution neural network for malignancy detection and classification in microscopic uterine cervix cell images. Asian Pacific J. Cancer Prevention: APJCP **20**(11), 3447 (2019)
22. Shi, X., Su, H., Xing, F., Liang, Y., Qu, G., Yang, L.: Graph temporal ensembling based semi-supervised convolutional neural network with noisy labels for histopathology image analysis. Medical Image Anal. **60**, 101624 (2020)
23. Simonyan, K., Zisserman, A.: Very deep convolutional networks for large-scale image recognition. arXiv preprint arXiv:1409.1556 (2014)
24. Szegedy, C., et al.: Going deeper with convolutions. In: Proceedings of the IEEE conference on computer vision and pattern recognition, pp. 1–9 (2015)

25. Tan, M., Pang, R., Le, Q.V.: Efficientdet: Scalable and efficient object detection. In: Proceedings of the IEEE/CVF Conference on Computer Vision and Pattern Recognition, pp. 10781–10790 (2020)
26. Teramoto, A., Tsukamoto, T., Kiriyama, Y., Fujita, H.: Automated classification of lung cancer types from cytological images using deep convolutional neural networks. In: BioMed Research International 2017 (2017)
27. Teramoto, A., et al.: Automated classification of benign and malignant cells from lung cytological images using deep convolutional neural network. Inform. Med. Unlocked **16**, 100205 (2019)
28. Vaswani, A., et al.: Attention is all you need. In: Advances in Neural Information Processing Systems, vol. 30 (2017)
29. Wei, Z., Cheng, S., Liu, X., Zeng, S.: An efficient cervical whole slide image analysis framework based on multi-scale semantic and spatial deep features. arXiv preprint arXiv:2106.15113 (2021)
30. William, W., Ware, A., Basaza-Ejiri, A.H., Obungoloch, J.: Cervical cancer classification from pap-smears using an enhanced fuzzy c-means algorithm. Inform. Med. Unlocked **14**, 23–33 (2019)
31. Woo, S., Park, J., Lee, J.Y., Kweon, I.S.: Cbam: Convolutional block attention module. In: Proceedings of the European Conference on Computer Vision (ECCV), pp. 3–19 (2018)
32. Xiang, Y., Sun, W., Pan, C., Yan, M., Yin, Z., Liang, Y.: A novel automation-assisted cervical cancer reading method based on convolutional neural network. Biocyberne. Biomed. Eng. **40**(2), 611–623 (2020)
33. Xue, Y., et al.: Synthetic augmentation and feature-based filtering for improved cervical histopathology image classification. In: Shen, D. (ed.) MICCAI 2019. LNCS, vol. 11764, pp. 387–396. Springer, Cham (2019). https://doi.org/10.1007/978-3-030-32239-7_43
34. Ye, H., Song, T., Zeng, X., Li, L., Hou, M., Xi, M.: Association between genital mycoplasmas infection and human papillomavirus infection, abnormal cervical cytopathology, and cervical cancer: a systematic review and meta-analysis. Archives Gynecol. Obstetrics **297**(6), 1377–1387 (2018). https://doi.org/10.1007/s00404-018-4733-5
35. Zeiler, Matthew D.., Fergus, Rob: Visualizing and understanding convolutional networks. In: Fleet, David, Pajdla, Tomas, Schiele, Bernt, Tuytelaars, Tinne (eds.) ECCV 2014. LNCS, vol. 8689, pp. 818–833. Springer, Cham (2014). https://doi.org/10.1007/978-3-319-10590-1_53
36. Zhang, C., et al.: DCCL: a benchmark for cervical cytology analysis. In: Suk, Heung-Il., Liu, Mingxia, Yan, Pingkun, Lian, Chunfeng (eds.) MLMI 2019. LNCS, vol. 11861, pp. 63–72. Springer, Cham (2019). https://doi.org/10.1007/978-3-030-32692-0_8
37. Zhang, L., et al.: Automation-assisted cervical cancer screening in manual liquid-based cytology with hematoxylin and eosin staining. Cytometry Part A **85**(3), 214–230 (2014)
38. Zhang, L., Lu, L., Nogues, I., Summers, R.M., Liu, S., Yao, J.: Deeppap: deep convolutional networks for cervical cell classification. IEEE J. Bbiomed. Health Inform. **21**(6), 1633–1643 (2017)

DSGRAE: Deep Sparse Graph Regularized Autoencoder for Anomaly Detection

Shicheng Li[1], Xiaoguo Yang[2], Haoming Zhang[1], Chaoyu Zheng[1], and Yugen Yi[1($\boxtimes$)]

[1] School of Software, Jiangxi Normal University, Nanchang, China
{lsc_learning,202140100838,chaoyuzheng,yiyg510}@jxnu.edu.cn
[2] Jiangxi Vocational College of Industry and Engineering, Pingxiang, China

Abstract. Anomaly detection aims to distinguish significant deviation data from an observed dataset, which has wide applications in various fields. Autoencoder (AE) is an effective approach, which maps the original data into latent feature space, and then identifies the anomalies with higher reconstruction errors. However, the performance of autoencoder-based approach heavily relies on feature representations in the latent space, which requires the feature representations be captured as much essential as possible. Therefore, a graph regularization constraint term is first introduced into Deep Autoencoder (DAE) to explore the geometric structure information. Moreover, to avoid the problem of overfitting and enhance the ability of feature representations, a constraint term is imposed and then a Deep Sparse Graph Regularized Autoencoder (DSGRAE) approach is proposed. Finally, we carry out extensive experiments on 14 widely used datasets and compare them with other state-of-the-art methods, which demonstrate the effectiveness of the proposed method.

Keywords: Anomaly detection · Deep Autoencoder · Graph regularization · DSGRAE

1 Introduction

With the rapid development of Internet and computer technologies, data have permeated everywhere to affect the development of the modern economy and society, which contains tremendous information and value. These massive collected data may contain many abnormal data, which do not conform to the expected behavior. For instance, an illegal traffic behavior in video surveillance [1], abnormal pixel blocks in retinal images [2], and suddenly tends of enormous network flow [3]. Therefore, how to identify abnormal data for further discovering the underlying information is very necessary, which is called as anomaly detection, also known as novelty detection or outlier detection. At present, the applications of anomaly detection has also increased in various areas such as cyber security [4], health risk [5] and financial risk management [6], etc. Thus, how to extract the important and significant information to detect anomalies from the collected data has becomes a challenging task [7].

Y. Xu et al. (Eds.): ML4CS 2022, LNCS 13656, pp. 254–265, 2023.
https://doi.org/10.1007/978-3-031-20099-1_21

Recently, deep learning has attracted enormous attention in various fields due to its tremendous capabilities of feature representation learning, such as anomaly detection [8]. Deep learning-based anomaly detection methods can be roughly divided into three categories, including end-to-end anomaly score learning, deep learning for feature extraction, and learning feature representations of normality [9]. The third type combines feature representation learning and anomaly score learning, making it flexible and versatile in practical applications [9]. It also can be further categorized into two groups, such as anomaly measure-dependent feature learning and generic feature learning [9]. The former introduces a designed measure into the objective function to learn specific feature representations in the low-dimensional subspace. Therefore, how to define and select the measure will affect the performance of feature representation. The latter aims to learn a generic feature representation while preserving the main regularity of underlying information [10]. Thus, the learned feature representation is still capable to detect anomalies even if the feature representation is not designed to be specific. Specially, generative adversarial network (GAN) and autoencoder (AE) are two representative approaches.

Compared with GAN, AE has a more straightforward structure and a concise theory, which can overcome the problems of difficult training and collapse to some extent. There are many autoencoder-based approaches have been proposed, which considered that abnormal instances are difficult to reconstruct from the low-dimensional latent space [11]. For example, RandNet [12] first introduced an ensemble learning to train a set of AE as ensemble components, and then randomly connected different architectures to reduce computational cost. Moreover, an adaptive sample strategy is incorporated into the ensemble framework for diversity enhancement and faster training. Inspired by robust principal component analysis (RPCA), Zhou et al. [13] proposed a robust deep AE (RDAE), which split input data into clean and noise or outlier parts to improve the robustness. RandNet and RDA are designed to deal with the data with simple structure and achieved better performance. In addition, many diverse models have been designed to handle complex data, such as sequence data [12, 14–18]. These methods ignore the geometric structure of data during feature representation learning. However, capturing the geometric structure of data is very important for feature representation learning. To overcome this drawback, Liao et al. [19] proposed graph regularized AE (GAE), which constructed a graph regularization to maintain local connections of the original data in feature representation spaces. By penalizing the weighted Frobenius norm of the latent representations' Jacobian matrix, the local property of feature representations can be captured well. Particularly, the graph regularization is only introduced into the last layer during the down sampling process of the encoder. Therefore, the representation and discriminative ability of feature representations are not well revealed. In this paper, we propose a deep sparse graph regularized AE (DSGRAE) for anomaly detection. First, different from GAE, the graph regularization term is incorporated into each layer of the encoder so that the feature map of each layer can preserve the local properties of the original data. Second, a sparse constraint term is imposed to avoid the problem of overfitting and enhance the ability of feature representations. Finally, a series of experiments have been conducted on 14 widely datasets for anomaly detection, and the proposed DSGRAE indicates a competitive performance compared with other methods.

The remainder of this paper is organized as follows. Section 2 briefly summarizes the preliminary knowledge. Section 3 describes the proposed method in detail and extensive experiments are conducted in Sect. 4. Finally, we present the conclusion and future work in Sect. 5.

2 Preliminary Knowledge

AE is a widely used algorithm that consists of an encoder and a decoder [20]. For convenience, here we just introduce the case that each layer is a feed-forward neural network. Suppose we have an encoder $e(\cdot)$, the encoding process can be formulated as follows:

$$
\begin{aligned}
H_1 &= f(W_1 X + b_1) \\
H_2 &= f(W_2 H_1 + b_2) \\
&\cdots \\
H_i &= f(W_i H_{i-1} + b_i)
\end{aligned}
\tag{1}
$$

where H_i is the feature representation for ith layer, W_i and b_i denote corresponding weight and bias, respectively. $f(\cdot)$ is a activation function and X represents the input original data. The whole process can be simplified as:

$$
H_l = e(X)
\tag{2}
$$

where l is the preset number of layers in encoder. Since AE always has a symmetrical structure, we suppose the decoder has the same number of layers.

Then, the decode process is defined as:

$$
\begin{aligned}
N_l &= f(M_l H_l + c_l) \\
N_{l-1} &= f(M_{l-1} U_l + c_{l-1}) \\
&\cdots \\
X' &= f(M_1 U_1 + c_1)
\end{aligned}
\tag{3}
$$

where U_i is the feature representation in the up sampling, M_i and c_i denote corresponding weight and bias, respectively. Let $d(\cdot)$ be a decoder and we can formulate the reconstructed input X' as:

$$
X' = d(H_l)
\tag{4}
$$

Here, Frobenius norm is used to measure the reconstruct error for learning effective feature representations, and the loss function can be represented as:

$$
\min_{\theta} J(X, X') = ||X - X'||_F^2
\tag{5}
$$

where $\theta = \{W, M, b, c\}$ are the parameters in the network.

3   The Proposed Method

AE aims to learn an effective latent feature representation and reconstruct the input data, and the obtained reconstruction only captures the limited essential information of original data, leading to poor performance for anomaly detection. To overcome this drawback, a deep sparse graph regularized AE (DSGRAE) is proposed for anomaly detection, which imposes a graph regularize term on each layer of the encoder to capture the comprehensive essential information of original data. Moreover, a constraint term is imposed to avoid the problem of overfitting and enhance the ability of feature representations. Figure 1 shows the structure of the proposed DSGRAE method.

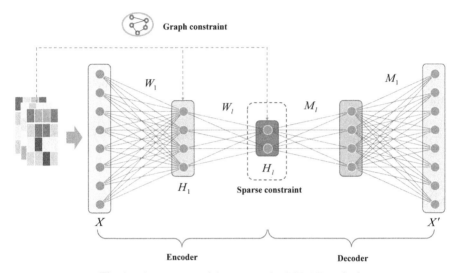

Fig. 1. The structure of the proposed DSGRAE method.

3.1   Graph Regularization Term

Manifold learning is an effective feature representation method, which assumes that the high-dimensional data lies on the low-dimensional manifold embedded in a high-dimensional space. To obtain better low-dimensional features, manifold learning methods preserve the local structure of data unchanged as much as possible when they map the high-dimensional data into a low-dimensional space. Therefore, the local geometrical information structure of the high-dimensional data is introduced into AE to increase the capability of feature representation. Similar to manifold learning methods, a graph regularization term is explored to depict the local geometrical information structure.

First, to depict the local geometrical structure of the high-dimensional data, a graph similarity matrix S is defined. There are several methods to compute the similarity matrix, which are defined as follows:

Binary weighting (BW)

$$S_{ij} = \begin{cases} 1 \text{ if nodes } i \text{ and } j \text{ are connected} \\ 0 \text{ otherwise} \end{cases} \tag{6}$$

Heat kernel weighting (HW)

$$S_{ij} = \begin{cases} e^{-\frac{\|x_i-x_j\|^2}{\sigma}} & \text{if nodes } i \text{ and } j \text{ are connected} \\ 0 & \text{otherwise} \end{cases} \tag{7}$$

where σ is a hyper parameter.

Cosine weighting (CW)

$$S_{ij} = \begin{cases} x_i^T x_j & \text{if nodes } i \text{ and } j \text{ are connected} \\ 0 & \text{otherwise} \end{cases} \tag{8}$$

Then, a graph regularization term is used to measure the smoothness, which is formulated as:

$$R_1 = \frac{1}{2} \sum_{i,j=1}^{n} ||h_i - h_j||^2 S_{ij} = tr(HDH^T) - tr(HSH^T)$$
$$= tr(HLH^T) \tag{9}$$

where $D_{ii} = \sum_j S_{ij}$ is a diagonal matrix, $L = D - S$ is a graph Laplacian matrix, $tr(\cdot)$ denotes the trace of the matrix, x_i, x_j, h_i, h_j represent the column vectors for X and H, respectively. By minimizing the graph regularization term, the local geometry information can be preserved well.

3.2 Sparse Constraint Term

To prevent overfitting and obtain more discriminative information of feature representations, a sparse constraint is added to regularize the hidden feature H^l. Given n input samples, we formulate the average activation $\hat{p}_j$ for j-th hidden neuron as:

$$\hat{p}_j = \frac{\sum_{i=1}^{n} z_{i,j}}{n} \tag{10}$$

where z is output of the hidden layer and $z_{i,j}$ denotes the j-th element for the i-th feature representation z_i, $j = 1, ..., d$. The sparse constraint term R_s is defined by using the Kullback-Leibler divergence, as follows:

$$R_s = \sum_{j=1}^{d} p \log \frac{p}{\hat{p}_j} + (1 - p) \log \frac{1 - p}{1 - \hat{p}_j} \tag{11}$$

where p is a pre-determined sparsity proportion.

3.3 Deep Sparse Graph Regularized Autoencoder

To guide AE to learn essential characteristics from original high-dimensional data, a graph regularization term is incorporated to constraint the feature representation. Then, we have the loss function:

$$\varphi = \min ||X - X'||_F^2 + Tr(H_i L H_i^T) \tag{12}$$

However, the graph regularization term is only introduced into the last layer of the encoder and the local geometrical structure in the shallow layer of the encoder is ignored. It is observed that AE could not capture the underlying manifold structure information well. Therefore, to capture the comprehensive essential information of original data, the graph regularize term is imposed on each layer of the encoder. Hence, the Eq. (13) can be redefined as:

$$\varphi = \min ||X - X'||_F^2 + \sum_{i=1}^{l} Tr(H_i L H_i^T) \tag{13}$$

In addition, a constraint term is imposed to avoid the overfitting and enhance the ability of feature representations. We rewrite the loss function as:

$$\varphi = \min ||X - X'||_F^2 + \sum_{i=1}^{l} Tr(H_i L H_i^T) + R_s \tag{14}$$

In this work, we adopt the back-propagation (BP) algorithm to optimize the loss function.

3.4 Anomaly Detection

To realize the anomaly detection task, it assumes that anomalies are considered to have different underlying characteristics and are hard to reconstruct. Consequently, the reconstruction error is exactly taken as the evaluation function to derive the anomaly score, which is defined as:

$$O = ||X - X'||_F^2 \tag{15}$$

For each observation, we calculate the anomaly score according to Eq. (15) and then sort the scores $\{O_i, i = 1, 2, ..., n\}$ in a descending order, where data points with high scores are flagged as anomalies. Unfortunately, the choice of one threshold value is a puzzled problem, and a simple solution is to flag N samples with top scores as anomalies. The detailed process of the proposed DSGRAE algorithm is described in Algorithm 1.

Algorithm 1 DSGRAE for anomaly detection
Input: original data X, unit number for each layer
Training the net 　　1: Calculate the graph Laplacian matrix L; 　　2: Initialize all the parameters for the model; 　　3: **for** i=1:2l **do** 　　4: 　Update all the trainable parameters W and M using BP algorithm 　　5: **end for** **Anomaly detection** 　　1: Calculate the anomaly score O_i by Eq. 15 　　2: Sort the anomaly score O_i in descending order 　　3: Flag top N samples with higher scores as anomalies
Output: the anomalies $\{x^a\}$

4 Experiments

In this section, we conduct extensive experiments to validate the performance of DSGRAE on the anomaly detection task. The comparison experiments with state-of-the-art methods demonstrate our proposed method obtains the competitive performance.

4.1 Benchmark Datasets

In the experiments, 14 benchmark datasets are utilized to evaluate the comparison performance. All datasets are preprocessed in terms of the route of literature [21], and characteristics are summarized in Table 1.

4.2 Evaluation Criteria

As a common metric in anomaly detection, the precision at N ($P@N$) is adopted for performance evaluation in this study. $P@N$ is straightforward and easy to understand, which is defined as follows:

$$P@N = \frac{\#\{o \in O | rank(o) \leq N\}}{N}. \tag{16}$$

Given a dataset DB, where $O \subset DB$ is an anomaly set and $N = |O|$ is the number of anomalies. $P@N$ indicates the percentage of true anomalies in the top N sorted predicted values. In our experiments, we flag top N instances as anomalies based on the corresponding sorted anomaly score set $\{O_i, i = 1, 2, ..., n\}$ for all methods. When the number of anomalies in each dataset is constant, we just report the true detected anomalies.

Table 1. The details of benchmark datasets

Dataset	Dimension	Anomalies	Samples	Contamination (%)
Annthyroid	21	347	7200	4.82
Arrhythmia	259	12	450	2.67
Cardiotocography	21	86	2126	4.05
Glass	7	9	214	4.21
HeartDisease	13	7	270	2.59
Ionosphere	32	126	351	35.90
Lymphography	19	6	148	4.05
Parkinson	22	5	195	2.56
Page Blocks	10	99	5473	1.81
Pima	8	26	768	3.39
Spambase	57	280	4601	6.09
WBC	9	10	454	2.20
WDBC	30	10	367	2.72
WPBC	33	47	198	23.74

4.3 Experimental Results

We conduct three experiments to demonstrate the effectiveness of DSGRAE. In the first experiment, we choose GAE and ordinary AE as the compared method to compare the effectiveness of the multiple graph regularizers. In addition, to explore the effects of the graph similarity matrix, we test three weighting models and add them for comparison. It is well known that hyperparameters have a great impact on the performance, and most deep learning methods struggle in adjusting these parameters, which leads to difficulties in applying. The results are listed in Table 2, which indicates that the proposed method achieves superior performance in most of the datasets. Compared with GAE and AE, the proposed DSGRAE have more effective graph regularization in the encoding process, and the deep feature representations is more discriminative for enhancing the detection performance. From Table 2, we can see that GAE performs better than ordinary AE, which demonstrates the significance of graph regularization again. Among the three weighting approaches, cosine similarity and heat kernel perform exactly the same, and the performance of binary distance is slightly lacking in WPBC.

Table 2. Comparisons with GAE and AE

Datasets	DSGRAE (BW)	DSGRAE (HW)	DSGRAE (CW)	GAE	AE
Annthyroid	13	13	13	11	7
Arrhythmia	3	3	3	3	2
Cardiotocography	29	29	29	29	27
Glass	1	1	1	0	0
HeartDisease	4	4	4	3	2
Ionosphere	75	75	75	74	63
Lymphography	5	5	5	2	1
Parkinson	2	2	2	1	0
Page Blocks	19	19	19	19	12
Pima	2	2	2	1	2
Spambase	50	50	50	47	28
WBC	8	8	8	8	6
WDBC	6	6	6	6	3
WPBC	9	10	10	6	7

In the second experiment, two distance-based methods, local minimum spanning tree (LoMST) and connectivity outlier factor (COF) are used to indicate the effectiveness of obtained deep feature representation. LoMST model the data samples as a network of nodes based on minimum spanning tree, and flag the less connected one as anomalous. COF uses the shortest path connecting the k neighbors as the "chaining distance", which quantify the "isolativity" and overcome the shortcoming of local outlier factor (LOF). We take the outputs of the encoder as the input data and feed them into LoMST and COF respectively, to detect anomalies in low-dimensional space. The results are shown in Table 3, which presents the comparison results of LoMST and COF. It is can be seen that although LoMST can achieve fine performance, the reconstruction error-based approach such as the proposed DSGRAE, has impressive superiority.

Finally, we also test other distance-based methods (i.e., Isolate Forests (IF) and LOF) using the original data instead of low-dimensional feature representations to further evaluate the effectiveness of our proposed structure. The experimental results are summarized in Table 4. From Table 4, we find that DSGRAE, which use the low-dimensional feature representations, achieve better performance in most datasets than IF and LOF, which use the original high-dimensional data. This result demonstrates the superiority of the low-dimensional feature representation obtained by DSGRAE. It is proved that the feature representation can capture more essential information and help to detect anomalies.

Table 3. Comparisons with two distance-based methods

Datasets	DSGRAE	LoMST	COF
Annthyroid	13	17	**31**
Arrhythmia	3	**4**	**4**
Cardiotocography	**29**	17	15
Glass	1	**3**	1
HeartDisease	**4**	2	1
Ionosphere	75	**89**	87
Lymphography	**5**	3	3
Parkinson	**2**	1	1
Page Blocks	19	**24**	**24**
Pima	**2**	1	1
Spambase	**50**	48	39
WBC	**8**	5	5
WDBC	6	6	6
WPBC	10	**12**	10

Table 4. Comparisons with the other baseline approaches

Datasets	DSGRAE	IF	LOF
Annthyroid	13	12	**26**
Arrhythmia	**3**	**3**	2
Cardiotocography	**29**	12	17
Glass	1	1	1
HeartDisease	**4**	0	1
Ionosphere	**75**	33	36
Lymphography	**5**	2	1
Parkinson	**2**	1	2
Page Blocks	**19**	15	9
Pima	**2**	1	0
Spambase	**50**	31	28
WBC	**8**	3	3
WDBC	**6**	2	3
WPBC	**10**	4	1

5   Conclusions

In this paper, we propose a novel unsupervised model named deep sparse graph regularized autoencoder (DSGRAE) for anomaly detection. Different from the existed model, the proposed DSGRAE model introduces a graph regularization term into each layer of the encoder to capture more essential information. Moreover, a constraint term is imposed on the bottleneck to avoid the overfitting and enhance the ability of feature representations. Finally, we carry out extensive experiments on 14 common datasets, and the experiment results demonstrate that our method can achieve better performance than compared methods. In future works, we will focus on the decoding process with graph regularization.

Acknowledgment. This work is supported in part by grants from the National Natural Science Foundation of China (No. 62062040), the Outstanding Youth Project of Jiangxi Natural Science Foundation (No. 20212ACB212003), the Jiangxi Province Key Subject Academic and Technical Leader Funding Project (No. 20212BCJ23017).

References

1. Xie, X., Wang, C., Chen, S., et al.: Real-time illegal parking detection system based on deep learning. In: Proceedings of the 2017 International Conference on Deep Learning Technologies, pp. 23–27 (2017)
2. Kaur, M., Kamra, A.: Detection of retinal abnormalities in fundus image using transfer learning networks. Soft Computing 1-15 (2021)
3. Shone, N., Ngoc, T.N., Phai, V.D., et al.: A deep learning approach to network intrusion detection. IEEE Trans. Emerging Topics Computational Intelligence 2(1), 41–50 (2018)
4. Pan, K., Palensky, P., Esfahani, P.M.: From static to dynamic anomaly detection with application to power system cyber security. IEEE Trans. Power Syst. 35(2), 1584–1596 (2019)
5. Venkataramanaiah, B., Kamala, J.: ECG signal processing and KNN classifier-based abnormality detection by VH-doctor for remote cardiac healthcare monitoring. Soft. Comput. 24(22), 17457–17466 (2020)
6. Pourhabibi, T., Ong, K.L., Kam, B.H., et al.: Fraud detection: a systematic literature review of graph-based anomaly detection approaches. Decis. Support Syst. 133, 113303 (2020)
7. Boukerche, A., Zheng, L., Alfandi, O.: Outlier detection: methods, models, and classification. ACM Comput. Surv. 53(3), 1–37 (2020)
8. Pang, G., Shen, C., Cao, L., et al.: Deep learning for anomaly detection: a review. ACM Comput. Surv. 54(2), 1–38 (2021)
9. Chalapathy, R., Chawla, S.: Deep Learning for Anomaly Detection: A Survey. arXiv preprint arXiv:1901.03407 (2019)
10. Lu, W., Cheng, Y., Xiao, C., et al.: Unsupervised sequential outlier detection with deep architectures. IEEE Trans. Image Process. 26(9), 4321–4330 (2017)
11. Hyperspectral image classification using k-sparse denoising autoencoder and spectral–restricted spatial characteristics. Applied Soft Computing 74, 693–708 (2019)
12. Chen, J., Sathe, S., Aggarwal, C., et al.: Outlier detection with autoencoder ensembles. In: Proceedings of the 2017 SIAM International Conference on Data Mining. Society for Industrial and Applied Mathematics, pp. 90–98 (2017)

13. Zhou, C., Paffenroth, R.C.: Anomaly detection with robust deep autoencoders. In: Proceedings of the 23rd ACM SIGKDD International Conference on Knowledge Discovery and Data Mining. pp. 665–674 (2017)

14. Xu, D., Ricci, E., Yan, Y., et al.: Learning Deep Representations of Appearance and Motion for Anomalous Event Detection. arXiv preprint arXiv: 1510.01553 (2015)

15. Hasan, M., Choi, J., Neumann, J., et al.: Learning temporal regularity in video sequences. In: Proceedings of the IEEE Conference on Computer Vision and Pattern Recognition, pp. 733–742 (2016)

16. Zhang, C., Song, D., Chen, Y., et al.: A deep neural network for unsupervised anomaly detection and diagnosis in multivariate time series data. Proceedings of the AAAI Conference on Artificial Intelligence **33**(01), 1409–1416 (2019)

17. Malhotra, P., Ramakrishnan, A., Anand, G., et al.: LSTM-Based Encoder-Decoder for Multi-Sensor Anomaly Detection. arXiv preprint arXiv: 1607.00148 (2016)

18. Luo, W., Liu, W., Gao, S.: Remembering history with convolutional LSTM for anomaly detection. In: 2017 IEEE International Conference on Multimedia and Expo, pp. 439-444 (2017)

19. Liao, Y., Wang, Y., Liu, Y.: Graph regularized auto-encoders for image representation. IEEE Trans. Image Process. **26**(6), 2839–2852 (2016)

20. Zhai, J., Zhang, S., Chen, J., et al.: Autoencoder and its various variants. In: 2018 IEEE International Conference on Systems, Man, and Cybernetics. IEEE, pp. 415–419 (2018)

21. Campos, G.O., et al.: On the evaluation of unsupervised outlier detection: measures, datasets, and an empirical study. Data Min. Knowl. Disc. **30**(4), 891–927 (2016)

A Lattice-Based Aggregate Signature Based on Revocable Identity

Yang Cui[1], Huayu Cheng[1], Fengyin Li[1(✉)], and Domenico Santaniello[2]

[1] Qufu Normal University, Qufu, China
lfyin318@qfnu.edu.cn
[2] University of Salerno, Fisciano, Italy
dsantaniello@unisa.it

Abstract. In the practical application of identity-based aggregated signature schemes, the problems of singer's key loss and signer's identity invalidation often occur. This makes the identity-based aggregate signature scheme need to realize the revocation of the signer, and the existing revocation of identities method needs to rebuild the system master key. Combined with the revocation method proposed by Boldyreva [1], this paper improves the aggregated signature scheme to realize the dynamic revocation of singer's identities. At the same time, in order to deal with the threat brought by the development of quantum computer to the traditional cryptosystem, a lattice-based aggregate signature scheme based on revocable identity is proposed in this paper.

Keywords: Revocable identity based · Lattice · Aggregated signature

1 Introduction

Aggregate signatures can effectively reduce the computational overhead of data authentication , and are especially suitable for resource-constrained and computationally inefficient working environments [2]. The aggregated signature technology can compress the signed messages of multiple users into one signed message for processing, thereby improving the authentication efficiency of the message. Aggregate signature achieves compression of signature size and reduction of signature verification times, so aggregated signature is a signature scheme that can effectively improve time efficiency and reduce communication overhead. Li et al. proposed an efficient model-heterogenous aggregation training scheme, which utilizes Knowledge Distillation (KD) for information aggregation [4].

Most of the existing aggregate signature schemes are based on large integer factorization and discrete logarithm problems, and these problems are no longer safe in the quantum computer environment (Shor proposed a quantum algorithm that can effectively solve large integer factorization and discrete logarithm problem). Therefore, quantum-resistant cryptography has received extensive attention. Lattice cryptography is a recognized quantum-resistant cryptography. This paper attempts to construct an aggregated signature scheme based on the RSIS

© The Author(s), under exclusive license to Springer Nature Switzerland AG 2023
Y. Xu et al. (Eds.): ML4CS 2022, LNCS 13656, pp. 266–274, 2023.
https://doi.org/10.1007/978-3-031-20099-1_22

problem on lattice to ensure the security of our scheme in the quantum computer environment.

Lattice-based cryptosystems, like any public key cryptosystem, suffer from the user revocation problem. Identity-based cryptography (IBE) was first proposed by Shamir in 1984 [9]. IBE solves the problem of high public key certificate management overhead, but when IBE revokes a user's identity, it needs to update the private keys of all legitimate users. This revocation mechanism requires multiple transmissions of the user's private key in the secure channel, which increases communication overhead and computational overhead. Boldyreva et al. proposed an IBE scheme that can efficiently revoke user identities by publishing key updates over an open channel [1]. Tsai et al. proposed the first RIBS (Revocable Identity Based Signature) scheme, which solved the problem of user revocation in the signature scheme. Xiang et al. firstly propose a lattice-based RIBS scheme [10]. Li et al. propose a new SSE(Searchable Symmetric Encryption) scheme by developing the hidden pointer technique (HPT), and their SSE scheme has forward search privacy [5].

Aiming at the problems of high cost of identity revocation, quantum attack and low efficiency of identity authentication in resource-constrained environment, this paper introduces the user revocation method based on KUNode algorithm into the identity aggregation signature scheme. We propose a lattice-based aggregate signature scheme based on revocable identity. The security of the proposed scheme can be reduced to the difficulty of the RSIS problem on the lattice, so the proposed scheme can resist quantum attacks. The security of the proposed scheme has been proved in the random oracle model.Efficiency analysis shows that the scheme in this paper can improve the efficiency of signature verification, and the aggregated signature has the advantage of space efficiency compared to the single signature before aggregation.

Contribution

For the first time, we propose a lattice-based aggregate signature based on revocable identity. Through the proposed scheme, we realize the aggregation of different message signatures by different signers, reduce the size of the signature and improve the verification efficiency.

2 Preliminary

2.1 Lattice

If $B = (b_1, b_2, \cdots, b_m)$ by R^n is composed of linearly independent vectors, then the lattice $L(B)$ is defined as the linear combination of all integer coefficients of this group of vectors, denoted as

$$\Lambda = L(B) = \{\sum_{i=1}^{m} x_i b_i x_i \in Z\} \tag{1}$$

Let n be the dimension of the lattice $L(B)$, m is the rank, and B is a set of bases of the lattice [8].

2.2   RSIS

Given a security parameter n and a uniform random matrix $A = [a_1, a_2, \cdots, a_m] \in R_q^{1 \times m}$, find a solution u that satisfies the following conditions non-zero vector $u = (u_1, u_2, \cdots, u_m)^T \in R^m$,

$$Au = 0 \quad \mod q, ||x||_\infty \leq \beta. \tag{2}$$

2.3   Basic Algorithm in Lattice Signature

In 2008, Gentry et al. proposed a variety of "trapdoor" cryptographic tool [3], which are used by most lattice signature schemes. We use an improved trapdoor algorithm MP12 [7]. The trapgen algorithm can generate a one-way function and the corresponding trapdoor information (A, T_A), where A is the trapdoor problem matrix, and T_A is the trapdoor information. In the case of only having A, u and no trapdoor information, it is computationally infeasible to obtain an e that satisfies the condition $Ae = u$. In the case of having A, u and having trapdoor information T_A, it is simple to computer an e that satisfies the condition $Ae = u$.

TrapGen. Let n be a positive integer, $q \geq 2, m > 5n \log q$, there is a polynomial time trapgen algorithm $TrapGen(q, n)$, output $A \in Z_q^{n \times m}$ and $T_A \in Z_q^{n \times m}$, where A satisfies statistical uniformity over the range, T_A is the trapdoor basis of the lattice $\Lambda_q^\perp(A)$, And satisfy $T_A \leq O(n \log q)$.

SamplePre. Let n be a positive integer, $q \geq 2, m > 5n \log q$, $A \in Z_q^{nm}$, $T_A \in Z_q^{nm}$ and T_A is the trapdoor basis of the lattice $\Lambda_q^\perp(A)$, the Gaussian parameter $s \leq T_A \times \omega(\sqrt{\log m})$. $u \in R_q^n$ satisfies the following conditions:

- $\Pr[x > s\sqrt{m}x \in D_{(\Lambda_q^\perp(A), s)}] \leq negl(n)$ (negligible probability).
- There exists a polynomial-time preimage sampling algorithm $Sample$ (A, T_A, u, s), which outputs a lattice vector e that is statistically close to $D_{\Lambda_q^\perp(A), s}$ in $\Lambda_q^\perp(A)$.

Rejection Sampling. Rejection sampling was first proposed by Lyubasevsky [6], and the method was subsequently applied to most lattice signature schemes. In the signing process, the signature is output with a certain probability to make sure the distribution of the signature and the private key of the signature are independent of each other. By the above method, the private key of the signature can be effectively prevented from leaking.

The following Definition 1 shows that the signature output using the rejection sampling algorithm is indistinguishable from the original signature algorithm output. That is, for any $v \in Z^m, \sigma = \omega(v\sqrt{\log m})$, there is $Pr[\frac{D_\sigma^m(z)}{D_{v,\alpha}^m(z)} = O(1)$: $z_m^D] = 1 - 2^{\omega(\log m)}$.

Definition 1. *Let* $V = v \in Z^m : v < t, \sigma = \omega(t\sqrt{\log m}), h : VR$ *be a probability distribution , then there is a constant* $M = O(1)$, *so that the statistical distance of the output distribution of the following two algorithms is less than* $2^{-\omega(\log m)}/M$.

Algorithm 1. *Sampling* $v \leftarrow h; z \leftarrow D^m_{v,\alpha}$: *with probability* $\min(\frac{D^m_\alpha(z)}{MD^m_{v,\alpha}(z)}, 1)$ *output* (z, v).

Algorithm 2. *Sample* $v \leftarrow h; z \leftarrow D^m_\alpha$: *Output* (z, v) *with probability* $1/M$.

The probability that Algorithm 1 has an output is at least $\frac{1-2^{-\omega(\log m)}}{M}$.

2.4   KUNode Algorithm.

Boldyreva et al. proposed an IBE scheme that can efficiently revoke user identities by publishing KeyUpdates over an open channel. At the same time, Boldyreva proposed a KUNode algorithm implementation to improve the efficiency of KeyUpdate production for legitimate users. The algorithm takes binary tree Tr, revocation list rl and time T as input, and outputs the minimum node set KU^T containing all legal user ancestor nodes. If a user's ancestor node or itself is in KU^T, the user is considered to be a legitimate user. The specific algorithm steps are shown in Fig. 1.

$KUNodes(Tr, rl, T)$
    $X, Y \leftarrow \emptyset$
    $\forall (v_i, t_i) \in rl$
        if $t_i \le T$ then add $Path(v_i)$ to X
    $\forall x \in X$
        if $x_l \notin X$ then add x_l to Y
        if $x_r \notin X$ then add x_r to Y
    If $Y \notin \emptyset$ then root to Y
    Return Y

Fig. 1. KUNode Algorithm

3   Lattice-Based Aggregated Signature Scheme Based on Revocable Identity

In this section we propose a lattice-based aggregated signature scheme based on revocable identities. First, we introduce the workflow of the scheme in this paper. Second, we present the lattice-based aggregation signature scheme based on revocable identity proposed in this paper. Through our scheme, the aggregation of different message signatures by different signers is realized, which reduces the size of the signature and improves the verification efficiency. At the same time, our scheme has an efficient user revocation method and the ability to resist quantum attacks.

3.1   Revocable Identity-Based Aggregate Signature Model

The revocable identity-based aggregate signature scheme proposed in this paper realizes the dynamic revocation of user identities through PKG server publishing KeyUpdate. In Fig. 2, user 3 is a legal user, and the KeyUpdate contains the information of user 3, so user 3 can generate a signature key to complete the signature of the message. In Fig. 3, the legal identity of user 3 is invalid, and the KeyUpdate issued by PKG no longer contains the information required by user 3 to generate the signature key, even if user 3 receives the newly released KeyUpdate, the signature key cannot be generated. From this we achieve dynamic revocation of identity.

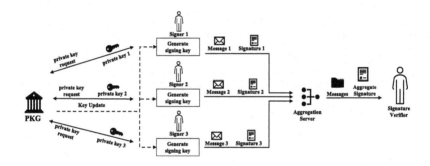

Fig. 2. Signature process before revocation of signer 3

3.2   Our Aggregate Signature Scheme

In the scheme of this paper, we set the following parameters: n, m are positive integers, q is a prime number, α is a positive real number that is a parameter of Gaussian distribution, $H_c : \{0,1\}^* \rightarrow Z_q^m, H : \{0,1\}^* \rightarrow Z_q^n$ is a hash function, $L_{id} = \{id_0, \ldots, id_{|L_{id}|}\}$ is the signer identity list, $rl = \{(id_0, T_0), \ldots, (id_n, T_n)\}$, is revocation user list, T_{cu} is the current time.

- $Setup(1^\lambda) \rightarrow (mpk, msk)$: PKG runs the TrapGen function to output trapdoor $T_A \in Z^{m \times m}$ and matrix $A \in Z_q^{n \times m}$. Set $msk = T_A, mpk = A$, the public parameters of the PKG broadcasting system and the master public key.

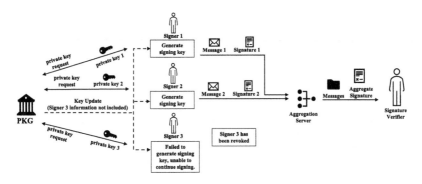

Fig. 3. Signature process after revocation of signer 3

- $GenSK(msk, mpk, id) \rightarrow (sk_{id})$: after receiving the signer's private key request, PKG enters the signer identity $id \in L_{id}$ and the system master key pair, and computers $u_{id} = H(id)$. Run the SamplePre function to output

$$e_{id} = SamplePre(A, T_A, u_{id}, \alpha) \tag{3}$$

Output the private key corresponding to the signer identity $sk_{id} = e_{id} \in Z_q^n$. Finally, the private key is transmitted to the signer through a secure channel, and the signer identity id acts as the signer's public key.

- $KeyUpdate(msk, mpk, rl_T) \rightarrow (ku^T)$: When the user list needs to be adjusted, PKG runs the KUNodes algorithm, inputs $msk, mpk, rl_{T_{cu}}$, and outputs the minimum set of legal users $KU^{T_{cu}} = KUNode(L_{id}, rl_T, T_{cu})$, the legitimacy of all user identities can be judged by $KU^{T_{cu}}$. PKG generates KeyUpdates for all valid $userid_{\theta_j}$:
  - PKG computer $u_{id_i, T^{cu}} = H(id_i, T^{cu})$.
  - PKG runs the SamplePre function output: $e_{\theta_j, T^{cu}} = SamplePre(A, T_A, u_{\theta, T^{cu}}, \alpha)$.
  - The final output KeyUpdate $ku^T\{e_{\theta_0, T}, e_{\theta_1, T}, \cdots, e_{\theta_{L_{id}}, T}\}, e_{\theta_j, T} \in Z_n^q$, PKG sends the KeyUpdate ku^T to all signers.

- $GenSignKey(sk_{id}, ku^T) \rightarrow (sik \ or \ \perp)$: after the signer receives the KeyUpdate issued by PKG, θ_j finds $e_{\theta_j, T}$ from ku^T, and computers the signature key $sik = e_{\theta_j} + e_{theta_j, T}$. In this stage, if the signer's identity has been revoked, the $e_{id, T}$ corresponding to the identity cannot be found in the KeyUpdate, and the algorithm will be exited directly.

- $Sign(mpk, sik, m) \rightarrow \sigma$: the signature algorithm is executed by the signer. When the signer needs to sign the message m, run the algorithm to generate the signature σ
  - Randomly choose $y \leftarrow D_\alpha^m$.
  - computer $r \leftarrow Ay, c \leftarrow H_c(m, r, T_{cu})$.
  - $z \leftarrow sik^T \cdot c + y$
  - Output the signature with the probability of $\min(\frac{D_\alpha^m(z)}{M \cdot D_{sik \cdot c}^m}(z))$, $\sigma = (z, r, c)$.

- $Verify(\sigma_i, mpk, id_i) \rightarrow$ (0 or 1): the verification algorithm is executed by the verification signer, and the verification signer determines whether the signature is legal or not according to the following two steps.
    - Verify $\|z_i\| \leq \alpha\sqrt{m_i}$, output 0 if not satisfied.
    - Whether c_i is equal to $H_c(A \cdot z_i - id_i \cdot c_i, m_i, T)$. Output 0 if it is not satisfied, otherwise output 1.
- $AggSign(\sigma_j, m_j) \rightarrow \Sigma$: the aggregation server runs the aggregation signature algorithm, and the signer sends the signature and message that needs to be aggregated to the aggregation server. The aggregation server follows the steps below to generate the aggregation signature Σ.
    - Computer $Z = \sum_i^{L_{id}} z_i (= \sum_i^{L_{id}} sik_i^T \cdot c_i + y_i)$.
    - The signature aggregator packs c_i and r_i in the signature, $C = (c_0, c_1, \cdots, c_{L_{id}})$, $R = (r_0, r_1, \cdots, r_{L_{id}})$.
    - Computer $\Sigma = (Z, C, R)$. $M = (m_0, m_1, \ldots, m_{L_{id}})$.
- $AggVerify(\Sigma, mpk, L_{id}) \rightarrow$ (0 or 1): the verifier verifies the aggregated signature and message, and the aggregated message only needs one verification to confirm the correctness of all messages.
    - Computer $u_{id_j} = H(id_j)$, $u_{id_j,T} = H(id_j, T)$, the value range of j is $0 \leq j \leq \|L_{id}\|$.
    - Verify that the equation holds $A \cdot Z \stackrel{?}{=} \sum_i^{L_{id}} (u_{id_i} + u_{id_i,T}) \cdot c_i + \sum_i^{L_{id}} r_i$. If not hold, output 0, otherwise output 1.

4   Performance Analysis

4.1   Correctness

The verifier uses the master public key A and the user public key id_i in the signer list L_{id} to verify the aggregated signature, and the verifier computers the $(u_{id_i} + u_{id_i,T})$, then computer $\sum_i^{L_{id}} (u_{id_i} + u_{id_i,T}) \cdot$ according to C, R in the aggregated signature $c_i + \sum_i^{L_{id}} r_i$. According to the definition of the pre-image sampling algorithm, $u_{id_i} = A \cdot e_{id_i}$, $u_{id_i,T} = A \cdot e_{id_i,T}$, and $sik_i = e_{id_i} + e_{id_i,T}$, $r_i \leftarrow Ay_i$. So $\sum_i^{L_{id}} (u_{id_i} + u_{id_i,T}) \cdot c_i + \sum_i^{L_{id}} r_i$ and $A \cdot \sum_i^{L_{id}} (sik_i \cdot c_i + y)$ is equivalent. The aggregated signature is $\Sigma = (Z, C, R)$, where $C = (c_0, c_1, \ldots, c_{L_{id}})$, $R = (r_0, r_1, \ldots, r_{L_{id}})$, L_{id} is the list of signers. The calculation process of Z in the aggregation process is $Z = \sum_i^{L_{id}} z_i$. Since the single signature is composed of $z_i \leftarrow sik_i^T \cdot c_i + y_i$, Z in the aggregate signature is equivalent to $\sum_i^{L_{id}} (sik_i \cdot c_i + y)$. To sum up, the result generated by running the signature aggregation signature scheme correctly satisfies $A \cdot Z = \sum_i^{L_{id}} (u_{id_i} + u_{id_i,T}) \cdot c_i + \sum_i^{L_{id}} r_i$.

The correctness of our scheme is proved by the transformation relation of the following equations:

$$A \cdot Z = A \cdot \sum_i^{L_{id}} z \tag{4}$$

$$= A \cdot \sum_i^{L_{id}} sik \cdot c + y \tag{5}$$

$$= \sum_i^{L_{id}} A \cdot (e_{id_i} + e_{id_i,T}) \cdot c_i + \sum_i^{L_{id}} A \cdot y \tag{6}$$

$$= \sum_i^{L_{id}} (u_{id_i} + u_{id_i,T}) \cdot c_i + \sum_i^{L_{id}} r_i \tag{7}$$

4.2   Efficiency Analysis

This section will analyze the efficiency of the revocable identity-based lattice-based aggregate signature proposed in this paper through theoretical analysis and specific experiments. The space efficiency analysis is mainly carried out through theoretical analysis, and the time efficiency analysis is mainly carried out through experiments.

Comparing the total signature size without aggregated signature and the aggregated signature size. In this paper, the aggregated signature size does not grow linearly with the number of signers. If aggregated signatures are not used, the total signature size will increase approximately linearly with the number of signers. The asymptotic complexity analysis is as follows(NU is the number of signers) Table 1.

Table 1. Signature size analysis after using aggregated signatures

Scheme	Size		
	Public key	Private key	Total message
Aggregate signatures	$n \log q$	$2n \log q$	NU $\times (m+n) \log q + m \log q$
Single signature	$n \log q$	$2n \log q$	NU $\times (2m+n) \log q$

5   Conclusion

Based on the lattice difficulty problem (RSIS), this paper introduces the user revocation method based on the KUNode algorithm into the identity-based aggregated signature scheme, and proposes a revocable identity-based lattice-based aggregated signature scheme. Our proposed scheme can protect the integrity of aggregated messages in a quantum computer environment, and it is proved in the random oracle model that its security can be reduced to the difficulty of the RSIS problem. At the same time, due to the realization of signature aggregation, the signature size of our scheme is relatively small and the verification time is short.

References

1. Boldyreva, A., Goyal, V., Kumar, V.: Identity-based encryption with efficient revocation. In: Proceedings of the 14th ACM Conference on Computer and Communications Security, CCS 2008, ACM Press, 2008. ACM (2012). https://www.microsoft.com/en-us/research/publication/identity-based-encryption-efficient-revocation/
2. Boneh, D., Gentry, C., Lynn, B., Shacham, H.: Aggregate and verifiably encrypted signatures from bilinear maps. In: Biham, E. (ed.) EUROCRYPT 2003. LNCS, vol. 2656, pp. 416–432. Springer, Heidelberg (2003). https://doi.org/10.1007/3-540-39200-9_26
3. Gentry, C., Peikert, C., Vaikuntanathan, V.: Trapdoors for hard lattices and new cryptographic constructions. In: Proceedings of the Fortieth Annual ACM Symposium on Theory of Computing. pp. 197–206. STOC '08, Association for Computing Machinery, New York, NY, USA (2008). https://doi.org/10.1145/1374376.1374407
4. Hu, L., Yan, H., Li, L., Pan, Z., Liu, X., Zhang, Z.: Mhat: an efficient model-heterogenous aggregation training scheme for federated learning. Inf. Sci. **560**, 493–503 (2021)
5. Li, J., et al.: Searchable symmetric encryption with forward search privacy. IEEE Trans. Dependable Secure Comput. **18**(1), 460–474 (2019)
6. Lyubashevsky, V.: Lattice signatures without trapdoors. vol. 2011, p. 537 (2011). https://doi.org/10.1007/978-3-642-29011-4_43
7. Micciancio, D., Peikert, C.: Trapdoors for lattices: simpler, tighter, faster, smaller. In: Pointcheval, D., Johansson, T. (eds.) EUROCRYPT 2012. LNCS, vol. 7237, pp. 700–718. Springer, Heidelberg (2012). https://doi.org/10.1007/978-3-642-29011-4_41
8. Peikert, C., et al.: A decade of lattice cryptography. Found. Trends® Theor. Comput. Sci. **10**(4), 283–424 (2016)
9. Shamir, A.: Identity-based cryptosystems and signature schemes. In: Blakley, G.R., Chaum, D. (eds.) Adv. Cryptol., pp. 47–53. Springer, Berlin Heidelberg, Berlin, Heidelberg (1985). https://doi.org/10.1007/3-540-39568-7_5
10. Xinyin, X.: Adaptive secure revocable identity-based signature scheme over lattices. Comput. Eng. **10**, 25 (2015)

Research and Design of an Emergency Supply Assurance Monitoring System in the Post-epidemic Context

Yongbo Li[✉]

Guangdong University of Science and Technology, Dongguan 523083, Guangdong, China
17039636@qq.com

Abstract. At present, the COVID-19 epidemic is still ravaging the world, and the domestic epidemic is still recurring and continues to affect people's life and work. The research and design of an emergency supply assurance monitoring system in response to the epidemic and other emergencies, which provides the competent authorities with monitoring alert and trend data of supply, demand and price of essential goods market, is of great significance to stabilize people's basic essential goods materials. Based on the data of essential goods under epidemic, the system carries out the construction and application of monitoring and warning model and RNN-SARIMA hybrid model. Through the research and design of the system, monitoring and warning of abnormal fluctuations of essential goods and predicting price trends are realized.

Keywords: Monitoring alerts · Indicators of daily necessities · RNN-SARIMA hybrid model

1 Introduction

With the normalized development of the domestic epidemic, the market supply, demand and prices of important livelihood commodities such as grain, oil, meat, eggs, vegetables, and milk, and other related supplies for epidemic prevention, which are closely related to people's lives, are changing every day. The impact of the work is very large. In order to monitor and warn the abnormal fluctuations of the daily necessities market in time for emergencies such as the epidemic, through research and design of an emergency supply guarantee monitoring system, a monitoring and warning model for daily necessities is constructed, and RNN-SARIMA hybrid is used. It monitors, warns and forecasts the supply and demand ratio and price trend of daily necessities, and provides powerful emergency insurance reference data for the government and relevant departments to make quick decisions.

1.1 Research Background and Purpose

Research Significance. The previous international epidemic continued to spread, the epidemic situation in some parts of the country was severe and complex, and the risk of epidemic transmission still existed. It is impossible for epidemic prevention and control to end in a short period of time. It is very likely that the epidemic will be in a state of epidemic prevention and control for a long time. Under the normalization of the COVID-19 epidemic, unprecedented pressures have been faced to ensure the living materials of residents, the supply and price of grain and oil, and the urgently needed prevention and control materials to prevent from the epidemic.

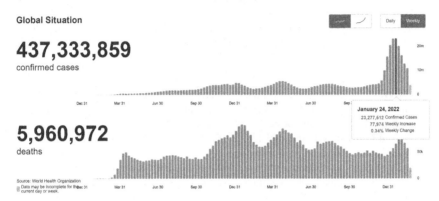

Fig. 1. WHO Global Situation of the COVID-19 Confirmations and Deaths

The COVID-19 epidemic poses a huge life-safety risk to people's food, housing and transportation. According to WHO statistics, as of now (March 26, 2022) (see Fig. 1), 437,333,859 cases have been confirmed worldwide, resulting in 5,960,972 deaths. With the recurrence of the epidemic, especially in those places where medical conditions are backward, most of the cases are in lack of epidemic prevention items to keep up with, and patients do not receive effective care, causing life threatens. On the other hand, according to the judgment and consensus of experts in the industry, the epidemic will exist in the longer term. Although the overall international and domestic food supply has been relatively stable for many years, during the epidemic, some major food supplying countries have slowed down or stopped food exports, China has a large demand for food with the overall economic development, and in the case of the continued epidemic, all regions are in urgent need to ensure the necessities of life for the residents. Some emergent problems of the basic life are essential to stabilize market prices and supply and demand. Therefore, it is very important and necessary to quickly understand and grasp the supply, demand and price changes in the market of important commodities such as food, oil, meat, eggs, vegetables, milk and epidemic prevention-related supplies through information technology, so as to monitor and warn of abnormal fluctuations in the market of essential commodities in unexpected events such as epidemics, and provide powerful reference data for the government and relevant departments to make quick decisions, which is essential to improve the government's ability to respond to unexpected epidemics and improve the quality of people's life. In view of this problem and the opportunities, this project researches and designs an emergency supply monitoring system in the post-epidemic context - research and design of an emergency supply monitoring system in the post-epidemic context.

Domestic and International Research Background. The research and design of the emergency supply assurance monitoring system in the context of post-epidemic situation mainly obtains the data of household necessities from monitoring enterprises through the data submission collector, automatically aggregates and integrates business rules and multi-dimensional statistical analysis based on these data, uses the monitoring and warning model for risk identification and monitoring and warning, and can take prospective trend analysis model for trend research and comparison of monitoring indicators.

Regarding the selection of necessity categories in the data reported by monitoring enterprises, some literature shows that necessity items should mainly include meat, vegetables, edible oil, eggs, dairy products, dry food, drinking water, paper towels, paper cups, towels and other categories [1], but the epidemic situation is different everywhere, so we need to combine the actual situation in the region, through flexible custom configuration of categories and regional expert advice, so as to select the appropriate main categories.

Regarding the design of data reporting collectors, some researchers have two acquisition methods through monitoring data with direct collection and data fusion. The former can be achieved by direct data reporting from monitoring points and intelligent data pumping, while the latter is advisable to use techniques such as network data capture data sharing, and the exchange between systems [2].

With regard to the market supply and demand indicators of essential commodities in the monitoring alert model, according to previous studies, the government reserves of essential commodities are mainly physical reserves, contract reserves and capacity reserves, from which quantifiable reserve indicators are extracted for monitoring, mainly the storage capacity, storage plan, actual storage quantity, incoming information, outgoing information, reserve ratio, and the name, specification, registered trademark, unit, and name of commodities operated by production and circulation enterprises. The indicators include the name, specification, registered trademark, unit, unit price, current sales volume, closing stock, current closing stock, current total sales volume, enterprise inventory capacity, and current production volume, current total production volume, shift capacity, daily capacity, and annual capacity of production enterprises [3], which enable the risk identification [4] determination and monitoring analysis of the emergency supply assurance system.

Regarding forward-looking trend analysis, Chen Yanhong et al. used the trend analysis model ARIMA model in China's grain supply and demand balance and forecast [5], Yang Zhenhao et al. used SARIMA model and exponential smoothing model in China's aquatic products consumer price index forecast based on SARIMA model [6], and Xu Yaqing et al. established exponential smoothing model, ARIMA in the construction of agricultural price forecasting model (summation and autoregressive moving average) model and a combined forecasting model based on both [7], and Zheng et al. applied neural network models in the combination of principal components and BP neural networks in grain yield forecasting [8], all of which achieved better trend forecasting results.

1.2   The Main Problems that Need to Be Solved at Present

The project research and design of the emergency supply monitoring system in the context of the post-epidemic situation, timely understanding, monitoring and mastering of the main emergency supply of essential goods information, the measures for monitoring the main essential goods for emergency supply aim to solve the following three types of problems.

The first, through the design of a good scalability and more practical emergency supply data collector, the system flexible configuration of the necessities of life category, to meet the emergency supply category adjustment, while monitoring enterprises to report missing data to remind.

The second, through the selection of monitoring and warning model indicators and set indicator thresholds, the establishment of the risk rating rules based on the category weighting system of essential goods, risk identification and monitoring and warning.

The third, through the trend analysis model, based on the cleaned data of supply and demand of essential goods and other categories of supply and demand ratios, demand, price trends and other forecasts.

1.3   Research Direction and Goals

We research and design an emergency supply monitoring system, and pay close attention to the market supply, demand and price changes of important livelihood commodities such as grain, oil, meat, eggs, vegetables, milk, and epidemic prevention-related supplies, so as to prevent abnormal fluctuations in the market of daily necessities in emergencies such as epidemics. Monitoring and warning, combined with Echarts [9], Tableau data visualization and tool technology for visual display, provide powerful reference data for the government and related departments to make quick decisions.

1.4   The Main Content of the Research

The system automatically processes, summarizes and statistically analyzes the data based on the data obtained from the monitored daily necessities, as well as the category price, supply and other emergency supply guarantee data, and finally monitors and warns against abnormal market fluctuations.

Establishment of Monitoring and Warning Model and Risk Identification of Emergency Supply Guarantee Monitoring System, and Visualization of Monitoring and Warning. To build a monitoring and warning model, the first thing is how to select the monitoring category, which is long-term and requires constant adjustment of the verification process, the selection of the category is based on historical data in the emergency supply, to derive the monitoring category and the degree of importance, the second is given by the industry experts' experience judgment, selected products and given weights. For risk identification, one is to be based on the government to develop the risk level of emergency supply, the second is to actively combine regional expert opinion or the use of emergency supply has been the results of research to define the risk rating rules of the category weighting system. Further is the use of the monitoring category data over the years, the monitoring and warning model is constantly revised, so as to improve the monitoring and warning model, the accuracy of the epidemic and other emergencies necessities of life market abnormal fluctuations.

Trend Analysis of the Emergency Supply Guarantee Monitoring System to Predict Trends in Inventory, Price and Other Trends. Through the trend analysis model, based on the data of supply and demand of the cleaned essential goods and other categories of supply and demand ratios, demand, price trends, etc. to forecast. One is the selection of monitoring indicators, based on the market supply and demand in essential goods mainly on the supply (sales volume, purchase volume, inventory, pre-saleable days), price (sales price) and other indicators, the second is that we can choose SARIMA model, time trend model, using RNN-SARIMA hybrid model, the trend prediction of the indicator trend situation, and the results of the superposition type data visualization and comparison analysis, and then determine the better model, and finally improve the accuracy of the forecast.

1.5   Research and Solve from the Following Three Key Issues

Category Selection. Based on the COVID-19 epidemic normalization of the category selection of essential goods, so as to design a good scalability and more practical emergency supply data collector.

Indicator System Construction. Monitoring the selection of indicators, indicator threshold settings, and risk identification of the warning model, the establishment of the risk rating rules based on the category weighting system of essential goods.

Model Building. Forward-looking trend analysis will be collected by the supply and demand data of essential commodities and other data will be converted and then serialized to form a basic data set of different frequencies, and use the construction model to forecast the supply and demand ratios, demand, price trends and so on. Common trend analysis models include ARIMA/SARIMA model, multiple regression model, time trend model, neural network model, and combined forecasting model, etc. The trend results are also displayed in a visual comparison analysis with superimposed data. In order to improve the accuracy of the forecast and early warning, the model can be further improved by combining expert consultation and social survey on the basis of the model analysis results.

1.6   Project Features and Innovations

This project focuses on the research and design of the emergency supply monitoring system under the background of the post-epidemic situation, takes the price and supply changes of daily necessities as the monitoring object, and pays close attention to important livelihood commodities such as grain, oil, meat, eggs, vegetables, milk, and other related epidemic prevention. Supply and demand and price changes in the supplies market, so as to monitor and warn the abnormal fluctuations in the daily necessities market, and provide powerful reference data for the government and relevant departments to make quick decisions, including the following three aspects.

First, combined with the normalization of the epidemic, reasonably select the categories of daily necessities, and support flexible custom configuration and online and offline submission of categories.

Second, automatic aggregation and multi-dimensional analysis of data submitted by monitoring companies, and use the monitoring and warning model to identify and monitor the risks of abnormal fluctuations in the daily necessities market.

Third, based on trend analysis models: SARIMA model, time trend model, using RNN-SARIMA hybrid model, etc., continue to analyze the sales volume, purchase volume, inventory volume, pre-sale days, sales price and other indicators of daily necessities. Trend research and comparison, superimposed data visualization comparison analysis and display of trend results, to provide forward-looking reference data for emergency protection of emergencies such as epidemics.

1.7 System Implementation Plan

It mainly involves the collection of data source data for monitoring of daily necessities information. The system provides configurable data collectors to collect data submitted by different monitoring companies and provides feedback reminders for missing category data. Based on the collected data, the first is to collect, transform and aggregate into statistical report data according to the business statistical rules of the categories of necessities of life; the second is to collect and integrate the data according to the monitoring and warning data model indicators, and at the same time, according to the risk level assessment rules, risks are identified, monitored, and warned; the third is to clean and collect data related to the supply and demand ratio, demand, price and other indicators of categories according to the supply and demand data of daily necessities, and finally use the SARIMA model, the time trend model, and RNN-SARIMA hybrid model. And other trend analysis models to predict the trend, and finally use the visual chart to display on the data application (see Fig. 2).

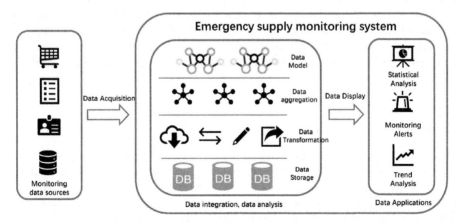

Fig. 2. System design

1.8 Research Technology Route

The technical route of research mainly includes the technical route of building a monitoring and warning model and the technical route of forward-looking trend analysis.

Technical Route to Build a Monitoring and Warning Model. Based on the experience of experts in the industry, we select the indicators of daily necessities for the monitoring and warning model. Set risk thresholds for market supply and demand indicators of daily necessities, such as supply (sales volume, purchase volume, inventory volume), demand (pre-sale days), price (sales price), etc. Define risk levels based on risk thresholds. Build a monitoring and warning model based on the above to realize the risk identification and monitoring and warning of the emergency supply guarantee system.

Forward-Looking Trend Analysis Technical Route. Selection of market supply and demand indicators for trend analysis models. Selection of trend analysis model, choose SARIMA model, time trend model, based on neural network-SARIMA model, study RNN-SARIMA hybrid model, etc. Check and process the historical data of the indicator. Based on the trend analysis model, select indicators and their related data for training, and compare trends. Verify the results of trend analysis and optimize the trend analysis model. Visual display of forward-looking trend analysis results.

1.9 Application Prospects and Social Benefits

The system designed by this research institute has distinctive technical advancement and foresight, which can quickly understand and grasp the abnormal fluctuation of the market of essential commodities through the system when natural disasters, accidents and disasters, epidemics and other sudden public health events and sudden social security events cause or may cause sudden changes in the market supply and demand of food, edible oil, meat, vegetables, eggs, hygiene and cleaning products, and make the system to monitor and warn, provide powerful reference data for the government and related departments to make quick decisions and intervene effectively, thus improving the government's ability to respond to emergencies, which is promising and socially beneficial to stabilize society and pacify people's lives.

The monitoring and warning role can respond emergencies. First, after the event, the system can effectively monitor and grasp the abnormal fluctuations in the market of essential commodities, second, it can alert the imbalance between supply and demand of categories of essential commodities, and third, it can analyze the category inventory and price trend, etc., so that the government can respond to the emergency more effectively.

Acknowledgements. Guangdong University of Science and Technology "Innovation and Strengthening School Project", Key Platform Construction Leapfrog Program: Platform Construction - Intelligent Computing Innovation and Application Center (GKY-2020CQPT-2). 2020 University-level Research Project of Guangdong University of Science and Technology - Analysis and Research on Online Learning Behavior of College Students under the Environment of Big Data (GKY-2020KYZDK-11). 2020 Innovative and Strengthening School Project - Comprehensive Data Management and Application Research Center (GKY-2020CQJG-1).

References

1. Zhao, Y.: Determination of emergency necessities reserve in response to public emergencies: the case of Shenzhen Pingshan New District. Logistics Technol. **36**(09) (2017)
2. Shi, Q.: Research on the risk management system of market supply of essential commodities. J. Liaoning Teachers College (Social Science Edition). (02) (2020)
3. Zhao, L., Li, N., Peng, T.: Research and application of monitoring technology for emergency reserve channel of essential commodities. China Safety Production Science and Technology. **9**(05) (2013)
4. Zhao, Y.: Research on food price early warning model and risk prevention mechanism. Economic Economics. (01) (2007)
5. Chen, Y., Hu, S., Shen, Q.: China's grain supply and demand balance and forecast based on ARIMA model. Guangdong Agricultural Science. **40**(05) (2013)
6. Yang, Z., Zhang, J., Yang, C.: Forecast of China's aquatic products consumer price index based on SARIMA model. Marine Lake and Marsh Bulletin. **43**(02) (2021)
7. Xu, Y., Wei, Y., Li, X.: Construction of agricultural product price forecasting model. Statistics and Decision Making. (12) (2017)
8. Zheng, J.: Combined application of principal components and BP neural network in grain yield forecasting. Computer System Applications **25**(11) (2016)
9. Echars Homepage. https://echarts.apache.org. Accessed 26 Mar 2022

Face Presentation Attack Detection Based on Texture Gradient Enhancement and Multi-scale Fusion

Fei Peng[1]([✉]), Shao-hua Meng[2], and Min Long[3]

[1] Institute of Artificial Intelligence and Blockchain, Guangzhou University, Guangzhou 510000, Guangdong, China
eepengf@gmail.com
[2] School of Computer Science and Electronic Engineering, Hunan University, Changsha 410082, China
[3] School of Computer and Communication Engineering, Changsha University of Science and Technology, Changsha 410114, China

Abstract. To make full use of image spatial detail information and further improve the detection performance, a face presentation attack detection method based on texture gradient enhancement and multi-scale fusion (FPAD-TGE) is proposed. Depth separable residual gradient enhancement block (DSRGEB) is first designed to obtain more texture-discriminative features. Subsequently, features containing rich contextual information are obtained at low cost through a designed multi-scale dilated convolution block (MDCB). Experiments and analysis on Oulu-NPU, CASIA-MFSD and Replay-Attack datasets show that the proposed method can achieve overall better performance in intra-dataset experiments and good generalization performance in cross-datasets experiments compared with some stat-of-the-art methods.

Keywords: Image forensics · Deep learning · Face presentation attack detection · Texture gradient enhancement · Multi-scale fusion

1 Introduction

Face recognition is one of the most frequently used and widely used biometric identification technologies with good convenience, security and accuracy. However, as the face recognition system is becoming more and more popular, the security of face recognition system have also attracted much attention. With the rapid development of Internet technology, criminals can steal and copy face images or videos of target objects at low cost. In this case, the face recognition system has become the main target of presentation attacks (PAs), where criminals try to deceive the face recognition system through various PAs, so as to achieve the purpose of illegal profit. Therefore, face presentation attack detection (FPAD) (also known as face liveness detection or face anti-spoofing) came into being [40].

At present, the common face PAs methods mainly include printing attack, video replay attack and 3D mask attack. Due to the complex acquisition process, high manufacturing cost, and the requirements of cooperation from the target object, the frequency of 3D mask attack is still far lower than that of printing attack and video replay attack. With the development of the Internet and the popularization of high-definition devices, photos and videos of the target objects are easily obtained by criminals, so printing attack and video replay attack have become the most common spoofing attacks. The printing attack and video replay attack capture the face image from the live face image, and both are regarded as recaptured images. Compared with the live face image, there are obvious differences in texture characteristics and image quality such as lack of mid-to-high frequency information [44], discrepancies between 2D plane and 3D stereo, lower resolution, generating noisy signals, moiré [35] and color distortion. These factors were proved to be useful cues for distinguishing live and fake faces.

In the existing FPAD, deep learning-based methods can learn to extract relatively high-level semantic features with the help of the good representation ability of models such as Convolutional Neural Networks (CNN), and they outperforms handcrafted features-based methods. Intuitively, the live face has more detailed and richer texture feature information than that of the fake face. However, most of the existing FPAD methods ignore the important role of low-level texture gradient information in distinguishing live faces from prosthetic faces, and does not fully utilize the image spatial details, Thus, the performance of FPAD is affected. Meanwhile, when auxiliary information such as timing information, depth information, and reflection information are implemented for FPAD, additional auxiliary labels or models need to be generated, it will result in high cost. Therefore, there are high requirements for the practical applications of such FPAD methods.

Based on this, a face presentation attack detection method based on texture gradient enhancement (FPAD-TGE) is proposed in this paper. The main contributions of this work are summarized as follows.

- A depth separable residual gradient enhancement block (DSRGEB) is proposed. The texture gradient of each level feature extracted from a single image is enhanced to obtain features with more texture discrimination.
- A multi-scale dilated convolution block (MDCB) is designed. It stacks multiple atrous convolutions with different expansion coefficients to capture contextual information.
- Experiments on three popular FPAD benchmark datasets Oulu-NPU [5], CASIA-MFSD [50], Replay-Attack [7] show that FPAD-TGE can achieve good performance both single dataset classification and generalization performance across datasets.

2   Related Work

2.1   Handcrafted Feature-Based Methods

Handcrafted feature-based methods usually extract features from various color spaces (RGB, HSV, and YCbCr), and Support Vector Machine (SVM), Quadratic Discriminant Analysis (QDA), Linear Discriminant Linear discriminant analysis (LDA) and other classifiers are used to train models for FPAD. Handcrafted feature-based methods can be further divided into three categories: (1) life activity-based methods, (2) texture-based methods, and (3) 3D geometry-based methods.

Life Activity-Based Methods. Life activity-based methods aim to detect dynamic life sign states or characteristics for FPAD. Typical dynamic life sign states include facial or head movements, facial expression changes, and subtle physiological signals. In 2007, Kollreider et al. first proposed an interactive method to detect print attacks and video replay attacks by reading the lips of a human face when the user is prompted to speak a randomly determined sequence of numbers [19]. After that, Tirunagari et al. adopted a dynamic pattern decomposition algorithm to capture facial expression changes [41]. In 2016, Remote Photoplethysmography (rPPG) is first applied to FPAD by Li et al. [26]. The lower half of the input face is used as the region of interest to extract rPPG data. After denoising and fourier transform, important features are obtained for classification. Afterward, the rPPG signal is leveraged by Liu et al. to detect whether the object has a heart rate, and judged whether the object is a living face [27].

Texture-Based Methods. Texture-based methods accomplish FPAD by detecting subtle differences in face texture. In 2004, Li et al. first proposed to detect face presentation attack by using static texture cues [22]. The frequency representation (two-dimensional Fourier spectrum) of the live face image and the corresponding printed image is utilized to analyze their difference in light reflectance. After extracting the difference features, classification is performed to determine the liveness of the face image . In 2011, multi-scale local binary patterns (LBP) was first proposed by Määttä et al. for FPAD [32]. After that, LBP texture features from luminance and chrominance channels in YCbCr color space was utilized by Boulkenafet et al. for FPAD [4].

3D Geometry Based Methods. 3D geometry based methods generally perform FPAD using the difference between a living face with a 3D structure and a fake face with a 2D plane. In 2012, De et al. first proposed to use 3D geometric invariants for FPAD [9]. After that, a 3D geometric feature is constructed by multiple 2D faces with different perspectives for detecting printing attack [42]. Meanwhile, Lagorio et al. put forward to use a 3D scanner to obtain the 3D model of the object to be measured, the 3D living face and the 2D fake face was determined by analyzing the surface curvature of the object [20].

2.2   Deep Learning Based Methods

End-to-End Methods. With the powerful representation capabilities of deep learning, end-to-end methods directly learn the distinct features from the input face images to perform FPAD, and the network model is mainly CNN. In 2014, Yang et al. first utilized an 8-layer shallow CNN for feature representation of FPAD [45]. However, since it is trained from the scratch, it is restricted by the scale and diversity of FPAD datasets, which may result in overfitting problems. To alleviate the problem of overfitting, transfer learning based on a pre-trained model for fine-tuning was addressed by Lucena et al. [31]. Besides CNN, a pre-trained Transformer model is also used for FPAD [12]. Nevertheless, the existing deep learning based FPAD is still dominated by CNN. Recently, long short-term memory (LSTM) was implemented by Ge et al. for the integration of temporal dynamic cues to distinguish between live and fake faces [11], and relative good performance is achieved.

Methods Combining Handcrafted Features. Methods combining handcrafted features generally distinguish live faces and fake faces with the extracted features or fused feature through classifiers such as fully connected layers, SVM, and Softmax. A 3D face mask presentation attack detection method based on intrisic image analysis was proposed by Li et al. [25]. The distinct features include the intensity difference distribution histogram extracted from the reflection image, and the illumination change captured by CNN. Besides, color LBP features extracted from convolutional feature maps was also utilized for FPAD in [1]. In [24], intensity variation features extracted by CNN and the width of motion blur extracted from motion-amplified face videos using local similar pattern are first fused, and then they are classified for detecting replayed video attack.

Generalization Methods. Generalization methods mainly include domain adaptation and domain generalization. Domain adaptation alleviates the difference between the source and the target domains. Domain adaptation-based methods require unlabeled target domain data to participate in model learning. A semi-supervised learning FPAD method was put forwarded by Quan et al. [38]. It only uses a small amount of labeled training data for pre-training, and unlabeled data in the target domain is gradually added during the training process, which can increase the diversity of the training data and narrow the domain gap. After that, a unified unsupervised and semi-supervised domain adaptation network was designed for FPAD by Jia et al. [17]. It aligns marginal and conditional distributions between source and target domains, and a domain-invariant feature space is achieved. While for domain generalization, it assumes that there exists a generalized feature space under multiple visible source domains and unseen but related target domains. Considering the large distribution difference between the fake faces in different domains, Jia et al. proposed to learn a generalized feature space for FPAD [16]. The fundamental principle is that the feature distribution of the fake faces is scattered in various fields, and it is compact within each field.

From the above anlaysis, the existing FPAD methods ignore the important role of low-level texture gradient information in distinguishing live and fake faces, and the use of auxiliary information increase the compuation cost.Therefore, a face presentation attack detection scheme based on texture gradient enhancement and multi-scale fusion is created in this paper.

3   Preliminaries

3.1   ConvNeXt Network Structure

ConvNeXt [30] is a pure convolutional neural network. It uses the strategies and methods of Swin Transformer [29] for reference to train the original ResNet model [14]. Compared with Transformer, ConvNeXt requires less computation time, higher accuracy, and it outperforms most existing image classification methods.

In this paper, FPAD-TGE uses the transfer-learned ConvNeXt as the backbone network for feature extraction, and more discriminative deep features can be obtained.

3.2   Sobel Operator

Sobel operator [18] can create images with prominent edges. Given an original image A, G_x and G_y represent the images for edge detection in the horizontal and vertical directions, respectively. It is calculated by

$$G_x = \begin{bmatrix} -1 & 0 & +1 \\ -2 & 0 & +2 \\ -1 & 0 & +1 \end{bmatrix} * A, \tag{1}$$

$$G_y = \begin{bmatrix} +1 & +2 & +1 \\ 0 & 0 & 0 \\ -1 & -2 & -1 \end{bmatrix} * A, \tag{2}$$

where $*$ represents a two-dimensional convolution operation. For each pixel in the image, the magnitude of the gradient G can be obtained by

$$G = \sqrt{G_x^2 + G_y^2}. \tag{3}$$

The direction of the gradient θ is calculated by

$$\theta = tan^{-1}(\frac{G_y}{G_x}). \tag{4}$$

Inspired by FAS-SGTD [43], Sobel operator is introduced in this paper to calculate the gradient size of the image, and it combines other convolution operations to analyze and express the unique attributes of the re-acquired face image.

3.3   Depthwise Separable Convolution

Depthwise separable convolution (DSC) [15] is lightweight, and significantly improves the computing efficiency of network models. Moreover, it can achieve the same level of performance as the standard convolution. DSC uses the idea of convolution decomposition for reference, and it is essentially a grouped convolution, which decomposes standard convolution into depthwise-wise convolution (DC) and point-wise convolution (PC). The convolution kernel of the standard convolution is performed to all channels. Thus, when an additional attribute detection is required, a convolution kernel must be increased. For each convolution operation of DC, it only involves one channel of the input layer. While for PC, it is very similar to the standard convolution, and the difference is that the size of the convolution kernel is $1 \times 1 \times M$, where M is the channel number. As for DSC, it first uses DC to convolve each channel, and then utilizes PC to weight these features to achieve the effect of standard convolution, which greatly reduces the calculation amount and model parameters with little loss of accuracy. For a convolutional layer with a convolution kernel size of 3×3, DSC can reduce the model calculation amount by 8 to 9 times comparing with the model calculation amount of the standard convolution. In practical models such as MobileNet [15], DSC, batch normalization (BN) and activation function ReLU together form the modules of the specific model.

In this paper, taking into account the performance and model calculation amount, DSRGEB is proposed. It combines DSC with the Sobel operator and residual operation, and it can make more full use of the detailed information of the image in the space domain.

3.4   Dilated Convolution

Dilated convolution [47] can increase the receptive field on the output unit at low cost without losing information, and it is very effective when multiple dilated convolutions are stacked together.

Taking a convolution kernel size of 3×3 and an expansion coefficient of 1 as an example, the schematic diagram of the dilated convolution is shown in the left part of Fig. 1. The range of each convolution operation of the dilated convolution is 9×9 (red frame area), and a receptive field of size 7×7 (blue area) is finally obtained. While for the standard convolution with the same convolution kernel size of 3×3, the schematic diagram of the standard convolution is shown in the right part of Fig. 1. The range of each convolution operation of the standard convolution is 3×3 (red frame area), a receptive field (blue area) with a size of 5×5 is finally obtained.

Indeed, the receptive field can be improved by using a pooling layer, increasing the stride of the convolution operation and the size of the convolution kernel. However, the use of a pooling layer and the increase of the stride of the convolution operation may cause the feature map to lose useful information, and the increase of the size of the convolution kernel will significantly increase the computational cost. In contrast, dilated convolution [47] can obtain large receptive

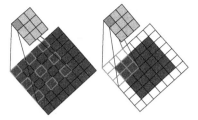

Fig. 1. The illustration of dilated convolution. The left is a diagram of a dilated convolution, and the right is a diagram of a standard convolution. (Color figure online)

field at low cost by only changing the expansion coefficient. Meanwhile, it can output a feature map with the same size. Besides the contextual information other than the face, such as background, hair, neck, etc., these contextual information is very beneficial to distinguish the live faces from the fake faces.Thus, dilated convolution can effectively capture contextual information at low cost. Therefore, in this paper, MDCB is proposed to stack multiple dilated convolutions with different expansion coefficients to capture contextual information, expand the feature receptive field without losing texture information, and obtain a more discriminative image context information.

4 The Proposed Scheme

4.1 Architecture of FPAD-TGE

The architecture of the proposed FPAD-TGE is shown in Fig. 2. It uses an RGB face image as the input, and then a ConvNeXt module adopting transfer learning is utilized for feature extraction. After that, DSRGEB is implemented to enhance the low-level, middle-level and high-level features, respectively. With the features of texture gradient enhancement, they are fused by MDBC, and the feature maps of multiple scales are spliced and convolved to obtain the features containing rich context information. Finally, they are utilized for the final classification prediction.

As DSRGEB are MDCB are two important modules of the proposed FPAD-TGE, they are respectively elaborated in the following.

4.2 Depth Separable Residual Gradient Enhancement Block

To make full use of the image details in the spatial domain, obtain more texture-discriminative face edge features, and take into account the computation cost, DSRGEB is designed in this paper to capture the discriminative information with different gradient sizes, and it combines the learnable convolution features with the gradient size. The illustration of DSRGEB is shown in Fig. 2, where the detailed structure of the point-wise conv layer, the Sobel filter conv layer and the

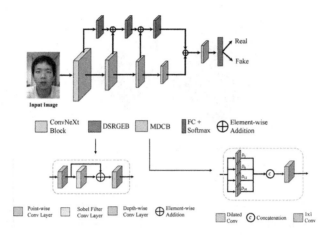

Fig. 2. Overall architecture diagram of FPAD-TGE.

depth-wise conv layer is also shown in Fig. 3. As seen from Fig. 2, DSRGEB is composed of DSC, Sobel filter convolution layer, and residual operation. Different from the traditional DSC which first passes through DC and then passes through PC, the DSC in this paper first passes through PC and then passes through DC, which is inspired by Xception [8] and Network Decoupling [13]. For the Sobel filter convolution layer, it uses Sobel operator to calculate the gradient size of the image, and the convolution operation is set as DC. The residual operation is consistent with the skip connection structure in ResNet [14], and the element-wise addition operation is performed to the convolutional graph.

4.3   Multi-scale Dilated Convolution Block

To obtain features that contain rich contextual information without losing information, MDCB is designed in this paper by stacking four dilated convolutional layers with different expansion coefficients (1, 6, 12, and 18) together and connecting a convolution layer with a kernel size of 1 × 1, as shown in Fig. 2, where the detailed structure of the dilated conv layer and the 1 × 1 conv layer is shown in Fig. 4. Because the dilated convolution can be regarded as filling '0' in the standard convolution kernel, the receptive field size of the dilated convolution can be calculated by using the standard convolution kernel. The calculation of the size of the dilated convolution receptive field is defined as

$$F_r = (k + (k - 1) * (r - 1)) \times (k + (k - 1) * (r - 1)), \tag{5}$$

where F_r is the size of the receptive field, k is the size of the convolution kernel, and r is the expansion coefficient. The range of the convolution kernel size and the expansion coefficient is a positive integer, which is greater than or equal to 1. The expansion coefficients in four dilated convolutional layers are 1, 6, 12, and 18, respectively. According to Eq.(5), the corresponding receptive field sizes are 3 × 3, 13 × 13, 25 × 25, 37 × 37.

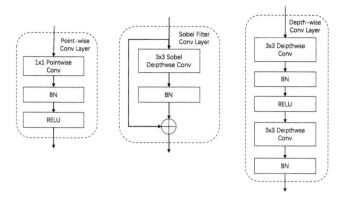

Fig. 3. The detailed structure of point-wise conv layer, Sobel filter conv layer and depth-wise conv layer.

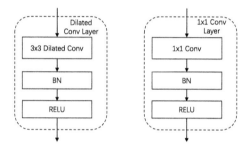

Fig. 4. The detailed structure of atrous conv layer and 1×1 conv layer.

5   Experiment and Analysis

5.1   Experiment Preparation

Datasets. To evaluate the performance of the proposed FPAD-TGE, experiments are conducted on three publicly used benchmark datasets, and they are OULU-NPU [5], CASIA-FASD [50] and Replay-Attack [7] datasets.

Evaluation Metrics. The following metrics are used to evaluate the Oulu-NPU dataset: (1) attack presentation classification error rate (APCER), (2) bona fide presentation classification error rate (BPCER), (3) average classification error rate (ACER). Here, ACER is the average of APCER and BPCER. As for CASIA-FASD and Replay-Attack datasets, half total error rate (HTER) and equal error rate (EER) are used as evaluation metrics. As for the above metrics, the lower the values are, the better the performance is.

Experimental Setup. The ConvNeXt model (convnext-base-in22ft1k) pre-trained on the ImageNet-22k dataset is adopted, RGB face images are taken as input, and the pre-trained model is fine-tuned by the images of FPAD. The entire network is trained end-to-end by using SGD. The optimizer is AdamW, the learning rate is 0.00005, the Batchsize is set to 32, the maximum epoch is set to 10, the loss function is a binary cross-entropy loss function, and the classifier is a fully connected layer and a Softmax classifier. The network architecture of FPAD-TGE is built by using PyTorch software library, and an RTX 2080Ti GPU is utilized for accelerated training. MTCNN [49] is used for face detection. The size of the input image is scaled to 224×224.

5.2   Experimental Results and Analysis

Intra-dataset Experiments. For Oulu-NPU dataset, the intra-dataset performance of the proposed FPAD-TGE is compared with some existing methods such as FAS-SGTD [43], STASN [46], Auxiliary [28], CDCN [48], CDCN++ [48] and TSViT [37]. The comparative results are listed in Table 1. From the results, it can be found that FPAD-TGE achieves ACERs of 1.0%, 0.9%, 1.9% ± 0.8% and 4.2% ± 1.5% in four protocols of OULU-NPU dataset. Specifically, the ACER in protocol 1 is third to CDCN++ [48] and TSViT [37], and the ACER in protocol 3 is slightly second to CDCN++ [48]. While for the ACERs in protocol 2 and protocol 4, they outperform those of FAS-SGTD [43], STASN [46], Auxiliary [28], CDCN [48], CDCN++ [48], and TSViT [37]. Furthermore, different from the comparative methods, FPAD-TGE can achieve very competitive results without additionally generating auxiliary information such as timing information, depth information and MSRCR images. This demonstrates that FPAD-TGE performs well in model robustness, and maintains stable intra-dataset test performance.

For CASIA-FASD and Replay-Attack dataset, the intra-dataset performance of the proposed FPAD-TGE is compared with some existing methods such as [2, 3, 6, 10, 21, 23, 34, 37, 39, 51], and the results are listed in Table 2. From the results, it can be found that FPAD-TGE and TSViT [37] can achieve EER of 0.00% in CASIA-FASD and Replay-Attack datasets, and HTER of 0.00% in Replay-Attack dataset, which outperforms the rest methods. Furthermore, compared with the two-stream structure of TSViT [37] , FPAD-TGE adopts a single-stream structure, which is simpler and and does not need to generate additional MSRCR images.

The above analysis indicates that the proposed FPAD-TGE can achieve good intra-dataset test performance.

Cross-datasets Experiments. Cross-datasets experiments are made to compare the performance of FPAD-TGE and that of [6, 28, 36, 37, 43, 46, 48], and the evaluation index is HTER(%), and two cross-database testing protocols are utilized. One is trained by the CASIA-FASD dataset and tested by the Replay-Attack dataset, which is called protocol CR. The other is trained by the Replay-Attack dataset and tested by the CASIA-FASD dataset, which is called protocol RC. The results are listed in Table 3, where Average represents the average value

Table 1. Experimental results on the OULU-NPU dataset

Prot.	Method	APCER(%)	BPCER(%)	ACER(%)
1	STASN [46]	1.2	2.5	1.9
	Auxiliary [28]	1.6	1.6	1.6
	FAS-SGTD [43]	2.0	0.0	1.0
	CDCN [48]	0.4	1.7	1.0
	CDCN++ [48]	0.4	0.0	**0.2**
	TSViT [37]	1.7	0.0	0.9
	FPAD-TGE (Proposed)	1.6	0.5	1.0
2	Auxiliary [28]	2.7	2.7	2.7
	STASN [46]	4.2	0.3	2.2
	FAS-SGTD [43]	2.5	1.3	1.9
	CDCN [48]	1.5	1.4	1.5
	CDCN++ [48]	1.8	0.8	1.3
	TSViT [37]	0.8	1.3	1.1
	FPAD-TGE (Proposed)	0.1	1.7	**0.9**
3	Auxiliary [28]	2.7±1.3	3.1±1.7	2.9±1.5
	STASN [46]	4.7±3.9	0.9±1.2	2.8±1.6
	FAS-SGTD [43]	3.2±2.0	2.2±1.4	2.7±0.6
	CDCN [48]	2.4±1.3	2.2±2.0	2.3±1.4
	CDCN++ [48]	1.7±1.5	2.0±1.2	**1.8±0.7**
	TSViT [37]	2.4±2.6	1.4±2.2	1.9±1.3
	FPAD-TGE (Proposed)	2.9±2.2	0.9±1.9	1.9±0.8
4	Auxiliary [28]	9.3±5.6	10.4±6.0	9.5±6.0
	STASN [46]	6.7±10.6	8.3±8.4	7.5±4.7
	CDCN [48]	4.6±4.6	9.2±8.0	6.9±2.9
	CDCN++ [48]	4.2±3.4	5.8±4.9	5.0±2.9
	FAS-SGTD [43]	6.7±7.5	3.3±4.1	5.0±2.2
	TSViT [37]	7.4±5.0	1.2±2.2	4.3±1.9
	FPAD-TGE (Proposed)	3.5±4.4	4.9±4.5	**4.2±1.5**

of the HTER of two protocols CR and RC. From the results, FPAD-TGE achieves HTER of 18.1% in the protocol CR and 21.9% in the protocol RC. Although the result in the protocol CR only ranks the fourth among the comparative counterparts, that in the protocol RC outperforms the rest methods with a significant margin. From an overall, the Average is 20.0%, which in only slightly second to CDCN++ [48]. However, the HTERs of CDCN++ [48] in two protocols are significantly unbalanced, which does not occur in the proposed FPAD-TGE.

From the above, FPAD-TGE can achieve competitive results in cross-datasets evaluation, and the results are relatively stabel in differnt protocols.

Table 2. Experimental results in the CASIA-FASD and Replay-Attack datasets

Method	CASIA-FASD	Replay-Attack	
	EER(%)	EER(%)	HTER(%)
Color-LBP [3]	6.20	0.40	2.90
Deep LBP [23]	2.30	0.10	0.90
ST Mapping [21]	1.10	0.78	0.80
VLBC [51]	6.50	1.70	0.80
Patch+depthCNN [2]	2.70	0.80	0.70
DSGN [34]	3.42	0.13	0.63
TSCNN-ResNet18 [6]	3.15	0.21	0.39
TSCNN-MobileNetV2 [6]	4.18	0.13	0.25
SSD+SPMT [39]	0.04	0.04	0.06
Multi-cues integration + NN [10]	5.83	0.83	**0.00**
TSViT [37]	**0.00**	**0.00**	**0.00**
FPAD-TGE (Proposed)	**0.00**	**0.00**	**0.00**

Table 3. Cross-datasets experimental results between CASIA-FASD and Replay-Attack HTER(%)

Method	CR	RC	Average
TS-FEN [36]	27.0	38.3	32.7
TSCNN-ResNet18 [6]	36.2	34.7	35.5
TSCNN-MobileNetV2 [6]	30.0	33.4	31.7
STASN [46]	31.5	30.9	31.2
Auxiliary [28]	27.6	22.8	25.2
FAS-SGTD [43]	17.0	22.8	19.9
CDCN [48]	15.5	32.6	24.1
CDCN++ [48]	**6.5**	29.8	**18.2**
TSViT [37]	19.5	27.7	23.6
FPAD-TGE (Proposed)	18.1	**21.9**	20.0

6   Conclusions

In this paper, a face presentatin attack detection method named as FPAD-TGE is proposed. It performs texture gradient enhancement on the features of each layer extracted by the pre-trained ConvNeXt module through the designed DSRGEB module to obtain texture-enhanced features, and obtains features containing rich contextual information at low cost through the designed MDCB module. The detection is carried out by classifing these features. Experimental results on Oulu-NPU, CASIA-MFSD and Replay-Attack show that FPAD-TGE can achieve good detection performance in a intra-dataset testing, and also achieves good generalization performance in cross-datasets testing. However, its performance of across-datasets is still far from satifactory. The improvement of the generalization performance of FPAD will be our future research direction.

Acknowledgments. This work was supported in part by project supported by National Natural Science Foundation of China (Grant No. U1936115,62072055, 92067104).

References

1. Agarwal, A., Vatsa, M., Singh, R.: Chif: Convoluted histogram image features for detecting silicone mask based face presentation attack. In: 2019 IEEE 10th International Conference on Biometrics Theory, Applications and Systems (BTAS), pp. 1–5 IEEE (2019)
2. Atoum, Y., Liu, Y., Jourabloo, A., Liu, X.: Face anti-spoofing using patch and depth-based CNNs. In: 2017 IEEE International Joint Conference on Biometrics (IJCB), pp. 319–328 IEEE (2017)
3. Boulkenafet, Z., Komulainen, J., Hadid, A.: Face anti-spoofing based on color texture analysis. In: 2015 IEEE International Conference on Image Processing (ICIP), pp. 2636–2640 IEEE (2015)
4. Boulkenafet, Z., Komulainen, J., Hadid, A.: Face spoofing detection using colour texture analysis. IEEE Trans. Inf. Forensics Secur. **11**(8), 1818–1830 (2016)
5. Boulkenafet, Z., Komulainen, J., Li, L., Feng, X., Hadid, A.: OULU-NPU: a mobile face presentation attack database with real-world variations. In: 2017 12th IEEE International Conference on Automatic Face & Gesture Recognition (FG 2017), pp. 612–618 IEEE (2017)
6. Chen, H., Hu, G., Lei, Z., Chen, Y., Robertson, N.M., Li, S.Z.: Attention-based two-stream convolutional networks for face spoofing detection. IEEE Trans. Inf. Forensics Secur. **15**, 578–593 (2019)
7. Chingovska, I., Anjos, A., Marcel, S.: On the effectiveness of local binary patterns in face anti-spoofing. In: 2012 BIOSIG-Proceedings of the International Conference of Biometrics Special Interest Group (BIOSIG), pp. 1–7 IEEE (2012)
8. Chollet, F.: Xception: deep learning with depthwise separable convolutions. In: Proceedings of the IEEE Conference on Computer Vision and Pattern Recognition, pp. 1251–1258 (2017)
9. De Marsico, M., Nappi, M., Riccio, D., Dugelay, J.L.: Moving face spoofing detection via 3D projective invariants. In: 2012 5th IAPR International Conference on Biometrics (ICB), pp. 73–78. IEEE (2012)
10. Feng, L., et al.: Integration of image quality and motion cues for face anti-spoofing: a neural network approach. J. Vis. Commun. Image Represent. **38**, 451–460 (2016)
11. Ge, H., Tu, X., Ai, W., Luo, Y., Ma, Z., Xie, M.: Face anti-spoofing by the enhancement of temporal motion. In: 2020 2nd International Conference on Advances in Computer Technology, Information Science and Communications (CTISC), pp. 106–111 IEEE (2020)

12. George, A., Marcel, S.: On the effectiveness of vision transformers for zero-shot face anti-spoofing. In: 2021 IEEE International Joint Conference on Biometrics (IJCB), pp. 1–8 IEEE (2021)

13. Guo, J., Li, Y., Lin, W., Chen, Y., Li, J.: Network decoupling: from regular to depthwise separable convolutions. arXiv preprint arXiv:1808.05517 (2018)

14. He, K., Zhang, X., Ren, S., Sun, J.: Deep residual learning for image recognition. In: Proceedings of the IEEE Conference on Computer Vision and Pattern Recognition, pp. 770–778 (2016)

15. Howard, A.G., et al.: MobileNets: efficient convolutional neural networks for mobile vision applications. arXiv preprint arXiv:1704.04861 (2017)

16. Jia, Y., Zhang, J., Shan, S., Chen, X.: Single-side domain generalization for face anti-spoofing. In: Proceedings of the IEEE/CVF Conference on Computer Vision and Pattern Recognition, pp. 8484–8493 (2020)

17. Jia, Y., Zhang, J., Shan, S., Chen, X.: Unified unsupervised and semi-supervised domain adaptation network for cross-scenario face anti-spoofing. Pattern Recogn. **115**, 107888 (2021)

18. Kanopoulos, N., Vasanthavada, N., Baker, R.L.: Design of an image edge detection filter using the sobel operator. IEEE J. Solid-State Circ **23**(2), 358–367 (1988)

19. Kollreider, K., Fronthaler, H., Faraj, M.I., Bigun, J.: Real-time face detection and motion analysis with application in liveness assessment. IEEE Trans. Inf. Forensics Secur. **2**(3), 548–558 (2007)

20. Lagorio, A., Tistarelli, M., Cadoni, M., Fookes, C., Sridharan, S.: Liveness detection based on 3D face shape analysis. In: 2013 International Workshop on Biometrics and Forensics (IWBF), pp. 1–4 IEEE (2013)

21. Lakshminarayana, N.N., Narayan, N., Napp, N., Setlur, S., Govindaraju, V.: A discriminative spatio-temporal mapping of face for liveness detection. In: 2017 IEEE International Conference on Identity, Security and Behavior Analysis (ISBA), pp. 1–7 IEEE (2017)

22. Li, J., Wang, Y., Tan, T., Jain, A.K.: Live face detection based on the analysis of fourier spectra. In: Biometric Technol. Human Ident. vol. 5404, pp. 296–303. SPIE (2004)

23. Ma, H., Wang, L., Zhang, C., Wu, F., Tan, T., Wang, Y., Lai, J., Zhao, Y. (eds.): PRCV 2021. LNCS, vol. 13021. Springer, Cham (2021). https://doi.org/10.1007/978-3-030-88010-1

24. Li, L., Xia, Z., Hadid, A., Jiang, X., Zhang, H., Feng, X.: Replayed video attack detection based on motion blur analysis. IEEE Trans. Inf. Forensics Secur. **14**(9), 2246–2261 (2019)

25. Li, L., Xia, Z., Jiang, X., Ma, Y., Roli, F., Feng, X.: 3D face mask presentation attack detection based on intrinsic image analysis. IET Biometrics **9**(3), 100–108 (2020)

26. Li, X., Komulainen, J., Zhao, G., Yuen, P.C., Pietikäinen, M.: Generalized face anti-spoofing by detecting pulse from face videos. In: 2016 23rd International Conference on Pattern Recognition (ICPR), pp. 4244–4249 IEEE (2016)

27. Liu, S.-Q., Lan, X., Yuen, P.C.: Remote photoplethysmography correspondence feature for 3D mask face presentation attack detection. In: Ferrari, V., Hebert, M., Sminchisescu, C., Weiss, Y. (eds.) ECCV 2018. LNCS, vol. 11220, pp. 577–594. Springer, Cham (2018). https://doi.org/10.1007/978-3-030-01270-0_34

28. Liu, Y., Jourabloo, A., Liu, X.: Learning deep models for face anti-spoofing: binary or auxiliary supervision. In: Proceedings of the IEEE Conference on Computer Vision and Pattern Recognition, pp. 389–398 (2018)

29. Liu, Z., et al.: Swin transformer: hierarchical vision transformer using shifted windows. In: Proceedings of the IEEE/CVF International Conference on Computer Vision, pp. 10012–10022 (2021)
30. Liu, Z., Mao, H., Wu, C.Y., Feichtenhofer, C., Darrell, T., Xie, S.: A convnet for the 2020s. arXiv preprint arXiv:2201.03545 (2022)
31. Lucena, O., Junior, A., Moia, V., Souza, R., Valle, E., Lotufo, R.: Transfer learning using convolutional neural networks for face anti-spoofing. In: Karray, F., Campilho, A., Cheriet, F. (eds.) ICIAR 2017. LNCS, vol. 10317, pp. 27–34. Springer, Cham (2017). https://doi.org/10.1007/978-3-319-59876-5_4
32. Määttä, J., Hadid, A., Pietikäinen, M.: Face spoofing detection from single images using micro-texture analysis. In: 2011 International Joint Conference on Biometrics (IJCB), pp. 1–7 IEEE (2011)
33. Ming, Z., Visani, M., Luqman, M.M., Burie, J.C.: A survey on anti-spoofing methods for facial recognition with RGB cameras of generic consumer devices. J. Imaging **6**(12), 139 (2020)
34. Ning, X., Li, W., Wei, M., Sun, L., Dong, X.: Face anti-spoofing based on deep stack generalization networks. In: ICPRAM. pp. 317–323 (2018)
35. Patel, K., Han, H., Jain, A.K., Ott, G.: Live face video vs. spoof face video: use of moiré patterns to detect replay video attacks. In: 2015 International Conference on Biometrics (ICB), pp. 98–105. IEEE (2015)
36. Peng, D., Xiao, J., Zhu, R., Gao, G.: Ts-Fen: Probing feature selection strategy for face anti-spoofing. In: ICASSP 2020–2020 IEEE International Conference on Acoustics, Speech and Signal Processing (ICASSP), pp. 2942–2946 IEEE (2020)
37. Peng, F., Meng, S.h., Long, M.: Presentation attack detection based on two-stream vision transformers with self-attention fusion. J. Vis. Commun. Image Represent. **85**, 103518 (2022)
38. Quan, R., Wu, Y., Yu, X., Yang, Y.: Progressive transfer learning for face anti-spoofing. IEEE Trans. Image Process. **30**, 3946–3955 (2021)
39. Song, X., Zhao, X., Fang, L., Lin, T.: Discriminative representation combinations for accurate face spoofing detection. Pattern Recogn. **85**, 220–231 (2019)
40. Souza, L., Oliveira, L., Pamplona, M., Papa, J.: How far did we get in face spoofing detection? Eng. Appl. Artif. Intell. **72**, 368–381 (2018)
41. Tirunagari, S., Poh, N., Windridge, D., Iorliam, A., Suki, N., Ho, A.T.: Detection of face spoofing using visual dynamics. IEEE Trans. Inf. Forensics Secur. **10**(4), 762–777 (2015)
42. Wang, T., Yang, J., Lei, Z., Liao, S., Li, S.Z.: Face liveness detection using 3D structure recovered from a single camera. In: 2013 International Conference on Biometrics (ICB), pp. 1–6. IEEE (2013)
43. Wang, Z., et al.: Deep spatial gradient and temporal depth learning for face anti-spoofing. In: Proceedings of the IEEE/CVF Conference on Computer Vision and Pattern Recognition, pp. 5042–5051 (2020)
44. Wen, D., Han, H., Jain, A.K.: Face spoof detection with image distortion analysis. IEEE Trans. Inf. Forensics Secur. **10**(4), 746–761 (2015)
45. Yang, J., Lei, Z., Li, S.Z.: Learn convolutional neural network for face anti-spoofing. arXiv preprint arXiv:1408.5601 (2014)
46. Yang, X., et al.: Face anti-spoofing: model matters, so does data. In: Proceedings of the IEEE/CVF Conference on Computer Vision and Pattern Recognition, pp. 3507–3516 (2019)
47. Yu, F., Koltun, V.: Multi-scale context aggregation by dilated convolutions. arXiv preprint arXiv:1511.07122 (2015)

48. Yu, Z., et al.: Searching central difference convolutional networks for face anti-spoofing. In: Proceedings of the IEEE/CVF Conference on Computer Vision and Pattern Recognition, pp. 5295–5305 (2020)
49. Zhang, K., Zhang, Z., Li, Z., Qiao, Y.: Joint face detection and alignment using multitask cascaded convolutional networks. IEEE Sign. Process. Lett. **23**(10), 1499–1503 (2016)
50. Zhang, Z., Yan, J., Liu, S., Lei, Z., Yi, D., Li, S.Z.: A face antispoofing database with diverse attacks. In: 2012 5th IAPR international conference on Biometrics (ICB), pp. 26–31 IEEE (2012)
51. Zhao, X., Lin, Y., Heikkilä, J.: Dynamic texture recognition using volume local binary count patterns with an application to 2D face spoofing detection. IEEE Trans. Multimedia **20**(3), 552–566 (2017)

Optimal Revenue Analysis of the Stubborn Mining Based on Markov Decision Process

Yiting Zhang[1], Ming Liu[1], Jianan Guo[1], Zhaojie Wang[1], Yilei Wang[1(✉)],
Tiancai Liang[2], and Sunil Kumar Singh[3]

[1] School of Computer Science, Qufu Normal University, Rizhao, China
wang_yilei2019@qfnu.edu.cn
[2] China Institute of Artificial Intelligence and Blockchain,
Guangzhou University, Guangzhou, China
[3] CCET, Panjab University, Chandigarh, India
sksingh@ccet.ac.in

Abstract. As one of the most popular cryptocurrencies, Bitcoin is essentially a decentralized ledger. Each node maintains the security of the blockchain through the workload proof mechanism, and the block that obtains the accounting right will receive a block reward in the form of Bitcoin. Because the Bitcoin system follows the "longest legal chain" principle, when a fork occurs, orphan blocks will inevitably be generated, and some miners' computing power will be a waste. In recent years, researchers have discovered that miners can obtain profits disproportionate to their own computing power by deviating from Bitcoin's honest mining. Selfish Mining (SM1) is a case in dishonest mining strategy, and dishonest miners (attackers) can obtain higher returns by retaining the blocks they create and selectively delaying their release. The stubborn mining strategy is a generalized form of selfish mining. It increases the revenue of the stubborn miner by adopting a wider range of parameters. Its three mining strategies are: Lead-Stubborn, Equal Fork stubborn and Trail stubborn.

The mining problem can be formulated as a Markov Decision Process (MDP), which can be resolved to give the optimal mining strategy. This work describes the three mining strategies of stubborn mining as a Markov decision process, solves it and gives the lower bound of the highest return under the optimal stubborn mining strategy. Our experimental results demonstrate that the revenue of the optimal stubborn mining strategy is higher than SM1 under certain circumstances, and this strategy allows dishonest miners (stubborn miners) to obtain revenue that does not match the actual computing power paid.

Keywords: Blockchain · Selfish mining · Stubborn mining · MDP

1 Introduction

In 2008, the financial crisis broke out all over the world. On November 1 of the same year, a person named Satoshi Nakamoto published "Bitcoin: A peer-to-peer electronic cash system" on the P2P foundation website [1], this article is also known as the Bitcoin

Y. Xu et al. (Eds.): ML4CS 2022, LNCS 13656, pp. 299–308, 2023.
https://doi.org/10.1007/978-3-031-20099-1_25

White Paper. The content of the book mainly states his new vision for electronic currency, and Bitcoin, a new type of electronic currency, was born. In January of the following year, the Bitcoin genesis block was born. After that, cryptocurrencies like Ethereum and Litecoin appeared in people's lives one after another, opening a new era of modern payment methods. In order to prevent the failure of a single node to cause problems for the entire Bitcoin system, the Bitcoin system is designed as a decentralized system [5].

The successful operation of the Bitcoin system is based on blockchain technology. The chain data structure of the blockchain, peer-to-peer (p2p) network protocols and distributed consensus algorithms have become the cornerstones of ensuring the security of the Bitcoin system [11]. The blockchain network does not have a central server, it is composed of many full nodes and light nodes, which form a decentralized p2p network. In the blockchain, each transaction occurs directly between the two parties, and both parties will broadcast the transaction information to the entire blockchain network through the Gossip protocol [2]. Miners are required to prove their workload by constantly trying to solve a cryptographic problem and obtain bookkeeping rights. Say in other words, in the blockchain network, miners use the POW (Proof of Work) consensus mechanism to determine the selection of accounting nodes in the network, and to ensure that the ledger data forms a correct and consistent consensus in the entire network [6].

The main contributions of this work can be described as the following three points:

1. This work conducts an in-depth analysis of three strategies of stubborn mining, and finds that the stubborn mining problem has Markov properties.
2. A Markov decision process includes action space, state space, objective function, transition and probability matrix. This work analyzes the process of stubborn mining, and describes the action space, state space, objective function, transition and probability matrix of the mining process.
3. This work uses python to build a Bitcoin mining simulator, the purpose is to simulate the mining income of Bitcoin after stubborn mining is described as MDP. Using the functions in the library to solve the MDP, the optimal return of stubborn mining based on the Markov decision process can be obtained.

2 Related Work

In the original Bitcoin system, people generally adopted the honest mining strategy and believed that this strategy is the most profitable, and these nodes that mine according to the protocol are called honest miners. Once a POW problem is solved, honest miners will broadcast to other miners immediately, so as to get a profit that matches the proportion of their computing power. Supposing that the ratio of the computing power of an honest miner to the sum of the computing power of all miners in the Bitcoin network is α, then the probability that he can solve the POW problem in each block is also α. In the long run, the Bitcoin reward that an honest miner can get should be $1/\alpha$ of the total rewards issued since the Bitcoin system was established. That is to say, the Bitcoin mining protocol can basically guarantee that miners can obtain matching income according to the proportion of their computing power to the total network computing power [3]. Consequently, the traditional view is that Bitcoin's mining protocol is incentive-compatible, which can resist collusive attacks by minority groups and incentivize miners to mine in the way specified by the protocol [22].

However, in 2014, Ittay Eyal and Emin Gün Sirer [4] proposed a mining strategy that deviates from the protocol. They proved that the Bitcoin mining protocol is not incentive-compatible, and named the mining strategy "Selfish Mining" (SM1), and the miners who adopted this strategy were called selfish miners. When a POW problem is solved by a selfish miner, the miner does not broadcast immediately like an honest miner, but hides the new block it mined, thereby constructing a private branch that it controls. Honest miners who abide by the mining protocol do not know the existence of the private chain, so they will only maintain a public chain. If the public branch is close to the length of the private branch, the selfish miner will publish the hidden private chain. According to the principle of the longest legal chain, honest miners will give up the public chain, and this attack directly causes the previous calculations of honest miners to become invalid calculations.

After this, some research work on the expansion and optimization of the "selfish mining" strategy has been put forward. In 2016 Ayelet Sapirshtein et al. found that SM1 is not the optimal best response to honest behavior, hence they proposed "Optimal Selfish Mining" [7], an algorithm to find the optimal strategy of the attacker in the model is presented.Kartik Nayak et al. proposed a generalized selfish mining strategy "Stubborn Mining" in the same year [8]. They expanded the mining strategy space and proposed two new strategies, namely "the Equal Fork Stubborn Mining" and "Trail Stubborn Mining". The "Trail stubborn" strategy defines a threshold j, if the attacker is T_j-stubborn, then only when it is behind honest j + 1 blocks will it choose to accept the public chain and thus give up its own private chain. Otherwise, it will silently continue to produce blocks on its own private chain. Depending on the difference in length between public and private chains, different mining strategies are adopted. Stubborn Mining employs a wider range of parameters, leading to more revenue for miners.

Immediately afterwards, researchers from all over the world have launched intense discussions on mining attacks in the Bitcoin system. For example, Tao Li et al. proposed semi-selfish mining attacks and formulated them as a Hidden Markov Decision Process (SMHMDP) to make certain improvements to selfish mining [9, 10]. Bonneau J et al. proposed "Bribery Attack", in which the attacker generates a fork by bribery, so as to achieve the purpose of "reverse" transaction [13]. The concept of bribery selfish mining attacks (BSM) was further proposed by Gao S et al. [14]. In 2020 Yang Get al. proposed a new selfish mining algorithm: intelligent bribery selfish mining (IPBSM), rational attackers increase their revenue by leveraging reinforcement learning to optimize their strategies [12].

3   Blockchain Mining Model

In this subsection, we introduce the Markov Decision Process (MDP) model for Stubborn Mining, mainly based on Kartik Nayak et al. [8]. First of all, we assume that the Bitcoin network is divided into two parts:

- *Hashpower of attacker (Alice): a* fraction of the computing power in the overall network controlled by the attacker, α.
- *Hashpower of the honest (Bob): a* network controlled by honest miners accounts for $(1-\alpha)$ of the computing power of the entire network (here we define $\beta = 1-\alpha$).

Since the information dissemination in the Bitcoin network is completed by the Gossip protocol, it will cause inevitable message delay [18, 21]. If attackers and honest miners release new blocks they just mined into the Bitcoin network at the same time, the message delay will also prevent other miners from receiving these blocks at the same time. Therefore, we highlight that:

· *Alice's network influence* γ: When Alice and Bob release a block around the same time, resulting in a fork of the same length, a small portion of Bob's network will mine Alice's block (Fig. 1).

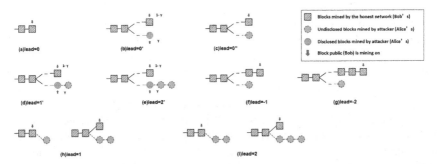

Fig. 1. Representation of Alice and Bob's blockchains in different Markov chain states, where lead = length (Alice's chain) − length (Bob's chain).

If the other miners involved in mining all abide by the protocol, the attacker faces an one-man decision-making problem. We model the problem as a one-person MDP M = < S, A, P, R >, where S is the state space, A is the action space, P is the transition probability matrix, and R is the reward matrix. If a state transition is Markov, it means that the next state of a state depends only on its current state, and has nothing to do with the state before its current state. The attacker's goal is a higher reward than the ratio of its computing power in the entire system. Depending on the current state, miners will choose different mining strategies, and the action space that needs to be defined is also different. Next, we first explain the state space, and then give the action space under three different situations of stubborn mining. The last list gives the transition probability matrix and the reward matrix.

3.1 State Space

Each state in the state space is composed of a ternary form *(a, h, fork),* where a and h are the lengths of the private chain maintained by the attacker and the public chain maintained by the honest after the most recent fork, respectively. There are three forms of fork are Relevant, Irrelevant and Active.

Relevant: It means that the latest block was mined by the honest network.

Irrelevant: It means that the latest block was mined by attacker.

Active: It means that the attacker just performed the action LMatch and the blockchain is now split into two forks.

3.2 Action Space

We start by describing the action space A, and the attacker's choice of actions will directly affect the state space S.

Lead Stubborn Mining: At This Time a > h.

- *LMatch:* If the latest block is mined by the honest (Relevant). Then the attacker immediately announces the chain of the same length as the honest, resulting in two forks of the same length, and the status becomes Active.
- *LWait:*

  1. If the latest block is mined by the attacker (Irrelevant) and h = 0. At this time only the private chain of the attacker is connected to the public chain, then the attacker does not disclose any blocks but continues to dig on the private chain secretly.
  2. If the attacker has just taken action LMatch and is in Active state, there are two public forks of equal length. Then the attacker does not disclose any blocks but continues to dig on the private chain secretly.

Equal-Fork Stubborn Mining: At This Time a = h.

- *FWait:* If the attacker has just taken action LMatch and is in Active state, there are two public forks of equal length. Then the attacker does not disclose any blocks but continues to dig on the private chain secretly.

Trail Stubborn Mining: At This Time a < h.

- *TAdopt:* If the attacker is a T_j-stubborn miner, and the latest block is mined by the honest (relevant), at this time h−a > j, then the attacker will give up its entire private chain and accept the public chain.
- *TWait:* If the attacker is a T_j-stubborn miner and h−a ≤ j, the attacker continues to dig the private chain secretly.
- *TOverride:* Once a > h occurs, the attacker immediately announces its entire private chain.

3.3 Transition and Reward Matrices

In order to make the rewards evenly distributed in time, we define that each new block corresponds to a state transition, blocks can be created by attacker or honest (Blocks are created at a rate of about 10 min per block in the Bitcoin system [18, 20]). We do an in-depth analysis of the action space and state space of stubborn mining. Taking Lead stubborn mining (a > h) as an example, the attacker can take two actions, L-Match and L-Wait. If the latest block is mined by the honest (the status is relevant), the attacker takes the action L-Match, immediately announces the chain of the same length as the honest network, and deliberately creates two forks of the same length, so that the state of the blockchain becomes Active. By analyzing the three strategies of stubborn mining consistent with the above, we can get its Transition and Reward Matrices. The transition matrix P and reward matrix R of Stubborn mining are briefly described in Tables 1, 2 and 3. Among them, reward R is described as a two-tuple *(A, H)*, the first parameter A represents the number of blocks of the attacker that have been accepted by each miner, and the second parameter H represents the number of blocks mined by the honest.

Table 1. State transition and reward matrices for MDP mining models for Lead stubborn.

State x Action	State	Probability	Reward
(a, h, Relevant), LMatch (a, h, Active), LWait	(a + 1, h, Active)	α	(0, 0)
	(a−h, 1, Relevant)	$\beta\gamma$	(H, 0)
	(a, h + 1, Relevant)	$\beta(1-\gamma)$	(0, 0)
(a, h, Irrelevant), LWait	(a + 1, h, Irrelevant)	α	(0, 0)
	(a, h, Relevant)	β	(0, 0)

Table 2. State transition and reward matrices for MDP mining models for Equal fork stubborn mining.

State x Action	State	Probability	Reward
(a, h, Active), FWait	(a + 1, h, Active)	α	(0, 0)
	(a−h, 1, Relevant)	$\beta\gamma$	(H, 0)
	(a, h + 1, Relevant)	$\beta(1-\gamma)$	(0, 0)

Table 3. State transition and reward matrices for MDP mining models for Trail stubborn mining.

State x Action	State	Probability	Reward
(a, h, Relevant), TAdopt	(1, 0, Irrelevant)	α	(0, H)
	(0, 1, Relevant)	β	
(a, h, Irrelevant), TWait (a, h, Relevant), TWait	(a + 1, h, Irrelevant)	α	(0, 0)
	(a, h, Relevant)	β	(0, 0)
(a, h, ·), TOverride	(a − h, 0, Irrelevant)	α	(H + 1, 0)
	(a − h − 1, 1, Relevant)	β	

3.4 Objective Function

In this article, attackers aim to reward rewards higher than the ratio of their computing power to the overall system. Specifically, the attacker should waste the blocks mined by the honest as much as possible, and ensure that its own blocks are not wasted to the greatest extent possible. In the literature [7], Ayelet Sapirshtein et al. defined the objective function of attacker in blockchain mining as relative mining gain (RMG). The specific calculation formula of RMG is given below:

$$RMG = E\left[\lim_{T\to\infty}\frac{\sum_{T=t}^{t+T-1} r_{T+1}^{(a)}}{\sum_{T=t}^{t+T-1} r_{T+1}^{(a)} + \sum_{T=t}^{t+T-1} r_{T+1}^{(h)}}\right] \tag{1}$$

where $r_t^{(a)}$ and $r_t^{(h)}$ are reward tuples issued in block interval t, represent the rewards of attacker and honest respectively, and T is the size of the observation window.

4 Experimental Evaluation

In this section, we use the simulation method in [4] to build a Bitcoin simulator to simulate the proposed optimal stubborn mining strategy. Although this method can realize the block generation process of the Bitcoin system, it does not actually solve the POW problem. In the simulation experiments, we define the longest length of the fork as 36 blocks, and the number of iterations is 1000, that is, 1000 miners mine at the same rate. A minor fraction (α) of 1000 miners are attackers who do not follow the rules of the protocol, but instead implement a strategy that deviates from the protocol. And the remaining part of the pool (β) miners are honest miners who mine in the way prescribed by the protocol.

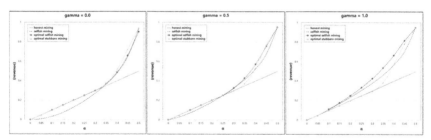

Fig. 2. The relevant revenue obtained by various mining strategies with low, medium and high communication capabilities.

First, we compare the performance of honest mining, selfish mining, optimal selfish mining and optimal stubborn mining. Figures 2 indicate the relative revenue of attackers when $\gamma = 0.0$, $\gamma = 0.5$, and $\gamma = 1.0$, respectively. Since γ represents the influence of the attacker in the network, we use $\gamma = 0.0$, $\gamma = 0.5$, and $\gamma = 1.0$ to represent the low, medium, and high communication capabilities of the attacker, respectively. It can be observed in the experimental results that under the same communication capability, as the computing power (α) of the attacker increases, the relative revenue that the attacker can obtain is also higher. And it can be clearly seen in Fig. 2 that when $\gamma = 0.0$, $\alpha \geq 0.35$ or $\gamma = 0.5$, $\alpha \geq 0.45$, the relative revenue of miners implementing the optimal stubborn mining strategy exceed what was previously considered to be the most profitable optimal selfish mining. And in most cases, the relative revenue obtained by the optimal stubborn mining strategy are higher than SM1. Moreover, with the increase of the communication capability of the attacker, the relative revenue that the attacker can obtain is likewise gradually increasing.

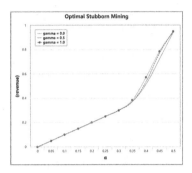

Fig. 3. The relevant revenue of optimal stubborn mining with low, medium, and high communication capabilities.

Then, our experiment compares the relative revenue of the attackers adopting the optimal stubborn mining strategy under the conditions of low, medium and high communication capabilities. As can be seen from Fig. 3, as the communication capabilities of the attackers increase, the relative revenue that the attackers can obtain is likewise gradually increasing.

5 Conclusion

The traditional Bitcoin mining protocol is considered to be incentive compatible, but since Ittay Eyal and Emin G"un Sirer proposed selfish mining, the Bitcoin mining protocol is not incentive compatible. It has been endorsed by everyone. Scholars from various countries have also focused on obtaining higher revenue by designing various mining strategies that deviate from the protocol. Strategies such as optimal selfish mining and stubborn mining have gradually come out. This work simulates the stubborn mining strategy by describing it as a Markov Decision Process to obtain the optimal strategy. Our experiments prove that the relative revenue obtained by the optimal stubborn mining strategy proposed in this paper is formally higher than that of honest mining. It is also more profitable for attackers to adopt our strategy than optimal selfish mining under certain circumstances.

Acknowledgement. This study is supported by the Foundation of National Natural Science Foundation of China (Grant No.: 62072273, 72111530206, 61962009, 61873117, 61832012, 61771231, 61771289); The Major Basic Research Project of Natural Science Foundation of Shandong Province of China (ZR2019ZD10); Natural Science Foundation of Shandong Province (ZR2019MF062); Shandong University Science and Technology Program Project (J18A326); Guangxi Key Laboratory of Cryptography and Information Security (No: GCIS202112); The Major Basic Research Project of Natural Science Foundation of Shandong Province of China (ZR2018ZC0438); Major Scientific and Technological Special Project of Guizhou Province (20183001), Foundation of Guizhou Provincial Key Laboratory of Public Big Data (No. 2019BD-KFJJ009), Talent project of Guizhou Big Data Academy. Guizhou Provincial Key Laboratory of Public Big Data. ([2018]01).

References

1. LNCS Homepage. http://www.springer.com/lncs. Accessed 21 Nov 2016
2. Nakamoto, S.: Bitcoin: a peer-to-peer electronic cash system. Decentralized Business Review 21260 (2008)
3. Böhme, R., Christin, N., Edelman, B., et al.: Bitcoin: economics, technology, and governance. J. Econ. Perspectives **29**(2), 213–238 (2015)
4. Tang, C., Wu, L., Wen, G., et al.: Incentivizing honest mining in blockchain networks: a reputation approach. IEEE Trans. Circuits Syst. II Express Briefs **67**(1), 117–121 (2019)
5. Eyal, I., Sirer, E.G.: Majority is not enough: Bitcoin mining is vulnerable. In: International Conference on Financial Cryptography and Data Security. Springer, Berlin, Heidelberg, pp. 436–454 (2014). https://doi.org/10.1007/978-3-662-45472-5_28
6. Tschorsch, F., Scheuermann, B.: Bitcoin and beyond: a technical survey on decentralized digital currencies. IEEE Communications Surveys Tutorials **18**(3), 2084–2123 (2016)
7. Wang, W., Hoang, D.T., Hu, P., et al.: A survey on consensus mechanisms and mining strategy management in blockchain networks. IEEE Access **7**, 22328–22370 (2019)
8. Sapirshtein, A., Sompolinsky, Y., Zohar, A.: Optimal selfish mining strategies in bitcoin. In: International Conference on Financial Cryptography and Data Security. Springer, Berlin, Heidelberg, pp. 515–532 (2016). https://doi.org/10.1007/978-3-662-54970-4_30
9. Nayak, K., Kumar, S., Miller, A., et al.: Stubborn mining: generalizing selfish mining and combining with an eclipse attack. In: 2016 IEEE European Symposium on Security and Privacy (EuroS&P). IEEE, pp. 305–320 (2016)
10. Li, T., Wang, Z., Chen, Y., et al.: Is semi-selfish mining available without being detected?. International Journal of Intelligent Systems (2021).https://doi.org/10.1002/int.22656
11. Li, T., Wang, Z., Yang, G., et al.: Semi-selfish mining based on hidden Markov decision process. Int. J. Intell. Syst. **36**(7), 3596–3612 (2021)
12. Swan, M.: Blockchain: Blueprint for a New Economy. O'Reilly Media, Inc.; (2015)
13. Yang, G., Wang, Y., Wang, Z., et al.: IPBSM: an optimal bribery selfish mining in the presence of intelligent and pure attackers. Int. J. Intell. Syst. **35**(11), 1735–1748 (2020)
14. Bonneau, J., Felten, E.W., Goldfeder, S., Kroll, J.A., Narayanan, A.: Why Buy When You Can Rent? Bribery Attacks on Bitcoin Consensus (2016)
15. Gao, S., Li, Z., Peng, Z., et al.: Power adjusting and bribery racing: novel mining attacks in the bitcoin system. In: Proceedings of the 2019 ACM SIGSAC Conference on Computer and Communications Security, pp. 833-850 (2019)
16. Dong, X., Wu, F., Faree, A., et al.: Selfholding: a combined attack model using selfish mining with block withholding attack. Comput. Secur. **87**, 101584 (2019)

17. Wang, T., Liew, S.C., Zhang, S.: When blockchain meets AI: optimal mining strategy achieved by machine learning. Int. J. Intell. Syst. **36**(5), 2183–2207 (2021)
18. Zheng, Z., Xie, S., Dai, H.N., et al.: Blockchain challenges and opportunities: a survey. Int. J. Web Grid Serv. **14**(4), 352–375 (2018)
19. Decker, C., Wattenhofer, R.: Information propagation in the bitcoin network. In: IEEE P2P 2013 Proceedings. IEEE, pp. 1-10 (2013).
20. Wang, Y., Wang, Z., Zhao, M., et al.: BSM-ether: bribery selfish mining in blockchain-based healthcare systems. Inf. Sci. **601**, 1–17 (2022)
21. Zhang, X., Wang, Y., Geng, G., Yu, J.: Delay-optimized multicast tree packing in software-defined networks. IEEE Transactions on Services Computing, Early Access, pp. 1–14 (2021). https://doi.org/10.1109/TSC.2021.3106264
22. Yuan, F., Chen, S., Liang, K., Xu, L.: Research on the coordination mechanism of traditional Chinese medicine medical record data standardization and characteristic protection under big data environment. Shandong:Shandong People's Publishing House (2021)

Bipolar Picture Fuzzy Graph Based Multiple Attribute Decision Making Approach-Part II

Shu Gong[1,2(✉)], Gang Hua[2], and Xiaomei Zhang[3]

[1] Department of Computer Science, Guangdong University of Science and Technology, Dongguan 523083, China
gongshu_gk@126.com
[2] School of Information and Control Engineering, China University of Mining and Technology, Xuzhou 221116, China
[3] Dongguan Nancheng People's Hospital, Dongguan 523000, China

Abstract. In Gong and Hua [1], two bipolar picture fuzzy graph based multiple attribute decision making algorithms have been proposed, labelled as Algorithm A and Algorithm B respectively. Furthermore, a case study is presented to explain how to implement Algorithm A for a specific multiple attribute decision making problem. This paper is a continue work of [1], in which a case study on medical diagnosis is manifested to show how to use Algorithm B for a specific multiple attribute decision making problem.

Keywords: Bipolar fuzzy set · Bipolar picture fuzzy set · Bipolar picture fuzzy graph · Multiple attribute decision making

1 Introduction

In Gong and Hua [1], we presented two algorithms for multiple attribute decision making problem based on bipolar picture fuzzy graph framework. However, only one case study in this paper conducted as numerical experiment for Algorithm A, and there is no instance to show how to implement Algorithm B. This paper is the continue work of [1] in which we mainly present a case study to show how to implement Algorithm B for a detailed multiple attribute decision making problem.

All the notations and terminologies on bipolar picture fuzzy set, bipolar picture fuzzy graph and bipolar picture fuzzy relation can be referred to [1], and we skip the settings here. Moreover, the statement of Algorithm B also can be found in Gong and Hua [1]. In this paper, we show the numerical example directly in the next section.

2 A Case Study

IN this section, we explain how to implement the Algorithm B in [1] by showing the following instance. The data of the simulation experiments in this paper are mainly adapted from Ye [2] and Amanathulla et al. [3].

© The Author(s), under exclusive license to Springer Nature Switzerland AG 2023
Y. Xu et al. (Eds.): ML4CS 2022, LNCS 13656, pp. 309–320, 2023.
https://doi.org/10.1007/978-3-031-20099-1_26

In this instance, we consider the medical diagnosis problem with a set of diagnosis $A = \{A_1, A_2, A_3, A_4, A_5\}$ and a set of symptoms $C = \{C_1, C_2, C_3, C_4, C_5\}$, where A_1: viral fever; A_2: malaria; A_3: typhoid; A_4: gastritis; A_5: stenocardia; C_1: temperature; C_2: headache; C_3: stomach pain; C_4: cough; C_5: sttenocardia.

The positive weight vector and negative weight vector of the symptoms are assumed to be $w^P = (0.2, 0.2, 0.1, 0.2, 0.3)$ and $w^N = (-0.2, -0.2, -0.3, -0.2, -0.1)$, respectively. The performance values of these diseases are featured by bipolar picture fuzzy set, and are presented in the following 5×5 matrix.

$$
\begin{bmatrix}
(0.4, 0.3, & (0.5, 0.1, & (0.1, 0.2, & (0.4, 0.3, & (0.4, 0.2, \\
0.2, -0.1, & 0.2, -0.4, & 0.7, -0.4, & 0.2, -0.1, & 0.2, -0.3, \\
-0.2, -0.5) & -0.2, -0.3) & -0.3, -0.1) & -0.2, -0.5) & -0.3, -0.1) \\
(0.4, 0.1, & (0.1, 0.6, & (0.6, 0.1, & (0.5, 0.2, & (0.4, 0.2, \\
0.3, -0.1, & 0.1, -0.3, & 0.1, -0.1, & 0.3, -0.3, & 0.1, -0.1, \\
-0.5, -0.2) & -0.1, -0.3) & -0.6, -0.3) & -0.3, -0.2) & -0.2, -0.4) \\
(0.2, 0.4, & (0.4, 0.1, & (0.3, 0.2, & (0.1, 0.6, & (0.2, 0.1, \\
0.1, -0.4, & 0.3, -0.2, & 0.1, -0.1, & 0.2, -0.6, & 0.5, -0.4, \\
-0.1, -0.4) & -0.5, -0.2) & -0.2, -0.4) & -0.2, -0.1) & -0.5, -0.1) \\
(0.1, 0.3, & (0.3, 0.3, & (0.4, 0.3, & (0.1, 0.2, & (0.4, 0.5, \\
0.5, -0.4, & 0.2, -0.2, & 0.2, -0.1, & 0.6, -0.5, & 0.1, -0.1, \\
-0.4, -0.2) & -0.2, -0.4) & -0.2, -0.5) & -0.2, -0.3) & -0.1, -0.7) \\
(0.8, 0.1, & (0.1, 0.7, & (0.3, 0.3, & (0.2, 0.3, & (0.4, 0.1, \\
0.1, -0.1, & 0.1, -0.3, & 0.3, -0.3, & 0.2, -0.3, & 0.4, -0.1, \\
-0.4, -0.4) & -0.2, -0.4) & -0.3, -0.3) & -0.2, -0.3) & -0.7, -0.2)
\end{bmatrix}
$$

Assume that there is a patient A having all symptoms is represented by the following bipolar fuzzy information:

$A = \{\langle C_1, 0.7, 0.2, 0.1, -0.2, -0.4, -0.4 \rangle, \langle C_2, 0.6, 0.1, 0.2, -0.4, -0.3, -0.3 \rangle$
$\langle C_3, 0.2, 0.0, 0.7, -0.1, -0.7, -0.2 \rangle, \langle C_4, 0.5, 0.1, 0.2, -0.1, -0.2, -0.6 \rangle$
$\langle C_5, 0.1, 0.1, 0.5, -0.4, -0.4, -0.1 \rangle\}$

Suppose the bipolar picture fuzzy edges represent the relation among the symptoms (refer to Fig. 1), which are denoted by

$$f_{12} = (0.2, 0.4, 0.1, -0.3, -0.1, -0.5),$$
$$f_{13} = (0.1, 0.1, 0.7, -0.4, -0.4, -0.1),$$
$$f_{14} = (0.3, 0.4, 0.1, -0.2, -0.1, -0.6),$$
$$f_{15} = (0.2, 0.1, 0.6, -0.3, -0.4, -0.1),$$
$$f_{23} = (0.0, 0.1, 0.7, -0.1, -0.3, -0.6),$$
$$f_{24} = (0.4, 0.4, 0.1, -0.3, -0.2, -0.4),$$
$$f_{25} = (0.1, 0.1, 0.6, -0.3, -0.4, -0.2),$$
$$f_{34} = (0.1, 0.1, 0.8, -0.4, -0.3, -0.1),$$
$$f_{35} = (0.1, 0.2, 0.7, -0.5, -0.4, -0.1),$$
$$f_{45} = (0.1, 0.2, 0.6, -0.1, -0.1, -0.5).$$

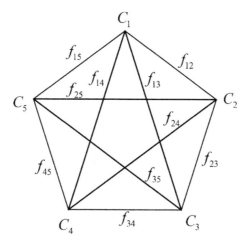

Fig. 1. The relationship expression graph for 5 attributes.

The bipolar impact coefficient among symptoms are determined by.

$$\eta_{12}^{P} = \frac{\mu_{12}^{P} + (1 - v_{12}^{P})(1 - \iota_{12}^{P})}{3} = \frac{0.2 + (1 - 0.4)(1 - 0.1)}{3} = \frac{37}{150},$$

$$\eta_{12}^{N} = \frac{\mu_{12}^{N} + (-1 - v_{12}^{N})(-1 - \iota_{12}^{N})}{3} = \frac{-0.3 - (-1 + 0.1)(-1 + 0.5)}{3} = -\frac{1}{4},$$

$$\eta_{13}^{P} = \frac{\mu_{13}^{P} + (1 - v_{13}^{P})(1 - \iota_{13}^{P})}{3} = \frac{0.1 + (1 - 0.1)(1 - 0.7)}{3} = \frac{37}{300},$$

$$\eta_{13}^{N} = \frac{\mu_{13}^{N} + (-1 - v_{13}^{N})(-1 - \iota_{13}^{N})}{3} = \frac{-0.4 - (-1 + 0.4)(-1 + 0.1)}{3} = -\frac{47}{150},$$

$$\eta_{14}^{P} = \frac{\mu_{14}^{P} + (1 - v_{14}^{P})(1 - \iota_{14}^{P})}{3} = \frac{0.3 + (1 - 0.4)(1 - 0.1)}{3} = \frac{37}{150},$$

$$\eta_{14}^{N} = \frac{\mu_{14}^{N} + (-1 - v_{14}^{N})(-1 - \iota_{14}^{N})}{3} = \frac{-0.2 - (-1 + 0.1)(-1 + 0.6)}{3} = -\frac{14}{75},$$

$$\eta_{15}^{P} = \frac{\mu_{15}^{P} + (1 - v_{15}^{P})(1 - \iota_{15}^{P})}{3} = \frac{0.2 + (1 - 0.1)(1 - 0.6)}{3} = \frac{14}{75},$$

$$\eta_{15}^{N} = \frac{\mu_{15}^{N} + (-1 - v_{15}^{N})(-1 - \iota_{15}^{N})}{3} = \frac{-0.3 - (-1 + 0.4)(-1 + 0.1)}{3} = -\frac{37}{150},$$

$$\eta_{23}^{P} = \frac{\mu_{23}^{P} + (1 - v_{23}^{P})(1 - \iota_{23}^{P})}{3} = \frac{0.0 + (1 - 0.1)(1 - 0.7)}{3} = 0.09,$$

$$\eta_{23}^{N} = \frac{\mu_{23}^{N} + (-1 - v_{23}^{N})(-1 - \iota_{23}^{N})}{3} = \frac{-0.1 - (-1 + 0.3)(-1 + 0.6)}{3} = -\frac{19}{150},$$

$$\eta_{24}^{P} = \frac{\mu_{24}^{P} + (1 - v_{24}^{P})(1 - \iota_{24}^{P})}{3} = \frac{0.4 + (1 - 0.4)(1 - 0.1)}{3} = \frac{47}{150},$$

$$\eta_{24}^{N} = \frac{\mu_{24}^{N} + (-1 - v_{24}^{N})(-1 - \iota_{24}^{N})}{3} = \frac{-0.3 - (-1 + 0.2)(-1 + 0.4)}{3} = -\frac{13}{50},$$

$$\eta_{25}^{P} = \frac{\mu_{25}^{P} + (1 - \nu_{25}^{P})(1 - \iota_{25}^{P})}{3} = \frac{0.1 + (1 - 0.1)(1 - 0.6)}{3} = \frac{23}{150},$$

$$\eta_{25}^{N} = \frac{\mu_{25}^{N} + (-1 - \nu_{25}^{N})(-1 - \iota_{25}^{N})}{3} = \frac{-0.3 - (-1 + 0.4)(-1 + 0.2)}{3} = -\frac{13}{50},$$

$$\eta_{34}^{P} = \frac{\mu_{34}^{P} + (1 - \nu_{34}^{P})(1 - \iota_{34}^{P})}{3} = \frac{0.1 + (1 - 0.1)(1 - 0.8)}{3} = \frac{7}{75},$$

$$\eta_{34}^{N} = \frac{\mu_{34}^{N} + (-1 - \nu_{34}^{N})(-1 - \iota_{34}^{N})}{3} = \frac{-0.4 - (-1 + 0.3)(-1 + 0.1)}{3} = -\frac{103}{300},$$

$$\eta_{35}^{P} = \frac{\mu_{35}^{P} + (1 - \nu_{35}^{P})(1 - \iota_{35}^{P})}{3} = \frac{0.1 + (1 - 0.2)(1 - 0.7)}{3} = \frac{17}{150},$$

$$\eta_{35}^{N} = \frac{\mu_{35}^{N} + (-1 - \nu_{35}^{N})(-1 - \iota_{35}^{N})}{3} = \frac{-0.5 - (-1 + 0.4)(-1 + 0.1)}{3} = -\frac{26}{75},$$

$$\eta_{45}^{P} = \frac{\mu_{45}^{P} + (1 - \nu_{45}^{P})(1 - \iota_{45}^{P})}{3} = \frac{0.1 + (1 - 0.2)(1 - 0.6)}{3} = \frac{7}{50},$$

$$\eta_{45}^{N} = \frac{\mu_{45}^{N} + (-1 - \nu_{45}^{N})(-1 - \iota_{45}^{N})}{3} = \frac{-0.1 - (-1 + 0.1)(-1 + 0.5)}{3} = -\frac{11}{60}.$$

Now, we compute the bipolar associated weighted values of disease as follows:

$$\tilde{b}_{11} = [\frac{w_1^{P}}{3}(\eta_{11}^{P} b_{11}^{P} + \eta_{21}^{P} b_{12}^{P} + \eta_{31}^{P} b_{13}^{P} + \eta_{41}^{P} b_{14}^{P} + \eta_{51}^{P} b_{15}^{P}),$$

$$\frac{w_1^{N}}{3}(\eta_{11}^{N} b_{11}^{N} + \eta_{21}^{N} b_{12}^{N} + \eta_{31}^{N} b_{13}^{N} + \eta_{41}^{N} b_{14}^{N} + \eta_{51}^{N} b_{15}^{N})]$$

$$= \frac{0.2}{3}[1 \times (0.4, 0.3, 0.2) + \frac{37}{150}(0.5, 0.1, 0.2) + \frac{37}{300}(0.1, 0.2, 0.7) + \frac{37}{150}(0.4, 0.3, 0.2)$$

$$+ \frac{14}{75}(0.4, 0.2, 0.2)], -\frac{0.2}{3}[-1 \times (-0.1, -0.2, -0.5) - \frac{1}{4}(-0.4, -0.2, -0.3)$$

$$- \frac{47}{150}(-0.4, -0.3, -0.1) - \frac{14}{75}(-0.1, -0.2, -0.5) - \frac{37}{150}(-0.3, -0.3, -0.1)]$$

$$= (0.0473, 0.0307, 0.0282, -0.0303, -0.0328, -0.0491),$$

$$\tilde{b}_{12} = [\frac{w_2^{P}}{3}(\eta_{12}^{P} b_{11}^{P} + \eta_{22}^{P} b_{12}^{P} + \eta_{32}^{P} b_{13}^{P} + \eta_{42}^{P} b_{14}^{P} + \eta_{52}^{P} b_{15}^{P}),$$

$$\frac{w_2^{N}}{3}(\eta_{12}^{N} b_{11}^{N} + \eta_{22}^{N} b_{12}^{N} + \eta_{32}^{N} b_{13}^{N} + \eta_{42}^{N} b_{14}^{N} + \eta_{52}^{N} b_{15}^{N})]$$

$$= \frac{0.2}{3}[\frac{37}{150}(0.4, 0.3, 0.2) + 1 \times (0.5, 0.1, 0.2) + 0.09(0.1, 0.2, 0.7) + \frac{47}{150}(0.4, 0.3, 0.2)$$

$$+ \frac{23}{150}(0.4, 0.2, 0.2)], -\frac{0.2}{3}[-\frac{1}{4}(-0.1, -0.2, -0.5) - 1 \times (-0.4, -0.2, -0.3)$$

$$- \frac{19}{150}(-0.4, -0.3, -0.1) - \frac{13}{50}(-0.1, -0.2, -0.5) - \frac{13}{50}(-0.3, -0.3, -0.1)]$$

$$= (0.0530, 0.0211, 0.0270, -0.0386, -0.0279, -0.0396),$$

$$\tilde{b}_{13} = [\frac{w_3^{P}}{3}(\eta_{13}^{P} b_{11}^{P} + \eta_{23}^{P} b_{12}^{P} + \eta_{33}^{P} b_{13}^{P} + \eta_{43}^{P} b_{14}^{P} + \eta_{53}^{P} b_{15}^{P}),$$

$$\frac{w_3^N}{3}(\eta_{13}^N b_{11}^N + \eta_{23}^N b_{12}^N + \eta_{33}^N b_{13}^N + \eta_{43}^N b_{14}^N + \eta_{53}^N b_{15}^N)]$$

$$= \frac{0.1}{3}[\frac{37}{300}(0.4, 0.3, 0.2) + 0.09(0.5, 0.1, 0.2) + 1 \times (0.1, 0.2, 0.7) + \frac{7}{75}(0.4, 0.3, 0.2)$$

$$+ \frac{17}{150}(0.4, 0.2, 0.2)], -\frac{0.3}{3}[-\frac{47}{150}(-0.1, -0.2, -0.5) - \frac{19}{150}(-0.4, -0.2, -0.3)$$

$$- 1 \times (-0.4, -0.3, -0.1) - \frac{103}{300}(-0.1, -0.2, -0.5) - \frac{26}{75}(-0.3, -0.3, -0.1)]$$

$$= (0.0092, 0.0099, 0.0261, -0.0620, -0.0561, -0.0501),$$

$$\tilde{b}_{14} = [\frac{w_4^P}{3}(\eta_{14}^P b_{11}^P + \eta_{24}^P b_{12}^P + \eta_{34}^P b_{13}^P + \eta_{44}^P b_{14}^P + \eta_{54}^P b_{15}^P),$$

$$\frac{w_4^N}{3}(\eta_{14}^N b_{11}^N + \eta_{24}^N b_{12}^N + \eta_{34}^N b_{13}^N + \eta_{44}^N b_{14}^N + \eta_{54}^N b_{15}^N)]$$

$$= \frac{0.2}{3}[\frac{37}{150}(0.4, 0.3, 0.2) + \frac{47}{150}(0.5, 0.1, 0.2) + \frac{7}{75}(0.1, 0.2, 0.7) + 1 \times (0.4, 0.3, 0.2)$$

$$+ \frac{7}{50}(0.4, 0.2, 0.2)], -\frac{0.2}{3}[-\frac{14}{75}(-0.1, -0.2, -0.5) - \frac{13}{50}(-0.4, -0.2, -0.3)$$

$$- \frac{103}{300}(-0.4, -0.3, -0.1) - 1 \times (-0.1, -0.2, -0.5) - \frac{11}{60}(-0.3, -0.3, -0.1)]$$

$$= (0.0480, 0.0301, 0.0270, -0.0277, -0.0298, -0.0483),$$

$$\tilde{b}_{15} = [\frac{w_5^P}{3}(\eta_{15}^P b_{11}^P + \eta_{25}^P b_{12}^P + \eta_{35}^P b_{13}^P + \eta_{45}^P b_{14}^P + \eta_{55}^P b_{15}^P),$$

$$\frac{w_5^N}{3}(\eta_{15}^N b_{11}^N + \eta_{25}^N b_{12}^N + \eta_{35}^N b_{13}^N + \eta_{45}^N b_{14}^N + \eta_{55}^N b_{15}^N)]$$

$$= \frac{0.3}{3}[\frac{14}{75}(0.4, 0.3, 0.2) + \frac{23}{150}(0.5, 0.1, 0.2) + \frac{17}{150}(0.1, 0.2, 0.7) + \frac{7}{50}(0.4, 0.3, 0.2)$$

$$+ 1 \times (0.4, 0.2, 0.2)], -\frac{0.1}{3}[-\frac{37}{150}(-0.1, -0.2, -0.5) - \frac{13}{50}(-0.4, -0.2, -0.3)$$

$$- \frac{26}{75}(-0.4, -0.3, -0.1) - \frac{11}{60}(-0.1, -0.2, -0.5) - 1 \times (-0.3, -0.3, -0.1)]$$

$$= (0.0619, 0.0336, 0.0375, -0.0195, -0.0181, -0.0143),$$

$$\tilde{b}_{21} = [\frac{w_1^P}{3}(\eta_{11}^P b_{21}^P + \eta_{21}^P b_{22}^P + \eta_{31}^P b_{23}^P + \eta_{41}^P b_{24}^P + \eta_{51}^P b_{25}^P),$$

$$\frac{w_1^N}{3}(\eta_{11}^N b_{21}^N + \eta_{21}^N b_{22}^N + \eta_{31}^N b_{23}^N + \eta_{41}^N b_{24}^N + \eta_{51}^N b_{25}^N)]$$

$$= \frac{0.2}{3}[1 \times (0.4, 0.1, 0.3) + \frac{37}{150}(0.1, 0.6, 0.1) + \frac{37}{300}(0.6, 0.1, 0.1) + \frac{37}{150}(0.5, 0.2, 0.3)$$

$$+ \frac{14}{75}(0.4, 0.2, 0.1)], -\frac{0.2}{3}[-1 \times (-0.1, -0.5, -0.2) - \frac{1}{4}(-0.3, -0.1, -0.3)$$

$$- \frac{47}{150}(-0.1, -0.6, -0.3) - \frac{14}{75}(-0.3, -0.3, -0.2) - \frac{37}{150}(-0.1, -0.2, -0.4)]$$

$$= (0.0464, 0.0231, 0.0286, -0.0191, -0.0546, -0.0337),$$

$$\tilde{b}_{22} = [\frac{w_2^P}{3}(\eta_{12}^P b_{21}^P + \eta_{22}^P b_{22}^P + \eta_{32}^P b_{23}^P + \eta_{42}^P b_{24}^P + \eta_{52}^P b_{25}^P),$$

$$\frac{w_2^N}{3}(\eta_{12}^N b_{21}^N + \eta_{22}^N b_{22}^N + \eta_{32}^N b_{23}^N + \eta_{42}^N b_{24}^N + \eta_{52}^N b_{25}^N)]$$

$$= \frac{0.2}{3}[\frac{37}{150}(0.4, 0.1, 0.3) + 1 \times (0.1, 0.6, 0.1) + 0.09(0.6, 0.1, 0.1) + \frac{47}{150}(0.5, 0.2, 0.3)$$

$$+ \frac{23}{150}(0.4, 0.2, 0.1)], -\frac{0.2}{3}[-\frac{1}{4}(-0.1, -0.5, -0.2) - 1 \times (-0.3, -0.1, -0.3)$$

$$- \frac{19}{150}(-0.1, -0.6, -0.3) - \frac{13}{50}(-0.3, -0.3, -0.2) - \frac{13}{50}(-0.1, -0.2, -0.4)]$$

$$= (0.0314, 0.0485, 0.0195, -0.0294, -0.0287, -0.0363),$$

$$\tilde{b}_{23} = [\frac{w_3^P}{3}(\eta_{13}^P b_{21}^P + \eta_{23}^P b_{22}^P + \eta_{33}^P b_{23}^P + \eta_{43}^P b_{24}^P + \eta_{53}^P b_{25}^P),$$

$$\frac{w_3^N}{3}(\eta_{13}^N b_{21}^N + \eta_{23}^N b_{22}^N + \eta_{33}^N b_{23}^N + \eta_{43}^N b_{24}^N + \eta_{53}^N b_{25}^N)]$$

$$= \frac{0.1}{3}[\frac{37}{300}(0.4, 0.1, 0.3) + 0.09(0.1, 0.6, 0.1) + 1 \times (0.6, 0.1, 0.1) + \frac{7}{75}(0.5, 0.2, 0.3)$$

$$+ \frac{17}{150}(0.4, 0.2, 0.1)], -\frac{0.3}{3}[-\frac{47}{150}(-0.1, -0.5, -0.2) - \frac{19}{150}(-0.3, -0.1, -0.3)$$

$$-1 \times (-0.1, -0.6, -0.3) - \frac{103}{300}(-0.3, -0.3, -0.2) - \frac{26}{75}(-0.1, -0.2, -0.4)]$$

$$= (0.0250, 0.0069, 0.0062, -0.0307, -0.0942, -0.0608),$$

$$\tilde{b}_{24} = [\frac{w_4^P}{3}(\eta_{14}^P b_{21}^P + \eta_{24}^P b_{22}^P + \eta_{34}^P b_{23}^P + \eta_{44}^P b_{24}^P + \eta_{54}^P b_{25}^P),$$

$$\frac{w_4^N}{3}(\eta_{14}^N b_{21}^N + \eta_{24}^N b_{22}^N + \eta_{34}^N b_{23}^N + \eta_{44}^N b_{24}^N + \eta_{54}^N b_{25}^N)]$$

$$= \frac{0.2}{3}[\frac{37}{150}(0.4, 0.1, 0.3) + \frac{47}{150}(0.1, 0.6, 0.1) + \frac{7}{75}(0.6, 0.1, 0.1) + 1 \times (0.5, 0.2, 0.3)$$

$$+ \frac{7}{50}(0.4, 0.2, 0.1)], -\frac{0.2}{3}[-\frac{14}{75}(-0.1, -0.5, -0.2) - \frac{13}{50}(-0.3, -0.1, -0.3)$$

$$- \frac{103}{300}(-0.1, -0.6, -0.3) - 1 \times (-0.3, -0.3, -0.2) - \frac{11}{60}(-0.1, -0.2, -0.4)]$$

$$= (0.0495, 0.0300, 0.0286, -0.0300, -0.0441, -0.0328),$$

$$\tilde{b}_{25} = [\frac{w_5^P}{3}(\eta_{15}^P b_{21}^P + \eta_{25}^P b_{22}^P + \eta_{35}^P b_{23}^P + \eta_{45}^P b_{24}^P + \eta_{55}^P b_{25}^P),$$

$$\frac{w_5^N}{3}(\eta_{15}^N b_{21}^N + \eta_{25}^N b_{22}^N + \eta_{35}^N b_{23}^N + \eta_{45}^N b_{24}^N + \eta_{55}^N b_{25}^N)]$$

$$= \frac{0.3}{3}[\frac{14}{75}(0.4, 0.1, 0.3) + \frac{23}{150}(0.1, 0.6, 0.1) + \frac{17}{150}(0.6, 0.1, 0.1) + \frac{7}{50}(0.5, 0.2, 0.3)$$

$$+1 \times (0.4, 0.2, 0.1)], -\frac{0.1}{3}[-\frac{37}{150}(-0.1, -0.5, -0.2) - \frac{13}{50}(-0.3, -0.1, -0.3)$$

$$- \frac{26}{75}(-0.1, -0.6, -0.3) - \frac{11}{60}(-0.3, -0.3, -0.2) - 1 \times (-0.1, -0.2, -0.4)]$$

$$= (0.0628, 0.0350, 0.0225, -0.0097, -0.0204, -0.0223),$$

$$\tilde{b}_{31} = [\frac{w_1^P}{3}(\eta_{11}^P b_{31}^P + \eta_{21}^P b_{32}^P + \eta_{31}^P b_{33}^P + \eta_{41}^P b_{34}^P + \eta_{51}^P b_{35}^P),$$

$$\frac{w_1^N}{3}(\eta_{11}^N b_{31}^N + \eta_{21}^N b_{32}^N + \eta_{31}^N b_{33}^N + \eta_{41}^N b_{34}^N + \eta_{51}^N b_{35}^N)]$$

$$= \frac{0.2}{3}[1 \times (0.2, 0.4, 0.1) + \frac{37}{150}(0.4, 0.1, 0.3) + \frac{37}{300}(0.3, 0.2, 0.1) + \frac{37}{150}(0.1, 0.6, 0.2)$$

$$+ \frac{14}{75}(0.2, 0.1, 0.5)], -\frac{0.2}{3}[-1 \times (-0.4, -0.1, -0.4) - \frac{1}{4}(-0.2, -0.5, -0.2)$$

$$- \frac{47}{150}(-0.1, -0.2, -0.4) - \frac{14}{75}(-0.6, -0.2, -0.1) - \frac{37}{150}(-0.4, -0.5, -0.1)]$$

$$= (0.0265, 0.0411, 0.0219, -0.0461, -0.0299, -0.0412),$$

$$\tilde{b}_{32} = [\frac{w_2^P}{3}(\eta_{12}^P b_{31}^P + \eta_{22}^P b_{32}^P + \eta_{32}^P b_{33}^P + \eta_{42}^P b_{34}^P + \eta_{52}^P b_{35}^P),$$

$$\frac{w_2^N}{3}(\eta_{12}^N b_{31}^N + \eta_{22}^N b_{32}^N + \eta_{32}^N b_{33}^N + \eta_{42}^N b_{34}^N + \eta_{52}^N b_{35}^N)]$$

$$= \frac{0.2}{3}[\frac{37}{150}(0.2, 0.4, 0.1) + 1 \times (0.4, 0.1, 0.3) + 0.09(0.3, 0.2, 0.1) + \frac{47}{150}(0.1, 0.6, 0.2)$$

$$+ \frac{23}{150}(0.2, 0.1, 0.5)], -\frac{0.2}{3}[-\frac{1}{4}(-0.4, -0.1, -0.4) - 1 \times (-0.2, -0.5, -0.2)$$

$$- \frac{19}{150}(-0.1, -0.2, -0.4) - \frac{13}{50}(-0.6, -0.2, -0.1) - \frac{13}{50}(-0.4, -0.5, -0.1)]$$

$$= (0.0359, 0.0280, 0.0315, -0.0382, -0.0488, -0.0268),$$

$$\tilde{b}_{33} = [\frac{w_3^P}{3}(\eta_{13}^P b_{31}^P + \eta_{23}^P b_{32}^P + \eta_{33}^P b_{33}^P + \eta_{43}^P b_{34}^P + \eta_{53}^P b_{35}^P),$$

$$\frac{w_3^N}{3}(\eta_{13}^N b_{31}^N + \eta_{23}^N b_{32}^N + \eta_{33}^N b_{33}^N + \eta_{43}^N b_{34}^N + \eta_{53}^N b_{35}^N)]$$

$$= \frac{0.1}{3}[\frac{37}{300}(0.2, 0.4, 0.1) + 0.09(0.4, 0.1, 0.3) + 1 \times (0.3, 0.2, 0.1) + \frac{7}{75}(0.1, 0.6, 0.2)$$

$$+ \frac{17}{150}(0.2, 0.1, 0.5)], -\frac{0.3}{3}[-\frac{47}{150}(-0.4, -0.1, -0.4) - \frac{19}{150}(-0.2, -0.5, -0.2)$$

$$- 1 \times (-0.1, -0.2, -0.4) - \frac{103}{300}(-0.6, -0.2, -0.1) - \frac{26}{75}(-0.4, -0.5, -0.1)]$$

$$= (0.0131, 0.0109, 0.0072, -0.0595, -0.0537, -0.0620),$$

$$\tilde{b}_{34} = [\frac{w_4^P}{3}(\eta_{14}^P b_{31}^P + \eta_{24}^P b_{32}^P + \eta_{34}^P b_{33}^P + \eta_{44}^P b_{34}^P + \eta_{54}^P b_{35}^P),$$

$$\frac{w_4^N}{3}(\eta_{14}^N b_{31}^N + \eta_{24}^N b_{32}^N + \eta_{34}^N b_{33}^N + \eta_{44}^N b_{34}^N + \eta_{54}^N b_{35}^N)]$$

$$= \frac{0.2}{3}[\frac{37}{150}(0.2, 0.4, 0.1) + \frac{47}{150}(0.4, 0.1, 0.3) + \frac{7}{75}(0.3, 0.2, 0.1) + 1 \times (0.1, 0.6, 0.2)$$

$$+ \frac{7}{50}(0.2, 0.1, 0.5)], -\frac{0.2}{3}[-\frac{14}{75}(-0.4, -0.1, -0.4) - \frac{13}{50}(-0.2, -0.5, -0.2)$$

$$- \frac{103}{300}(-0.1, -0.2, -0.4) - 1 \times (-0.6, -0.2, -0.1) - \frac{11}{60}(-0.4, -0.5, -0.1)]$$

$$= (0.0220, 0.0508, 0.0265, -0.0556, -0.0339, -0.0255),$$

$$\tilde{b}_{35} = [\frac{w_5^P}{3}(\eta_{15}^P b_{31}^P + \eta_{25}^P b_{32}^P + \eta_{35}^P b_{33}^P + \eta_{45}^P b_{34}^P + \eta_{55}^P b_{35}^P),$$

$$\frac{w_5^N}{3}(\eta_{15}^N b_{31}^N + \eta_{25}^N b_{32}^N + \eta_{35}^N b_{33}^N + \eta_{45}^N b_{34}^N + \eta_{55}^N b_{35}^N)]$$

$$= \frac{0.3}{3}[\frac{14}{75}(0.2, 0.4, 0.1) + \frac{23}{150}(0.4, 0.1, 0.3) + \frac{17}{150}(0.3, 0.2, 0.1) + \frac{7}{50}(0.1, 0.6, 0.2)$$

$$+ 1 \times (0.2, 0.1, 0.5)], -\frac{0.1}{3}[-\frac{37}{150}(-0.4, -0.1, -0.4) - \frac{13}{50}(-0.2, -0.5, -0.2)$$

$$-\frac{26}{75}(-0.1, -0.2, -0.4) - \frac{11}{60}(-0.6, -0.2, -0.1) - 1 \times (-0.4, -0.5, -0.1)]$$

$$= (0.0347, 0.0297, 0.0604, -0.0232, -0.0254, -0.0136),$$

$$\tilde{b}_{41} = [\frac{w_1^P}{3}(\eta_{11}^P b_{41}^P + \eta_{21}^P b_{42}^P + \eta_{31}^P b_{43}^P + \eta_{41}^P b_{44}^P + \eta_{51}^P b_{45}^P),$$

$$\frac{w_1^N}{3}(\eta_{11}^N b_{41}^N + \eta_{21}^N b_{42}^N + \eta_{31}^N b_{43}^N + \eta_{41}^N b_{44}^N + \eta_{51}^N b_{45}^N)]$$

$$= \frac{0.2}{3}[1 \times (0.1, 0.3, 0.5) + \frac{37}{150}(0.3, 0.3, 0.2) + \frac{37}{300}(0.4, 0.3, 0.2) + \frac{37}{150}(0.1, 0.2, 0.6)$$

$$+ \frac{14}{75}(0.4, 0.5, 0.1)], -\frac{0.2}{3}[-1 \times (-0.4, -0.4, -0.2) - \frac{1}{4}(-0.2, -0.2, -0.4)$$

$$-\frac{47}{150}(-0.1, -0.2, -0.5) - \frac{14}{75}(-0.5, -0.2, -0.3) - \frac{37}{150}(-0.1, -0.1, -0.7)]$$

$$= (0.0215, 0.0369, 0.0494, -0.0400, -0.0383, -0.0457),$$

$$\tilde{b}_{42} = [\frac{w_2^P}{3}(\eta_{12}^P b_{41}^P + \eta_{22}^P b_{42}^P + \eta_{32}^P b_{43}^P + \eta_{42}^P b_{44}^P + \eta_{52}^P b_{45}^P),$$

$$\frac{w_2^N}{3}(\eta_{12}^N b_{41}^N + \eta_{22}^N b_{42}^N + \eta_{32}^N b_{43}^N + \eta_{42}^N b_{44}^N + \eta_{52}^N b_{45}^N)]$$

$$= \frac{0.2}{3}[\frac{37}{150}(0.1, 0.3, 0.5) + 1 \times (0.3, 0.3, 0.2) + 0.09(0.4, 0.3, 0.2) + \frac{47}{150}(0.1, 0.2, 0.6)$$

$$+ \frac{23}{150}(0.4, 0.5, 0.1)], -\frac{0.2}{3}[-\frac{1}{4}(-0.4, -0.4, -0.2) - 1 \times (-0.2, -0.2, -0.4)$$

$$-\frac{19}{150}(-0.1, -0.2, -0.5) - \frac{13}{50}(-0.5, -0.2, -0.3) - \frac{13}{50}(-0.1, -0.1, -0.7)]$$

$$= (0.0302, 0.0360, 0.0363, -0.0312, -0.0269, -0.0516),$$

$$\tilde{b}_{43} = [\frac{w_3^P}{3}(\eta_{13}^P b_{41}^P + \eta_{23}^P b_{42}^P + \eta_{33}^P b_{43}^P + \eta_{43}^P b_{44}^P + \eta_{53}^P b_{45}^P),$$

$$\frac{w_3^N}{3}(\eta_{13}^N b_{41}^N + \eta_{23}^N b_{42}^N + \eta_{33}^N b_{43}^N + \eta_{43}^N b_{44}^N + \eta_{53}^N b_{45}^N)]$$

$$= \frac{0.1}{3}[\frac{37}{300}(0.1, 0.3, 0.5) + 0.09(0.3, 0.3, 0.2) + 1 \times (0.4, 0.3, 0.2) + \frac{7}{75}(0.1, 0.2, 0.6)$$

$$+ \frac{17}{150}(0.4, 0.5, 0.1)], -\frac{0.3}{3}[-\frac{47}{150}(-0.4, -0.4, -0.2) - \frac{19}{150}(-0.2, -0.2, -0.4)$$

$$-1 \times (-0.1, -0.2, -0.5) - \frac{103}{300}(-0.5, -0.2, -0.3) - \frac{26}{75}(-0.1, -0.1, -0.7)]$$

$$= (0.0165, 0.0146, 0.0116, -0.0457, -0.0454, -0.0959),$$

$$\tilde{b}_{44} = [\frac{w_4^P}{3}(\eta_{14}^P b_{41}^P + \eta_{24}^P b_{42}^P + \eta_{34}^P b_{43}^P + \eta_{44}^P b_{44}^P + \eta_{54}^P b_{45}^P),$$

$$\frac{w_4^N}{3}(\eta_{14}^N b_{41}^N + \eta_{24}^N b_{42}^N + \eta_{34}^N b_{43}^N + \eta_{44}^N b_{44}^N + \eta_{54}^N b_{45}^N)]$$

$$= \frac{0.2}{3}[\frac{37}{150}(0.1, 0.3, 0.5) + \frac{47}{150}(0.3, 0.3, 0.2) + \frac{7}{75}(0.4, 0.3, 0.2) + 1 \times (0.1, 0.2, 0.6)$$

$$+ \frac{7}{50}(0.4, 0.5, 0.1)], -\frac{0.2}{3}[-\frac{14}{75}(-0.4, -0.4, -0.2) - \frac{13}{50}(-0.2, -0.2, -0.4)$$

$$- \frac{103}{300}(-0.1, -0.2, -0.5) - 1 \times (-0.5, -0.2, -0.3) - \frac{11}{60}(-0.1, -0.1, -0.7)]$$

$$= (0.0208, 0.0311, 0.0546, -0.0453, -0.0276, -0.0494),$$

$$\tilde{b}_{45} = [\frac{w_5^P}{3}(\eta_{15}^P b_{41}^P + \eta_{25}^P b_{42}^P + \eta_{35}^P b_{43}^P + \eta_{45}^P b_{44}^P + \eta_{55}^P b_{45}^P),$$

$$\frac{w_5^N}{3}(\eta_{15}^N b_{41}^N + \eta_{25}^N b_{42}^N + \eta_{35}^N b_{43}^N + \eta_{45}^N b_{44}^N + \eta_{55}^N b_{45}^N)]$$

$$= \frac{0.3}{3}[\frac{14}{75}(0.1, 0.3, 0.5) + \frac{23}{150}(0.3, 0.3, 0.2) + \frac{17}{150}(0.4, 0.3, 0.2) + \frac{7}{50}(0.1, 0.2, 0.6)$$

$$+ 1 \times (0.4, 0.5, 0.1)], -\frac{0.1}{3}[-\frac{37}{150}(-0.4, -0.4, -0.2) - \frac{13}{50}(-0.2, -0.2, -0.4)$$

$$- \frac{26}{75}(-0.1, -0.2, -0.5) - \frac{11}{60}(-0.5, -0.2, -0.3) - 1 \times (-0.1, -0.1, -0.7)]$$

$$= (0.0524, 0.0664, 0.0331, -0.0126, -0.0119, -0.0361),$$

$$\tilde{b}_{51} = [\frac{w_1^P}{3}(\eta_{11}^P b_{51}^P + \eta_{21}^P b_{52}^P + \eta_{31}^P b_{53}^P + \eta_{41}^P b_{54}^P + \eta_{51}^P b_{55}^P),$$

$$\frac{w_1^N}{3}(\eta_{11}^N b_{51}^N + \eta_{21}^N b_{52}^N + \eta_{31}^N b_{53}^N + \eta_{41}^N b_{54}^N + \eta_{51}^N b_{55}^N)]$$

$$= \frac{0.2}{3}[1 \times (0.8, 0.1, 0.1) + \frac{37}{150}(0.1, 0.7, 0.1) + \frac{37}{300}(0.3, 0.3, 0.3) + \frac{37}{150}(0.2, 0.3, 0.2)$$

$$+ \frac{14}{75}(0.4, 0.1, 0.4)], -\frac{0.2}{3}[-1 \times (-0.1, -0.4, -0.4) - \frac{1}{4}(-0.3, -0.2, -0.4)$$

$$- \frac{47}{150}(-0.3, -0.3, -0.3) - \frac{14}{75}(-0.3, -0.2, -0.3) - \frac{37}{150}(-0.1, -0.7, -0.2)]$$

$$= (0.0644, 0.0255, 0.0177, -0.0233, -0.0503, -0.0466),$$

$$\tilde{b}_{52} = [\frac{w_2^P}{3}(\eta_{12}^P b_{51}^P + \eta_{22}^P b_{52}^P + \eta_{32}^P b_{53}^P + \eta_{42}^P b_{54}^P + \eta_{52}^P b_{55}^P),$$

$$\frac{w_2^N}{3}(\eta_{12}^N b_{51}^N + \eta_{22}^N b_{52}^N + \eta_{32}^N b_{53}^N + \eta_{42}^N b_{54}^N + \eta_{52}^N b_{55}^N)]$$

$$= \frac{0.2}{3}[\frac{37}{150}(0.8, 0.1, 0.1) + 1 \times (0.1, 0.7, 0.1) + 0.09(0.3, 0.3, 0.3) + \frac{47}{150}(0.2, 0.3, 0.2)$$

$$+ \frac{23}{150}(0.4, 0.1, 0.4)], -\frac{0.2}{3}[-\frac{1}{4}(-0.1, -0.4, -0.4) - 1 \times (-0.3, -0.2, -0.4)$$

$$- \frac{19}{150}(-0.3, -0.3, -0.3) - \frac{13}{50}(-0.3, -0.2, -0.3) - \frac{13}{50}(-0.1, -0.7, -0.2)]$$

$$= (0.0299, 0.0574, 0.0184, -0.0311, -0.0381, -0.0445),$$

$$\tilde{b}_{53} = [\frac{w_3^P}{3}(\eta_{13}^P b_{51}^P + \eta_{23}^P b_{52}^P + \eta_{33}^P b_{53}^P + \eta_{43}^P b_{54}^P + \eta_{53}^P b_{55}^P),$$

$$\frac{w_3^N}{3}(\eta_{13}^N b_{51}^N + \eta_{23}^N b_{52}^N + \eta_{33}^N b_{53}^N + \eta_{43}^N b_{54}^N + \eta_{53}^N b_{55}^N)]$$

$$= \frac{0.1}{3}[\frac{37}{300}(0.8, 0.1, 0.1) + 0.09(0.1, 0.7, 0.1) + 1 \times (0.3, 0.3, 0.3) + \frac{7}{75}(0.2, 0.3, 0.2)$$

$$+ \frac{17}{150}(0.4, 0.1, 0.4)], -\frac{0.3}{3}[-\frac{47}{150}(-0.1, -0.4, -0.4) - \frac{19}{150}(-0.3, -0.2, -0.4)$$

$$-1 \times (-0.3, -0.3, -0.3) - \frac{103}{300}(-0.3, -0.2, -0.3) - \frac{26}{75}(-0.1, -0.7, -0.2)]$$

$$= (0.0157, 0.0138, 0.0128, -0.0507, -0.0762, -0.0648),$$

$$\tilde{b}_{54} = [\frac{w_4^P}{3}(\eta_{14}^P b_{51}^P + \eta_{24}^P b_{52}^P + \eta_{34}^P b_{53}^P + \eta_{44}^P b_{54}^P + \eta_{54}^P b_{55}^P),$$

$$\frac{w_4^N}{3}(\eta_{14}^N b_{51}^N + \eta_{24}^N b_{52}^N + \eta_{34}^N b_{53}^N + \eta_{44}^N b_{54}^N + \eta_{54}^N b_{55}^N)]$$

$$= \frac{0.2}{3}[\frac{37}{150}(0.8, 0.1, 0.1) + \frac{47}{150}(0.1, 0.7, 0.1) + \frac{7}{75}(0.3, 0.3, 0.3) + 1 \times (0.2, 0.3, 0.2)$$

$$+ \frac{7}{50}(0.4, 0.1, 0.4)], -\frac{0.2}{3}[-\frac{14}{75}(-0.1, -0.4, -0.4) - \frac{13}{50}(-0.3, -0.2, -0.4)$$

$$-\frac{103}{300}(-0.3, -0.3, -0.3) - 1 \times (-0.3, -0.2, -0.3) - \frac{11}{60}(-0.1, -0.7, -0.2)]$$

$$= (0.0342, 0.0391, 0.0227, -0.0345, -0.0372, -0.0412),$$

$$\tilde{b}_{55} = [\frac{w_5^P}{3}(\eta_{15}^P b_{51}^P + \eta_{25}^P b_{52}^P + \eta_{35}^P b_{53}^P + \eta_{45}^P b_{54}^P + \eta_{55}^P b_{55}^P),$$

$$\frac{w_5^N}{3}(\eta_{15}^N b_{51}^N + \eta_{25}^N b_{52}^N + \eta_{35}^N b_{53}^N + \eta_{45}^N b_{54}^N + \eta_{55}^N b_{55}^N)]$$

$$= \frac{0.3}{3}[\frac{14}{75}(0.8, 0.1, 0.1) + \frac{23}{150}(0.1, 0.7, 0.1) + \frac{17}{150}(0.3, 0.3, 0.3) + \frac{7}{50}(0.2, 0.3, 0.2)$$

$$+ 1 \times (0.4, 0.1, 0.4)], -\frac{0.1}{3}[-\frac{37}{150}(-0.1, -0.4, -0.4) - \frac{13}{50}(-0.3, -0.2, -0.4)$$

$$-\frac{26}{75}(-0.3, -0.3, -0.3) - \frac{11}{60}(-0.3, -0.2, -0.3) - 1 \times (-0.1, -0.7, -0.2)]$$

$$= (0.0627, 0.0302, 0.0496, -0.0121, -0.0330, -0.0187).$$

The similarity between patient A and A_k ($k \in \{1, \cdots, 5\}$) are determined as follows: $S(A, A_1)$.

$$= 1 - \frac{1}{30}\sum_{j=1}^{5}(|\mu_j^P - \tilde{\mu}_{1j}^P| + |v_j^P - \tilde{v}_{1j}^P| + |\iota_j^P - \tilde{\iota}_{1j}^P| + |\mu_j^N - \tilde{\mu}_{1j}^N| + |v_j^N - \tilde{v}_{1j}^N| + |\iota_j^N - \tilde{\iota}_{1j}^N|)$$

$$= 1 - \frac{1}{30}[|0.7 - 0.0473| + |0.2 - 0.0307| + |0.1 - 0.0282| + |0.2 - 0.0303| + |0.4 - 0.0328| + |0.4 - 0.0491|$$

$$+ |0.6 - 0.053| + |0.1 - 0.0211| + |0.2 - 0.027| + |0.4 - 0.0386| + |0.3 - 0.0279| + |0.3 - 0.0396|$$

$$+ |0.2 - 0.0092| + |0.0 - 0.0099| + |0.7 - 0.0261| + |0.1 - 0.062| + |0.7 - 0.0561| + |0.2 - 0.0501|$$

$$+ |0.5 - 0.0480| + |0.1 - 0.0301| + |0.2 - 0.0270| + |0.1 - 0.0277| + |0.2 - 0.0298| + |0.6 - 0.0483|$$

$$+ |0.1 - 0.0619| + |0.1 - 0.0336| + |0.5 - 0.0375| + |0.4 - 0.0195| + |0.4 - 0.0181| + |0.1 - 0.0143|]$$

$$= 0.7305.$$

$$S(A, A_2) = 1 - \frac{1}{30} \sum_{j=1}^{5} \left(\left| \mu_j^P - \tilde{\mu}_{2j}^P \right| + \left| v_j^P - \tilde{v}_{2j}^P \right| + \left| \iota_j^P - \tilde{\iota}_{2j}^P \right| + \left| \mu_j^N - \tilde{\mu}_{2j}^N \right| + \left| v_j^N - \tilde{v}_{2j}^N \right| + \left| \iota_j^P - \tilde{\iota}_{2j}^N \right| \right)$$

$$= 1 - \frac{1}{30}[|0.7 - 0.0464| + |0.2 - 0.0231| + |0.1 - 0.0286| + |0.2 - 0.0191| + |0.4 - 0.0546| + |0.4 - 0.0337|$$

$$+|0.6 - 0.0314| + |0.1 - 0.0485| + |0.2 - 0.0195| + |0.4 - 0.0294| + |0.3 - 0.0287| + |0.3 - 0.0363|$$

$$+|0.2 - 0.025| + |0.0 - 0.0069| + |0.7 - 0.0062| + |0.1 - 0.0307| + |0.7 - 0.0942| + |0.2 - 0.0608|$$

$$+|0.5 - 0.0495| + |0.1 - 0.03| + |0.2 - 0.0286| + |0.1 - 0.03| + |0.2 - 0.0441| + |0.6 - 0.0328|$$

$$+|0.1 - 0.0628| + |0.1 - 0.035| + |0.5 - 0.0225| + |0.4 - 0.0097| + |0.4 - 0.0204| + |0.1 - 0.0223|]$$

$$= 0.7299.$$

$$S(A, A_3) = 1 - \frac{1}{30} \sum_{j=1}^{5} \left(\left| \mu_j^P - \tilde{\mu}_{3j}^P \right| + \left| v_j^P - \tilde{v}_{3j}^P \right| + \left| \iota_j^P - \tilde{\iota}_{3j}^P \right| + \left| \mu_j^N - \tilde{\mu}_{3j}^N \right| + \left| v_j^N - \tilde{v}_{3j}^N \right| + \left| \iota_j^P - \tilde{\iota}_{3j}^N \right| \right)$$

$$= 1 - \frac{1}{30}[|0.7 - 0.0265| + |0.2 - 0.0411| + |0.1 - 0.0219| + |0.2 - 0.0461| + |0.4 - 0.0299| + |0.4 - 0.0412|$$

$$+|0.6 - 0.0359| + |0.1 - 0.028| + |0.2 - 0.0315| + |0.4 - 0.0382| + |0.3 - 0.0488| + |0.3 - 0.0268|$$

$$+|0.2 - 0.0131| + |0.0 - 0.0109| + |0.7 - 0.0072| + |0.1 - 0.0595| + |0.7 - 0.0537| + |0.2 - 0.062|$$

$$+|0.5 - 0.022| + |0.1 - 0.0508| + |0.2 - 0.0265| + |0.1 - 0.0556| + |0.2 - 0.0339| + |0.6 - 0.0255|$$

$$+|0.1 - 0.0347| + |0.1 - 0.0297| + |0.5 - 0.0604| + |0.4 - 0.0232| + |0.4 - 0.0254| + |0.1 - 0.0136|]$$

$$= 0.7301.$$

$$S(A, A_4) = 1 - \frac{1}{30} \sum_{j=1}^{5} \left(\left| \mu_j^P - \tilde{\mu}_{4j}^P \right| + \left| v_j^P - \tilde{v}_{4j}^P \right| + \left| \iota_j^P - \tilde{\iota}_{4j}^P \right| + \left| \mu_j^N - \tilde{\mu}_{4j}^N \right| + \left| v_j^N - \tilde{v}_{4j}^N \right| + \left| \iota_j^P - \tilde{\iota}_{4j}^N \right| \right)$$

$$= 1 - \frac{1}{30}[|0.7 - 0.0215| + |0.2 - 0.0369| + |0.1 - 0.0494| + |0.2 - 0.04| + |0.4 - 0.0383| + |0.4 - 0.0457|$$

$$+|0.6 - 0.0302| + |0.1 - 0.036| + |0.2 - 0.0363| + |0.4 - 0.0312| + |0.3 - 0.0269| + |0.3 - 0.0516|$$

$$+|0.2 - 0.0165| + |0.0 - 0.0146| + |0.7 - 0.0116| + |0.1 - 0.0457| + |0.7 - 0.0454| + |0.2 - 0.0959|$$

$$+|0.5 - 0.0208| + |0.1 - 0.0311| + |0.2 - 0.0546| + |0.1 - 0.0453| + |0.2 - 0.0276| + |0.6 - 0.0494|$$

$$+|0.1 - 0.0524| + |0.1 - 0.0664| + |0.5 - 0.0331| + |0.4 - 0.0126| + |0.4 - 0.0119| + |0.1 - 0.0361|]$$

$$= 0.7329.$$

$$S(A, A_5) = 1 - \frac{1}{30} \sum_{j=1}^{5} \left(\left| \mu_j^P - \tilde{\mu}_{5j}^P \right| + \left| v_j^P - \tilde{v}_{5j}^P \right| + \left| \iota_j^P - \tilde{\iota}_{5j}^P \right| + \left| \mu_j^N - \tilde{\mu}_{5j}^N \right| + \left| v_j^N - \tilde{v}_{5j}^N \right| + \left| \iota_j^P - \tilde{\iota}_{5j}^N \right| \right)$$

$$= 1 - \frac{1}{30}[|0.7 - 0.0644| + |0.2 - 0.0255| + |0.1 - 0.0177| + |0.2 - 0.0233| + |0.4 - 0.0503| + |0.4 - 0.0466|$$

$$+|0.6 - 0.0299| + |0.1 - 0.0574| + |0.2 - 0.0184| + |0.4 - 0.0311| + |0.3 - 0.0381| + |0.3 - 0.0445|$$

$$+|0.2 - 0.0157| + |0.0 - 0.0138| + |0.7 - 0.0128| + |0.1 - 0.0507| + |0.7 - 0.0762| + |0.2 - 0.0648|$$

$$+|0.5 - 0.0342| + |0.1 - 0.0391| + |0.2 - 0.0227| + |0.1 - 0.0345| + |0.2 - 0.0372| + |0.6 - 0.0412|$$

$$+|0.1 - 0.0627| + |0.1 - 0.0302| + |0.5 - 0.0496| + |0.4 - 0.0121| + |0.4 - 0.033| + |0.1 - 0.0187|]$$

$$= 0.7323.$$

We have

$$S(A, A_4) > S(A, A_5) > S(A, A_1) > S(A, A_3) > S(A, A_2).$$

Hence, the patient A can be diagnosed with the diseases A_4 by means of the recognition principle.

Acknowledgements. This work is supported by 2021 Guangdong Basic and Applied Basic Youth Fund Project (No. 2021A1515110834), Guangdong University of Science and Technology University Major Scientific Research Achievement Cultivation Program Project 2020 (No. GKY-2020CQPY-2), 2022 Special Projects in Key Fields of Higher Education Institutions in Guangdong Province, and Guangdong Provincial Department of Education Project (No. 2020KTSCX166).

References

1. Gong, S., Hua, G.: Bipolar Picture Fuzzy Graph Based Multiple Attribute Decision Making Approach-Part I. ML4CS (2022)
2. Ye, J.: Cosine similarity measures for intutistic fuzzy sets and their applications. Math. Comput. Model. **53**, 19–97 (2011)
3. Amanathulla, S.K., Muhiuddin, G., Al-Kadi, D., Pal, M.: Multiple attribute decision-making problem using picture fuzzy graph. Mathematical Problems in Engineering, 9937828 (2021). https://doi.org/10.1155/2021/9937828

Machine Learning Based Method for Quantifying the Security Situation of Wireless Data Networks

Jie Xu[✉]

Gansu Medical College, Pingliang 744000, China
`xxjj210@126.com`

Abstract. Wireless data networks are vulnerable to Trojans, viruses, malware and other attacks, resulting in important data being leaked and tampered with. Therefore, a quantitative evaluation method of wireless data network security situation based on machine learning is proposed. Based on the principles of independence, completeness and scientificity, network security situation assessment indicators are selected, combined with CVSS scoring standards, and network security situation assessment indicators are quantitatively processed to obtain time series of wireless data networks. Based on machine learning and support vector machine algorithm, the process of security situation quantification is established and the parameters of support vector machine algorithm are optimized. Experimental results show that the minimum delay of the proposed method is 4 s, the result is consistent with the actual result, and the minimum error is 5.6%, which fully proves the effectiveness of the proposed method.

Keywords: Machine learning · Wireless data network · Security situation · Quantitative evaluation · Network data processing

1 Introduction

In recent years, the attack targets of network attackers are not limited to the network attacks against the general public, such as obtaining passwords, malicious advertising, seeking ill gotten gains and so on. These cyber attackers have begun to target networks with national and organizational backgrounds [1]. The concept of situational awareness was first proposed in the military field, including three levels: perception, understanding and prediction. With the rapid development of network technology, situational awareness has been upgraded to network security situational awareness [2]. The important point of network security situational awareness is to pay more attention to the status and development trend of network security, make an effective quantitative evaluation of the current network security status, and provide a reliable data basis for network security personnel, so as to make timely decision-making and implementation. In this way, the threat and risk of network security can be minimized as far as possible, so as to improve the security of wireless data network.

© The Author(s), under exclusive license to Springer Nature Switzerland AG 2023
Y. Xu et al. (Eds.): ML4CS 2022, LNCS 13656, pp. 321–334, 2023.
https://doi.org/10.1007/978-3-031-20099-1_27

To solve the above problems, the method of reference [3] takes BP neural network as the decision engine to analyze the data of each data source, uses exponential weighted D-S evidence theory to fuse the output results of each decision engine, and evaluates the network threat status based on the hierarchical network threat assessment method. This method can effectively evaluate the status of network threats, but the recognition accuracy is low. The method of reference [4] uses the information fusion method based on the improved D-S evidence theory to fuse the attack generation consent probability of multiple detection devices to realize the comprehensive evaluation of external attack information; Vulnerability assessment system (CVss) is used to evaluate the vulnerability of wireless network, and the vulnerability assessment of internal nodes is realized; By integrating external attack information assessment and internal node vulnerability assessment, network security situation assessment is realized. This method has high recognition accuracy, but low recognition efficiency.

Therefore, a quantitative evaluation method of wireless data network security situation based on machine learning is proposed. According to the three principles, the network security situation assessment indicators are determined by combining quantitative indicators and qualitative indicators. The CVss scoring standard is adopted to quantify the indicators and improve the quality of the indicators. The time series of wireless data network are obtained directly, and the quantitative evaluation of wireless data network security situation is realized based on machine learning support vector machine algorithm, so as to improve the stability of wireless data network operation.

2 Research on Quantitative Assessment of Network Security Situation

2.1 Selection of Network Security Situation Assessment Indicators

The selection of network security situation assessment index is an important link in the quantitative assessment of network security situation. It is not only the expression of the internal meaning of network security situation, but also the reflection of the overall network in the security situation.

In the quantitative assessment of network security situation, the selection of indicators is an indispensable link. The selected indicators directly reflect the evaluator's evaluation perspective and ideas, and to a certain extent affect the application of quantitative assessment results and indicator system.

The selection of indicators shall be taken into account in many aspects as follows:

First, the indicators should be independent of each other and be comprehensive in their entirety [5]. When there is too much redundancy or duplicated information between indicators, the accuracy of network security situation assessment results will be affected by the increase of indicators. Because the factors affecting the network state are complex and changeable, we should choose indexes from multi-dimension and multi-level, and try our best to find comprehensive indexes.

Secondly, dynamic index and static index should be considered synthetically. Among them, the selected static indexes, such as the key host operating system type and the important grade of each device, may not change much in a certain period of time, but can reflect the basic performance of some important devices in the network environment. Through these basic indexes, the network situation can be analyzed more comprehensively and objectively. The selected dynamic index not only works at a certain time or node, but also has a lasting impact on the network situation through its own dynamic changes. Therefore, the combination of dynamic and static indicators can better reflect the overall network security situation;

Thirdly, the selection of indicators should follow the scientific basis and proceed from the actual situation, according to the network scale, network environment and network security requirements to select appropriate indicators to ensure the scientific selection of indicators;

Fourth, quantitative and qualitative indicators should be combined. Facing the complex and changeable network security status in practice, the qualitative index based on some empirical knowledge can make the use of index elements more comprehensive and balanced.

Based on the above description, in addition to the principles of independence, completeness and scientificity, the combination of quantitative and qualitative indicators shall be considered under the conditions of operability and feasibility.

Table 1. Table of indicators for network security situation assessment

Primary indicators	Secondary indicators	Tertiary indicators
Cyber Security Situation Assessment Indicators	Threat subsituation	Severity of attack
		Number of alarms
		Security incident frequency
		TCP packet distribution
		UDP packet distribution
		ICMP packet distribution
	Fragile subsituation	Vulnerability severity
		Total number of open ports
		Total number of security devices
		Device Operating System Security Status
		Topological structure
	Basic operating subsituation	Rate of intra-network traffic variation
		Peak intra-network traffic
		Total intra-network traffic
		Bandwidth utilization
		Device Service Status
		Asset value

The network security situation assessment indicators selected according to the above principles are shown in Table 1.

As shown in Table 1, Threat Subposture: The threat to a network is an assessment of the security posture of the network itself from various external threats. Often the behaviors that most affect network security are external threats that result in network service interruptions or data loss [6]. External threats are usually composed of various network attacks and triggered network security events, and the distribution of data packets can provide the corresponding threat distribution trend. Therefore, the attack severity, the number of alarms, the frequency of security events and the distribution of various packets are selected as the secondary indicators.

Vulnerability subsituation: Network vulnerability focuses on describing the security defects of the network itself, so its main carrier is the configuration of each device in the network topology environment.

Basic Operation Sub-situation: The basic operation sub-situation of the network reflects the operation state of the current network, and shows a continuous network operation state through the change trend of this index. When the basic operation sub-situation fluctuates violently, it shows that the operation state of the previous moment has changed greatly from the current state. Therefore, the basic operation of the network is closely related to the time, and at the same time, the assets of the host computer in the network system determines the safe operation of the network to a certain extent. Therefore, this paper selects the traffic change, bandwidth utilization rate, equipment service status and equipment asset value that has a certain impact on the network operation status as the secondary indicator under the first indicator of the basic operation situation [7].

The above process completes the selection of security situation evaluation index of wireless data network, and lays a solid foundation for the follow-up evaluation index quantification.

2.2 Steps of Quantitative Assessment of Network Security Situation

2.2.1 Quantification of network security situation assessment indicators.

Based on the above selected wireless data network security situation assessment indicators, combined with CVSS scoring standard, the indicators are quantified to facilitate follow-up security situation assessment.

Attack severity: This index is a priority index to measure the degree of network system damage. The higher the attack severity score is, the more serious the target network system damage is. In the network system, the importance, the number and the type of attack of the host are different, so this paper comprehensively considers many factors to determine the severity of attack as a secondary indicator. The quantitative formula is as follows:

$$
\begin{cases}
Y = \dfrac{\sum\limits_{e=1}^{n} \sum\limits_{j=1}^{m} 10^{P_{ej}} Q_j C_{ej}}{K} \\[4mm]
Q_j = \dfrac{I_j}{\sum\limits_{j=1}^{m} I_j} \\[4mm]
I_j = \begin{cases} 1.0 & \text{confidential} \\ 0.7 & \text{important} \\ 0.4 & \text{ordinary} \end{cases}
\end{cases}
\tag{1}
$$

In formula (1), Y is the severity of the attack; n is the number of types of attacks; m is the total number of hosts; P_{ej} is the attack rank factor of the j host under attack e, which can be obtained from the attack severity score; Q_j is the importance of the j host; C_{ej} is the number of attacks against the j host e; K is the total number of attacks detected in a certain time period; and I_j is the importance score of the information contained in the host.

Number of alerts: This indicator refers to the number of alerts per unit time, which can be directly obtained by the analysis tool.

Frequency of Security Events: The total number of Security Events is the total number of attacks, anomalies, etc. The frequency of security events refers to the number of security events in different time periods of the same time interval, which can reflect the time period when network security is most affected. The frequency quantization formula for security events is

$$
f = \frac{E_\tau}{\tau}
\tag{2}
$$

In formula 2, f represents the frequency of security incidents; E_τ represents the total number of security incidents; and τ represents the unit time period.

Data Packet Distribution: Network attacks are complex, but any network attack requires data packets to achieve its objectives [8]. Therefore, the change of the packets in the network can reflect whether the network is attacked or the situation of being attacked. This paper selects TCP packet, ICMP packet and UDP packet distribution as the secondary indicators, the quantitative formula is as follows:

$$
R_l = \frac{b_l}{\sum_{l=1}^{p} b_l} \times 100\%
\tag{3}
$$

In formula (3), R_l represents the quantification of packet distribution; b_l represents the total number of packets using the protocol in l; and p represents the total number of packet types.

Due to the limitation of research space, it is impossible to demonstrate the quantification process of all assessment indicators. Instead, only the severity of subsequent vulnerabilities, the security status of the device operating system, the topology and the quantification formula for the traffic within the network are demonstrated as follows:

$$
L = \frac{\sum\limits_{i=1}^{n} \sum\limits_{j=1}^{m} 10^{W_{ij}} Q_j D_{ij}}{M}
\tag{4}
$$

$$O = \begin{cases} 1 & \text{boot} \\ 0 & \text{shutdown} \end{cases} \tag{5}$$

$$A = \begin{cases} 1.0 & 0 \le nodes < 3 \\ 0.5 & 3 \le nodes < 5 \\ 0.1 & nodes > 3 \end{cases} \tag{6}$$

$$Q_t = \sum_{t=1}^{T} d_t \tag{7}$$

In formula (4), L represents the quantification of vulnerability severity; W_{ij} represents the vulnerability rating factor for Type i vulnerability of the j host; D_{ij} represents the number of Type i vulnerabilities of the j host; and M represents the total number of all vulnerabilities detected in a certain time period.

In formula (5), O represents the quantified result of the security status of the equipment operating system.

In Formula (6), A represents the quantified result of topology structure; *nodes* represents the score of network topology structure.

In formula (7), Q_t represents the quantification result of the flow within the network; d_t represents the total number of bytes in the network data flow of time t; and T represents the total network start time.

The above process completes the quantification of the security situation assessment index of wireless data network, and provides help for obtaining time series of wireless data network.

2.3   Wireless Data Network Time Series Acquisition

Based on the quantitative results of the above-mentioned wireless data network security situation assessment indicators, a time series of wireless data networks is obtained to provide a data basis for the implementation of the follow-up quantitative network security situation assessment [9].

Time series is a kind of prediction method based on the extension of historical data or called historical extended prediction. It mainly studies the change relationship between the predicted object and time process. Firstly, by compiling and analyzing historical data, it can predict the degree or level that can be achieved in the next period of time according to the development process, evolution direction and trend information reflected by time, and its application range is particularly wide. In this paper, time series model is mainly applied to the domain of network security situation prediction.

The network security situation system evaluates the network security periodically, and the network attacks a potential relationship, so the time series have certain relevance, and belong to short time series.

According to the characteristics of time series, the prediction methods of time series can be divided into two types. One is the linear method. The traditional methods of time series prediction are generally linear regression, such as moving average method, decomposition method, exponential smoothing method and so on. They are all based on the correlation among each variable, while the other is nonlinear method of time series prediction. In fact, the above methods of linear regression are generally nonlinear. At this time, the above methods of linear regression are basically not used.

According to the characteristics of time series, the prediction methods of time series can be divided into two types. One is linear method. The traditional time series prediction is generally linear regression, such as moving average method, decomposition method, exponential smoothing method, etc., which are based on the correlation between various variables. The other is a non-linear time series prediction method, which is generally non-linear in practice. At this time, the above linear regression methods are basically useless. At this time, machine learning methods are widely used, such as support vector machines, genetic algorithms, neural networks, and so on. Many research results have been achieved [10].

According to the requirement of quantitative evaluation of wireless data network security situation, the time series of wireless data network can be obtained by direct method. The expression is

$$X = \{x_1, x_2, \cdots, x_t\} \tag{8}$$

In formula (8), X represents the time series of the wireless data network; XX represents the operation data of the time TT wireless data network.

The above process completes the acquisition of time series of wireless data network, and provides support for the realization of the final quantitative assessment of network security situation.

2.4 Implementation of Quantitative Assessment of Cyber Security Situation

Based on the acquired time series of wireless data networks, the security situation of wireless data networks is quantitatively evaluated by machine learning and support vector machine algorithm.

The quantitative assessment of network security situation is to evaluate each index in the network comprehensively, and divide the situation quantitative assessment level according to the assessment value. With reference to the National Contingency Plan for Cyber Security Incidents, the quantitative assessment of cyber security situation can be divided into five grades: security, light danger, general danger, medium danger and high danger. So cybersecurity posture assessment is a multi-category problem [11].

Support Vector Machine Algorithm (SVM) has two kinds of ideas when dealing with multi-classification problems. The first kind is to optimize the objective function of SVM to solve multi-classification problems directly. This method needs only one solution, but it has high computational complexity and computational complexity, so it is rarely used in practical applications. The second is to transform multi-classification problems into multi-binary classification problems, construct multi-SVM models, and decompose complex problems into simple ones. Common algorithms for the second category are:

(1) One-Versus-One (OVO), the basic idea is to design an SVM model between any two types of samples. For problems with z categories, $z(z-1)/2$ SVM models

need to be constructed. For classification, there will be $z(z - 1)/2$ logos. Using the voting method, the logo with the most votes is the category of the sample;.

(2) One-Versus-All (OVA), the basic idea is that for samples with z categories, all samples of the $g(g = 1, 2, \cdots, z)$ class are marked as positive, and all remaining samples are marked as negative. Therefore, it is necessary to build z SVM models, and there are z decision functions. When classifying a sample, the sample belongs to the category to which the larger decision function value belongs;

(3) Binary Tree (BT), whose basic idea is to first divide all samples into two groups, one for the positive group and the other for the parent group, construct the root node's SVM model, and then continue to divide each group into two smaller groups and build the child node's SVM model until all the categories are divided.

Compared with traditional SVM, TWSVM has the advantages of fast training speed and accuracy. This research combines the binary tree idea TWSVM to construct a new multi-classification model BT-TWSVM. Based on the number of security situational awareness levels, the topology of the model is shown in Fig. 1.

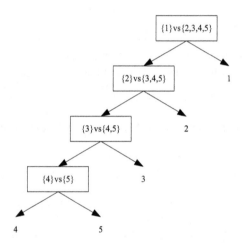

Fig. 1. BT-TWSVM model structure diagram

According to Fig. 1, Because of the problem of error accumulation in the multi-classification model based on binary tree, the error will continue in the later stage for the samples with errors in the earlier stage. Therefore, it is very important to determine the classification order of nodes, and the clustering algorithm can be introduced to optimize the model. The basic idea of the algorithm is as follows: Firstly, K-means algorithm is used to compute the cluster centers of each class of all samples.

The steps of network security situational awareness assessment based on the improved AFSA-TWSVM binary tree multi-classification model are as follows:

Step 1: Calculate the average characteristic values of all kinds of samples in the network security situational awareness dataset as the clustering center. Get the cluster centers of five categories $o_i(i = 1, 2, 3, 4, 5)$;

Step 2: Separately calculate the sum of the distances from each cluster center to other clusters centers, sort the values, put the category to which the sum belongs to the maximum value in the first place and record its cluster center as o_1, then repeat the previous steps to calculate the sum of the distances from each cluster center to the remaining cluster center, take the maximum value and record it as o_2, and so on, until all 5 reordered cluster centers are obtained, and the order is o_1, o_2, o_3, o_4, o_5;

Step 3: Mark the samples corresponding to the center o_1 in the cluster as 1 class, and the samples corresponding to the o_2, o_3, o_4, o_5 cluster center as -1 class.The improved AFSA-TWSVM algorithm is used to train the classification model and obtain the classifier of the root node. Using the same operation, we construct the classifiers of the subnodes of the binary tree in o_i order until all classifiers are constructed.

The parameters of AFSA-TWSVM algorithm are the key to evaluate the security situation of wireless data network, so PSO algorithm is used to optimize the parameters of AFSA-TWSVM algorithm.

There are three main parameters of AFSA-TWSVM algorithm: firstly, penalty coefficient χ, which is used to tradeoff the smoothness of regression curve and empirical risk in the determined feature space, controls the robustness of regression model, determines the complexity of support vector machine and the degree of punishment for fitting difference larger than ε, which is too large to cause over-learning and too small to cause under-learning; secondly, insensitive loss coefficient χ, which determines the number of support vectors of the model, indirectly affects the accuracy of fitting, represents the expectation for estimating the error of the function in the sample data, ε increases, the number of support vectors decreases, the expression of solution tends to be sparse, the regression curve becomes flat and slow, and the accuracy of calculation will be lowered if the value is too small; and thirdly, kernel function width parameter σ, which controls the complexity of the optimal solution to the nonlinear planning problem corresponding to the support vector machine, determines the precise structure of high-dimensional feature space, which is too large or too small to reduce the generalization capability of the support vector machine.

The selection of the above three parameters is the key to the performance of the algorithm and directly affects the prediction accuracy. At present, there is no strict theory to determine these three parameters directly, usually using empirical determination method, grid search method and genetic algorithm intelligent optimization methods to determine. This paper uses particle swarm optimization algorithm to optimize SVM parameters.

Particle Swarm Optimization (PSO) is an evolutionary algorithm developed by Eberhart and Kennedy, which is a swarm intelligence algorithm with strong global optimization ability. At first, PSO was used to solve continuous optimization problems, but now it has been applied to combinatorial optimization problems, which is simple and effective. Rather than the "Crossover" and "Mutation" operations of the genetic algorithm, PSO works like a gradient descent algorithm, allowing each chromosome to swarm in the direction with the highest fitness. Compared with other optimization algorithms, PSO not only has the ability of global optimization, but also is easy to program and popularize.

The basic idea of PSO is that each solution of the optimization problem is called a particle, that is, the position of each particle is a potential solution. PSO randomly initializes a swarm of particles and their velocities, and each particle travels in a swarm based on its "flight experience" with other particles to search for the optimal solution from full space.

In the specific search process, each particle approaches two points at the same time in the solution space. The first point is the optimal solution reached by all particles in the whole particle swarm in the course of historical search, which is called the global optimal solution of the population. The other point is the optimal solution reached by the particle itself in the course of historical search, which is called the individual optimal solution. Because of the simultaneous action of these two points, the particle trajectory has memory property, so the particle can express to reach the final optimal position and obtain the optimal solution [12, 13].

Three parameters (χ, ε and σ) of AFSA-TWSVM are optimized, and the steps of PSO-AFSA-TWSVM model algorithm are given:

Step 1: Randomly construct the initial population of b particles, initialize the settings, including setting the population size, iteration times, randomly given the initial particle s_b^0 and particle initial velocity v_b^0. The particle vector represents a SVM model which corresponds to different SVM parameters.

Step 2: The parameters of particle vectors determine a support vector machine model, which is used to test the test samples and calculate the fitness $u(s)$ of each individual.

Step 3: Compare u_b with p_{best}, if $u_b < p_{best}$, replace the previous optimal solution with a new fitness, replace the previous round with a new particle, namely $p_{best} = u_b$;

Step 4: Compare the best fitness p_{best} for each particle with the best fitness g_{best} for all particles. If $p_{best} < g_{best}$, the best fitness of the particle replaces the global best fitness, $g_{best} = p_{best}$, while preserving the particle's current state;

Step 5: Determine whether the fitness or the number of iterations meet the requirements. If the requirements are not met, a new round of calculation will be carried out, and the particles will be moved according to the rules to generate a new particle (i.e. a new solution) and return to Step 2. If the requirements are met, the calculation ends.

The optimal solution of the parameters can be input into the AFSA-TWSVM algorithm, and then the security situation of the wireless data network can be evaluated quantitatively.

3 Experiment and Result Analysis

3.1 Preparation for Experiment

The experimental test environment is Debian 7.8wheel system, with 6 GB memory and 2.2 GHz CPU speed. According to the requirement of the experiment, the contents of the preparation stage are the determination of the wireless data network topology structure, the formulation of the network security situation grade standard and data processing. UNSW-NB15 (The UNSW-NB15 Dataset Description) is used as the experimental data set.

The wireless data network topology is shown in Fig. 2.

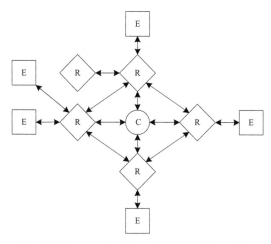

Fig. 2. Diagram of wireless data network topology

In Fig. 2, C represents the coordinator, R the routing device, and E the terminal device.

The results of the development of standards for cyber security posture levels are shown in Table 2.

Table 2. Cyber security situation grade standard table

Rank	Security situation description	Safe situation number
1	Safety	0.00–0.20
2	Minor danger	0.21–0.40
3	General danger	0.41–0.60
4	Moderate danger	0.61–0.80
5	Highly dangerous	0.81–1.00

In order to reduce the influence of different data in the same dimension on model training, the formula (9) is used to normalize the sample data.

$$y' = \frac{y - y_{min}}{y_{max} - y_{min}} \tag{9}$$

In formula (9), y and y' represent the sample data before and after normalization respectively; y_{min} and y_{max} represent the minimum and maximum values of the sample data respectively.

The above process completes the preparation of the experiment, and facilitates the smooth implementation of the follow-up experiment.

3.2   Analysis of Experimental Results

Carry out the wireless data network security situation quantification assessment experiment based on the above experimental preparation contents. In order to clearly show the application performance of the proposed method, according to the subjective experience method, the time delay of security situation quantification assessment, the results of security situation quantification assessment and the error of security situation quantification assessment are selected as evaluation indicators. The specific experimental result analysis process is as follows:

Delay Analysis of Quantitative Assessment of Security Posture
The delay data of security situation quantification assessment obtained by experiment is shown in Fig. 3.

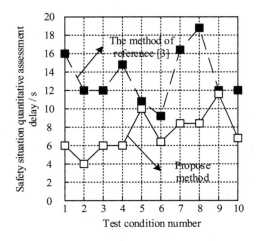

Fig. 3. Security posture quantification assessment delay data graph

As shown in Fig. 3 data, the latency of security situation quantification assessment obtained by the proposed method is lower than the method of reference [3] and the minimum is 4s.

Analysis of Quantitative Assessment Results of Security Posture
The results of quantitative assessment of safety situation are shown in Table 3.

As shown by the data in Table 3, during the quantitative assessment of the security situation for 100 experimental samples, the safety situation quantitative assessment results obtained by the proposed method are consistent with the actual results, the accuracy of the evaluation results is high, which proves the effectiveness of the proposed method.

Error Analysis of Security Situation Quantification Assessment
The error data of safety situation quantification assessment obtained by experiment is shown in Fig. 4.

Table 3. Results of quantitative assessment of security

Numbering of experimental condition	Propose a method	Actual result
1–10	Safety	Safety
11–20	Minor danger	Minor danger
21–30	Moderate danger	Moderate danger
31–40	Highly dangerous	Highly dangerous
41–50	Safety	Safety
51–60	Moderate danger	Moderate danger
61–70	Minor danger	Minor danger
71–80	Highly dangerous	Highly dangerous
81–90	Safety	Safety
91–100	Moderate danger	Moderate danger

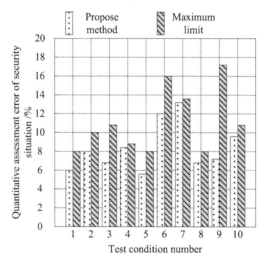

Fig. 4. Error data graph of security situation quantification assessment

As shown in Fig. 4, the average error of the proposed method is 8.35%, and the average error of the given maximum limit is 11.05%. The error of quantitative assessment of security situation obtained by using the proposed method is 2.7% lower than the average error of the given maximum limit.

The experimental results show that the time delay is lower than the maximum value, the result is consistent with the actual result, and the error is lower than the maximum value.

4 Conclusions

In this study, a new method of security situation quantification based on machine learning and support vector machine is designed, which greatly shortens the delay of security situation quantification, reduces the error of security situation quantification, improves the precision of security situation quantification assessment, provides more effective method support for network security situation assessment, and provides some reference for related research.

References

1. Liu, S., et al.: Human memory update strategy: a multi-layer template update mechanism for remote visual monitoring. IEEE Transactions on Multimedia, **23**, 2188-2198 (2021)
2. Zhang, R., Liu, M., Yin, Y., et al.: Prediction algorithm for network security situation based on BP neural network optimized by SA-SOA. Int. J. Performability Eng. **16**(8), 1171 (2020)
3. Liwei, C., Xiaoxiong, T., Yuqing, Z., et al.: Network security situation assessment architecture based on multi-source heterogeneous data fusion. CAAI Trans. Intelligent Syst. **16**(01), 38–47 (2021)
4. Wei, W.: Data driven security situation assessment of wireless network. Foreign Electronic Measurement Technol. **39**(07), 22–26 (2020)
5. Liu, S., Liu, D., Muhammad, K., Ding, W.: Effective template update mechanism in visual tracking with background clutter. Neurocomputing **458**, 615–625 (2021)
6. Liu, Q., Zeng, M.: Network security situation detection of internet of things for smart city based on fuzzy neural network. Int. J. Reasoning-based Intelligent Systems **12**(3), 222 (2020)
7. Zhang, H., Kang, C., Xiao, Y.: Research on network security situation awareness based on the LSTM-DT model. Sensors **21**(14), 4788 (2021)
8. Zheng, R., Ma, H., Wang, Q., et al.: Assessing the security of campus networks: the case of seven universities. Sensors **21**(1), 306 (2021)
9. Shuai, L., Shuai, W., Xinyu, L., et al.: Fuzzy detection aided real-time and robust visual tracking under complex environments. IEEE Trans. Fuzzy Syst. **29**(1), 90–102 (2021)
10. Wang, K., Tong, M., Yang, D., et al.: A web-based honeypot in IPv6 to enhance security. Information (Switzerland) **11**(9), 440 (2020)
11. Ren, J.: Network security situation assessment model based on information quality control. Int. J. Performability Eng. **16**(4), 673 (2020)
12. Vajjha, H., Sushma, P.: Techniques and limitations in securing the log files to enhance network security and monitoring. Solid State Technol. **64**(2), 1–8 (2021)
13. Gopal, A., Sultani, M.M., Bansal, J.C.: On stability analysis of particle swarm optimization algorithm. Arab. J. Sci. Eng. **45**(4), 2385–2394 (2020)

Overlapping Community Discovery Algorithm Based on Three-Level Neighbor Node Influence

Shishuang Chen[1], Guanru Huang[1], Sui Lin[1], Wenchao Jiang[1(⊠)], and Zhiming Zhao[2]

[1] Guangdong University of Technology, Guangzhou 510006, China
2112105230@mail2.gdut.edu.cn
[2] University of Amsterdam, Amsterdam, The Netherlands

Abstract. In view of the high time complexity of the current overlapping community discovery algorithm and the low stability, an overlapping community discovery algorithm OCDITN based on three-level neighbor influence is proposed. The algorithm uses three-level neighbor node influence measurement method TIM (Three-level Influence Measurement) to calculate the node influence, and determines the order of selecting and updating nodes according to the node influence; the similarity between the nodes is determined by the update sequence of neighbor node labels, and finally the label membership of each node is calculated to discover the overlapping communities. The experiment is performed based on the artificial simulation network data set and the real world network data set. Compared with the SLPA, LPANNI, and COPRA algorithms, the performance of this algorithm is improved by 7% and 12% on the two evaluation standards EQ and Qvo respectively.

Keywords: Label propagation · Community division · Overlapping communities · Node influence · Node proximity

1 Introduction

Complex network [1, 2] is an abstraction of various entities in the real world and their relationships with each other. In the real world, there are often overlaps and intersections between community entities composed of complex associated entities, and a complex network is composed of many community networks. There are many ways to discover overlapping communities, such as the faction filtering CPM algorithm of overlapping community discovery [3, 4], which treats the community as a fully connected subgraph in the entire complex network; Lancchinetti et al. [5] proposed LFM to discover overlapping communities based on extended functions and local optimization, sets an F value list for each node, and deletes nodes with an F value less than 0 in each iteration; Wang Bin et al. [6] proposed an edge graph-based algorithm Overlapping community discovery algorithm, which uses calculated similarity of each edge to realize division and discovery of overlapping communities. COPRA is a community discovery algorithm proposed by Gregory et al. [7] based on label propagation. This algorithm assigns an initial label to each node, and iterates through label propagation until the node label is stable; Xie et al.

[8] proposed SLPA algorithm, which adds a label for each iteration of each node, and then filters the label through a threshold r; Lu et al. [9] developed the LPANNI algorithm through neighbor node influence, which calculates new label membership based on label propagation algorithm.

However, the current overlapping community discovery algorithm still has problems of low efficiency and low accuracy. For example, time complexity is a major problem with the CPM algorithm; COPRA algorithm is low and unstable for dividing community quality; SLPA algorithm is high in the space complexity. To solve the above problems, an overlapping community discovery algorithm is proposed, we named it OCDITN algorithm, this algorithm based on influence measurement TIM [10] and large-scale network graph. Finally actual network datasets are used to evaluate the effectiveness of OCDITN. Compared with the SLPA, LPANNI, and COPRA algorithms, the OCDITN algorithm is more stable, better in quality, and more efficient in the divided community.

2   OCDITN Algorithm

2.1   Influence Measurement Based on Three Level Neighbors

Set up the network $G = (V, E, pu, v)$, V and E respectively represent the node set and edge set in complex network, pu and v represent the activation probability of node u to v. The second and third level neighbor nodes whose propagation influence gradually weakens are regarded as a whole, which is recorded as M_{23} If the level 2 neighbor is active, then M_{23} Third level neighbors of may also be activated at this time M_{23} The probability of activation is shown in formula (1).

$$\varphi = \sum_{w \in N(v)} \sum_{v \in N(u)} p_{u,v} p_{v,w} \tag{1}$$

For node u, the number of its first level neighbors is the same as that of the first level neighbors M_{23} Compared with the total number of neighbor nodes, M_{23} It may be several times of level 1 neighbor. As shown in Fig. 1, for node u, the first to third level neighbors are V, W, and X, respectively. According to Fig. 1, the nodes marked W and X are M_{23} A whole with three times the number of nodes labeled v.

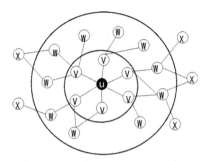

Fig. 1. Example of u neighbor node

The influence of node u in Fig. 1 on the neighbors of level 2 and level 3 neighbors is obviously greater than that on level 1 neighbors, which is in contradiction with the feature that the influence of node u gradually decays with the deepening of propagation level. Therefore, it is necessary to strengthen the influence of level 1 neighbor nodes and adjust the proportion between the overall influence of node u on M_{23} and the influence of level 1 neighbor nodes. According to the exponential function $y = ex$, when $x > 0$, $y > 1$, the propagation influence of the first level neighbor node is strengthened, and the parameter is introduced θ And parameters φ Adjust the impact gap. The calculation of Tim node influence is shown in formula (2).

$$T(u) = \theta \cdot e^{\sum_{v \in N(u)} p_{u,v}} + \varphi \cdot |M_{23}| \tag{2}$$

Among them, $p_{u,v}$ Indicates the activation probability of node u to v, and the parameter θ And parameters φ, adjusting the influence gap. The values are 0.5 and 0.2 respectively, $|M_{23}|$ represents the number of level 2 and level 3 neighbors of node u.

2.2 Label Updating of OCDITN Algorithm

COPRA algorithm is an overlapping community discovery algorithm based on label propagation proposed in 2010. The main step of COPRA algorithm is to initialize the initial ID of each node, which is usually its own number; then the node determines its own community according to the distribution of the neighborhood node's community. This process is called the community membership process of the node, which can be expressed by the node membership degree; finally, the algorithm determines whether the number of nodes or tags in the community remains unchanged after two iterations change, to decide whether to stop execution. The calculation method of node membership is shown in formula (3).

$$b_t(c, u) = \frac{\sum_{y \in N(u)} b_{t-1}(c,v)}{|N(u)|} \tag{3}$$

Among $N(u)$ it represents the set of neighbor node for node u. $b_t(c, u)$ represents the membership degree of node u and community c in the t number iterations.

OCDITN algorithm reoptimizes and defines the similarity calculation model between the node and its neighbors in the node label update stage, as shown in formula (4).

$$O_v(u) = \frac{NS(u,v)}{|k(u)-k(v)| \cdot |T(u)-T(v)|} \tag{4}$$

Among them, $T(u)$ represents Tim value of node u in the array, and represents the influence of node U; $NS(u, v)$ is common node numbers between node u and neighbor v; $k(u)$ represents the node u degree. $O_v(u)$ the larger the value is, the stronger the correlation between node u and neighbor v is, and the smaller the influence of neighbor on node is. To solve the problem of low quality and instability of community discovery caused by COPRA algorithm randomly selecting nodes to update labels, nodes effects is sorted in descending order, the sequence is recorded as sq as the sequence of updating labels. Refer to the node membership in COPRA algorithm $b_t(c, u)$ as shown in formula (3), overlapping communities are found again. In the label updating process after selecting node to update, the neighbor node propagates the main label sequence to node u, and uses the LS_N expression, as shown in formula (5).

$$LS_N = \{ls(c_1, b_1), ls(c_2, b_2), \cdots, ls(c_v, b_v)\} \tag{5}$$

Among them, $ls(c_v, b_v)$ represents the primary label of neighbor node v, b_v indicates that node v belongs to the community c_v the membership degree of the system. Among $v \in N(u)$, $N(u)$ represents sequence of neighbor u nodes.

Referring to the LPANNI algorithm to calculate the membership of the label, formula (6) calculates the membership model of updating node label.

$$b'(c, u) = \frac{\sum_{ls(c_v, b_v) \in LS_N, v \in N(u), c_v = c} b(c_v, v) \cdot O_v(u)}{\sum_{ls(c_v, b_v) \in LS_N, v \in N(u)} b(c_v, v) \cdot O_v(u)} \tag{6}$$

The new label membership degree sequence of nodes is obtained by formula (6), which is recorded as LS'_N, delete LS'_N if the membership degree of tags in the sequence is less than the threshold p, the tag sequence can be obtained again LS''_N.

The label sequence normalization model of LPANNI algorithm is used to process the sorted node label sequence as shown in formula (7) LS''_N and get the new tag sequence LS''_N.

$$b''(c, u) = \frac{b'(c, u)}{\sum_{ls(c, b') \in LS''_N} b'(c, u)}, \sum b''(c, u) = 1 \tag{7}$$

After label normalization model processing node label sequence LS_u, node u selects the label with the largest label membership as the main label.

2.3 OCDITN Algorithm

OCDITN algorithm first initializes each node, uses the its label as its own ID. At the same time, TIM value of each node and influence value its neighbors are calculated. Secondly, in label propagation stage, node will receive the main label from its neighbors and form a label sequence LS_N after iterative processing, a new tag sequence is formed LS_N as the final label sequence updated by the node, and finally output the label sequence LS_N,the nodes with multiple tags are overlapping nodes, which constitute overlapping communities. The algorithm flow is as follows.

Input: Undirected and unauthorized network $G = (V, E, pu, v)$, compute nodes TIM value θ set to 1000, pu, v set the value to 0.5, the maximum number of iterations in the label propagation process T.

Output: node u label collection for LS_u.

Step 1: initialize the tag ID of each node as its own number, and the membership degree of the tag is 1;

Step 2: calculate the TIM value of each node through formula (2), and sort all nodes according to the descending order of TIM value to get the node update sequence SQ;

Step 3: calculate the similarity between each node and its neighbors by formula (4);

When t iterations are less than the maximum iterations T, label updates of each node in the node update sequence SQ continue to cycle from step 4 to step 8 until the maximum iterations T.

Step 4: calculate node membership of each neighbor node through formula (3), and add all its primary tags $b_t(c, u)$ propagate to node u to get the node u label set LS_N;

Step 5: recalculate the node label membership degree through formula (6) to get the node label set again LS'_N;

Step 6: by discarding LS'_N if the membership degree of labels in the set falls below the threshold value p, the label set is updated to LS''_N;

Step 7: normalize the nodes by formula (7) to get a new set of node labels LS'_N;

Step 8: in the label set LS'_N the label with the largest membership degree is choose as final primary label of the node;

Step 9: output label set LS'_N the nodes with multi-tags as overlapping node, which constitute overlapping communities.

3 Experiment and Analysis

To verify the effectiveness of OCDITN algorithm, we test OCDITN based on artificial simulation network and real network data sets. For synthetic networks, the NMI index is used to judge the similarity between overlapping communities found in test environment and overlapping communities in real network. The definition of NMI index is shown in formula (8).

$$NMI(X|Y) = 1 - \frac{1}{2}[H(X|Y) + H(X|Y)] \tag{8}$$

Among them, X represents the set in real networks; Y represents the overlapping community set found in experimental tests; H(X|Y) represents the conditional entropy of community X on community Y, and represents the divergence indicator between community X and community Y. NMI index range is [0, 1]. The NMI index tends to 0, this indicates that the overlapping community discovered by the detection algorithm are significantly different from the real networks. On the contrary, the NMI index tends to 1, it shows that the difference between the overlapping community discovered by the algorithm and the actual community is small, find effective improvements in overlapping communities.

For the community distribution of real network datasets with fuzzy real values, we can use the modularity function as the evaluation standard. To test the performance of each algorithm more comprehensively, we use the extended modularity function EQ and the overlapping modularity index Qov as evaluation criteria for test algorithm.

3.1 Experimental Results and Analysis of Real Data Sets

Real social network is a molecular set of intercepting the real structure of social network. Because it truly reflects the real network structure and data characteristics, the analysis results of real network data have direct and important reference significance for the effectiveness of network community discovery algorithm. In this paper, we test OCDITN algorithm on several complex real network datasets and compared with SLPA, LPANNI and COPRA algorithms. The experimental datasets are shown in Table 1, including Dolphin social network, Zachary's club network, Polbooks network, Blogs network, Lesmis network, PGP network and Internet snapshot network.

Table 1. Real social network data set

Network	Spot	Edge	Describe
Dolphins	62	159	Dolphin social network
Karate	34	78	Karate club network
Polbooks	105	441	American politics book network
Blogs	3982	6803	Blog network
Lesmis	44	254	Les miserables network
PGP	10680	24316	Trust network
Internet	22964	48466	Internet snapshot network

In the experiment, the parameter $\mu = 0.2$ was set. Table 2 and Table 3 show the EQ and Qov values of OCDITN, SLPA, LPANNI and COPRA algorithms tested on each data set, respectively. Table 2 shows the evaluation results in the datasets of Dolphins, Karate, Polbooks, Blogs, Lesmis, PGP and Internet. The EQ value of OCDITN algorithm is higher than that of SLPA, LPANNI, COPRA algorithm, which indicates that OCDITN algorithm has good overlapping community partition effect.

Table 2. Experimental results of EQ value of each algorithm

Network	OCDITN	SLPA	LPANNI	COPRA
Dolphins	0.6233	0.5862	0.4268	0.5462
Karate	0.4236	0.3966	0.3258	0.3762
Polbooks	0.3122	0.3045	0.3086	0.2916
Blogs	0.6862	0.6231	0.5986	0.6424
Lesmis	0.8040	0.6822	0.7826	0.7264
PGP	0.9224	0.9064	0.8644	0.8824
Internet	0.4224	0.3688	0.3924	0.2836

3.2 Experimental Results and Analysis of Simulated Data Sets

In the research of complex network community discovery, LFR benchmark network is a typical artificial simulation dataset. It is often used in the experimental test of discovering overlapping communities and has important properties of real-world network. LFR benchmark network mainly includes the following fields: N is the node number; K is the average degree of nodes; maxk is the maximum degree of nodes; min is the nodes number in minimum community; maxc is the nodes number in maximum community; on is overlapping nodes number between communities; OM is overlapping nodes number. mu represents the degree of mixing between communities, and the larger its value, the more fuzzy the division of community structure [14].

Table 3. Rour different LFR benchmark network parameters

Id	N	K	mark	minc	maxc	on	om	mu
N1	1000	10	40	20	40	100	2	0–0.6
N2	2000	10	40	20	40	100	2	0–0.6
N3	1000	10	40	20	40	200	2	0–0.6
N4	2000	10	40	20	40	200	2	0–0.6

The experimental results of OCDITN, SLPA, LPANNI and COPRA algorithms in four groups of LFR network data are shown in Figs. 2, 3, 4 and 5. The abscissa is the mixture coefficient mu, and the ordinate is the community discovery quality NMI. The found quality of the community decreases because the NMI values of OCDITN, SLPA, LPANNI and COPRA algorithms decrease with the increase of the hybrid coefficient.

According to Fig. 2, except for the NMI value of LPANNI algorithm is larger than that of OCDITN algorithm when mu = 0.4, the NMI value of OCDITN algorithm is the largest under other Mu parameters, which indicates that OCDITN algorithm is more effective than other algorithms.

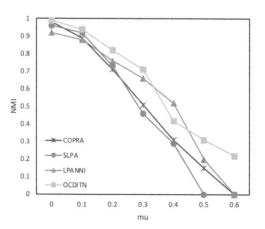

Fig. 2. NMI value of N1 network

As shown in Fig. 3, from the N2 network test results, OCDITN algorithm is only slightly better than SLPA algorithm, and the effect between the two algorithms is very close.

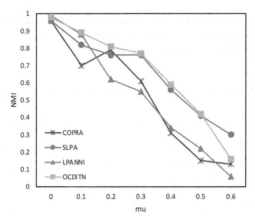

Fig. 3. NMI value of N2 network

As shown in Fig. 4, from the test results of N3 network, OCDITN algorithm is superior to SLPA, LPANNI and COPRA algorithms, especially when mu = 0.4, OCDITN algorithm is obviously superior to SLPA, LPANNI and COPRA algorithms.

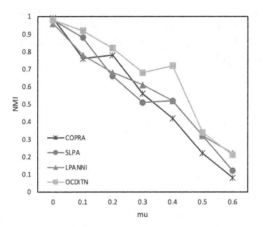

Fig. 4. NMI value of N3 network

Figure 5 depicts the N4 network test results. The effects of the four algorithms are very close, and OCDITN algorithm is still slightly better than SLPA, LPANNI and COPRA algorithms.

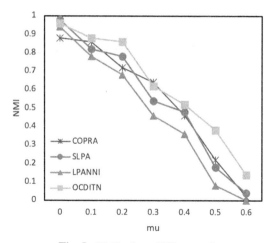

Fig. 5. NMI value of N4 network

The above comparative experimental results show that the OCDITN algorithm is effective for SLPA, LPANNI and COPRA algorithms in all indexes.

4   Conclusion

OCDITN, an overlapping community discovery algorithm based on the influence of three-level neighbors, is proposed in this paper. This algorithm combined with the latest node influence algorithm to rank the importance of nodes, which is better than COPRA algorithm and robustness and efficiency and accuracy of overlapping communities. Through the experiments based on artificial networks and actual networks and comparison between OCDITN and COPRA, the results show that OCDITN algorithm can effectively detect overlapping communities, and the overlapping communities have better quality.

Acknowledgment. This study was funded by Guangdong Natural Science Fund Project (2021A1515011243), Guangzhou Science and Technology Plan Project (201902020016), Yunfu Science and Technology Plan Project S2021010104 and Guangdong Science and Technology Plan Project (2019B010139001, 2021B1212100004).

References

1. Shen Hao, A., Rong Huan, Y.: Review of complex network theory. Comput. Syst. Appl. **29**(09), 26–31 (2020)
2. Schmitt, R., Ramos, P., Santiago, R., et al.: Novel Clique enumeration heuristic for detecting overlapping clusters. In: IEEE Congress on Evolutionary Computation, pp. 1390–1397. IEEE (2017)
3. Zhou, B.: Applying the Clique Percolation Method to analyzing cross-market branch banking network structure: the case of Illinois. Soc. Netw. Anal. Min. **6**(1), 1–14 (2016). https://doi. org/10.1007/s13278-016-0318-0

4. Lancichinetti, A., Fortunato, S., Kertész, J.: Detecting the overlapping and hierarchical community structure in complex networks. New J. Phys. **11**(3), 033015 (2009)
5. Hu, L., Guo, G., Ma, C.: Overlapping community discovery method based on symmetric nonnegative matrix factorization. Comput. Appl. **35**(10), 2742–2746 (2015)
6. Wang, B., Li, Q., Sheng, J., Sun, Z.: Overlapping community discovery algorithm for linear flow based on edge graph. Comput. Eng. Appl. **55**(02), 60–66 (2019)
7. Gregory, S.: Finding overlapping communities in networks by label propagation. New J. Phys. **12**(10), 103018 (2010)
8. Xie, J., Szymanski, B.K., Liu, X.: SLPA: uncovering overlapping communities in social networks via a speaker-listener interaction dynamic process. In: 2011 IEEE 11th International Conference on Data Mining Workshops, pp. 344–349. IEEE (2011)
9. Lu, M., Zhang, Z., Qu, Z., Kang, Y.: LPANNI: overlapping community detection using label propagation in large-scale complex networks. IEEE Trans. Knowl. Data Eng. **31**(9), 1736–1749 (2018)
10. Sun, H., Liu, J., Huang, J., Wang, G., Jia, X., Song, Q.: LinkLPA: a link-based label propagation algorithm for overlapping community detection in networks. Comput. Intell. **33**(2), 308–331 (2017)
11. Shuxin, Y., Wen, L., Kaili, Z.: Measurement method of node influence in complex networks based on three-level neighbors. Acta Electron. Sin. **42**(05), 1140–1148 (2020)
12. Shen, H., Cheng, X., Cai, K., Hu, M.B.: Detect overlapping and hierarchical community structure in networks. Phys. A Stat. Mech. Appl. **388**(8), 1706–1712 (2009)
13. Nicosia, V., Mangioni, G., Carchiolo, V., Malgeri, M.: Extending the definition of modularity to directed graphs with overlapping communities. J. Stat. Mech. Theory Exp. **2009**(03), P03024 (2009)
14. Lancichinetti, A., Fortunato, S., Radicchi, F.: Benchmark graphs for testing community detection algorithms. Phys. Rev. E **78**(4), 046110 (2008)

Content-Aware Deep Feature Matching

Weice Wang[1], Zuoyong Li[2], Xiangpan Zheng[3], Taotao Lai[2(✉)],
and Pantea Keikhosrokiani[4]

[1] College of Computer and Information Sciences, Fujian Agriculture and Forestry
University, Fuzhou 350002, China
[2] Fujian Provincial Key Laboratory of Information Processing and Intelligent
Control, College of Computer and Control Engineering, Minjiang University, Fuzhou
350121, China
laitaotao@gmail.com
[3] College of Physics and Electronic Information Engineering, Minjiang University,
Fuzhou 350121, China
[4] School of Computer Sciences, Universiti Sains Malaysia, 11800 Gelugor, Penang,
Malaysia

Abstract. Feature matching is a fundamental and critical step for many
tasks of computer vision. In recent years, many methods for feature
matching have been proposed. However, the image alignment algorithm
used in the state-of-the-art matching method is not robust enough, and
the number of the features extracted from the images are insufficient,
thus the performance obtained by the state-of-the-art matching method
is unsatisfactory. To address these issues, firstly, we use a more robust
geometric estimation algorithm to align image pairs. Secondly, based
on aligned image pairs, we design a content-aware block to more focus
on effective features by using a feature extractor and a mask predictor. Experimental results show that our method achieves more superior
results, and outperforms several classical and deep learning methods on
the HPatches dataset.

Keywords: Feature matching · Image alignment · Content-aware

1 Introduction

Feature matching is a job of finding correct correspondences in two images, as
shown in Fig. 1. It is also the basis for high-level tasks in the field of computer
vision. Improving the performance of matching methods will make some tasks
(e.g., 3D reconstruction, image stitching, simultaneous localization and mapping
and lane line detection) better developed.

Classical feature matching methods usually include three steps in a pipeline:
feature detection, feature description and feature matching. Before the deep
learning methods proposed, most of the methods are based on the above pipeline.
The authors of these methods improve these methods' performance by improving one step in the pipeline usually. For example, Sadder detector [1], brightness comparison-based FAST detector [2] and its developed version FAST-ER

Y. Xu et al. (Eds.): ML4CS 2022, LNCS 13656, pp. 345–354, 2023.
https://doi.org/10.1007/978-3-031-20099-1_29

Fig. 1. An example of feature matching.

[3] improve the performance of the feature detection step. Methods proposed in [4,5] concentrate on the feature description step. Famous classical methods such as SIFT [6], SURF [7], KAZE [8], AKAZE [9] try to improve the first two steps simultaneously. For the last step, classical model fitting methods including RANSAC [10] and its differentiable substitute DSAC [11] improve matching accuracy by estimating geometric transformation such as epipolar geometry and homography.

With the advent of the deep learning, recently proposed matching methods have used neural networks to improve their matching performance. Part of these learning-based methods [12,13] follow the classical pipeline, while others [14,15] are end-to-end. SuperPoint [12] jointly detects key points and computes relevant descriptor vectors. SuperGlue [13] basically improves the descriptor vectors considering the cross and self-attention by the help of a graph neural network. In different scenarios, trying to improve the performance of one or two steps of the methods is not optimal, and thus many end-to-end methods have been proposed. D2-Net [14] uses pre-trained VGG-16 as feature extractor to obtain feature maps. DFM [15] uses pre-trained VGG-19 as a feature extractor to get deep features and perform matching. At the same time, the image pairs are pre-aligned before matching. This step improves the performance of the method. However, the numbers of feature points extracted by D2-Net and DFM are insufficient, resulting in fewer correct matches on non-planar images. Additionally, the geometric estimation algorithm used in DFM is not efficient enough.

To address the above issues, we propose a two-stage feature matching method in this paper. There are two main motivations for our method. Firstly, because the geometric estimation algorithm used in the existing two-stage matching method has unsatisfactory precision for pre-alignment of images pairs, we perform a pre-alignment of image pairs in the first stage using state-of-the-art model fitting algorithms. The pre-aligned image is used as the input of the second stage. Secondly, because of insufficient number of features, the accuracy obtained by the existing method in non-planar images is not enough. In view of this, we use a block consisting of a feature extractor and a mask predictor before perform-

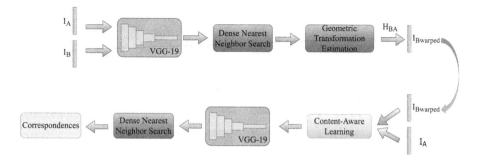

Fig. 2. The proposed two-stage architecture.

ing VGG-19 to improve the ability to extract local effective features. Our work uses the above techniques outperforms many classical and deep feature matching methods in accuracy.

2   Method

In this section, we propose an improved two-stage method to find correct correspondences between image pairs, as shown in Fig. 2. The first stage includes three steps. Firstly, a pre-trained feature extractor (VGG-19) is used to extract the features from the input images I_A and I_B. Secondly, Dense Nearest Neighbor Search (DNNS) is used on the last layer's feature map to initialize the correspondences. Thirdly, these correspondences are then used for homography matrix estimation for pre-alignment. The second stage includes two steps. Firstly, the pre-aligned results are input into a feature extractor, which is composed of a content-aware block and VGG-19 to extract features. Secondly, DNNS is used for feature matching, and hierarchical refinement is used to refine the matching results. The first highlight of our work is the use of a better model fitting algorithm to obtain more accurate homography matrix for image alignment. The second highlight is that a content-aware block is used to predict a probability map, which is used to guide for feature extraction. This effectively reduce the sensitivity to local content compared to the existing feature extraction methods.

2.1   Pre-alignment

In the feature matching tasks, preprocessing the input image is important to improve the probability of finding the correct correspondences. Mental Rotation [16] indicated that the human brain performs an initial rotation of the target when looking for the similarity of two objects. Inspired by this theory, when performing feature matching, DFM [15] performs initial alignment of input image pairs, which is performed in the first stage in its architecture. DFM first uses the pre-trained network to extract features and then dose preliminary matching. DFM uses this matching result to obtain a homography matrix by using

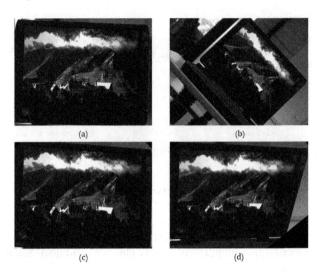

(a)   (b)

(c)   (d)

Fig. 3. This figure shows the comparisons of the effectiveness of aligning image pairs by two homography estimation methods. (a) and (b) are the input images, where (a) is the reference image. (c) is the alignment result using MAGSAC++ for homography estimation, (d) is the alignment result using RANSAC.

RANSAC to achieve pre-alignment of image pairs. However, the RANSAC used in DFM has poor performance in the challenging scenarios, as shown in Fig. 3(d), and thus the alignment result obtained by DFM is not satisfactory.

Different from DFM using RANSAC to estimate homography matrix to do pre-alignment of image pairs, the proposed method uses the recently proposed robust model fitting method MAGSAC++ [17] to estimate the homography matrix H_{BA}, and the H_{BA} is used to process the image I_B to obtain the warped image $I_{B_{warped}}$ (as shown in Fig. 2). Using MAGSAC++, the proposed method can more effectively align the two images and then look for more correct correspondences. In this stage, as shown in Fig. 3(c), the MAGSAC++ algorithm achieves better result than RANSAC in the homography estimation task.

2.2 Content-Aware Learning

Feature-based matching methods usually achieve satisfactory performance on popular test benchmarks, but they are highly dependent on the number and the quality of features. They may obtain poor performance because of insufficient feature number, when images include challenging scenarios such as non-planar images, repeating images or lighting change images. Hence, feature matching requires more effective features.

We will address the above issue in this section. Before performing VGG-19, a content-aware learning block is performed. The content-aware learning block consists of a feature extractor and a mask predictor, which can improve the quantity and quality of useful features. The feature extractor is used to initially

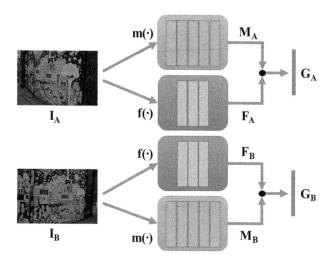

Fig. 4. The composition of the content-aware block.

Table 1. Feature extractor.

Layer no.	1	2	3
Type	conv	conv	conv
Kernel	3	3	3
Stride	1	1	1
Channel	4	8	1

extract the feature map of the input images. The mask predictor is used to predict the probability map, i.e., the location with more contributing content has a higher probability value, and then the probability map is used to initially weight the above feature map. The content-aware block is shown in Fig. 4.

Feature Extractor. To enable the network to learn deep features of image pairs autonomously, we use a fully convolutional network to compose a feature extractor whose structural details are shown in Table. 1. It takes an input of size $H * W * 1$ and produces a feature map of size $H * W * C$. For input images I_A and I_B, the feature extractor shares weights and generates feature maps F_A and F_B, i.e.

$$F_i = f(I_i), i \in \{A, B\} \tag{1}$$

Mask Predictor. In non-planar scenes, especially those involving moving objects, it is difficult to effectively align two views. In traditional methods, RANSAC is widely applied to find the inliers for homography estimation, so as to solve most approximate matrix for the scene alignment. Following the similar

Table 2. Mask predictor.

Layer no.	1	2	3	4	5
Type	conv	conv	conv	conv	conv
Kernel	3	3	3	3	3
Stride	1	1	1	1	1
Channel	4	8	16	32	1

idea, we build a network to automatically learn the locations of useful features, and details are shown in Table. 2. Specifically, the network m(·) generates an inlier probability map, highlighting what has more contributing content in the feature map. The size of the mask is the same as the sizes of the feature maps F_A and F_B. We further weight the features extracted by f(·) through the mask, and then feed two weighted feature maps G_A and G_B into VGG-19, i.e.

$$M_i = m(I_i), G_i = F_i M_i, i \in \{A, B\} \qquad (2)$$

3   Experiments

In this section, we evaluate standard feature matching tasks based on image sequences with illumination and viewpoint changes. The proposed method is evaluated on the HPatches [18] dataset, which contains 116 sets of images. Each set includes 6 images of the same scene. The 6 images were captured at different viewpoints or under different lighting conditions, including planar or non-planar image pairs. At the same time, each set also has a ground-truth homography matrix. In experiments, we compare with classical methods SIFT [6], SURF [7], ORB [19], KAZE [8], AKAZE [9] and learning-based methods SuperPoint [12], Patch2Pix [20] and DFM [15]. We also remove the content-aware block in the proposed method (without C-A) to verify the influence of this block. We use Mean Match Accuracy (MMA) to measure the performance of the competing method, where MMA describes the average of the percentage of correctly matched features (i.e., inliers). If the value of the re-projection error (computed between the ground-truth homography matrix and a match) is less than a given threshold, we consider the match as an inlier.

In this paper, we do two experiments to measure the effectiveness of the proposed method. (1) All competing methods employ a mutual nearest neighbor search with a bidirectional ratio test to find correct correspondences between the extracted features. We measure the performance of different ratio from 0.1 to 1.0 with a step size of 0.1. (2) For thresholds of 1 pixel to 10 pixels, fixing a ratio for each method when the method obtains the best performance, we report MMAs for all methods.

Figure 5 shows the MMAs of 9 feature matching methods for HPatches dataset with different ratios. We can observe from Fig. 5 that the curves of all the

Table 3. The MMAs obtained by all competing methods with different pixel thresholds.

Method	Mean Matching Accuracy (MMA)			
	$\leq 1\,px$	$\leq 3\,px$	$\leq 5\,px$	$\leq 10\,px$
SIFT	0.60	0.87	0.93	0.95
SURF	0.52	0.82	0.89	0.93
ORB	0.37	0.68	0.73	0.74
KAZE	0.52	0.83	0.90	0.94
AKAZE	0.50	0.80	0.87	0.89
SuperPoint	0.50	0.87	0.93	0.95
Patch2Pix	0.48	0.88	**0.94**	0.96
DFM	0.50	0.83	0.91	0.96
Ours (without C-A)	0.67	0.88	0.93	0.95
Ours	**0.69**	**0.89**	**0.94**	**0.97**

compared methods change significantly during the ratio change. This indicates that the ratio change has a more significant impact on all the methods, while the proposed method suffers less.

With different pixel thresholds, we list the MMA of each method in Table. 3, from which it can be seen that the proposed algorithm is highly competitive. Compared with other methods (SIFT, SURF, ORB, KAZE, AKAZE, Super-Point, Patch2Pix and DFM), the proposed method has the highest accuracy in the case of arbitrary pixel thresholds. The MMA obtained by the proposed method is significantly higher than that obtained by the second best method at the threshold of 1. When the threshold is set to 5, the MMA obtained by the proposed method is equal to that obtained by Patch2Pix. When the thresholds are set to 1, 3, 5 and 10, the MMAs of our method exceeds those of the end-to-end method DFM by 0.19, 0.06, 0.03 and 0.01, respectively. With the threshold of 1, SIFT achieves the second best performance (i.e., 0.60). With the threshold of 3, the second best method is Patch2Pix (i.e., 0.88). When the threshold is 10, the second best method is Patch2Pix and DFM (i.e., 0.96).

As shown in Table 3, without the content-aware block, our method also exhibits its superiority, where it outperforms the second best method (SIFT) by 0.07 at the pixel threshold of 1. When pixel thresholds are set to 3 and 5, the proposed method is on par with the second best method. But after introducing content-aware blocks, the superiority of our method further enlarge. Therefore, the proposed content-aware block can effectively improve the performance of the proposed method.

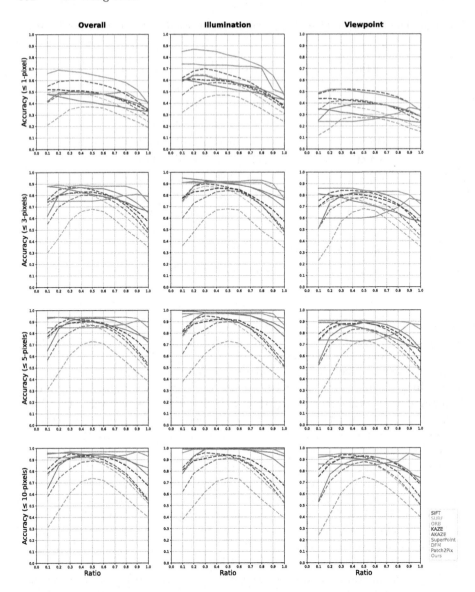

Fig. 5. This figure shows the evaluation results of the feature matching methods on the HPatches dataset, and the scenes include illumination, viewpoint, and overall. Classical methods are represented by dashed lines, while deep learning methods are represented by solid lines.

4   Conclusions

In this paper, we introduce a content-aware deep feature matching method. The proposed method uses an advanced model fitting algorithm to pre-align the image pairs, and then extracts more effective features for matching through a content-aware block and a pre-trained VGG-19 network. The experimental results in this paper show that the proposed method can achieve better results.

Acknowledgement. This work was partially supported by the National Natural Science Foundation of China (62172197, 61972187), and the Natural Science Foundation of Fujian Province (2020J02024).

References

1. Aldana-Iuit, J., Mishkin, D., Chum, O., Matas, J.: In the saddle: chasing fast and repeatable features. In: 2016 23rd IEEE International Conference on Pattern Recognition (ICPR), pp. 675–680 (2016)
2. Trajković, M., Hedley, M.: Fast corner detection. Image Vis. Comput. **16**(2), 75–87 (1998)
3. Rosten, E., Porter, R., Drummond, T.: Faster and better: a machine learning approach to corner detection. IEEE Trans. Pattern Anal. Mach. Intell. **32**(1), 105–119 (2008)
4. Gong, Y., Kumar, S., Rowley, H.A., Lazebnik, S.: Learning binary codes for high-dimensional data using bilinear projections. In: Proceedings of the IEEE Conference on Computer Vision and Pattern Recognition, pp. 484–491 (2013)
5. Trzcinski, T., Lepetit, V.: Efficient discriminative projections for compact binary descriptors. In: Fitzgibbon, A., Lazebnik, S., Perona, P., Sato, Y., Schmid, C. (eds.) ECCV 2012. LNCS, vol. 7572, pp. 228–242. Springer, Heidelberg (2012). https://doi.org/10.1007/978-3-642-33718-5_17
6. Lowe, D.G.: Distinctive image features from scale-invariant keypoints. Int. J. Comput. Vision **60**(2), 91–110 (2004). https://doi.org/10.1023/B:VISI.0000029664.99615.94
7. Bay, H., Tuytelaars, T., Van Gool, L.: SURF: speeded up robust features. In: Leonardis, A., Bischof, H., Pinz, A. (eds.) ECCV 2006. LNCS, vol. 3951, pp. 404–417. Springer, Heidelberg (2006). https://doi.org/10.1007/11744023_32
8. Alcantarilla, P.F., Bartoli, A., Davison, A.J.: KAZE features. In: Fitzgibbon, A., Lazebnik, S., Perona, P., Sato, Y., Schmid, C. (eds.) ECCV 2012. LNCS, vol. 7577, pp. 214–227. Springer, Heidelberg (2012). https://doi.org/10.1007/978-3-642-33783-3_16
9. Alcantarilla, P.F., Solutions, T.: Fast explicit diffusion for accelerated features in nonlinear scale spaces. IEEE Trans. Pattern Anal. Mach. Intell. **34**(7), 1281–1298 (2011)
10. Fischler, M.A., Bolles, R.C.: RANdom SAmple consensus: a paradigm for model fitting with applications to image analysis and automated cartography. Commun. ACM **24**(6), 381–395 (1981)
11. Brachmann, E., et al.: DSAC-differentiable RANSAC for camera localization. In: Proceedings of the IEEE Conference on Computer Vision and Pattern Recognition, pp. 6684–6692 (2017)
12. DeTone, D., Malisiewicz, T., Rabinovich, A.: SuperPoint: self-supervised interest point detection and description. In: Proceedings of the IEEE Conference on Computer Vision and Pattern Recognition Workshops, pp. 224–236 (2018)
13. Sarlin, P.E., DeTone, D., Malisiewicz, T., Rabinovich, A.: SuperGlue: learning feature matching with graph neural networks. In: Proceedings of the IEEE/CVF Conference on Computer Vision and Pattern Recognition, pp. 4938–4947 (2020)

14. Dusmanu, M., et al.: D2-Net: a trainable CNN for joint description and detection of local features. In: Proceedings of the IEEE/CVF Conference on Computer Vision and Pattern Recognition, pp. 8092–8101 (2019)

15. Efe, U., Ince, K.G., Alatan, A.: DFM: a performance baseline for deep feature matching. In: Proceedings of the IEEE/CVF Conference on Computer Vision and Pattern Recognition, pp. 4284–4293 (2021)

16. Shepard, R.N., Metzler, J.: Mental rotation of three-dimensional objects. Science **171**(3972), 701–703 (1971)

17. Barath, D., Noskova, J., Ivashechkin, M., Matas, J.: MAGSAC++, a fast, reliable and accurate robust estimator. In: Proceedings of the IEEE/CVF Conference on Computer Vision and Pattern Recognition, pp. 1304–1312 (2020)

18. Balntas, V., Lenc, K., Vedaldi, A., Mikolajczyk, K.: HPatches: a benchmark and evaluation of handcrafted and learned local descriptors. In: Proceedings of the IEEE Conference on Computer Vision and Pattern Recognition, pp. 5173–5182 (2017)

19. Rublee, E., Rabaud, V., Konolige, K., Bradski, G.: ORB: an efficient alternative to SIFT or SURF. In: 2011 International Conference on Computer Vision, pp. 2564–2571. IEEE (2011)

20. Zhou, Q., Sattler, T., Leal-Taixe, L.: Patch2Pix: epipolar-guided pixel-level correspondences. In: Proceedings of the IEEE/CVF Conference on Computer Vision and Pattern Recognition, pp. 4669–4678 (2021)

F2DLNet: A Face Forgery Detection and Localization Network Based on SSIM Error Maps

Fei Peng[1(✉)], Xin-lin Zhang[2], and Min Long[3]

[1] Institute of Artificial Intelligence and Blockchain, Guangzhou University, Guangzhou 510000, Guangdong, China
eepengf@gmail.com
[2] School of Computer Science and Electronic Engineering, Hunan University, Changsha 410082, China
[3] School of Computer and Communication Engineering, Changsha University of Science and Technology, Changsha 410114, China

Abstract. Aiming to counteract the negligence of structural distortion of face swapped videos in the existing face forgery methods, a novel face forgery detection and localization network named as F2DLNet is proposed based on structural similarity (SSIM) error maps. It consists of Adjacent Layer Aggregation Module (ALAM), Dilated Convolution Module (DCM), and Gradient-enhanced Block (GEB). The ALAM is proposed to extract features from multiple levels and estimate SSIM error maps through attention residual learning. The DCM is introduced to deal with multi-scale manipulation regions. Finally, the Sobel stream which consists of three GEBs is capable to enhance forgery artifact and manipulation region contours. Experimental results and analysis on large-scale benchmark datasets show that F2DLNet can effectively perceive artifacts and their strength of Deepfake videos and thoroughly predict manipulation regions. It outperforms the existing methods in face forgery detection and localization accuracy. It has great potential to be applied for forgery detection and localization of Deepfake videos.

Keywords: Deep learning · Deepfakes · Face forgery detection · Face manipulation localization

1 Introduction

Recently, some social problems caused by face-swapped videos have aroused wide attention. With the development of deep learning, it is difficult to distinguish synthetic media with human's eyes. Moreover, the rapid development of hardware, the massive growth of social media data, and the open-source and commercialization of face editing software have also aggravated the uncontrollability of Deepfakes.

Currently, some methods for distinguishing synthetic videos from natural ones have been proposed. According to the difference of detection objects [19], it

Y. Xu et al. (Eds.): ML4CS 2022, LNCS 13656, pp. 355–369, 2023.
https://doi.org/10.1007/978-3-031-20099-1_30

can be divided into data-driven detection methods [1,23,26], special artifacts detection methods [15,17] and abnormal biological signal detection methods [5,8,16]. Although these methods have achieved encouraging results in forgery detection, there still have apparent shortages in manipulation localization. The main reasons come from two aspects. The first is that not all datasets provide standard localization maps, which makes it hard to carry out quantitative evaluation between different methods. The error-threshold method has been successfully used in manipulation localization [6,10], but it is tough to find a universal threshold suitable for different datasets to generate localization maps with good visual effect. Moreover, the threshold may destroy the integrity of manipulation regions and enhance unnecessary background noise. The second is that multiscale manipulation regions and high similarity of colour and texture near the boundaries of manipulation regions make localization tasks extremely challenging. These issues require the network to understand the global context of images and pay attention to the local details. As the existing manipulation localization networks [6,22] do not explicitly solve these problems, the accuracy of estimated regions is very limited.

Toward the artifact contamination caused by video compression, it is hard to effectively distinguish between the real and the fake faces only by spatial information. At present, the mainstream method is to obtain high-frequency information by transforming the domain, such as DCT and DFT, and then combine the spatial domain for dual-stream learning. Usually, these two streams have the same number of parameters and require pre-processing. Therefore, how to extract high-frequency information from images by adding a small amount of parameters is still unexplored for face forgery detection.

To address the aforementioned issues, this paper proposes a novel face forgery detection and localization network based on SSIM error maps. The main contributions are summarized as follows.

- A novel **Face Forgery Detection and Localization Net**work F2DLNet is proposed. The network uses both classification labels and SSIM error maps for multi-task learning. Different from the previous methods, the SSIM error maps consider the structural distortion caused by face swapping, and have more complete forged signals, which is helpful for improving the detection performance.
- An light-weight auxiliary Sobel stream which consists of three Gradient-enhanced Blocks (GEBs) is proposed to enhance forgery artifact and manipulation contours. It combines features from Adjacent Layer Aggregation Module (ALAM) and finally merges with the encoder, and then input Dilated Convolution Module (DCM), which can alleviate the problem of artifact contamination caused by compression.
- Experimental results and analysis show that F2DLNet outperforms the existing methods in forgery detection and localization accuracy on four Deepfake benchmark datasets FaceForensics++ [26], FaceShifter [14], Celeb-DF [18], and Deepfake Detection Challenge [7].

The rest of the paper is organized as follows. Related work is introduced in Sect. 2. Localization map generation based on SSIM is described in Sect. 3. The proposed F2DLNet is depicted in Sect. 4. Experimental results and analysis are provided in Sect. 5. Finally, some conclusions are drawn in Sect. 6.

2   Related Work

2.1   Face Forgery Detection

Most data driven based methods train neural networks in the spatial or temporal domain by using many static images or video frames. Afchar *et al.* [1] utilized shallow network MesoNet to reduce the impact of image and video compression for Deepfake detection. Nguyen *et al.* [23] detected various spoofs by employing a capsule network. Due to the limited performance of the used backbone networks, the above methods cannot achieve satisfactory results on the latest datasets. To make use of temporal information of video, literatures [9,20], and [27] adopted a strategy of extracting the spatial features and the temporal features by CNN and RNN, respectively. However, it may increase the inference time and cannot be applied to a single Deepfake image. To address the problem of contaminated forgery artifacts caused by image compression, a number of methods [3,13,25] transform images from spatial domain to frequency domain to mine clues, and complement each other's information through two stream neural network.

2.2   Face Manipulation Localization

Comparing with forgery detection, only few efforts have been put on face manipulation localization. Furthermore, not all datasets provide standard localization maps, and the acquisition of localization maps also varies from one to another. Nguyen *et al.* [22] proposed a multi-task learning framework for Deepfake detection and segmentation. In this method, the localization maps used for training are provided by FaceForensics++. Dang *et al.* [6] pointed out that multi-task learning did not necessarily improve the detection performance, and the attention mechanism was proposed. Simultaneously, the attention map is used to automatically locate the manipulation regions of the fake faces. A new dataset is built and the error-threshold method is utilized to generate localization maps. However, the estimated attention maps are tiny, and they only roughly describe the tampered location. For GAN-based face attribute editing and entire face synthesis, Huang *et al.* [10] proposed a universal pipeline to locate manipulation regions of the tampered faces. It collects many fake faces based on GANs and uses the absolute error maps as localization maps. However, its localization maps have poor visual perception, and the semantic segmentation framework is not well suitable for manipulation localization tasks.

Based on the above analysis, the existing methods still have limitations in the performance of forgery detection and manipulation localization. To countermeasure these problems, a novel face forgery detection and localization network

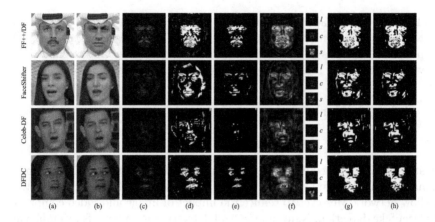

Fig. 1. Comparison of different localization map generation methods on Face-Forensics++/DeepFakes, FaceShifter, Celeb-DF, and Deepfake Detection Challenge datasets. From left to right: (a) real faces, (b) fake faces, (c) absolute error maps between original faces and fake faces, (d) absolute error maps when $\tau = 0.05$, (e) absolute error maps when $\tau = 0.1$, (f) SSIM error maps of the original face and the fake face, and l, c, s components of SSIM error maps, (g) SSIM error maps when $\tau = 0.2$, (h) SSIM error maps when $\tau = 0.25$. **Conclusion: SSIM error maps have more complete and salient forgery signals.**

F2DLNet is put forward. It belongs to data-driven methods, and it implements SSIM error maps for guiding the network to learn the semantics of structural distortion.

3　Generation of Localization Map

Since it lacks standard ground truth maps for manipulation localization task in some popular datasets and the methods for obtaining localization maps are different, a localization map generation method based on SSIM is proposed. Here, the error-threshold method is first briefly introduced and analyzed.

3.1　Error-Threshold Method

In a typical pipeline of synthesizing Deepfakes, it first has a target face $\mathbf{A}$, and then a fake face $\mathbf{A}'$ is generated after different manipulation operations such as face identity replacement, face attribute editing, and etc. The real face $\mathbf{A}$ and the fake face $\mathbf{A}'$ are consistent except for the manipulation region, as shown in Figs. 1(a) and 1(b). Therefore, a ground truth map can be obtained. It first calculates the absolute error between the original face and the fake face, and then it is converted into a grayscale image [10]. Finally, a threshold is introduced to transform the map into a binary map [6], which can be formulated as

$$\mathbf{M}(i,j) = \text{Gray}(|\mathbf{A}(i,j,k) - \mathbf{A}'(i,j,k)|)/255.0, \tag{1}$$

$$\mathbf{M}_{binary}(i,j) = \begin{cases} 0, & \text{if } \mathbf{M}(i,j) < \tau \\ 1, & \text{otherwise} \end{cases}, \tag{2}$$

where function $\text{Gray}(\cdot)$ converts a colour image into a grayscale image, and τ is a manually selected threshold.

The above method is named as the error-threshold method. Figure 1(c) shows some samples generated by this method. From these figures, the absolute error maps are hard to be visually perceived. The reason is that it only compares the difference of each pixel, while the difference in structure between two images is ignored. If the original portrait's skin colour is similar to the target, the skin colour of the fake portrait tampered by Deepfake technology will be close to the original one. Thus, it is hard to obtain localization maps with good visual perception through absolute error. With different thresholds $\tau = 0.05$ and $\tau = 0.1$, the error maps are shown in Fig. 1(d) and 1(e), respectively. From Fig. 1(d), the background noise is enhanced because the threshold is relatively small. While for Fig. 1(e), the background noise is almost eliminated because of the large threshold.

From the above analysis, the error-threshold method may bring two problems: (1) The threshold may enhance the noise and eliminate some manipulation regions. (2) Different datasets may require different thresholds. Since the incompleteness of manipulation regions may mislead the network, more tampered regions will be misclassified as non-tampered regions in the forgery localization. Moreover, it is hard to generalize to different datasets because of the variation of thresholds.

3.2 Localization Map Generation Based on SSIM

To overcome the above issues, SSIM error maps are utilized as the ground truth maps of manipulation localization. The calculation of pixel-wise SSIM [31] between images $\mathbf{A}$ and $\mathbf{A}'$ is formulated as

$$\text{SSIM}(x,y) = \Big(l(x,y)\Big)^{\alpha}\Big(c(x,y)\Big)^{\beta}\Big(s(x,y)\Big)^{\gamma}, \tag{3}$$

where l, c and s are brightness, contrast and structure, respectively, and $\alpha, \beta, \gamma > 0$ are parameters for adjusting the importance of three components. To calculate the mean, variance and covariance in a pixel neighborhood, a Gaussian filter with $\sigma = 1.5$ is used. Let $\mu_{\mathbf{A}}$, $\sigma_{\mathbf{A}}^2$ be the mean, variance of $\mathbf{A}$, $\sigma_{\mathbf{A}\mathbf{A}'}$ be the covariance of $\mathbf{A}$ and $\mathbf{A}'$, three components brightness, contrast and structure are formulated as

$$l(x,y) = \frac{2\mu_{\mathbf{A}}\mu_{\mathbf{A}'} + C_1}{\mu_{\mathbf{A}}^2 + \mu_{\mathbf{A}'}^2 + C_1}, c(x,y) = \frac{2\sigma_{\mathbf{A}}\sigma_{\mathbf{A}'} + C_2}{\sigma_{\mathbf{A}}^2 + \sigma_{\mathbf{A}'}^2 + C_2}, s(x,y) = \frac{\sigma_{\mathbf{A}\mathbf{A}'} + C_3}{\sigma_{\mathbf{A}}\sigma_{\mathbf{A}'} + C_3}, \tag{4}$$

where $C_1 = (K_1 L)^2$, $C_2 = (K_2 L)^2$, $C_3 = C_2/2$, $K_1 \ll 1$, $K_2 \ll 1$. For images represented in 8-bits, $L = 255$. Generally, the expression is simplified by setting $\alpha = \beta = \gamma = 1$ in Eq. (3). After simplification, it can obtain

$$\text{SSIM}(x,y) = \frac{(2\mu_{\mathbf{A}}\mu_{\mathbf{A}'} + C_1)(2\sigma_{\mathbf{A}\mathbf{A}'} + C_2)}{(\mu_{\mathbf{A}}^2 + \mu_{\mathbf{A}'}^2 + C_1)(\sigma_{\mathbf{A}}^2 + \sigma_{\mathbf{A}'}^2 + C_2)}. \tag{5}$$

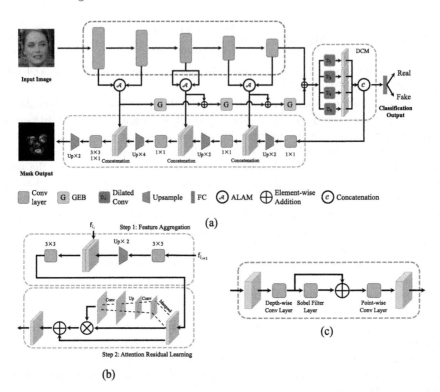

Fig. 2. Detailed network architecture of the suggested F2DLNet. (a) Network architecture. (b) Illustration of Adjacent Layer Aggregation Module. (c) Illustration of Gradient-enhanced Block.

Since the value of SSIM(x, y) directly generated by Eq. (5) is in the range of $[0, 1]$, it means that they are the same when SSIM$(x, y) = 1$, and they are different when SSIM$(x, y) = 0$. To obtain the location map where the pixel values of the tampered area are 1 and the non-tampered area are 0, contrast inversion is needed, and it can be formulated as

$$\overline{\text{SSIM}}(x, y) = 1 - \text{SSIM}(x, y), \tag{6}$$

where $\overline{\text{SSIM}}(x, y)$ is an image with three channels. To obtain a single-channel ground truth map, it is converted to a grayscale image as

$$\mathbf{S} = \text{Gray}(\overline{\text{SSIM}}(x, y) \times 255)/255. \tag{7}$$

The visual effect of SSIM maps is shown in Fig. 1(f). Comparing with Fig. 1(d) and 1(e), the SSIM maps can achieve better visual perception. The main reason is that a face image is structured, and the adjacent pixels in space are highly dependent. However, face-swapping will lead to structural distortion. Therefore, the difference of each pixel cannot accurately reflect the structural difference. On the contrary, the SSIM map evaluates the differences between two images from three aspects: brightness, contrast and structure. As seen from the brightness, contrast and structural components on the right side of Fig. 1(f), the structural difference plays a leading role in highlighting manipulation regions. Figures 1(g) and 1(h) show SSIM error maps whose thresholds are 0.2 and 0.25, respectively. The integrity is better than that of Figs. 1(d) and 1(e) after setting the thresholds. Through observation and analysis on multiple datasets, SSIM maps can achieve more complete and salient forgery signals. Even if the threshold is set, the integrity of manipulation regions can be guaranteed and the background noise can be ignored.

4   The Proposed F2DLNet

4.1   Network Architecture

The network architecture is shown in Fig. 2(a). It consists of an encoder, a Sobel stream and a decoder. Since the encoder performs five times of downsampling, F2DLNet extracts feature maps from five levels of the backbone network to effectively utilize the features from low to high. Feature maps from the encoder can be denoted by $\mathbf{F} = \{\mathbf{f}_{l_i}\}(i = 1, 2, 3, 4, 5)$. As the resolution of the input image $\mathbf{X}_i$ is 256×256, the resolution of feature maps is $w_i \times h_i = \frac{256}{2^i} \times \frac{256}{2^i}$. $\mathbf{F}$ is a feature set extracted from multiple levels, and it contains low-level visual cues and high-level semantic information with different resolutions, which can guide the network to pay attention to both the global context and the local details of images. Even if the colour and the texture near the manipulation regions' boundaries are highly similar, the network still can distinguish them. $\mathbf{F}$ is further transferred to the decoder module and Sobel stream through the Adjacent Layer Aggregation Module (ALAM) to integrate these features. The Sobel stream consists of three Gradient-enhanced Blocks (GEB) which is capable to enhance forgery artifact and manipulation region contours. Moreover, to deal with multi-scale manipulation regions, the feature maps output from the last level of the encoder will first merges with the Sobel stream, and then input into the Dilated Convolution Module (DCM). DCM obtains receptive fields with different sizes by paralleling dilated convolution with different ratios. Thus, it can process features with different scales. Here, the dilated rates of DCM is setting as $\{1, 3, 6, 9\}$. Finally, the decoder module restores the manipulation regions from bottom to top using the feature set extracted from the backbone network.

4.2   Adjacent Layer Aggregation Module

To reduce parameters of the decoder, preserve the spatial structure of the input image and enhance the global context information, the feature maps extracted from multiple levels of the backbone network are further divided into high, middle and low three levels. High-level, middle-level, and low-level features are aggregated and transferred to the decoder by their respective ALAMs. As shown in Fig. 2(b), ALAM mainly composes of two steps. In the first step, feature maps

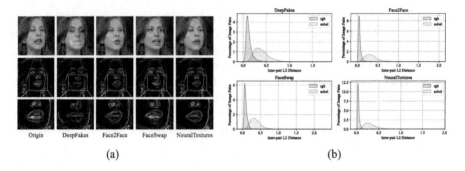

(a)   (b)

Fig. 3. Motivation of the proposed GEB. (a) Exapmle of Image gradient generated from FaceForensics++ displaying difference between the origin and four types of manipulation. (b) Distributions of mean L2 distance between real and fake image pairs of different manipulation types before and after using GEB, which can indicate the discriminative-ability of GEB.

$\mathbf{f}_{l_i}$ and $\mathbf{f}_{l_{i+1}}$ from two adjacent levels of the backbone network are delivered to ALAM and carried out aggregation, which can be formulated as

$$h(\mathbf{f}_{l_i}, \mathbf{f}_{l_{i+1}}) = \delta_{3\times3}(\mathrm{Cat}(\mathbf{f}_{l_i}, \mathrm{Up}_{\times2}(\delta_{3\times3}(\mathbf{f}_{l_{i+1}})))), \tag{8}$$

where δ represents convolution layer composed of the convolution kernel, batch normalization and ReLU activation function, and its subscript is the size of convolution kernel. Up denotes two-dimensional bilinear upsampling, and its subscript denotes scaling factor. Cat denotes the concatenation of two input feature maps in the same channel.

After feature aggregation, to make the network pay more attention to the manipulation regions and reduce the influence of background noise, ALAM introduces bottom-up and top-down attention residual learning [30], which is shown in the second step of Fig. 2(b). The advantage of bottom-up top-down is that it can obtain a larger receptive field while only a small number of parameters are increased, which helps the network to obtain more global context at a low level. Different from [30], no convolution operation is performed to the trunk branch. While for the second step, it can be formulated by

$$h(\mathbf{f}_{l_i}, \mathbf{f}_{l_{i+1}}) = (1 + \mathrm{M}(h(\mathbf{f}_{l_i}, \mathbf{f}_{l_{i+1}}))) \times h(\mathbf{f}_{l_i}, \mathbf{f}_{l_{i+1}}), \tag{9}$$

where $\mathrm{M}(\cdot)$ represents the branch of generating attention map. By combining Eqs. (8) and (9), the output features of high, middle and low levels are $\mathbf{H}_{hi} = h(\mathbf{f}_{l_4}, \mathbf{f}_{l_5})$, $\mathbf{H}_{mid} = h(\mathbf{f}_{l_3}, \mathbf{f}_{l_3})$, and $\mathbf{H}_{lo} = h(\mathbf{f}_{l_1}, \mathbf{f}_{l_2})$.

4.3 Gradient-Enhanced Block

To alleviate the problem of artifact contamination caused by video compression, different from the previous method of transforming images from spatial domain to frequency domain, this paper combines Sobel filter [11] and convolution layer to extract features from the perspective of image gradient enhancement. Figure 3 shows the difference of image gradient between fake face and real face. In this paper, Sobel operator is used to calculate the gradient of the image in vertical and horizontal directions, which is expressed as

$$\mathbf{Grad}_{hor} = \begin{bmatrix} +1 & 0 & -1 \\ +2 & 0 & -2 \\ +1 & 0 & -1 \end{bmatrix} * \mathbf{f}, \ \mathbf{Grad}_{ver} = \begin{bmatrix} +1 & +2 & +1 \\ 0 & 0 & 0 \\ -1 & -2 & -1 \end{bmatrix} * \mathbf{f}, \tag{10}$$

where $*$ denotes the depth-wise convolution operation and $\mathbf{f}$ denotes the input feature. The Sobel stream consists of three Gradient-enhanced Blocks (GEB) and receives low, middle and high input from encoder. As shown in Fig. 2(c), the GEB is a Depthwise Separable Convolution layer [28]. Besides, a depth-wise sobel filter and a skip connection are inserted between depthwise convolution and pointwise convolution to enhance the gradients of these features, which can be formulated as

$$\hat{\mathbf{f}} = \mathbf{f} \oplus \sqrt{\mathbf{Grad}_{hor}^2 + \mathbf{Grad}_{ver}^2}, \tag{11}$$

where $\oplus$ refers to channel-wise addition between input feature and gradient feature.

4.4 Loss Functions

As mentioned above, F2DLNet conducts end-to-end supervised learning with the training dataset $\mathbf{D} = \{\mathbf{X}_i, y_i, \mathbf{S}_i\}_{i=1}^N$. The total loss is defined as

$$\mathcal{L} = \mathcal{L}_{Cls} + \lambda \mathcal{L}_{Mask}, \tag{12}$$

where $\mathcal{L}_{Cls}$ is the cross-entropy loss for forgery detection, $\mathcal{L}_{Mask}$ is the loss for manipulation localization, and the weight is λ. $\mathcal{L}_{Cls}$ is defined as

$$\mathcal{L}_{Cls} = - \sum_{(x,y) \sim \mathbf{D}} [y \log(\mathrm{C}(\mathrm{F}_{l_5}(x))) + (1 - y) \log(1 - \mathrm{C}(\mathrm{F}_{l_5}(x)))], \tag{13}$$

where $\mathrm{F}_{l_5}(\cdot)$ represents the output of the fifth level of the decoder, and $\mathrm{C}(\cdot)$ represents the output of the classifier.

The loss of manipulation localization is defined as

$$\mathcal{L}_{Mask} = \sum_{(x,\mathbf{S}) \sim \mathbf{D}} \|\mathrm{D}(\mathbf{H}) - \mathbf{S}\|^2, \tag{14}$$

where $\mathbf{H} = \{\mathbf{H}_{hi}, \mathbf{H}_{mid}, \mathbf{H}_{lo}, \mathbf{H}_{DCM}\}$ represents the feature map set output by high, middle and low levels and DCM module, $\mathrm{D}(\cdot)$ represents the decoder, and $\mathbf{S}$ represents the ground truth map.

Table 1. Comparison of forgery detection results of different methods on FaceForensics++ dataset with High-Quality and Low-Quality settings, respectively.

Method	FF++ (c23)		FF++ (c40)	
	ACC	AUC	ACC	AUC
MesoNet [1]	83.10	–	70.47	–
Xception [4]	95.73	96.30	86.86	89.30
Face X-ray [15]	–	87.40	–	61.60
Two Branch [21]	96.43	98.70	86.34	86.59
F3-Net [25]	97.52	98.10	**90.43**	93.30
FDFL [13]	96.69	99.28	89.00	92.39
MultiAtt [33]	97.60	99.29	88.69	90.40
EffNet-B4 [29]	96.10	99.23	83.95	89.65
F2DLNet (Proposed)	**98.04**	**99.77**	86.85	**94.31**

5 Experimental Results and Analysis

5.1 Implementation Details

In the experiments, EfficientNet-B4 [29] is chosen as the backbone network to balance the parameters and performance, which has been pre-trained on ImageNet. The whole network adopts Stochastic Gradient Descent learning for end-to-end training. The loss weight λ is set to 1, The optimizer is Adam [12], the learning rate is 0.0002, the batch size is set to 32, and the maximum epoch is set to 20. The proposed F2DLNet is implemented with PyTorch [24] framework, and one GTX 1080 Ti GPU is used to accelerate training. As mentioned above, this method is frame-based. For every video, 20 frames are sampled from each video. The face detector is MTCNN [32]. Because the extracted face images' width and height are inconsistent, the longer side of the input image will be scaled to 256, and the shorter side will be equally scaled and then filled with zero before training and testing.

5.2 Datasets and Evaluation Metrics

To evaluate the performance of the proposed method, experiments are conducted on four widely used benchmark datasets: FaceForensics++ (FF++) [26], Faceshifter (FSH) [14], Celeb-DF [18] and Deepfake Detection Challenge (DFDC) [7]. FF++ dataset contains four types of manipulation techniques, *i.e.*, DeepFakes, Face2Face, FaceSwap and NeuralTextures. The latest FaceForensics++ also includes a new GAN-based dataset Faceshifter [14]. Celeb-DF [18] dataset includes 590 original videos and 5639 related Deepfake videos. DFDC dataset contains 23654 real videos and 104500 fake videos.

Accuracy (ACC) and Area Under Curve(AUC) are adopted to evaluate the forgery detection performance of different methods. Intersection over Union (IoU) and Mean Absolute Error (MAE) are used to evaluate different methods'

Table 2. Comparison of manipulation localization results of different methods on four benchmark datasets. ↓ denotes the lower is better.

Method	FF++ (c23)			FSH			Celeb-DF			DFDC		
	AUC	IoU	MAE↓	AUC	IoU	MAE↓	AUC	IoU	MAE↓	AUC	IoU	MAE↓
MTDS [22]	76.07	54.14	0.023	96.15	54.03	0.030	58.76	56.85	0.023	73.08	56.77	0.023
Xception+Reg [6]	98.41	58.24	0.019	99.88	57.18	0.031	99.82	57.24	0.019	94.49	58.57	0.023
FakeLocator [10]	99.44	59.61	0.018	99.91	58.84	0.031	99.82	60.71	0.018	93.88	60.68	0.022
F2DLNet (Proposed)	**99.77**	**60.71**	**0.016**	**99.97**	**59.09**	**0.027**	**99.86**	**61.81**	**0.016**	**97.38**	**61.62**	**0.021**

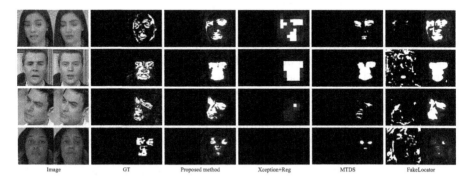

Image   GT   Proposed method   Xception+Reg   MTDS   FakeLocator

Fig. 4. Visual comparison between the proposed method and other methods on the benchmark datasets.

manipulation localization performance. For the evaluation of the manipulation localization performance, binary maps transformed from SSIM error maps and prediction maps are used, because SSIM error maps and prediction maps are not binary maps, and they cannot be used for calculating IoU directly. The transformation threshold is empirically set to 0.25.

5.3   Experiments and Performance Analysis

Forgery Detection Performance. To analyze the forgery detection performance, the proposed F2DLNet is firstly compared with state-of-the-art methods on c23(HQ) version and c40(LQ) version of FF++, respectively. The experimental results are listed in Table 1. From the results, the proposed F2DLNet outperforms the existing methods on c23 version of FF++. It is worth noting that F2DLNet can effectively improve the forgery detection performance compared with EfficientNet-B4 [7], which only focuses on forgery detection. In c40 version of FF++, our model lags behind the method based on frequency domain in terms of accuracy, but obtains highest AUC score than other methods. This is mainly because the proposed model needs to pay attention to both forgery detection and manipulation localization, while manipulation localization require pure localization ground truth. However, the background noise of high compression rate video will be mixed up with manipulation regions, which makes it much more difficult to distinguish.

Table 3. Ablation study on the effectiveness of different model components.

No.	GEB	ALAM	DCM	FF++ (c40)		Param (M)
				AUC	IoU	
0				89.65	–	17.55
1	✓			93.28	–	17.72
2		✓		92.43	57.44	18.35
3		✓	✓	93.34	58.43	20.15
4	✓	✓	✓	**94.31**	**58.64**	20.93

Manipulation Localization Performance. To analyze the manipulation localization performance, the proposed F2DLNet is compared with MTDS [22], Xception+Reg [6], and FakeLocator [10]. All methods are implemented according to the existing codes, and they are retrained by the same datasets. For the localization task, Intersection over Union (IoU) and Mean Absolute Error (MAE) are both used to compare the performance of F2DLNet with other methods, and the results are listed in Table 2. From the results, it can be found that the performance of the proposed F2DLNet is the best compared with the existing methods on all datasets. The improvements are always kept about 1% in IoU, except FaceShifter dataset which has small data volume. The results indicate the good performance of manipulation localization of the proposed F2DLNet.

Visualization of Localization Map. Here, experiments are also made to illustrate the visualization of the proposed F2DLNet and the other methods with four benchmark datasets, and the results are shown in Fig. 4. It can be seen that the prediction of the manipulation regions of F2DLNet is more accurate than those of Xception+Reg [6], MTDS [22], and FakeLocator [10]. For Xception+Reg [6], it only roughly depicts the manipulation regions, because the estimated maps are very small. As MTDS [22] is a pixel-level localization method, and the network structure is relatively simple which does not consider the multi-scale and multi-level information, the final predicted regions are not complete. The closest visual effect to F2DLNet is FakeLocator [10], whose backbone network is DeeplabV3 [2]. However, it incorrectly predicts a large number of backgrounds as tampered regions. The above results indicate the good visualization of the localization map of the proposed F2DLNet.

Analysis of Effectiveness of Model Components. To analyze the effectiveness of GEB, ALAM, and DCM , ablation experiments are carried out on these three modules. F2DLNet will degenerate into a EfficientNet when all model components is not used. Here, experiment is only conducted on FF++ (c40) for simplification, and the results are listed in Table 3. From the results, the second, and the third rows show add-on effectiveness of GEB and ALAM, respectively. Moreover, Compared to the baseline model with only the backbone, GEB improves the performance by over 3% while only increase the parameter amount by less 0.2M. With GEB, ALAM, and DCM, it can achieve the best performance. The above ablation experiments illustrate the effectiveness of GEB, ALAM, and DCM.

6   Conclusion

In this paper, a face forgery detection and localization network is proposed based on SSIM error map. SSIM map explicitly considers the spatial structure difference between the original image and the fake image, so the ground truth map with good visual effect can be directly obtained. F2DLNet can learn to locate manipulation regions from multiple levels and scales by combining ALAM, DCM, and GEB. Extensive experiments on four datasets show that F2DLNet outperforms the existing methods in forgery detection and manipulation localization. Our future work will be concentrated on the improvement of the generalization of F2DLNet.

Acknowledgments. This work was supported in part by project supported by National Natural Science Foundation of China (Grant No. U1936115, 62072055, 92067104), and the authors would like to thank for the authors of the previous works for sharing their codes.

References

1. Afchar, D., Nozick, V., Yamagishi, J., Echizen, I.: MesoNet: a compact facial video forgery detection network. In: Proceedings of the IEEE International Workshop Information Forensics and Security, pp. 1–7 (2018)
2. Chen, L.C., Papandreou, G., Schroff, F., Adam, H.: Rethinking atrous convolution for semantic image segmentation. arXiv preprint arXiv:1706.05587 (2017)
3. Chen, S., Yao, T., Chen, Y., Ding, S., Li, J., Ji, R.: Local relation learning for face forgery detection. In: Proceedings of the AAAI Conference on Artificial Intelligence, vol. 35, pp. 1081–1088 (2021)
4. Chollet, F.: Xception: deep learning with depthwise separable convolutions. In: Proceedings of the IEEE Conference on Computer Vision and Pattern Recognition, pp. 1251–1258 (2017)
5. Ciftci, U.A., Demir, I., Yin, L.: FakeCatcher: detection of synthetic portrait videos using biological signals. IEEE Trans. Pattern Anal. Mach. Intell. (2020). https://doi.org/10.1109/TPAMI.2020.3009287
6. Dang, H., Liu, F., Stehouwer, J., Liu, X., Jain, A.K.: On the detection of digital face manipulation. In: Proceedings of the IEEE/CVF Conference on Computer Vision and Pattern Recognition, pp. 5781–5790 (2020)
7. Dolhansky, B., et al.: The deepfake detection challenge dataset. arXiv preprint arXiv:2006.07397 (2020)
8. Fernandes, S., et al.: Predicting heart rate variations of deepfake videos using neural ode. In: Proceedings of the IEEE Conference on Computer Vision Pattern Recognition Workshops (2019)

9. Güera, D., Delp, E.J.: Deepfake video detection using recurrent neural networks. In: Proceedings of the 15th IEEE International Conference on Advanced Video Signal Based Surveillance, pp. 1–6 (2018)

10. Huang, Y., Juefei-Xu, F., Guo, Q., Liu, Y., Pu, G.: Fakelocator: robust localization of GAN-based face manipulations. IEEE Trans. Inf. Forensics Secur. **17**, 2657–2672 (2022)

11. Kanopoulos, N., Vasanthavada, N., Baker, R.L.: Design of an image edge detection filter using the Sobel operator. IEEE J. Solid-State Circuits **23**(2), 358–367 (1988)

12. Kingma, D.P., Ba, J.: Adam: a method for stochastic optimization. arXiv preprint arXiv:1412.6980 (2014)

13. Li, J., Xie, H., Li, J., Wang, Z., Zhang, Y.: Frequency-aware discriminative feature learning supervised by single-center loss for face forgery detection. In: Proceedings of the IEEE Conference Computer Vision and Pattern Recognition, pp. 6458–6467 (2021)

14. Li, L., Bao, J., Yang, H., Chen, D., Wen, F.: Advancing high fidelity identity swapping for forgery detection. In: Proceedings of the IEEE Conference on Computer Vision and Pattern Recognition, pp. 5074–5083 (2020)

15. Li, L., et al.: Face x-ray for more general face forgery detection. In: Proceedings of the IEEE Conference on Computer Vision and Pattern Recognition, pp. 5001–5010 (2020)

16. Li, Y., Chang, M.C., Lyu, S.: In ictu oculi: exposing AI created fake videos by detecting eye blinking. In: Proceedings of the IEEE International Workshop on Information Forensics and Security, pp. 1–7 (2018)

17. Li, Y., Lyu, S.: Exposing deepfake videos by detecting face warping artifacts. arXiv preprint arXiv:1811.00656 (2018)

18. Li, Y., Yang, X., Sun, P., Qi, H., Lyu, S.: Celeb-DF: a large-scale challenging dataset for deepfake forensics. In: Proceedings of the IEEE Conference on Computer Vision and Pattern Recognition, pp. 3207–3216 (2020)

19. Lyu, S.: Deepfake detection: current challenges and next steps. In: Proceedings of the IEEE International Conference on Multimedia Expo Workshops, pp. 1–6 (2020)

20. Mas Montserrat, D., et al.: Deepfakes detection with automatic face weighting. In: Proceedings of the IEEE Conference on Computer Vision and Pattern Recognition Workshops, pp. 668–669 (2020)

21. Masi, I., Killekar, A., Mascarenhas, R.M., Gurudatt, S.P., AbdAlmageed, W.: Two-branch recurrent network for isolating deepfakes in videos. In: Vedaldi, A., Bischof, H., Brox, T., Frahm, J.-M. (eds.) ECCV 2020. LNCS, vol. 12352, pp. 667–684. Springer, Cham (2020). https://doi.org/10.1007/978-3-030-58571-6_39

22. Nguyen, H.H., Fang, F., Yamagishi, J., Echizen, I.: Multi-task learning for detecting and segmenting manipulated facial images and videos. In: Proceedings of the IEEE 10th International Conference on Biometrics Theory, Applications and Systems, pp. 1–8 (2019)

23. Nguyen, H.H., Yamagishi, J., Echizen, I.: Capsule-forensics: using capsule networks to detect forged images and videos. In: Proceedings of the IEEE International Conference on Acoustics Speech and Signal Processing, pp. 2307–2311 (2019)

24. Paszke, A., et al.: Automatic differentiation in PyTorch (2017)

25. Qian, Y., Yin, G., Sheng, L., Chen, Z., Shao, J.: Thinking in frequency: face forgery detection by mining frequency-aware clues. In: Vedaldi, A., Bischof, H., Brox, T., Frahm, J.-M. (eds.) ECCV 2020. LNCS, vol. 12357, pp. 86–103. Springer, Cham (2020). https://doi.org/10.1007/978-3-030-58610-2_6

26. Rossler, A., Cozzolino, D., Verdoliva, L., Riess, C., Thies, J., Nießner, M.: Face-Forensics++: learning to detect manipulated facial images. In: Proceedings of the IEEE International Conference on Computer Vision, pp. 1–11 (2019)

27. Sabir, E., Cheng, J., Jaiswal, A., AbdAlmageed, W., Masi, I., Natarajan, P.: Recurrent convolutional strategies for face manipulation detection in videos. Interfaces (GUI) **3**(1), 80–87 (2019)

28. Sandler, M., Howard, A., Zhu, M., Zhmoginov, A., Chen, L.C.: MobileNetV 2: inverted residuals and linear bottlenecks. In: Proceedings of the IEEE Conference on Computer Vision and Pattern Recognition, pp. 4510–4520 (2018)

29. Tan, M., Le, Q.: EfficientNet: rethinking model scaling for convolutional neural networks. In: Proceedings of the International Conference on Machine Learning, pp. 6105–6114 (2019)

30. Wang, F., et al.: Residual attention network for image classification. In: Proceedings of the IEEE Conference on Computer Vision and Pattern Recognition, pp. 3156–3164 (2017)

31. Wang, Z., Bovik, A.C., Sheikh, H.R., Simoncelli, E.P.: Image quality assessment: from error visibility to structural similarity. IEEE Trans. Image Process. **13**(4), 600–612 (2004)

32. Zhang, K., Zhang, Z., Li, Z., Qiao, Y.: Joint face detection and alignment using multitask cascaded convolutional networks. IEEE Signal Process. Lett. **23**(10), 1499–1503 (2016)

33. Zhao, H., Zhou, W., Chen, D., Wei, T., Zhang, W., Yu, N.: Multi-attentional deepfake detection. In: Proceedings of the IEEE Conference Computer Vision and Pattern Recognition, pp. 2185–2194 (2021)

An Eye-Gaze Tracking Method Based on a 3D Ocular Surface Fitting Model

Zhang Ling[1], Ma Zongxin[1(✉)], Yan MingYu[2], Jiang Wenchao[1], and Muhammad[3]

[1] Computer Faculty, Guangdong University of Technology, Guangzhou, China
2112005123@mail2.gdut.edu.cn
[2] State Key Laboratory of Computer Architecture, Institute of Computing Technology, Chinese Academy of Sciences, Beijing, China
[3] University of Management and Technology, Lahore 54770, Pakistan

Abstract. Nowadays gaze tracking systems have several common drawbacks: low suitability, high complexity and low accuracy. To solve these problems, this paper presents a novel gaze tracking method, which improves the performance of gaze tracking system in two aspects. A 3D ocular quadratic surface model is constructed with eyeball's point cloud data, which are collected by a pair of binocular cameras in a free space, allowing head movement and without any wearable devices. Geometrical features of ocular surface, including principal direction, Gaussian curvature and radius are exploited to calculate ocular optical axis direction and person-specific parameters, and then to estimate ocular visual axis direction, i.e. gaze direction without any personal calibration procedures. For this purpose, two person-specific parameters, the radius of cornea curvature and the distance between the center of cornea curvature and the pupil on the ocular model, are inputted into a GRNN network to estimate the value of kappa angle, which is an angle between ocular optical axis and visual axis and has important effect on estimation accuracy of the ocular visual axis direction by the ocular optical axis direction. Compared with the pupil center cornea reflection method, the following experimental results show that the method presented in this paper is effective and accurate in kappa angle estimating and gaze tracking.

Keywords: Gaze tracking · Quadratic surface fitting · Personal calibration · Kappa angle estimation

1 Introduction

In recent years, the detection and tracking of eye-gaze has been recognized as an active research field because it increases the convenience of various applications. Robust eye detection and tracking algorithms need to be developed to implement and design attentive user interfaces, human-computer interaction systems, assistive technologies, and human emotional state analysis systems.

Y. Xu et al. (Eds.): ML4CS 2022, LNCS 13656, pp. 370–381, 2023.
https://doi.org/10.1007/978-3-031-20099-1_31

At present, the methods for estimating the sight are divided into three categories [1]: (1) biological indicators, (2) infrared corneal reflection, (3) Photo-OculoGraphy (POG) or Video-OculoGraphy (VOG). The first category measures biological indicators, such as electrooculography (EOG) [2, 3, 10] to analyze eye movement using induced electromotive force (EMF). Disadvantages of this type include being harmful to the eyes and being susceptible to eye conditions. The second category is Pupil Center Cornea Reflection (PCCR), which determines the direction of the line of sight through the different angles of the infrared light reflected by the experimenter's cornea [6, 8, 11–14]. The third categories is to extract the features of the experimenter from the 2D/3D image or video based on the digital image or video processing algorithm, and then establish the gaze model according to the extracted features. Compared with the other two category, this category is nonintrusive to the experimenters' body and it is easily implemented. However, the accuracy of this method is limited by the light and the posture of the head relative to the camera.

References [7, 9, 15] estimate the direction of eye gaze with 2D gaze model, using one monocular camera combining with the infrared pupil-corner technique. They believed that there is a geometric mapping relationship between pupil movement and direction of gaze, so eye-gaze direction can be estimated by a camera and a reference infrared light source. In order to solve the problem of head motion limitation, [16–18] proposed a line of sight tracking method combined with head pose estimation. In these systems, when matching feature points, the relative head angle is calculated using dual view geometry. Although the two-dimensional models have the characteristics of low complexity and easy implementation, they are still in low robustness.

3D image method can estimate the intersection of the line of sight and the object surface immediately, and has been widely used without being affected by the head movement. Boumbarov [19] proposed a 3D eye gaze direction estimation method using one camera and multiple reference light sources. Auvinet [20] modeled the eyeball cornea as a convex mirror and established a three-dimensional geometric eye gaze estimation mechanism. Nagamatsu [21] proposed an eye gaze detection system, which establishes a geometric gaze model in 3D space through two cameras and two light sources. Ling [22] proposed an eye gaze estimation method based on eyeball parameters, which uses two stereo cameras to model the eyes in three-dimensional space. Craig heekyung [23] proposed an eye-gaze detection method, which uses a camera set composed of wide-angle and narrow-angle cameras and infrared equipment to build a 3D eye model to detect the line of sight direction. The 3D model method has no limitation on the movement of the experimenter's head. However, it is complex and requires repeated calibration. In addition, when the head moves, the pre calibrated parameters will easily fail.

In order to overcome this limitation, we propose a new system, which eliminates the need for gaze calibration through the geometric structure of the eye and its binocular image. It requires only two person-specific parameters to perform the necessary calibration. Three steps are included: 1) 3D point cloud data of human's eye are collected using a binocular stereo imaging system. 2) With quadratic surface fitting method, they are fitted to reconstruct a 3D eye image. 3) From the reconstructed 3D eye image, the eigen gaze features are obtained to track gaze in a stereo space. In order to evaluate the proposed system, several experiments were designed and carried out with two objectives:

(a) To collect a binocular imaging database of people with different facial orientation and distance cameras. (b) In order to verify the 3D model method proposed in this paper, compared with other methods based on 2D images or 3D monocular images proposed in references, and point of gaze (POG) test results mentioned in references [4, 5] are taken as ground-truth.

The rest of the paper is organized as follows. The Sect. 2 introduces the theory and basis of binocular stereo imaging. In Sect. 3, the method of obtaining gaze direction and estimating person-specific parameters based on 3D eyeball surface fitting is introduced in detail. In Sect. 4, an experiment on kappa angle estimation is conducted, and experimental results associated with three distances 350, 450, and 550 mm between the person's eye and the screen surface with motionless and free head posture respectively are given. Comparison with the ground truth and relative analysis and discussion are also shown in this section. Finally, in Sect. 5, the conclusions and future work are presented.

2   Eye Point Cloud Data Acquisition Based on Binocular Stereo Vision

Binocular stereo vision is an important form of machine vision based on binocular vision parallax theory. That is, human's two eyes would view two slightly different pictures of a same object, and this difference would help humans to perceive the object's depth [5].

Two digital cameras with the same parameters are used to build a binocular stereo imaging platform, which is responsible for taking pairs of images simultaneously of a person's eye. At first, kernel parameters, distortion matrices of two cameras, and reconstructing matrices of both left and right eyes are obtained one by one through a system's calibration process, and then, they are used to correct distorted images of left and right cameras and match the left view image with right view image based on semi-global block matching (SGBM) algorithm. Finally, disparity maps are obtained to reconstruct stereo images of the eye within 180-degree range, based on the imaging surface of the left view of Fig. 1a), and after all, a 3D point cloud model within 180 degree range of eyeball surface is obtained, as shown in Fig. 1b).

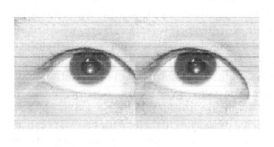
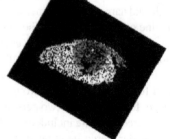

a) A pair of binocular vision images   b) 3D ocular surface point cloud map

Fig. 1. Acquisition of point cloud data of eye based on binocular vision

3 Acquisition of Gaze Direction Based on 3D Ocular Surface Fitting

3.1 Ocular Geometrical and Optical Structure Analysis

Eyeball's optical model is shown in Fig. 2, which is composed of front and back two spheres with different size. The front sphere is transparent cornea, whose center of curvature is Ocornea, while the back one with bigger size is non-transparent eyeball, whose center of curvature is Oeyeball. The line connecting point Ocornea to point Oeyeball is defined as the optical axis of eyeball. Small concave point in the middle of retina is called Fovea, which is the most sensitive and well-developed area of eye. The line connecting Fovea point to corneal center point Ocornea is defined as visual axis, whose angle deviation with optical axis is kappa, as shown in Fig. 2. The values of angle kappa of two eyes are the same, about 5° or so.

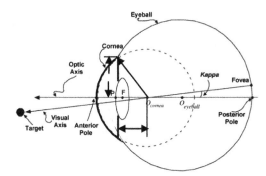

Fig. 2. Eyeball structure and gaze optical model

In most existing systems, gaze direction, or the visual axis, can be estimated by adding a kappa angle to the optical axis, which is obtained through location of pupil center point P and corneal center point Ocornea. This kind of method usually needs a beforehand personal calibration procedure to obtain the person-specific eye parameters, for the kappa angle's value changes a little among different persons. There are two personal parameters R and L of eyeball model, as shown in Fig. 2.

R ------ radius of cornea curvature.

L ------ distance between pupil and center of cornea curvature.

In general, R and L vary depending on the different persons, if we use the same values R and L for all persons, gaze direction error may remains. However, such a personal calibration is often cumbersome and unnatural.

3.2 Ocular Surface Fitting and Feature Extraction

Suppose that the front and back spheres of eyeball both have curved surfaces, a two-step surface fitting process is developed to realistically model the two spheres shape of the eyeball from the 3D ocular point cloud data. 1° All point data are fitted into a quadric surface, which closely model the geometry of the two spheres, as shown in formula (1):

$$ax^2 + by^2 + cz^2 + 2fyz + 2gzx$$
$$+2hxy + 2px + 2qy + 2rz + d = 0 \tag{1}$$

The size of two spheres is different. Therefore, their fitted quadric surface equations are different with each other.

2° A subdivision surface is employed to refine the quadric surface. It is through a repeated iteration procedure, and then mesh smoothing of the quadric surface is performed.

In order to obtain the ocular parameters, the equation in formula (1) is transformed to the format in formula (2):

$$z = f(x, y) = \frac{c \cdot (y^2 + x^2)}{1 + \sqrt{1 - (k+1) \cdot c^2 \cdot (x^2 + y^2)}} \tag{2}$$

where $c = 1/r$ is the paraxial curvature, and k is the conic constant of quadric surface. Utilizing Eq. (2), point (x, y, z) in formula (1) is transformed to the format $(x, y, f(x, y))$, whose corresponding Gaussian curvature K is described as the following formula [22]:

Gaussian curvature:

$$K = \frac{f_{xx}f_{yy} - f_{xy}^2}{(1 + f_x^2 + f_y^2)^2} \tag{3}$$

$f_x, f_y, f_{xx}, f_{xy}, f_{yy}$ represent 1st and 2nd order derivative at point (x, y) of the function f. Since the 2nd order derivative is very sensitive to noise, it is necessary to smooth the surface S first. Before calculating the Gaussian curvature, the depth data is noise removed by a Gaussian filter.

Considering the existence of some corneal deformation, the multi region model of Gaussian curvature is used for corneal analysis and feature extraction. The idea is to divide the corneal surface into multiple regions, and then apply the standard model to analyze each region independently. The total surface is the union of different regions. Gaussian curvature topography of corneal surface with 3 zones is shown in Fig. 3, including 1. Optical region, 2. Transition region and 3. Periphery region.

In the transition zone, points with the biggest Gaussian curvature consist of the corneal boundary. These points are fitted into a circle equation to extract the pupil's radius r, which is used to calculate the person-specific parameter L, combined with parameter R obtained from the fitted corneal surface equation.

In the optical zone, points with the biggest Gaussian curvature consist of the pupil central region, whose centroid is considered as pupil center point, marked with symbol "†", also shown in Fig. 3.

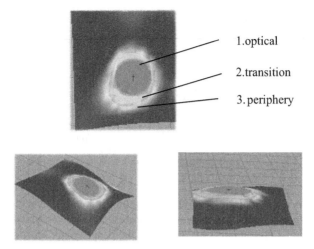

1. optical

2. transition

3. periphery

Fig. 3. Gaussian curvature topography of corneal surface

3.3 Estimation of Optical Axis and Acquisition of Gaze Direction

It is assumed that the fitted surface of the corneal sphere is an ellipsoid, and one vertex of the ellipsoid is the same as the pupil center point. According to the fitting curve and surface equation, the principal direction equation can be obtained, as shown in formula (4):

$$\begin{cases} aX + hY + gZ = \lambda X \\ hX + bY + fZ = \lambda Y \\ gX + fY + cZ = \lambda Z \end{cases} \tag{4}$$

where X: Y: Z represents the main direction of the fitting surface. The secular equation of the quadric surface can be derived from formula (4), and its root is called the root of the quadric surface. Three non-zero characteristic roots are obtained by solving the characteristic equation, and two of them are the same. Solving two principal direction equations with the same eigenvalues can only get the plane equation of the principal direction, but can not get the required line of sight. On the other hand, solving the principal direction equations with different eigenvalues will obtain a unique principal direction, that is, the optical axis direction X: Y: Z. With the 3D coordinates P(x0, y0, z0) of the pupil center, ocular optical axis direction is estimated.

For different persons, there is a little difference in the kappa angle, which is in relation to axial length, corneal curvature and anterior chamber depth [24, 25]. However, it is difficult to use accurate models to describe these relationships. Given sufficient kappa angle and parameters R and L, we used generalized regression neural network (GRNN) to realize a unique function that relates kappa angle's value to different personal-specific parameters.

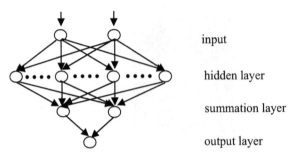

input

hidden layer

summation layer

output layer

Fig. 4. GRNN architecture used for kappa angle estimation

As shown in Fig. 4, GRNN architecture topology consists of input layer, hidden layer, summation layer and output layer. Wherein the input layer contains two specific parameters R and L. The output layer represents the kappa angle. The number of hidden nodes is the same as the training samples, and one hidden node is added for each group of training samples. The number of nodes in the summation layer is the number of output nodes plus 1.

4 Experiments of Gaze Tracking and Results Analysis

4.1 Experimental Devices and Parameters Acquisition

To test the effect of the algorithm, we designed a series of experiments to compare the gaze deviation based on the 3D eyeball surface fitting model and the 2D image processing algorithm. During experiments, 37 specified points are designed to scatter over a 1440 × 900 pixels screen at first, as shown in Fig. 5. Then, the observed person is required to gaze at these points one by one according to prompts on the screen, in two different head posture: motionless mode and free motion, respectively. Two cameras with essentially the same parameters are used in binocular vision platform, with each camera first installed on a 180°rotating base, then both of them are installed on a 90-cm-long horizontal guide rail to guide two camera sliding horizontally. Length and width size of the screen is 410 × 320 mm. Resolution ratio of the two cameras is 3872 × 2592 pixels, which are controlled by one single electronic synchronization controller to take a pair of images of the observed person's eye, to make sure that the left and right views are taken simultaneously.

In order to find out how the distance between the human eye and the screen surface affects the line of sight tracking accuracy, three distances: 350, 450, and 550 mm are set between the person's eye and the screen surface for gaze tracking experiments, each with motionless and free motion head posture, respectively.

105 sets of training data under motionless head posture were collected for kappa angle estimation. When collecting data, users are required to fix their eyes on the gaze area. At each fixation, two input parameters were calculated according to the fitted corneal surface equation to subsequently identify outliers. After preprocessing (e.g., nonlinear filtering to remove outliers) and normalization, the training data is used to train the GRNN. GRNN uses a single learning algorithm for training, so it is very fast.

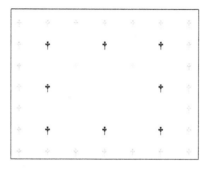

Fig. 5. Diagram of test points distribution on the screen

4.2   Establishment of 3D Coordinate System

The guide rail with two cameras is fixed right over the screen, and the 3D coordinate system is set up according to the following steps:

1° Center point of the left camera's imaging surface is considered as the origin point of the 3D coordinate system.

2° Two imaging surfaces of two cameras are adjusted to coincide with the screen surface that displays 37 specified points, and in the mean time, the line connecting two center points of two imaging surfaces is in parallel with the line connecting the specified points of the screen on the same row.

3° Calculating the distance between two center points of the two cameras' imaging surfaces.

4° Calculating the distances between the specified points on the screen and the origin point of the 3D coordinate system.

Among the 2nd step discussed previously, the checkerboard stereo calibration method is used to make two cameras' imaging surfaces coincide with the screen surface. The practice is described as follows: a black and white checkerboard is put ahead of two cameras, whose grid is 1 mm wide and 2 mm long, and the total cells are about 40×50 or so. The distance between the checkerboard surface and the screen surface is measured and recorded as L1. Then, the binocular stereo images of the checkerboard are taken and used to calculate the depth data of the checkerboard, and with the camera's focal parameter f, the distance between the cameras' imaging surface and the checkerboard surface is obtained and recorded as L2. Finally, based on the requirement that L2==L1, cameras are adjusted to capture an image on the coincided surface after many times of operations of data sampling and iteration of the 3D calibrating process. After that, the camera's imaging surface with the origin point, the screen surface with specified points, person's eye coordinates, and the actual gaze's fixation points on the screen are linked into a uniform 3D coordinate system.

4.3   Experimental Results and Analysis

To quantitatively characterize the accuracy of our system in kappa angle measurement, the first experiment studies the performance of GRNN used in estimating kappa angle from personal-specific parameters. The output layer of GRNN has only one node, kappa angle's value which is measured accurately by an apparatus, made by ourselves and consisting of one high-resolution camera, one circular IR light source, two point light sources and a reflector glass. Through calibration process of pupil axis, the measurement of kappa angle is obtained by using an attached vernier caliper, whose accuracy degree reaches $0.01°$. The input layer of GRNN includes two inputs, personal-specific parameters R and L, obtained from the corneal fitted equation, described in Sect. 3.2. Table 1 summarizes the estimation results of kappa angle of 9 testees, age from 20 years old to 60 years old.

Table 1. Estimation results of kappa angle

No.	R/mm	L/mm	kappa/°	Accuracy/%
1	6.023	3.891	4.227	98.52
2	7.822	4.509	5.088	98.77
3	5.641	3.056	4.116	99.44
4	8.155	5.262	6.172	98.73
5	7.336	4.103	5.625	99.99
6	8.724	5.506	6.014	98.21
7	4.925	2.905	3.787	99.36
8	6.835	4.216	4.534	98.15
9	7.614	4.369	4.891	98.22

The eye images are separated by segmentation of facial left view and right view and used to acquire the 3D point cloud data of the observed person's eyes by binocular vision method described in Sect. 2 of this paper. Finally, gaze directions of the eyes are acquired through the 3D gaze modeling method, as described in Sect. 3 of this paper. Some gaze extracting results are shown in Fig. 6.

After that, gaze line equations are acquired in the established 3D coordinate system mentioned in Sect. 4.2, and then, each fixation point of each gaze line on the screen is acquired by calculating the crossover point of each gaze line and the screen surface. Compared with the specified points on the screen to measure their horizontal and vertical direction's errors. The average errors of 37 points are shown in Table 2.

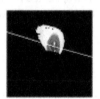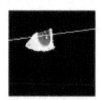

Fig. 6. Some gaze extracting results by this paper's method

From Table 2, it is shown that when head posture is motionless, the accuracy of gaze's fixation (mm) decreases gradually with the increase of distance between the person's eye and the screen, and the average error is between 2.20% and 2.83%. When head posture is in free motion, the accuracy of gaze's fixation (mm) is slightly lower than that in head motionless posture, and the average error is between 3.31% and 3.90%. Therefore, it can be concluded that estimating the accuracy of gaze is effected to some degree by the head's movement. Another conclusion is that, although estimating errors of gaze in free motion is slightly bigger than that in motionless posture with the same eye-screen distance, they increase slightly with the increase of eye-screen distance, which indicates that the 3D gaze estimating model presented by this paper has good adaptability to head's free motion. It can be found in Table 1, estimating the accuracy of gaze fixation in vertical direction is always lower than that in horizontal direction under equal conditions, for vertical resolution of a display device is usually lower than its horizontal resolution.

Table 2. Estimating errors of gaze's fixation points with different head postures

Head posture	Distance of eyes and camera (mm)	Average errors (mm)	
		Horizontal direction	Vertical direction
Motionless	350	8.04	9.41
	450	9.89	11.21
	550	12.36	15.56
Free motion	350	12.73	13.65
	450	14.90	15.83
	550	18.63	21.46

Compared with 2D PCCR method, estimating the accuracy of gaze's fixation by this paper's method is better than that by 2D PCCR method [2–4, 7], and at the meantime, no additional auxiliary equipment is needed, improving the adaptability of gaze tracking system to the head's movement.

5   Conclusions

The pupil center cornea reflection method uses additional infrared light source in gaze tracking, which needs a user, keeping the head absolutely or relatively motionless. To reduce the use of auxiliary sources and improve the adaptability of the system to the head's movement, a gaze tracking method based on binocular vision is presented in this paper. On the grounds of physiological structure feature of the eyeball, the 3D eyeball curvature surface is fit by its stereo point cloud data, upon which, the kappa angle and the ocular optical axis direction is calculated, and then gaze direction, i.e. the ocular visual axis direction of the observed person is acquired in a stereo space.

The following experiment on kappa angle estimation shows that the GRNN method presented in this paper could estimates accurately kappa angle from personal-specific parameters. The experiment on gaze fixation points estimation with different head postures show that, regardless of the head in motionless posture or in free motion posture, the gaze tracking errors of this paper's method are in the range of tracking accuracy requirements with no limitations on the user and convenient in use, robustness, promoting gaze tracking system, and technology to more advanced applications.

Acknowledgment. This study was funded by Guangdong Natural Science Fund Project (2021A1515011243), Guangzhou Science and Technology Plan Project (201902020016), Yunfu Science and Technology Plan Project S2021010104 and Guangdong Science and Technology Plan Project (2019B010139001, 2021B1212100004).

References

1. Li, X., Li, Z.L., Qin, J.L.: An improved gaze tracking technique based on eye model. In Proceedings of the 33rd Chinese Control Conference, vol. 6, pp. 7286–7291. IEEE (2014)
2. Lopez-Gordo, M., Pelayo, F., Prieto, A., Fernandez, E.: An auditory brain-computer interface with accuracy prediction. Int. J. Neural Syst. **22**(3), 1250009 (2012)
3. Ghahari, A., Enderle, J.D.: A neuron-based time-optimal controller of horizontal saccadic eye movements. Int. J. Neural Syst. **24**(6), 1450017 (2014)
4. Xinming, Y., Qijie, Z., Dawei, T., Hui, S.: A novel approach to estimate gaze direction in eye gaze HCI system. In: The 5th International Conference on Intelligent Human-Machine Systems and Cybernetics (IHMSC), vol. 8, pp. 588–591 (2013)
5. Pauwels, K., Van, H., Marc, M.: Head-centric disparity and epipolar geometry estimation from a population of binocular energy neurons. Int. J. Neural Syst. **22**(3), 1250007 (2012)
6. Dong-Chan, C., Whoi-Yul, K.: Long-range gaze tracking system for large movements. IEEE. Trans. Biomed. Eng. **60**(12), 3432–3440 (2013)
7. Hansen, D.W., Qiang, J.: In the eye of the beholder: a survey of models for eyes and gaze. IEEE Trans. Pattern Anal. Mach. Intell. **32**(3), 478–500 (2010)
8. Dong-Chan, C., Wah-Seng, Y., Heekyung, L., Injae, L.: Long range eye gaze tracking system for a large screen. IEEE Trans. Consum. Electron. **58**(4), 1119–1128 (2013)
9. Enderle, J.D., Sierra, D.A.: A new linear muscle fiber model for neural control of saccades. Int. J. Neural Syst. **23**(2), 1350002 (2013)
10. Lopez, A., Rodriguez, I., Ferrero, F.J., Valledor, M.: Low-cost system based on electro-oculography for communication of disabled people. In: The 11th International Multi-Conference on Systems, Signals & Devices (SSD), vol. 2, pp. 1–6 (2014)
11. Chumerin, N., Gibaldi, A., Sabatini, S.P., Van Hulle, M.M.: Learning eye vergence control from a distributed disparity representation. Int. J. Neural Syst. **20**(4), 267–278 (2010)
12. Jian-nan, C., Peng-yi, Z., Si-yi, Z., Chuang, Z., Ying, H.: Key techniques of eye gaze tracking based on pupil corneal reflection. In: WRI Global Congress on Intelligent Systems (GCIS), vol. 2, pp. 133–188 (2009)
13. Ji, W.L., Chul, W.C., Kwang, Y.S., Eui, C.L., Kang, R.P.: 3D gaze tracking method using purkinje images on eye optical model and pupil. Opt. Lasers Eng. **50**(5), 736–751 (2012)
14. Chuang, Z., Jiannan, C., Chaohui, Z.: A novel eye gaze tracking technique based on pupil center cornea reflection technique. Chin. J. Comput. **33**(7), 1273–1285 (2010)

15. Ince, I.F., Kim, J.W.: A 2D eye gaze estimation system with low-resolution webcam images. EURASIP J. Adv. Signal Process. **2011**, 40 (2011). https://doi.org/10.1186/1687-6180-201 1-40
16. Valenti, R., Sebe, N., Gevers, T.: Combining head pose and eye location information for gaze estimation. IEEE Trans. Image Process. **21**(2), 802–815 (2012)
17. Siriteerakul, T., Sato, Y., Boonjing, V.: Estimating change in head pose from low resolution video using LBP-based tracking. In: 2011 International Symposium on Intelligent Signal Processing and Communications Systems (ISPACS), vol. 12, pp. 1–6 (2011)
18. Wi, N.T.N., Loo, C.K., Chockalingam, L.: Biologically inspired face recognition: toward pose-invariance. Int. J. Neural Syst. **22**(6), 1–17 (2012)
19. Boumbarov, O., Panev, S., Paliy, I., Petrov, P., Dimitrov, L.: Homography-based face orientation determination from a fixed monocular camera. In: The 6th International Conference on IEEE Intelligent Data Acquisition and Advanced Computing Systems (IDAACS), vol. 1, pp. 399–403 (2011)
20. Auvinet, E., Meunier, J., Ong, J., Durr, G., Gilca, M., Brunette, I.: Methodology for the construction and comparison of 3D models of the human cornea. In: Annual International Conference of the IEEE Engineering in Medicine and Biology Society (EMBC), pp. 5302–5305 (2012)
21. Nagamatsu, T., Sugano, R., Iwamoto, Y., Kamahara, J.: User-calibration-free gaze estimation method using a binocular 3D eye model. IEICE Trans. Inf. Syst. **E94D**(9), 1817–1829 (2011)
22. Ling, Z., Mingyu, Y., Yanjun, Z.: Fatigue detection with 3D facial features based on binocular stereo vision. Integr. Comput. Aided Eng. **21**(4), 387–397 (2014)
23. Heekyung, L., SeongYong, L., Injae, L., Jihun, C., Dong-Chan, C., Sunyoung, C.: Multi-modal user interaction method based on gaze tracking and gesture recognition. Signal Process. Image Commun. **28**, 114–126 (2013)
24. Eghosasere, I., Joy, I., Christian, I.O.: The role of axial length-corneal radius of curvature ratio in refractive state categorization in a Nigerian population. ISRN Ophthalmol. **2011**, ID: 138941 (2011)
25. Marta, K., Frantisek, P., Petr, M., Ondrej, V., Martin, S., Klara, M.: The importance of angle kappa evaluation for implantation of diffractive multifocal intra-ocular lenses using pseudophakic eye model. Acta Ophthalmol. **93**(2), e123–e128 (2015)

A Certificateless-Based Blind Signature Scheme with Message Recovery

Xiao Li, Mengwen Wang, and Fengyin Li[(✉)]

School of Computer Science, Qufu Normal University, Rizhao 276826, China
lfyin318@126.com

Abstract. Blind signature is a digital signature technology that enables the signature requester to obtain the valid signature of the signer without revealing the identity and content of the message to the signer. It is widely used in electronic cash, electronic voting and other fields. The message recovery technology is a technology that can hide the message in the signature, and only pass the signature without passing the message when it is delivered. In this paper, a blind signature scheme based on certificateless message recovery is proposed based on the combination of blind signature and message recovery technology, and based on certificateless public key cryptosystem. The signer can sign the blinded message under the certificateless cryptosystem, and the final blind signature result can only transmit the signature to reduce the conmmunication bandwidth. Security analysis shows that the scheme satisfies correctness, blindness, and unforgeability.

Keywords: Certificateless · Blind signature · Message recovery

1 Introduction

At a time when the network is inseparable from people's lives, there are many security risks in the data that users transmit through the network every day, and the issue of data privacy protection has attracted more and more attention. Digital signatures ensure the integrity and verifiability of data sent by users over the network. Diffie and Hellman first proposed the traditional public key cryptography (PKC) scheme in 1976 [1]. In traditional PKC, the user's public key is bound to a certificate issued by a trusted certificate authority, and a large number of user certificates are concentrated in the certificate authority, which brings the problem of certificate management. For certificate management, Shamir proposed the identity-based public key cryptography (ID-PKC) system in 1984 [2]. In ID-PKC, the user's public key can be directly generated from the user's name, email address and other information that can uniquely identify the user. The user's identity is the certificate, but this cryptosystem requires a trusted third-party organization called KGC, and the user's private key is generated by KGC. Therefore, although ID-PKC eliminates the problem of certificate management existing in traditional PKC, it also brings about the problem of

Y. Xu et al. (Eds.): ML4CS 2022, LNCS 13656, pp. 382–389, 2023.
https://doi.org/10.1007/978-3-031-20099-1_32

key escrow, that is, KGC knows the private keys of all users, and it can forge the signatures of these users, threatening the data security of users. For the key escrow problem, AI-Riyami and Paterson first proposed a certificateless public key cryptography (CL-PKC) system in 2003 [3]. In CL-PKC, the user's public key is independently generated by the user and does not need to be authenticated by a certificate authority, and the user's private key is a combination of a partial private key generated by KGC and a secret value selected by the user. Therefore, CL-PKC solves both the certificate management problem of PKC and the key escrow problem of ID-PKC.

In 1983, Chaum first proposed the concept of blind signature [4]. In blind signatures, users can obtain the signer's message-signature pair without revealing their identity information and message content, and the signer cannot link any signature to the previous signature transmission script. Therefore, blind signatures [5] provide user anonymity and can effectively protect user privacy. Blind signature can effectively protect user privacy, which makes it widely used in electronic cash, electronic voting, electronic government and other fields. When designing communication systems for these applications, more secure, more efficient, and smaller-scale signature schemes are required. Therefore, smaller-scale, more secure blind signatures in low-bandwidth and high-security applications have become a research hotspot.

The message recovery technology can hide the message in the signature, and only pass the signature during delivery without passing the message-signature pair, which can effectively reduce the bandwidth overhead during signature delivery and improve the efficiency of signature delivery. The message recoverable blind signature is to use the message recoverable technology in the blind signature, so that the message can be embedded in the signature without having to be transmitted together with the signature, which reduces the size of the message-signature pair. Various efficient blind signature schemes [6–8] for realizing different functions have been proposed one after another. In 2017, Verma et al. [9] first proposed an efficient identity-based message recovery blind signature scheme, in which the message is not transmitted with the signature and recovered during the verification phase. In 2021, Wen et al. [10] pointed out that the scheme of Verma et al. [9] could not satisfy the untraceability of signatures, and proposed a new identity-based message recovery blind signature scheme to achieve the untraceability of signatures. However, the existing blind signature schemes for message recovery are based on traditional PKC or ID-PKC systems. The inherent overhead and security defects brought by these cryptosystems greatly limit the application of blind signatures.

This paper aims to propose a message recoverable blind signature scheme based on certificateless cryptosystem(CL-BS-MR). Message recoverability is used to solve the high bandwidth problem caused by the need to propagate the message-signature together in the delivery of existing blind signatures. The certificateless feature can solve the key escrow problem existing in the existing identity-based message recoverable blind signature schemes.

2   Preliminaries

In this section we introduce the knowledge of bilinear pairing and the framework of the CL-BS-MR scheme proposed in this paper. Some symbols used in this paper are shown in Table 1.

Table 1. Notations.

Notation	Descriptions
KGC	The key generation center
$\mathbb{G}_1$	The cyclic additive group
$\mathbb{G}_T$	The cyclic multiplicative group
q	The large prime
$|q|$	The bit length of q
$_{l_1}|u|$	The first l_1 bits to the left of u
$|u|_{l_2}$	The first l_2 bits to the left of u
$\oplus$	X-OR computation
$[\theta]_{10}$	The decimal representation of $\theta \in \{0,1\}^*$
$[\alpha]_2$	The binary representation of $\alpha \in \mathbb{Z}$
$s_1||s_2$	The concatenation of two bit strings s_1 and s_2

2.1   Billinear Pairing

Suppose $\mathbb{G}_1$ is cyclic additive groups with prime order q, and $\mathbb{G}_T$ is a cyclic multiplicative group with prime order q. $e : \mathbb{G}_1 \times \mathbb{G}_1 \rightarrow \mathbb{G}_T$ is called a bilinear map if it satisfies the following conditions:

(1) Bilinearity: For $\forall X, Y \in \mathbb{G}_1$, and $a, b \in \mathbb{Z}_q^*$, $e(aX, bY) = e(X, Y)^{ab}$.
(2) Computability: Giving $\forall X, Y \in \mathbb{G}_1$, it is easy to compute $e(X, Y)$.
(3) Non-degeneracy: There exits $X, Y \in \mathbb{G}_1$ to make $e(X, Y) \neq 1_{\mathbb{G}_T}$.

2.2   Framework of an Efficient CL-BS-MR

A CL-BS-MR scheme consists of the following seven algorithms:

(1) **Setup.** Input the security parameter λ, the algorithm is executed by the key generation center KGC, and generates the system master key msk, the master public key mpk and the public system parameter $params$.
(2) **Partial-Private-Key-Extract.** Input the system parameter $params$ and the user identity ID, the algorithm is executed by KGC to generate the partial private key D_{ID} corresponding to the user.

(3) **Set-Secret-Value.** Input the system parameter $params$ and the user identity ID, the algorithm is executed by the user to generate the secret value x corresponding to the user.

(4) **Set-Public-Key.** Input the system parameter $params$, the user identity ID and the user's secret value x, the algorithm is executed by the user to generate the public key PK_{ID} corresponding to the user.

(5) **Set-Private-Key.** Input the system parameter $params$, the user identity ID, the user's secret value x, the partial private key D_{ID} and the public key PK_{ID}, the algorithm is executed by the user to generate the public key SK_{ID} corresponding to the user.

(6) **Blind-Signature-Generation.** This is an interactive algorithm between the requester and the signer who provided the message. Input the system parameter $params$, message m, signer's private key SK_{ID}, the algorithm generates blind signature σ of the message m, the specific steps are as follows:

   (a) Committing: The signer first computes a promise R and send it to requester;

   (b) The requester randomly selects a blinding factor to blind the message m, and sends the blinded message to the signer;

   (c) Signing: The signer signs the blinded message with his private key SK_{ID}, and sends the signature result $\tilde{\sigma}$ to the requester;

   (d) After the requester gets out of blindness, the signer's blind signature σ of the message m is obtained.

(7) **Blind-Signature-Verify.** Input the system parameter $params$, the signer's public key PK_{ID} and the signer's blind signature σ to the message m, the algorithm restores the message m and verifies the validity of the blind signature σ, if it is valid, output 1; otherwise, output 0.

3   A Certificateless-Based Blind Signature Scheme with Message Recovery

In this section, we describe the specific steps of the CL-BS-MR protocol. The CL-BS-MR scheme includes seven algorithms, namely, the system initialization algorithm **Setup**, the partial private key generation algorithm **Set-Partial-Private-Key**, the setting secret value algorithm **Set-Secret-Value**, and the public key generation algorithm **Set-Public-Key**, private key generation algorithm **Set-Private-Key**, blind signature generation algorithm **Blind-Signature-Generation**, blind signature verification algorithm **Blind-Signature-Verification**. The specific algorithm is as follows:

Setup. Given safety parameter λ, KGC performs the following steps:

(a) Select bilinear pairing parameters $PP_{bp} = \{\mathbb{G}_1, \mathbb{G}_T, P, q, e, g\}$, where $(\mathbb{G}_1, +)$ is cyclic group of prime order q, and $P_1 \in \mathbb{G}_1$ is the generator. $(\mathbb{G}_T, \cdot)$ is a cyclic group whose order is prime q. $e : \mathbb{G}_1 \times \mathbb{G}_1 \to \mathbb{G}_T$ is a bilinear pairing.

(b) Choose the hash function as $H_1 : \{0,1\}^* \to \mathbb{Z}_q^*, H_2 : \mathbb{G}_1 \to \mathbb{Z}_q^*, H_3 : \mathbb{G}_T \to \{0,1\}^{|q|}. F_1 : \{0,1\}^{l_2} \to \{0,1\}^{l_1}, F_2 : \{0,1\}^{l_1} \to \{0,1\}^{l_2}$, where l_1, l_2 are positive integers, and $l_1 + l_2 = |q|$.

(c) Randomly choose $s \in \mathbb{Z}_q^*$ as the master key and compute $P_{pub} = sP_2$ as the master public key.

(d) Publish public parameters $params = \{pp_{bp}, l_1, l_2, H_1, H_2, H_3, F_1, F_2, P_{pub}\}$ and save the master key $msk = s$.

Set-Partial-Private-Key. The KGC generates a partial private key $D_{ID_i} = (s + H_1(ID_i))^{-1}P$ for the user with identity $ID_i \in \{0,1\}^*$ and sends it to the user.

Set-Secret-Value. A user with identity ID_i randomly chooses $x_i \in \mathbb{Z}_q^*$ as his secret value.

Set-Public-Key. User ID_i calculates $Q_i = P_{pub} + H_1(ID_i)P$ and $PK_{ID_i} = x_iQ_i$, and PK_{ID_i} is his public key.

Set-Private-Key. ID_i calculates $y_i = H_2(PK_{ID_i})$ and $SK_{ID_i} = (x_i + y_i)^{-1}D_{ID_i}$, and SK_{ID_i} is his private key.

Blind-Signature-Generation. The message provider with identity ID_m interacts with the signer with identity ID_S to obtain the signature of message $m \in \{0,1\}^{l_2}$. The process of generating a blind signature is shown in Fig. 1 (see Fig. 1), and the specific steps are as follows:

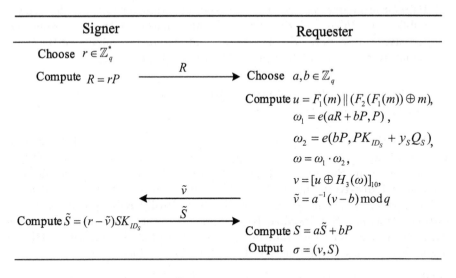

Fig. 1. Blind signature generation process

(a) Committing. Signer ID_S randomly chooses $r \in \mathbb{Z}_q^*$, and computes $R = rP_1$, sending R to message provider ID_m.

(b) Blinding. Provider ID_m randomly chooses $a, b \in \mathbb{Z}_q^*$, computes $u = F_1(m) \| (F_2(F_1(m)) \oplus m)$, $\omega_1 = e(aR + bP, P)$, $\omega_2 = e(bP, PK_{ID_S} + y_S Q_S)$, $\omega = \omega_1 \cdot \omega_2$, $v = [u \oplus H_3(\omega)]_{10}$. Then, the message provider sends $\tilde{v} = a^{-1}(v - b) \bmod q$ to the signer.

(c) Signing. Signer ID_S computes $\tilde{S} = (r - \tilde{v}) SK_{ID_S}$ and sends it to the message provider.

(d) Unblinding. Message provider ID_m computes $S = a\tilde{S} + bP$, and outputs signature $\sigma = (v, S)$.

Blind-Signature-Verification. Input the signature $\sigma\prime = (v\prime, S\prime)$ of the signer ID_S to the message $m \in \{0, 1\}^{l_2}$ provided by the message provider ID_m, and the verifier uses the public key PK_{ID_S} of the signer ID_S to calculate $\omega\prime = e(S\prime, PK_{ID_S} + y_i Q_i) \cdot e(P, P)^{v\prime}$, $u\prime = [v\prime]_2 \oplus H_3(\omega\prime)$, $m\prime = F_2(_{l_1} |u\prime|) \oplus |u\prime|_{l_2}$. The verifier then checks if $_{l_1} |u\prime|$ is equal to $F_1(m\prime)$. If equal, the signature is valid and $m\prime$ is the extracted message. Otherwise, the signature is invalid.

4   Analysis of Proposed CL-BS-MR Scheme

In this section we demonstrate the correctness, blindness and unforgeability of our proposed CL-BS-MR scheme.

4.1   Correctness Analysis

Theorem 1 *(Correctness). Our proposed CL-BS-MR scheme is correct.*

Proof.

$$
\begin{aligned}
\omega\prime &= e(S\prime, PK_{ID_S} + y_S \cdot Q_S) \cdot e(P, P)^{v\prime} \\
&= e(a \cdot \tilde{S} + b \cdot P, PK_{ID_S} + y_S \cdot Q_S) \cdot e(P, P)^{v} \\
&= e(a \cdot (r - \tilde{v}) \cdot SK_{ID_S} + b \cdot P, PK_{ID_S} + y_S \cdot Q_S) \cdot e(P, P)^{v} \\
&= e((a \cdot r - v + b) \cdot SK_{ID_S}, PK_{ID_S} + y_S \cdot Q_S)) \cdot e(b \cdot P, PK_{ID_S} + y_S \cdot Q_S) \cdot e(P, P)^{v} \\
&= e((a \cdot r - v + b) \cdot (x_S + y_S)^{-1} \cdot DID_S, (x_S + y_S) \cdot Q_S)) \cdot \omega_2 \cdot e(P, P)^{v} \\
&= e((a \cdot r - v + b) \cdot DID_S, Q_S) \cdot \omega_2 \cdot e(P, P)^{v} \\
&= e((a \cdot r - v + b) \cdot (s + H_1(ID_S))^{-1} \cdot P, P_{pub} + H_1(ID_S) \cdot P) \cdot \omega_2 \cdot e(P, P)^{v} \\
&= e((a \cdot r - v + b) \cdot P, P) \cdot \omega_2 \cdot e(P, P)^{v} \\
&= e(a \cdot R + b \cdot P, P) \cdot e(P, P)^{-v} \cdot \omega_2 \cdot e(P, P)^{v} \\
&= \omega_1 \cdot \omega_2 \\
&= \omega
\end{aligned}
$$

Therefore, $u\prime = [v\prime]_2 \oplus H_3(\omega\prime) = u \oplus H_3(\omega) \oplus H_3(\omega\prime) = u$, from $u = F_1(m) \| (F_2(F_1(m)) \oplus m)$ we know $_{l_1} |u| = F_1(m)$, from $|u|_{l_2} = F_2(F_1(m)) \oplus m$ we know $m\prime = F_2(_{l_1} |u|) \oplus |u|_{l_2}$. Then, check $F_1(m\prime) = _{l_1} |u|$ to know the correctness of the signature.

4.2   Security Analysis

Theorem 2 *(Blindness). Due to the difficulty of the ECDLP problem, our proposed CL-BS-MR scheme satisfies the unlinkability or untraceability (blindness).*

Proof. If (v, S) is a valid blind signature and $(R, \tilde{v}, \tilde{S})$ is any view of the signer, there must be a unique blinding factor $a, b \in \mathbb{Z}_q^*$ that makes them match. Because the valid signature is $v = [u \oplus H_3(\omega)]_{10}$, $S = a\tilde{S} + bP$, and the view of the signer is $R = rP$, $\tilde{v} = a^{-1}(v - b) \bmod q$, $\tilde{S} = (r - \tilde{v})SK_{ID_S}$. The blinding factor $a, b \in \mathbb{Z}_q^*$ always exists. To link the valid signature and the signer's view, the value of the blind factor must be calculated. To calculate the value of the blind factor, the ECDLP problem must be solved, but the ECDLP problem is difficult, so the scheme in this paper satisfies the blindness.

Theorem 3 *(unforgeability). The CL-BS-MR scheme proposed in this paper is unforgeable.*

Proof. Because in the CL-BS-MR scheme the signer's private key is calculated by the signature itself, no one except the signer can obtain the signer's private key. The adversary cannot obtain the private key of the signer and cannot forge the signature, so the CL-BS-MR scheme proposed in this paper is unforgeable.

5   Conclusion

In this paper, a certificateless message recovery blind signature scheme is proposed, which combines certificateless public key cryptosystem with blind signature primitives and message recovery technology. The signer can blind the requester under the certificateless cryptosystem to sign. And the final blind signature result can only transmit the signature without transmitting the message-signature pair during transmission, which successfully realizes the message recoverable blind signature in the certificateless system. Subsequent analysis of the scheme shows that the proposed CL-BS-MR scheme satisfies correctness, blindness, and unforgeability.

References

1. Diffie, W., Hellman, M.: New directions in cryptography. IEEE Trans. Inf. Theory **22**(6), 644–654 (1976)
2. Shamir, A.: Identity-based cryptosystems and signature schemes. In: Blakley, G.R., Chaum, D. (eds.) CRYPTO 1984. LNCS, vol. 196, pp. 47–53. Springer, Heidelberg (1985). https://doi.org/10.1007/3-540-39568-7_5
3. Al-Riyami, S.S., Paterson, K.G.: Certificateless public key cryptography. In: Laih, C.-S. (ed.) ASIACRYPT 2003. LNCS, vol. 2894, pp. 452–473. Springer, Heidelberg (2003). https://doi.org/10.1007/978-3-540-40061-5_29
4. Chaum, D.: Blind signatures for untraceable payments. In: Chaum, D., Rivest, R.L., Sherman, A.T. (eds.) Advances in Cryptology, pp. 199–203. Springer, Boston, MA (1983). https://doi.org/10.1007/978-1-4757-0602-4_18

5. Islam, S.H., Obaidat, M.S.: Design of provably secure and efficient certificateless blind signature scheme using bilinear pairing. Secur. Commun. Netw. **8**(18), 4319–4332 (2015)
6. Verma, G.K., Singh, B.B.: Efficient message recovery proxy blind signature scheme from pairings. Trans. Emerg. Telecommun. Technol. **28**(11), 3167 (2017)
7. James, S., Gayathri, N.B., Reddy, P.V.: Pairing free identity-based blind signature scheme with message recovery. Cryptography **2**(4), 29 (2018)
8. Elkamchouchi, H., Abouelseoud, Y.: A new blind identity-based signature scheme with message recovery. Cryptology ePrint Archive (2017)
9. Verma, G.K., Singh, B.B.: Efficient identity-based blind message recovery signature scheme from pairings. IET Inf. Secur. **12**(2), 150–156 (2018)
10. Wen, Y., Peng, C., Wang, S., Li, L., Luo, M.: An identity-based blind signature scheme with message recovery from pairings. In: Zhou, J., et al. (eds.) ACNS 2021. LNCS, vol. 12809, pp. 42–55. Springer, Cham (2021). https://doi.org/10.1007/978-3-030-81645-2_4

Fault Detection of Rolling Bearings by Using a Combination Network Model

Tingting Chen, Guanhong Zhang$^{(\boxtimes)}$, and Tong Wu

Department of Artificial Intelligence and Big Data, Hefei University, Hefei, China
`xishazgh@163.com`

Abstract. Bearings are one of the core components used in the mechanical equipment. However, mechanical failures caused by rolling bearing failures account for around 20%–40%. The convolutional neural network model is effective at detecting the fault of rolling bearings, but it suffers overfitting problem. In this paper, we propose a combined network model for the fault detection of rolling bearings by combining the convolutional neural network model and the random forest algorithm. Experiment results show that the combined network model can achieve the expected results in the classification accuracy of rolling bearing mechanical faults.

Keywords: Rolling bearings · Fault detection · Convolutional neural network · Random forest · Combined network model

1 Introduction

Large-scale mechanical equipment is widely used in the artificial devices, and the safe operation of mechanical equipment has become an important problem. Bearings are one of the components commonly used in mechanical equipment (e.g. gearboxes and steam turbines) and are known as the "joints" of the mechanical system. However, mechanical failures caused by rolling bearing failures account for 30% of the total failures; about 40% of induction motor failures are caused by rolling bearing failures; bearing faults ranked second after gear faults, accounting for about 20% [1].

Much work for fault detection of the mechanical equipment is mainly based on the computer-centered fault detection system. Commonly used systems include neural network [2], support vector machine [3], expert system [4], etc. Typically, the fault detection of rolling bearings consists of two main steps: fault feature extraction and pattern recognition. Fault feature extraction is mainly to convert some original high-dimensional data into low-dimensional data through certain mathematical transformations, or to update some original features, reducing the data dimension and extracting effective features for the subsequent usages. Pattern recognition, also known as pattern classification, is the computational method of classifying test sets into specific categories based on the characteristics of the training sets. The convolutional neural network model is effective

© The Author(s), under exclusive license to Springer Nature Switzerland AG 2023
Y. Xu et al. (Eds.): ML4CS 2022, LNCS 13656, pp. 390–399, 2023.
https://doi.org/10.1007/978-3-031-20099-1_33

at detecting the fault of rolling bearings, but is not to generalize well from the training data, making it overfitting (Due to the lack of training set samples, the effect is better during training, and the effect is poor during sample testing).

In this paper, a combined convolutional neural network and random forest is used as a combined network model to alleviate the overfitting phenomenon and improve the accuracy of fault detection for rolling bearings. To this end, we introduce random forest which utilizes ensemble learning that can reduce the overfitting of datasets and increase the accuracy of machine learning algorithms.

2   Methodology

2.1   Convolutional Neural Network

The convolutional neural network (CNN) has been used in many fields such as image processing, object detection, speech semantic analysis, etc. [5]. Compared with the fully connected neural networks, CNN can largely reduce the numbers of model parameters and the complexity of the network model, thus improving the efficiency of the model.

A CNN model mainly consists of an input layer, a convolutional layer, a ReLU layer, a pooling layer, and a fully connected layer. The convolutional layer is the core component of a CNN, and the high-level features of the input samples can be extracted using the convolutional layer through convolutional operations. The element involved in carrying out the convolution operation in the part of a convolutional layer is called the kernel/filter which corresponds to weights and biases. The parameters of the convolution layer include the size of the convolution kernel, the step size, and the padding, which together determine the size of the output feature map of the convolution layer. The pooling layer follows the convolutional layer, mainly performing feature selection and information filtering. The convolutional layer and the pooling layer, together form the i-th layer of a CNN. After multiple convolutional and pooling layers, one or more fully connected layers are connected. Each neuron in a fully connected layer is fully connected to all neurons in its previous layer, and the output of the last fully connected layer is passed to an output layer [6]. The parameters in the CNN model are trained by the gradient descent method.

In this paper, we consider a simple 1D CNN model where the input data is a one-dimensional vector. The model is depicted in Fig. 1. Batch Normalization (BN) serves to normalize the mean α and variance β of the output values after 1-dimensional convolution, effectively alleviating the occurrence of overfitting in the feature extraction process. ReLU is used as activation function, and 1-dimensional global average pooling is used to improve the ability of extracting features. The softmax layer normalizes the data of the previous layer and converts it into a value between zero and one.

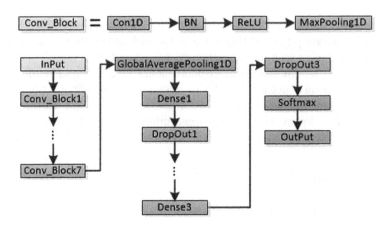

Fig. 1. A simple 1D CNN model.

2.2   Random Forest

A Random Forest (RF) is a supervised machine learning algorithm that is constructed from decision tree algorithms [7]. It has been applied to many fields [8]. A random forest algorithm consists of many decision trees. The decision tree needs to be "trimmed" in the process of training, avoiding overfitting of the decision results.

Following, we generate a random forest as follows:

(1) Bootstrap resampling method is applied to randomly select L samples from N original training samples. The selected L samples are used to construct L decision trees, and the remaining samples form N-L out-of-bag (OOB) data each time.

(2) We assume that each sample (decision tree) has M attributes. Each node of a decision tree needs to be split, and m attributes are randomly selected from these M attributes ($m \leq M$). Each node of a decision tree is split until it cannot be split, and no pruning is done during the entire process.

(3) Then, the information of each attribute is calculated, and one of the m attributes is selected as the attribute of the split node.

(4) A large number of decision trees are build by using step (1) to (3), and the generated decision trees form a random forest. Each individual tree in the random forest spits out a class prediction and the class with the most votes becomes our model's prediction (see Fig. 2).

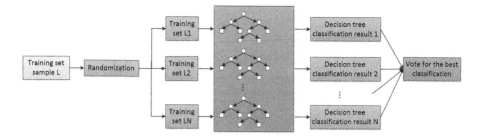

Fig. 2. The structure of random forest algorithm.

2.3   Combined Network Model

We propose a combined network model based on the convolutional neural network model and the random forest algorithm. Figure 3 presents the pipeline of the model. The model consists of two main parts: a CNN model is trained to extract features and predict the fault (see Fig. 4), and a random forest is generated to detect the fault (see Fig. 5).

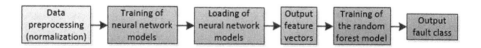

Fig. 3. The pipeline of the combined model.

3   Experiments

3.1   Data Sources

The experimental data used in this paper comes from the "Mechanical Equipment Health Monitoring Joint Laboratory" [9]. The test data is obtained from the XJTU-SY bearing data set, and the test bearing selected is LDK UER204 rolling bearing. The relevant parameters of this bearing are shown in Table 1.

Three types of working conditions are designed in the experiment, as shown in Table 2, and the XJTU-SY rolling bearing test dataset are used for working condition 1 and 2. The details are shown in Table 3.

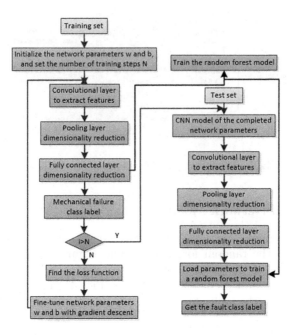

Fig. 4. The training process of CNN.

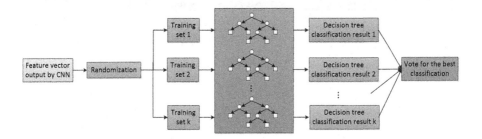

Fig. 5. A RF model makes a prediction.

Table 1. The parameters of LDK UER204 bearing.

Parameter name	Numerical value	Parameter name	Numerical value
Inner ring raceway diameter/mm	29.30	Ball diameter/mm	7.92
Outer ring raceway diameter/mm	39.80	Number of balls	8
Bearing diameter/mm	34.55	Contact angle/(°)	0
Basic dynamic load rating/N	12820	Basic static load rating/kN	6.65

Table 2. Bearing test working conditions.

Working condition number	1	2	3
Rotational speed (r/min)	2100	2250	2400
Radial force/kN	12	11	10

Table 3. Details of bearings for working condition 1 and 2.

Working condition	Data set	Total number of samples	Basic rated life	Actual life	Failure position
1	Bearing 1_1	123	5.600–9.677 h	2 h 3 min	Outer ring
	Bearing 1_2	161		2 h 41 min	Outer ring
	Bearing 1_3	158		2 h 38 min	Outer ring
	Bearing 1_4	122		2 h 2 min	Cage
	Bearing 1_5	52		52 min	Inner ring, Outer ring
2	Bearing 2_1	491	6.786–11.726 h	8 h 11 min	Inner ring
	Bearing 2_2	161		2 h 41 min	Outer ring
	Bearing 2_3	533		8 h 53 min	Cage
	Bearing 2_4	42		42 min	Outer ring
	Bearing 2_5	339		5 h 39 min	Outer ring

3.2   Experiments and Results

Firstly, the time domain diagrams of the horizontal and vertical vibration signals of the bearings are drawn, respectively. The normal and abnormal datasets in the rolling bearing are determined according to the time domain diagram of the bearing. The time domain diagram of the horizontal and vertical vibration signals in different rolling bearing life cycles and different working conditions are drawn in Fig. 6(a) and Fig. 6(b).

As shown in Fig. 6(a), the horizontal vibration signal of Bearing1_1 is the time domain diagram of the horizontal vibration signal of the outer ring of a rolling bearing under working condition 1. The normal interval of the data set is [1, 70], and the abnormal interval is [86, 123]. The interval [71, 85] is the data interval of the transition period from the normal condition to the abnormal condition for the outer ring of the rolling bearing. Some normal data and abnormal data under each working condition are selected for experiments. The selection of data sets and their class labels are shown in Table 4.

The data is randomly selected from the processed data set and split into the training and test sets. The number of training sets is i * N and the number of test sets is $(1 - i) * N$, where $(0 < i < 1)$ and N refers to the total number of samples. The CNN model and the combined network model are trained using selected training sets, and the comparison results on the test sets are shown in Table 5, 6, 7 and 8.

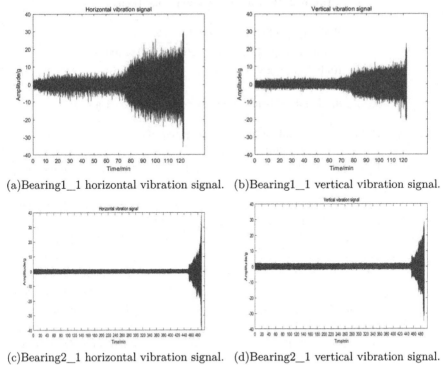

(a)Bearing1_1 horizontal vibration signal. (b)Bearing1_1 vertical vibration signal.

(c)Bearing2_1 horizontal vibration signal. (d)Bearing2_1 vertical vibration signal.

Fig. 6. Time domain diagram of some bearing vibration signals.

Table 4. Datasets used in the experiment.

Working conditions	Data set	Sample	Class label
Working condition1	Bearing1_1	1–70	0
		86–123	1
	Bearing1_2	1–40	2
		86–161	3
	Bearing1_3	1–60	4
		148–158	5
	Bearing1_4	1–85	6
		120–122	7
	Bearing1_5	1–35	8
		50–52	9
Working condition2	Bearing2_1	1–255	0
		481–491	1
	Bearing2_2	1–50	2
		86–161	3
	Bearing2_3	1–130	4
		331–533	5
	Bearing2_4	1–30	6
		36–42	7
	Bearing2_5	1–120	8
		241–339	9

Table 5. Comparison results of the fault detection models on the horizontal vibration signals for working condition 1 (%).

	Epochs	100	200	300	400	500	600
i = 0.2	CNN	71.31	93.75	**95.74**	**95.74**	**95.74**	95.45
	CNN+RF	95.51	95.79	**96.35**	95.79	95.79	95.51
i = 0.4	CNN	97.27	98.05	73.05	97.27	**98.44**	**98.44**
	CNN+RF	98.50	98.50	96.64	97.38	**98.88**	98.50

Table 6. Comparison results of the fault detection models on the vertical vibration signals in working condition 1 (%).

	Epochs	100	200	300	400	500	600
i = 0.2	CNN	45.17	94.03	95.17	95.23	**96.88**	96.31
	CNN+RF	94.95	94.95	95.23	96.63	**96.91**	96.63
i = 0.4	CNN	96.88	**97.27**	**97.27**	93.36	95.70	**97.27**
	CNN+RF	97.01	**97.38**	**97.38**	96.26	97.01	**97.38**

Table 7. Comparison results of the fault detection models on the horizontal vibration signals in working condition 2 (%).

	Epochs	100	200	300	400	500	600
i = 0.2	CNN	96.61	96.88	97.66	97.92	**98.18**	97.53
	CNN+RF	98.59	98.08	98.34	98.34	98.47	**98.85**
i = 0.4	CNN	98.09	98.09	98.61	98.26	**98.78**	98.44
	CNN+RF	**99.32**	98.98	**99.32**	99.15	98.98	98.98

Table 8. Comparison results of the fault detection models on the vertical vibration signals in working condition 2 (%).

	Epochs	100	200	300	400	500	600
i = 0.2	CNN	97.79	97.27	97.66	**97.92**	97.53	97.40
	CNN+RF	97.96	97.83	97.96	**98.21**	97.83	98.08
i = 0.4	CNN	97.40	97.74	97.74	**98.26**	97.92	98.09
	CNN+RF	98.47	98.81	98.64	98.47	98.98	**99.15**

As can be seen from the above tables, when i = 0.2 or i = 0.4, the number of epochs varies from 100 to 600, the performance of CNN model is lower than the combined network model in the vibration signal dataset in the same direction under the same working condition. When the number of epochs is from 100 to 600, i = 0.2 or i = 0.4, the higher accuracy of the model for the fault detection of rolling bearings is achieved by the combined network model.

As shown in Table 8, when i = 0.2, the CNN model achieves higher accuracy (97.92) when the number of iterations is 400 epochs. When the number of iterations is 400 epochs, the highest fault detection accuracy is obtained using the combined network model with a value of (98.21), which is 0.29 higher than the accuracy rate using CNN. However, the CNN model has the highest fault accuracy with (98.26) when i = 0.4. When the number of iterations is 600 epochs, the combined network model has the highest fault detection accuracy (99.15), which is 0.89 higher than the classification accuracy using the CNN model.

Under working condition 1, when i = 0.2 and epochs = 100, it can be seen from Table 5 and Table 6 that the classification accuracy of rolling bearing using the combined network model is significantly higher than that of CNN on both the horizontal and vertical vibration signal datasets. The main reason for this is that the data distribution of the standard sample under the condition 1 is more balanced than that under condition 2.

In general, under different working conditions, the accuracy of rolling bearing fault detection using only the CNN model is lower than the combined network model. It seems that the combined network model benefit from the CNN which has the strong self-learning ability for features and the RF algorithm which is helpful for high classification accuracy by alleviating the overfitting.

4 Conclusion

This paper proposed a combined network model using the convolutional neural network model and the random forest algorithm to improve the performance of the rolling bearing fault detection system. It is an end-to-end model. Self-learning features can be extracted by using the convolutional neural network model and the results from the CNN model is fed to a random forest algorithm, detecting the fault of the rolling bearing. Our results on the XJTU-SY bearing data set showed that the combined network model can effectively improve the classification accuracy of rolling bearing fault detection.

Acknowledgement. The authors acknowledge the Key Research and Development Plan of Anhui Province (202104d07020006), the Natural Science Foundation of Anhui Province (2108085MF223), University Natural Sciences Research Project of Anhui Province (KJ2021A0991), the Key Research and Development Plan of Hefei (2021GJ030).

References

1. Li, X.: Current situation and development of rolling bearing fault diagnosis technology. In: Proceedings of the 2009 National Youth Tribology Academic Conference, pp. 56–62 (2009)
2. Oka, M., Enokizono, M.: Space resolution of adjacent reverse-side cracks using rotational magnetic flux sensor and neural network. In: AIP Conference Proceedings, vol. 509, no. 1 (2000)

3. Osuna, E., Freund, R., Girosi, F.: Training support vector machines: an application to face detection. In: Proceedings/CVPR, IEEE Computer Society Conference on Computer Vision and Pattern Recognition. IEEE Computer Society Conference on Computer Vision and Pattern Recognition (2000)

4. Reinstein, H.C.: Expert systems—a technology for intelligent assistance. ACM SIGAPL APL Quote Quad, vol. 2, no. 1 (1981)

5. Nan, Y.: Research on convolutional neural network based on caffe deep learning framework. Hebei Normal University (2016)

6. Zhou, F., Jin, L., Dong, J.: A review of convolutional neural network research. Chin. J. Comput. **40**(6), 1229–1251 (2017)

7. Breiman, L.: Bagging predictors. Mach. Learn. **24**(2), 123–140 (1996)

8. Li, M.: Research on optimization and improvement of random forest algorithm. Jinan University (2016)

9. Wang, B., Lei, Y., Li, N., et al.: A hybrid prognostics approach for estimating remaining useful life of rolling element bearings. IEEE Trans. Reliab. **69**, 1–12 (2018)

zkChain: An Efficient Blockchain Privacy Protection Scheme Based on zk-SNARKs

Jiahui Huang, Teng Huang$^{(\boxtimes)}$, and Jiehua Zhang

Institute of Artificial Intelligence and Blockchain, Guangzhou University,
Guangzhou, China
{2112006105,2112106265}@e.gzhu.edu.cn, huangteng1220@buaa.edu.cn

Abstract. As a distributed public ledger technology in a peer-to-peer network, blockchain has been significantly adopted in a variety of Internet interaction systems in the past few years, such as market supervision, copyright protection, digital identity, etc. However, most blockchain-based applications remain susceptible to privacy attacks. In the blockchain environment, all historical transactions are open access and transparent, and adversaries may illegally access private data, including transaction amounts, account addresses, and account balances. In this paper, we present an efficient blockchain privacy protection scheme based on zk-SNARKs, called zkChain. In zkChain, we construct zero-knowledge proof based on one-way hash function and zk-SNARKs scheme. The proof is publicly recorded in the ledger after verification by miners, and users use proofs to transfer digital assets. In the above process, zkChain can achieve strong privacy guarantee on account balance, transaction amount and account address. To demonstrate the practicality of zkChain, we conduct experiments based on libsnark and FISCO BCOS. Our empirical results demonstrate the practicality and effectiveness of zkChain, which takes about 5.9 s to generate a pair of keys, about 1.7 s to generate a proof, and about 0.005 s to verify a proof.

Keywords: Blockchain · Zero-knowledge proof · Privacy protection · zkSNARKs

1 Introduction

With the help of core technologies such as distributed ledgers, asymmetric encryption, smart contracts, and consensus mechanisms, blockchain can realize functions such as point-to-point, anonymity, traceability, and anti-tampering, ensuring security and trust in the transaction process. In recent years, blockchain technology has been extended to digital finance [1], internet of things (IoT) [2,3], edge computing [4], artificial intelligence (AI) [5], supply chain management (SCM) [6] and other fields. At present, many countries in the world are accelerating the development of blockchain technology.

Based on peer-to-peer network, encryption technology and consensus mechanism, blockchain is a decentralized, immutable, traceable ledger that exists

Y. Xu et al. (Eds.): ML4CS 2022, LNCS 13656, pp. 400–410, 2023.
https://doi.org/10.1007/978-3-031-20099-1_34

across a network, and the ledger is used to record all historical transaction data on the blockchain. The transaction data generally includes the specific information of the transaction, such as transaction amount, account address, account balance, etc. However, in order to reach a consensus, nodes in the network need to disclose the transaction information in the ledger, which brings serious privacy issues to users, that is, the blockchain itself cannot ensure that user data remains private. In order to deal with the privacy challenges in blockchain, in recent years, there have been many blockchain privacy protection technologies and typical applications, which can prevent privacy theft or tampering attacks from different angles. At present, a variety of encryption methods have been applied to blockchain applications, such as ring signature [7], mixing service [8], homomorphic encryption [9] and zero-knowledge proof [10].

Zero-Knowledge Proof (ZKP) is an interactive verification protocol. In this protocol, based on the execution of a series of predefined operations, the verifier can be confident that the prover has some secret data without revealing the prover's secret data, which the verifier only knows that the prover has. This feature enables zero-knowledge proof technology to guarantee the validity and authenticity of the data in the ledger without revealing any sensitive information about the data. The implementation of the zero-knowledge proof protocol does not require a complex public key, and the protocol supports repeated implementation, and will not reveal any additional useful information to the adversary during the process of repeated implementation. ZKP is often used to realize anonymous verifiable voting, secure exchange of digital assets, secure remote biometric authentication, and secure auctions.

In order to ensure the privacy and security of the blockchain, inspired by the security and efficiency of ZKP in privacy protection, we present zkChain, an efficient blockchain privacy protection scheme based on zk-SNARKs. More specifically, we present to use one-way hash chain to denote account balances, and generate zero-knowledge proofs of account balances based on one-way hash chain and the zk-SNARKs scheme. In addition, in order to achieve a complete transfer process with privacy awareness, four types of transactions are constructed based on zero-knowledge proofs. This scheme can effectively ensure the privacy of account balances and the anonymity of account addresses.

1.1   Related Work

The protection of the anonymity of users and the confidentiality of transactions attracts widespread interest in the scientific community. Therefore, ZKP has been well studied in the blockchain environment, and many researchers have presents schemes that can efficiently and safely implement ZKP in the blockchain environment. Most of these schemes work on public blockchains, enabling any party to join the blockchain network, submit transactions and become a verifier.

Zerocoin [13] aims to achieve completely anonymous currency transactions in Bitcoin. Zerocoin is a cryptographic extension of Bitcoin to improve the privacy of transactions. In Zerocoin, transaction privacy is not compromised. However, due to the large number of applications of discrete logarithm problems,

Zerocoin has a large amount of proofs and a slow verification speed. Zerocash [14] provides a cryptocurrency protocol based on SNARKs for fully anonymous transactions that protects the source, destination and amount of funds. Compared to Zerocoin, the size of transactions used to pay for coins is reduced by 97.7%. Verification time is reduced by 98.6%, but a common string must be generated beforehand. Hawk [15] implements a transaction privacy protection protocol based on decentralized smart contracts. The protocol hides transaction data between pseudonyms and allows the use of programmable logic to bind these transactions for offline computation. In Hawk, non-interactive ZKPs are used to verify the correctness of smart contract executions and the validity of funds transfers, handled by a trusted third party, but the third party can see the user's input.

1.2 Our Contributions

In this work, we present an efficient blockchain privacy protection scheme based on zk-SNARks, which dramatically reduce the time costs and storage sizes of zero-knowledge transaction. In summary, the main contributions of this paper are as follows:

- We present zkChain, a blockchain privacy protection scheme based on zk-SNARKs non-interactive zero-knowledge proof, which can ensure the anonymity of transaction participants and the privacy of account balances. The scheme is independent of smart contracts and consensus mechanisms, and does not require changes to the underlying design of the blockchain. Therefore, zkChain can be applied to other account-model blockchains.
- We present a method to denote account balances using one-way hash chain, and construct a zero-knowledge proof of account balances based on one-way hash chain. The Zk-proof can prove the validity of the account balance and can be used to send transactions, which can dramatically improve the execution efficiency of zero-knowledge transaction.
- We implement zkChain based on libsnark, a C++ library for building SNARKs, and consortium blockchain FISCO BCOS. In practice, we use libsanrk to construct zero-knowledge proofs and evaluate storage performance and computational performance. Then, we use FISCO BCOS to build a blockchain network and evaluate the transmission performance of the zero-knowledge transaction constructed by the zkChain scheme in the blockchain network.

2 Preliminaries

The cryptographic techniques used in zkChain is the Succinct Non-interactive Argument of Knowledge (SNARK) technology. More specifically, we use a publicly verifiable preprocessing zero-knowledge SNARK, or zk-SNARK for short.

The zk-SNARK zero-knowledge proof scheme we use can be represented by a tuple of polynomial-time algorithms. We informally define zk-SNARK, the formal definition can be found in [16].

$$zk - SNARK = (KeyGen, GenProof, VerProof) \qquad (1)$$

- $KeyGen(1^\lambda, C) \rightarrow (pk, vk)$. Input the security parameter λ and the arithmetic circuit C, the key generator KeyGen randomly samples a proving key pk and a verification key vk. pk denotes a proving key used to generate proofs, and vk denotes a verification key used to verify proofs. Both keys are published as public parameters and can be used any number of times to prove or verify the relation R_C constructed by the circuit C.
- $GenProof(pk, \overrightarrow{x}, \overrightarrow{a}) \rightarrow \pi$. The algorithm generates a zero-knowledge proof π. pk denotes a proving key, $\overrightarrow{x}$ denotes a public input of circuit C, $\overrightarrow{a}$ denotes a auxiliary input of circuit C, and π denotes a zero-knowledge proof that the relationship R_C between $\overrightarrow{x}$ and $\overrightarrow{a}$ constructed by the circuit C can be proved. $\overrightarrow{x}$ and π are publicly available to anyone.
- $VerProof(vk, \overrightarrow{x}, \pi) \rightarrow b$. The algorithm verify a zero-knowledge proof. It outputs 1 if the zero-knowledge proof is verified successfully, otherwise, it outputs 0. vk denotes the verification key, π denotes the zero-knowledge proof generated in GenProof, and x denotes the public input in GenProof used to generate π.

According to the above zk-SNARK scheme, we construct zero-knowledge proofs using arithmetic circuits provided by the libsnark library, a C++ library for SNARKs. It implements circuit construction tools and general proof systems. Circuit building components can be used to construct R1CS or polynomial equation systems for zero-knowledge protocols. In this scheme, we create zero-knowledge proofs for the following statement:

$$\begin{aligned} ST : \{(R_1, R_2) : &H_1 = SHA256(R_1), \\ &H_2 = SHA256(R_2), \\ &R_1 = R_2 \wedge X\} \end{aligned} \qquad (2)$$

In Eq. (2), $H1$, $H2$ and X are public inputs, R_1 and R_2 are auxiliary inputs, and the prover generates the proof π, which can prove that prover knows the plaintext of the private auxiliary inputs R_1 and R_2. Where R_1 is the preimage of H_1, R_2 is the preimage of H_2, and $\wedge$ is XOR operation.

3   Architecture

As show in Fig. 1, zkChain's architecture is divided in two major components: the zk-SNARK scheme and the privacy protection scheme.

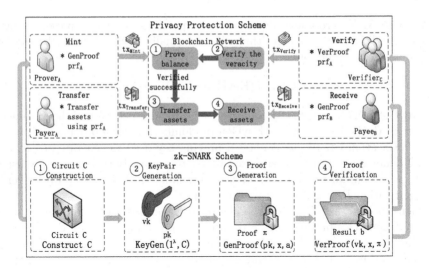

Fig. 1. System architecture of zkChain

3.1 zk-SNARK Scheme

As shown in Fig. 1, we use the zk-SNARK scheme to construct zero-knowledge proofs. It is mainly divided into four steps: In step 1, we build an arithmetic circuit $\mathcal{C}$ using the libsnark library. In step 2, we generate the Proving key pk and verification key vk corresponding to the arithmetic circuit $\mathcal{C}$. In step 3, we use the Proving key pk, the public input x, and the auxiliary input a to generate our zero-knowledge proof π. In step 4, we verify the zero-knowledge proof π with the verification key vk and the public input x.

3.2 Privacy Protection Scheme

As shown in Fig. 1, in the privacy protection scheme, there are four main roles, namely **Prover**, **Verifier**, **Payer** and **Payee**. In general, an account acts as both Prover and Payee. For convenience, we assume three roles: payer **A(Alice)** and payee **B(Bob)** and trusted authority **C(Charles)**. The following is the definition of the above four roles.

Prover. We utilize $Prover_A$ to denote a prover A(Alice). $Prover_A$ constructs a hash chain of length equal to the balance of the digital asset she own, and generates a zero-knowledge proof prf_A at the tail of the hash chain. By sending a tx_{Mint} to publicly record the proof prf_A in the ledger, the $prover_A$ can claim its digital assets through the public record of the proof prf_A recorded in the ledger. Since the length of the hash chain is only privately known to $Prover_A$, the proof prf_A in the ledger does not reveal any information about $Prover_A$'s assets.

Verifier. We utilize $Verifier_C$ to denotes a verifier C(Charles). Any third party authority $Verifier_C$ can send a transaction tx_{Verify_C} to verify the authenticity of the balance proof prf_A issued by $Prover_A$, if the proof prf_A is successfully verified, the signature of $Verifier_C$ will be appended On the proof prf_A and record it in the ledger to increase the authority of the asset. The proof prf_A does not reveal any useful information about the digital asset, and is traceable and immutable.

Payer. We utilize $Payer_A$ to denote a payer A(Alice). $Payer_A$ with a proof of balance prf_A sends a transaction $tx_{Transfer}$ to pledge balance it holds to the ledger. More specifically, $Payer_A$ pays assets by disclosing a private hash chain node. After that, $Payer_A$ subtracts the amount of payouts from the length of the private hash chain. And update the proof of balance prf_A at the tail of the new hash chain. The miner verify the authenticity of $tx_{Transfer}$, and the verified spending asset can be received by $Payee_B$.

Payee. We utilize $Payee_B$ to denote a payee B(Bob). After $Payee_A$ sends the transaction $tx_{Transfer}$, $Payee_B$ generates a new balance proof prf_B to receive a disposable asset. prf_B is publicly recorded in the ledger after verification by miners, and is traceable and non-tamperable. The proof prf_B in the ledger does not reveal any information about $Payee_B$'s account.

4 Proposed zkChain Scheme

In this section, we give an overview of zkChain's scheme, and then describe the specific construction process of zkChain in detail. For convenience, we still assume three roles: payer **A(Alice)** and payee **B(Bob)** and trusted authority **C(Charles)**. The key pair and account address of payer A(Alice) are denoted as (sk_A, pk_A) and $addr_A$ respectively. The key pair and the account address of the payee B(Bob) are denoted as (sk_B, pk_B) and $addr_B$ respectively. This scheme can be represented by a polynomial-time algorithm:

$$\prod = (\textbf{Mint}, \textbf{Verify}, \textbf{Transfer}, \textbf{Receive}) \tag{3}$$

4.1 Mint

The account balance of $Prover_A$ is denoted by a one-way hash chain $\mathbb{H}_A = \cup h_{Ai}$ with $i \in \{1, 2, ..., n\}$, h_{Ai} denotes i-th node, n denotes the length of the one-way hash chain $\mathbb{H}_A$. When a function SHA256($\cdot$) is iteratively applied i times to an argument $sk_A \| addr_A$, the result will be h_{Ai}, $\|$ denotes concatenation, that is:

$$h_{Ai} = \text{SHA256}(\text{SHA256}(\cdots \text{SHA256}(sk_A \| addr_A) \cdots)) \tag{4}$$

If the balance held by $Prover_A$ is v, the corresponding hash chain is $\mathbb{H}_A = \cup h_{Ai}$ with $i \in \{1, 2, ..., v\}$. To construct a zero-knowledge proof of account balance,

$Prover_A$ disclose the last hash chain node h_{Av}. Now, $\forall h_{Ai} \in \{h_{A1}, ..., h_{Av-1}\}$ is only visible $Prover_A$, $\exists h_{Av} \in \mathbb{H}_A$ is visible to anyone. Then, generate a proof prf_A with public h_{Av} as public input and private $h_{A(v-1)}$ as private auxiliary input. Since $Prover_A$ only discloses the last node h_{Av}, the length of $\mathbb{H}_A$ is not disclosed, which means that the amount of balance v of $Prover_A$ is unknown to others. $Prover_A$ uses prf_A to prove that he knows the preimage $h_{A(v-1)}$ of the public input h_{Av}. Since $h_{A(v-1)} \in \mathbb{H}_A$ is only visible to asset owner $Prover_A$, a verifier can verify the authenticity of prf_A to confirm that $Prover_A$ is the owner of asset $\mathbb{H}_A$. More formally, $Prover_A$ generates proof prf_A to prove the following statement:

$$ST_{Mint} : \{(R_1 = h_{A(v-1)} \wedge sn_A, R_2 = h_{A(v-1)}) :$$
$$H_1 = \text{SHA256}(R_1) = \text{SHA256}(h_{A(v-1)} \wedge sn_A),$$
$$H_2 = \text{SHA256}(R_2) = \text{SHA256}(h_{A(v-1)}) = h_{Av},$$
$$R_1 = R_2 \wedge X = R_2 \wedge sn_A\}$$

(5)

In Eq. (5), public input sn_A is a unique serial number associated with the transaction tx_{Mint} sent by $Prover_A$. $sn_A = CRH(sk_A \| r)$. sk_A is the private key of $Prove_A$, r is a random number, $CRH(\cdot)$ is a collision-resistant hash function, $\|$ denotes concatenation. Miners defend against double-spending attacks by confirming the uniqueness of serial number during transaction verification.

4.2   Verify

Any verifier $Verifier_C$ can verify the proof prf_A using the public h_{Av}, the verification key vk of prf_A, and the serial number sn_A uniquely associated with prf_A. Then the miner verifies the zero-knowledge proof prf_A, if the check is successful, it outputs $b = 1$, otherwise it outputs $b = 0$. The zero-knowledge proof prf_A and its associated verification result b are publicly recorded in the ledger to support public traceability and verification operations, as shown in Fig. 2. All successfully verified balance proofs (i.e. prf_A with $b = 1$) can be used to send $tx_{Transfer}$.

4.3   Transfer

Firstly, $Payer_A$ holding proof prf_A discloses a private hash chain node $h_{A(v-p)} \in \mathbb{H}_A$ to pay amount of p balance. $Payee_B$ generates a private hash chain $\mathbb{H}_B = \cup h_{Bi}$ with $i \in \{1, 2, ..., p\}$ locally to replace the public $\{h_{A(v-p)}, ..., h_{Av}\}$, and generates random numbers $\{r_1, r_2, ..., r_p\}$ of length p to mask the private $\mathbb{H}_B$, that is:

$$\mathbb{H}'_B = \{h_{B1} \wedge r_1, h_{B2} \wedge r_2, ..., h_{Bp} \wedge r_p\} = \{h'_{B1}, h'_{B2}, ..., h'_{Bp}\}$$

(6)

$Payee_B$ sends $\mathbb{H}'_B$ and r_p to $Payer_A$ via off-chain channel, then $Payer_A$ inputs $h_{A(v-p)}$, $\mathbb{H}'_B$ and r_p to send the transaction $tx_{Transfer}$. Secondly, the miners calculates $h_{A(v-p)}$ iteratively through the SHA256($\cdot$) function. If the corresponding

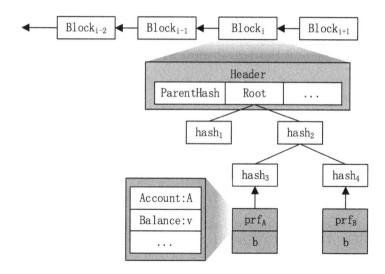

Fig. 2. Traceability of zero-knowledge proofs in blockchain

public $h_{Av} \in H_A$ can be calculated, then compare the lengths of p and $\mathbb{H}'_B$, if the lengths are equal, the transaction $tx_{Transfer}$ is verified successfully. Finally, $Payer_A$ updates his proof of balance prf_A to prove the following statement:

$$
\begin{aligned}
\text{ST}_{\text{Transfer}} : \{ (R_1 &= h_{A(v-p-1)} \wedge sn'_A, R_2 = h_{A(v-p-1)}) : \\
H_1 &= \text{SHA256}(R_1) = \text{SHA256}(h_{A(v-p-1)} \wedge sn'_A), \\
H_2 &= \text{SHA256}(R_2) = \text{SHA256}(h_{A(v-p-1)}) = h_{A(v-p)}, \\
R_1 &= R_2 \wedge X = R_2 \wedge sn'_A \}
\end{aligned} \tag{7}
$$

4.4 Receive

$Payee_B$ uses the locally generated $\mathbb{H}_B$ to generate a new proof of balance prf_B, which means that he received a disposable asset. More formally, $Payee_B$ generates proof prf_B to prove the following statement:

$$
\begin{aligned}
\text{ST}_{\text{Receive}} : \{ (R_1 &= h_{B(p-1)} \wedge sn_B, R_2 = h_{B(p-1)}) : \\
H_1 &= \text{SHA256}(R_1) = \text{SHA256}(h_{B(p-1)} \wedge sn_B), \\
H_2 &= \text{SHA256}(R_2) = \text{SHA256}(h_{B(p-1)}) = h_{Bp}, \\
R_1 &= R_2 \wedge X = R_2 \wedge sn_B \}
\end{aligned} \tag{8}
$$

Miners compute $h_{Bp} \wedge r_P \overset{?}{=} h'_{Bp}$ using $h'_{Bp} \in \mathbb{H}'_B$ and r_P publicly recorded in the ledger, if $h_{Bp} \wedge r_P = h'_{bp}$, then verified successfully. The verified prf_B is publicly recorded in the ledger to represent a disposable asset, which means that $Payee_B$ has received the asset from $Payer_A$.

5 Experiments

5.1 Computing and Storage Performance of zkSNARK

We implemented the zkSNARK scheme based on libsnark [11], which is a C++ library that implements the zk-SNARK scheme. We use the zk-SNARK scheme to construct zero-knowledge proof. We serialize the proof through object serialization technology and store the serialized string in the ledger through the smart contract. We conduct our experiments on 64-bit Ubuntu 16.04LTS with 12 GB RAM in a notebook with Intel Core i7-8750CPU@2.20 GHz*6 and a notebook with Intel Core i5-4200HCPU@2.80 GHz*4, and evaluate the related computing performance and storage performance. The experimental results are shown in Table 1.

The experimental results show that zkChain has high computing efficiency in the Intel Core i7-8750CPU@2.20 GHz*6 laptop. It takes about 5.9 s to generate a pair of keys, about 1.7 s to generate a proof, and about 0.005 s to verify a proof.

Table 1. Computing and storage performance of zkChain

zkChain		Intel Core i7-8750CPU@2.20 GHz*6 12 GB of RAM	Intel Core i5-4200HCPU@2.8 GHz*4 12 GB of RAM
KeyGen	Time	5.931780 s	8.966478 s
	Proving key	12.1932192 MB	
	Verification key	573.25 B	
Prove	Time	1.789675 s	2.788520 s
	Proof	286.75 B	
Verify	Time	0.005211 s	0.006772 s

5.2 Processing Performance Based on FISCO BCOS

We built a blockchain network based on FISCO BCOS [12], and tested the processing performance of the zero-knowledge transactions in the blockchain network. Specifically, we use serialization technology to persistently store the zero-knowledge proof constructed by libsanrk, and then broadcast the proof in the blockchain network through solidity smart contracts.

The experimental results are shown in Fig. 3. Firstly, we tested the effect of different node numbers on transaction latency. We set the transaction sending rate to 1000 TPS, and sent a total of 10,000 transactions. As shown in Fig. 3(a), the figure shows the maximum transaction delay rate, the average transaction delay rate, and the minimum transaction delay rate under different numbers of nodes. As the number of nodes increases, transaction latency shows an upward trend. Secondly, we tested the effect of different number of nodes on transaction

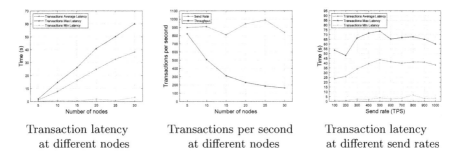

| Transaction latency at different nodes | Transactions per second at different nodes | Transaction latency at different send rates |

Fig. 3. The performance of zkChain based on FISCO BCOS.

throughput, we set the transaction sending rate to 1000 TPS, and sent a total of 10000 transactions. As shown in Fig. 3(b), the red line is the actual transaction sending rate, and the blue line is the transaction throughput. With the increase of the number of nodes, the transaction throughput shows a downward trend. Finally, we tested the effect of different transaction sending rates on transaction latency. We set the number of nodes to 30 and sent a total of 10,000 transactions. As shown in Fig. 3(c), with the increase of the transaction sending rate, the transaction delay shows an upward trend, and then tends to be stable, which indicates that when a certain transaction sending rate is reached, the transaction delay is mainly affected by the number of nodes constraints.

6   Conclusion

In this work, we present zkChain, an efficient blockchain privacy protection scheme based on zk-SNARks. In zkChain, firstly, we use a one-way hash chain to denote the account balance, and build the account asset balance proof based on the one-way hash chain and the zk-SNARKs scheme. The proof is publicly recorded in the ledger after being verified by the miners. Prover claim the authenticity of their account balances through the proofs recorded in the ledger. Secondly, payers with proof of balance can pledge their assets to the ledger, and the pledge amount is limited by the length of the one-way hash chain, which can effectively prevent over-consumption attacks. Finally, Payees can receive an asset pledged in the ledger in an anonymous identity. We implemented the zkChain scheme based on libsnark. The experimental results show the excellent performance of zkChain. It takes about 5.9 s to generate a pair of keys, about 1.7 s to generate a proof, and about 0.005 s to verify a proof.

References

1. Treleaven, P., Brown, R.G., Yang, D.: Blockchain technology in finance. Computer **50**(9), 14–17 (2017)

2. Minoli, D., Occhiogrosso, B.: Blockchain mechanisms for IoT security. Internet Things **1**, 1–13 (2018)
3. Wang, Q., Zhu, X., Ni, Y., Gu, L., Zhu, H.: Blockchain for the IoT and industrial IoT: a review. Internet Things **10**, 100081 (2020)
4. Xu, J., Wang, S., Bhargava, B.K., Yang, F.: A blockchain-enabled trustless crowd-intelligence ecosystem on mobile edge computing. IEEE Trans. Industr. Inf. **15**(6), 3538–3547 (2019)
5. Salah, K., Rehman, M.H.U., Nizamuddin, N., Al-Fuqaha, A.: Blockchain for AI: review and open research challenges. IEEE Access **7**, 10127–10149 (2019)
6. Dutta, P., Choi, T.M., Somani, S., Butala, R.: Blockchain technology in supply chain operations: applications, challenges and research opportunities. Transp. Res. Part E Logist. Transp. Rev. **142**, 102067 (2020)
7. Rivest, R.L., Shamir, A., Tauman, Y.: How to leak a secret. In: Boyd, C. (ed.) ASIACRYPT 2001. LNCS, vol. 2248, pp. 552–565. Springer, Heidelberg (2001). https://doi.org/10.1007/3-540-45682-1_32
8. Chaum, D.L.: Untraceable electronic mail, return addresses, and digital pseudonyms. Commun. ACM **24**(2), 84–90 (1981)
9. Rivest, R.L., Adleman, L., Dertouzos, M.L.: On data banks and privacy homomorphisms. Found. Secur. Comput. **4**(11), 169–180 (1978)
10. Ben-Sasson, E., Chiesa, A., Tromer, E., Virza, M.: Succinct non-interactive zero knowledge for a von Neumann architecture. In: 23rd USENIX Security Symposium (USENIX Security 2014), pp. 781–796 (2014)
11. SCIPR Lab: Libsnark: a C++ library for zkSNARK proofs. https://github.com/scipr-lab/libsnark. Accessed 29 Mar 2022
12. FISCO BCOS. https://github.com/FISCO-BCOS/FISCO-BCOS. Accessed 03 Apr 2022
13. Miers, I., Garman, C., Green, M., Rubin, A.D.: Zerocoin: anonymous distributed e-cash from bitcoin. In: 2013 IEEE Symposium on Security and Privacy, pp. 397–411. IEEE (2013)
14. Sasson, E.B., et al.: Zerocash: decentralized anonymous payments from bitcoin. In: 2014 IEEE Symposium on Security and Privacy, pp. 459–474. IEEE (2014)
15. Kosba, A., Miller, A., Shi, E., Wen, Z., Papamanthou, C.: Hawk: the blockchain model of cryptography and privacy-preserving smart contracts. In: 2016 IEEE Symposium on Security and Privacy (SP), pp. 839–858. IEEE (2016)
16. Bitansky, N., Chiesa, A., Ishai, Y., Paneth, O., Ostrovsky, R.: Succinct non-interactive arguments via linear interactive proofs. In: Sahai, A. (ed.) TCC 2013. LNCS, vol. 7785, pp. 315–333. Springer, Heidelberg (2013). https://doi.org/10.1007/978-3-642-36594-2_18

Research on Influential Factors of Online Learning Behavior Based on Big Data

Fangqin Ma[1(✉)] and JunHan Qiu[2]

[1] College of General Education, Xi'an Eurasia University, Xi'an, China
syzasmfq@126.com
[2] School of Cyber Science and Technology, Beihang University, Beijing, China
20231056@buaa.edu.cn

Abstract. Online learning is becoming more and more popular in today's world. Through the online learning platform for the vast amounts of data information analysis, analysis of online learners' learning and learning behavior, try to online learners' internal influence factors and external influence factors of online learning make a comprehensive analysis, finally for learners to provide a higher quality of learning resources, to provide support for effective learning.

Keywords: Online learning · Influencing factors · The future education

At the 2019 AI and Education Big Data Summit, Professor Ronghuai Huang pointed out that the current problem of Education in China is how to balance large-scale education and personalized training under the background of Ai and big data [1]. And International Conference on Artificial Intelligence education 2020(AIED) discusses how to deeply integrate AI and education. Based on the big data of online education as the research background, the study on the influencing factors of learners' learning behavior will provide a scientific research basis for the decision-making of online education in China.

1 Introduction

In recent years, our country invested enough attention for online teaching, have issued a series of documents and clear requirements to advanced information technology such as large data used in the teaching management, teaching informatization construction and development for the future pointed out the development direction [2].

Project Description: This project is the periodical research results of xi 'an 2021 Basic education Research Major Subject (Subject No. 2021ZB-ZY17), The periodical research results of Xi 'an 2021 Basic education Research Key topic (Subject No. 2021ZB-GG08), The phased research results of 2021 university-level educational reform (Project No. 2021YB025), This project is the periodical research results of 2022 university-level Ideological and political demonstration course (Project No. 2022KS011).

Y. Xu et al. (Eds.): ML4CS 2022, LNCS 13656, pp. 411–421, 2023.
https://doi.org/10.1007/978-3-031-20099-1_35

Since the outbreak of the COVID-19 epidemic, universities have successively carried out online teaching activities with the help of different platforms. The online platform will record all the learning behavior data and behavior tracks of learners during the whole process from login to exit from the platform. And the fact which how to participate in, how to evaluate etc., have become the problems that need in-depth discussion and practice under the new teaching mode. Therefore, it is particularly necessary to systematically analyze and process the massive data generated by online platform operation.

This article mainly through to the relevant data of online learning and influencing factors of comprehensive and system analysis, understand the basic elements of online teaching and learning activities, to optimize the design and implementation of online teaching, gradually improve the existing teaching system, eventually to promote learners' learning efficiency and learning effect.

2 Research Review

At this time, the mode of massive online teaching has gradually become a good supplement to traditional teaching. The learning data of online learners that can be obtained through big data technology is more rich and diversified. Domestic and foreign scholars have different research emphases. They study online teaching from different research perspectives, and their research methods and research categories are also different (Fig. 1).

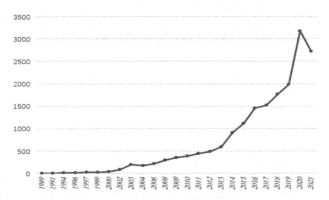

Fig. 1. Number of relevant publications in past years

The author looked up studies on online learning on CNKI, and found that relevant studies have increased significantly since 2003, especially since the outbreak of COVID-19, the annual number of published papers has exceeded 3000, and it is expected that the total number of published papers will continue to increase in 2022 (Fig. 2).

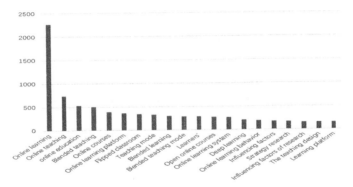

Fig. 2. Number of articles published on major topics

Data from CNKI show that there are a lot of research achievements on online learning in recent years, which will provide new research ideas and directions for exploring new education and teaching modes.

The author further researches the existing achievements from the following aspects:

Research on learning behavior: The research on online learning behavior was initially started by foreign scholars Anna Hummel et al. Their research mainly used mobile devices to track and record students' learning behavior in real time, Teachers or managers can obtain students' learning information, and timely feedback and evaluation for students [4]. To simplify the teaching process, the United States has also created an online student achievement management platform, which includes nine functions such as testing, management, homework and evaluation. Teachers can view students' learning status at any time and adjust teaching plans accordingly. Teaching resources are reused and teaching efficiency is improved [5].The research on online learning behavior analysis in China is relatively later than that in foreign countries. In 2004, Zhiwu Gong sed the distance education network teaching platform for empirical research, Xiaoxue Wang and others all kinds of data based on big data in college students' learning behavior, integrating the research and management practice of students' behavior [6].

Research on personalized learning and intelligent service: Chih Ming Chen and others designed a personalized learning system to infer the strength of learners' learning ability according to learners' response to courseware learning, and recommend learning content with difficulty coefficient consistent with learners' learning ability [7]. Hongyan Wu builds a personalized online learning system based on intelligent learning theory and learning analysis theory, according to learners' needs and learning laws, and recommends learning resources and learning paths suitable for different learners. Teachers can predict learning effects and intervene students' learning [8]. Research on learning behavior analysis model: Chia-hua chang, etc. Based on the traditional RTI(Responseto Intervention, or RTI) model to construct the Intervention model of online learning [9].

Based on the analysis of the associated factors and driving forces of online learning behavior based on the current situation of artificial intelligence, Li Yang et al. constructed the overall framework of online learning behavior analysis model and designed the horizontal and vertical flow of online learning behavior analysis [10]. Based on the research on the life cycle of big data, long Yang and Jin Yao put forward the reference architecture of big data ecosystem [11].

Research on complex network and big data analysis: Hong Sheng et al.proposed a resistance factor which can characterize the impact of individual's difference on the propagation dynamics in complex dynamical network, which are helpful to the understanding of epidemic spreading mechanism [12]. Besides, Hong Sheng et al. modeled the interdependent network with the strength of embedding length, which can improve the robustness of real-world network systems big data analysis [13]. The study in modeled inter-dependencies among networks to describe functional and logical relations among components in different systems. In the field of big data and deep learning [14], some feature extraction and analysis methods, such as Gaussian nonlinear feature association mapping [15], combined LLE –Isomap [16] and integrating autoencoder [17] have significant value for the studying of learner behavior and related data key features analysis.

Based on the above research, we can see that: (1) In the future education model, the public will accept online learning more and more; (2) In the online learning mode, learners' learning needs show a trend of diversification. In the future, online learning services and learning types will be more abundant. (3) The learner behavior analysis and related data of online learning will provide powerful data support and technical support for online learning providers and managers; (4) The process management of online learning has become a key link to improve the effect of online learning. Researchers have built reasonable online teaching models according to the data of learners' learning process. Researchers have constructed a reasonable online teaching model based on learners' learning process data. In online learning mode based on big data, learners are not only the producer of learning behavior, but also the ultimate beneficiary of learning behavior analysis. In the future, online teaching needs to be gradually constructed with the construction idea of "data acquisition -- data analysis -- result feedback". While data is constantly updated iteratively, the analysis mechanism also needs to be updated constantly, finally realizing a virtuous cycle of online courses. In the future, online teaching needs to be gradually constructed with the construction idea of "data acquisition -- data analysis -- result feedback". While data is constantly updated iteratively, the analysis mechanism also needs to be updated constantly, finally realizing a virtuous cycle of online courses.

3 Analysis of Online Learning Behavior Status Quo

3.1 Value Analysis of Online Learning Data

McKinsey, a world-renowned research institute, once defined big data as a collection of data so large that its acquisition, storage, management and analysis and other aspects are far beyond the scope of previous database software tools. Online learning behavior is mainly reflected in the following aspects (Table 1):

Table 1. Comparison of students' online learning behaviors

Learning phase	Learning behavior
Before class	Query learning task lists, watch teaching videos, search learning materials, complete pre-class tests, post and discuss boards
during class	Listening, online group discussion, online simulation training, online practice, group online sharing, online test
after class	Online practice, online test, simulation practice

These data associated with the occurrence of learning and produce huge amounts of information, these data. Teachers and the teaching researchers can through these data mining valuable and consistency of information, analysis of learners' learning styles and learning habits, understand students' learning behavior model.

3.2 Takeholder Analysis of Online Learning

The openness and sharing of online learning can promote the construction of learners' thinking habits and knowledge framework. Online teaching mode can truly build a student-centered online teaching mode and provide learners with more free learning space, which will promote the realization of personalized teaching in the future. The stakeholders involved in online learning mode mainly include learners, teachers and platform managers [18].

For learners, the nonlinear and related characteristics of online course structure enable learners to participate in various senses and get exercise and learning from it, thus realizing the transfer to diversified learning behaviors. Online learning has a new communication mechanism, through the establishment of learning communities to help users and peers and course organizers to fully interact and communicate. In the context of big data, it is crucial for educational researchers to select targeted learning behavior attributes and characteristics from the massive original learning data for analysis to monitor and guide learners' learning behavior.

The author found in the survey that there are great differences in the attitudes and opinions of learners towards online learning. About learners' attitudes towards online learning, About 62% of the surveyed learners support online learning, about 25% of the surveyed learners are neutral, and about 4% are against it (Fig. 3).

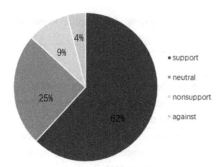

Fig. 3. Learners' attitudes towards online learning

As for the overall feedback of online learning, about 88.2% of learners participating in the survey think that online learning requires strong autonomy, about 53.2% of learners participating in the survey think that online learning experience is not strong, about 41.4% of learners participating in the survey think that online classroom is not interactive, about 51.2% of learners participating in the survey think that online learning is underrated, about 75% of learners participating in the survey think that classroom group activities are limited, and about 70% of learners participating in the survey think that classroom learning feedback is not timely enough. It can be seen that although online learning is convenient, its disadvantages are gradually revealed. There is a long way to go to explore and popularize online learning (Fig. 4).

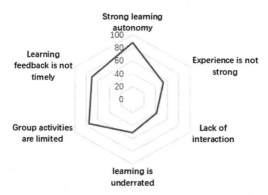

Fig. 4. Learner overall feedback on the online learning process

For teachers, they make use of the data of online learning behavior to conduct cluster analysis, fully understand and identify students' learning dynamics, analyze the difficulties and key points of the course, the blind spots of learners' learning, and reasonably adjust the course content, teaching structure and teaching video rhythm. At the same time, teachers can based on data from online learning platform, and carry out online teaching in a more orderly way [19].

As for the implementation of online teaching, more than 83% of the surveyed teachers have tried online teaching since 2020. Among them, about 15% of teachers participating in the survey think it is not difficult, about 67% of teachers participating in the survey think it is difficult but can be overcome through learning, about 13% of teachers participating in the survey think there are many difficulties and about 5% of teachers participating in the survey think online teaching should not be used as much as possible. It can be seen that there are also differences in teachers' attitudes towards online teaching, which may be caused by some teachers' own barriers in using relevant technologies. However, in general, the free and flexible online teaching has won the recognition of the vast majority of teachers. In the future, online education is likely to become one of the main teaching modes in modern education (Fig. 5).

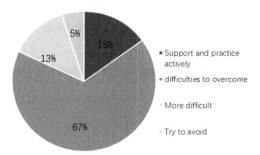

Fig. 5. Teachers' attitudes towards online teaching

For the platform manager, the trajectory of learning data stored on the online teaching platform can be used to comprehensively analyze the learning behavior of learners, on the one hand to promote the improvement the platform functions, and on the other hand, the platform manager can better guide learners' learning behavior.

4   Construction of Influencing Factors Model of Online Learning Behavior in the Big Data

4.1   Construction of Online Learning Learner's Own Literacy Factor Model

Online learning behavior is a multi-dimensional complex system, and learners' basic literacy affects the experience and learning effect of online learning. Online learning mode requires learners to have certain information literacy, to be able to use information learning means and skillfully operate the learning platform [20]. Online learning platform helps learners to select and utilize learning resources and enhance their experience of learning process. The learner's old knowledge can help stimulate new knowledge; Learners' learning styles and habits are related to the learning effect. Learners' original preferred learning strategies and learning styles need to be gradually adapted to online learning mode. Learning motivation and learning efficiency are the internal driving forces that drive learners to engage in learning, the confidence of the skills necessary to achieve learning goals and beliefs. In short, the construction of learner literacy model under online learning mode can clearly understand the basic elements of online learning, facilitate teachers to design more appropriate teaching activities [21] (Fig. 6).

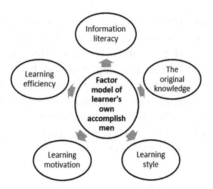

Fig. 6. Construction of learning learner's own literacy factor model

4.2 Modeling of External Influencing Factors Related to Online Learning Behavior

(See Fig. 7).

Fig. 7. Modeling of external influencing factors related to online learning behavior

4.2.1 Online Learning Platform of Choice

Well-known overseas MOOCs mainly includes Coursera, Udacity and edX. Representative domestic MOOCs platforms include: Chinese university MOOCs, MOOCs Institute, Super star MOOCs, etc. Online learning platform have diversified and open teaching mode of learners' effective learning behavior have a major impact, choose suitable for online learning platform can maximum limit satisfy all types of learners' study demand,

Improve the effect of online learning and facilitate the recording, storage and analysis of data related to learning behavior [22].

4.2.2   Ability and Level of Online Teaching

Online teaching for traditional teaching mode has brought the unprecedented challenge, which requires the organizers of the course and education researchers in a timely manner to explore online teaching mode, and to be the leader of class, to encourage class participation and learning motivation, improving learning self-discipline, Strengthen the design of teaching scaffold in online learning or mixed environment; Consciously identify the differences in online learning behaviors of different types of learners and carry out personalized learning guidance.

4.2.3   Push Online Learning Resources

Online learning is a long process. Abundant and diversified online learning resources can help learners selectively learn according to their learning needs. Short online resources can avoid mental fatigue or absentmindedness caused by long-term investment, so they win the favor of learners. The managers and teachers of the platform regularly push relevant learning resources and tasks to learners, so that students can keep learning fresh in the rhythm of relaxation and ensure effective intake of online resources within a limited time.

4.2.4   Design and Participation of Online Learning Activities

Online learning is different from the traditional communicative learning mode where learners have face-to-face learning seminars. The design of online learning activities should closely follow the learning objective and content, and pay attention to the feasibility and realization effect of the course objective. And the course activity designer also needs to design relevant activity plans, paying attention to online learners' acceptance level, participation mode, learning activity results and the displayability of the results. All these factors involve the online learning experience of learners and stimulate the occurrence of real learning behaviors.

4.2.5   Evaluation of the Online Learning Process

Online learning mode depends on learners' self-discipline to a great extent, so it is necessary to pay high attention to learners' procedural learning in the construction of course evaluation system. Therefore, in the process of strengthening the evaluation system of online courses, it is necessary to focus on the evaluation of learning process, such as the length of learning, the completion and submission times of homework, the number of questions and discussions on the discussion board, and the frequency of communication and interaction in the q&A area. Establish learning quality evaluation index system for each chapter, objectively evaluate the learning quality of learners in each chapter, realize the whole process of online course evaluation, find those who fall behind, give more supervision, reminder and encouragement in time, enhance their self-discipline, avoid perfunctory response.

4.2.6 Feedback on the Effectiveness of Online Learning

Online learning platform from login learners learning platform will be detailed records the learner's behavior, such as watching video, job submission, online discussion participation behavior, teachers through the analysis of the behavior of trajectory for the learners to understand students' learning behavior, learners' study demand and the possible problems in the learning process, adjust teaching strategy and activity design, Focus on the supervision of problematic learning behaviors, timely feedback and communication of learners' learning effects, improve online learning behaviors, and finally realize the improvement of online teaching quality [23].

5 Conclusion

The big data era of "data-driven schools and analysis to transform education" has come. Online learning has become a common way of learning. The research on the influencing factors of online learning behavior will help teachers and educational researchers systematically analyze the characteristics of learners' online learning, provide ideas for the organic combination of traditional learning methods and emerging learning methods, and expect to create a new model for future education.

References

1. He, W., Zhang, M., Lu, L.: Human-machine collaborative information technology education of application of the new concept of. J. Educ. Dev. Res (2021)
2. Yang, X., Yao, J., Huang, D.: Online learning behavior analysis model based on big data architecture. Comput. Knowl. Technol (2020)
3. Curran, C., Bramble, W.J., Panda, S.: Online Learning and University in Economics of Distance and Online Learning: Theory, Practice and Research. Routledge, NewYork (2008)
4. Hummel, K.A., Hlavacs, H.: Anytime, anywhere learning behavior using a web-based platform for a universty lecture. In: Proceedings of the SSGRR 2003 Winter Confernce(2003)
5. Engrade IK-12 Instructional Management Platform [DB/OL]. https://www.engrade.com
6. Wang, X.: Application of big data in college students' learning behavior pattern mining, intelligent computer and application (2017)
7. Zhao, Z., Zhen, L., Zhou, D., Zhong, S.: Research on learning behavior analysis and recommendation system in intelligent learning space Mod. Educ. Technol. (2016)
8. Wu, H.: Design and application of personalized online learning system from the perspective of intelligent learning. China Audio Visual Educ. (2015)
9. Zhang, J., Zou, Q., Zhu, Z.: Application of online learning intervention model from the perspective of learning analysis. Mod. Dist. Educ. Res. (2017)
10. Zhang, H., Li, N.: Research and analysis of learning behavior Data Model based on online learning platform. Sci. Technol. Inf. (2020)
11. Yang, L., Yao, J., Huang, D., et al.: online learning behavior analysis model based on big data architecture. Comput. Knowl. Technol. (2020)
12. Sheng, H., et al.: Epidemic spreading model of complex dynamical network with the heterogeneity of nodes. Int. J. Syst. Sci. (2016)
13. Sheng, H., et al.: Cascading failure and recovery of spatially interdependent networks. J. Stat. Mech. Theory Exp. **2017**(10), 103208 (2017)

14. Sheng, H., et al.: Cascading failure analysis and restoration strategy in an interdependent network. J. Phys. A Math. Theor. **49**, 195101 (2016)
15. Sheng, H., et al.: Vehicle energy system active defense: a health assessment of lithium-ion batteries. Int. J. Intell. Syst. (2020)
16. Sheng, H., et al.: A health assessment framework of lithium-ion batteries for cyberdefense. Appl. Soft Comput. (2021)
17. Sheng, H., et al.: Remaining useful life prediction for lithium-ion battery: a deep learning approach. IEEE Access (2018)
18. Li, T., Dou, X., Xiong, J.: Study on students' learning behavior and strategies for improving learning quality. Educ. Teach. Forum (2021)
19. Yu, S., Wang, H.: How to better organize online learning in COVID-19 and other extreme environments. China Electron. Educ. (2020)
20. Li, Y.: Research on Online learning Behavior Analysis Model in Big Data Environment. Harbin University of Science and Technology (2017)
21. Xie, S.: Analysis of higher vocational students' learning behavior and effect based on big data. Comput. Telecommun. (2018)
22. Luo, L., Huang, X., Yuan, W.: A longitudinal learning behavior prediction model based on online learning data. Sci. Technol. Innov. Appl. (2021)
23. Chen, W.: Construction of higher vocational students' learning behavior model based on big data. Educ. Modern (2018)

Short Speech Key Generation Technology Based on Deep Learning

Zhengyin Lv◉, Zhendong Wu$^{(\boxtimes)}$◉, and Juan Chen◉

Hangzhou Dianzi University, Hangzhou, China
{201270022,wzd,212270048}@hdu.edu.cn

Abstract. With the increasing popularity of biometric identity authentication in important key authentication applications, biometric key generation technology has attracted more and more attention. How to extract secure, stable and high-strength keys from biometrics has become a key research direction of biometric key generation technology. However, the proposed biometric key generation technology can not meet the security requirements as a key, that is, the key is easy to be cracked, resulting in unpredictable consequences. This paper presents a framework of voiceprint key generation based on deep neural network, which is mainly composed of voiceprint feature extraction model and fuzzy extraction model. The voiceprint feature extraction model is based on the deep neural network, and the sigmoid layer is added at the end of the neural network. This operation makes the features extracted by the neural network have high accuracy and low error recognition rate after binary quantization. The voiceprint database used in this paper is aishell-wakeup-1 wakeup word database. The voiceprint key generation model proposed in this paper generates the key on the voiceprint database with the generation intensity of more than 1000bit, the accuracy rate of more than 93%, and the error recognition rate of less than 0.001%. These data can prove that the voiceprint key generation model proposed in this paper can meet the needs of users for generation strength and security.

Keywords: Deep learning · Voiceprint bio-key · Fuzzy extraction

1 Introduction

In recent years, due to the rapid development of deep neural network, the biometric recognition rate has also reached a very high level. In addition, biometrics are easy to carry without storage and easy to use. Voiceprint recognition is a new technology. It has been proposed that biometric technology must store the user's voiceprint feature on the server or local security domain and other media for registration, and match it with the user's input voiceprint feature to realize the role of authentication. Unlike memory keys, human voice print features are unique. Once leaked, it can no longer be used for identity authentication. However, voiceprint templates stored in media are easy to be targeted by hackers, and often face the risk of disclosure. Because the existing biometric technology can not completely avoid the risk of template leakage, researchers are trying to develop a key generation technology that does not store biometric information.

Wu et al. [4] proposed a biological key generation method based on double-layer deep neural network has high accuracy, but the structure of the model is complex and the biological key generation time is long.

Therefore, this paper proposes a new voiceprint biokey generation framework. The framework combines the deep neural network model with the fuzzy extraction model. Compared with the above methods, the framework can extract voiceprint features and generate voiceprint keys faster and more accurately, and it is also easier to train and implement. The voiceprint biological key generated by the framework has the characteristics of high strength, high accuracy and strong robustness. The generated voiceprint biological key has more than 1000 bits and high strength. At the same time, the length of the bio-key generated by different voiceprints is also different, which further increases the randomness and intensity. In addition, the voiceprint biokey generation framework proposed in this paper does not need to save the collected voiceprint information. The collected voiceprint information is destroyed after being trained by the deep neural network model, which reduces the risk of voiceprint privacy information disclosure.

The main contributions of this study are as follows:

1) A new voiceprint biokey generation framework is proposed, including voiceprint feature extraction and key fuzzy extraction. This framework can well integrate the voiceprint features learned by deep neural network and fuzzy extraction in cryptography to obtain voiceprint keys with high strength, high accuracy and strong robustness.
2) After simple binary quantization and error correction, the fuzzy extraction model proposed in this paper can effectively stabilize the instability between deep neural network voiceprint features, and can greatly speed up the generation of stable keys at the same time.

The rest of this paper is arranged as follows. Section 2 discusses related work. The third section introduces the voiceprint biokey generation framework. The experimental results are presented and analyzed in Sect. 4. Finally, Sect. 5 presents concluding observations.

2   Related Work

In recent years, the research of biological key mainly focuses on template protection, key generation and key application. In 2012, Wang et al. [1] proposed a two-step hybrid method, which used random projection and hash points to generate cancelable voiceprint templates. In 2014, Wang et al. [2] used cyclic convolution to reduce the length of binary fingerprint feature vector and construct fingerprint template. The cyclic convolution process is unidirectional and irreversible; Therefore, the fingerprint template can be calibrated to make it scalable and diverse. In 2014, Kaur integrated iris, retina and finger vein, and introduced a new multi-functional fuzzy database framework [5]. In addition, Kaur used the minimum entropy method to measure and prove the security of the framework. In 2015, Lu and Teoh proposed a hybrid scalable palmprint coding cryptosystem called row independent and row symbiotic fuzzy library [6]. In the same year, sandhya et al. [7] used the k-order nearest neighbor structure and the user random matrix to build a secure fingerprint template for fingerprint feature points to protect the security of the original fingerprint data. Various formwork protection methods have limitations.

In order to improve the security of identity authentication, researchers began to use multiple biological information for identity authentication. In 2017, MOI and Pang proposed an identity authentication framework combining iris and face [8]. In 2018, Wu et al. Proposed a fingerprint and voiceprint multi-mode authentication framework based on dynamic Bayes [9]. In 2020, Gupta et al. Proposed a new revocable multi-mode biometric system [10]. The system generates revocable features from feature points, and then focus multiple feature data.

With the development of deep learning technology, Choudhury et al. [11] proposed an identity authentication method based on deep learning. Roy et al. [12] proposed a retinal feature extraction and identity authentication method based on deep learning. Wang et al. [13] proposed a fingerprint recognition algorithm based on deep neural network. Wu et al. [14] proposed a fingerprint depth neural network recognition algorithm based on the fusion of fingerprint feature point radial basis vector and fine image.

Varini et al. [15] studied speaker verification tasks related to small footprint texts using deep neural networks in 2014. Boles et al. [16] proposed a speaker recognition and verification scheme based on deep learning support vector machine model. Sun et al. [17] proposed a voiceprint recognition method based on the depth migration hybrid model in 2018. The model is a convolutional neural network hybrid restricted Boltzmann machine based on transfer learning, which makes it easier to realize voiceprint recognition in the case of small samples. Gulati et al. [18] proposed a convolution enhancement converter for speech recognition, named Transformer. Transformer is obviously superior to the previous models based on transformer and CNN, and achieves the most advanced accuracy. The above research work is still in the biometric stage, and the research on voiceprint biometric key generation has not been carried out.

Sheng et al. [19] proposed a semi supervised clustering scheme optimized by niche meme algorithm is proposed to effectively simulate the changes within and between users at the same time. This method used a single feature and feature subset to model the changes of biological information, so as to recover the feature elements for key generation. On this basis, a key generation method is proposed. Wu et al. [3] proposed a method to extract the biological key, projected the biological feature vector into the high-dimensional space, and stabilized the feature vector of the same finger vein within a certain fluctuation range in the high-dimensional space. In general, the success rate and strength of biological key generation is not high enough, the error rate is not low enough, and the security cannot be guaranteed. Wang et al. [20] proposed a deep neural network biological key generation model based on senet structure. The test result of this model in the actual biometric database is not ideal. Wang et al. proposed a fingerprint key generation method based on feature distance and generation interval [21]. This method used the fingerprint feature distance and generation interval mechanism to generate the user's fingerprint key, which avoids the direct disclosure of fingerprint information to a certain extent. The double-layer error correction technology and sha256 function are combined to ensure the accuracy and fault tolerance of the fingerprint key. In the process of fingerprint key generation, the method preserves fingerprint features and key information, such as fingerprint feature distance, generation interval and segmented biological key. The information must be stored in the local security domain; Therefore, the security of the whole method depends on the vulnerable local security domain. The existing schemes of fingerprint biometric key generation are based on classical fingerprint feature point extraction; However, feature point extraction does not achieve high stability. Therefore, all types of fingerprint key generation schemes can not achieve the desired accuracy and robustness. Ibrahim et al. [22] proposed a biometric encryption scheme for speech recognition data based on software architecture in 2021. This scheme uses dynamic time warping (DTW) technology to solve the problem that the duration of speech biometric recognition changes with nonlinear scaling. Then, the method uses a database to store a single binding key into the user's equivalent biometric enhancement template. The identity of the key will remain hidden unless the biometric is successfully verified by the target.

Recently, several studies have been carried out on the application of biometric encryption. Zhang et al. [26] proposed a hierarchical group key agreement protocol based on direct attributes, and applied biological keys to group key agreement to save computing overhead. Zhang et al. [27] combined the biological key with attribute encryption and applied it to vehicular ad hoc networks (VANETs), which can better protect the privacy group user information. Panchal et al. [28] designed a new biometric based authentication protocol to provide secure access to remote cloud servers. Zhang et al. [29] applied biological key to proxy pre encryption technology, proposed an identity based anonymous data storage scheme in fog computing scenario, and proved its security in random predictor. Tian et al. [30] used the biological key to audit the shared data in the cloud environment, and used the random masking method to blind prove the data, which has better data privacy protection. Sammoud et al. [31] applied the biological key to the secure communication system of wireless body area network, which can effectively reduce the cost of key negotiation. Mahendran et al. [32] applied the key technology of biometrics to the motion sensor network (BSN) and developed a secure fuzzy extractor combined with fuzzy vault to provide higher security by using biometric key authentication scheme. Hong et al. [33] proposed a a new health assessment framework for lithium-ion batteries to construct an efficient defense mechanism. The framework could mitigate the effects of variable operation conditions to the evaluating process. Ren et al. [34]

proposed an integrated deep learning approach for RUL prediction of lithium-ion battery by integrating autoencoder with deep neural network.

3   Voiceprint Key Generation Model

This paper presents a voiceprint biological key generation model, which is composed of three parts: fbank feature extraction model, deep neural network and voiceprint biological key fuzzy extraction model. The voiceprint key generation framework is shown in Fig. 1. The framework can effectively perform normal voiceprint biological key generation. The generated key has the characteristics of strong randomness and long key length, which can meet the security needs of users.

Fig. 1. Overall flow chart of voiceprint key generation model.

In this paper, the filter bank algorithm is used to preprocess the 80 dimensional fbank features extracted from voiceprints. This method can contain more voiceprint information, which is helpful for the training of deep neural network. Figure 2 shows the extraction process of fbank features.

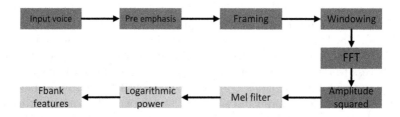

Fig. 2. Fbank

The depth feature extraction model learns through the depth neural network, and then extracts the deep features from the fbank features. Figure 3 shows the structure of the fuzzy extraction model.

The deep neural network model combines ECAPA-TDNN with the encoder structure of transformer to build a more lightweight model, transformer TDNN. Convolutional neural network has very advanced computer vision tasks, such as image classification, object detection and instance segmentation. This is largely due to convolution, which collects local features in a hierarchical manner as a powerful image representation. Although CNN has advantages in local feature

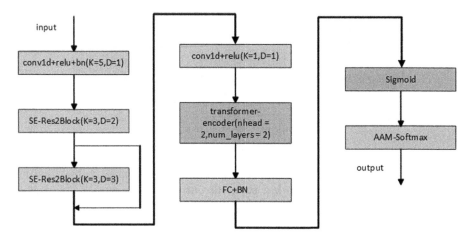

Fig. 3. Improved voiceprint recognition depth neural network with transformer encoder and sigmoid function.

extraction, it has difficulties in capturing global representations, such as the relationship between remote information elements, which is usually very important for speaker recognition tasks. Attention mechanism can also solve this problem, so we introduce attention mechanism into deep neural network and add transformer encoder module to the network structure. The res2net module in ECAPA-TDNN introduces compression and excitation blocks to clarify the interdependence of modeling channels. The module extends the time context of the frame layer by rescaling the channels according to the recorded global attributes. Secondly, convolutional neural network can learn depth and shallow features. The complexity of each feature layer is different, and the information expressed is also different. To take advantage of this complementary information, we aggregate and disseminate features at different levels. Shallower feature mapping also contributes to more robust speaker embedding. We use jump connection to combine deep and shallow features, which makes the model more powerful. Note that the number of operations required by the mechanism to calculate the correlation between two locations is independent of distance. In addition, self attention can produce a more explanatory model. We can examine the distribution of attention from the model. Each attention leader can learn to perform different tasks. Just like the deep features and shallow features in convolutional neural networks, the features learned by each attention head can complement each other and complete the accurate output of features, which is more helpful for the key generation task. Figure 4 shows the bottle2neck structure.

Because the deep neural network is trained and output end-to-end, and its interpretability is weak, the output of neural network on untrained new samples may exceed the prediction of the output of training set. This output can be used for identification tasks, but can not be used as a biological bond. Therefore, this paper adds a sigmoid activation function before the output layer of the neural

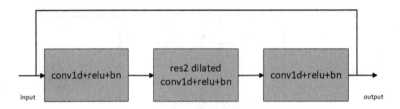

Fig. 4. Improved se-res2block module.

network to control the output of the neural network between 0–1, thus limiting the output of the neural network. Fixing the output of the neural network in a controllable range can reduce the risk, and then taking 0.5 as the boundary, the output of the neural network is used as the voiceprint key.

Transformer TDNN simplifies and processes the classical ECAPA-TDNN [25] model, introduces attention mechanism, adds sigmoid function at the end of the model, and uses AAM softmax [23] as the loss function for training. The training sample set is composed of voiceprint features processed by fbank algorithm. After training the training set samples, the output vector of sigmoid activation function is extracted as the depth feature. The depth feature is a vector composed of 0–1 elements. Using this vector as a 0.5 boundary, we can get a 01 bit string that can be used as a key. However, the current 01 bit string can not meet the requirements of high security of biological key, and the accuracy is not high enough. The fuzzy extraction model needs to generate a more stable bit string as a stable voiceprint key.

Alg1 describes the key generation process of deep neural networks. The whole biokey generation framework based on deep learning first uses the training data set to train the neural network, and then generates the key through the training data set. For the key generated from the training data set is not stable enough, we should continue to select the stable position in the key, and finally use the test data set to generate the key.

The fuzzy extraction model studied in this paper uses error correcting code technology to correct 8 bits of the key with a length of more than 1000 bits, so as to further reduce the instability of voiceprint features. Error correcting codes can obtain higher data reliability with less data redundancy, but the coding method is complex and the amount of computation is large. Error correcting codes can only tolerate data loss, but not data tampering. This is the name of the error correction code. Error code is a coding technique that can add m data to N original data and recover to the original data through any n data in n+m. That is, if any data less than or equal to m fails, it can still be recovered from the remaining data.

Algorithm 1. Voiceprint key generation algorithm

Input: voice
Output: bio-key
    train_ds=$train_1, train_2, ..., train_n$ # The training dataset of the voiceprint
    test_ds=$test_1, test_2, ..., test_n$ # The testing dataset of the voiceprint
    Model # The transformer-tdnn
    Function Train(model, dataset):
        for e in range(epoch)
            for $data_i$ in dataset
                z_i=model($data_i$)
                y'=sigmoid(z_i)
                loss=AAM-softmax(y',y_i)
                loss.backward()
            endfor
        endfor
    Function Selection(bio-vector):
        for e,e+1 in bio-vectors
            for j in range(len(e))
                if e[j]=e+1[j]:
                    store
                else:
                    delete
            endfor
        endfor
    Q1=Train(Model, train_ds)
    bio-vector-train = Q1(train_ds)
    bio-vector-test=Q1(test_ds)
    S1 = Selection(bio-vector-train)
    bio-key = S1(bio-vector-test)
Return: bio-key

4 Experiment

The voiceprint database used in the experiment is the open source wake-up word database aishell-wakeup-1 [24]. Aishell-wakeup-1 voice database has a total of 3936003 wake-up words, 1561.12 h. Recording language, Chinese and English; Recording area, China. The recording text is "Hello, Mia" and "Hi, Mia", and the time of each recording is about 1 s. 290 speakers were invited to participate in the recording. In the recording process, seven recording bits are set in the real home environment, and six circular 16 channel PDM microphone array recording boards are used for far speaking pickup (16KHz, 16bit) and one high fidelity microphone for near speaking pickup (44.1KHz, 16bit). The database has been transcribed and marked by professional voice proofreaders, and has passed strict quality inspection. The word accuracy is 100%. It can be used in voiceprint recognition, voice wake-up recognition and other research. In this paper, 100 kinds of voiceprints are used to train the deep neural network. 60% of these 100 kinds of voiceprints are used as the training set, 40% as the test set to verify the accuracy, and together with the other 190 kinds of voiceprints, they are used as the sample set of error recognition rate. The other 190 voiceprints do not participate in the training and are completely used as the sample set to test the error rate. In the laboratory environment, the experimental model runs in x64 computing environment with i9-9900k CPU, 32 GB ram and 2080ti GPU with 11 GB ram. All algorithms run on the same aishell-wakeup-1 voiceprint database. After the voiceprint is processed by the model, the voiceprint biological key is obtained. The accuracy and loss of the model training proposed in this paperare shown in Figs. 5 and 6.

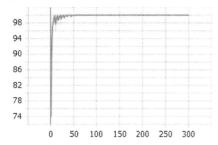

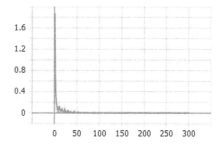

Fig. 5. The speech recognition accuracy of transformer TDNN on the verification data set.

Fig. 6. Transformer TDNN's loss during training.

The comprehensive accuracy of the experiment is shown in Table 1. The average accuracy rate is the test result of 40% test set of 100 training set samples. The lowest accuracy rate is the result with the lowest accuracy rate of 100 voiceprints. The same is true for the highest accuracy rate. The comprehensive error rate is shown in Table 2. The average false recognition rate is the result of using 100 training set samples to remove this kind of samples, and the other 99 test sets plus 190 kinds of all voiceprints. The test false recognition rate of each kind of samples should be tested with other 289 kinds of samples. The lowest error rate is the test result of the sample with the lowest error rate among 100 types of samples, and the highest error rate is the same. The model proposed in this paper is modified based on ECAPA-TDNN. Wang et al. [20] proposed a deep neural network bio-key generation model based on the Senet structure, which mainly generates bio-keys for human faces. We apply this method to voiceprint, use feature extraction models suitable for different samples to extract features, and then map the features directly to the customized key for training, so as not to let the neural network train the feature vector by itself. Chung, Joon son et al. [35] proposed a deep neural network recognition model based on RESNET structure with fewer parameters, which mainly recognizes voiceprints and has high accuracy. We use this model to replace the neural network in the framework proposed in this paper to generate voiceprint biological keys. We compare the key generation capabilities of the comparative models from many aspects. Table 1 and Table 2 show these comparisons.

Table 1. Accuracy of transformer-tdnn compared with other models

Model	Average precision	Min precision	Max precision
ECAPA-TDNN [25]	0.913	0.818	1.0
SENet-DNN [20]	0	0	0
resnet-2d-cnn [35]	0.999	0.987	1.0
transformer-tdnn	0.92	0.855	1.0

Table 2. Err of transformer-tdnn compared with other models

Model	Average err	Min err	Max err
ECAPA-TDNN [25]	8.682e−07	0.0	8.68e−05
SENet-DNN [20]	0	0	0
resnet-2d-cnn [35]	0.645	0.195	0.997
transformer-tdnn	8.68e−07	0	4.341e−05

Through two groups of comparative experiments, the advantages of the voice key generation model proposed in this paper in accuracy and error recognition rate are compared. The lowest accuracy indicates the stability of the voiceprint key generation model in generating keys, and the stability of key generation will not be reduced due to the disturbance caused by voiceprint recording. The highest accuracy indicates the highest ability of the voiceprint key generation model. Table 1 shows that the voiceprint key generation model has high ability. In terms of the error rate, the key output from the voiceprint key generation model has a high discrimination. It can be seen from the above table that resnet-2d-cnn has a high accuracy and error recognition rate. This is because the output vectors of resnet-2d-cnn are not differentiated, and the model output vectors corresponding to each type of voiceprint have high similarity after passing through the sigmoid layer. After error correction, the similarity is further increased, making the error recognition rate reach 64.5%, and high stability keys cannot be generated. The accuracy, error rate and time comparison of the four models are shown in Table 3.

It can be seen from Table 3 that the accuracy of the output of convolutional neural network is directly mapped into a key is not as good as the voiceprint key generation model proposed in this paper. By mapping the output of the model directly to the user-defined key to calculate the loss, the training neural network has great limitations on the training of the model. The self-defined key can not make the neural network learn the deep relationship between data sets, so the

Table 3. The proposed model compared with other models.

Model	Precision	Err	Time	Classify accuracy
ECAPA-TDNN [25]	0.913	8.682e−07	0.033	0.995
SENet-DNN [20]	0	0	0.033	0.992
resnet-2d-cnn [35]	0.999	0.645	0.009	0
transformer-tdnn	0.92	8.682e−07	0.025	0.995

training effect is not good, and the accurate key cannot be generated. SENet-DNN method has a high error recognition rate, and the security performance of the generated key is not very high, which can be further improved. When comparing the output keys of the training set, only the keys with a length of about 150 bits in the 1024 bit keys are stable. The accuracy of the three network training is more than 99%, but it can be seen from the key generation results that the accuracy can not reflect the ability of the model key generation. When calculating the accuracy, the one hot vector is used. The one hot vector can only ensure the stability of a certain element on the whole vector, but can not ensure the stability of the whole vector. The model proposed in this paper limits the output of the deep neural network and enhances the stability of the output vector to a certain extent. Although resnet-2d-cnn has a good effect in recognizing voiceprints, after we modify the network to generate voiceprint keys, this model will lose the ability to recognize voiceprints. After training, the original resnet-2d-cnn outputs vector values between 0.5–1. Although the difference between vector values is not large, the recognition accuracy can still reach 98%. After adding the sigmoid layer, the value of the output vector cannot be trained to be balanced between 0–1, and is still concentrated between 0.5–1, which makes most of the output vector values after binary quantization are 1, and the average 1000 bit vector is only about 10 bit 0. The distribution of 0 in each type of voiceprint output vector is relatively similar. We use an 8 bit error correction 1000 bit vector, This eliminates the generated key failure caused by the difference between the distribution of a small number of zeros in the output vector and the target key. Therefore, the effect of resnet-2d-cnn generated key is unstable.

5   Conclusion and Future Work

The voiceprint recognition framework proposed in this paper combines the deep learning model with the biological key generation, uses the deep neural network to extract the features with certain stability, and then quantizes and fuzzy extracts the features to generate the biological key with high stability. The performance of the voiceprint recognition framework proposed in this paper is mainly related to the recognition ability of deep neural network. The recognition ability of the existing ECAPA-TDNN network has a good recognition effect on specific voiceprints. The next step is to improve the generalization ability of the network and make it have strong recognition ability for all voiceprints. The goal of subsequent research is to reduce the generation time of voiceprint key to less than 0.01 s. In the next stage of work, we will continue to optimize the model to further reduce the error recognition rate, and expand the model to various fields of biological key generation, including face, finger vein and signature handwriting. For applications requiring higher security, we will also study multimodal biometric key recognition, integrate various human features, and generate biometric keys with higher strength. Our goal is to help people avoid using high-intensity memory in daily life.

Acknowledgements. This research is supported by Key Projects of NSFC Joint Fund of China (No. U1866209), National Natural Science Foundation of China (No. 61772162), National Key R&D Program of China (No. 2018YFB0804102).

References

1. Zhu, H.H., He, Q.H., Li, Y.X.: A two-step hybrid approach for voiceprint-biometric template protection. In: 2012 International Conference on Machine Learning and Cybernetics, vol. 2, pp. 560–565. IEEE (2012)
2. Wang, S., Hu, J.: Design of alignment-free cancelable fingerprint templates via curtailed circular convolution. Pattern Recogn. **47**(3), 1321–1329 (2014)
3. Wu, Z., Tian, L., Li, P., et al.: Generating stable biometric keys for flexible cloud computing authentication using finger vein. Inf. Sci. **433**, 431–447 (2018)
4. Wu, Z., Lv, Z., Kang, J., et al.: Fingerprint bio-key generation based on a deep neural network. Int. J. Intell. Syst. **37**(7), 4329–4358 (2021)
5. Kaur, M.: Multimodal based fuzzy vault using iris retina and fingervein. In: 2013 Fourth International Conference on Computing, Communications and Networking Technologies (ICCCNT), pp. 1–5. IEEE (2013)
6. Leng, L., Teoh, A.B.J.: Alignment-free row-co-occurrence cancelable palmprint fuzzy vault. Pattern Recogn. **48**(7), 2290–2303 (2015)
7. Sandhya, M., Prasad, M.V.N.K.: k-Nearest Neighborhood Structure (k-NNS) based alignment-free method for fingerprint template protection. In: 2015 International Conference on Biometrics (ICB), pp. 386–393. IEEE (2015)
8. Moi, S.H., Yong, P.Y.: A modified reed Solomon error correction codes for multimodal biometrics recognition. In: 2017 3rd International Conference on Control, Automation and Robotics (ICCAR), pp. 418–422. IEEE (2017)
9. Wu, Z., Yang, J., Zhang, J., et al.: Multibiometric fusion authentication in wireless multimedia environment using dynamic Bayesian method. Secur. Commun. Netw. **2018**, 1–12 (2018)
10. Gupta, K., Walia, G.S., Sharma, K.: Novel approach for multimodal feature fusion to generate cancelable biometric. Visual Comput. **37**(6), 1401–1413 (2021)
11. Choudhury, S.H., Kumar, A., Laskar, S.H.: Biometric authentication through unification of finger dorsal biometric traits. Inf. Sci. **497**, 202–218 (2019)
12. Roy, N.D., Biswas, A.: Fast and robust retinal biometric key generation using deep neural nets. Multimedia Tools Appl. **79**(9), 6823–6843 (2020)
13. Wang, R., Han, C., Wu, Y., et al.: Fingerprint classification based on depth neural network. arXiv preprint arXiv:1409.5188 (2014)
14. Wu, Z., Wang, Y., Zhang, J.: Fouling and damaged fingerprint recognition based on deep learning. J. Electron. Inf. Technol. **39**(7), 1585–1591 (2017)

15. Variani, E., Lei, X., McDermott, E., et al.: Deep neural networks for small footprint text-dependent speaker verification. In: 2014 IEEE International Conference on Acoustics, Speech and Signal Processing (ICASSP), pp. 4052–4056. IEEE (2014)
16. Boles, A., Rad, P.: Voice biometrics: deep learning-based voiceprint authentication system. In: 2017 12th System of Systems Engineering Conference (SoSE), pp. 1–6. IEEE (2017)
17. Sun, C., Yang, Y., Wen, C., et al.: Voiceprint identification for limited dataset using the deep migration hybrid model based on transfer learning. Sensors **18**(7), 2399 (2018)
18. Gulati, A., Qin, J., Chiu, C.C., et al.: Conformer: convolution-augmented transformer for speech recognition. arXiv preprint arXiv:2005.08100 (2020)
19. Sheng, W., Chen, S., Xiao, G., et al.: A biometric key generation method based on semisupervised data clustering. IEEE Trans. Syst. Man Cybern. Syst. **45**(9), 1205–1217 (2015)
20. Wang, Y., Li, B., Zhang, Y., et al.: A secure biometric key generation mechanism via deep learning and its application. Appl. Sci. **11**(18), 8497 (2021)
21. Wang, P., You, L., Hu, G., et al.: Biometric key generation based on generated intervals and two-layer error correcting technique. Pattern Recogn. **111**, 107733 (2021)
22. Ibrahim, A.J., Jauro, U.A.: Bio-metric encryption of data using voice recognition. Autom. Control Intell. Syst. **9**(3), 89 (2021)
23. Deng, J., Guo, J., Xue, N., et al.: Arcface: additive angular margin loss for deep face recognition. In: Proceedings of the IEEE/CVF Conference on Computer Vision and Pattern Recognition, pp. 4690–4699 (2019)
24. Qin, X., Bu, H., Li, M.: HI-MIA: a far-field text-dependent speaker verification database and the baselines. In: 2020 IEEE International Conference on Acoustics, Speech and Signal Processing (ICASSP), ICASSP 2020, pp. 7609–7613. IEEE (2020)
25. Desplanques, B., Thienpondt, J., Demuynck, K.: ECAPA-TDNN: emphasized channel attention, propagation and aggregation in TDNN based speaker verification. arXiv preprint arXiv:2005.07143 (2020)
26. Zhang, Q., Wang, X., Yuan, J., et al.: A hierarchical group key agreement protocol using orientable attributes for cloud computing. Inf. Sci. **480**, 55–69 (2019)
27. Zhang, Q., Gan, Y., Liu, L., et al.: An authenticated asymmetric group key agreement based on attribute encryption. J. Netw. Comput. Appl. **123**, 1–10 (2018)
28. Panchal, G., Samanta, D., Das, A.K., et al.: Designing secure and efficient biometric-based secure access mechanism for cloud services. IEEE Trans. Cloud Comput. **10**, 749–761 (2020)
29. Zhang, J., Bai, W., Wang, X.: Identity-based data storage scheme with anonymous key generation in fog computing. Soft. Comput. **24**(8), 5561–5571 (2020)
30. Tian, H., Nan, F., Jiang, H., et al.: Public auditing for shared cloud data with efficient and secure group management. Inf. Sci. **472**, 107–125 (2019)
31. Sammoud, A., Chalouf, M.A., Hamdi, O., et al.: A new biometrics-based key establishment protocol in WBAN: energy efficiency and security robustness analysis. Comput. Secur. **96**, 101838 (2020)
32. Mahendran, R.K., Velusamy, P.: A secure fuzzy extractor based biometric key authentication scheme for body sensor network in Internet of Medical Things. Comput. Commun. **153**, 545–552 (2020)
33. Hong, S., Zeng, Y.: A health assessment framework of lithium-ion batteries for cyber defense. Appl. Soft Comput. **101**, 107067 (2021)

34. Ren, L., Zhao, L., Hong, S., et al.: Remaining useful life prediction for lithium-ion battery: a deep learning approach. IEEE Access **6**, 50587–50598 (2018)
35. Chung, J.S., Huh, J., Mun, S., et al.: In defence of metric learning for speaker recognition. arXiv preprint arXiv:2003.11982 (2020)

Domain Adversarial Interaction Network for Cross-Domain Fault Diagnosis

Weikai Lu[1,2], Jian Chen[1,2], Hao Zheng[3], Haoyi Fan[3], Eng Yee Wei[4], Xinrong Cao[2], and Deyang Zhang[5(✉)]

[1] School of Electronic, Electrical Engineering and Physics,
Fujian University of Technology, Fuzhou 350118, China
[2] Fujian Provincial Key Laboratory of Information Processing and Intelligent
Control, College of Computer and Control Engineering, Minjiang University,
Fuzhou 350121, China
[3] School of Computer and Artificial Intelligence, Zhengzhou University,
Zhengzhou 450001, China
[4] School of Computer Sciences, Universiti Sains Malaysia, Penang 11800, Malaysia
[5] Henan Provincial Institute of Scientific and Technical Information,
Zhengzhou 450003, China
zhdy@qq.com

Abstract. Intelligent fault diagnosis has been widely used in the industry and plays a crucial role in the health management of machinery. In recent years, unsupervised domain adaptation (UDA) has been applied to fault diagnosis, showing excellent performance under variable working conditions. However, most existing UDA-based methods do not consider the temporal relations in the fault signal, resulting in sub-optimal performance. In this paper, we proposed a domain adversarial interaction network (DAIN) to solve this problem. By downsampling sub-sequences of fault signals and interacting with their features, DAIN can obtain feature representations containing the temporal relations. In addition, domain adversarial learning and maximum mean discrepancy (MMD) are applied to DAIN to align the domain discrepancy and distribution discrepancy of source and target domains. We conducted extensive experiments on the public Paderborn University (PU) dataset, and the results demonstrate that the proposed method can achieve higher cross-domain fault diagnosis accuracy than the existing methods.

Keywords: Fault diagnosis · Unsupervised domain adaptation · Adversarial learning

1 Introduction

As one of the key parts of a rotating machine, the status monitoring of the rotating bearing is important to the safe running of the rotating machine [12, 20].

Y. Xu et al. (Eds.): ML4CS 2022, LNCS 13656, pp. 436–446, 2023.
https://doi.org/10.1007/978-3-031-20099-1_37

Fault diagnosis, aims to judge the classes of the early fault of rotating bearing, so as to prevent the paralysis of the whole system, ensuring the safety and reliable operation of the system [11]. In recent years, with the development of artificial intelligence technology, intelligent fault diagnosis technology has been widely used in modern industries, serving the real-time monitoring of devices and health status management.

The traditional machine learning-based fault diagnosis method, including support vector machine [7], logistic regression [17], has been extensively studied and applied in real-world scenarios. However, traditional methods rely on manual features and advanced signal processing techniques, which makes their application difficult and expensive. With the explosive growth of data volume, deep learning technology [4,5], which does not require manual features as input, has become a research hotspot and has achieved higher diagnostic accuracy. For example, Jillian et al. [2] proposed a multiscale convolutional neural network, which can capture more rich diagnosis information, and achieve better performance. Yin et al. [21] proposed an optimized long short term memory network with cosine loss, which converts the loss from Euclidean space to angular space, reducing the impact of signal strength.

Traditional fault diagnosis methods assume that training samples and testing samples are independent and identically distributed. However, such assumptions are often not valid in real application scenarios, such as large distribution differences in data collected from bearings under different working conditions. Collecting enough training data for each different working condition is labor-intensive and expensive, which greatly reduces the practical significance of these methods. To solve the above problem, some unsupervised domain adaptation (UDA) based methods, which aim to transfer knowledge from a labeled domain to an unlabeled domain, have emerged. Existing UDA-based methods mainly include mapping-based methods [1,13,15,19] and adversarial-based methods [6,14]. The Mapping-based method minimizes the distribution distance of the features extracted by the feature extractor so that the feature extractor can map the source domain and the target domain into a shared feature space. The maximum mean discrepancy (MMD) is the most commonly used mapping-based method, which maps the representation into the Reproducing Kernel Hilbert Space (RKHS) space and minimizes the kernel embedding distance between different domains. The adversarial-based method adds a domain discriminator for adversarial training so that the feature extractor can extract features that the domain discriminator cannot distinguish. Recently, Li et al. [9] have combined mapping-based and adversarial-based methods, modeled the data structure information of signals via a graph convolution neural network, and achieved excellent performance in cross-domain diagnosis.

Although existing methods have been able to achieve encouraging cross-domain fault diagnosis results, they fail to take into account the temporal relations in the time series, resulting in sub-optimal diagnostic accuracy. The odd and even sub-sequences of a time series are offsets with a unit time interval, and their relationship reflects the slight variation pattern of the signal. To capture this pattern, we propose a new cross-domain fault diagnosis method, called DAIN. Specifically, We first construct an interaction network to extract feature embedding including temporal relation between signal sub-sequences, then distinguish the fault classes by classifier and domain labels by domain discriminator, all of which make up an end-to-end network structure. To align the feature distributions of the source and target domains, we introduced MMD loss and domain adversarial loss to participate in the training of the network.

In sum, the main contributions of this paper are as follows:

- We propose an interaction network to extract the temporal relations of signals. By downsampling sub-sequences of signals and feature interaction, the slight variation pattern in a signal can be more easily obtained.
- We introduce MMD loss and domain discriminator for end-to-end domain adaptation. By joint training with the interaction network, more domain-invariant representation can be captured.
- We conduct experiments on the PU dataset, and the experimental results show the superiority of the proposed method.

2   Methodologies

In this section, we provide an overview of the proposed method, which is depicted in Fig. 1. Firstly, we feed the raw data to the interaction network to extract the feature representation containing the temporal relation information. Then, the obtained features are input into the classification network for fault classification. In addition, the domain discriminator is designed to perform adversarial training with the feature extractor, and the MMD loss is added for aligning the feature distribution discrepancy between the two domains. The detailed structure of the proposed method is shown in Table 1.

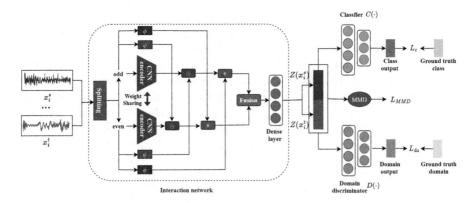

Fig. 1. The framework of the proposed method.

2.1   Problem Statement

In this work, we investigate the UDA fault diagnosis problem. Suppose we have a labeled dataset $D_s = \{x_i^s, y_i^s\}_{i=1}^{|D_s|}$ sampled from source domain P^s and a unlabeled dataset $D_t = \{x_i^t\}_{i=1}^{|D_t|}$ sampled from target domain P^t, where samples in P^s and P^t share the same label space but with different probability distribution. Given D_s and D_t, our goal is to train a function $f(\cdot)$ to predict fault classes of the samples from P^t.

Table 1. Structures of the proposed method

Network	Layer	Filter	Output size
CNN Encoder $F(\cdot)$	Input	/	N×1024
	Conv1D, BN, LeakyReLU	8×4×1	N×8×512
	Conv1D, BN, LeakyReLU	16×4×1	N×16×256
	Conv1D, BN, LeakyReLU	32×4×1	N×32×128
	Conv1D, BN, LeakyReLU	64×4×1	N×64×64
	Pooling	1×1 Adaptive max-pooling	N×64×1
$\phi(\cdot)$ and $\psi(\cdot)$	Conv1D, BN, LeakyReLU	32×4×1	N×32×512
	Conv1D, BN, LeakyReLU	64×4×1	N×64×256
	Pooling	1×1 Adaptive max-pooling	N×64×1
Classifier $C(\cdot)$	Linear, Softmax	64×n_class	N×n_class
Domain Discriminator $D(\cdot)$	Linear, ReLU, Dropout	64×64	N×64
	Linear, ReLU, Dropout	64×64	N×64
	Linear, Sigmoid	64×1	N×1

2.2   Feature Extractor

Inspired by the work of [10], We designed an interaction network as feature extractor $Z(\cdot)$. For an original signal X from source or target domains, we first split it into odd sub-sequence X_{odd} and even sub-sequence X_{even}. Figure 2 shows the detailed process of the splitting module.

Next, we extracted features from X_{odd} and X_{even} using a four-layer CNN encoder with shared weights, and the obtained features are represented by F_{odd} and F_{even}. Due to the information loss in the two sub-sequences, the feature interaction between the two sequences is carried out by learning affine transformation functions. The process can be defined as:

$$F'_{odd} = F_{odd} \odot \exp(\phi(F_{even})) + \psi(F_{even}), \qquad (1)$$

$$F'_{even} = F_{even} \odot \exp(\phi(F_{odd})) + \psi(F_{odd}), \qquad (2)$$

where $\odot$ is the Hadamard product, ϕ and ψ are two projection functions that project the sequence to two hidden states for multiplication and addition transformations of another sequence. Finally, two sub-sequence features are fused through a nonlinear transformation to achieve the overall feature:

$$F = ReLU(W[F'_{odd}, F'_{even}] + b), \qquad (3)$$

where $ReLU(\cdot)$ is nonlinear activation function, W and b are trainable weight matrix and bias vector, respectively.

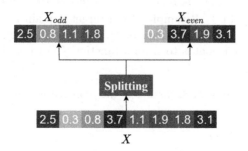

Fig. 2. The detailed process of splitting module.

2.3 Fault Classifier

To identify the fault classes of extracted feature representation, a fully connection layer with a softmax activation function is used as a classifier. During the training phase, only the labeled source domain data are used as input for the classifier. To measure the discrepancy between the predicted classes and the ground truth labels, the cross-entropy loss is regarded as classification loss:

$$L_C = E_{\left(x_i^s, y_i^s\right) \sim P^s} L\left(C\left(Z\left(x_i^s\right)\right), y_i^s\right), \tag{4}$$

where $L(\cdot)$ is the cross-entropy loss, $C(\cdot)$ is the classifier, $E(\cdot)$ is the mathematical expectation.

2.4 Domain Discriminator

Due to the large distribution discrepancy between source and target domains, the feature extractor that only trains with the source domain samples cannot provide a valid feature representation for the target domain samples, resulting in low classification accuracy. To solve that problem, a domain discriminator consisting of a multi-layer perceptron is used for determining whether feature representation comes from a source or target domain, and conducting adversarial training to deceive the feature extractor and domain discriminator from each other. Intuitively, the domain discriminator is trained to better distinguish domain sources, while the feature extractor is trained to generate feature representation that cannot be identified by the discriminator. After adversarial training, the feature extractor can extract domain-invariant features. We use the cross-entropy loss as the adversarial loss, which can be defined as:

$$\min_{D} \max_{Z} L_D = E_{x_i^s \sim P^s} \log\left(1 - D\left(Z\left(x_i^s\right)\right)\right) + E_{x_j^t \sim P^t} \log\left(D\left(Z\left(x_j^t\right)\right)\right), \quad (5)$$

where $D(\cdot)$ represent the domain discriminator.

2.5 Feature Distribution Alignment

To align the feature distribution discrepancy from the source and target domains, the MMD loss is applied to the proposed method, which can be defined as:

$$L_{MMD} = \left\| E_{x_i^s \sim P_s} Z\left(x_i^s\right) - E_{x_j^t \sim P_t} Z\left(x_j^t\right) \right\|_{\Omega}^2, \quad (6)$$

where Ω represents the RKHS.

2.6 Objective Funtion

Combining classification loss, domain adversarial loss, and feature distribution alignment loss, the ultimate optimization objective of the proposed method can be defined as:

$$L = L_C + \alpha L_D + \beta L_{MMD}, \quad (7)$$

where α and β are adjustable parameters.

3 Experiments

3.1 Data Description

The PU dataset was collected from the Paderborn University rig test and it consists of artificially induced and real damages. The PU dataset includes four different working conditions under different drive system speeds, radial forces on the test bearings, and load torque on the drive systems, as shown in Table 2. Thirteen failure classes KA04, KA15, KA16, KA22, KA30, KB23, KB24, KB27, KI14, KI16, KI17, KI18, and KI21, are adopted according to [22]. Figure 3 shows the experimental scenario of the PU dataset.

3.2 Compared Approaches

To demonstrate the superiority of the proposed DAIN method, Six methods including MLP, CNN, CORAL [19], JMMD [15], CDANN [14], CDANN+E [14] are implemented. Both MLP and CNN are simply training with source domain samples and testing with target domain samples, and others are UDA-based methods. In addition, MLP uses four full connection layers as the backbone network, while the others use a four-layer CNN encoder the same as the proposed method.

Table 2. The parameters for different working conditions on the PU dataset

Conditions	Load Torque	Radial Force	Speed
0	0.7	1000	1500
1	0.7	1000	900
2	0.1	1000	1500
3	0.7	400	1500

Fig. 3. The experimental scenario of the PU dataset. [8]

3.3   Experimental Setting

The experiments were coded with PyTorch(v1.10.0) [18] and conducted on one workstation with an Intel Xenon Silver 4210 CPU and an NVIDIA GeForce RTX 3080 Ti GPU. In model training, each method is trained with 1000 epochs, of which the first 20 epochs are pre-training without target domain samples. The Adam optimizer [3] was used in all experiments. The initial learning rate is set to 0.005 and divided by 10 at epochs 300 and 600. The L2 regularization coefficient is set to 1e-5. The evaluation metrics of all experiments are classification accuracy. To minimize the impact of randomness on the experimental results, all the experimental results are shown as the average results of 5 runs.

3.4   Experimental Results

Quantitative Results. Table 3 shows the experimental results of the proposed DAIN method and comparison methods. It is observed that DAIN performs best among all comparison methods in all tasks, and its average accuracy outperforms the best baseline CDANN+E by 9.39%. Notably, in Task 1-0, the diagnostic accuracy of DAIN increased by 18.43% compared to the best baseline. These high-precision performances demonstrate the superiority of DAIN in cross-domain fault diagnosis tasks.

Ablation Analysis. To explore the rationality of the design of each component, two variants of DAIN are designed for comparison: 1)DACNN: DAIN without

Table 3. The experimental results of all comparison methods

Approachs	Tasks												Average
	0-1	0-2	0-3	1-0	1-2	1-3	2-0	2-1	2-3	3-0	3-1	3-2	
DAIN	**0.7245**	**0.9292**	**0.7362**	**0.7401**	**0.7631**	0.4206	**0.9303**	**0.7163**	**0.7486**	0.6882	0.4890	**0.7472**	**0.7188**
MLP	0.2945	0.4644	0.3498	0.2811	0.2690	0.1870	0.4544	0.2991	0.3455	0.3339	0.2298	0.3447	0.3211
CNN	0.5552	0.8699	0.5359	0.5330	0.5472	0.3646	0.8578	0.5862	0.5392	0.5521	0.4086	0.5780	0.5773
JMMD [15]	0.6439	0.8867	0.6324	0.6157	0.6394	0.4466	0.9023	0.6101	0.6297	0.6424	0.4531	0.6278	0.6442
CORAL [19]	0.5779	0.8942	0.6566	0.5349	0.5502	0.3707	0.8783	0.5776	0.6514	0.6243	0.4242	0.6116	0.6127
CDANN [14]	0.6377	0.9029	0.7201	0.5942	0.6134	**0.4678**	0.8869	0.6098	0.6505	0.67	0.419	0.6748	0.6539
CDANN+E [14]	0.6592	0.9044	0.6947	0.6249	0.6431	0.4324	0.8823	0.6374	0.6533	0.6826	0.4071	0.6632	0.6571

downsampling and feature interaction. 2)TIN: DAIN without feature distribution alignment loss.

Table 4 shows the experimental results of different sub-methods. As we can see, the average accuracy of DAIN is improved by 10.98% over DACNN, which indicates that consideration of signal internal relations is critical to improving performance. In addition, DAIN outperforms TIN by 6.82%, which shows that aligning the feature distribution from different domains can also provide performance improvements.

Table 4. The performance comparison of different sub-methods.

Approachs	Tasks												Average
	0-1	0-2	0-3	1-0	1-2	1-3	2-0	2-1	2-3	3-0	3-1	3-2	
DAIN	**0.7245**	**0.9292**	**0.7362**	**0.7401**	**0.7631**	0.4206	**0.9303**	**0.7163**	**0.7486**	**0.6814**	**0.4890**	**0.7472**	**0.7188**
DACNN	0.6528	0.8846	0.6539	0.6332	0.6229	**0.4333**	0.8897	0.6365	0.6360	0.6366	0.4761	0.6171	0.6477
TIN	0.6672	0.9133	0.6496	0.6955	0.7090	0.3912	0.9192	0.6923	0.7271	0.6369	0.4417	0.6321	0.6729

Visualization. To further understand the performance differences between DAIN and other fault diagnosis methods, we use the t-SNE tool [16] to visualize the features extracted by the trained feature extractor for task 2-0, and the results are shown in Fig. 4. Here, each sample from the source domain and target domain is displayed as a node, and the domain and class information can be distinguished by color. As we can see, compared with other approaches, nodes that have the same class from different domains are clustered together better by DAIN, while nodes of different classes are separated better by DAIN, which demonstrates that DAIN can capture domain-invariant features and class-distinguishing features. The feature visualization result also shows why the proposed DAIN can achieve better performance on cross-domain fault diagnosis tasks.

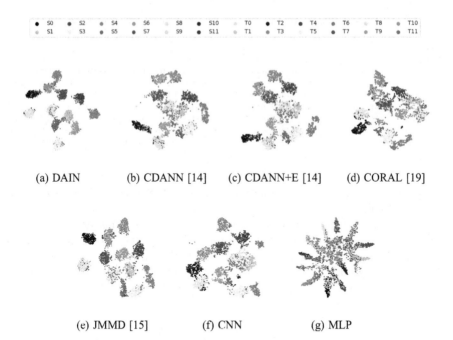

Fig. 4. The feature visualization results via t-SNE for task 2-0. Subgraph (a)–(g) corresponds to seven baselines. In the legend, S and T represent the source domain and target domain, respectively, and the numbers correspond to fault classes.

4   Conclusion

In this paper, we investigate the cross-domain fault diagnosis task from a novel perspective of taking temporal relations between odd and even subsequences into consideration and proposed an end-to-end DAIN method. Specifically, DAIN first extracts the feature representation including temporal relations between signal sub-sequences via an interaction network, then uses a classifier and a domain discriminator to distinguish fault classes and domain labels, respectively, and finally combines classification loss, MMD loss, and domain adversarial loss to achieve domain adaptation fault diagnosis. By comparing with the existing methods, we demonstrate the superiority of the proposed method in the PU dataset. By visualizing the features extracted by the feature extractor, we verify that the proposed method can extract domain-invariant and class-distinguishing features.

Acknowledgement. This work is partially supported by the Open Fund Project of Computer Science and Technology Application-Oriented Discipline of Minjiang University under Grant MJUKF-JK202004.

References

1. Borgwardt, K.M., Gretton, A., Rasch, M.J., Kriegel, H.P., Schölkopf, B., Smola, A.J.: Integrating structured biological data by kernel maximum mean discrepancy. Bioinformatics **22**(14), e49–e57 (2006)
2. Chen, Z., Gryllias, K., Li, W.: Mechanical fault diagnosis using convolutional neural networks and extreme learning machine. Mech. Syst. Signal Process. **133**, 106272 (2019)
3. Diederik, K., Jimmy, B., et al.: Adam: a method for stochastic optimization. arXiv preprint arXiv:1412.6980 pp. 273–297 (2014)
4. Fan, H., Zhang, F., Gao, Y.: Self-supervised time series representation learning by inter-intra relational reasoning. arXiv preprint arXiv:2011.13548 (2020)
5. Fan, H., Zhang, F., Wang, R., Xi, L., Li, Z.: Correlation-aware deep generative model for unsupervised anomaly detection. In: Lauw, H.W., Wong, R.C.-W., Ntoulas, A., Lim, E.-P., Ng, S.-K., Pan, S.J. (eds.) PAKDD 2020. LNCS (LNAI), vol. 12085, pp. 688–700. Springer, Cham (2020). https://doi.org/10.1007/978-3-030-47436-2_52
6. Ganin, Y., et al.: Domain-adversarial training of neural networks. J. Mach. Learn. Res **17**(1), 2030–2096 (2016)
7. Gu, Y.-K., Zhou, X.-Q., Yu, D.-P., Shen, Y.-J.: Fault diagnosis method of rolling bearing using principal component analysis and support vector machine. J. Mech. Sci. Technol. **32**(11), 5079–5088 (2018). https://doi.org/10.1007/s12206-018-1004-0
8. Lessmeier, C., Kimotho, J.K., Zimmer, D., Sextro, W.: Condition monitoring of bearing damage in electromechanical drive systems by using motor current signals of electric motors: a benchmark data set for data-driven classification. In: PHM Society European Conference, vol. 3 (2016)
9. Li, T., Zhao, Z., Sun, C., Yan, R., Chen, X.: Domain adversarial graph convolutional network for fault diagnosis under variable working conditions. IEEE Trans. Instrum. Meas. **70**, 1–10 (2021)
10. Liu, M., Zeng, A., Xu, Z., Lai, Q., Xu, Q.: Time series is a special sequence: forecasting with sample convolution and interaction. arXiv preprint arXiv:2106.09305 (2021)
11. Liu, R., Yang, B., Zio, E., Chen, X.: Artificial intelligence for fault diagnosis of rotating machinery: a review. Mech. Syst. Signal Process. **108**, 33–47 (2018)
12. Liu, Z.H., Jillian, L.B., Wei, H.L., Chen, L., Li, X.H.: Optimal transport-based deep domain adaptation approach for fault diagnosis of rotating machine. IEEE Trans. Instrum. Meas. **70**, 1–12 (2021)
13. Long, M., Cao, Y., Wang, J., Jordan, M.: Learning transferable features with deep adaptation networks. In: International Conference on Machine Learning, pp. 97–105. PMLR (2015)
14. Long, M., Cao, Z., Wang, J., Jordan, M.I.: Conditional adversarial domain adaptation. In: 31st Proceedings of the conference on Advances in Neural Information Processing Systems (2018)
15. Long, M., Zhu, H., Wang, J., Jordan, M.I.: Deep transfer learning with joint adaptation networks. In: International Conference on Machine Learning, pp. 2208–2217. PMLR (2017)
16. Van der Maaten, L., Hinton, G.: Visualizing data using t-SNE. J. Mach. Learn. Res. **9**(11) (2008)

17. Pandya, D., Upadhyay, S.H., Harsha, S.P.: Fault diagnosis of rolling element bearing by using multinomial logistic regression and wavelet packet transform. Soft. Comput. **18**(2), 255–266 (2014)
18. Paszke, A., et al.: Pytorch: an imperative style, high-performance deep learning library. In: 32nd Proceedings Conference on Advances in Neural Information Processing Systems (2019)
19. Sun, B., Saenko, K.: Deep CORAL: correlation alignment for deep domain adaptation. In: Hua, G., Jégou, H. (eds.) ECCV 2016. LNCS, vol. 9915, pp. 443–450. Springer, Cham (2016). https://doi.org/10.1007/978-3-319-49409-8_35
20. Wang, X., Liu, F.: Triplet loss guided adversarial domain adaptation for bearing fault diagnosis. Sensors **20**(1), 320 (2020)
21. Yin, A., Yan, Y., Zhang, Z., Li, C., Sánchez, R.V.: Fault diagnosis of wind turbine gearbox based on the optimized lSTM neural network with cosine loss. Sensors **20**(8), 2339 (2020)
22. Zhao, Z., et al.: Applications of unsupervised deep transfer learning to intelligent fault diagnosis: a survey and comparative study. IEEE Trans. Instrum. Measur. **70** (2021)

A Vehicle Data Publishing System with Privacy-Awares in VANETs Based on Blockchain

Xueqing Sun, Xiao Li, and Fengyin Li[✉]

School of Computer Science, Qufu Normal University, Rizhao 276826, China
lfyin318@126.com

Abstract. Vehicles generate a large amount of data every day. Through Vehicular ad-hoc networks, vehicles exchange and aggregate data, and deliver the data to data centers for data analysis to extract valuable information. In order to solve the problems of privacy leakage and insufficient security when vehicles publish data, this paper proposes a vehicle data publishing system with Privacy-awares in Vehicular ad-hoc networks based on blockchain to ensure the anonymity, traceability and safety of vehicle communication in Vehicular ad-hoc networks. While publishing data to the blockchain, solves the problem of data tampering. The results of security and performance analysis show that the scheme can resist common attacks, with low computational complexity and low communication cost, safe, efficient and practical.

Keywords: Ring signature · VANETs · Privacy protection

1 Introduction

Vehicle Internet of Things (VANETs) is an ad hoc network that connects various entities on the road [1]. In VANETs, each vehicle broadcasts traffic-related information such as its speed, location, road conditions, etc. through the VANETs, and a large amount of data is shared between vehicles and roadside units (RSUs) in real-time [2]. The application of VANETs reduces the incidence of traffic accidents and traffic congestion, thereby greatly improving road safety and efficiency.

However, due to the open nature of the VANETs environment, attackers may send bogus messages to confuse nearby drivers, which can lead vehicles in the vehicle network to be guided by misinformation, creating a potential traffic hazard. In order to maintain system security, the validity of information must be verified in the vehicle network. At the same time, the Internet of Vehicles also faces the problem of vehicle privacy leakage. Once the vehicle driving information is exposed, it will bring certain risks to the vehicle and the driver. The use of ring signature technology can protect the real identity information of vehicles in the vehicle network. However, complete anonymity has the potential to be disastrous for the system. Therefore, it is necessary to design a method for tracking the real identity of malicious users in the system. A traceable ring signature scheme

Y. Xu et al. (Eds.): ML4CS 2022, LNCS 13656, pp. 447–454, 2023.
https://doi.org/10.1007/978-3-031-20099-1_38

is proposed [3,4], which ensures the conditional anonymity of the signer in the system, and provides a method for tracking the real identity of the signer, which improves the security of the system. In addition, batch verification allows the verifier to verify multiple signatures with a single bilinear pairing, shortening the verification time and improving the efficiency of signature verification [5].

VANET improves traffic efficiency and reliability by sharing road events and traffic information in a timely manner. However, the issues of insufficient data storage capacity and vehicle selfish behavior need to be addressed [6]. The traditional data storage mechanism involves a third party for data management, which is opaque, unreliable, untrustworthy, and unsafe. Blockchain technology originated from a paper published by Satoshi Shigemoto in 2008 [7]. Blockchain is a distributed ledger, which can store a large amount of data with better performance [8]. At the same time, it also has the advantages of distributed and tamper-proof [9]. The application of blockchain technology to the vehicle network can protect the relevant data of the vehicle and improve the security of the system [10].

The remainder of this article is organized as follows. In Sect. 1, we introduce the research background of this paper. In Sect. 2, we introduce the preliminary of this paper. In Sect. 3, we propose the vehicle data publishing system with privacy-aware in vehicular ad-hoc networks based on blockchain. In Sect. 4, we analyze the performance of the vehicle data publishing system with privacy-aware. Finally, we conclude the paper in Sect. 5.

2 Preliminary

2.1 Bilinear Pairings

G_1 and G_2 are two multiplicative cyclic groups of prime order p. g_1 is a generator of G_1. g_2 is a generator of G_2. G_T is a multiplicative group of order n. Let $e : G_1 \times G_2 = G_T$ be a map with the following three properties:

(1) Bilinear: for all $a, b \in Z_n$ and $u \in G_1, v \in G_2$, $e(u^a, v^b) = e(u,v)^{ab}$.
(2) Nondegenerate: for any $u \in G_1, v \in G_2, e(u,v) \neq O$, where O means the identity of G_T.
(3) Computability: for all $u \in G_1, v \in G_2$, there is an efficient algorithm to compute $e(u,v)$.

2.2 DLP Hard Problem

Discrete Logarithm Problem (DLP): Given three points $P, aP, bP \in G_1$ on E/Fq, where $a, b \in Z_q$, it is computationally infeasible to compute abP from aP, bP and P.

3 A Vehicle Data Publishing System with Privacy-Awares in VANETs Based on Blockchain

In this section, we combine the Internet of Vehicles and blockchain technology to propose a privacy-aware vehicle data publishing system. The system realizes the anonymous release of vehicle data in the Internet of Vehicles. The released data will be stored in the blockchain by the sensing node, and analyzed and processed by the data center. At the same time, in order to ensure the security of the system, the system provides a user tracking function. For malicious vehicles existing in the system, the audit node can obtain the real identity of the user through user tracking and take punitive measures. The system model proposed in this paper is shown in Fig. 1 (see Fig. 1).

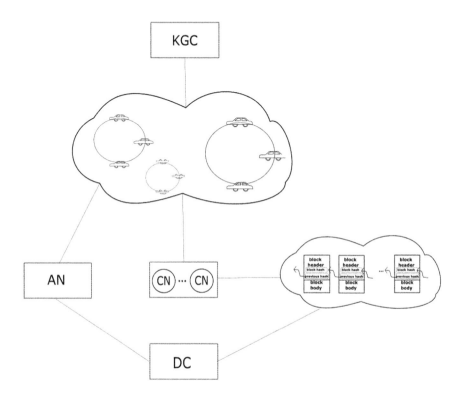

Fig. 1. The system model of the vehicle data publishing system with privacy-awares.

3.1 The Entities in the System

In the vehicle data publishing system proposed in this paper, there are six kinds of entities, including Auditing nodes, data center, vehicles, key generation centers, consensus nodes, and blockchain.

The work of each entity of the system is described next.

Auditing nodes (AN) are responsible for tracking down malicious nodes in the system.

Data center (DC) is responsible for analyzing the data uploaded to the blockchain, and predicting the occurrence of traffic congestion through big data analysis.

Vehicles are responsible for generating the data, signing the data using ring signature technology, and publishing the generated ring signature.

Key generation centers (KGC) are responsible for generating partial keys for vehicles.

Consensus nodes (CN) are responsible for verifying the signature of the vehicle and uploading the successfully verified data to the blockchain.

Blockchain is responsible for storing the data generated by the vehicle.

The symbols and definitions of the parameters used in the system are shown in Table 1.

Table 1. The symbols and definitions of the parameters used in the system.

Symbols	Definitions
G_1	A cyclic additive group with prime number p
G_T	A cyclic multiplicative group with prime number p
p	A large prime
g	The generator of G_1
e	A bilinear pairing mapping
H_1	A hash function
H_2	A hash function
(SPK, SSK)	The public key and private key of KGC
u_i	A user in the system
u_s	The real user signed the ring signature
ID_i	The real identity of u_i
psk_i	The partly private key of u_i
x_i	The secure value of u_i
$pk_i = (pka_i, pkb_i)$	The public key of u_i
$U_N = u_1, ..., u_s, ..., u_n$	The user set of ring

3.2   Design Goals

In the blockchain-based vehicle data release system with privacy awareness in the Internet of Vehicles, the vehicle needs to publish the data it generates anonymously, and at the same time, it is necessary to ensure the availability and security of the system. Therefore, the system needs to satisfy message authentication and integrity, public key certificateless, conditional anonymity, and batch verification.

Message Authenticity and Integrity: In the system, all traffic-related messages broadcast by vehicles should be authenticated to ensure that the messages are complete and generated by legitimate vehicles.

Public key without certificate: In order to simplify certificate management and facilitate deployment on resource-constrained vehicles, the system uses a certificateless public key system.

Conditional anonymity: Since the data generated by the vehicle in the system involves a large amount of vehicle privacy information, the real identity of the vehicle must be protected; and since the system is vulnerable to network attacks, in the event of a dispute, the audit node must identify the real identity of the malicious node and impose penalties, so the Internet of Vehicles needs to satisfy the conditional anonymity. That is, the real identity of the signer is unknown to the vehicle, but is known to the audit node.

Bulk verification of messages: Due to the huge amount of data in the system, it is unrealistic for the verifier to verify the validity of the information broadcast by the vehicle one by one. Therefore, the verifier needs to verify multiple signatures at a time, and the system needs to meet the batch verification of signatures.

3.3 System Initialization

In this section, we describe the process of system initialization.

The key generation centers(KGC) chooses a cyclic additive group G_1, where g is a generation of G_1. KGC chooses a cyclic multiplicative group G_T and a bilinear pairing mapping $e : G_1 \times G_1 \rightarrow G_T$. KGC also chooses two hash function $H_1 : \{0,1\}^* \rightarrow Z_q$ and $H_2 : \{0,1\}^* \times G_1 \rightarrow Z_q$ and an integer $SSK \in Z_q$ as KGC's private key, and computes KGC's public key $SPK = SSK \cdot g \in G_1$. The parameters $SystemP = (p, G_1, G_T, g, e, H_1, H_2, SPK)$ as the system parameter in this system.

Data center(DC) chooses the private key $SK_DC \in Z_q$, and computes the public key $PK_DC = SK_DC \cdot g \in G_1$.

The vehicle u_i computers $d_i = H_1(SSK||ID_i) \in Z_q$,$D_i = d_i \cdot g \in G_1$, and send to KGC.

For all vehicles in the system, KGC computes the vehicle's partial private key $psk_i = SSK \cdot d_i \cdot g \in G_1$, and sends psk_i to the vehicle u_i.

The vehicle u_i randomly selects the secret value $x_i \in Z_q$, computes the private key $sk_i = (d_i + x_i)^{-1} \cdot psk_i \in G_1$, and computes the public key of himself $pk_i = (pka_i, pkb_i)$, where, $pka_i = (d_i + x_i)^{-1} \cdot g \in G_1$, $pkb_i = (d_i + x_i)^{-1} \cdot D_i \in G_1$.

3.4 Publishing Data

In this section, we describe the process of publishing data.

The vehicle u_s selects the n-1 users in the system to form a ring with himself. The ring user set is $U_N = u_1, ..., u_s, ..., u_n$, and the corresponding ring public key set is $pk_N = pk_1, ..., pk_s, ..., pk_n$.

The vehicle u_s chooses random values $r_i(i = 1, ..., n)$ for each vehicles in the ring user set.

The vehicle u_s computes $R_i = r_i \cdot g$, $T_i = r_i \cdot pkb_i$, $h_i = H_2(m||pk_i||R_i||T_i)$, $i = 1, ..., n, i \neq s$.

The vehicle u_s chooses $R_s = r_s \cdot g - \sum_{i=1, i \neq s}^{n}(R_i + h_i \cdot pkb_i)$, $T_s = r_s \cdot pkb_i - \sum_{i=1, i \neq s}^{n} T_i$, $h_s = H_2(m||pk_s||R_s||T_s)$, $F = r_s \cdot SPK + (h_s + r_s) \cdot sk_s$.

Letting $R_N = \{R_1, ..., R_s, ..., R_n\}$, $T_N = \{T_1, ..., T_s, ..., T_n\}$.

The vehicle u_s generates a ring signature $\sigma = (m, pk_N, R_N, T_N, F, T_t)$, and sends the ring signature σ to Consensus nodes(CN).

After receiving the single ring signature σ, the CN verifies the ring signature.

Consensus nodes(CNs) compute $h_i = H_2(m||pk_i||R_i||T_i)$, verify whether the equation $e(\sum_{i=1}^{n}(R_i + h_i \cdot pkb_i), SPK) = e(F, g)$ is true. If the equation is true, the signature is valid and "true" is output; otherwise the signature is invalid, output "false".

After receiving the multiple single ring signatures, CNs verify the signatures in batches, calculates, and verifies the equation $e(\sum_{i=1}^{k}(\sum_{j=1}^{n_i}(R_{ij} + h_{ij} \cdot pkb_{ij} + T_{ij})), SPK) = e(\sum_{j=1}^{k} F_i, g)$. If the equation is true, the signature is valid and "true" is output, otherwise, there is an invalid signature, and "false" is output.

CNs package and send the successfully verified data to the blockchain. The data in the blockchain is read and analyzed by the DC.

3.5   Tracking Vehicle

In this section, we describe the process of tracking vehicle.

If a malicious user appears in the system, the auditing node (AN) sends the tracking requests to the vehicles according to the user public key list in the ring signature.

AN sends T_i to each user in the ring user set.

The vehicle u_i computes $T_i' = d_i^{-1} \cdot T_i$, and returns T_i' to AN.

AN verifies $e(T_i', g) = e(R_i, pka_i)$. If the equation holds, u_i is not a real signer. If the equation does not hold, u_i is the real signer, AN outputs the public key of the real signer u_i, and the system will prohibit the signer from continuing to publish messages.

4   Performance Analysis

4.1   Correctness Proof

In this section, we prove the correctness of the equations used in verifying the single ring signature, verifying the ring signatures with batch and tracing vehicle.

(1) Verifying the single ring signature.

$e(\sum_{i=1}^{n}(R_i + h_i \cdot pkb_i + T_i), SPK) = e(r_s \cdot g + h_s \cdot pkb_s + r_s \cdot pkb_s, SSK \cdot g) = e(SSK \cdot r_s \cdot g + SSK \cdot (h_s + r_s) \cdot pkb_s, g) = e(r_s \cdot SPK + (h_s + r_s) \cdot sk_s, g) = e(F, g)$

(2) Verifying the ring signatures with batch.

$e(\sum_{i=1}^{k}(\sum_{j=1}^{n_i}(R_{ij} + h_{ij} \cdot pkb_{ij} + T_{ij})), SPK) = e(\sum_{i=1}^{k}(R_{is} + h_{is} \cdot pkb_{is} + r_{is} \cdot pkb_{is}), SPK) = e(\sum_{i=1}^{k}(R_{is} + h_{is} \cdot pkb_{is} + r_{is} \cdot pkb_{is}), SSK \cdot g) = e(\sum_{i=1}^{k}(SSK \cdot R_{is} + SSK \cdot (h_{is} + r_{is}) \cdot pkb_{is}), g) = e(\sum_{i=1}^{k}(r_{is} \cdot SPK + (h_{is} + r_{is}) \cdot sk_{is}), g) = e(\sum_{i=1}^{k} F_i, g)$

(3) Tracing vehicle

$e(T_i', g) = e(d_i^{-1} \cdot T_i, g) = e(d_i^{-1} \cdot r_s \cdot pkb_i, g) = e(r_s \cdot pka_i, g) = e(R_i, pka_i)$

4.2   Efficiency Analysis

Suppose the time cost of a bilinear pairing is T_b, the time cost of a hash is T_h, the time cost of a group addition is T_a, the time cost of a group multiplication is T_m, and the time cost of the interaction between the audit node and the user is T_t. Then in the traceable ring signature scheme with batch verification proposed in this paper, the time cost of generating a ring signature containing n users' public keys is $2nT_a + nT_h$, and the time cost of k ring signatures containing n users' public keys is $nk(2T_a + T_h)$. The time cost of a single ring signature verification containing n user public keys is $nT_h + T_b$. The time cost of verifying k ring signatures containing n user public keys at a time is $knT_h + T_b$. The time cost of a user tracking is $T_t + nT_b$.

5   Conclusions

In this paper, combined with blockchain technology, we propose a blockchain-based vehicle data publishing system with privacy awareness in the Internet of Vehicles. The system uses a traceable certificateless ring signature method with batch verification, and vehicles can publish data anonymously, which protects vehicle privacy information in the system. At the same time, the system provides a signer tracking method, and audit nodes can track malicious vehicles, which ensures the security of the system. At the same time, the system also provides the function of batch verification of vehicle signatures, which can verify multiple ring signatures at one time, which improves the efficiency of the system. Finally, we analyze the performance of the system. The performance analysis shows that the privacy-aware vehicle data publishing system can resist common attacks, and at the same time, it has low computational complexity and low communication cost, and is safe, efficient and practical.

References

1. Khalid, A., Iftikhar, M.S., Almogren, A., et al.: A blockchain based incentive provisioning scheme for traffic event validation and information storage in VANETs. Inf. Process. Manage. **58**(2), 102464 (2016)
2. Mundhe, P., Verma, S., Venkatesan, S.: A comprehensive survey on authentication and privacy-preserving schemes in VANETs. Comput. Sci. Rev. **41**, 100411 (2021)
3. Fujisaki, E., Suzuki, K.: Traceable ring signature. In: Okamoto, T., Wang, X. (eds.) PKC 2007. LNCS, vol. 4450, pp. 181–200. Springer, Heidelberg (2007). https://doi.org/10.1007/978-3-540-71677-8_13
4. Tang, F., Pang, J., Cheng, K., et al.: Multiauthority traceable ring signature scheme for smart grid based on blockchain. Wirel. Commun. Mob. Comput. (2021). https://doi.org/10.1115/2021/5566430
5. Liu, F., Wang, Q.: An Identity-based Batch Verification Scheme for VANETs Based on Ring Signature with Efficient Revocation. arXiv preprint arXiv:2103.07653 (2021)
6. Ali, I., Hassan, A., Li, F.: Authentication and privacy schemes for vehicular ad hoc networks (VANETs): a survey. Veh. Commun. **16**, 45–61 (2019)

7. Nakamoto, S.: Bitcoin: a peer-to-peer electronic cash system. Decentralized Bus Rev. 21260 (2008)
8. Sun, X., Li, X., Li, F.: An agricultural traceability permissioned blockchain with privacy-aware. In: Tan, Y., Shi, Y., Zomaya, A., Yan, H., Cai, J. (eds.) DMBD 2021. CCIS, vol. 1453, pp. 218–229. Springer, Singapore (2021). https://doi.org/10.1007/978-981-16-7476-1_20
9. Lai, C., Ma, Z., Guo, R., et al.: Secure medical data sharing scheme based on traceable ring signature and blockchain. Peer-to-Peer Netw. Appl. **15**(3), 1562–1576 (2022). https://doi.org/10.1007/s12083-022-01303-w
10. Li, F., Sun, X., Liu, P., et al.: A traceable privacy-aware data publishing platform on permissioned blockchain. Trans. Emerg. Telecommun. Technol. **33**(5), e4455 (2022). https://doi.org/10.1002/ett.4455

Highsimb: A Concrete Blockchain High Simulation with Contract Vulnerability Detection for Ethereum and Hyperledger Fabric

Pengfei Huang[1], Wanqing Jie[1], Arthur Sandor Voundi Koe[1,2(✉)], Ruitao Hou[1], Hongyang Yan[1], Mourad Nouioua[3], Phan Duc Thien[4], Jacques Mbous Ikong[5], and Camara Lancine[6]

[1] Institute of Artificial Intelligence and Blockchain, Guangzhou University, Guangzhou 510006, China
2517482859@qq.com
[2] Pazhou Lab, Guangzhou 510330, China
[3] Faculty of Mathematics and Computer Science, University of Mohamed Bachir El Ibrahimi, 34030 Bordj Bou Arreridj, Algeria
[4] Faculty of Information Technology, Nam Dinh University of Technology Education, Nam Dinh 420000, Vietnam
[5] Department of Electrical and Telecommunications Engineering, National Advanced School of Engineering - University of Yaounde I, Yaounde 337, Cameroon
[6] Department of Computer Science, University of Social Sciences and Management, Bamako 2575, Mali

Abstract. Blockchain testing plays a critical role in the maturation of blockchain technology by ensuring the quality of implemented functional and non-functional requirements. In the new global economy, rapid time to market has become a central issue: developers fail to scrutinize their blockchain designs prior to deployment and customers undergo negative experiences that hurt the widespread adoption of the blockchain technology. Previous published studies aimed for effective blockchain simulators. However, existing solutions exhibit several drawbacks: they rely on guesswork, conceal low-level implementation details, lack expected realistic outcomes and automated testing, as well as lag in smart contract vulnerability analysis. In this paper, we introduce highsimb: the first concrete blockchain high simulation platform for Ethereum and Hyperledger Fabric that supports smart contract vulnerability detection. Unlike a testnet, the blockchain tester can customize any low-level detail to achieve realistic expected results under automated testing. Theoretical analysis demonstrates our concrete simulator is highly observable, supports realistic feedback, is scalable, detects smart contract vulnerabilities, has strong white-box testing capabilities and automates experiments. Our framework complements existing blockchain simulators and introduces a novel development paradigm for blockchain testing.

Keywords: Blockchain · Bitcoin · Simulator · Ethereum · Hyperledger Fabric

Y. Xu et al. (Eds.): ML4CS 2022, LNCS 13656, pp. 455–468, 2023.
https://doi.org/10.1007/978-3-031-20099-1_39

1   Introduction

The blockchain technology, which first proof of concept - by the pseudonym Satoshi Nakamoto - supports the Bitcoin cryptocurrency [27], has attracted a diverse range of stakeholders in recent years: businesses, academicians and practitioners. In the new global economy, blockchain technology plays a key role and its application spans across many domains: healthcare [6,34], artificial intelligence [32,40], government affairs [20,33], project management [37], power battery systems [13,14], etc. Recent trends predict that global spending on blockchain technology will reach 19 billion U.S. dollars by 2024 [23]: such soaring statistics forecast a growing number of blockchain applications that address a broad range of functional and non-functional requirements.

Security, scalability and decentralization issues impact negatively upon the wide adoption of blockchain technology and the applicability of blockchain solutions [21]. What is interesting is the phenomenal growth in the number of blockchain projects that fail to stand the test of time: developers prioritize time to market over rigorous testing prior to software release and such behavior leads to poor overall product implementation and lack of widespread customer adoption. Another consequence is the increasing rate of vulnerabilities within smart contracts that are aggravated by the properties of immutability and asset holders [4]. Evidence suggests that such vulnerabilities persist as a result of smart contract code reuse [7] and it is paramount to capture them prior to deploying smart contracts on real chains [41]. We hypothesize that early detection and testing will boost the community's trust in the validity and effectiveness of the proposed blockchain solutions.

There are several challenges inherent to the area of blockchain testing.

- *Inadequate understanding of blockchain technology and relatively little experience in designing blockchain applications*: Blockchain technology requires a clear understanding and standardization of concepts and associated terminologies, as well as a technical, non-technical, and legal expertise, in order for blockchain solutions to be widely adopted.
- *Unavailability of tools to implement an automated system under test*: Blockchain technology requires a system under test that accurately replicates the production environment. Furthermore, with so many smart contract programming languages available, debugging and testing tools, as well as automation in blockchain network design and deployment, should be prioritized.
- *Lack of standardization of testing strategies*: Guidelines for developing blockchain solutions are required by blockchain technology. Furthermore, the high complexity and heterogeneity of the blockchain environment should be considered when designing and testing blockchain applications.
- *Blockchain technology's immutability*: Blockchain technology is essentially a collection of append-only logs organized into blocks. In other words, once a transaction has been deployed, it is impossible to reverse it under normal

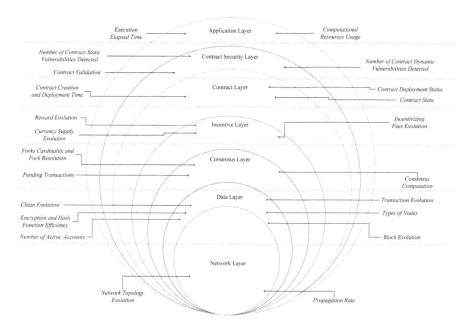

Fig. 1. Our blockchain abstraction model with the associated metrics

circumstances. Such a situation therefore calls for smart contracts validation and vulnerability analysis before their deployment on the chain.

- *High complexity in performance evaluation*: It is time-consuming to generate real-world traffic, including workload and faultload. Furthermore, developing and deploying a system under evaluation that mimics a real production environment is required, but this comes at a high cost in terms of effort and time.
- *Dependability assessment*: It is critical to ensure that the blockchain testing environment remains consistent and exhibits liveness and safety properties when various types of faultload are fed into one or more levels of the blockchain abstraction model depicted in Fig. 1.

In this paper, we present highsimb, the first concrete blockchain high simulation platform for Ethereum and Hyperledger Fabric that supports smart contract vulnerability detection and allows the blockchain tester to customize any low-level detail to achieve realistic expected results, a property known as experimental analysis [11,18]. To achieve our goals, this work follows a hybrid approach between simulation and concrete execution. It incorporates automation in blockchain system deployment at multiple levels of the abstraction model detailed in Fig. 1. Furthermore, highsimb supports smart contracts static and dynamic vulnerability analysis, and can scale to thousands of nodes depending on the available computing resources. Our contributions are as follows.

1. We adopt a concrete execution model while allowing the tester to simulate their own blockchain deployment using our proposed semantic metamodel. Furthermore, our blockchain semantic metamodel can be extended to simulate any blockchain model.
2. Our scheme enables the automatic deployment and testing of the blockchain network using professional-grade tools. As a result, we do not bother explicitly simulating the network layer because it is managed automatically. Instead, we concentrate on the higher layers of our blockchain abstraction model. In light of the above, our scheme falls under the category of blockchain high simulation framework.
3. We extend Blockperf [31]'s blockchain abstraction model. As a result, we introduce a new layer known as the contract security layer, as shown in Fig. 1, and move the contract validation task to the contract security layer. Moreover, our scheme introduces novel metrics we think are important in blockchain testing, and enables support for static and dynamic smart contract vulnerability analysis.
4. Our construction simulation can be expanded over a thousand nodes regarding the availability of computing resources.
5. We employ the Python programming language to implement our metamodel, then use the Docker engine and Kubernetes to build our framework and perform automated deployment and testing under strong white-box capabilities. In fact, the tester has the ability to alter the majority of the parameters both before and during the blockchain simulation.

The remainder of our work is organized as follows: Section 2 explores the related works; Section 3 delves into our blockchain abstraction model and our high simulation platform semantic metamodel; Section 4 describes the methodology of empirical experiments; Section 5 concludes our work and outlines avenues for future research.

2   Related Works

This section goes over the existing blockchain testing methods in the literature. To evaluate a blockchain design, three approaches are commonly used: emulators, test networks, and simulators. Emulators, in general, tend to completely replicate the hardware and software of a guest blockchain platform within a host system [39]. Developers who want to create an emulator for the hyperledger sawtooth consensus mechanism, for example, can use the open source TEE (trusted execution environment) emulator [28]. Furthermore, blockchain emulators are closely related to blockchain benchmarking [10]. However, the disadvantages of using emulators include high resource consumption and the necessity for a standardized test scenario restricting access for the tester, to specific workloads or faultloads. Nevertheless testing scenarios under emulation are usually well documented. A blockchain test network, on the other hand, is commonly referred to as an alternative to a main chain that employs the same technology and software. There are several examples of blockchain testnets ready products available, such as [5,8]. Furthermore, the token used on a blockchain testnet has no real-world value, and self-designed workloads or faultloads can be provided as test network inputs. However, while blockchain testnets provide concrete expected results based on inputs, they generally abstract the network layer, do not provide automation for all supported functionalities, conceal low level implementation details, do require high complexity to modify some source code features, and are further typically limited in terms of the available set of testing features which rely primarily on monitoring and performance evaluation. Given the aforementioned, it is generally difficult to provide, for experimentation and testing purposes, a complete automatic and detail-oriented implementation of the exact proposed system at its full envisioned scale, along with the full set of operating parameters [22]. As a result, the authors in [3,9,17,22,38] advocate the use of abstract working models known as simulators to obtain a reproducible empirical evaluation as well as to allow for cost and time efficiency in designing of the blockchain under test, while removing the existing challenges inherent to blockchain testing. Such challenges are depicted in Sect. 1. Moreover, the work in [22] recommends using the best software engineering practices in designing a simulator, and proposes a domain meta-model and an object-oriented framework for developing efficient and reliable blockchain network simulators. Such best practices are usually based on configurability and design transparency. Furthermore, model driven development [16] and software product line engineering [24,30] can be considered as the two best software engineering approaches. However, while having a blockchain system under test that mimics the production environment is desirable, a blockchain simulator does not generally provide realistic expected results. Nevertheless, according to the authors of [12], concrete blockchains lack the flexibility to extend or replace the blockchain model under test, and they cannot easily simulate other blockchains using different protocols or consensus models.

As using simulators appears to be a commendable approach, there are however numerous drawbacks to such a creative process. First, the inability to accurately reflect the production environment, i.e. the lack of concrete execution of smart contracts as in [31]. Second, there is a scarcity of automation because parameters are typically specified in configuration files prior to deployment and cannot be changed automatically during the blockchain model simulation, via scripts or IT (information technology) execution tools. Third, when developing a generic blockchain simulator framework capable of simulating multiple types of blockchains, specific low-level details related to the heterogeneity and complexity of the blockchain ecosystem are typically overlooked. Fourth, most of the existing blockchain simulation platforms do not simultaneously provide static and dynamic vulnerability analysis of the smart contract source code. In fact, implementing dynamic analysis necessitates the inclusion of a smart contract execution environment, which in most cases relates to concrete execution. For example, [31] provides a simulator that does not cover the contract layer because doing so obviously requires concrete execution.

3 Our Concrete Blockchain High Simulation Model

3.1 Our Blockchain Abstraction Model

Despite the fact that there are numerous blockchain abstraction layered models in the literature [1,2], we adhere to the work in [31]. Unlike the Blockperf semantic model [31], however, our blockchain abstraction model implements the contract layer and introduces a novel contract security layer in charge of contract security analysis. Furthermore, this work introduces several novel metrics that we believe are critical for evaluating the preciseness and effectiveness of the blockchain system under test. The roles of the various layers of our blockchain abstraction model depicted in Fig. 1 are described below.

1. **Application layer**: In our blockchain abstraction model, the application layer serves as the interface between the tester and the simulator. It provides a set of functionalities through an application programming interface that allows the tester to interact with the simulator both before and during the simulation. Our research takes into account the following desirable metrics measurable at the application layer level: the simulation execution time and the computational resource usage, such as the amount of CPU, memory, or storage capacity available.
2. **Contract security layer**: The contract security layer is in charge of contract codification, also known as contract validation, which is concerned with providing optimized and correct contracts as well as of contract security through vulnerability detection analysis. This work focuses primarily on contract security, with contract validation left out of scope. The number of vulnerabilities linked to contract static analysis, and the number of uncovered vulnerabilities through contract dynamic analysis are the desirable metrics at this layer.
3. **Contract layer**: The contract layer manages smart contract execution in a concrete, emulated, or simulated contract execution virtual environment. Moreover, such a layer would embed the Ethereum virtual machine (EVM) in the case of Ethereum blockchain simulation. At this stage, the metrics of interest are the contract creation and execution time, the contract state storage, and the contract deployment status, i.e., whether the contract was successfully deployed or rolled back.
4. **Incentive layer**: The incentive layer monitors and manages incentives to keep the majority of nodes honest. There are numerous metrics of interest. First, we consider the current reward, the history of reward values, and the process of generating rewards. Second, there are incentive fees, such as the amount of resources required to execute a contract, namely the gas price or

the amount of gas in an Ethereum blockchain concrete high simulation. Third, the currency supply mechanism, with Bitcoin having a maximum supply of 21 million BTC and Ethereum having an infinite maximum supply. However, we need to mention for clarity, that an infinite market cap does not always insinuate a high inflationary currency.

5. **Consensus layer**: Depending on the type of blockchain being tested, the consensus layer will implement a specific consensus algorithm. Measurable metrics at the consensus layer include the number of pending transactions, the number of hard and soft forks that have occurred, the frequency of forks, and the global consensus computation history.

6. **Data layer**: The data layer, also known as the node layer, is in charge of structuring transactions and blocks prior to their inclusion on the chain. It is also in charge of data storage in distributed databases, as well as access control in permissioned blockchains. The metrics of interest at the data layer are numerous. First, we consider transaction evolution, which includes the number of transactions, the frequency with which they are generated, and the time required to process a transaction or set of transactions. Second, there is the block evolution, which includes the number of blocks added to the chain, the frequency of block validation, mining, and addition to the main chain, the block size, and the number of transactions included per block. Third, there is the chain evolution, which is the number of blocks on the main chain over time, as well as the node's level of synchronization. Fourth, in the case of hosted accounts, the number of accounts created. Fifth, the node types, i.e., the number of lightweight or full nodes. The sixth metric of interest is the efficiency and effectiveness of the encryption techniques and hash functions implemented.

7. **Network layer**: In our blockchain abstraction model, the network layer is a network logical topology built on a physical peer-to-peer (P2P) topology. This network layer is in charge of defining blockchain nodes and establishing node intercommunication. At the network layer level of our blockchain abstraction layer, there are two primary metrics of interest. First, the network graph evolution, which handles node addition and deletion, simulates nodes going offline and back online, as well as managing the communication protocol between nodes. For the network graph evolution, Ethereum, for example, relies on the Kademlia protocol [15]. Second, throughput, also known as propagation rate, is a key aspect of blockchain that measures the number of valid transactions that can be inserted into the main chain per second (TPS).

3.2   Our High Simulation Platform Semantic Metamodel

In this paper, we follow the model view controller (MVC) design pattern [26]. Moreover, we leverage the unified modeling language (UML 2) [29] to define our high simulation platform metamodels. We further adopt a necessary and sufficient subset of UML diagrams based on the unified process model (UP) described in [35] and the agile modeling (AM) detailed in [19] to achieve reliable fast source code production. To be more specific, we use the UML class diagram to depict our high simulation platform semantic metamodel. Furthermore, we depict our semantic metamodel, the various entities being leveraged, and the important relationships between those entities in Fig. 2.

4   Our Concrete Blockchain High Simulation Empirical Construction

4.1   Concrete Design Methodology

Our work follows a hybrid approach that combines simulation and concrete execution. As a result, it incorporates automation in the blockchain model under testing, particularly in the network layer of our blockchain abstraction model depicted in Fig. 1. Furthermore, our framework enables testers to define their own code and deploy it using automation. To accomplish our objectives, we structured our source code around nine main packages, as shown in Fig. 3, and implemented them as microservices in Python 3.6.2 under Ubuntu 20.04. In addition, we defined several base classes based on the semantic metamodel shown in Fig 2. Each microservice is free to extend and redefine such base classes. Then, we adopt a physical and local server to power our network of 30 ethereum nodes (miners and transaction forwarders) and 30 hyperledger fabric nodes (i.e., endorsers and peers). A server of this type has the following characteristics: To begin, the processor is an Intel (R) Xeon (R) Gold 6240R CPU running at 2.40 GHz. Second, the internal memory (RAM) is bounded to 32 GB. Finally, the total storage capacity is 6.5 terabytes. Furthermore, in order to facilitate interaction with the blockchain system under test, we used web interfaces to depict the presentation layer in each microservice. Table 1 summarizes the tools or technologies used, as well as their utilities, for automated concrete execution of our blockchain high simulation for ethereum and hyperledger fabric.

4.2   Personalized Blockchain Model Simulation Strategy

This section describes the deployment methodology of the concrete high simulation of one's own blockchain model using our proposed framework. To attain this purpose, we outline the four steps in the lines below. However, the order in which the suggested steps are implemented is not rigid and is left to the tester's discretion. Furthermore, the simulated blockchain source code must be ready and correct before proceeding. As a result, the approach for obtaining a concrete high simulation of one's personalized blockchain is as follows.

1. The tester must select a docker base image specified in a dockerfile and customize it using the docker image layering approach. This step will be repeated as more different types of nodes are used in the blockchain under test. Each node, however, must be customized based on the functional and non-functional requirements of the blockchain to be tested. Furthermore, as described in [36], the tester should ensure the security of the base image. Once an image is ready, the tester can either push it to a docker registry or save it locally in a file.

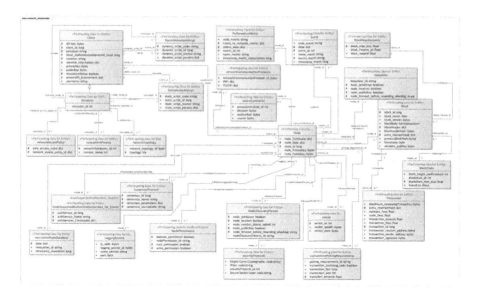

Fig. 2. Semantic metamodel of our high simulation platform

Table 1. Summary of tools and technology used together with their utilities

Tool/Technology	Version	Utility
Devspace	5.18.4	Fast and automated kubernetes deployment tool through the manifest file *devspace.yaml*
Nginx	1.18.0	Proxy Server to redirect traffic from kubernetes cluster internal service port to server port
Minikube	1.25.2	Local kubernetes cluster environment with docker driver
Kubectl	1.23.3	Kubernetes command line tool to manage the cluster together with the number of replicas
Npm	6.14.4	Package manager for Javascript programming language
Nodejs	10.19.0	Javascript backend runtime environment
docker	20.10.14	Operating system level virtualization for easy and portable application development
docker-compose	1.29.2	Docker container orchestration limited to a single host (contrarily to kubernetes)
Slither-analyzer	0.8.3	Solidity static analysis framework for smart contract vulnerabilities detection
Mythril	0.23.0	Solidity dynamic analysis framework for smart contract vulnerabilities detection
Flask	0.12.2	Web backend microframework to support our nine microservices
Bulma CSS	0.9.3	Front-end css library for web development
Chaincode analyzer	*None*	Chaincode static analysis command-line tool for chaincode vulnerabilities detection

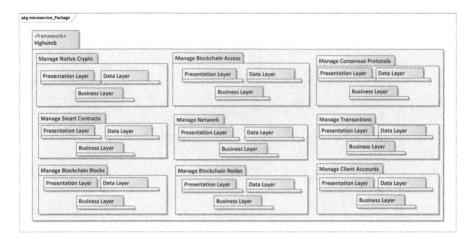

Fig. 3. Highsimb microservices architecture

2. The tester can use docker-compose or kubernetes to automate network policies, hardware resources, port forwarding, replica count, and so on. In our
   experiments, we utilized docker-compose to deploy hyperledger fabric and
   the minikube kubernetes local cluster to deploy ethereum.
3. The tester can either extend our proposed user interface, which uses the flask
   microweb framework in conjunction with bulma css, or use any other web
   framework of their choice. However, completely redefining a new presentation
   layer from scratch comes at a high cost in terms of time and deployment
   complexity.
4. The tester can integrate automated state-of-the-art network monitoring tools
   such as prometheus [25], centralized or decentralized state-of-the-art database
   storage systems, or existing blockchain implementations into the concrete high
   simulation experiments thanks to the flexibility and automation capabilities
   of docker-compose and kubernetes.

5 Conclusion and Future Works

This paper addresses the shortcomings of existing blockchain simulations. Specifically, the lack of concrete execution of smart contracts, the lack of automation in blockchain simulators, the reliance on guesswork, which translates into
the inability to obtain expected realistic results, the non-consideration of low
level simulation details, and the scarcity of smart contract vulnerability analysis. To address the aforementioned deficiencies, and in light of the existing
challenges in the blockchain testing research field, this paper takes a hybrid approach between concrete execution and simulation, and introduces highsimb, a
concrete blockchain high simulation with contract vulnerability detection, for
both ethereum and hyperledger fabric. Our design leverages the unified modeling language and focuses on a combination of unified process and agile model-

ing software development methods to realize a good software product. Furthermore, we provide an extensible testing framework based on a novel blockchain abstraction layered model that supports realistic expected results, smart contract vulnerability detection, testing deployment automation, active interaction with the blockchain under test even during simulation, and self-designed testing experiments. As a result, our concrete high simulation is adaptable and can be thought of as a novel development framework for blockchain testing in comparison to existing blockchain simulators. As future works, we intend to integrate the majority of existing blockchain schemes into our approach, as well as provide several ready-to-use black box and white box tests while allowing the tester to define its own set of testing strategies and to interact with any entity within our framework. Moreover, we plan to support cross-chain testing and endorse smart contract codification, which will address the need for writing optimized and correct contracts. Furthermore, the majority of the source code has already been written, and we intend to make empirical performance analysis details as well as our framework's source code available.

Acknowledgements. This work was supported by the Joint Funds of the National Natural Science Foundation of China (No.U20A20176), the National Key Project of China (No.2020YFB1005700), and the National Key Research and Development Program of China (No.2021YFA1000600).

References

1. Albshri, A., Alzubaidi, A., Awaji, B., Solaiman, E.: Blockchain simulators: a systematic mapping study. In: 2022 IEEE International Conference on Services Computing (SCC), pp. 284–294 (2022)
2. Alharby, M., van Moorsel, A.: BlockSim: an extensible simulation tool for blockchain systems. Front. Blockchain **3**, 28 (2020). https://doi.org/10.3389/fbloc.2020.00028
3. Aoki, Y., Otsuki, K., Kaneko, T., Banno, R., Shudo, K.: SimBlock: a blockchain network simulator. In: INFOCOM 2019 - IEEE Conference on Computer Communications Workshops, INFOCOM WKSHPS 2019, pp. 325–329. Institute of Electrical and Electronics Engineers Inc. (2019). https://doi.org/10.1109/INFCOMW.2019.8845253
4. Bartoletti, M., Pompianu, L.: An empirical analysis of smart contracts: platforms, applications, and design patterns. In: Brenner, M., et al. (eds.) FC 2017. LNCS, vol. 10323, pp. 494–509. Springer, Cham (2017). https://doi.org/10.1007/978-3-319-70278-0_31
5. Biryukov, A., Tikhomirov, S.: Transaction clustering using network traffic analysis for bitcoin and derived blockchains. In: INFOCOM 2019 - IEEE Conference on Computer Communications Workshops, INFOCOM WKSHPS 2019, pp. 204–209. Institute of Electrical and Electronics Engineers Inc. (2019). https://doi.org/10.1109/INFCOMW.2019.8845213
6. Chelladurai, U., Pandian, S.: A novel blockchain based electronic health record automation system for healthcare. J. Ambient Intell. Humanized Comput. **13**(1), 693–703 (2022). https://doi.org/10.1007/s12652-021-03163-3

7. Chen, X., Liao, P., Zhang, Y., Huang, Y., Zheng, Z.: Understanding code reuse in smart contracts. In: Proceedings - 2021 IEEE International Conference on Software Analysis, Evolution and Reengineering, SANER 2021, pp. 470–479. Institute of Electrical and Electronics Engineers Inc. (2021). https://doi.org/10.1109/SANER50967.2021.00050

8. Choi, W., Hong, J.W.K.: Performance evaluation of Ethereum private and Testnet networks using hyperledger caliper. In: 2021 22nd Asia-Pacific Network Operations and Management Symposium, APNOMS 2021, pp. 325–329. Institute of Electrical and Electronics Engineers Inc. (2021). https://doi.org/10.23919/APNOMS52696.2021.9562684

9. Deshpande, A., Nasirifard, P., Jacobsen, H.A.: Demo abstract: eVIBES: configurable and interactive ethereum blockchain simulation framework. In: Middleware 2018 - Proceedings of the 2018 ACM/IFIP/USENIX Middleware Conference (Posters), pp. 11–12. Association for Computing Machinery, Inc (2018). https://doi.org/10.1145/3284014.3284020

10. Dinh, T.T.A., Wang, J., Chen, G., Liu, R., Ooi, B.C., Tan, K.L.: BLOCKBENCH: a framework for analyzing private blockchains. In: Proceedings of the ACM SIGMOD International Conference on Management of Data, pp. 1085–1100. Association for Computing Machinery, New York, NY, USA (2017). https://doi.org/10.1145/3035918.3064033

11. Fan, C., Khazaei, H., Chen, Y., Musilek, P.: Towards a scalable DAG-based distributed ledger for smart communities. In: IEEE 5th World Forum on Internet of Things, WF-IoT 2019 - Conference Proceedings, pp. 177–182. Institute of Electrical and Electronics Engineers Inc. (2019). https://doi.org/10.1109/WF-IoT.2019.8767342

12. Faria, C., Correia, M.: BlockSim: blockchain simulator. In: Proceedings - 2019 2nd IEEE International Conference on Blockchain, Blockchain 2019, pp. 439–446. Institute of Electrical and Electronics Engineers Inc. (2019). https://doi.org/10.1109/Blockchain.2019.00067

13. Hong, S., Yue, T., Liu, H.: Vehicle energy system active defense: a health assessment of lithium-ion batteries. Int. J. Int. Syst. (2020). https://doi.org/10.1002/int.22309

14. Hong, S., Zeng, Y.: A health assessment framework of lithium-ion batteries for cyber defense. Appl. Soft Comput. **101**, 107067 (2021). https://doi.org/10.1016/j.asoc.2020.107067

15. Kanemitsu, H., Nakazato, H.: KadRTT: routing with network proximity and uniform ID arrangement in Kademlia. In: 2021 IFIP Networking Conference, IFIP Networking 2021. Institute of Electrical and Electronics Engineers Inc. (2021). https://doi.org/10.23919/IFIPNetworking52078.2021.9472816

16. Karaduman, B., Mustafiz, S., Challenger, M.: FTG+PM for the model-driven development of wireless sensor network based IoT systems. In: Companion Proceedings - 24th International Conference on Model-Driven Engineering Languages and Systems, MODELS-C 2021, pp. 306–316. Institute of Electrical and Electronics Engineers Inc. (2021). https://doi.org/10.1109/MODELS-C53483.2021.00052

17. Kreku, J., Vallivaara, V., Halunen, K., Suomalainen, J.: Evaluating the efficiency of blockchains in IoT with simulations. In: IoTBDS 2017 - Proceedings of the 2nd International Conference on Internet of Things, Big Data and Security, pp. 216–223. SciTePress (2017). https://doi.org/10.5220/0006240502160223

18. Kuzlu, M., Pipattanasomporn, M., Gurses, L., Rahman, S.: Performance analysis of a hyperledger fabric blockchain framework: throughput, latency and scalability. In:

Proceedings - 2019 2nd IEEE International Conference on Blockchain, Blockchain 2019, pp. 536–540. Institute of Electrical and Electronics Engineers Inc. (2019). https://doi.org/10.1109/Blockchain.2019.00003

19. Lano, K., Fang, S., Alfraihi, H., Kolahdouz-Rahimi, S.: Simplified specification languages for flexible and agile modelling. In: Proceedings - 2019 ACM/IEEE 22nd International Conference on Model Driven Engineering Languages and Systems Companion, MODELS-C 2019, pp. 460–467. Institute of Electrical and Electronics Engineers Inc. (2019). https://doi.org/10.1109/MODELS-C.2019.00074

20. Lee, S., Kim, S.: Blockchain as a cyber defense: opportunities, applications, and challenges. IEEE Access **10**, 2602–2618 (2022). https://doi.org/10.1109/ACCESS.2021.3136328

21. Li, T.,et al.: Rational protocols and attacks in blockchain system. Secur. Commun. Netw. 2020 (2020). https://doi.org/10.1155/2020/8839047

22. Liaskos, S., Anand, T., Alimohammadi, N.: Architecting blockchain network simulators: a model-driven perspective. In: IEEE International Conference on Blockchain and Cryptocurrency, ICBC 2020. Institute of Electrical and Electronics Engineers Inc. (2020). https://doi.org/10.1109/ICBC48266.2020.9169413

23. Liu, S.: ● Global spending on blockchain solutions 2024 | Statista (2020). https://www.statista.com/statistics/800426/worldwide-blockchain-solutions-spending/ Published by Statista Research Department U.S. dollars by 2024

24. Made Satvika Iswari, N., Budiardjo, E.K., Hasibuan, Z.A.: Aspect oriented programming approach for variability feature implementation in software product line engineering. In: 2020 5th International Conference on Informatics and Computing, ICIC 2020. Institute of Electrical and Electronics Engineers Inc. (2020). https://doi.org/10.1109/ICIC50835.2020.9288558

25. Mart, O., Negru, C., Pop, F., Castiglione, A.: Observability in kubernetes cluster: automatic anomalies detection using prometheus. In: Proceedings - 2020 IEEE 22nd International Conference on High Performance Computing and Communications, IEEE 18th International Conference on Smart City and IEEE 6th International Conference on Data Science and Systems, HPCC-SmartCity-DSS 2020, pp. 565–570. Institute of Electrical and Electronics Engineers Inc. (2020). https://doi.org/10.1109/HPCC-SmartCity-DSS50907.2020.00071

26. Mufid, M.R., Basofi, A., Al Rasyid, M.U.H., Rochimansyah, I.F., Rokhim, A.: Design an MVC model using python for flask framework development. In: IES 2019 - International Electronics Symposium: The Role of Techno-Intelligence in Creating an Open Energy System Towards Energy Democracy, Proceedings, pp. 214–219. Institute of Electrical and Electronics Engineers Inc. (2019). https://doi.org/10.1109/ELECSYM.2019.8901656

27. Nakamoto, S.: A peer-to-peer electronic cash system. J. Gen. Philos. Sci. (2008)

28. Nehal, A., Ahlawat, P.: Securing IoT applications with OP-TEE from hardware level OS. In: Proceedings of the 3rd International Conference on Electronics and Communication and Aerospace Technology, ICECA 2019, pp. 1441–1444. Institute of Electrical and Electronics Engineers Inc. (2019). https://doi.org/10.1109/ICECA.2019.8822040

29. Pathak, N., Singh, B.M., Sharma, G.: UML 2.0 based framework for the development of secure web application. Int. J. Inf. Technol. **9**(1), 101–109 (2017). https://doi.org/10.1007/s41870-017-0001-3

30. Pohl, K., Böckle, G., Van Der Linden, F.: Software product line engineering: Foundations, principles, and techniques. Springer, Heidelberg (2005). https://doi.org/10.1007/3-540-28901-1

31. Polge, J., Ghatpande, S., Kubler, S., Robert, J., Le Traon, Y.: BlockPerf: a hybrid blockchain emulator/simulator framework. IEEE Access **9**, 107858–107872 (2021). https://doi.org/10.1109/ACCESS.2021.3101044

32. Qu, Y., Pokhrel, S.R., Garg, S., Gao, L., Xiang, Y.: A blockchained federated learning framework for cognitive computing in industry 4.0 networks. IEEE Trans. Ind. Inform. **17**(4), 2964–2973 (2021). https://doi.org/10.1109/TII.2020.3007817

33. Ranjan, P., Sharma, B., Mittal, A., Gupta, H., Singh, A.K.: Blockchain powered government financial system, pp. 1–6. Institute of Electrical and Electronics Engineers (IEEE) (2022). https://doi.org/10.1109/iconat53423.2022.9726095

34. Ray, P.P., Dash, D., Salah, K., Kumar, N.: Blockchain for IoT-based healthcare: background, consensus, platforms, and use cases. IEEE Syst. J. **15**(1), 85–94 (2021). https://doi.org/10.1109/JSYST.2020.2963840

35. Sarkar, D., Bhalla, M., Singal, S.M.: Enhancing unified process workflows using UML. In: Proceedings of the 7th International Conference Confluence 2017 on Cloud Computing, Data Science and Engineering, pp. 788–792. Institute of Electrical and Electronics Engineers Inc. (2017). https://doi.org/10.1109/CONFLUENCE.2017.7943257

36. Sengul, O., Ozkilicaslan, H., Arda, E., Yavanoglu, U., Dogru, I.A., Selcuk, A.A.: Implementing a method for docker image security. In: 14th International Conference on Information Security and Cryptology, ISCTURKEY 2021 - Proceedings, pp. 34–39. Institute of Electrical and Electronics Engineers Inc. (2021). https://doi.org/10.1109/ISCTURKEY53027.2021.9654383

37. Sonmez, R., Sönmez, F.Ö., Ahmadisheykhsarmast, S.: Blockchain in project management: a systematic review of use cases and a design decision framework. J. Ambient Intell. Humanized Comput. 3 (2021). https://doi.org/10.1007/s12652-021-03610-1

38. Stoykov, L., Zhang, K., Jacobsen, H.A.: Demo: VIBES: fast blockchain simulations for large-scale peer-to-peer networks. In: Middleware 2017 - Proceedings of the 2017 Middleware Posters and Demos 2017: Proceedings of the Posters and Demos Session of the 18th International Middleware Conference, pp. 19–20. Association for Computing Machinery Inc, New York, NY, USA (2017). https://doi.org/10.1145/3155016.3155020

39. Wang, X., Al-Mamun, A., Yan, F., Zhao, D.: Toward accurate and efficient emulation of public blockchains in the cloud. In: Da Silva, D., Wang, Q., Zhang, L.-J. (eds.) CLOUD 2019. LNCS, vol. 11513, pp. 67–82. Springer, Cham (2019). https://doi.org/10.1007/978-3-030-23502-4_6

40. Xiao, W., et al.: Blockchain for secure-GaS: blockchain-powered secure natural gas IoT system with AI-enabled gas prediction and transaction in smart city. IEEE Internet Things J. **8**(8), 6305–6312 (2021). https://doi.org/10.1109/JIOT.2020.3028773

41. Xu, J., Dang, F., Ding, X., Zhou, M.: A survey on vulnerability detection tools of smart contract bytecode. In: Proceedings of 2020 IEEE 3rd International Conference on Information Systems and Computer Aided Education, ICISCAE 2020, pp. 94–98. Institute of Electrical and Electronics Engineers Inc. (2020). https://doi.org/10.1109/ICISCAE51034.2020.9236931

Research on Key Technologies for the Trusted Perception of Network Information for Big Data

Yuxiang Li[1(✉)] and Fakariah Hani Mohd Ali[2]

[1] Department of Computer Science, Guangdong University of Science and Technology, 523083
Dongguan, China
gdliyuxiang@qq.com
[2] School of Computer Science, Universiti Teknologi Mara (UiTM),
50250 Kuala Lumpur, Malaysia

Abstract. With the rapid development of modern computer and network technology, the rapid growth of the number of network users, the exponential growth of data information between users, the complexity and variety of network threats are mixed in network information in the big data environment, including viruses, botnets, backdoors, advanced persistent threats, and other traditional network attacks. The study of the trusted perception of such network threat information has become one of the main directions of information security and has attracted much attention. In this paper, through the study of the behavior of scenario-based network entities, a global trust assessment method of network nodes based on context awareness is proposed to improve the credibility of network information--the key technologies of network information trust perception oriented to scenario awareness in big data environment are discussed and studied.

Keywords: Trusted perception · Cyber threats · Big data network

1 Introduction

With the explosive development of computer and network technology, the number of Internet users has grown rapidly, network information has grown exponentially and rapidly, and there are more and more types of network threats mixed in network information in the big data environment, including viruses, botnets, backdoors, advanced persistent threats and other traditional network attacks. Network attacks are increasingly sophisticated, continuous, organized, armed, and intelligent, and it is difficult to identify the credibility of information by relying on the strength of a single organization. The traditional static security control measures that rely on border defense are gradually being replaced by intelligent security means based on big data analysis. Information security technology is gradually evolving from passive after-the-fact analysis to active pre-defense, and mastering the network threat posture is gradually evolving from a single force of the organization to a multi-organization cooperation. At present, in the face of an increasingly complex network security environment, adopting a dynamic trust assessment method based on situational awareness to ensure the security of the network is also an effective way to enhance the credibility of network information. "Cyber threat intelligence-driven information security defense" has become a recognized future development direction of information security in the industry, and threat intelligence in the big data environment has received widespread attention from academia and industry. More and more organizations and institutions in the world have begun to share known threat information and defense means with other organizations and institutions, form intelligence cooperation and sharing, linkage defense effects, complete linkage analysis and attack traceability, and obtain a rapidly evolving network threat posture. Figure 1 below is a statistical chart of the network security time in various provinces in China.

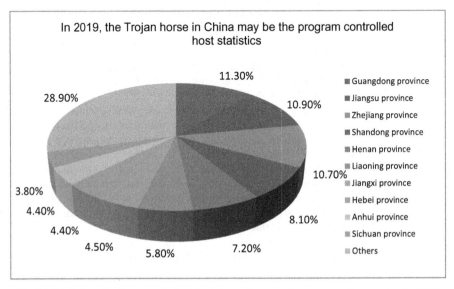

Fig. 1. Statistics of cyber security incidents in various provinces across the country in 2019.

While the internet brings convenience to people's work, study and life, it also brings huge security risks. According to statistics, among all network threat attacks, network security incidents account for 79%, and data protection will be the key defense direction of future network security. In the face of the development trend of globalization and information technology in the world today, compared with the traditional information network, the credible perception research of network threat intelligence has just started, and many problems are still in the early stage of exploration, and there is still a lack of accurate threat intelligence source credibility assessment methods, basic intelligence content trust perception mechanisms, and effective threat intelligence infrastructure node threat type intelligent identification methods. Figure 2 below is statistics of various types of network security incidents in China.

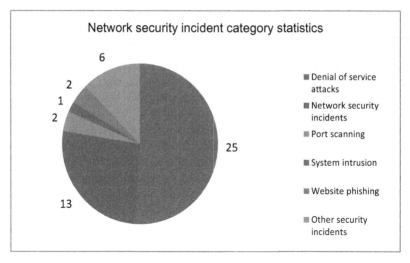

Fig. 2. Statistics of Network security incident category.

Facing the development trend of globalization and information technology in the world today, compared with the traditional information network, the credible perception research of network threat intelligence has just started, and many problems are still in the early stage of exploration, and there is still a lack of accurate threat intelligence source credibility assessment methods, basic intelligence content trust perception mechanisms, and effective threat intelligence infrastructure node threat type intelligent identification methods. Aiming at this problem and the opportunities faced, this paper proposes a global trust assessment method of network nodes based on context-aware through the study of context-based network entity behavior, and improves the credibility of network information--the key technology of network information trust perception oriented to scenario awareness in big data environment is discussed and studied.

With the rapid development of the Internet, the network is facing more and more serious security threats, and the traditional network security mechanism based on static authorization has been unable to meet the requirements of the current network security situation. On the one hand, due to the complexity of the network structure and the fragility of the network, the network itself faces internal security threats, on the other hand, due to the improper operation of users and malicious attacks by hackers, the network is also facing increasingly serious external security threats. Therefore, it is necessary to adopt a new security mechanism based on trust assessment to evaluate the security of computer networks in the form of dynamic assessments, so as to establish a high-trust network based on dynamic trust.

In China, Scientist Lin Chuang was the first to put forward the concept of trusted network, and he claimed that in a trusted network can be expectable, manageable and detectable, behavior results can be evaluated, and the behavior abnormalities can be managed [1]. The essence of the trusted relationship is the most complex social relationship, with a series of complex attributes such as uncertainty, ambiguity, and dynamics, and is an abstract psychological cognitive process that involves assumptions, expectations, behaviors, and environmental factors, and is difficult to define and quantify [2]. The reason why human society can operate smoothly is that it depends on trusted relationships between individuals and organizations. Similarly, trust is the foundation of various computer network security technologies. Kamvar et al. of Stanford University proposed a global reputation model [3], which calculates the global reputation of a node to be evaluated by calculating the credibility of all relevant nodes in the network to a node to be evaluated. Zeng Jianbo et al. proposed a trust model based on DS evidence theory [4], which solves the shortcomings of incomplete information provided by a single node, and uses recommendation information to supplement trust evidence, but does not distinguish the difference between the amount of information contained in recommended nodes.

The domestic guarantee mechanism for network information security is also continuously improved, but in view of the rapid growth of the network, the quantification of network information, and the complexity of the network layout environment, and most of the existing models do not consider the impact of the situation on trust, which will lead to the inaccuracy of trust assessment, so a new trust assessment method based on situational perception is proposed.

2   Analysis and Research of Key Technical Models

At present, scholars have proposed a variety of evaluation models for the evaluation of network trust, and the basis of its modeling is mainly based on people's cognition of trust, and people use a variety of mathematical methods to model and study trust, through the development of these models, enrich people's understanding of trust relationships, and effectively promote the development of trust assessment.

2.1   Analysis and Comparison of Mainstream Models

Based on the scenario-aware network information credibility assessment method, through the collection of context-aware information, the model representation of scenario-aware information, and then the relevant processing and application of scenario information to related scenarios, the credibility assessment results of relevant network nodes are finally obtained [5]. At present, there are the following models commonly used in mainstream scenario awareness research: trust evaluation model based on cloud model, trust model based on fuzzy decision analysis, trust model based on Bayesian network, trust model based on DS evidence theory, and global trust model. As shown in Fig. 3 below:

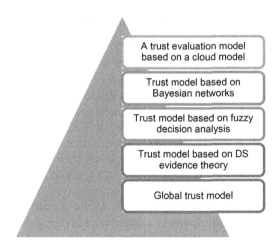

Fig. 3. Mainstream model of situational awareness.

For the multi-trust model that has been proposed so far, the trust calculation and measurement are carried out in different scenarios. For the above-mentioned models, this paper comprehensively compares the types of trusts, theoretical basis, computational complexity, and modeling factors of the model. The specific comparison results are shown in Table 1 [6, 7]:

Table 1. Comparison of trust models.

Model category	Trust category	Modeling fundamentals	Computational complexity	Model trust source
Trust evaluation model based on cloud model	Direct trust plus indirect trust	Cloud model theory	More complex	User feedback evaluation, historical trust, and evaluation subject trust
Trust model based on fuzzy decision analysis	Subjective trust	Fuzzy decision theory	Relatively simple and easy to implement	Evidence of user behavior
Trust model based on Bayesian network	Direct trust plus indirect trust	Bayesian theory	Compares complex	Node properties themselves
Trust model based on DS evidence theory	Subjective trust	DS Evidence Theory	The reasoning process is very complex	Node history interaction record
A global trust model for P2P networks	Global trust	Matrix theory	General	Node history interaction record
Similarity-weighted global trust model	Global trust	Matrix theory	General	Node behavior similarity

2.2 Multi-dimensional Analysis of Intelligence Source Credibility Assessment Method

In this paper, the multi-dimensional intelligence source credibility assessment method is also studied. Studies have shown that the level of trust in sources in social media is related to the identity of the source [8], and that disinformation is likely to be generated and spread by network bots [9, 10]. In general, certified sources of information are more trustworthy than anonymous sources of information. Therefore, this topic quantifies the degree of trust based on whether the intelligence source s_i has been authenticated by a real name or anonymously, and defines the authentication score of the intelligence source s_i as AS (s_i), with a value range [0, 1]. If the s_i is certified, the as (s_i) is 1; If the s_i is anonymous, the $AS(s_i)$ is 0.2 (a lower score). In general, the longer an intelligence source is registered, the more credible it is. We use the registration time score of the intelligence source s_i as an assessment factor for the credibility of the intelligence source, and the registration time score of the intelligence source s_i can be defined as follows:

$$RS(s_i) = \frac{|R(s_i) - \mu_R|}{\sigma_R} \tag{1}$$

where $R(s_i)$ represents the registration time of the intelligence source s_i, μ_R represents the average registration time of all intelligence sources, and σ_R represents the standard deviation of the registration time of all intelligence sources.

In the network of intelligence-sharing communities, the historical publication behavior of intelligence sources is an important basis for assessing the credibility of intelligence sources. Although there is no significant difference between the untrusted intelligence source and the trusted intelligence source in the characteristics of "the number of likes per intelligence post" and the "number of shares per intelligence post", the false intelligence and trusted intelligence released by them are significantly different in these two characteristic dimensions. In info-Trust, the behavioral trust factor of the intelligence source, which is referred to as T_i^B, considers the number and influence of the false intelligence history of the intelligence source s_i, and the calculation model formula is as follows:

$$T_i^B = 1 - \frac{\sum_{f \in Q_i} I_{i,f}}{\sum_{i=1}^{N} \sum_{f \in Q_i} I_{i,f}} \tag{2}$$

Among them Q_i is a collection of false intelligence s_i intelligence sources, f is a piece of false intelligence in the Q_i, and I_f is the influence of false intelligence f.

In intelligence-sharing community networks, trusted intelligence sources often have strong network structure associations with other intelligence sources. In contrast, untrusted intelligence sources often blindly focus on other intelligence sources and have weak network structure associations with other intelligence sources [11]. From Fig. 4 below, it can be seen that untrusted intelligence sources have a lower local agglomeration coefficient value than trusted intelligence sources.

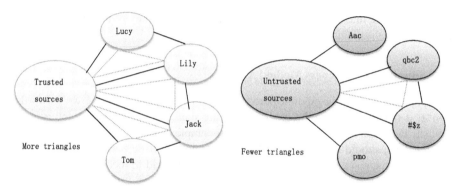

Fig. 4. Schematic diagram of the difference in local agglomeration coefficients between trusted and untrusted intelligence sources.

3   Specific Analysis of Situational Awareness

The research in this paper starts from the credibility of network nodes, introduces contextual information into the trust evaluation of network nodes by defining related concepts and establishing relevant models, so as to realize the trust assessment of network nodes based on situational awareness, on this basis, by studying the correlation degree between network nodes and studying its quantitative methods, the credibility of each node is reasonably combined, so as to achieve a combined trust assessment based on the multidimensional characteristics of the network, and evaluate the trust value of the entire network or subnet.

3.1   Situational Awareness Method Proposed

The research on the credibility perception of network information in the big data environment is mainly from the research, perception and discrimination of the trust assessment method of network nodes based on situational awareness to the characteristics of the network's own attributes, using trusted computing and appropriate models for selection, integrating the scenario information of the network itself, further evaluating the credibility of existing network nodes, obtaining the credibility results of network nodes, and completing the assessment [12]. In view of the threat intelligence in network information, this paper mainly analyzes whether the specific content of threat intelligence itself is credible, whether the network threat intelligence content itself is credible, and the lack of credibility assessment mechanism for network intelligence information content itself.

According to the specific environment of the network, the context-related information of situational awareness is introduced to assess the credibility of the current network nodes, so as to achieve the judgment and processing of the credibility of the network information intelligence transmitted by the current network nodes. The analysis of the network environment includes the analysis of the situational characteristics of the network nodes, as well as the comprehensive analysis and evaluation of the network's own attribute characteristics, such as network traffic, the number of successes and failures of network node interactions, etc., and the evaluation and study of the credibility of the network nodes is obtained.

3.2 Situational Awareness Method Analysis

This paper focuses on the credible perception of threat intelligence in network information. It is mainly based on the credibility of the source of cyber threat intelligence to evaluate the research. Trust, as one of the most complex and dynamic concepts in social relationships, should consider the trust factor from a holistic perspective. Ignoring a trust factor, such as a user feedback factor, is likely to lead to incorrect or unfair trust decisions. In this project, we will integrate multi-dimensional trust factors to solve the problem of confidence assessment of threat intelligence sources, and solve the problem of inaccurate trust decision-making problems in the dynamic allocation of weights to multiple trust factors through the combined algorithm of ordered weighted average and weighted moving average.

The intelligence data obtained by perception has the characteristics of heterogeneity, massiveness, dispersion, and real-time. The reliability, validity, security and stability of threat intelligence data have become difficulties in the research of credible perception of threat intelligence. Judging the credibility of the information content itself in massive, decentralized, heterogeneous, and real-time data is also one of the key issues to be solved in this course. In general, the credibility of threat intelligence includes multiple dimensions such as intelligence relevance, intelligence timeliness, intelligence completeness, intelligence accuracy, intelligence compatibility, and intelligence consistency, and this topic will analyze and discuss the feasibility of intelligence content itself from multiple dimensions.

3.3 Results and Analysis

Starting from the situational awareness analysis, this paper integrates the analysis of the scenario environment, integrates the scenario information into the credibility analysis of network information, and improves the credibility perception of network information. Feature 1 of this paper: The contextual information and network trust assessment are effectively combined, and the global trust of the node is calculated through a more detailed quantitative analysis of the existing global trust model. This method can dynamically assess the credibility of nodes in different contexts, and meet the dynamic adaptability of the situation of trusted assessment. Feature 2: In this study, we conducted an in-depth study on the problem of insufficient consideration of trust factors in the credibility assessment of threat intelligence sources is conducted and the subjective allocation of trust factor weights in this project, and considered the integration of multi-dimensional credibility factors to solve such problems and improve the credibility perception evaluation effect of threat intelligence sources. Feature 3: This paper conducts in-depth research on the problems of low efficiency and low accuracy of infrastructure node threat type marking in threat intelligence, and considers the use of explicit relationships between threat intelligence and intelligent algorithms to automatically and accurately identify threat types of infrastructure nodes.

This paper intends to study and discuss the "key technology of network information trust perception for big data", which has certain application values: and the main application value has the following two points: Firstly, In view of the increasingly severe network security situation, the original network security mechanism based on static authorization must be changed to a dynamic network security mechanism based on trust, and under the trust-based mechanism, a high-trust network with user and network behavior status can be monitored, behavior results can be evaluated, and abnormal behavior can be managed. The research scheme of "Global Trust Assessment Method for Network Node Entities Based on Context Awareness" proposed in this paper provides a certain basis for the subsequent research on the trust perception of network information. Secondly, the credibility analysis of network information intelligence sources. Aiming at the problem of insufficient consideration of trust factors in the credibility assessment of intelligence sources, a multi-dimensional threat intelligence source credibility assessment method is proposed. This method evaluates the credibility of intelligence sources from four perspectives: identity trust factor, behavioral trust factor, relationship trust factor and feedback trust factor, and dynamically allocates weights to the four trust factors by using the combined algorithm of ordered weighted average and weighted moving average. The integration of multi-dimensional trust factors to analyze the credibility of network information intelligence sources provides a new idea and direction for future research in this regard.

4   Conclusion

In this paper, the credibility perception of network information in the big data environment is mainly from the research, perception and discrimination of the trust assessment method of network nodes based on situational awareness to the characteristics of the network's own attributes, using trusted computing and appropriate models for selection, integrating the scenario information of the network itself, further evaluating the credibility of existing network nodes, obtaining the credibility results of network nodes, and completing the assessment. In view of the threat intelligence in the network information, the specific content of the threat intelligence itself is the focus of this paper, and the relevant research can be carried out are on whether the network threat intelligence content itself is credible or not, and the lack of a credible assessment mechanism for the network intelligence information content itself. Starting from the analysis of various threats to current network information, this paper analyzes the six key technical models of the current trust perception of network information. The research on the credibility assessment method of network information and the improvement of credibility have reached the goal of improving the security of the entire network, for the entire society, the whole country, as small as each individual, the study of the credibility perception of network information in the big data environment can reduce the occurrence of network security incidents to a certain extent, which has very far-reaching significance.

Acknowledgements. This work is supported by 2021 Guangdong Basic and Applied Basic Youth Fund Project (No. 2021A1515110834), Guangdong University of Science and Technology University Innovative Strong School Project 2020-Integrated Data Management and Application

Research Center (No. GKY-2020CQJG-1), Guangdong University of Science and Technology Natural Science Research General Project in 2020 (No. GKY-2020KYYBK-31).

References

1. Lin, C., Peng, X.: Trusted network research. Chin. J. Comput. **28**(5), 751–758 (2005)
2. Li, X.: Research on the Key Technology of Trusted Perception of Cyber Threat Intelligence Oriented to Big Data. Beijing University of Posts and Telecommunications, Beijing (2020)
3. Tang, H., Sun, Q.: Research and Design of Real-Time Network Credibility Assessment Based on Situational Awareness. Beijing University of Posts and Telecommunications, Beijing (2018)
4. Li, X., Ma, H., Yao, W., Gui, X.: Data-driven and feedback-enhanced trust computing pattern for large-scale multi-cloud collaborative services. IEEE Trans. Serv. Comput. **11**(4), 671–684 (2018)
5. Wang, X., Hu, S., Ye, Q., et al.: Credible probability assessment method based on bayesian network. J. Huazhong Univ. Sci. Technol. (Nat. Sci. Ed.) (s1), 79–82 (2012)
6. Li, X., Ma, H., Zhou, F., Gui, X.: Service operator-aware trust scheme for resource matchmaking across multiple clouds. IEEE Trans. Parallel Distrib Syst **26**(4), 1419–1429 (2014)
7. Li, X., Ma, H., Zhou, F., Yao, W.: T-broker: a trust-aware service brokering scheme for multiple cloud collaborative services. IEEE Trans. Inf. Forensics Secur. **10**(7), 1402–1415 (2015)
8. SHu, K., Wang, S., Liu, H.: Understanding user profiles on social media for fake new detection. In: Proceedings of IEEE Conference on Multimedia Information Processing and Retreival (MIPR), pp. 430–435 (2018)
9. Shu, K., Sliva, A., Wang, S., Tang, J., Liu, H.: Fake news detection on social media: a data mining perspective. ACM SIGKDD Explor. Newslett **19**(1), 22–36 (2017)
10. Shao, C., Ciampaglia, G.L., Varol, O., Flammini, A., Menczer, F.: The spread of fake news by social bots (2017). https://arxiv.org/abs/1707,07592
11. Yang, C., Harkreader, R., Gu, G.: Empirical evaluation and new design for fighting evolving Twitter spammers. IEEE Trans. Inf. Forensics Secur. **8**(8), 1280–1293 (2013)
12. Samtani, S., Abate, M., Benjamin, V., Li, W.: Cybersecurity as an industry: a cyber threat intelligence perspective. In: Holt, T.J., Bossler, A.M. (eds.) The Palgrave Handbook of International Cybercrime and Cyberdeviance, pp. 135–154. Springer, Cham (2020). https://doi.org/10.1007/978-3-319-78440-3_8

Micro-expression Recognition Method Combining Dual-Stream Convolution and Capsule Network

Lanwei Zeng[1], Yudong Wang[1], Chang Zhu[1(✉)], Wenchao Jiang[1], and Jiaxing Li[2]

[1] School of Computers, Guangdong University of Technology, Guangzhou 510006, China
464036181@qq.com

[2] The Hong Kong Polytechnic University, Hong Kong, China

Abstract. Aiming at the problem that the existing micro-expression recognition methods do not comprehensively consider the facial spatial structure information and the single input feature, which leads to the low recognition rate of accuracy, the method combining dual-stream convolution and capsule network is proposed. An improved dual-stream convolutional shallow network is used to extract feature, and CapsNet is used for micro-expression identification. This method first takes the image with the magnified motion amplitude and the optical flow image as dual feature input, and uses attention mechanism and dual-stream convolutional network to extract the spatiotemporal features. Dynamic routing between capsules is used to encode features for better expression. Finally, the squashing function for classification. Experiments are used CASME II, SAMM and SMIC datasets. Contrast with existing advanced methods, accuracy of micro-expression i identification is increased by 3.34%, 3.71%, and 4.13%, respectively, indicating the advanced nature and effectiveness of this method.

Keywords: Micro-expression recognition · Capsules network · Dual-stream convolutional network · Dynamic routing mechanism · Attention mechanism

1 Introduction

Micro-expressions is an unconscious facial movement that appear in small local areas within a short period of time. It is usually generated when a person tries to conceal the inner expression. It can neither be faked nor suppressed, reflecting the real emotional state of the person [1]. The shortness and Low range facial motion make it difficult to be recognized by the human eye in real time. Therefore, recognition method has developed from manual discrimination to the use of technological means.

Micro-expression identification initially used based on traditional feature extraction recognition methods. Pfister et al. [2] proposed LBP-TOP, which extending dimensionality to three dimensions, and performs micro-expression identify by extracting features by combining local binary mode in three orthogonal planes. Aiming at low-amplitude problem of micro-expression facial motion, Li et al. [3] applied EVM to micro-expression recognition, amplifying the motion amplitude. For the sake of leverage micro-expression

Y. Xu et al. (Eds.): ML4CS 2022, LNCS 13656, pp. 479–494, 2023.
https://doi.org/10.1007/978-3-031-20099-1_41

motion information in videos, scholars began to introduce optical flow features into micro-expression identification method. Liu et al. [4] presented MDMO Flow Feature, and Liong et al. [5] proposed Bi-WOOF with global weighting of optical strain and local weighting of optical flow intensity. However, Traditional methods are difficult to perform in improving the recognition rate of micro-expressions.

Micro-expression recognition starts using deep learning. Li et al. [6] applied VGG-16 to a micro-expression recognition task and achieved higher accuracy than traditional recognition methods, which became a benchmark method based on deep learning methods. But training traditional deep convolutional networks requires a lot of data, and does not utilize spatial and temporal between image frames. Meanwhile, the small number of micro-expression datasets can easily lead to overfitting and cannot be directly applied to traditional deep network models. In response to the above problems, scholars first preprocess the raw micro-expression video to extract information between image frames before applying it to the training network. Gan et al. [7] presented OFF-ApexNet, in micro-expression tasks used the optical flow image into shallow convolutional network. While Khor et al. [8] used dual-stream shallow convolutional neural network. Xia et al. [9] used EVM for micro-expression image sequences and then fed the extracted feature images to a network for micro-expression identification. In addition, for the localization of micro-expressions, Wang et al. [10] presented micro-expression identification network based on micro-attention and residual networks. The network integrates micro-attention units in the residual block, which makes the network focus on the regions where micro-expression movements occur during the feature extraction phase. Li et al. [11] presented a feature learning network combining global and local information to recognize micro-expressions.

However, convolutional neural networks have limitations in representing the whole-part relationship. These convolutional neural network approaches do not take into account both facial structural features and feature orientation information, and ignore the relative relationship between Action Units (AUs). Sabour et al. [12] proposed capsule networks to deeply understand the relationship between the whole and the parts of an image, with rotational invariance, and explore the relationship between features through dynamic routing mechanisms, which are considered as promising methods for image classification. Quang et al. [13] first use of capsule networks in the field of micro-expressions and performed micro-expression identification by extracting feature relationships between the part and the whole. But there are problems of single input feature and the lack of temporal information. Liu et al. [14] input optical flow images to a multi-stream convolutional network to extract features, and finally use a capsule network to complete micro-expression recognition. However, only optical flow characteristics are considered, which is easy to lose the key information in the original image.

Inspired by these works, author presented micro-expression identification method combining dual-stream convolution and capsule network. The modified dual-stream convolutional network is used a micro-expression feature extraction network, and images after Eulerian videos amplification and optical flow images are selected as the input to extract spatiotemporal information, solving the problem of single feature input. Considering the localization of micro-expression motion, AU attention mechanism is hint at in spatial convolutional network, which makes network dedicated on the region where micro-expression motion occurs. Finally, the dynamic routing mechanism of the capsule network is used to leverage face structure information to improve accuracy. Experiments were carried out on the micro-expression data sets SMIC [15], CASME II [16] and SAMM [17]. Compared with the existing advanced methods, the accuracy of micro expression recognition increased by 3.34%, 3.71% and 4.13%, respectively. At the same time, it also proves the validity of face structure information and multi-feature information input.

2 Proposed Methods

The framework of this paper is shown in Fig. 1. Dual-stream convolutional network is splited into two parts: spatial convolution and temporal convolution. It takes individual frames and optical flow images as input to obtain temporal and spatial information of the face. Micro-expression recognition is a recognition task for subtle information. Therefore, during the input stage, preprocessing the start frame and vertex frame of micro expression image sequence, images amplified by EVM and optical flow images extracted are used to enhance the quality of network input image. AU attention mechanism is introduced in spatial convolutional network to withdrawal locally valid information of micro-expressions. Dual feature information is fused and input to the capsule network, encoded by decoded by the full connection layer, then decoded by fully connected layer. Final result of micro-expression classification is obtained using the squeeze function.

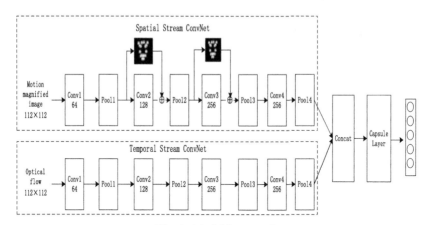

Fig. 1. Model framework

2.1 Preprocessing

2.1.1 Face Detection and Cropping

For sake decrease influence of irrelevant background on the model learning effect, it is necessary to perform positioning detection and cropping on the face image. First, we use the face detector [18] for each frame to locate feature points for face detection, and use these key points to divide the rectangular recognition frame of the face area. Secondly, since the face image has multiple poses and angles, The following actions must be performed face-face alignment on the image to eliminate the facial and sequence differences in the expressionless state. Finally we get the face image with size 112×112.

2.1.2 Amplify Facial Movements

It is difficult to observe the small movement amplitude of the muscle with the naked eye, so we used Eulerian video motion amplification [19] to make micro-expression more visible. First, we decompose the micro-expression sequences into different spatial frequencies by multi-resolution pyramids, and then perform time-domain band-pass filtering on each image to obtain the target frequency band. Due to the small range of facial muscle movement of micro expression, the target frequency band is a low-frequency region. First, we decompose the micro-expression sequences into different spatial frequencies by multi-resolution pyramids, target frequency band is obtained by doing time-domain band-pass filter processing on the image with the purpose. This is because the amplitude of facial muscle movements is small in the case of micro-expressions, the target frequency band is a low-frequency region. Then the frequency band after approximation filtering with Taylor series is multiplied by the amplification factor α to linearly amplify the signal in the target area. Finally, we reconstruct the image by synthesizing the original signal with the amplified signal.

2.1.3 Optical Flow Feature Extraction

Optical flow method is to study the changes between video images. It can describe the small movements of facial muscles [20], clearly reflect the region where micro-expression movements occur, and enhance image feature extraction. In this paper, the TV-L1 [21] optical flow algorithm is used to computed motion information between micro-expression frame and vertex frame.

Suppose pixel value at position (x, y) of face image at time t is $I(x, y, t)$, and distance of point moves in Δt time is $(\Delta x, \Delta y)$. Based on the principle of constant pixel intensity of the optical flow method, the pixel values before and after the movement are considered constant, as shown in Eq. (1):

$$I(x, y, t) = I(x + \Delta x, y + \Delta y, t + \Delta t) \tag{1}$$

According to Taylor extension, the following equations can be obtained.

$$I(x, y, t) = I(x, y, t) + \frac{\partial I}{\partial x}\Delta x + \frac{\partial I}{\partial y}\Delta y + \frac{\partial I}{\partial t}\Delta t + \varepsilon \tag{2}$$

where ε on behalf a negligible second order infinitesimal term, When Δt tends infinity, Eq. 3 obtained by combining Eq. (1–2):

$$\frac{\partial I}{\partial x}\frac{\Delta x}{\Delta t} + \frac{\partial I}{\partial y}\frac{\Delta y}{\Delta t} + \frac{\partial I}{\partial x} = 0 \tag{3}$$

u and v be the horizontal and vertical parts of optical flow field, defined as shown in Eq. (4):

$$u = \frac{\Delta x}{\Delta t}, v = \frac{\Delta y}{\Delta t} \tag{4}$$

The final equation obtained is shown below:

$$u\frac{\partial I}{\partial x} + v\frac{\partial I}{\partial y} + \frac{\partial I}{\partial t} = 0 \tag{5}$$

where partial derivative of the pixel (x, y, t) along each direction is obtained from image data. u and v which are used to represent micro-expression samples.

2.2 Dual-Stream Convolutional Feature Extraction Network

As shown in Fig. 1, this paper uses an improved dual-stream convolutional shallow network as the micro-expression feature extraction network. Convolutional layer can extract multi-dimensional features from images by convolution operation, and different convolutional layers extract detail different features. Pooling layers not only can reduce the dimensionality of output features. Therefore, convolution part of the feature extraction network uses 4 convolutional layers and 4 pooling layers. Specific parameters and structure are shown in Table 1. All convolutional kernels are of size 3 × 3 with a step size of 1. A 2 × 2 convolutional kernel with stride = 2 is applied convolutional layers for pooling operation. Finally author can obtain 7 × 7 feature map.

Table 1. Parameters and structure.

Layer	Filter	Stride	Output
Input			3 × 112 × 112
	—	—	
Conv1	3 × 3	1	64 × 112 × 112
Pool1	2 × 2	2	64 × 56 × 56
Conv2	3 × 3	1	128 × 56 × 56
Pool2	2 × 2	2	128 × 28 × 28
Conv3	3 × 3	1	256 × 28 × 28
Pool3	2 × 2	2	256 × 14 × 14
Conv4	3 × 3	1	256 × 14 × 14
Pool4	2 × 2	2	256 × 7 × 7

As shown in Fig. 1, AU attention mechanism of the spatial convolutional network is similar to Residual Net. The attention layer is applied on the convolution layer, and the low-level features are first multiplied with the attention layer. Then it is added with the convolved high-level features, so that both low-level and high-level characteristics can be represented.

For a single AU region, different locations have different importance. The change of the AU center point and part within the region have a large impact on the detection result, for which AU attention maps need to be constructed based on key facial landmarks. The key points of facial landmarks shown in Fig. 2(a) are necessary conditions for obtaining the attention map. The AU center cannot use the detected facial key points directly, but define a scaled distance as consult for face pixel movement by calculating the distance. For make the movement distance more suitable for all face images, for sake to facilitate the positioning of the AU center, the inner angle distance is used zoom distance. Due to symmetry of face, AU centers are paired, so each AU defines a pair of points. The attention map shown in Fig. 2(b) is built based on AU centers.

(a) landmark on a face   (b) attention map of the face

Fig. 2. Attention map generation

The face image size was resized to 100×100 to ensure that all images share the same scale. We used 7 pixels near the center of each AU, so AU size area is 15×15. The closer the point is to the center of the AU, the greater its weight. The relationship equation is shown as bellow:

$$W_a = 1 - 0.07d_m \qquad (6)$$

d_m is Manhattan distances of a location from the center of AU. The regions with higher weight values in the attention graph correspond to active regions of AU in the facial micro-expression images, and higher weight values enhance the active regions of AU.

As shown in Fig. 1, The feature map generated by the pooling layer in the second stage is multiplied with attention graph, in parallel with convolution operation in the third stage. The convolution result of the third stage is summed element by element to the pooled layer1 in this stage. Similarly, in the fourth stage, attention map performs the same operation together with the convolution layer, and its generated model is directly applied to the active region of micro-expression.

2.3 Capsule Network Layer

The parameters and structure of capsule network are shown in Fig. 3. Main work is to use the dynamic routing mechanism to encode the feature graph accessed by dual-stream convolution module. Feature map size after the dual-stream convolution feature extraction network is $512 \times 7 \times 7$, and the 2×2 convolution kernel with stride $= 1$ is used to gain a $256 \times 6 \times 6$ feature map. Finally, the classification of micro-expressions is obtained through squash function.

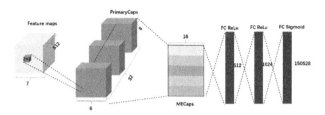

Fig. 3. Structure and parameters

Dynamic routing process between Primary-Caps layer and the ME-Caps layer is shown in Fig. 4. The current input layer of capsules comes from the output of the previous layer of capsules. The bottom layer capsule unit is connected to the high layer capsule unit through a weight matrix. We dynamically update the weight matrix by calculating and judging the correlation between the capsule layers. Repeat this process until convergence, and update the coupling coefficient. Where the coupling coefficient is obtained by SoftMax calculation with the following equation:

$$c_{ij} = soft \max(b_i) = \frac{\exp(b_{ij})}{\sum_k \exp(b_{ik})} \tag{7}$$

where b_{ij} denotes the log possibility of coupling from the capsule i to capsule j in the main capsule layer. B_{ij} is initially set to 0, and c_{ij} is iteratively refined by a dynamic routing. The input vector x_j for the j calculated as below:

$$x_j = \sum_i c_{ij} W_{ij} u_i \tag{8}$$

We apply the output vector obtained by applying the "squash" function for normalization. The modal length of output capsule can be made to represent the possibility, ensuring that output vector lies in the interval [0,1] and the direction remains constant. The v_j calculated as follows:

$$v_j = squash(x_j) = \frac{x_j}{\|x_j\|} \times \frac{\|x_j\|^2}{1 + \|x_j\|^2} \tag{9}$$

After the MECaps layer, there are three fully layers for image decoding. In training, we use real labels as reconstruction targets.

Network loss function L^{net} contains the marginal loss L^{margin} and reconstruction loss L_{rec}. In this paper, the reconstruction loss increases proportionally to 0.0005. Loss function is calculated as shown below:

$$L^{net} = \sum_k L_k^{m \arg in} + 0.0005 L_{rec} \tag{10}$$

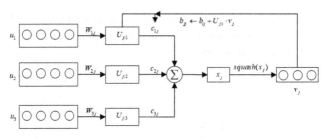

Fig. 4. Structure and dynamic routing

$$L_k^{m\,\arg\,in} = T_k \max(0, m^+ - \|v_k\|)^2 + \lambda(1 - T_k)\max(0, \|v_k\| - m^-)^2 \qquad (11)$$

$$L_{rec} = (x_{rec} - x)^2 \qquad (12)$$

The value of T_k is 1 when k exists and 0 if it not exist. m^+ denotes the boundary of correct classification, and m^- denotes the boundary of incorrect classification. x denotes the original image and x_{rec} denotes reconstructed image. λ denotes loss due to presence or absence of micro-expressions in conditioning image. In experiments, the values of m^+ and m^- are 0.9 and 0.1, and λ is set to 0.5 to control their effects.

3 Experiments

3.1 Dataset and Experimental Evaluation Metrics

SMIC recorded 164 micro-expression sequences of 16 subjects.

CASME II recorded 255 micro-expression sequences of 26 subjects. Micro-expression samples were encoded by AU with onset frame. The micro-expression dataset can be classified into 7 categories: happy, disgusted, depressed, fearful, sad, surprised, and other.

SAMM recorded 159 micro-expression sequences of 32 subjects. The micro-expression samples were coded using AU with 8 categories: happy, surprised, angry, contempt, disgusted, fearful, sad and other.

Due to the differences in micro-expression classification categories and sample sizes of the dataset, we take different sample classifications for the dataset. In the CASME II dataset, the sample amount of two categories, fear and sadness, is too small to be trained for feature learning. So we chose samples from 5 categories of happy, disgusted, surprised, depressed and other for the experiment. In SAMM dataset, we choose samples of angry, happy, surprised, contempt and other for the experiment. The specific expression categories and the number of samples are shown in Table 2.

Table 2. Samples categorization reference

Label	CASME II	Label	SAMM	Label	SMIC
Happy	63	Happy	26	Positive	51
Disgust	32	Anger	57	Negative	70
Surprise	25	Surprise	15	Surprise	43
Repression	27	Contempt	12		
Other	99	Other	26		

The evaluation metrics used for the experiments are accuracy and the composite metric F1-Score. Calculation is as follows:

$$Acc = \frac{TN + TP}{TN + TP + FN + FP} \tag{13}$$

$$F1 - Score = \frac{2 \times TP}{TP + FP + FN} \tag{14}$$

where TN is true negative. TP means a true positive is predicted to be a positive category, actual category is a positive. FN is false negative, predicted category is negative, actual category is positive. FP means false positive, predicted category is positive, actual category is negative.

Experiments use the LOSO protocol. The data of a subject is taken as test and the remaining subjects as training, average value is taken evaluation result. LOSO validation method maintains the diversity of subjects and prevents subject bias during training.

3.2 Experimental Setup and Preprocessing

In the image preprocessing process, the amplification band chosen for the EVM method is [0.2 Hz, 2.4 Hz]. A reasonable amplification factor needs to be set by comparing effects of different amplification factors on the results, otherwise it will amplify the noise and even lead to distortion of facial expressions. This experiment is conducted to study the effect of the amplification factor α on the test results to determine the value of α. From Fig. 5, obtain accuracy of all three data sets showed an increasing trend when the parameter was less than 10. The best results are obtained with a parameter of 10, after which a decreasing trend is observed. The noise in the images affects the feature extraction of the network and leads to decreased recognition rate, so the value of α is set to 10.

All input images for the network are resized to 112×112. We choose an image with a magnification factor of 10 and normalize it to 50 frames using the TIM method. We select middle frame as apex frame. Where learning rate $= 0.0001$, $\beta1 = 0.9$, $\beta2 = 0.999$, and $\varepsilon = 10^{-8}$. The batch size, the maximum iteration are set to 16 and 200.

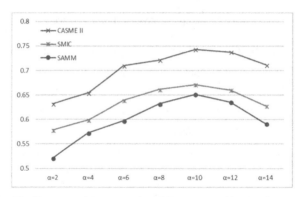

Fig. 5. Recognition rate using different magnification factor

3.3 Experimental Results and Analysis

3.3.1 Network Contrast

We compared the single-stream spatial capsule network (SC-CapsNet) and the single-stream temporal convolutional capsule network (TC-CapsNet) with our proposed dual-stream input capsule network. Table 3 shows effects of different network structures on accuracy. In Table 3, present method outperforms the single feature input on all three datasets.

In Table 3, we can derive the Acc and F1-Score data corresponding to CASME II, SMIC, and SAMM. The results show that dual-stream feature input network enhance feature extraction ability of model, which enable model learn more discriminative features and enhance recognition ability of micro expression.

Table 3. Comparison of single-stream input network with dual-stream input network

Method	CASME II		SMIC		SAMM	
	Acc. (%)	F1-Score (%)	Acc. (%)	F1-Score (%)	Acc. (%)	F1-Score (%)
Single-stream (SC-CapsNet)	64.52	63.02	58.89	57.15	56.58	55.39
Single-stream (TC-CapsNet)	67.81	66.12	61.18	60.01	58.67	58.07
proposed	74.34	73.28	67.12	66.47	65.15	63.22

In addition, we compared the recognition effects of different network structures for each emotion on this dataset. The results are shown in Fig. 6, where (a), (b), and (c) indicate classification effects of different emotions on the SMIC, SAMM, and CASME II datasets, respectively. In Fig. 6, the recognition rate of each emotion shows an overall increasing trend in the three datasets. However, Fig. 6(a) shows that the rate of "positive" is higher than that of "surprise" in the SMIC dataset by SC-CapsNet. Rate of "surprise" is lower than that of "positive" in TC-CapsNet. Similarly, as shown in Fig. 6(b) and Fig. 6(c), the rate of "happy" is higher than that of "negative" in SC-CapsNet, while TC-CapsNet performs the opposite, with the best recognition rate in proposed network. In conclusion, SC-CapsNet and TC-CapsNet are complementary and mutually reinforcing in the recognition of emotions in micro-expressions. The proposed network combines two modules to achieve the best performance.

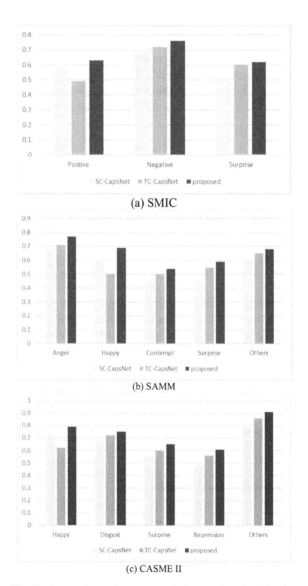

(a) SMIC

(b) SAMM

(c) CASME II

Fig. 6. Comparison of two networks in emotion classification

3.3.2 Ablation Experiment

The model presented in paper combines dual-stream network and a capsule network, and the dual-stream network is integrated with the AU attention module. The effectiveness of the dual-stream network has been discussed in 2.3.1.Large number of samples and classifications of CASME II, for the verification of the effectiveness of the AU attention mechanism and dynamic routing mechanism, three sets of comparison experiments were chosen to be conducted on CASME II.

We use the dual-stream feature extraction network with the AU attention module removed as the base network. The first group adds the AU attention module to the basic network, connecting to fully connected layer for micro-expression classification. Second group connects to the capsule network module. The third group adds AU attention module and capsule network module, which is the proposed model in this paper. Comparison results of the three groups of experiments are shown in Table 4.

Table 4. Ablation experiment results on CASME II

Method	Acc(%)	F1-Score(%)
Basic + Attention map	69.38	68.76
Basic + CapsNet	72.53	70.75
Basic + Attention map + CapsNet (proposed)	74.34	73.28

As shown in Table 4, the third set of experiments get the best performance on CASME II. Compared to the first group, the accuracy of the network by 4.96% and F1-Score by 4.52%. Compared to the second group, the introduced AU attention mechanism improves the accuracy by 1.81% and F1-Score by 2.53%. Comparison results of the first and third groups validate the effectiveness of dynamic routing. AU attention mechanism cloud capture subtle muscle movements better than model without the attention mechanism. The comparison results of the second and third groups validate the effectiveness of AU-aware attention. Therefore, both capsule network and the AU attention map generated based on face landmarks are beneficial to enhance accuracy of micro-expression recognition.

3.3.3 Comparison With Other Methods

To verify effectiveness of model, this paper is compared with the mainstream algorithms, and results are shown in Table 5. LBP-TOP [2], Bi-WOOF [5] are traditional extraction feature methods, and VGG-16 [6], DSSN [8], STRCN [9], Micro-Attention [10], LGCon [11], and CapsuleNet [13] are methods based on deep learning.

As shown in Table 5, highest accuracy of micro-expression recognition among traditional feature methods is Bi-WOOF. Compared with Bi-WOOF, the accuracy of presented method on CASME II, SMIC and SAMM is improved by 16.45%, 5.53% and 5.4%, and F1-Score is improved by 12.03%, 5.37% and 4.12%.

Table 5. Comparison of experimental results of different methods

Method	CASME II		SMIC		SAMM	
	Acc. (%)	F1-Score (%)	Acc. (%)	F1-Score (%)	Acc. (%)	F1-Score (%)
LBP-TOP	46.46	42.41	43.38	34.21	36.98	35.89
Bi-WOOF	57.89	61.25	61.59	61.10	59.75	59.10
VGG-16	71.00	48.62	59.64	50.25	47.93	29.11
DSSN	70.78	73.00	63.41	64.61	57.35	46.44
STRCN	63.37	62.00	64.63	63.00	53.48	36.00
Micro-Attention	51.70	53.90	46.60	47.30	34.00	40.30
LGCon	62.14	60.00	63.41	62.00	35.29	23.00
CapsuleNet	70.18	70.68	58.77	58.20	59.89	59.09
Proposed	**74.34**	**73.28**	**67.12**	**66.47**	**65.15**	**63.22**

VGG-16 is the benchmark method. Compared with it, the proposed method enhance accuracy by 3.34%, 7.48% and 17.22% on three datasets. The proposed method and DSSN both use dual-stream shallow convolution to get better recognition results compared to VGG-16 which uses deep convolutional structure. The proposed method and DSSN both use dual-stream shallow convolution to get better recognition results compared to VGG-16 which uses deep convolutional structure. The experimental results show that shallow layer network is more suitable for micro-expression classification with fewer dataset.

In the comparison method, VGG-16, DSSN and CapsuleNet get the best performance on CASME II, SMIC and SAMM with an increase of 3.34%, 3.71% and 4.13%. Presented method outperforms above methods on all three datasets. Where DSSN is an improved network based on dual-stream convolutional network. Compared with it, the proposed method enhanced accuracy by 3.56%, 3.71% and 7.8% on three datasets, and the F1-Score by 0.28%, 1.86% and 16.78%, respectively. CapsuleNet is a micro-expression recognition method using capsule network. The proposed method improves accuracy by 4.16%, 8.35%, and 5.26% and F1-Score by 2.6%, 8.27%, and 4.13% on the three datasets compared with it. Overall, combining dual-stream network and capsule network can improve network performance.

We calculated the confusion matrix to further measure the recognition ability of the model, as shown in Fig. 7. The columns of the matrix represent the prediction category, and the rows represent the prediction results of the category. The diagonal line of the matrix is the ratio of number of correctly classified emotions in the category of emotions. As shown in Fig. 7, in the three datasets, the SAMM dataset has the lowest accuracy of micro-expression classification. The reason is that SAMM has a small amount of data and a large number of classification tasks. In SAMM, the "angry" category has a larger proportion and the best recognition performance. "Contempt" and "surprise" have less sample and lower accuracy.

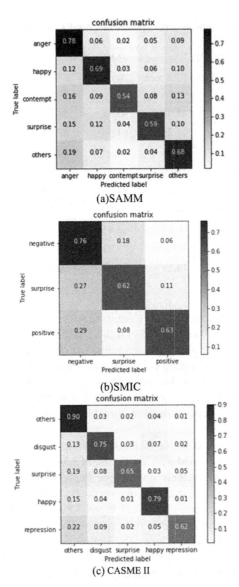

Fig. 7. Confusion matrix

Furthermore, on SMIC, the sample categories are evenly distributed, so the classification performance is better. But " negative" and "surprise" use similar AU, which makes them easily confused in classification. In CASME II, the recognition rate of "happy" is higher due to the strong facial movement intensity when generating happy expressions. Most of the micro-expressions in "other" are natural expressions. It has the largest proportion of samples, so it gets the best performance. While disgust and depression have many similarities between the two emotions, the differentiation degree is low and the sample distribution is unbalanced. Experimental results show the distribution and amplitude of sample sizes in each affective category of facial movements of micro-expressions are important factors influencing the recognition effect in the micro-expression recognition task.

4 Conclusion

To solve the problems that current micro-expression identify methods based on convolutional networks use a single feature and have insufficient feature extraction capability for face spatial structure information, we propose a method combining dual-stream convolution and capsule networks. The proposed method uses dual feature information input. Where the input images are the images with amplified motion magnitude using EVM and optical flow features of onset frame and apex frame extracted using TV-L1. AU attention mechanism is introduced in dual-stream convolutional network, which enables network to extract high-dimensional features and micro-expression active region features. Finally, dynamic routing mechanism of capsule network is utilized, which enables the network extract spatial structure features to further improve the micro-expression classification ability. Experimental results show that model accuracy reaches 74.34%, 67.12%, and 65.15% on CASME II, SMIC, and SAMM datasets, which increases 3.34%, 3.71%, and 4.13% compared with existing advanced methods, verifying effectiveness of the model. However, problems of small dataset and unbalanced distribution of categories are still the main reasons for the low accuracy. Investigation of how to spot micro-expressions in long videos to expand the micro-expression dataset is the next step that can be explored.

References

1. Zhou, L., Shao, X., Mao, Q.: A survey of micro-expression recognition. Image Vis. Comput. **105**, 104043 (2021)
2. Pfister, T., Li, X., Zhao, G., et al.: Recognising spontaneous facial micro-expressions. In: International Conference on Computer Vision, pp. 1449–1456. IEEE (2011)
3. Li, X., Hong, X., Moilanen, A., et al.: Towards reading hidden emotions: a comparative study of spontaneous micro-expression spotting and recognition methods. IEEE Trans. Affect. Comput. **9**(4), 563–577 (2017)
4. Liu, Y.J., Zhang, J.K., Yan, W.J., et al.: A main directional mean optical flow feature for spontaneous micro-expression recognition. IEEE Trans. Affect. Comput. **7**(4), 299–310 (2016)
5. Liong, S.T., See, J., Wong, K.S., et al.: Less is more: Micro-expression recognition from video using apex frame. Signal Process.: Image Commun. **62**, 82–92 (2018)
6. Li, Y., Huang, X., Zhao, G.: Can micro-expression be recognized based on single apex frame. In: 2018 25th IEEE International Conference on Image Processing (ICIP), pp. 3094–3098. IEEE (2018)
7. Gan, Y.S., Liong, S., Yau, W., et al.: OFF-ApexNet on micro-expression recognition system. Signal Process.-Image Commun. **74**, 129–139 (2019)
8. Khor, H.Q., See, J., Liong, S.T., et al.: Dual-stream shallow networks for facial micro-expression recognition. In: 2019 IEEE International Conference on Image Processing(ICIP), pp. 36–40. IEEE (2019)

9. Xia, Z., Hong, X., Gao, X., et al.: Spatiotemporal recurrent convolutional networks for recognizing spontaneous micro-expressions. IEEE Trans. Multimedia **22**(3), 626–640 (2020)
10. Wang, C., Peng, M., Bi, T., et al.: Micro-attention for micro-expression recognition. Neurocomputing, 354–362 (2020)
11. Li, Y., Huang, X., Zhao, G.: Joint local and global information learning with single apex frame detection for micro-expression recognition. IEEE Trans. Image Process. **30**, 249–263 (2021)
12. Sabour, S., Frosst, N., Hinton, G.E.: Dynamic routing between capsules. In: Proc of the 2017 Neural Information Processing Systems, Long Beach, CA, USA, NIPS, pp. 3856–3866 (2017)
13. Quang, N.V., Chun, J., Tokuyama, T.: CapsuleNet for micro-expression recognition. In: 2019 14th IEEE International Conference on Automatic Face & Gesture Recognition (FG 2019). IEEE (2019)
14. Liu, N., Liu, X., Zhang, Z., et al.: Offset or onset frame: a multi-stream convolutional neural network with CapsuleNet module for micro-expression recognition. In: 2020 5th International Conference on Intelligent Informatics and Biomedical Sciences (ICIIBMS) (2020)
15. Li, X., Pfister, T., Huang, X., et al.: A spontaneous micro-expression data-base: inducement, collection and baseline. In: 10th IEEE International Conference and Workshops on Automatic Face and Gesture Recognition(FG), pp. 1–6. IEEE (2013)
16. Yan, W.J., Li, X., Wang, S.J., et al.: CASME II: an improved spontaneous micro-expression database and the baseline evaluation. PLoS ONE **9**(1), e86041 (2014)
17. Davison, A.K., Lansley, C., Costen, N., et al.: SAMM: a spontaneous micro-facial movement dataset. IEEE Trans. Affect. Comput. **9**(1), 116–129 (2018)
18. Adam, G.: Face Recognition[EB/OL]. https://github.com/ageitgey/facerecognition
19. Wu, H.Y., Rubinstein, M., Shih, E., et al.: Eulerian video magnification for revealing subtle changes in the world. ACM Trans. Graph. **31**(4), 65–83 (2012)
20. Li, Q., Yu, J., Kurihara, T., et al.: Deep convolutional neural network with optical flow for facial micro-expression recognition. J. Circ. Syst. Comput. **29**(1), 1–7 (2020)
21. Zach, C., Pock, T., Bischof, H.: A duality based approach for realtime TV-L1 optical flow. In: Hamprecht, F.A., Schnörr, C., Jähne, B. (eds.) DAGM 2007. LNCS, vol. 4713, pp. 214–223. Springer, Heidelberg (2007). https://doi.org/10.1007/978-3-540-74936-3_22

Security Scheduling Method of Cloud Network Big Data Cluster Based on Association Rule Algorithm

Teng Peng[(✉)] and Xiaohong Wang

Yichun Vocational and Technical College, Yichun 336000, China
`pttt20@yeah.net`

Abstract. In order to avoid unreasonable deployment and realize the orderly deployment of big data cluster nodes, a cloud network big data cluster security scheduling method based on association rule algorithm is proposed. According to the execution steps of association rule mining algorithm, the connection form of hadoop/mapreduce framework is determined, and then the security mapping conditions are jointly solved to complete the security performance analysis of cloud network based on association rule algorithm. Combine the obtained big data information parameters, set the link bandwidth time list structure, and solve the specific value of packet routing index according to the connection form of SDN scheduling system. The experimental results show that the cloud network big data information migration amount of the method in this paper reaches 6.50×107 MB, and the continuous occupation time of cluster nodes is less than 0.7 ms, which increases the unit migration amount of big data information and reduces the continuous occupation time of cluster nodes. It can solve the problem of unreasonable allocation of information parameters and realize the orderly deployment of big data cluster nodes.

Keywords: Association rule algorsithm · Cloud network · Big data cluster · Safety dispatching · Mining confidence · Link bandwidth time list

1 Introduction

Cloud service operators provide pay-as-you-go, easy-to-maintain computing resources to machine learning users in enterprises or research institutions in the form of virtual machine instances [1, 2]. The machine learning cluster environment based on cloud computing platform has become the best choice for enterprises or research institutions to efficiently deploy big data and artificial intelligence applications. Even with the use of large-scale computing resource clusters, it still takes a lot of time for machine learning algorithms to go from beginner level to expert level. The way to alleviate the above problems is to reasonably allocate and schedule cluster resources for machine learning algorithms to improve the utilization efficiency of cluster resources.

Reference [3] proposes a fault-tolerant control method for cloud platform security monitoring big data cluster scheduling. A stepped C/S cloud platform monitoring framework is constructed, and the CPU signal strength fluctuation algorithm in the $3+1$ integration method is used to perform scheduling calculations on data clusters. Stability analysis of nonlinear switching system in big data cluster, realize fault-tolerant control of big data cluster scheduling. Reference [4] proposes a balanced scheduling method for DNS network traffic big data based on set pair analysis strategy. Reconstructs the network link in the environment of static domain name resolution (DNS), designs a network traffic load information, the information is analyzed according to the directional controller to ensure the matching of routes and links, and to achieve balanced scheduling of network traffic. However, the above methods cannot effectively avoid the appearance of unreasonable allocation behavior, so the deployment effect of big data cluster nodes is not good. Therefore, a cloud network big data cluster security scheduling method based on association rule algorithm is proposed. Determine the connection form of the Hadoop/MapReduce framework based on the association rule mining algorithm, solve the security mapping conditions, and complete the cloud network security performance analysis; combine the acquired big data information parameters, set the link bandwidth-time list structure, and follow the SDN scheduling system. The connection form is used to solve the specific value of the packet routing index, and realize the orderly deployment of the big data cluster nodes. The experimental results prove the contribution of the method in this paper: the unit migration amount of cloud network big data information is significantly increased, while the continuous occupation time of cluster nodes is shortened. The orderly deployment is more in line with the actual application needs.

2 Analysis of Cloud Network Security Performance Based on Association Rule Algorithm

The analysis of cloud network security performance based on association rule algorithm includes three processing steps: improvement of mining steps, design of hadoop/mapreduce framework, and solution of security mapping conditions. This chapter will study the above contents.

2.1 Association Rule Mining Steps

Association rule mining algorithms have many categories according to different classification methods. According to the dimension of processing data, association rule mining algorithms are divided into single-dimensional operations and multi-dimensional operations [5, 6]. Each classification has a variety of algorithms, among which the typical ones are apriori, FP growth and Eclat. However, the basic mining steps are the same regardless of the algorithm of each category, which is mainly divided into the following two steps.

(1) Mining the frequent item set. This step is the core of the whole association rule mining, so the research is mostly based on this stage. According to the set minimum support degree α, establish the frequent item set $\Im$ from the thing database, and solve the expression as follows:

$$\Im = \left\{ q|q = \alpha \frac{\sqrt{e_1^2 + e_2^2 + \cdots + e_n^2}}{(n-1)! \times |\Delta E|} \right\} \tag{1}$$

In the formula, q represents the correlation frequency coefficient, $e_1, e_2, \cdots, e_n$ represent n different abstraction index, and ΔE represents the unit cumulant of the correlation abstract index.

(2) Generate strong association rules.Determine whether the mining rules can meet the actual application requirements.The strong association rule expression is:

$$W = \frac{\sum\limits_{\delta=1}^{+\infty}\left(w_1 \times w_2 - \overline{w}^2\right)}{\beta \cdot t} \tag{2}$$

In the formula, δ represents the initial assignment of the confidence vector, w_1, w_2 represent two unequal confidence association indicators, the value condition of its and $w_1 \in \mathfrak{I}$, $w_2 \in \mathfrak{I}$ hold simultaneously, $\overline{w}$ represents the average of the coefficients w_1 and w_2, t represents the unit action time of the association rule, and β indicates the confidence extraction coefficient.

The complete association rule mining process is shown in Fig. 1.

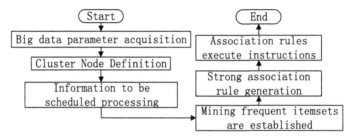

Fig. 1. Execution flow of association rule mining instructions

When faced with big data parameters in the cloud network environment, the running association rule algorithm must have strong inclusiveness[7]. On the one hand, it allows obvious differences between the information to be processed. On the other hand, it can also determine the security mapping relationship between the associated data according to the location of the mining node.

2.2 Hadoop/Mapreduce Framework

When establishing a cloud network big data cluster, it needs to be based on the hadoop/mapreduce framework. The information parameters to be processed can be fused together by combining metadata nodes, HDFS master nodes and network cloud nodes, so that Internet hosts can independently extract these data documents[8]. The complete hadoop/mapreduce framework connection form is shown in Fig. 2.

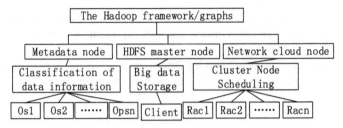

Fig. 2. Hadoop/mapreduce framework structure

Metadata node: this type of data node is almost distributed on each physical node of the Hadoop cluster and is responsible for storing real file data. The data node takes the block as the basic storage unit, and completes the distributed storage and retrieval of large files according to the specific scheduling of the client and the name node[9]. Each data node will regularly send its own stored data block list to the name node to ensure the consistency of storage information in the big data cluster of the whole cloud network.

HDFS master node: as the main connection node in the hadoop/mapreduce framework, the node object does not save the file data that needs to be stored, but records the metadata information of all stored files; When users read and write stored data, they first need to obtain the location information of the target file through the metadata in the name node, and then complete the subsequent operations.

The upper layer of the adoop/mapreduce framework is the MapReduce engine, through which cloud network users can process big data information parameters without knowing the execution of association rule mining instructions. The MapReduce engine consists of two modules, jobtracker and tasktracker:

Jobtracker: the main function of jobtracker in Hadoop system is to assign data processing tasks to tasktrackers on other nodes for execution. In order to ensure the i/o efficiency during the execution of big data applications, jobtracker will first query the information of the data node through the metadata in the name node, and allocate data processing tasks to the tasktracker node closest to the data node as far as possible to avoid data transmission across physical nodes.

Tasktracker: the tasktracker module is responsible for performing data processing tasks. Similar to the working mechanism of data nodes, the tasktracker module is deployed on almost all physical nodes of the Hadoop cluster, and regularly sends heartbeat information to jobtracker, so that jobtracker can control the status of all tasktracker modules and plan task allocation.

In the actual implementation process, hadoop/mapreduce framework has the following application advantages:

(1) The platform architecture is scalable[10]. The streaming big data processing system, whether it is a symmetric architecture or a master-slave system architecture, has good scalability, retains the status information of each node through middleware technology, and adds or deletes cluster nodes during operation.

(2) Low coupling design. By separating the computing logic from the underlying basic modules, the streaming big data processing system has a low degree of coupling, so that developers can easily carry out secondary development of the system according to actual needs.

(3) User defined applications. The streaming big data processing platform fully entrusts the computing logic to the user, enabling the user to design the corresponding topology according to the actual business scenario requirements. The data source, processing logic and result output are completely defined by the user, greatly improving the availability and universality of the streaming big data processing platform.

2.3 Security Mapping Conditions

After the deployment location of big data cluster is determined, the association rule algorithm can complete the definition and query of big data cluster nodes according to the connection of hadoop/mapreduce framework. The optimal mapping relationship between the communication agent and the virtual node can be obtained by optimizing the MapReduce job time span. The specific optimization process is: minimize the use of memory during the mapping process, avoid the continuous stacking of memory in the map, and ensure that map and reduce have enough memory to run business logic. On the map side, try to write tasks into a spill file. Set a reasonable job time span by estimating the output size of the map. At a certain time, when the load requests assigned to a specific cloud network big data cluster node cannot be fully processed, the unprocessed requests will be overstocked in the waiting queue for subsequent processing[11]. When different big data cluster processing requests arrive at the storage platform, if the application copy of the association rule cannot process the loading task temporarily, the requests will be temporarily stored in the logical waiting queue. The execution time of the entire request is determined by the request waiting time and the image loading time. Due to the different load conditions of different replica deployment nodes, the m/g/1 queue model can be used to analyze the request backlog of each mirror replica logical queue, and then the overall performance of the platform can be quantitatively modeled.

When defining the security mapping conditions based on the association rule algorithm, it is necessary to comprehensively consider the load of the current platform storage nodes and the storage network. On the one hand, it is necessary to analyze the degradation of average i/o performance after image deployment according to the load status of storage nodes[12]; On the other hand, it is necessary to comprehensively consider the load status of the storage network, analyze the bottleneck performance of application replica transmission in the current platform, and avoid excessive waste of network or node i/o performance. When the number of big data cluster nodes for concurrent transmission in the cloud network environment is small, the network transmission performance is not fully utilized. At this time, the loading rate of the scheduled replica is mainly limited by the i/o rate of the storage node, so the execution time of the data information loading operation is almost fixed. As the number of data and information copies transmitted concurrently in the storage network gradually increases, the network transmission rate allocated to each copy will gradually decrease. Compared with the i/o rate of the storage node, the network transmission rate has gradually become the bottleneck performance of scheduling instruction loading; At this time, the average transmission rate of the mirrored copy will decrease with the increase of the number of concurrent transmitted images in the network.

Let ε represent the initial value condition for the cloud network mapping parameter, χ represent the established correlation measure, and ΔR represent the unit cumulant of the cloud network big data parameter within the cluster node. Combining the above physical quantities, the basic expression of the association rule algorithm can be defined as:

$$I = \sum_{\varepsilon=1}^{+\infty} \frac{W}{\left(1 - \left|\frac{1}{\chi}\right|^2\right)} \cdot |\Delta R| \tag{3}$$

The applications of association rule mining mainly include but are not limited to these five aspects: classification data mining, clustering data mining, association rule data mining, prediction data mining and deviation (singularity) data mining. These five functions do not exist independently and will affect each other in the data mining project. First of all, we need to understand the root cause of the problem, so understanding the problem is naturally the basis of the whole data mining. The understanding of business data determines which aspects of data to collect and what kind of data to choose for data mining. These two steps are the same logic; Then the data mining work has entered the technical preparation stage, which is mainly to preprocess the prepared data. In the work of data mining on specific data, the data preprocessing work actually occupies a very large space, because the output of data preprocessing is the input of data mining, and the existing data mining mode has very strict requirements on the input data.

On the basis of formula (3), let β represent the big data information query parameter in the cloud network environment, and p_1, p_2, $\cdots$, p_n represent n different big data cluster node definition coefficient.

The expression of big data cluster in cloud network based on association rule algorithm is:

$$U = \left| \frac{\beta I}{p_1 + p_2 + \cdots + p_n} \right|^{n^2 - 1} \tag{4}$$

In order to arrange the cloud network big data cluster nodes according to the established query order, when solving the security mapping conditions, the association rule algorithm must be followed to constrain the actual storage form of the information parameters to be processed[13].

3   Security Scheduling and Processing of Big Data Cluster

With the support of association rule algorithm, the security scheduling and processing of cloud network big data cluster nodes can be realized according to the processing flow of link bandwidth time list setting, SDN scheduling system construction and packet routing coefficient solution.

3.1 Link Bandwidth - Time List

Simply put, in the cloud network environment, the link bandwidth of big data information is the transmission rate, which refers to the maximum number of bytes transmitted per second (mb/s), that is, how many megabytes are processed per second. High bandwidth means the high processing capacity of the system. In the analog signal system, bandwidth is used to identify the frequency width occupied by the transmission signal. This width is determined by the highest frequency and the lowest frequency of the transmission signal. The difference between the two is the bandwidth value. Therefore, it is also called signal bandwidth or carrier frequency bandwidth. Bandwidth is actually a measure of the spectrum occupied by a signal, which can be regarded as a space related quantity. In contrast, the signal transmission rate is a physical quantity related to space and time, which is defined as the amount of data transmitted on the channel in unit time.

The topology of $|A|$ high-performance network (HPN) with a node and $|S|$ links is represented as a graph $\gamma(A, S)$, where A represents the node set in the high-performance network, S represents the link set in the high-performance network, each link $\varphi \in S$, and link φ is numbered $0, 1, 2, \cdots, |S|$. . The bandwidth of each link is stored in a time-varying segment function list; A time bandwidth (TB) 3 tuple $(d_\iota[\iota], d_\iota[\iota + 1], g_\iota[\iota])$ is used to represent the available bandwidth $g_\iota[\iota]$ of link φ in time interval $(d_\iota[\iota], d_\iota[\iota + 1])$, where $\iota = 0, 1, 2, \cdots, T_{\iota-1}, T_\iota$ is the total number of time slots of link φ. When $\iota = 0$, $d_\iota[0]$ represents the current (initial) time; when $\iota \geq 1$, $d_\iota[\iota]$ represents the future time.

According to the time bandwidth table tb of each link, an aggregated TB (ATB) table including all links in the network can be established to store the bandwidth of all links in each time slot (including the newly divided time slot due to the intersection of each link time slot). The time slots of all links are combined into a series of new time slots. A time slot is actually the longest period in which the available bandwidth of all links in network G remains unchanged. The specific link bandwidth time list solution expression is as follows:

$$\begin{cases} |A| = \lambda U \\ |S| = \phi U \\ d_\iota[\iota + 1] = \left| G\dfrac{1}{T_\iota - T_{\iota-1}} \right| \times d_\iota[\iota] \end{cases} \tag{5}$$

In the formula, λ represents the transverse scheduling coefficient of the big data cluster nodes in the cloud network, and ϕ represents the longitudinal scheduling coefficient.

Under the action of the association rule algorithm, the definition conditions of the relevant node parameters involved in the link bandwidth-time list are shown in Table 1.

Table 1. Link Bandwidth-Time list definition conditions

Name	Step value / (bit)	Action position	Action form
Aggregated node	3.15	Big data cluster framework	Adjusting association rule algorithm
ATB node	3.15	Information input layer	Rectify cloud network connection form
TB node	3.15	Information coding layer	Rewrite big data information
Bandwidth node	3.15	Information output layer	Cluster node code
Big data node	3.15	Big data decoding layer	Big data information decoding

In general, the goal of resource allocation and scheduling of link bandwidth time list is usually to improve the execution time efficiency of clustered applications.

3.2 SDN Dispatching System

As a new network architecture, software defined network (SDN) can separate the network control plane from the data plane (forwarding plane) and program directly in the control plane. This separation helps to decouple specific applications from the underlying network, thus supporting a wider range of applications. Moreover, SDN can centrally control multiple network supply environments by the control plane, reduce the complexity of node equipment through the centralized control mechanism, and improve the innovation rate, network reliability and security, which is difficult to achieve in traditional networks.

The scenario of multi application mixing is not considered. According to the actual business scenario of the streaming big data processing platform, the streaming big data processing platform will have a variety of different types of applications in the same business field to mix and share the resources of the streaming big data processing platform.

Figure 3 is a schematic diagram of SDN architecture, which includes three layers from top to bottom: I) application layer, II) control layer, and III) forwarding layer. Each layer is responsible for different network services, which improves scalability and facilitates migration between different networks.

The application layer is composed of various user applications such as bandwidth scheduling, virtualization, cloud computing, etc. centralized network control is required to achieve quality of service and higher network utilization.

The control layer is the middle layer, which is composed of one or more controllers and can cover the entire network (including virtual machines and business traffic). It is the most critical layer in the SDN architecture. Network services such as routing and path calculation are provided to the application layer through northbound APIs. This layer is also responsible for: I) managing the underlying network devices by forwarding flow

Main application parts

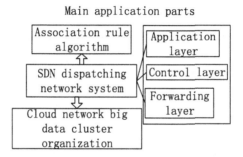

Fig. 3. Connection form of the S D N scheduling system

table entries; II) effectively select network routes for user requests from the application layer; III) maintain a real-time updated global network view (gnv) containing network topology, link status and other relevant information; IV) exchange status information with other controllers to maintain consistent gnv, etc.

The forwarding layer is the bottom layer, including SDN switches, routers and other devices. They use flow tables (FT) or forwarding information bases (fibs) to forward streams or packets, where these ft or fibs contain next hop information. At present, openflow switches are most commonly used in the forwarding layer and are assigned to one or more controllers, which are responsible for updating the flow table entries through openflow information.

Based on SDN technology, the centralized bandwidth scheduling function of high performance network (HPN) can be easily realized. The efficient and flexible network control function of SDN can make the network architecture intelligent, and make the control task run on the server with stronger computing power instead of the router. The controller can monitor the congestion status and load balance of the whole network. It is the control center of the whole network and various applications. With the rise of big data, cloud computing and data centers, SDN has been widely used by more and more operators, scientific research institutions, large data center hosting and cloud service providers in recent years.

The bandwidth scheduler of the control plane receives the user request input from the application layer, calculates the appropriate network path for it based on the global network view gnv, provides a dedicated transmission channel, and releases the occupied bandwidth in time when the transmission ends. The global network view gnv of the control plane can provide real-time network status information for the bandwidth scheduler, including node, link status, load status, etc. The bandwidth scheduler of the control plane calculates the appropriate network path according to the network status information of gnv, creates and manages the flow information table by using the openflow protocol, and sends it to the switch supporting openflow in the data plane. The openflow switch analyzes and processes the flow table entries, and sets the relevant network devices and ports according to the flow table information to realize data forwarding.

3.3 Packet Routing Coefficient

Firstly, the packet routing coefficient uses the instantaneous or average communication delay of the network link to give a "distance" measure to the network link, so as to model the network as a weighted graph with edge weights. Generally speaking, the goal of resource allocation and scheduling in cluster system is to improve the execution time efficiency of cluster applications. In essence, the resource allocation and scheduling problem of cluster system is a very challenging dynamic optimization problem to determine the resource allocation mode according to the load status of cluster resources. In related work, the solutions to such problems are mainly divided into two categories. One is to design resource allocation methods based on intuitive and reasonable artificial heuristics, such as task scheduling based on load balancing, small coflow priority scheduling based on priority, device placement based on graph division, or packet routing algorithm based on graph theory. The other is based on association rule algorithm to solve the near optimal resource allocation strategy.

The computing containers in the existing streaming big data processing platform perform resource scheduling based on the pre static configuration. Because it is impossible to ensure the actual demand of the computing container by dynamically scheduling resources, and if the resources are configured according to the highest load to ensure the quality of service, when the load of the application is low, it will bring inevitable waste of resources.

The solution expression of cloud network big data cluster packet routing coefficient based on association rule algorithm is:

$$M = \left| \frac{\sqrt{|A| \cdot |S|} / \xi \cdot d_\iota[\iota + 1]}{\sum\limits_{\omega=1}^{+\infty} (v_1 \times v_2)} \right| \Bigg\|_{\bar{v} \neq 1} \tag{6}$$

In the formula, ξ represents the cloud network routing nodes assignment indication, v_1 and v_2 represent two randomly selected routing feature parameters, and the inequality condition of $v_1 \neq v_2$ is constant, $\bar{v}$ represents the average of the coefficients v_1 and v_2, and ω represents the initial assignment of the correlation coefficient of the routing nodes.

After all the newly arrived tasks are put into the task queue, the first task of the task queue is executed in a time slot, so the remaining service time is reduced. If the first task of the queue completes the calculation in this time slot, the first task of the queue is removed from the task queue, and the next task in the queue becomes the first task of the queue and starts to execute. If the task queue becomes empty after the first task of the queue completes the calculation, the algorithm randomly extracts the index of a scheduler from the index number set of the scheduler and reports the index number of the idle computing resource to the selected scheduler.

When the solution result of packet routing coefficient is known, the scheduling of cloud network big data cluster nodes includes two processing forms: the first type of task is assigned to the resource by a scheduler according to the idle resource recorded in its storage unit. The second type of task is randomly assigned to a resource when the free resource record on a scheduler is empty. For an idle computing resource, its first arriving task may be either the first type of task or the second type of task. If the idle resource receives the second type of task, the idle resource status reported by the computing resource to a scheduler is no longer valid. To remove the invalid idle resource record, the computing resource sends a notification message to the corresponding scheduler to delete the idle record of the computing resource. Therefore, for a non idle computing resource, the tasks that arrive on it are the second type of tasks assigned randomly.

4 Example Analysis

To verify the practical application value of the cloud network big data cluster security scheduling method based on association rule algorithm, the following comparative experimental group is designed. The specific experimental execution process is as follows:

Select the cloud network big data cluster security scheduling method based on association rule algorithm as the application technology of the experimental group;

The Reference [3] method was selected as the control group application technique;

Minipc equipment is taken as the experimental object to ensure that other interference conditions do not change and improve the connection form of windows system;

Using the scheduling methods of the experimental group and the control group respectively, the host computer of the calculation and selection experiment is controlled;

Record the numerical changes of two physical quantities: the amount of big data information migration and the occupation time of cluster nodes in the experimental group and the control group;

Compare the experimental group and the control group, record the values, and summarize the experimental rules;

The distributed environment of the cloud network big data cluster adopts the Hadoop framework configuration, and the version is Cloudera Hadoop; the experimental platform is a Cluster composed of multiple nodes, and the nodes are composed of 18 GB RAM and 2.98G 8-core Intel Xeom X9870 CPU. Build a Hadoop node cluster, and the cluster communication is implemented based on the MPI library. Cloud network cluster data set Select the private cloud database of a technology company and store the data set in HDFS. The hardware configuration of the experimental environment is shown in Table 2:

Table 2. Experimental Environment Configuration

Name	Configure
Hardware environment	Intel i3 CPU
Network environment	100 M switch
Node connection network	Galaxy-1A
MPI	MPICH-2
Processing element	Intel Xeon 64 2.33GHz
Hadoop	Cloudera Hadop 5.0
Compiler	Ifort V10-O3
Number of nodes	80

In the cloud network environment, the amount of big data information migration and the continuous occupation time of cluster nodes can be used to describe the deployment ability of network hosts to big data cluster nodes. Generally, the larger the unit migration amount of big data information and the shorter the continuous occupation time of cluster nodes, the lower the probability of unreasonable deployment of data information. At this time, the network host has a relatively strong ability to deploy big data cluster nodes; On the contrary, if the unit migration amount of big data information is small and the continuous occupation time of cluster nodes is long, it means that the probability of unreasonable deployment of data information is high. At this time, the deployment ability of network hosts to big data cluster nodes is relatively weak. The numerical changes of the unit migration amount of big data information in the experimental and control groups are shown in Fig. 4.

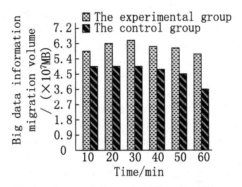

Fig. 4. Big Data information Migration Volume

Experimental group: under the action of the scheduling method of the experimental group, the amount of big data information migration first increases and then decreases. When the experimental time is equal to 30 min, the amount of big data information migration in the experimental group reaches a maximum of 6.50×10^7 MB.

Control group: under the control group's scheduling method, the amount of big data information migration is stable first and then decreased. When the experimental time is equal to 10 min, 20 min and 30 min, the amount of big data information migration in the control group reaches a maximum of 4.95×10^7 MB, decreased by 1.55×10^7 MB compared with the maximum value of the experimental group. The numerical changes in the occupation time of the cluster nodes in the experimental and control groups are shown in Table 3.

Table 3. Occuptime of cluster nodes

Big data information transmission volume/ × 107 MB	Cluster node occupancy time/ ms	
	Experimental group	Control group
1.0	0.2	0.2
2.0	0.2	0.3
3.0	0.2	0.5
4.0	0.4	0.6
5.0	0.5	0.7
6.0	0.7	0.8
7.0	0.8	0.9
8.0	0.6	1.1
9.0	0.5	1.2

It can be seen from Table 3 that with the increase of big data information transmission, the continuous occupation time of cluster nodes in the experimental group shows a numerical change state of first stable, then increasing and finally decreasing. During the whole experimental process, the maximum value of the experimental group reaches 0.7 MS; The continuous occupation time of cluster nodes in the control group kept increasing. During the whole experiment, the maximum value of the control group reached 1.2 MS, an increase of 0.5 ms compared with the maximum value of the experimental group.

To sum up, the experimental conclusion is:

(1) The traditional scheduling method can not improve the numerical level of the unit migration volume of big data information, and the matching cluster nodes occupy a relatively long time, which can not promote the network host to deploy the big data cluster nodes on demand, and does not meet the actual application requirements;

(2) Under the action of the cloud network big data cluster security scheduling method based on the association rule algorithm, the numerical accumulation trend of big data information migration has been effectively promoted, while the cluster node occupation time has significantly decreased, which can play a catalytic role in avoiding the occurrence of unreasonable data information allocation and improving the network host for the on-demand deployment of big data cluster nodes.

(3) The reason why the cloud network big data cluster security scheduling method based on the association rule algorithm designed in this paper can achieve advantageous results is that: based on the association rule mining algorithm, the connection form of the Hadoop/MapReduce framework is determined, the cloud network security performance analysis is realized, and the big data information is improved. Numerical level of unit migration. The link bandwidth-time list structure is set up, and the specific value of the packet routing index is solved according to the connection

form of the SDN scheduling system, which realizes the on-demand deployment of big data cluster nodes by network hosts.

5 Conclusion

Since the data source parameters in the big data cluster nodes in the cloud network environment are generated in real time, the load of applications in the system also changes with time. However, the resources required by the computing containers of various applications in the existing streaming big data processing platform are scheduled in a pre statically configured manner, and the amount of resources allocated during operation will not change. This leads to the application resources being unsatisfied when the load is high, and a waste of resources when the load is low.

To solve this problem, a cloud network big data cluster security scheduling method based on association rule algorithm is proposed. By analyzing the connection state of hadoop/mapreduce framework, the security mapping conditions are solved, and then the connection form of SDN scheduling system is improved according to the link bandwidth time list definition standard, so as to determine the specific numerical results of packet routing indicators.

However, due to limited conditions, this paper mainly studies the orderly deployment of big data cluster nodes, and the research on external virus attacks in cloud network big data cluster scheduling is insufficient and has research limitations. In the future, from the perspective of virus intrusion security defense in the big data scheduling process, in-depth research will be carried out to improve the big data cluster scheduling method.

References

1. Dehdouh, K., Boussaid, O., Bentayeb, F.: Big data warehouse: building columnar NoSQL OLAP cubes. Int. J. Decis. Supp. Syst. Technol. **12**(1), 1–24 (2020)
2. Liu, S., et al.: Human memory update strategy: a multi-layer template update mechanism for remote visual monitoring. IEEE Trans. Multim. **23**, 2188–2198 (2022)
3. Shan, Z.: Simulation of scheduling fault tolerant control of big data cluster for security monitoring of cloud platform. Comput. Simul. **38**(7), 486–490 (2021)
4. Wenting, W., Junshuang, J., Hao, Z.: Big data equalization scheduling method of network traffic based on set pair analysis. Autom. Instrum. **2**(1), 66–69 (2020)
5. Shuai, L., Shuai, W., Xinyu, L.: Fuzzy Detection aided real-time and robust visual tracking under complex environments. IEEE Trans. Fuzzy Syst. **29**(1), 90–102 (2021)
6. Liu, S., Liu, D., Muhammad, K., Ding, W.: Effective template update mechanism in visual tracking with background clutter. Neurocomputing **458**, 615–625 (2021)
7. Kumar, S., Mohbey, K.K.: Memory-optimized distributed utility mining for big data. J. King Saud Univ. Comput. Inf. Sci. **3**(12), 23–27 (2021)
8. Adnan, T.Z., Yohannes, C.: Performance evaluation of mini single board computer in Hadoop big data cluster. IOP Conf. Ser.: Mater. Sci. Eng. **875**, 120–125 (2020)
9. Khalemsky, A., Gelbard, R.: A dynamic classification unit for online segmentation of big data via small data buffers. Decis. Sup. Syst. **128**(1), 113157.1–113157.14 (2020)
10. Pasupathi, S., Shanmuganathan, V., Madasamy, K., Yesudhas, H.R., Kim, M.: Trend analysis using agglomerative hierarchical clustering approach for time series big data. J. Supercomput. **77**(7), 6505–6524 (2021). https://doi.org/10.1007/s11227-020-03580-9

11. Sardar, T.H., Ansari, Z.: Distributed big data clustering using Mapreduce-based fuzzy C-Medoids. J. Inst. Eng. (India): Ser. B **103**(1), 73–82 (2021). https://doi.org/10.1007/s40031-021-00647-w
12. Ramdane, Y., Kabachi, N., Boussaid, O.: A data mining approach to guide the physical design of distributed big data warehouses. Adv. Knowl. Discov. Manag. **1004**(15), 107–125 (2022)
13. Ramdane, Y., Boussaid, O., Boukraà, D.: Building a novel physical design of a distributed big data warehouse over a Hadoop cluster to enhance OLAP cube query performance. Parallel Comput. **111**(9), 102–109 (2022)

Towards Differentially Private Contrastive Learning

Wenjun Li[1], Anli Yan[2], Taoyu Zhu[1], Teng Huang[1(✉)], Xuandi Luo[1], and Shaowei Wang[1]

[1] Institute of Artificial Intelligence and Blockchain, Guangzhou University, Guangzhou 510006, China
huangteng1220@buaa.edu.cn
[2] School of Cyberspace Security (School of Cryptology), Hainan University, Haikou 570228, China

Abstract. With the surge of unlabeled data, increasing efforts have been put into unsupervised learning. As one of the most representative branches of unsupervised learning, contrastive learning has achieved great progress by the high efficiency. Unfortunately, privacy threats on contrastive learning have become sophisticated, making it imperative to develop effective technologies that are able to deal with such threats. To alleviate the privacy issue in contrastive learning, we propose some novel techniques based on differential privacy, which aim at reducing the high sensitivity of gradient in the private training caused by interactive contrastive learning. Specifically, we add differentially private protection to the connection point related to different per-example gradients, which decreases the sensitivity of the gradients significantly. Our experiments on SimCLR demonstrate the superiority of our approach with higher accuracy under the same privacy protection.

Keywords: Contrastive learning · Differential privacy · Sensitivity analysis

1 Introduction

In the wake of the increase in unlabeled data, it puts forward higher requirements for unsupervised learning. As one of the mainstream branches of unsupervised learning, contrastive learning (CL) has made great progress with its high efficiency [5,10,12]. However, some studies have exposed potential privacy

This work was supported by National Natural Science Foundation of China (No.62102107, 62072132, 62002074, 62072127, 62002076,62102108), the Joint Funds of the National Natural Science Foundation of China (No. U20A20176), National Natural Science Foundation of China for Joint Fund Project (No. U1936218), Natural Science Foundation of Guangdong Province of China (No.2022A1515010061), Guangzhou Basic and Applied Basic Research Foundation (No.202201010194, No.622191-098), Research Project of Guangzhou University (No.62295098, No.RQ2021006).

Y. Xu et al. (Eds.): ML4CS 2022, LNCS 13656, pp. 510–520, 2023.
https://doi.org/10.1007/978-3-031-20099-1_43

risks about contrastive learning [21], which shows that contrastive models are vulnerable to membership inference attacks and attribute inference attacks. For example, the image encoder trained by contrastive learning achieves unexpectedly high attack accuracy [15]. Due to the absence of the class label, most contrastive learning models depend on the supervision of examples within the same batch or a memory bank [12]. The calculation of the loss in contrastive models heavily relies on the similarity of each pair of images, which leads to excessive interaction and the potential of privacy issues. To mitigate these privacy issues of contrastive learning, some researchers have made efforts propose Talos [13], which tackles the privacy problem by applying adversarial training on contrastive models. This method has played a certain role to some extent, but it is not a powerful and theoretically rigorous privacy protection method. Therefore, it is significant and urgent to explore new technologies to make the training of contrastive models safer.

To conduct private training of the contrastive model, some challenges need to be overcome: 1) The contrastive model generally has a complex network including encoder, projection head and prediction head, which inevitably suffer from high sensitivity of gradient; 2) most contrastive models correlate augmented views of different images, i.e., The independence of examples is broken, and the change of a single example in batch processing may affect the gradient of other examples. Because differential privacy is a provable privacy guarantee [7] and has been applied extensively for privacy-preserving machine learning [1,3,19,21]. In this paper, we protect the privacy of contrastive model training by making rational use of differential privacy technology. Considering that the most influential factor in the model update is the gradient of the model, adding privacy protection to the gradient may be more efficient and general. However, the correlations among different examples incur a high sensitivity of gradient. To solve this problem, components that undermine the independence between examples should be replaced or given different privacy protection. Benefiting from that, the sensitivity of the gradient can be decreased to a relatively small value. Furthermore, to give that connection point appropriate protection, we analysed its sensitivity, and theoretically demonstrated an upper bound.

In summary, we make the following contributions:

- We discussed the necessity of differentially private contrastive learning and analyzed the main challenge, i.e., the high sensitivity of gradient.
- We proposed a novel contrastive learning method based on differential privacy, which makes the connection point between different per-example gradients differentially private to decrease the sensitivity of the gradient.
- We analyzed the sensitivity of similarity matrix which is the connection point in SimCLR, and provided the theoretical proof.
- The experiments on SimCLR indicated that our methods can effectively conduct differentially private training of the contrastive model.

2 Background and Related Work

In this section, we briefly introduce the background knowledge of contrastive learning and differential privacy.

2.1 Contrastive Learning

Contrastive learning [11] is a framework that learns similar/dissimilar representations from data which are organized into similar/dissimilar pairs [6]. As the most representative self-supervised learning paradigm, contrastive learning aims to train a contrastive model which can generate expressive representations to perform downstream supervised machine learning tasks [13]. Self-supervised learning mainly uses pretext to mine its own supervised information from large-scale unlabeled data.

InfoNCE [17] is a commonly used contrastive loss function, defined as

$$\mathcal{L}_{q,k^+,\{k^-\}} = -\log \frac{\exp(q \cdot k^+/\tau)}{\exp(q \cdot k^+/\tau) + \sum_{k^-} \exp(q \cdot k^-/\tau)} \tag{1}$$

where q is a query representation, k^+ is a positive example derived from the augmentation version of the same image, k^- is a negative example derived from the augmentation of other examples, τ is a temperature hyper-parameter.

From Eq. (1), we know that InfoNCE maximizes the similarity between positive examples, and minimizes the similarity between positive examples and negative examples. InfoNCE is mainly used in the contrastive model with negative examples such as SimCLR [5], MoCo [12] or one of its variants, e.g., JCL [4].

Furthermore, contrastive learning can also work without negative examples. BYOL [10] only uses positive examples' representations to compute mean squared error and gets comparable performance. W-MSE [9] uses a whitening transform to avoid degenerate solutions. Some contrastive models try to construct loss function from the perspective of the feature.

2.2 Differential Privacy

Differential privacy (DP) is a rigorous mathematical framework that can guarantee a randomized algorithm behaves similarly on similar input databases.

Definition 1 (Differential Privacy [8]). *A randomized algorithm $\mathcal{M}$ with domain $\mathbb{N}^{|\mathcal{X}|}$ is (ε, δ)-differentially private if for all $\mathcal{S} \subseteq Range(\mathcal{M})$ and for all $x, y \in \mathbb{N}^{|\mathcal{X}|}$ such that $\|x - y\|_1 \leq 1$:*

$$\Pr[\mathcal{M}(x) \in S] \leq \exp(\varepsilon)\Pr[\mathcal{M}(y) \in S] + \delta$$

If $\delta = 0$, $\mathcal{M}$ is ε−differentially private. ϵ, δ are generally called privacy budget parameters. The smaller they are, the stronger the privacy guarantee is [20].

A standard paradigm to provide privacy-preserving approximations to function $f : \mathcal{D} \to \mathcal{R}^d$ is to add noise proportional to the sensitivity $\mathcal{S}_f$ of function f [18]. The sensitivity of a function gives an upper bound on how much we must perturb its output to preserve privacy [8].

3   Differentially Private Contrastive Learning

This section shows how to conduct private training on the contrastive model. A popular way to differentially private machine learning is using Stochastic Gradient Descent (SGD) with differentially private releases of gradients evaluated on mini-batches of a dataset. Differentially private contrastive learning can partly imitate this way while some specific problems may be occurred caused by the characteristic of contrastive learning.

We firstly present the basic components of the contrastive model's private training, then concretely show how to differentially private train specific contrastive models such as SimCLR.

3.1   Basic Components of Private Training

To protect the privacy of training data, DPSGD needs to perform two operations: (1) limit the sensitivity of gradient by clipping the norm of per-example gradients, and (2) add noise to the gradient of a batch before updating the model's parameters. These two operations can be detailed following steps.

Per-example Gradient Computation. In general, gradients are computed for a batch of examples. To limit the influence of every example, the gradient with respect to every example $\nabla_\theta \mathcal{L}(\theta, x)$ ($g(x)$ for short) is needed.

Per-example Gradient Clipping. Once we have obtained all per-example gradients, the next step is clipping the per-example gradients as:

$$\bar{g}(x) = \begin{cases} g(x) & \text{if } \|g(x)\|_2 \leq C \\ g(x)/(\frac{\|g(x)\|_2}{C}) & \text{if } \|g(x)\|_2 > C \end{cases}$$

where C denotes the clipping threshold.

Adding Noise to the Gradient. Adding noise to the gradient needs to analyze its sensitivity. The gradient is calculated as $f(B) = \sum_{x \in B} \bar{g}(x)$ (B represents a mini-batch of examples). We have mentioned that per-example gradients within the same batch are correlated, which means that the sensitivity of the gradient is a high value. The gradient's sensitivity Δ can be calculated by $\Delta = \|f(B) - f(B')\|_2$. We choose the Gaussian mechanism $M(\cdot)$ to make the gradient differentially private.

Updating Model Parameters. Once we obtain the noisy gradient, The next step is to use the noise gradient to update the parameters of the model. As for the choice of the optimizer, original SGD or SGD with momentum is available.

Privacy Accounting. The composability of differential privacy makes it possible to implement an "accountant" procedure that calculates the privacy loss at every iteration. We use Rényi differential privacy, which is natural for composability to analyze the privacy loss of one training step. Because of the existence of subsampling, we need to consider the "privacy amplification".

3.2 Private Training of SimCLR

SimCLR [5] can be viewed as a representation of contrastive learning with negative examples. This subsection shows how to differentially private train the SimCLR model. Firstly, we briefly introduce the framework of SimCLR.

A base encoder $f(\cdot)$ which extracts representation vectors from augmented data examples, no constraint for the network architecture but commonly use ResNet. **A projection head** $g(\cdot)$ that maps representations to the space where contrastive loss is applied. **A contrastive loss function** $\mathcal{L}$ defined for a contrastive prediction task, the loss function $\mathcal{L}$'s formulation is $\mathcal{L} = \frac{1}{2N}\sum_{k=1}^{N}[\ell(2k-1,2k) + \ell(2k,2k-1)]$ and $\ell(i,j)$ is defined as

$$\ell(i,j) = -\log \frac{\exp(sim(z_i,z_j)/\tau)}{\sum_{k=1}^{2N} \mathbb{1}_{[k\neq i]}\exp(sim(z_i,z_k)/\tau)} \tag{2}$$

where $\mathbb{1}_{[k\neq i]} \in \{0,1\}$ is an indicator function evaluating to 1 if $k \neq i$ and τ denotes a temperature parameter.

In Eq. (2), the similarities between different representations are the connection point that makes per-example gradients correlated. So if this similarity can be made differentially private, the relationship between examples will be significantly weakened. For the private training of the SimCLR model, we adopt the original DPSGD and our improved DPSGD.

Original-DPSGD. The gradient of a batch can be seen as a gradient query function. We know from Eq. (2) that a single example's change can not change other examples' representations, but can change other per-example gradients. Hence two neighboring batches of examples B and B', which differ in one example, may have different similarity values and losses. Then it will generate two batches of totally different per-example gradients g_i and g_i'. So the sensitivity of gradient query function Δ_g can be analyzed as

$$\Delta_g = \|g_B - g_{B'}\|_2$$
$$= \|\sum_{i=1}^{n} g_i - \sum_{i=1}^{n} g_i'\|_2$$
$$\leq \|\sum_{i=1}^{n} g_i\|_2 + \|\sum_{i=1}^{n} g_i'\|_2$$
$$\leq \sum_{i=1}^{n}(\|g_i\|_2) + \sum_{i=1}^{n}(\|g_i'\|_2)$$
$$\leq 2 \cdot n \cdot C$$

where n represents the number of augmented views, so n is $2|B|$, C is the clipping threshold. The first inequality follows from the triangle inequality, the last inequality follows the fact that each per-example gradient's norm is at most C.

It can be known from the inequality that this sensitivity is related to the number of a batch of examples, which means a bigger batch size will lead to higher sensitivity of gradient.

We use a Gaussian mechanism $\mathcal{M}_g$ to make the model's gradient differentially private as $\mathcal{M}_g(g_B) = g_B + \mathcal{N}(0, \Delta_g^2 \sigma_g^2 I)$, where σ_g denotes the noise scale of gradient.

$\mathcal{M}_g(\cdot)$ adds independently drawn random noise distributed as $\mathcal{N}(0, \Delta_g^2 \sigma_g^2 I)$ to each dimension of g_B. According to the observation of $\mathcal{M}_g(\cdot)$, even the noise scale of the gradient σ_g is small, the overall variance of noise $\Delta_g^2 \sigma_g^2$ is big, which results that original DPSGD is hard to conduct efficient private training of the SimCLR model.

DPSGD with DP-Similarity. The similarity is the connection point that makes per-example gradients correlated, so the core to decrease the sensitivity of gradient is weakening the relationships between different per-example gradients. To this end, we propose to make the similarity differentially private by adding noise. As we mentioned above, the similarity is calculated by matrix operation, hence the real operation is on similarity matrix S. In general, the SimCLR model gives a L_2 normalization to representations output by the projection head. Let Z represents the representations of a batch of augmented batches (i.e. $|Z| = 2|B|$), the similarity matrix S can be calculated as

$$S(Z) = Z^T Z$$

Let B and B' represent two neighboring batches of examples which has the same size but differ in one example. Through data augmentation and encoding, we can obtain respective representations Z and Z', cause every example has two augmented views, so Z and Z' differ in two representations. To make the similarity matrix differentially private, we first prove the upper bound of the similarity matrix's sensitivity.

Theorem 1. *Let $Z = \{Z_1, \cdots, Z_N\}$ and $\|Z_i\|_2 = 1$, then $S(Z)$ has L_2 sensitivity Δ_S bounded above by $4\sqrt{(|Z| - 1)}$.*

Proof. The sensitivity of similarity matrix can be calculated as

$$\Delta_S = \|S(Z) - S(Z')\|_2$$
$$= \|Z^T Z - Z'^T Z'\|_2$$

while Z and Z' differ in two representations, then $Z^T Z$ and $Z'^T Z'$ differ in two rows and two columns, which are $(4|Z| - 4)$ elements, so there are $(4|Z| - 4)$ different similarities. Following the fact that the dot product between two l_2 normalized representations is at most 1, which also means the similarity is at most 1, then the difference between one similarity from $Z^T Z$ and one similarity from $Z'^T Z'$ is at most 2, so the sensitivity of similarity matrix Δ_S is at most $2\sqrt{(4|Z| - 4)} = 4\sqrt{(|Z| - 1)}$.

It can be known from **Theorem 1** that the sensitivity of similarity matrix Δ_S is $4\sqrt{(2|B| - 1)}$, σ_S denotes the noise scale of similarity matrix, and the

Gaussian mechanism $M_S(Z)$ that make similarity matrix differentially private is as

$$M_S(Z) = S(Z) + \mathcal{N}(0, \Delta_S^2 \sigma_S^2 I)$$

That means M_S adds independently drawn random noise distributed as $\mathcal{N}(0, \Delta_S^2 \sigma_S^2 I)$ to each output of $S(Z)$.

Through the noisy similarity matrix, we can significantly weaken the relationships between different per-example gradients, which means the change of single examples in a batch has limited influence on other per-example gradients.

With the assistance of a noisy similarity matrix, it can be thought that two neighboring batches of examples B and B' obtain two similar similarity matrixes and two similar losses. Furthermore, the per-example gradient of all examples excluding the example being changed can be seen unchanged. Hence two neighbouring batches of examples have two batches of per-example gradients which only differ in two per-example gradients, while each example has two augmented views. So the sensitivity of gradient query function Δ_g' can be analyzed as

$$
\begin{aligned}
\Delta_g' &= \|g_B' - g_{B'}'\|_2 \\
&= \|\sum_{i=1}^{n} g_i - \sum_{i=1}^{n} g_i'\|_2 \\
&= \|2(g_i - g_i')\|_2 \\
&= 2\|g_i - g_i'\|_2 \\
&\leq 2(\|g_i\|_2 + \|g_i'\|_2) \\
&\leq 4 \cdot C
\end{aligned}
$$

Then using a Gaussian mechanism $\mathcal{M}_g'$ to make the model's gradient differentially private as $\mathcal{M}'_g(g_B) = g_B' + \mathcal{N}(0, \Delta_g'^2 \sigma_g'^2 I)$, where σ_g' denotes the noise scale of gradient.

Original DPSGD has a sensitivity of gradient $4|B|C$, using DPSGD with DP-similarity has saved a factor of $2|B|$ in L_2 sensitivity. Although some privacy budgets are allocated for the similarity matrix, means fewer privacy budgets are allocated for the model's gradient. Although σ_g' is a little bigger than σ_g, $\Delta_g'^2 \sigma_g'^2$ is still smaller than $\Delta_g^2 \sigma_g^2$. Hence using DPSGD with DP-similarity to conduct efficient private training of the SimCLR model is promising.

4   Privacy Analysis

A fundamental component in a differentially private stochastic gradient descent algorithm is iteratively sampling a mini-batch of examples in the training dataset as the model's input. In privacy analysis of differentially private training algorithms, different subsampling methods have different privacy analysis frameworks. In this paper, we fix the batch size of a mini-batch, which is equivalent to a fixed size of a sample. For the sake of rigor, we adopt the analysis strategy of "sampling without replacement", proposed by Wang et al. [20].

4.1   Privacy Analysis of SimCLR

The privacy analysis of the SimCLR's private training can be forwarded as the steps we mentioned above. Due to that original DPSGD and DPSGD with DP-similarity have a difference in privacy loss, we analyzed the privacy loss respectively.

Original DPSGD. We only add noise to the sum of per-example gradients. Once the noise scale of gradient σ, sampling probability γ and the number of steps T are set. First, the RDP $\epsilon(\alpha, \sigma)$ of the Gaussian mechanism with noise scale σ for each order α is obtained through the corollary 3 in [16]. Second, the RDP $\epsilon'(\alpha)$ of the subsampled Gaussian mechanism with sampling probability γ for each α is calculated by Theorem 9 in [20]. Third, the RDP of T subsampled Gaussian mechanisms for each α is $T \cdot \epsilon'(\alpha)$. Lastly, through Theorem 21 in [2] calculating a series of DP i.e. $\{\epsilon_{(\alpha,\delta)}\}$ for each α and the same given δ and picking the smallest ϵ as the final privacy loss of this differentially private training.

DPSGD with DP-Similarity. We add noise not only to the sum of per-example gradients but also to the similarity matrix. There are two-part to privacy loss. The noise scale of gradients and similarity matrix is set to be σ_1 and σ_2 respectively. First, the RDP of Gaussian mechanism applying to gradient $\epsilon_1(\alpha, \sigma_1)$ and similarity matrix $\epsilon_2(\alpha, \sigma_2)$ are obtained according to the corollary 3 in [16]. Second, the subsampled version $\epsilon_1'(\alpha)$, $\epsilon_2'(\alpha)$ are calculated by Theorem 9 in [20]. Third, the overall RDP of T subsampled Gaussian mechanisms for each α is $(T \cdot (\epsilon_1'(\alpha) + \epsilon_2'(\alpha)))$. Lastly, the DP of differentially private SimCLR training with DP-similarity is picked among a series of DP $\{\epsilon_{(\alpha,\delta)}\}$, which are calculated through Theorem 21 in [2].

5   Implementation

This section conducts experiments on different differentially private training methods within the same privacy budget. The contrastive model we use is still SimCLR.

5.1   Experimental Setup

There are some settings for the differentially private training of SimCLR.

- **Dataset.** This paper aims to investigate different contrastive models' performances in different differentially private training. From a computational efficiency perspective, we conduct our experiments on the CIFAR10 dataset [14].
- **Data augmentation.** We use random crop, resize(with random flip), and color distortions, but without gaussian blur due to the low resolution of CIFAR-10 images.
- **Architecture setting.** A ResNet-18 as a base encoder to encode the image into a 512-dimensional representation, and a 2-layer MLP projection head to project the representation to a 128-dimensional latent space, the former has

512 hidden units and the latter has 128 hidden units. The batch normalization layer in ResNet-18 is replaced with a group normalization layer and weight standardization is used in the projection head.

- **Evaluation protocol.** The most common evaluation protocol for unsupervised feature learning is based on freezing the network encoder after unsupervised pre-training and then obtaining the accuracy of a k-nearest neighbors classifier (KNN, $k = 5$) [9].
- **Privacy parameters.** The privacy parameters (ϵ, δ) is $(1000, 10^{-5})$, while ϵ is the privacy budget and δ is the breaking probability.
- **Implementation details.** The learning rate is 0.1, weight decay = 1e−6, clipping threshold $C = 0.02$, the sampling ratio of each mini-batch $q = 0.00256$, and the number of epochs E is 200 (i.e., the number of steps is $T = E/q$), the optimizer is SGD with Momentum, the momentum is 0.9.

As the privacy loss is independent of the algorithm, once the sampling rate, privacy budget, and running epochs are deterministic, the noise scale for gradient and similarity matrix can be obtained.

Original DPSGD. According to the analysis in Sect. 3, the sensitivity of gradients is $(4 \cdot |B| \cdot C)$, then the minimum variance of noise to satisfy the privacy budget is $\sigma = 0.3812$.

DPSGD with DP-Similarity. With the assistance of the noisy similarity matrix, the gradient's sensitivity has been significantly decreased to $(4 \cdot C)$, which saves a factor of $|B|$ compared to the original DPSGD. We allocated the privacy budget equally to the gradient and similarity matrix. So the noise scale of similarity matrix and gradient is set to be the same value 0.4021, which is calculated by privacy analysis. Moreover, we choose the true loss in the visualization of training results, while the noisy loss can not reflect the true convergence situation.

5.2 Experimental Results

The experiment results of these two private training methods are presented in Figs. 1 and 2. For original DPSGD, the variation curve of training is similar to a straight line, we argued this phenomenon is that the gradient with momentum changes a little. The test accuracy changes randomly, we argued this reason is that the encoder can learn something but it's hard to get further improvement. Hence it's reasonable to argue that the original DPSGD can't effectively conduct differentially private training of SimCLR. For DPSGD with DP-similarity, the training loss steadily decreases and the test accuracy gradually increases. The test accuracy curve starts from a very low cardinality and the loss curve starts from a very high cardinality, which may be due to the interference of noisy similarity matrix. The comparison of the two methods shows that our method can effectively conduct differentially private training, and performs better than the original DPSGD.

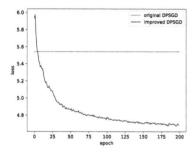

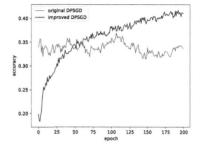

Fig. 1. The training loss of SimCLR

Fig. 2. The test accuracy of SimCLR

6 Conclusion

In this paper, we analyze the privacy risk of contrastive learning. Compared to the supervised model (i.e., it has independent per-example gradients), the contrastive model normally has correlated per-example gradients, which brings the challenge of the high sensitivity of the gradient. To solve this issue, we propose to add differentially private protection to the connection point related to different per-example gradients, which is able to decrease the sensitivity of the gradients significantly.

Specifically, we show our method on SimCLR and analyze the sensitivity of their connection points. More private points mean more privacy budgets, i.e., the noise scale for the gradient is bigger. To demonstrate the superiority of our method, we conduct a comprehensive and detailed evaluation on SimCLR. The results have verified that our improved private training methods can complete effective training while the original DPSGD can't. Although the training loss in our improved methods converged a little slowly, which is a common phenomenon in private training. Therefore, to achieve the same performance as no privacy protection, the version with privacy protection costs more time.

References

1. Abadi, M., et al.: Deep learning with differential privacy. In: Proceedings of the 2016 ACM SIGSAC Conference on Computer and Communications Security, pp. 308–318 (2016)
2. Balle, B., Barthe, G., Gaboardi, M., Hsu, J., Sato, T.: Hypothesis testing interpretations and renyi differential privacy. In: International Conference on Artificial Intelligence and Statistics, pp. 2496–2506. PMLR (2020)
3. Bassily, R., Smith, A., Thakurta, A.: Private empirical risk minimization: efficient algorithms and tight error bounds. In: 2014 IEEE 55th Annual Symposium on Foundations of Computer Science, pp. 464–473. IEEE (2014)
4. Cai, Q., Wang, Y., Pan, Y., Yao, T., Mei, T.: Joint contrastive learning with infinite possibilities. arXiv preprint arXiv:2009.14776 (2020)

5. Chen, T., Kornblith, S., Norouzi, M., Hinton, G.: A simple framework for contrastive learning of visual representations. In: International Conference on Machine Learning, pp. 1597–1607. PMLR (2020)
6. Chen, X., Fan, H., Girshick, R., He, K.: Improved baselines with momentum contrastive learning. arXiv preprint arXiv:2003.04297 (2020)
7. Dwork, C.: Differential privacy. In: Bugliesi, M., Preneel, B., Sassone, V., Wegener, I. (eds.) ICALP 2006. LNCS, vol. 4052, pp. 1–12. Springer, Heidelberg (2006). https://doi.org/10.1007/11787006_1
8. Dwork, C., Roth, A., et al.: The algorithmic foundations of differential privacy. Found. Trends Theor. Comput. Sci. **9**(3–4), 211–407 (2014)
9. Ermolov, A., Siarohin, A., Sangineto, E., Sebe, N.: Whitening for self-supervised representation learning. In: International Conference on Machine Learning, pp. 3015–3024. PMLR (2021)
10. Grill, J.B., et al.: Bootstrap your own latent: a new approach to self-supervised learning. arXiv preprint arXiv:2006.07733 (2020)
11. Hadsell, R., Chopra, S., LeCun, Y.: Dimensionality reduction by learning an invariant mapping. In: 2006 IEEE Computer Society Conference on Computer Vision and Pattern Recognition (CVPR'06), vol. 2, pp. 1735–1742. IEEE (2006)
12. He, K., Fan, H., Wu, Y., Xie, S., Girshick, R.: Momentum contrast for unsupervised visual representation learning. In: Proceedings of the IEEE/CVF Conference on Computer Vision and Pattern Recognition, pp. 9729–9738 (2020)
13. He, X., Zhang, Y.: Quantifying and mitigating privacy risks of contrastive learning. arXiv preprint arXiv:2102.04140 (2021)
14. Krizhevsky, A., Hinton, G., et al.: Learning multiple layers of features from tiny images. Technical Report (2009)
15. Liu, H., Jia, J., Qu, W., Gong, N.Z.: EncoderMI: membership inference against pre-trained encoders in contrastive learning. In: Proceedings of the 2021 ACM SIGSAC Conference on Computer and Communications Security, pp. 2081–2095 (2021)
16. Mironov, I.: Rényi differential privacy. In: 2017 IEEE 30th Computer Security Foundations Symposium (CSF), pp. 263–275. IEEE (2017)
17. Oord, A.V.D., Li, Y., Vinyals, O.: Representation learning with contrastive predictive coding. arXiv preprint arXiv:1807.03748 (2018)
18. Pichapati, V., Suresh, A.T., Yu, F.X., Reddi, S.J., Kumar, S.: AdaCliP: adaptive clipping for private SGD. arXiv preprint arXiv:1908.07643 (2019)
19. Shokri, R., Shmatikov, V.: Privacy-preserving deep learning. In: Proceedings of the 22nd ACM SIGSAC Conference on Computer and Communications Security, pp. 1310–1321 (2015)
20. Wang, Y.X., Balle, B., Kasiviswanathan, S.P.: Subsampled rényi differential privacy and analytical moments accountant. In: The 22nd International Conference on Artificial Intelligence and Statistics, pp. 1226–1235. PMLR (2019)
21. Yu, L., Liu, L., Pu, C., Gursoy, M.E., Truex, S.: Differentially private model publishing for deep learning. In: 2019 IEEE Symposium on Security and Privacy (SP), pp. 332–349. IEEE (2019)

Two-Stage High Precision Membership Inference Attack

Shi Chen and Yubin Zhong[✉]

Guangzhou University, Guangzhou 510006, China
zhong_yb@gzhu.edu.cn

Abstract. Most membership inference attacks (MIA) identify training set records by observing the particular behavior of machine learning models on training data, but these methods based only on overfitting are difficult to achieve high precision. Even though recent difficulty calibration techniques have alleviated this problem, calibrated attacks can still only identify a smaller number of memberships with high precision. In this work, we rethink the value of overfitting for MIA and we argue that overfitting can provide clear signals of non-membership to the adversary. In scenarios where the cost of an attack is high, such signals can prevent the adversary from launching unnecessary attacks. We propose a simple and efficient two-stage high-precision MIA that uses an overfitting-based attack to perform "membership exclusion" before performing the MIA. We show that this two-stage attack can significantly increase the number of identified members while guaranteeing high precision.

Keywords: Machine learning · Membership inference · Overfitting · Data privacy

1 Introduction

Machine learning methods rely on large amounts of data for training, and when training data contains sensitive information, one concern is whether the model will reveal private information about the training data. Unfortunately, recent research [2,3,11,12,14] has shown that attackers can gain access to models to steal sensitive information from datasets. One of the more representative of existing privacy attacks is the membership inference attack (MIA) [12], where the adversary aims to infer whether a record exists in the training set of the target model.

However, Rezaei et al. [9] discovered that previous MIAs tend to predict non-member samples as member samples and suffer from a high false positive rate (FPR). The previous attacks [11–13] are not suitable in attack scenarios where the false positive cost is high [8]. Some recent work [1,14] has considered the use of difficulty calibration to mitigate the high FPR problem, and this approach has also been shown to achieve high precision attacks on models that generalize well [8]. Nevertheless, identifying more members with high precision requirements is still a difficult task. For example, for a CNN that achieve 98.61%

© The Author(s), under exclusive license to Springer Nature Switzerland AG 2023
Y. Xu et al. (Eds.): ML4CS 2022, LNCS 13656, pp. 521–535, 2023.
https://doi.org/10.1007/978-3-031-20099-1_44

accuracy at MNIST, the C-Conf attack proposed by Watson et al. [14] is able to identify only 21 out of 10000 members with 100% precision. Although it is already a big improvement compared to the attack without considering the difficulty calibration, we still want to know how to identify more members with a high precision (Fig. 1) .

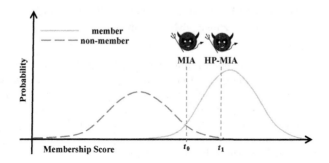

Fig. 1. The difference between HP-MIA and MIA.The aim of MIA is to find a suitable threshold that achieves the highest accuracy in distinguishing members from non-members, while the goal of HP-MIA is to find the threshold that identifies members with a high prediction rate.

Deep learning models have strong learning ability, even if the samples in the training set are contaminated, their Loss tend to be not too high [17]. Suppose the target model is overfitting so severely that the Loss of all members in the training set is less than a small real number ϵ, then we just need to mark all records with a Loss greater than ϵ as non-members and we can achieve a "membership exclusion attack" with 100% precision. However, easy-to-predict non-members may have very low Loss [14]. Therefore, we argue that **overfitting may not provide a valid basis for membership inference directly, but can provide an explicit non-membership signal to the adversary.**

In this paper, we focus on how to design a high precision MIA that can identify more members, and we name this type of attack as High Precision MIA (HP-MIA). As shown in the figure, the goal of the previous MIA was to obtain an optimal threshold for distinguishing members from non-members, and this threshold corresponded to a high accuracy rate. In contrast, the goal of HP-MIA is to determine a threshold such that most of the identified samples are members. We treat the construction of a high prediction rate MIA as an optimization problem with constraints, setting the number of members identified as the optimization objective and the high precision as the constraint. Instead of using overfitting-based attacks for direct membership inference, we use them as a "membership exclusiontechnique", specifically, we propose a simple and effective two-stage HP-MIA. We first exclude non-membership samples from the target dataset by traditional overfitting-based attack [16], and then use calibrated attack [14] to identify the true members.

Contribution. We summarize our contributions and key finding as follows :

- We propose a new perspective on designing MIAs based on overfitting. Specifically, we find that overfitting provides the adversary with a far more reliable non-membership signal than the membership signal. In scenarios where the cost of attack is high, such signals can help the adversary avoid unnecessary losses. We propose to use the overfitting-based membership exclusion technique to assist the adversary in achieving high precision inference.
- We propose a Two-stage High Precision MIA. Specifically, this attack is divided into two steps of exclusion and inference, using preemptive exclusion to further improve the performance of high-precision inference. Unlike the previous MIA attack, we use overfitting of neural networks to perform identification of non-members rather than identification of members. We deploy our attack on various datasets and on various models, and our evaluation results show that Two-stage HP-MIA is able to identify more memberships than other attacks while guaranteeing high precision.

Organization. We present the membership inference attack and some recent work on difficulty calibration techniques in Sect. 2. Section 3 shows our HP-MIA framework and a new two-stage attack. Experimental results are given in Sect. 4. In Sect. 5 we conclude this work.

2   Background

In this section, we give the definition of membership inference attack (MIA) and introduce the threshold-based MIA in Sect. 2.1. Then, we describe difficulty calibration techniques used to mitigate the high FPR problem of MIA in Sect. 2.2.

2.1   Membership Inference Attacks

Definition 1 (Membership Inference Attacks [12]). *Given a machine learning model h that has completed training on the training set $D \sim Q^n$, and a target sample $z = (x, y) \sim Q$, where Q denotes the probability distribution of the data points. The membership inference attack can be formalized as a binary classifier:*

$$\mathcal{A} : Z \times H \longrightarrow \{0, 1\} \tag{1}$$

where 0 means z does not belong to the training set D, otherwise it is 1. Z denotes the set of all samples $z \sim Q$ and H denotes the set of all classifiers trained on examples from a data distribution Q.

A common binary classification in membership inference problems is the threshold model, which distinguishes members from non-members by computing a particular score $s(h, z)$ and setting a threshold t.

$$\mathcal{A}_{score}(h, z, s, t) = I\left[s(h, z) > t\right] \tag{2}$$

where the indicator function $I\left[x\right]$ equals to 1 if x is true and 0 otherwise.

2.2   Calibrated Membership Inference Attacks

For non-member examples with low prediction difficulty, the target model may exhibit a high degree of confidence. Most of the early MIA attacks [11,12,16] implicitly assumed that the prediction difficulty of members and non-members is the same, which is believed to be the main reason for the high FPR problem. To address this problem, Watson et al. [14] proposed the difficulty calibration technique.

Specifically, we assume that the adversary has a reference dataset D_{ref} with the same distribution as the training set of the target model. He trains some reference models on the D_{ref} before performing the attack, then, he determines whether the example is a membership by comparing the membership score of the target example on the target model and reference models. Formally, we define the calibrated score as:

$$s_{cal}(h, z) = s(h, z) - E_{g \leftarrow T(D_{ref})} [s(g, z)] \tag{3}$$

where T denotes the randomized training algorithm. The calibrated attack is performed by setting a threshold on the calibrated score.

3   Methodology

In this section we introduce our two-stage High Precision Membership Inference Attack (Two-stage HP-MIA). In Sect. 3.1 we describe HP-MIA formally using a game and illustrate the setup of this paper on adversary knowledge. In Sect. 3.2 we introduce the attack procedure and technical details of Two-stage HP-MIA.

3.1   Threat Model

In contrast to the definition in Sect. 2.1, for HPMIA, the adversary is more interested in the precision of the attack, specifically, we consider the following HP-MIA game:

Definition 2 (HP-MIA game $G(\mathcal{Q}, \mathcal{A}, T, n)$). *Let $\mathcal{Q}$ be a distribution over data points, $\mathcal{A}$ be an attack, T be a randomized training algorithm, n be a positive integer. The game proceeds as follows:*

1. *The challenger chooses a secret bit $b \leftarrow \{0,1\}$ uniformly at random, and samples a training dataset $D \sim \mathcal{Q}^n$.*
2. *If $b = 1$, the challenger randomly selects a record z in the training set D. Otherwise, the challenger samples a record z from the distribution $\mathcal{Q}$.*
3. *The challenger trains a model $h \leftarrow T(D)$ on D and sends h and z to the adversary.*
4. *The adversary tries to infer the secret bit as b', and performs an attack only if $b' = 1$.*

5.

$$G(\mathcal{Q}, \mathcal{A}, T, n) = \begin{cases} 1 & b' = 1 \ and \ b = 1 \\ 0 & b' = 1 \ and \ b = 0 \end{cases}$$

In this paper, we assume that the adversary has only black-box access to the target model and has a shadow dataset D_{shadow} sampled from the same distribution as the training set of the target model, through which the adversary can train the shadow model to mimic the behavior of the target model. Given a target dataset $D_{target}, D_{shadow} \cap D_{target} = \emptyset$, the adversary aims to identify members of the target model from the target dataset D_{target} with as high a precision as possible. Our assumptions about the adversary's knowledge are similar to most prior work [11–13].

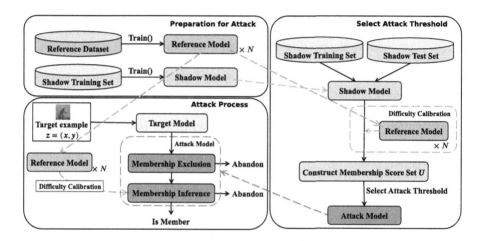

Fig. 2. Overall procedure of two-stage HP-MIA

3.2   Two-stage HP-MIA

Overview. For the above attack setup, the two important metrics we focus on are the precision(Pr) and recall(Recall) of the attack. We give a formal definition of HP-MIA by a constrained optimization problem:

Definition 3 (High-Precisionα Membership Inference Attack). *Given a target model h, a target dataset D_{target}, $\alpha \in [0, 1]$ is a precision constraint value. We call $\hat{\mathcal{A}}$ is a High-Precision α Membership Inference Attack (HPα-MIA) for h if $\hat{\mathcal{A}}$ satisfies:*

$$\hat{\mathcal{A}} = \underset{\mathcal{A}_{score}}{argmax} \, Recall(\mathcal{A}, D_{target})$$
$$s.t. Pr(\mathcal{A}, D_{target}) \geqslant \alpha$$

(4)

The formulae for Pr and Recall we will give in Sect. 4.1. We outline the whole process of Two-stage HP-MIA in Fig. 2. The adversary needs to build reference model and shadow model before conducting an attack. Then, the adversary select the attack threshold based on the shadow model. When performing membership inference, the attacker first excludes some examples by membership exclusion attack, and then uses high-precision membership inference for the remaining examples.

Preparation for Attack. Before the attack, the adversary needs to build a series of models to imitate the behavior of the target model, which will be used for membership score calibration and attack model training. These models can be divided into reference model and shadow model because of their different uses. We assume that the adversary has a adversary dataset D_{adv} which from the same distribution as the training set of the target model, so we can construct the reference dataset D_{ref} for training the reference model and the shadow dataset D_{shadow} for training the shadow model. Note that the two data sets should be disjoint, i.e. $D_{ref} \bigcap D_{shadow} = \emptyset$.

The reference model is used to construct the calibrated MIA, The calculation of the calibrated membership score is shown in (3). The basic idea of calibrated attack is to judge whether the target model has learned the target example by comparing the prediction of the target model with that of the reference model In general, the higher the number of reference models, the better the difficulty correction. We will discuss the effect of the number of reference models on the attack performance in Sect. 4.3.

The shadow model is used to mimic the behavior of the target model just like the reference model, but it is used for the determination of the attack model threshold. The shadow training set is constructed from the adversary dataset, and the shadow training set and the reference training set do not overlap because of the reliance on the reference model for difficulty correction in shadow training. For convenience, we refer to the setup of Salem et al. [11] which only trains a shadow model for the attack.

Algorithm 1: Two-stage High-Precision Membership Inference Attack

---

1 **Input:** target model h, target record z, membership score used s_0 in the first stage and its threshold t_0, membership score s_1 used in the second stage and its threshold t_1
2 **if** $s_0(h, z) < t_0$ **then**
3 $\quad$ **return** $\emptyset$
4 **else if** $s_1(h, z) < t_1$ **then**
5 $\quad$ **return** $\emptyset$
6 **else**
7 $\quad$ **return** 1

Attack Process. We propose a novel attack framework, which is divided into two steps: exclusion and inference. We adopt simple threshold model as the implementation of this attack, and therefore need to determine the membership scores(s_1 and s_2) and thresholds(t_1 and t_2) for both steps. The method for determining the thresholds will be shown in Sect. 7. We use the cross-entropy Loss score as an indicator of member exclusion, calculated as follows:

$$s_1(h, z) = -l(h, z) = log(h(x)_y) \tag{5}$$

where $z = (x, y)$ denotes the target example and h denotes the target model. We excluded examples with large Loss values as non-members in the first stage. This is a completely opposite approach to Yeom et al. [16] Our intuition is that the neural network is able to fit the training data well, so examples with large Loss values have a high probability of being non-members.

For the examples that are not excluded in the first stage, we further perform high-precision membership inference on them. Note that a score-based attack without considering the example difficulty makes it difficult to achieve a high-precision MIA. Therefore, we use the calibrated Loss as the membership score s_2 in the second stage, which is calculated in (3).

Algorithm 1 demonstrates the process of performing Two-stage HP-MIA on a single target example. Note that in this paper, we consider an extremely cautious adversary who only judges the target example as a member when he is very sure, otherwise he will abandon the attack.

Select Attack Threshold. In practice, we do not have access to the training set of the target model and thus cannot solve the optimization problem (4) on the real dataset D_{target}. According to our assumptions on adversary knowledge in Sect. 3.1, we can construct the member dataset D_{shadow}^{in} and non-member dataset D_{shadow}^{out} of the shadow model for supervised training of the attack model. As for the score-based attacks, the process of constructing a attack is actually finding an optimal threshold,and we choose the appropriate threshold in the following membership score set U:

$$U(h, s, D_{shadow}) = \left\{ u_i = \frac{s(h, z_i) + s(h, z_{i+1})}{2} : z_i \in D_{shadow} \right\} \tag{6}$$

where $s(h, z_i) \leqslant s(h, z_{i+1}), i = 1, 2, ..., m$, and m is the amount of members of the shadow data set. Specifically, we iterate through all elements in U and calculate the attack precision and recall corresponding to each element, select the subset U' that satisfies precision $\geqslant \alpha$, and return the element in U' that corresponds to the largest recall.

Two-stage HP-MIA needs to rely on two thresholds, the threshold t_0 for membership exclusion attack and the threshold t_1 for membership inference attack. Appendix Algorithm 2 shows our process of choosing the optimal threshold. We denote the precision constraint value of the membership inference attack as α and the precision constraint value of the membership exclusion attack as β. α is set by the adversary according to his requirements, and in order to construct the optimal attack, the adversary continuously adjusts the value of β through the well-trained shadow model to obtain the optimal threshold value. Eventually the adversary attacks the victim model through the two determined thresholds t_1 and t_0.

4   Experiments

4.1   Experimental Setup

Table 1. Accuracy of the target model

	MNIST	F-MNIST	CIFAR10	Purchase100	Texas100
Model	CNN	CNN	AlexNet	MLP	MLP
Train_Acc	100%	100%	100%	100%	100%
Test_Acc	98.59%	88.74%	70.61%	80.59%	43.89%

Dataset. We conducted experiments on several baseline datasets of different complexity: MNIST [7], Fashion-MNIST (F-MNIST) [15], CIFAR10 [5], Purchase100[1], and Texas100[2]. We randomly divide each of these datasets into six datasets, two of which are used as the training set D_{target}^{in} and test set D_{target}^{out} for the target model, two of which are used as the training set D_{shadow}^{in} and test set D_{shadow}^{out} for the shadow model, and the remaining two datasets are used as the reference training set for the training of the reference model.

For MNIST and F-MNIST, the target model test set has 10,000 images, and the remaining datasets have 12,000 images each. For CIFAR10, each dataset has 10,000 images. For Purchase100, each dataset has 20,000 records, and for Texas100, each dataset has 10,000 records.

Model Architectures. The target model for MNIST and Fashion-MNIST is a small CNN with two convolutional layers and a maximum pooling layer, two convolutional layers with 24 and 48 output channels, and a kernel size of 5, followed by a fully connected layer with 100 neurons as the classification head, and we use Tanh as the activation function. For CIFAR10, we use AlexNet [6] as the structure of the target model. For Purchase100 and Texas100, we refer to the work of Song et al. [13] and use a multilayer perceptron (MLP) as the target model with four hidden layers with the number of neurons of 1024, 512, 256, and 128, respectively, and use Tanh as the activation function.

---

[1] https://www.kaggle.com/c/acquire-valued-shoppers-challenge/data.
[2] https://www.dshs.texas.gov/THCIC/Hospitals/Download.shtm.

Model Training. We use Adam optimizer [4] to train the target model 200 epochs. For the target models of MNIST, F-MNIST, CIFAR10, Purchase100, and Texas100, we set the learning rates to 0.0005, 0.0005, 0.0001, 0.0002, and 0.0002, respectively, and the corresponding batch sizes to 100, 100, 50, 100, and 100, respectively. Table 1 shows the performance of several target models.

The shadow and reference models are trained using the same training algorithm and hyperparameters as the target model. For each dataset, we train a shadow model on the shadow dataset for attack model construction and 20 reference models on the reference dataset for calculating the calibrated score.

Success Metrics. We consider an extremely cautious MIA adversary who wants to identify as many members as possible with high precision. We use the following metrics to evaluate the attack performance: number of correctly identified members (TP), recall (Recall) and precision (Pr). Recall and Pr are calculated as follows:

$$\text{Recall} = \frac{\text{TP}}{|D_{target}^{in}|} \quad \text{Pr} = \frac{\text{TP}}{\text{TP} + \text{FP}}$$

where FP denotes the number of non-members identified as members by the attack model.

4.2 Attack Evaluation

Effectiveness of Two-Stage HP-MIA. To highlight the effect of Two-stage attack, we use two calibrated attacks, C-Loss and C-Conf, to compare with our attacks. These two attacks use Loss and Confidence as membership scores, respectively, and use difficulty calibration [14] to remove the effect of example difficulty. It is worth noting that C-Loss can be viewed as a direct HP-MIA without using the membership exclusion technique.

Table 2. Evaluation of various data sets, model structures, and MIA methods, $\alpha = 90\%$

		MNIST	F-MNIST	CIFAR10	Purchase100	Texas100
C-Loss	TP	41	224	100	4	1872
	Recall	0.41%	2.24%	1.00%	0.02%	18.72%
	Pr	91.11%	**92.18%**	**95.24%**	**100%**	88.83%
C-Conf	TP	111	686	1427	46	4087
	Recall	1.11%	6.86%	14.27%	0.23%	40.87%
	Pr	92.50%	88.98%	87.17%	93.88%	89.98%
Two-stage	TP	**590**	**1406**	**3866**	**8283**	**5792**
	Recall	**5.90%**	**14.06%**	**38.66%**	**41.42%**	**57.92%**
	Pr	**92.91%**	89.21%	85.34%	89.32%	**90.02%**
$\alpha = 90\%$						

Table 3. Evaluation of various data sets, model structures, and MIA methods, $\alpha = 94\%$

		MNIST	F-MNIST	CIFAR10	Purchase100	Texas100
C-Loss	TP	21	133	75	4	1142
	Recall	0.21%	1.33%	0.75%	0.02%	11.42%
	Pr	100%	96.38%	96.15%	100%	91.65%
C-Conf	TP	81	511	796	18	2489
	Recall	0.81%	5.11%	7.96%	0.09%	24.89%
	Pr	93.10%	93.76%	92.67%	94.74%	**94.42%**
Two-stage	TP	**390**	**1104**	**2301**	**3465**	**4022**
	Recall	**3.90%**	**11.04%**	**23.01%**	**17.33%**	**40.22%**
	Pr	97.74%	93.16%	90.84%	93.27%	94.18%
$\alpha = 94\%$						

Table 4. Evaluation of various data sets, model structures, and MIA methods, $\alpha = 98\%$

		MNIST	F-MNIST	CIFAR10	Purchase100	Texas100
C-Loss	TP	17	70	40	4	183
	Recall	0.17%	0.70%	0.40%	0.02%	1.83%
	Pr	100%	95.89%	93.02%	100%	**96.32%**
C-Conf	TP	49	195	353	8	678
	Recall	0.49%	1.95%	3.53%	0.04%	6.78%
	Pr	92.45%	97.01%	**96.45%**	100%	**99.41%**
Two-stage	TP	**258**	**461**	1059	**71**	1543
	Recall	**2.58%**	**4.61%**	10.59%	**0.36%**	15.43%
	Pr	100%	**97.26%**	96.27%	95.95%	97.84%
$\alpha = 98\%$						

We can only implement HP-MIA that satisfies the precision constraint on the shadow model, so the precision on the target model may be biased, and the bias size depends on how close the shadow model is to the target model. Most of the time, as the precision constraint value rises, the accuracy of the attack on the target model becomes higher. Tables 2, 3 and ,4 show the attack performance of the three attacks when α is set to 0.9, 0.94 and 0.98 respectively. The Two-stage attack consistently identifies the most members on all models at various precision constraint settings.

The precision of various attacks on the target model varies under the same precision constraint value setting. We compare the experimental results under different precision constraint values. For MNIST, Two-stage can identify 258 memberships with 100% accuracy, while other methods fail to identify more than 120 members at various precision constraint settings. For F-MNIST, Two-stage identified 461 memberships with 97.26% when $\alpha = 0.98$, C-Conf identified 689 memberships with only 88.98% precision when $\alpha = 0.9$, and 511 memberships with only 93.76% precision when $\alpha = 0.94$. For CIFAR10, Two-stage identified

1059 memberships with 96.27%. Although C-Conf was able to identify 1427 memberships when $\alpha = 0.9$, the precision was only 87.17%. On the other hand, Two-stage was able to identify 2301 memberships with 90.84% precision when $\alpha = 0.94$. For Purchase100, the precision of Two-stage is lower than the other two attacks, but identifies far more memberships than them. For Texas100, Two-stage consistently identifies more memberships than the other two methods, but with lower precision at $\alpha = 0.94$ and $\alpha = 0.9$. We believe that Two-stage is suitable for high-precision membership inference tasks that wish to identify a larger number of memberships.

Failure of the Direct Overfitting-Based MIA. MIA without the use of difficulty calibration fails under the requirement of high precision, so we did not compare these methods directly with our attacks in Sect. 4.1. We construct HP-MIA using three membership scores, Loss [16], Conf [11,12] and Mentr [13], respectively, and Table 5 shows the performance of these attacks on different datasets. Note that Algorithm1 will return a threshold that achieves the maximum accuracy when it finds that it cannot find a threshold that satisfies the accuracy requirement on the shadow model. We find that these attacks are completely unable to achieve the precision we require, even though we only set $\alpha = 0.9$. Specifically, for a model generalized on the MNIST dataset, the overfitting-based direct attack can only achieve up to 57.44% precision. Even for the simple MLP with only 43.89% accuracy on Texas100, it can only achieve 74.65% precision. In scenarios where the cost of the attack is high, these attacks are completely inappropriate.

Table 5. Performance of overfitting-based MIA under high-precision constraints

	MNIST	F-MNIST	CIFAR10	Purchase100	Texas100
Loss	56.56%	55.99%	68.00%	73.11%	74.32%
Conf	54.55%	55.99%	68.21%	73.11%	74.32%
Mentr	57.44%	57.22%	68.01%	74.50%	74.65%
$\alpha = 90\%$					

4.3 Ablation Experiments

l_2 **Regularization.** l_2 regularization is a relatively simple defense technique for member inference attacks [8,12]. We assume that the adversary is unknown to the defense used by the victim, and both the shadow model and the reference model are trained using the original algorithm. Table 6 shows the performance of the target model with the regularization technique and the inference effect of the Two-stage attack. As a common method to overcome overfitting, regularization can prevent the leakage of membership privacy to some extent.

Table 6. Two-stage experimental results on the target model using regularized defense,the datasets are F-MNIST and CIFAR10

Dataset	λ	Train_Acc	Test_Acc	TP	Pr
F-MNIST	0	100%	88.74%	1406	89.21%
	0.0001	100%	88.77%	283	84.99%
	0.0003	100%	88.16%	111	84.09%
	0.0005	99.96%	88.14%	83	81.37%
	0.0007	99.93%	88.34%	75	81.52%
	0.001	99.68%	87.87%	47	79.66%
	0.005	95.12%	88.50%	0	0
	0.01	89.68%	86.50%	0	0
CIFAR10	0	100%	70.61%	3866	85.34%
	0.0001	99.92%	67.88%	2044	92.57%
	0.0003	99.74%	69.13%	1781	90.77%
	0.0005	100%	68.85%	1531	92.79%
	0.0007	99.88%	70.23%	583	88.74%
	0.001	99.50%	66.59%	505	90.02%
	0.005	98.91%	69.26%	23	85.19%
	0.01	92.26%	62.26%	10	76.92%

In general, the number of memberships that can be inferred by Two-stage decreases significantly as λ grows. It is worth noting that lower levels of l_2 regularization may not reduce the attack precision as well. For CIFAR10, the attack precision at $\lambda < 0.001$ is instead higher than that without the l_2 regularization method.

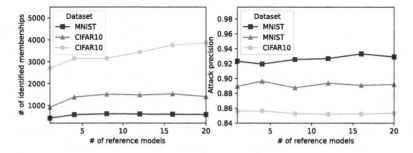

Fig. 3. The TP and Pr of Two-stage HP-MIA with different number of reference models. Attack precision receives little effect from the number of reference models. Using few reference models (e.g., one) may result in a low number of identified memberships.

Number of Reference Models. Figure 3 shows the TP and Pr of Two-stage HP-MIA with different number of reference models. we use the datasets MNIST, F-MNIST and CIFAR10. in general, the attack precision receives little effect from the number of reference models, and the difference between the maximum and minimum precision on MNIST, F-MNIST and CIFAR10 are 0.97%, 0.89% and 0.43%. Besides, using fewer reference models may lead to a lower number of identified memberships. The TP of Two-stage HP-MIA using only one reference model is the least on the target model of three datasets.

However, we found that the increase in the number of reference models did not significantly improve the TP except for CIFAR10. For MNIST,the highest number of identified members was for the attack using 8 reference models, with 621, while the attack using 20 reference models identified 590 memberships. For F-MNIST, the highest number of identified memberships was for the attack using 16 reference models, with 121 more members identified than when using 20 reference models. We do not recommend training too many reference models for calculating the calibrated score when not planning to spend too much time to deploy the attack.

5   Conclusion

In this work, we rethink the relationship between overfitting and membership inference attacks and demonstrate that using an overfitting-based approach for membership exclusion can effectively improve the performance of HP-MIA. Our evaluation results show that our attack is able to identify more members while guaranteeing high accuracy compared to other attacks.

Previous related work focused on how to perform effective direct inference, but in realistic scenarios where attacks are costly, a simple and reliable exclusion method can avoid many unnecessary losses. We have only done preliminary work for black-box scenarios, and we hope that future work will explore other more effective exclusion techniques and consider more scenarios. For example, in the white-box scenario, how can we use hidden layer information or gradient information to avoid launching unnecessary attacks ?

Appendix

A   Algorithm for the Selection of Attack Thresholds

Algorithm 2: Select attack threshold

---

1   **function** *Membership Exclusion threshold*:
2   **Input:** shadow dataset D_{shadow}, target model h, membership score s and precision constraint value β.
3   Initialize U' and $TPset$ to $\emptyset$
4   Construct the set $U(h, s, D_{shadow})$ according to Equation 6, $m \leftarrow |U|$
5   **for** $i \leftarrow 1 : m$ **do**
6   Judge examples in D_{shadow} with membership scores less than u_i as non-members
7   Calculate the number of correctly identified non-members (TP) and the precision (Pr) of non-member identification
8   **if** $Pr \geqslant \beta$ **then**
9          $U' \leftarrow U' \cup u_i$
10          $TPset \leftarrow TPset \cup TP$

11   **if** $U' == \emptyset$ **then**
12   **return** *fail*
13      $k \leftarrow \underset{k=1,2,\ldots,n}{max} TPset$
14      $t \leftarrow U'_k$
15   **return** t, TP

16   **function** *Membership Inference threshold*:
17   **Input:** shadow dataset D_{shadow}, target model h, membership score s and precision constraint value α.
18   Initialize U' and $TPset$ to $\emptyset$
19   Construct the set $U(h, s, D_{shadow})$ according to Equation 6, $m \leftarrow |U|$
20   **for** $i \leftarrow 1 : m$ **do**
21   Judge examples in D_{shadow} with membership scores greater than u_i as members
22   Calculate the number of correctly identified members (TP) and the precision (Pr) of member identification
23   **if** $Pr \geqslant \alpha$ **then**
24          $U' \leftarrow U' \cup u_i$
25          $TPset \leftarrow TPset \cup TP$

26   **if** $U' == \emptyset$ **then**
27   **return** *fail*
28      $TP, k \leftarrow \underset{k=1,2,\ldots,n}{max} TPset$
29      $t \leftarrow U'_k$
30   **return** t, TP

31   **function** *Two-stage threshold*:
32   **Input:** shadow dataset D_{shadow}, target model h, membership score used s_0 in the first stage, membership score s_1 used in the second stage and precision constraint value α.
33   Initialize TP^{opt}, t_0^{opt} and t_1^{opt} to 0
34   **for** $\beta \leftarrow 0, 1; step = 0.001$ **do**
35        $t_0 \leftarrow$ Membership Exclusion-threshold($D_{shadow}, h, s_0, \beta$)
36        $D_{remaining} \leftarrow \{z_i : z_i \in D_{shadow}, s(h, z_i) < t_0\}$
37        $t_1, TP \leftarrow$ Membership Inference-threshold($D_{remaining}, h, s_1, \alpha$)
38   **if** $TP > TP^{opt}$ **then**
39          $TP^{opt} \leftarrow TP$
40          $t_0^{opt} \leftarrow t_0$
41          $t_1^{opt} \leftarrow t_1$

42   **return** t_0^{opt}, t_1^{opt}

References

1. Carlini, N., et al.: Membership inference attacks from first principles. ArXiv, abs/2112.03570 (2021)
2. Carlini, N., Liu, C., Erlingsson, Ú., Kos, J., Song, D.: The secret sharer: evaluating and testing unintended memorization in neural networks. In: 28th USENIX Security Symposium (USENIX Security 19), pp. 267–284 (2019)
3. Carlini, N., et al.: Extracting training data from large language models, In: USENIX Security Symposium (2021)
4. Kingma Diederik, P., Adam, J.B.: A method for stochastic optimization. CoRR, abs/1412.6980 (2015)
5. Krizhevsky, A.: Learning multiple layers of features from tiny images. (2009)
6. Krizhevsky, A., Sutskever, I., Hinton, G.E.: Imagenet classification with deep convolutional neural networks. Commun. ACM **60**, 84–90 (2012)
7. LeCun, Y., Bottou, L., Bengio, Y., Haffner, P.: Gradient-based learning applied to document recognition. Proc. IEEE **86**, 2278–2324 (1998)
8. Long, Y.: Understanding membership inferences on well-generalized learning models. ArXiv, abs/1802.04889 (2018)
9. Rezaei, S., Liu, X.: On the difficulty of membership inference attacks. In: 2021 IEEE/CVF Conference on Computer Vision and Pattern Recognition (CVPR), pp. 7888–7896 (2021)
10. Sablayrolles, A., Douze, M., Schmid, C., Ollivier, Y., Jégou, H.: Bayes optimal strategies for membership inference. In: ICML, White-box vs black-box (2019)
11. Salem, A., Zhang, Y., Humbert, M., Fritz, M., Backes, M.: Ml-leaks: model and data independent membership inference attacks and defenses on machine learning models. ArXiv, abs/1806.01246 (2019)
12. Shokri, R., Stronati, M., Song, C., Shmatikov, V.: Membership inference attacks against machine learning models. In: 2017 IEEE Symposium on Security and Privacy (SP), pp. 3–18 (2017)
13. Song, L., Mittal, P.: Systematic evaluation of privacy risks of machine learning models. In: USENIX Security Symposium (2021)
14. Watson, L., Guo, C., Cormode, G., Sablayrolles, A.: On the importance of difficulty calibration in membership inference attacks. In: International Conference on Learning Representations (2022)
15. Xiao, H., Rasul, K., Vollgraf, R.: Fashion-MNIST: a novel image dataset for benchmarking machine learning algorithms. arXiv: Learning (2017)
16. Yeom, S., Giacomelli, I., Fredrikson, M., Jha, S.: Privacy risk in machine learning: analyzing the connection to overfitting. In: 2018 IEEE 31st Computer Security Foundations Symposium (CSF), pp. 268–282 (2018)
17. Zhang, C., Bengio, S., Hardt, M., Recht, B., Vinyals, O.: Understanding deep learning requires rethinking generalization. ArXiv, abs/1611.03530 (2017)

Secure Storage Method for Network Resources of Professional Works Based on Decision Tree Algorithm

Bomei Tan[✉] and Rong Yu

Nanning University, Nanning 530200, China
ttbm21@163.com

Abstract. Because the work network resources quantity are large, the storage difficulty is great, the security is very difficult to obtain safeguard. Therefore, a method of secure storage for network resources of professional works based on decision tree algorithm is proposed. According to the network resource storage requirements of professional works, the network layer, middleware layer and application layer of the network resource security storage system are constructed. On this basis, the secure storage network communication and its open network protocol are designed through CSocket class and CConsection class, the decision tree is constructed to predict the network load performance, and the work resource cache model is built. By encoding the transmitted work resources, complete the encryption and decryption process of network resources, find network resources based on POP3 protocol, and create the retransmission failure task of main thread and monitoring thread, so as to realize the safe storage of professional work network resources. Experimental results show that the maximum caching efficiency of the proposed method is 94.21%, and the maximum safety factor of the resource storage is 0.9.

Keywords: Decision tree algorithm · Design specialty · Network resources · Professional works · Safe storage · Resource management

1 Introduction

With the rapid development of network technology, the data volume of various resources on the Internet is also rapidly expanding, and the data volume of network resources of professional works increases exponentially, which has led to a greater demand for network storage services [1]. Network resources are information resources that use computer systems to spread through communication equipment and network software management. They are scientific and objective. While providing services for art colleges, their security is also paid more and more attention. Network storage is an important and valuable resource in the development of IT. Enterprises and network operators have put more and more money and energy into the development of network storage. It is predicted that with the rapid development of multimedia applications, data storage on the network will be more and more. Multimedia data is known as hard disk killer, which will eventually lead to further rapid growth of network storage. Network storage technology is becoming more and more important in network construction [2]. Only by solving the problems in network storage, can we provide good technical support for the huge amount of data resources in the network. Storage is what any enterprise needs. Now small and medium-sized enterprises, like large enterprises, are facing the pressure of enterprise capacity brought about by the sustainable development of enterprises, and all of them hope to solve the increasing pressure under the circumstance of reducing costs, and art universities are no exception.

In order to solve the above problems, domestic and foreign experts have conducted in-depth research. Reference [3] proposed block level cloud storage (blcs) architecture based on raptorq code, which can provide sufficient information access and transmission performance in cloud data storage system, with high storage security, but low storage efficiency. Reference [4] combines the threat analysis and literature research of cloud storage security of academic information resources, extracts the influencing factors of cloud storage security of academic information resources, and then uses the DEMATEL method to extract the key influencing factors This method can improve the integrity of data, but the security is low. Reference [5] proposes that using cloud computing to realize data storage, data usage and other types of services can improve the security of data storage, but the scope of application is small. Reference [6] proposes an authentication based protocol (A-MAC) for intelligent vehicle communication and a new framework for IOV architecture model. Using the concept of password to transmit messages between vehicles can improve the efficiency of data transmission, but this method is more complex and less feasible.

In view of the above problems, a secure storage method of network resources of professional works based on decision tree algorithm is proposed. The idea of hierarchical design is used to build the secure storage system of network resources, design the secure storage network communication and its open network protocol, and build the cache model based on the decision tree algorithm to improve the comprehensive performance of the storage system. Encrypt and decrypt network resources, improve the security of transmission, use POP3 protocol to find work resources, improve the transmission efficiency through the main thread and monitoring thread, and complete the safe storage of work resources.

2   Research on Secure Storage of Network Resources of Professional Works in Design

2.1   Building a Secure Storage System for Network Resources

Network resource security storage system integrates the use of idle resources on the network to provide durable and stable storage services for professional works. Using the idea of layered design [7], the secure storage system of network resources can adapt well to the requirements of dynamic changes, and facilitate the expansion of the storage system. The secure storage system of network resources consists of three layers: network layer, middleware layer and application layer [8].

Each layer has different responsibilities. The network layer is responsible for the normal and stable operation of server- related programs; the middleware layer is responsible for the client implementation and integration of different open network protocols; the application layer is responsible for providing users with relevant storage services and building a coverage network among users. Each layer is independent of and interrelated with each other. The indivisible group builds the whole open network protocol system. The change of any layer in the storage system will not directly lead to the change of other layers, and the responsibilities of each layer are clear, achieving good encapsulation and unloading, which mainly reflects the mutual independence of each layer; the upper layer in the storage system makes use of the interface provided by the lower layer, and the functional realization of the upper layer relies on the services provided by the lower layer, and the lower layer provides services for the upper layer, which mainly reflects the interconnection and indivisibility of each layer. When a new open network protocol is added, the storage system only needs to integrate it into the middleware layer.

The functional module diagram of network resource security storage system is shown in Fig. 1.

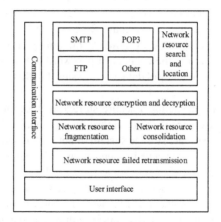

Fig. 1. Functional module diagram of network resource secure storage system

As shown in Fig. 1, the communication interface shall be responsible for the normal communication between the storage system and the remote server; the positioning module of network resources of professional works of design category shall be responsible for the accurate positioning of resources on the remote server; the encryption and decryption module of network resources of professional works of design category shall be responsible for the safe transmission of resources and the correct acquisition of resources in the process of network transmission; the sharing and merging module of network resources of professional works of design category shall be responsible for the sharding and merging functions of resources so as to enable the storage system to send and obtain network resources in the form of attachments; the module of failed retransmission shall be responsible for the retransmission function of network resources so as to greatly reduce the probability of failure of network resources transmission; and the user interface module shall be responsible for the interaction with users [9].

Through the above steps, build a secure storage system of network resources, which lays a solid foundation for the design of network resource security storage network communication.

2.2 Secure Storage Network Communication Design

Based on the secure storage system of network resources, the secure storage network communication and its open network protocol are designed to support the caching and storage of network resources.

Secure storage network communication mainly includes two parts: CSocket and CConsection. The CSocket class encapsulates the original network socket, and the client of the class only needs to care about its interface. In order to prevent the resource from being stolen when transmitting on the network, it is necessary to encrypt the resource during the transmission. The CSocket class can encrypt or transmit the resources according to the user's requirements, and the user only needs to provide the corresponding parameters when creating the class. When a user needs to encrypt a resource for transmission, the CSocket class uses a secure socket (SSL) -based method for transmission. Before SSL is transmitted, the authentication server is authenticated, and the client sends a start message to the server to start a new session connection. The server determines whether a new master key needs to be generated based on the client's information, and if so, the server will include the information needed to generate the master key in response to the client's information. The client generates a master key based on the response message received from the server and encrypts it to the server using the server's public key. The server recovers the master key and returns a message authenticated by the client using the master key to enable the client to authenticate the server. The server is then authenticated by the user, and the authenticated server sends a question to the customer, who returns the digitally signed question and its public key to provide authentication to the server.

The CConection class is a further encapsulation and extension of the CSocket class, which provides interfaces for sending data, parsing data, setting network timeouts, and user authentication. This class is well suited for different network protocols and provides the interfaces required by these different network protocols [10].

The open network protocol module mainly includes two parts: sending and receiving. Send sub-module core class, CSMTPBodyPart class is mainly used to deal with the design of professional works network resources, including text and attachments. This class contains many functions to set and get the network resource format, set the network resource theme, and so on. The storage system has carried on certain writing to the work main text, thus guaranteed that because the work main text will not be marked as the rubbish content by the server. The CSMTPMessage class is used to hold the resources returned by the server, including the artwork handler and the artwork receiver. The CSMTPAddress class is used for various processing of the work address. The CBase64Coder class is responsible for encoding and decoding the transport resources. The algorithm converts three 8-bit bytes into four 6-bit resources, then fills two zeros before the four 6-bit data to form four 8-bit bytes. These four 8-bit network resources are then encoded according to the encoder table, which can be stored in a character array of size 65, as shown in Table 1.

Table 1. Coding example table

Source network resource	After conversion	Corresponding decimal	Corresponding code table value
10010110	00100101	37	1
10100111	00101010	42	q
01011010	00011101	29	d
–	00011010	26	a

The algorithm uses lookup table method to encode data, and the running time is very fast. The algorithm encodes data in every three bytes and generates four bytes of encoded data. When the data read is not a three-byte multiple, the algorithm uses zeros to follow it to a three-byte multiple, then encodes it, and finally adds a specific number of characters to the encoded data.

When using this algorithm to decode, we need to check the inverse table. Decoding for every four bytes, by the encoding algorithm, decoding the source data must be four times the integer, but the last need to decode the data to determine whether there are special characters. If there is one, only the first two bytes of decoded data are written to the buffer; if there are two, only the first byte of decoded data is written to the buffer [11].

The receiving sub-module mainly deals with the received work resources, thus obtains the work resources which the user needs. When a user needs to obtain a work resource, he/she requests the corresponding triple from the index server. If the third item of the triple is not empty, the storage system directly locates to the designated resource of the designated account of the remote server based on the relevant information of the triple, and then directly sends the RETR command to obtain the work resource after being authenticated by the remote server; if the third item of the triple is empty, the system first locates to the designated account of the remote server, and then obtains the work resource information after being authenticated by the remote server, and then obtains the work resource information by sending the TOP command. Through the analysis of the works of resources and extract its 19 lines of subject content, and then compare with the target file. If the same, the RETR command is sent to retrieve the current work resource and the attachment is parsed and saved; if not, the TOP command is sent to retrieve the work resource for the account's other resources.

By integrating different network protocols, it provides unified write and read interfaces. When the user needs to store the works, the interface calls write. When the user needs to get the work resource, he calls the read interface, which selects the corresponding network service according to the storage location of the work resource. Read and write interface does not need to care about the underlying protocol implementation, storage system for different protocols to achieve a good package, each layer is independent of each other.

The above process completes the design of work resource secure storage network communication and its open network protocol, providing sufficient preparation for the subsequent professional work network resource caching.

2.3 Caching Model Construction Based on Decision Tree Algorithm

Based on the above design of network communication module, combined with the design of professional works network resources security storage needs, build a decision tree, based on this, set up work resources cache model, for the implementation of safe storage.

Decision tree is a machine learning technique for regression, classification and ranking tasks. It integrates multiple decision trees with weak learners to construct the final prediction model. When the decision tree algorithm is used alone, it is easy to overfit. But it can solve the problem of over-fitting by integrating multiple decision trees by gradient lifting. For a decision tree, it is impossible to enumerate all possible tree structures because of the large number of tree structures. Greedy strategy is usually used to generate every node of the decision tree. Gradient lifting decision tree is a decision tree model with iterative algorithm. The key elements of the tool are decision tree and gradient iteration. The concept of gradient iteration is introduced into decision tree analysis, which reduces the size of decision tree object, reduces processing workload and improves processing efficiency [12].

The decision tree build process is shown in Fig. 2.

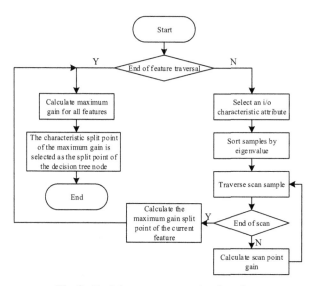

Fig. 2. Decision tree construction flowchart

As shown in Fig. 2, in order to find the maximum gain position of an eigenvalue, the samples are sorted according to the eigenvalue, then all the sample data are scanned in turn to calculate the revenue value of each split point, and finally the position of the maximum revenue value is used as the split point. The aim of each split is to obtain more information gain. If the information gain after the split is negative, then stop the split. Then the maximum eigenvalue of each eigenvalue is taken as the first split point, and the maximum eigenvalue of each eigenvalue is calculated. Finally, using the greed method, we can build a complete decision tree by repeating the above process. Compared with the traditional performance analysis methods, the iterative decision tree model based on machine learning algorithm has obvious advantages in convenience, accuracy, adaptability and cost. The decision tree model based on machine learning algorithm does not need to consider the internal structure and load characteristics of devices, so it can obtain the load performance prediction results more conveniently, quickly and accurately.

Based on the network load performance results predicted by decision tree, a work resource caching model is established. When the cache hit ratio for a particular access request is $h = C/Z$, the average access latency for that storage system can be calculated using the following formula:

$$h \approx C/Z \tag{1}$$

$$T_{avg} = h \times T_{cache} + (1 - h) \times T_{disk} \tag{2}$$

$$T_{avg} = (1 - h) \times T_{disk} \tag{3}$$

In Eqs. (1), (2) and (3), h represents the cache hit ratio; C represents the cache size; Z represents the range between the logical address minimum and maximum; T_{avg} represents the average access latency; T_{cache} and T_{disk} represent the latency that occurs when data read and write requests access the cache and storage device respectively.

In general, access latency with storage devices is much greater than cache access latency, so the effect of cache access latency on performance can be ignored and the average access latency for storage devices can be formulated as (3). Join the two formulas to obtain the basic cache allocation formula under the same access latency conditions, as follows:

$$\left(1 - \frac{C_1}{Z_1}\right)T_{disk1} = \left(1 - \frac{C_2}{Z_2}\right)T_{disk2} = \cdots = \left(1 - \frac{C_n}{Z_n}\right)T_{diskn} \tag{4}$$

In Formula (4), the parameters n, C and C_i represent the number of storage devices, cache size and the cache size corresponding to the i storage device, respectively. This algorithm dynamically adjusts the cache allocation according to the load characteristics and the performance of storage devices. The main function of this algorithm is to improve the cache allocation and reduce the performance difference between storage devices in the same heterogeneous storage system.

The above process completes the design of professional works network resource caching model, and provides support for the implementation of the ultimate network resource security storage.

2.4 Implementation of Secure Storage of Network Resources

Based on the above caching model, the secure storage of network resources is divided into three parts, including encryption and decryption of network resources, network resource lookup and failed retransmission of network resources, as follows:

Network Resources Encryption and Decryption

In order to prevent the work resources from being stolen or lost, it is necessary to guarantee the confidentiality of the work resources and the reliability of the transmission [13]. This paper adopts the method of coding the transmitted work resources to ensure that the whole work resources can not be lost due to the loss of some pieces during the transmission. In this paper, linear erasure code algorithm is adopted to achieve the above goal.

An (N, K) erasure code encodes K work resources into $N (N > K)$ pieces of data, so that the original K work resources can be reconstructed by using any K pieces of encoded data in the N data. The (N, K) linear erasure code can be expressed as:

$$Y = XG \tag{5}$$

In formula (5), $X = (x_0, x_1, \cdots, x_{K-1})$ represents the network resources of professional works in the original design category; $Y = (y_0, y_1, \cdots, y_{N-1})$ represents the linear erasure code; and G represents the $K \times N$ matrix, which is said to be the generating matrix of (N, K) linear erasure code by G. If the submatrix G' composed of any K column of G is reversible, the original K source work resources can be reconstructed with any m data received, and the algorithm guarantees that the source work resources can be reconstructed according to the inverse matrix $(G')^{-1}$ of G' when the data after obtaining the K encoded data fragments. The time complexity of the algorithm is mainly to find the inverse G' of the matrix. Selecting the appropriate matrix G is crucial to the performance of the algorithm.

Network Resource Lookup

The work resources are stored in the server of the open network protocol, and the remote server stores them in its file system according to certain rules. The local index server stores metadata information and has no idea about how the work resources are stored on the remote server and the path. Different service providers have different file systems on their servers, and this algorithm aims to find users' works with minimal interaction.

This section discusses resource discovery algorithms based on transfer protocols. The transmission protocol works in the application layer of the TCP/IP protocol, adopts the traditional client/server architecture, completes the transmission of work resources through the communication between the server and the client, and is mainly divided into two parts, the user agent (MUA) and the work resources transmission agent (MTA).

MUA provides users with read-write interface, that is, the client, MTA runs on the server, responsible for the complete transfer of works resources, mainly including SMTP, POP3 two parts. SMTP and POP3 are responsible for the delivery of work resources and the recipient's ability to receive work resources from the server. Users use MUA to send prepared works of resources, the use of SMTP protocol sent to their MTA. MTA judges the recipients of the works resources, and delivers the works resources directly to the recipient's mailbox if the users are local users; if the users are other server users, MTA connects the recipient's MTA and forwards the works resources by using SMTP protocol. Finally, the recipient uses MUA to receive the work resources to the local host using the POP3 protocol [14].

This algorithm is mainly based on POP3 protocol. POP3 is the user and the server to receive works of resources between the protocol is based on the TCP protocol application layer protocol, the default communication port number is 110. POP3 protocol adopts C/S working mode, namely client/server mode. The host providing the POP3 service is called the POP3 server, and the host requesting the POP3 service is called the POP3 client. The server first establishes an account for each mailbox, each of which consists of a username and password. Mailbox to save this account's works resources, the client through the POP3 protocol to collect works from the mailbox resources, and then processed on the local machine, POP3 is an offline protocol. Works of resources were taken away after the plane was deleted, the server does not retain copies of works of resources.

The POP3 protocol partial commands are shown in Table 2.

Table 2. POP3 protocol partial command table

Order	Parameter	Instructions
USER	Username	Enter the user name to use with the following PASS command
PASS	Password	User password
STAT	None	Returns the work resource data and the total size of the work resource
UIDL	[msgnum]	If there is a parameter, returns the unique identifier for the work resource specified by this parameter, otherwise returns the unique identifier for all work resources
LIST	[msgnum]	If there is a parameter, return the size of the work resource specified by this parameter, otherwise return the size of all work resources
RETR	Msgnum	Get the work resource for the specified ordinal
TOP	Msgnum [n]	Get the content of the first p line of the work resource specified by the first parameter. If the third parameter p is not specified, only part of the work resource information is returned. If p is greater than the number of original lines of the work resource, all work resources are returned
QUIT	None	Exit session, close connection

Based on the contents of Table 2, develop a network resource lookup process as follows:

Step 1: The client obtains access rights by sending user name and password;
Step 2: Determine whether the data is downloaded for the first time based on the ternary table returned by the index server. If this is the first download, proceed to the next step, otherwise go to step five;
Step 3: Send the STAT command to get the total number of work resources;

Step 4: Send the TOPi command to get the work resource information, extract and parse the topic. If the target download file, go to step six, otherwise, i automatically next step;

Step 5: Determine whether the i is greater than the total number of work resources in the account. If it is greater than the total number of object files, go to Step 7, otherwise go to Step 4.

Step 6: Send RETR command, get the whole work resources, extract the attachment data and save it locally;

Step 7: Check if there is any other sliced data in the account. If there is, go to Step 2, or proceed to the next step.

Step 8: Send the QUIT command to end the session.

The above process completes the formulation of network resource search, and provides support for safe storage and search of work resources.

Network Resource Transmission Failure Retransmission

This section from the user's point of view, analysis of the problems faced by the transmission of works resources and the problem of the transmission of works resources failed retransmission algorithm. Users will visit the storage server when they use the storage system to transfer works. When the user's data is very large, users will visit the remote server frequently. Server denial of service or temporary unavailability is inevitable for various reasons. For example, for a server, when a user needs to acquire a large work resource, if most of the work resource is stored on a single server, the user will access the server frequently. When the remote server detects the user's behavior, in order to avoid excessive consumption of resources, the corresponding measures will be taken, which will lead to the failure of the work resources.

The work resource transmission failure retransmission algorithm flow is as follows:

Step 1: The client program starts the main thread and creates two listening threads. Listening threads are primarily used to listen for tasks in waiting queues. The main thread creates a certain number of worker threads according to the current file size and local machine information, which is used to transfer multi-threaded work resources.

Step 2: If the transmission task fails in the process of work resource slicing transmission, the task of transmission failure is put into waiting queue 1 for the next step, otherwise, to step nine;

Step 3: Listen on thread 1 to see if there is a task in queue 1 that meets the conditions. If there is no task, repeat step 4, or the next step;

Step 4: Monitor thread 1 to start the transmission of work resources;

Step 5: If the transmission task fails in the process of the work resource slicing transmission, the transmission failed task is put into waiting queue 2 for the next step, otherwise, to step nine;

Step 6: Listen thread 1 listens to see if there is a task in queue 1 that meets the conditions. If there is no task, repeat step 6, or the next step;

Step 7: Monitor thread 2 begins to transfer work resources;

Step 8: If the transmission task fails during the sliced transmission of the work resource, the task with the transmission failure is put into the failure queue;

Step 9: End the resource transfer, close the connection.

The above process completes the safe storage of network resources of professional works, and provides effective help for the management of professional works.

3 Experiment and Result Analysis

3.1 Preparation for Experiment

In order to verify the application performance of the proposed method, 10 groups of professional design works were selected in the experimental preparation stage, and the number of works in each group was 100. Due to space constraints, only part of the design professional works are displayed, as shown in Fig. 3.

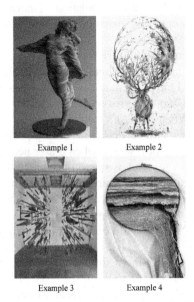

Example 1   Example 2

Example 3   Example 4

Fig. 3. Design professional work example diagram

The above process completes the selection of experimental objects and provides convenience for the subsequent experiments.

3.2 Analysis of Experimental Results

Based on the above experimental preparation stage, the experiment of secure storage of professional works network resources is carried out. In order to visually demonstrate the application performance of the proposed method, the work resource cache efficiency and resource storage safety factor are selected as evaluation indicators. The specific experimental results are analyzed as follows:

Analysis of Caching Efficiency of Works

The data of work resource caching efficiency obtained from experiments are shown in Table 3.

Table 3. Work resource cache efficiency data table

Experimental group	The proposed method	The method of reference [3]
1	89.15%	60.23%
2	90.10%	51.24%
3	85.24%	50.01%
4	78.15%	62.31%
5	80.32%	59.48%
6	91.45%	68.25%
7	86.25%	45.20%
8	80.02%	41.28%
9	89.61%	43.50%
10	94.21%	51.79%

As shown in Table 3, the work resource caching efficiency of the proposed method is between 78.15% and 94.21%, while that the method of reference [3] is between 41.28% and 68.25%, which is lower than that of the proposed method, which proves that the work resource caching efficiency of the proposed method is better than that the method of reference [3].

Analysis of Safety Factor of Resource Storage
The safety factor of resource storage obtained by experiment is shown in Fig. 4.

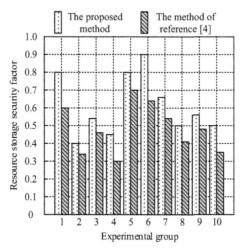

Fig. 4. Resource storage safety factor data graph

As shown in Fig. 4, the resource storage security coefficient of the proposed method is between 0.4 and 0.9, while the resource storage security coefficient of the method of reference [4] is between 0.3 and 0.7, the resource storage safety factor obtained by applying the proposed method (it should be noted that the greater the resource storage safety factor, the higher the resource storage safety factor) is greater than the method of reference [4], it is proved that the resource security storage effect of the proposed method is better.

The experimental results show that the proposed method is more efficient and safer than the given minimum value, which fully proves the effectiveness and feasibility of the proposed method.

4   Conclusions

In order to improve the caching efficiency and storage security coefficient of work resources, a secure storage method of professional work network resources based on decision tree algorithm is proposed. Build a secure storage system of network resources through the network layer, middleware layer and application layer, design secure storage network communication and its open network protocol, build a decision tree to predict network load performance, build a cache model of work resources, and store work resources through network resource encryption and decryption, network resource search and network resource transmission failure retransmission. This study introduces decision tree algorithm to propose a new safe storage method for professional works network resources, which improves the efficiency of caching and the safety factor of resources storage.

References

1. Shuai, L., Shuai, W., Xinyu, L., et al.: Fuzzy detection aided real-time and robust visual tracking under complex environments. IEEE Trans. Fuzzy Syst. **29**(1), 90–102 (2021)
2. Huang, C.: research on encryption simulation of attributes based on cloud labdatabase resource cloud storage. Comput. Simul. **37**(5): 115–118+123 (2020)
3. Fei, G., Na, Z.: Design of structure for network resource security cloud storage based on RaptorQ code. Comput. Eng. Softw. **42**(10), 135–137 (2021)
4. Yue, W., Qiu, R.: Research on security factors of cloud storage for academic information resources based on DEMATEL. Inf. Stud. Theory Appl. **43**(03), 53–58 (2020)
5. Praveen, S.P., Sindhura, S., Madhuri, A., et al:. A novel effective framework for medical images secure storage using advanced cipher text algorithm in cloud computing. In: 2021 IEEE International Conference on Imaging Systems and Techniques (IST), pp. 1–4. IEEE (2021)
6. Gupta, N., Manaswini, R., Saikrishna, B., et al.: Authentication-based secure data dissemination protocol and framework for 5G-enabled VANET. Future Internet **12**(4), 63 (2020)
7. Cao, S., Zhang, X., Xu, R.: Toward secure storage in cloud-based ehealth systems: a blockchain-assisted approach. IEEE Netw. **34**(2), 64–70 (2020)
8. Liu, S., et al.: Human memory update strategy: a multi-layer template update mechanism for remote visual monitoring. IEEE Trans. Multimedia **23**, 2188–2198 (2021)
9. Ayub, M.F., Shamshad, S., Mahmood, K., et al.: A provably secure two-factor authentication scheme for USB storage devices. IEEE Trans. Consum. Electron. **66**(4), 98–3063 (2020)

10. Hou, R., Liu, H., Hu, Y., et al.: Research on secure transmission and storage of energy IoT information based on Blockchain. Peer-to-Peer Netw. Appl. **13**(4), 1225–1235 (2020)
11. Arslan, S.S., Goker, T.: Compress-store on blockchain: a decentralized data processing and immutable storage for multimedia streaming. Clust. Comput. **25**(3), 1957–1968 (2022)
12. Liu, S., Liu, D., Muhammad, K., Ding, W.: Effective template update mechanism in visual tracking with background clutter. Neurocomputing **458**, 615–625 (2021)
13. Wang, Y., Zhang, T., Yang, W., et al.: Secure communication via multiple RF-EH untrusted relays with finite energy storage. IEEE Internet Things J. **7**(2), 1476–1487 (2020)
14. Ebinazer, S.E., Savarimuthu, N., Bhanu, S.: ESKEA: enhanced symmetric key encryption algorithm based secure data storage in cloud networks with data deduplication. Wirel. Pers. Commun. **117**(6), 1–17 (2021)

Vehicle CAN Network Intrusion Detection Model Based on Extreme Learning Machine and Feature Analysis

Jiaoxing Xu[✉]

Chongqing Vocational Institute of Tourism, Chongqing 409000, China
yaya52200@163.com

Abstract. The vehicle can bus is vulnerable to network attack, and the attack mode is complex, and the attack characteristics are relatively hidden. In order to ensure the safety and stability of automobile can network system, the limit learning machine and feature analysis algorithm are used to optimize the intrusion detection model of automobile can network. Simulate various intrusion behaviors of automotive CAN network, and set up intrusion detection standard features. Build the car CAN network structure, collect and process the car CAN network traffic data. The extreme learning machine is used to analyze the network traffic characteristics, and through the matching with the set standard characteristics, the intrusion detection results of the automobile CAN network are obtained. Through the performance test experiment, it is concluded that compared with the traditional intrusion detection model, the error detection rate and missed detection rate of the optimized design model are reduced by 0.86% and 0.52% respectively, and the running delay of the model is effectively reduced.

Keywords: Extreme Learning Machine · Feature analysis · Automotive CAN network · Network intrusion · Intrusion detection model

1 Introduction

The connotation of vehicle network mainly includes: vehicle equipment can effectively use all vehicle dynamic information in the information network platform by wireless communication technology to provide different function services. It can be found that the vehicle network shows the following characteristics: the vehicle network can provide protection for the distance between vehicles, reduce the probability of collision. The vehicle network can help the vehicle owner to navigate in real time and improve the efficiency of traffic by communicating with other vehicles and network systems. In the automotive industry, CAN bus is selected as the connection mode of vehicle networking for the requirements of safety, comfort, convenience, low power consumption and low cost [1]. CAN is a controller local area network, which provides powerful technical support for distributed control system to realize real-time and reliable data communication between nodes. Compared with the traditional network, the data communication

© The Author(s), under exclusive license to Springer Nature Switzerland AG 2023
Y. Xu et al. (Eds.): ML4CS 2022, LNCS 13656, pp. 550–564, 2023.
https://doi.org/10.1007/978-3-031-20099-1_46

between nodes of CAN network is more real-time and shorter, so it is widely used in the automotive field.

However, in practical application, the CAN protocol can only ensure reliable communication between ECUs, and has no defense against attacks. The attacker will attack the communication process of the CAN network in the vehicle by the security flaw of CAN protocol, disturb the transmission of normal ECU signal, and endanger the safe driving of the vehicle. According to incomplete statistics, car theft incidents caused by CAN network security problems can reach 35% of the total car theft incidents. The number of car crashes due to CAN network security problems reached 689 per month.

Aiming at the security problem of CAN bus network, this paper puts forward some measures to prevent malicious attacks. One is to ensure the privacy and integrity of messages through message encryption and message authentication. The other is to use firewall strategy to isolate the vehicular network from the potential attack interface. Third, the development and deployment of vehicular network to join IDS. In order to discover the intrusion behavior of automobile CAN network and defend it effectively, a network intrusion detection model is designed and developed. Intrusion detection is the fast detection of intrusion. He collects and analyzes information about several key points in a computer network or computer system. Discover whether the network or system in violation of security policies and the signs of attack. At present, the mature models of network intrusion detection include: network intrusion detection model based on BP algorithm, Bayesian network and immune principle. However, in the actual application process, it is found that the traditional detection model has the problems of delayed detection, high error detection rate and error detection rate. Therefore, the concepts of limit learning machine and feature analysis are introduced.

Extreme learning machine is a kind of machine learning system or method based on feedforward neural network, which is suitable for supervised learning and unsupervised learning. The core of Extreme Learning Machine is to complete the training of single hidden layer neural network by solving the least square problem. In this process, Moore-Penrose generalized inverse is used to calculate the output weight matrix, which avoids the huge time consumption caused by iteration of traditional feedforward network. It also guarantees the uniqueness of the numerical solution of the output weights. Limit learning machine algorithm is faster than the traditional learning algorithm, and the accuracy is not affected. However, the original data used for intrusion detection generally contain many characteristic attributes. These attributes describe the network connectivity from different aspects. There are some correlations and redundancies among different features. Some of them are noise attributes and should be removed completely. If these data are used directly for intrusion detection, the performance of detection system will be seriously affected. Therefore, it is necessary to minimize the correlation between these features and remove the redundancy and noise features. This is the first task before intrusion detection, that is, data preprocessing. Feature analysis is one of the effective ways of data preprocessing. Limit learning machine and feature analysis algorithm can reduce the error detection rate and miss detection rate of network intrusion detection, and effectively reduce the running delay of the model.

2   Design of Intrusion Detection Model for Automotive Can Network

In this paper, the limit learning machine and feature analysis algorithm are used to detect intrusion. The network traffic audit record is taken as the object to be analyzed, and data mining is conducted. Figure 1 shows the basic detection flow of the automobile CAN network intrusion detection model.

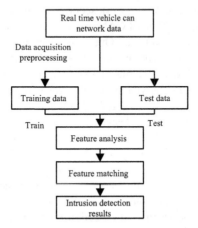

Fig. 1. Automotive CAN network intrusion detection process

After capturing the raw data of the network, we should preprocess the captured data and arrange them into multi-attribute connected records. Then the intrusion detection model is constructed by classification, clustering, or association analysis. Then the intrusion detection model is trained with preprocessed data. Finally, the trained model is used to detect the network traffic data.

2.1   Simulation of Car CAN Network Intrusion Behavior

Common car CAN network intrusion behaviors include DDoS attacks, fuzzing attacks, and spoofing attacks. The types of car CAN network intrusion behaviors are shown in Table 1.

Taking DDoS attack as an example, the intrusion principle is shown in Fig. 2.

Since no node is owned or controlled by the network manager, malicious nodes may not obey the protocol rules to gain unauthorized access [3]. DDoS network intrusion consists of four parts: the attacker, the main control machine, the attacking agent, and the attacked target host. The host computer and the attack agent are used as the control and the actual attack respectively. For the target computer, the attack packets come from the attack agent. But the main control machine only issues the order, does not participate in the actual attack. The attacker implants the attack program into the host machine and the attack agent machine, realizes to their control. In normal times, the attacker uses various means to hide itself from the attacker, waiting for instructions from the attacker.

Table 1. Classification of car CAN network intrusion behavior

Way of attack	Intrusion principle	Security incidents that may result from intrusion
DDoS	Attacker injects high-priority messages on the bus in a short amount of time	Active safety system DoS attack, throttle DoS attack, car door lock DoS attack, etc.
Fuzzy attack	Attackers use random data frames to increase the amount of data received by the network, resulting in network failures and abnormal vehicle functions	Steering wheel shakes violently, turn signals illuminate erratically, dashboard flashes in countless ways and shifts change automatically, etc.
Spoofing attack	The hidden target node has been maliciously attacked	Communication exception
Pause attack	Attacker hacks an in-vehicle ECU A to stop message passing	Communication exception

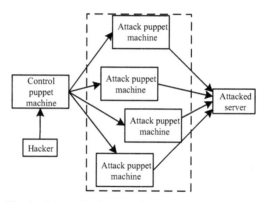

Fig. 2. Schematic diagram of DDoS network intrusion

Once the attacker connects to them and issues an attack command, the attacking agent begins to attack the target host. DDoS network intrusion can be divided into three stages in the process of execution, which are pre-attack stage, initial attack stage and attack stage [4].

In the pre-attack stage, the host computer scans available attack agents. An attacker implants various scanning tools and attacking programs on a host computer that obtains system administrator privileges. A wide range of networks is then scanned to identify potential targets. The characteristic of this attack stage is that there are a lot of request connection information in the target system or subnet in a short time. In the initial attack stage, the host computer sends control information to the attacking agent.After getting the list of target system, the program of attack is used to implement intrusion attack, listen on port, connect port and confirm whether the intrusion is successful. The characteristic of this stage is that there are many irregular random source addresses in the target system or subnet. In the attack phase, the attacking agent attacks the target system. The attacker runs the attack program through the host computer, and the attack agent is controlled by the attack program to attack the target system. Because attackers can control a large number of attacking agents, many attacking agents have high-speed bandwidth and high-end system configuration, so that attackers can launch high-intensity distributed attacks. This attack inevitably results in a large number of data streams occurring within a short time at the network boundary of the target host [5]. According to the above way, we can get the simulation results of other automobile CAN network intrusion behavior, and convert the different network intrusion behavior into the characteristic vector.

2.2 Construction of Automotive CAN Network Structure

The electronic equipments such as automobile sensor, ECU and actuator share data through vehicle communication network. Automobile manufacturers will adopt different on-board bus protocols depending on the communication requirements of different on-board electronic devices and the relationship between different modules [6]. Different bus protocols need to be interrelated through the central gateway. The basic architecture of an automotive CAN communication network is shown in Fig. 3.

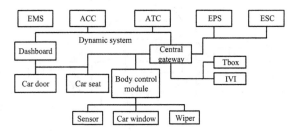

Fig. 3. Automotive CAN network structure diagram

The central gateway in Fig. 3 is used to realize the data interaction between different on-board bus protocols, and between the intra-vehicle network and the external network. The TBox is responsible for the interconnection between the in-vehicle network and the out-of-vehicle network. The TBox can directly communicate with the on-board CAN bus and send corresponding commands to the CAN bus. The functions that TBox can achieve are very powerful. Some low-end vehicles may not contain TBox, but TBox in some mid-to-high-end cars can achieve various functions. For example, it can send vehicle status information to the cloud platform in real time to realize remote diagnosis function, realize remote control of door opening and closing through mobile phone APP, query vehicle fuel and battery status, and alarm and rescue in emergency. IVI is an in-vehicle infotainment system, and OBD-II is an in-vehicle diagnostic system. In the car CAN network structure, due to the different models of cars connected, it supports various types of communication protocols such as LIN and MOST. The protocol stipulates that the communication speed is between 10 kbps and 1 Mbps. The CAN bus can meet the communication needs of up to 30 automotive nodes at the same time.

2.3   Collect and Process Automotive CAN Network Traffic Data

The traffic data acquisition of automobile CAN network can be divided into two parts. Firstly, each terminal node of automobile CAN network is set as the collection point of flow data, and the real-time flow data collector is installed. Set up the working parameters of the collector, and get the traffic data collection results of automobile CAN network. The second part is to transmit the real-time traffic data to the intrusion detection terminal, which is restricted by the NetFlow protocol. Through the analysis of IP packet characteristics, the data flow of various services in the network can be identified quickly, and the communication information such as route, arrival node, start and end time, message and number of bytes contained in service type can be recorded. Finally, the traffic data is rearranged according to the structure of NetFlow traffic statistics protocol, and is successfully received by the intrusion detection terminal [7]. First, the collected data is filtered. Because of the different characteristics of messages sent on the CAN bus, they all have ID fields representing identity. And the DATA field of each information under each ID identifier has control functions or other special functions. Just save the required frame ID field with the DATA field, as shown in Table 2.

Table 2. Automotive CAN network message ID and DATA field

Serial number	Network message ID	DATA
1	Ox2b6	ObOlOf0034090600
2	Ox2b6	ObOlOf00340a0600
3	Ox10d	ScOd5500a0ff0363
4	Ox30d	972300ca00020969
......	......	......

Then the data is further processed, grouped by the ID segment, stored in the corresponding file, and then DATA field hexadecimal conversion to decimal. According to the data message characteristics of CAN data frame, the DATA domain is divided into 8 feature bits, which are all distributed from 0 to 255. After dealing with the character features, the features in the data set are divided into two attributes, continuous and discrete. Therefore, it is necessary to normalize the eigenvalues of the data set to [0, 1] intervals and normalize them with min-max standardization. This only compresses the data and does not change the original information of the data [8]. The normalization process of real-time traffic data of automobile CAN network can be represented as follows:

$$x_{Unify} = \frac{x - x_{min}}{x_{max} - x_{min}} \tag{1}$$

In the formula, x is the sample of real-time network traffic data. x_{min} and x_{max} are the minimum and maximum values of network traffic data respectively.

After the basic preprocessing of the data, it enters the second stage. We separate a few training samples and input them into GAN model. In this paper, we combine the minority samples generated by GAN with the original training set to obtain a training set with balanced distribution. GAN is a generative model for learning real sample distribution in a confrontational manner. The model can generate high-quality new samples without premodeling. In the process of intrusion detection, due to the small amount of some abnormal data, the data set used in intrusion detection is unbalanced. Therefore, the use of GAN to generate minority training samples to reduce the impact of unbalanced training samples on detection accuracy [9]. Finally, the traffic data processed above are fused by clustering, and the similarity analysis method is based on Euclidean distance measure. The whole cluster was divided into k clusters with high similarity by random cluster number. Swarm intelligence algorithm is used to optimize the initial k value of K-Means clustering algorithm, and then the data set is divided into k classes. According to the similarity of objects, the sum distance S_{dis} of corresponding cluster centers is minimum. S_{dis} is calculated as follows:

$$S_{dis} = \sum_{i=1}^{k} \sum_{x_i \in s_j} D(x_i, c_j) \tag{2}$$

The above x_i and c_j data in the i-cluster and the j-cluster center are repectively by X and. $D(x_i, c_j)$ is the Euclidean distance between the data x_i in the i th cluster and the center c_j of the j th cluster. The overall quality $Z(\rho)$ of the clustering system is used to evaluate the final generated clusters. The calculation formula of the overall quality is as follows:

$$Z(S_{dis}) = 1 - [S_{dis} \times C_{crowd} + (1 - S_{dis})C_{close}] \tag{3}$$

where C_{crowd} and C_{close} are the aggregation degree coefficient and closure degree coefficient of flow data, respectively. Its specific value is:

$$\begin{cases} C_{Crowd} = \dfrac{1}{n \sum_{i=1}^{k} \left[\frac{var(c_i)}{var(D)} \right]} \\[4mm] C_{Close} = \dfrac{1}{[k(k-1)] \sum_{i=1}^{k} \sum_{j=1, j \neq i}^{k} \exp \left[-\frac{D^2(c_i, c_j)}{2\sigma^2} \right]} \end{cases} \tag{4}$$

The parameter n represents the number of final output clusters, and $var(c_i)$ and $var(D)$ are the variance of cluster c_i and the variance of network traffic data sample D respectively. $D^2(c_i, c_j)$ is the square of the distance between cluster center c_i and c_j Euclidean. σ is a Gaussian constant. Replace the results of formula 4 into formula 3. If the final result $Z(S_{dis})$ reaches the expected value of clustering, the clustering is valid. Otherwise, re-optimize the k value and cluster the data again.

2.4 Using Extreme Learning Machine to Analyze Network Traffic Characteristics

Based on the collected and processed traffic data of automobile CAN network, the limit learning machine is constructed to extract and analyze the traffic characteristics.

According to the definition of Extreme Learning Machine, Extreme Learning Machine is a feedforward neural network with a single implicit layer, including an input layer, an implicit layer and an output layer. The input layer and the hidden layer, the hidden layer and the output layer of neurons are all connected. The weights of connection between input layer and output layer and the threshold of hidden layer neurons are generated randomly, and the unique optimal solution can be obtained without any adjustment. ELM has fast learning ability and good generalization performance, its structure is shown in Fig. 4.

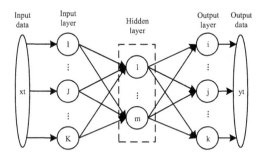

Fig. 4. Extreme learning machine structure

Suppose there are N samples, and the sample data has m feature attributes. The input and desired output data of the network are denoted as y_p and y_q, respectively. Where p and q represent the number of neurons in the input layer and output layer, respectively. And assuming that K is the number of neurons in the hidden layer, the actual output of the network can be expressed as:

$$u_i = \sum_{j=1}^{K} \beta_j g\left(w_j y_p + b_j\right) \tag{5}$$

In the above formula, w_j is the connection weight between each neuron node of the input layer and the j th hidden layer neuron node. β_j is the connection weight between the j th hidden layer neuron node and each neuron node in the output layer. b_j is the threshold of the j th neuron node in the hidden layer, and $g()$ is the excitation function. The excitation function selected this time is the sigmoid function, and its function expression is:

$$g(x) = \frac{1}{1 + e^{-x}} \tag{6}$$

Substitute the selection result of formula 6 into formula 5 to obtain the output result of the extreme learning machine. In the actual feature analysis process, the constructed extreme learning machine is used to extract according to the process of Fig. 5.

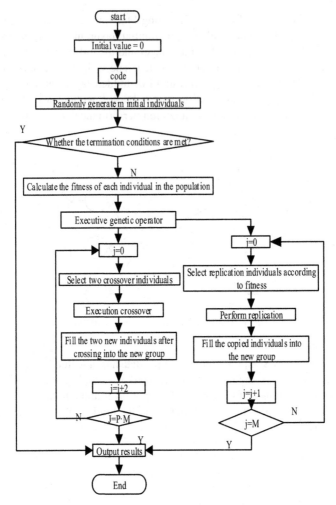

Fig. 5. Extreme learning machine learning process

Determine the number of neurons in the hidden layer, and randomly set the connection weights between the input layer and the hidden layer and the threshold of the neurons in the hidden layer. An infinitely differentiable function is selected as the activation function of neurons in the hidden layer, and then the output matrix of the hidden layer is calculated. Formula 7 is used to calculate the weight of output layer.

$$\beta = H^+Y \tag{7}$$

In the formula, H represents the output matrix of the hidden layer neurons. H^+ is the Moore-Penrose generalized inverse matrix of the output matrix H of the hidden layer neurons. Y represents the desired output matrix. In the process of traffic feature extraction of automobile CAN network, the collected network traffic data is substituted into the input layer of Extreme Learning Machine. The output of Extreme Learning Machine is the result of traffic feature extraction of automobile CAN network [10]. The extraction results of peak traffic characteristics of automobile CAN network can be expressed as follows:

$$\tau_{\text{peak}} = \max_i(x_i) \tag{8}$$

In Eq. 8, $\max_i(\cdot)$ is the maximum value solving function. The extraction results of network traffic skewness and kurtosis indices can be expressed as:

$$\begin{cases} \tau_\alpha = \dfrac{1}{N}\sum_{i=1}^{N}(x_i - \bar{x})^3 \\ \tau_\beta = \dfrac{1}{N}\sum_{i=1}^{N}(x_i - \bar{x})^4 \end{cases} \tag{9}$$

In the above equation, $\bar{x}$ is the average value of network traffic data. The results of the above feature extraction are fused to get the comprehensive feature extraction results of automobile CAN network traffic.

2.5 Realizing Intrusion Detection of Automotive CAN Network

Formula 10 is used to calculate the similarity between the traffic characteristics of CAN network and the standard characteristics of network intrusion attacks.

$$\mu = \sqrt{(\tau_{com} - \tau_{\text{standard}})^2} \tag{10}$$

In the formula, τ_{com} and τ_{standard} are the extracted comprehensive network traffic characteristics and the set network intrusion attack standard characteristics, respectively. The characteristics corresponding to different types of network intrusion types are inserted into Eq. 10 one by one. If the calculated feature similarity μ is higher than the set threshold μ_0, the current car CAN network has intrusion behavior. And the intrusion type corresponding to τ_{standard} is the detection result of the intrusion type of the car CAN network. If the current calculation result of μ is lower than μ_0, the matching calculation of the next attack standard feature needs to be performed until the threshold requirement is met. If the traffic characteristics of current automobile CAN network do not satisfy any intrusion type by matching calculation, it proves that the current automobile CAN network is in normal operation.

3 Performance Test Experimental Analysis

In order to test the detection performance of vehicle CAN network intrusion detection model based on limit learning machine and feature analysis, a performance test experiment is designed. Compared with the traditional intrusion detection model, the optimization design model has more advantages in performance.

3.1 Configuring the Automotive CAN Network

Set up 3.4 GHz main frequency CPU, 16.00GB RAM, 128GB SSD, 500GB SATA PC equipment as the main test computer. This experiment chooses GCAN201 as the model of the automobile CAN network central gateway equipment, and connects the automobile equipment altogether 300. The automobile terminal is connected to the CAN network as shown in Fig. 6.

Fig. 6. Car hardware device connection diagram

The software of collecting CAN information is CanTest software, and the hardware is Canalyst-II bus message transceiver. The transceiver is connected with the CAN bus inside the car, and then transmitted to the CanTest software to monitor the transmission information. The analyzer has 2 CAN interfaces, supports CAN2.0A and CAN2.0B protocols, supports standard frames and extended frames. USB interface can support USB2.0 and USB1.1 protocol, support two-way transmission, namely CAN send and CAN receive. Support for baud rate measurements in the 10 Kbps–1 Mbps range. Both CAN channels support traffic up to 8500 frames per second.

3.2 Prepare Experimental Data Samples

Prepare various types of attacks such as DDoS, fuzzy intrusion attacks, deception intrusion attacks, and pause intrusion attacks, and use coding tools to write corresponding intrusion attack codes. Apply it to the configured automotive CAN network environment. Through the acquisition of real-time data, the data samples prepared for the experiment are obtained. The prepared experimental data samples contain a total of 125,973 training data and 22,544 test data. And each piece of data belongs to one of the five attack types of Normal, DOS, Probing, R2L, and U2R. Table 3 shows the specific preparation of the experimental data samples.

In order to ensure the controllability of network intrusion attack program, it is necessary to add a forced termination button in the process of programming. After the experimental data samples are collected, the stop button is activated to restore the automobile CAN network to normal operation. To ensure the reliability of the experimental results, the sample data in Table 3 were divided into 10 groups on average. Each set of samples is the same in number, but contains different types of intrusion attacks.

Table 3. Experimental data sample

Types of car CAN network intrusion attacks	Amount of training data/bar	Test data volume/item
No intrusion attack	67543	9811
DDoS	45727	7067
Fuzzy intrusion attack	11456	2427
Spoofing intrusion attack	1095	3078
Pause intrusion attacks	152	167

3.3 Set the Operating Parameters of the Extreme Learning Machine Algorithm

Because the LLS algorithm is used in the CAN intrusion detection model, the parameters of the LLS algorithm are set to ensure the LLS algorithm can run normally in the experimental environment. Set the number of nodes in input layer to 144, the number of nodes in output layer to 5, the offset initialization of output layer to 0, the initialization of connection weight is the same as input layer. For pre-training, the learning rate of each layer is 3, and the number of iterations of the limit learning algorithm is 1000.

3.4 Describe the Performance Test Experiment Process

Taking the prepared experimental data sample as the initial data, it is substituted into the optimally designed vehicle CAN network intrusion detection model, and the corresponding detection results are obtained, as shown in Fig. 7.

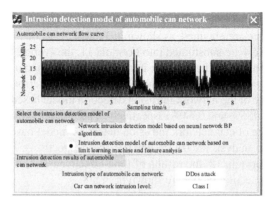

Fig. 7. Automotive CAN network intrusion detection results

In the experiment, the traditional network intrusion detection model based on neural network BP algorithm and the traditional network intrusion detection model based on Bayesian network are established as experimental comparison. The sample data processed by the comparison model are the same. In this experiment, the precision and aging performance of network intrusion detection are tested respectively. The error detection rate and miss detection rate are set as the quantitative test indexes of the performance precision. The numerical results of the two indexes are as follows:

$$
\begin{cases}
\eta_{err} = \dfrac{Num_{all} - N_{cor}}{Num_{all}} \times 100\% \\
\eta_{miss} = \dfrac{Num_{all} - N_{out}}{Num_{all}} \times 100\%
\end{cases}
\tag{11}
$$

In the above formula, Num_{all} represents the total number of samples set. N_{cor} and N_{out} are the number of correct samples for network intrusion detection and the number of detection results successfully output by the model, respectively. By comparing the model output result with the set sample data, it can be determined whether the current model output result is correct, thereby determining the specific value of N_{cor}. The value of N_{out} can be directly obtained through the output data volume of the statistical model. In addition, the timeliness test index of the detection model is set to the running delay, and the numerical results are:

$$
\Delta T = t_{out} - t_{in}
\tag{12}
$$

Among them, t_{out} and t_{in} are the output time of network intrusion detection results and the time of inputting the number of samples into the model, respectively. Finally, the lower the error detection rate and the miss detection rate, the better the detection accuracy of the corresponding model, and the greater the value of the running delay index.

3.5 Analysis of Results

Through the statistics of relevant data, the test results reflecting the model detection accuracy performance are obtained, as shown in Table 4.

The data in Table 4 are substituted into Formula 11, the average error detection rate and missed detection rate of the network intrusion detection model based on Bayesian network are 0.97% and 0.55% respectively, and the average error detection rate and missed detection rate of the network intrusion detection model based on neural network BP algorithm are 0.955% and 0.54% respectively. The average error detection rate and missed detection rate of can network intrusion detection model based on limit learning machine and feature analysis are 0.11% and 0.024%, respectively. In addition, through the calculation of formula 12, the results of time-effectiveness test and comparison of network intrusion detection model are shown in Fig. 8.

Table 4. Model checking accuracy performance test data

Experimental group	Network intrusion detection model based on Bayesian network		Network intrusion detection model based on neural network BP algorithm		Vehicle CAN network intrusion detection model based on extreme learning machine and feature analysis	
	$\eta_{err}/\%$	$\eta_{miss}/\%$	$\eta_{err}/\%$	$\eta_{miss}/\%$	$\eta_{err}/\%$	$\eta_{miss}/\%$
1	0.97	0.56	0.96	0.55	0.10	0.03
2	0.98	0.58	0.95	0.54	0.09	0.04
3	0.97	0.60	0.95	0.56	0.12	0.02
4	0.98	0.54	0.96	0.53	0.11	0.03
5	0.97	0.52	0.94	0.56	0.13	0.03
6	0.96	0.56	0.96	0.55	0.10	0.01
7	0.96	0.55	0.97	0.54	0.12	0.02
8	0.97	0.54	0.95	0.52	0.10	0.03
9	0.96	0.53	0.96	0.53	0.11	0.02
10	0.98	0.52	0.95	0.55	0.12	0.01

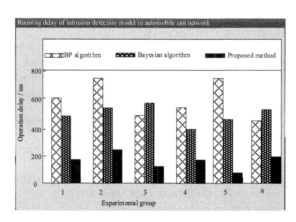

Fig. 8. Timeliness test comparison of network intrusion detection models

As shown in Fig. 8, the operation delay time of the network intrusion detection model based on neural network BP algorithm and the network intrusion detection model based on Bayesian network is between 500 ms and 800 ms, while the operation delay time of the can network intrusion detection model based on limit learning machine and feature analysis is less than 300 ms. It can be concluded that the runtime delay of the optimization design model is always lower than that of the comparison model. In conclusion, the can network intrusion detection model based on limit learning machine and feature analysis has obvious advantages in accuracy performance and aging performance.

4 Conclusion

At present, there is not much research on automobile CAN network intrusion detection, and there is no very effective network intrusion detection model in commercial application. Therefore, through the research of the limit learning machine and the characteristic analysis algorithm, it is designed as the network intrusion detection algorithm. It can automatically analyze and identify intrusions, and improve the efficiency of detection and the ability of fast response. At the same time, the algorithm has good expansibility, which makes the intrusion detection algorithm rise to an unprecedented new height, and provides technical support for automatization and intelligence.

References

1. Tang, Y., Li, C.: An online network intrusion detection model based on improved regularized extreme learning machine. IEEE Access **9**, 94826–94844 (2021)
2. Wang, Y., Jiang, Y., Lan, J.: A fast deep learning method for network intrusion detection without manual feature extraction. J. Phys.: Conf. Ser. **1738**(1), 012127 (2021)
3. Yang, Y., Zheng, K., Wu, B., et al.: Network intrusion detection based on supervised adversarial variational auto-encoder with regularization. IEEE Access **8**, 42169–42184 (2020)
4. Alagrash, Y., Drebee, A., Zirjawi, N.: Comparing the area of data mining algorithms in network intrusion detection. J. Inf. Secur. **11**(1), 1–18 (2020)
5. Wang, Z., Liu, J., Sun, L.: EFS-DNN: an ensemble feature selection-based deep learning approach to network intrusion detection system. Secur. Commun. Netw., 1–14 (2022)
6. Moualla, S., Khorzom, K., Jafar, A.: Improving the performance of machine learning-based network intrusion detection systems on the UNSW-NB15 dataset. Comput. Intell. Neurosci., 1–13 (2021)
7. Li, F.L., Wu, X.J.: Intelligent network communication terminal information security simulation method. Comput. Simul, **37**(5), 86–90 (2020)
8. Liu, S., Liu, D.Y., Muhammad, K., Ding, W.P.: Effective template update mechanism in visual tracking with background clutter. Neurocomputing **458**, 615–625 (2021)
9. Liu, S., Wang, S., Liu, X.Y., et al.: Fuzzy detection aided real-time and robust visual tracking under complex environments. IEEE Trans. Fuzzy Syst. **29**(1), 90–102 (2021)
10. Liu, S., et al.: Human memory update strategy: a multi-layer template update mechanism for remote visual monitoring. IEEE Trans. Multimedia **23**, 2188–2219 (2021)

A Broad Learning System Based on the Idea of Vertical Federated Learning

Junrong Ge[1], Xiaojiao Wang[1], Fengyin Li[1(✉)], and Akshat Gaurav[2]

[1] Qufu Normal University, Jining, China
lifyin318@qfnu.edn.cn
[2] Ronin Institute, Montclair, USA
akshat.gaurav@ieee.org

Abstract. As a new type of deep neural network, the broad learning system has been attracting attention since it was proposed. It shows good performance in image processing, face recognition, etc. To train a broad learning model requires comprehensive data. But the data on which the models are trained is often held by different companies and these companies are reluctant to share the data. To address this problem, we propose a broad learning system based on Vertical Federated Learning. Compared with the existing broad learning systems, it can integrate multi-party data to obtain comprehensive information, and realize the training of broad learning systems in the case of isolated data islands. This facilitates the application and advancement of broad learning systems.

Keywords: Broad learning system · Vertical federated learning · Deep neural network

1 Introduction

In recent years, with the advent of the era of big data, the amount of data has grown rapidly, and at the same time, the scale of data has expanded dramatically. Many models, such as linear regression or decision trees, can often achieve better generalization and smaller training errors than deep neural networks when the sample data is small. But the performance of these models tends to be flat when the amount of data is large, because these models cannot handle massive amounts of data. With the continuous breakthrough of computer hardware technology, deep neural network models have shown excellent performance in processing large amounts of data. For example, when the amount of labeled data is particularly large, the accuracy of large-scale neural networks is found to be stable and higher than other models. Therefore, deep neural networks are widely used in image recognition [1] and classification, target recognition, fault detection [2] and other fields.

Although neural networks show excellent performance in many fields, training deep neural network models is a very time-consuming process due to the multi-layer network structure of deep neural networks. Furthermore, the time-consuming training process is repeated many times when the model fails to achieve the expected performance [3]. The broad learning system based on Random vector link neural network overcomes this difficulty. The broad learning system does not expand in depth, but expands in the horizontal direction. After the width learning system is established, if the performance does not meet our needs, we can use the incremental learning algorithm to quickly rebuild without rebuilding the network from scratch. Therefore, in many cases, we need to train a broad learning system model [4].

In this era of big data, people are deeply aware of the authenticity of the phrase "whoever has data may create value", and at the same time, people are paying more and more attention to protecting their privacy. People value the data in their hands, and all parties are reluctant to share their data, and at the same time, they do not want to reveal their privacy when transmitting data. In such a situation, if the data required to train a model is in the hands of different data owners, it is unlikely that they will share the data to complete the model training. Vertical federated learning provides ideas for solving this problem, can solve the problem of data islands, and can complete the training of the model collaboratively without sharing data between all parties.

This paper proposes a broad learning system based on the idea of vertical federated learning, which can complete the training of the broad learning system model in the case of data fragmentation. At the same time, not only the generalization of the model is better, but also the model can protect the data privacy of the participant.

2   Research Background

In this section, we first give a brief introduction to vertical federated learning. After that, a brief introduction to the breadth learning system is given.

2.1   Vertical Federated Machine Learning

Federated Machine Learning aka Federated Learning [5]. There are three types of federated learning: vertical federated learning, Horizontal federated learning, and Federated Transfer learning. The vertical federation scenario is where participants have more overlap in training sample IDs and less overlap in data features. Generally, it is suitable for learning scenarios with the same sample space and different feature spaces on the dataset. Vertical federated learning can also be understood as federated learning divided by features.

For example, suppose there are two different companies A and B in the same location, and the users of their information are basically the same. Enterprises hold different information about users. For example, enterprise A has user consumption data; enterprise B has user income data and label data. Since companies want to ensure the privacy of users and want to use their unique data to create value, the two companies will not directly merge the data owned by both parties. Assuming that both parties build a task model, each task can be classification or prediction. The question is how to build high-quality models on the A and B sides [6]. Due to incomplete data or incomplete data, the models at each end may fail to build models or the model building effect is not ideal. Vertical federated learning is to solve this problem. It hopes to ensure that the own data of each enterprise is not local, and then the vertical federated system can exchange parameters under the encryption mechanism, that is, without violating data privacy regulations, common model. When building a virtual model, the data itself does not move, nor does it leak privacy and affect data compliance. It solves the problem of feature fragmentation and data silos [7]. It provides ideas for building good performance models where data features are in the hands of different owners.

2.2   Broad Learning System

The broad learning system is a new deep neural network, which is designed based on The random vector function-linked neural network (RVFLNN) [8]. First, let's introduce RVFLNN, and then introduce the broad learning system.

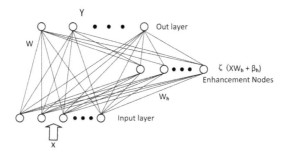

Fig. 1. Structure of random vector functions-link neural networks

The random vector function-linked to the neural network is shown in Fig. 1. The data X is fed into the neural network, the data X is multiplied by a weight matrix W_h and the bias matrix $_h$ of the same type is added, and then the hidden layer is obtained by nonlinear transformation through the activation function $\zeta(XW_h + \beta_h)$. Among them, the weight W_h and bias β_h matrices are of a scale that meets the computational requirements, and the elements of the matrices are randomly generated. The neurons of the hidden layer are called booster nodes. We horizontally concatenate the original data X with $\zeta(XW_h + \beta_h)$ to obtain the extended matrix $A = [X|\zeta(XW_h + \beta_h)]$. The expansion matrix A is connected to the output layer through the weight W to obtain the output value Y, that is, $Y = AW$. The output W can be obtained by computing the pseudo-inverse of A. Although RVFLNN has a simple structure and convenient weight solution, it has strong generalization ability.

The broad learning system is similar to the random vector function-linked neural network, with a slight difference, and its structure is shown in Fig. 2. First, the original data X is subjected to n nonlinear transformations to obtain the nth

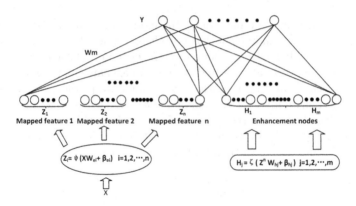

Fig. 2. Structure for the broad learning system

group of mapping features. The generation method of i group of mapped features is $Z_i = \varphi(XW_{ei} + \beta_{ei})$, $i = 1, 2, 3, ..., n$ where the matrix W_{ei} and the bias matrix β_{ei} are randomly generated matrices of suitable scale. The activation function is selected by the user, and the activation function we choose to generate each set of mapped features is the same, which is $\varphi()$ as the activation function. We horizontally connect the mapped features $Z_1, Z_2, ..., Z_n$ obtained by n nonlinear transformations to obtain $Z^n = [Z_1|Z_2|...|Z_n]$. At this time, Zn can be regarded as the data X of the input random vector function-linked the neural network. The j group of enhanced nodes $H_j = \zeta(Z^n W_{hj} + \beta_{ej})$ is obtained by nonlinear transformation of Z^n, where W_{hj} and β_{ej} are randomly generated matrices that meet certain computational requirements. The activation function $\zeta()$ used to generate the enhanced features is uniformly selected, which is different from the activation function of the mapped features. A total of m groups of enhanced nodes $H_1, H_2, H_3, ..., H_m$ are generated through m nonlinear transformations $\zeta(Z^n W_{hj} + \beta_{hj})$, $j = 1, 2, 3..., m$. We connect m groups of enhanced nodes horizontally to get $H^m = [H_1|H_2|, ..., |H_m]$. At this time, $Z^n and H^m$ are connected horizontally to obtain $A = [Z^n|H^m]$. The matrix A is multiplied by the output matrix Wm to obtain the output result Y of the output layer. The pseudo-inverse is a convenient tool for solving the output layer of the neural network, and Wm can be obtained by computing the pseudo-inverse. When the output weight is obtained, it is equivalent to the completion of initialization, and the prediction training can be performed. This way of generating augmented nodes takes all the mapped features as input data. I will introduce another way of generating boost nodes, which generates a set of boost nodes for each set of mapped features.

First, the original data X is subjected to n nonlinear transformations $Z_i = \varphi(XW_{ei} + \beta_{ei})i = 1, 2, ..., n$to generate n sets of mapping features. The elements of the weight matrix W_{ei} and the bias matrix β_{ei} are randomly generated, and the matrix size is a matrix that satisfies the above matrix operations. Afterwards, each set of mapped features generates a corresponding set of enhanced features. That is, $Hi = \zeta(Z_i W_{hi} + \beta_{hi})$, where W_{hi} and β_{hi} are randomly generated matrices that satisfy matrix operations. At the same time, the value of i is an integer from

1 to n. In this way, each group of mapping nodes generates a group of enhanced nodes, and each group of generated mapping nodes is horizontally connected with the corresponding enhanced nodes to form n matrices $[Z_i|H_i]i = 1, 2, ...n$. Concatenate these n matrices horizontally to get A= $[Z_1, \zeta(Z_1W_{h1} + \beta_{h1})|Z_2W_{h2} + \beta_{h2})|, ..., |Z_n, (Z_nW_{hn}+\beta_{hn})]$, which is equivalent to $[Z_1, Z_2, ..., Z_n|H_1, H_2, ..., H_n]$. These nodes are connected to the label through the output matrix W, that is, $Y = AW$.

3   Design Goals and System Models

In this section, we introduce the design goals and system model of a broad learning system based on the idea of vertical federation.

3.1   Design Goal

Suppose we want to build a broad learning system to classify the life stability of people within the Rizhao city system. The stability of life of institutional personnel depends not only on their income, but also on their consumption. For example, if Bank D has information on the salary and income of the personnel in the Rizhao City system, and Party C has information on the consumption of the personnel in the Rizhao City system. The large number of users owned by Banks D and C can overlap. If we need to classify the life stability of the residents of Rizhao City, we directly use the information of Bank D or Company C to establish a broad learning system to classify the life stability of the people in the Rizhao system and the retrograde classification. The information is not comprehensive enough. The results are quite different from the actual ones. In this paper, Bank D and Customer C are reluctant to directly share the characteristics of all their own data, but are willing to cooperate to establish a broad learning system without sharing the original data and ensuring the security of the original data. The model established in this way is based on the information of both C and D, the information is more comprehensive, and the effect of the model is better.

3.2   System Model

First, our model consists of three parts, bank D and institution C and trusted third parties, where trusted third parties are honest and curious, which is shown in Fig. 3. Bank D and institution C want to establish a broad learning system classification model with good classification effect. However, due to the limited data held by both parties and their unwillingness to share their own original data, this often leads to insufficient information for building the model. Model performance does not meet expectations. Therefore, Bank D and Institution C are willing to collaborate to build a better model without sharing the original data. The users of Bank D and Institution C are not exactly the same, but most of them overlap, and both parties have different information on these overlapping

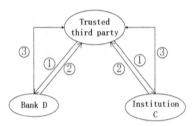

Fig. 3. System model diagram

users. For this problem, we select the information of the shared users of Bank D and Customer C, that is, the data corresponding to the selected overlapping sample IDs [9]. Then use the information of these shared users as training data to train the broad learning system. After Bank D and Institution C determine the data for training the model, they can perform subsequent pseudo-inverse calculations, output weight calculations, and train the model. The following is a brief description of the subsequent operations.

First, the trusted third party sends the task G(X) to the user, and the bank D and the institution C receive the task G(X), and generate corresponding mapping nodes and enhanced nodes through a corresponding number of nonlinear transformations according to the requirements of the task. Bank D and institution C perform horizontal splicing of the generated mapping features and enhanced features to form a matrix K1 and K2, and bank D and institution C transmit the spliced matrices K1 and K2 to a trusted third party. During transmission with a trusted third party, the third party may steal sensitive information, so it is necessary to ensure that the transmitted data is encrypted. The content we transmit in this paper is obtained from the original data after multiple nonlinear transformations. Even if the thief steals the data, he will not decipher the original data through the obtained data. After receiving the splicing matrices K1 and K2 of Bank D and Institution C, the trusted third party splices K1 and K2 horizontally to obtain matrix A. The trusted third party calculates the pseudo-inverse of matrix A, and after obtaining the pseudo-inverse of A, the third party calculates the output weight Wm according to the pseudo-inverse of A [10].

4   Analysis of Broad Learning System Based on Vertical Federation Idea

Next, we will analyze the security of the broad learning system based on the Vertical Federation idea and the tasks undertaken by each part [11], and finally introduce the shortcomings of the algorithm.

4.1   Security Analysis

First of all, the original data of the bank and the institution will not be transmitted to the outside, which can ensure the security of the original data of both parties [12]. At the same time, when the two parties interact with the trusted third party, the data transmitted by the two parties to the trusted third party is processed by calculation. The mapping feature of both sides is that the original data is first multiplied by the weight matrix W, plus a bias matrix b, and then generated by the activation function. In this process, the weight matrix W and the paranoid matrix b are randomly generated and stored locally, and other parties other than the two parties cannot obtain specific matrix information [13]. Since the matrices W and b are randomly generated, the probability of a trusted third party or malicious attacker deciphering the matrices is extremely low. At the same time, the choice of activation function is also decided by both parties, and the two parties do not publish the activation function they use. To sum up, the probability of an honest and curious third party obtaining the original data of both parties from the mapping node is very low. For the enhanced feature, it takes the map feature as input and is generated by the same nonlinear transformation as the map node. Therefore, it is very difficult to obtain the user's original data starting from enhanced features. Based on the above analysis, we can see that the broad learning system based on the Vertical Federation idea can well ensure the security of the original feature data of the data owner.

4.2   Analysis of the Tasks Undertaken by Each Part

In this section, we analyze the tasks of both data providers and the trusted third party [14]. For the data provider Bank D and Institution C, they need to generate the weight matrix and bias matrix for generating mapped features and enhanced features, respectively, which satisfy the matrix calculation requirements, and then save them. Next, Bank D and Institution C operate their own local data with the saved weight matrix and bias matrix to generate mapped features and enhanced features through activation functions. After that, the two sides will horizontally concatenate the mapped features and the enhanced features to form a matrix. After the two parties have generated the horizontal splicing matrix of the mapping matrix and the enhancement matrix, the two parties transmit the matrix to a trusted third party.

For trusted third parties, a four-step operation is required. First, the received matrices from both parties need to be horizontally spliced to form a matrix. The second step is to compute the pseudo-inverse of this concatenated matrix. After the pseudo-inverse is obtained, the output weight of the model is calculated according to the pseudo-inverse. Finally, the trusted third party should do the work of testing the accuracy of the model.

4.3   Inadequacies of the Proposed System

Here, we briefly analyze the shortcomings of the algorithm [15]. The broad learning system based on the idea of Vertical Federation proposed in this paper requires data only in the hands of both parties, and the actual situation is often more complicated. At the same time, the security we propose is only to ensure the security of the feature data, and the label data is to be given to a third party, so the privacy of the label data cannot be guaranteed. Therefore, this algorithm still has a lot of room for improvement.

5   Experimental Results

In this section, in order to verify the effectiveness of the bread learning system based on the idea of vertical federation, we conduct experiments and analyze the experimental results. All our experiments are implemented on the Pycharm platform using Python. In the experiments, we use the processed MNIST data set as experimental samples. First, the MNIST data set we specified is composed of handwritten digits collected by the National Institute of Standards and Technology from 250 different people, 50.

5.1   Experimental Process

First, we stipulate that the number of mapping nodes in each group is fifty, and the number of enhancement nodes in each group is fifty. After setting the number of mapping nodes and enhancement nodes, we set the number of groups to generate mapping nodes and enhancement nodes to be 8 to 21 groups each time. Next, we generate fourteen different groups of mapped nodes and enhanced node splicing matrices. After that, we perform the calculation of the pseudo-inverse of the spliced node matrix and the calculation of the output node matrix. Finally, we calculate the accuracy in the training data set and the test data set separately based on the output weight matrix we calculated.

5.2   Experimental Results and Analysis

Through experiments, we obtained the accuracy of fourteen map nodes and enhanced nodes with different group numbers. We found that when the number of groups of mapping nodes and augmentation nodes is controlled between eight and twenty groups, the accuracy of the training data set fluctuates between 0.94497 and 0.98062, while the accuracy on the test data set is between 0.83083 and 88500 floating between. It may be that there is a slight overfitting of the training results on the training dataset. At the same time, when the number of mapping nodes and enhancement node groups is between eight and twenty-one, with the increase of the number of node groups, the overall accuracy of the test data set increases continuously. However, for the test data set, the accuracy fluctuates around 0.86, but it is relatively stable as a whole and has no drastic changes. The specific fluctuations of the accuracy on the training data set and the test data set are shown in Fig. 4.

Through experiments, we can find that our proposed the broad learning system based on the idea of vertical federation is effective to a certain extent.

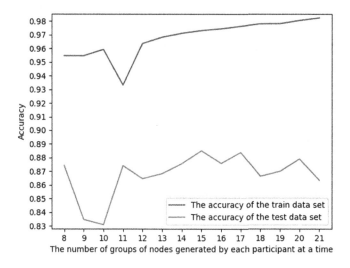

Fig. 4. Accuracy graph corresponding to different number of node groups

Its generalization ability is not particularly strong, but it is decent. The broad learning system based on the vertical federation idea proposed in this paper needs to be improved in the prediction and classification ability of non-training data.

6   Conclusion

The broad learning system based on the idea of Vertical Federation proposed in this paper can complete the training of the broad learning system model under the condition that the data required for training the model is held by different participants. At the same time, it guarantees the feature data security of all parties involved in training. In this case, the broad learning system can integrate data from multiple parties to obtain more comprehensive information. Therefore, the broad learning system model based on the Vertical Federation idea has better performance and stronger generalization ability [16].

References

1. Gong, M., et al.: Change detection in synthetic aperture radar images based on deep neural networks. IEEE Trans. Neural Netw. Learn. Syst. **27**(1), 125–138 (2015)
2. Zhao, H., et al.: Fault diagnosis method based on principal component analysis and broad learning system. IEEE Access **7**, 99263–99272 (2019)
3. Ba, J., Frey, B.: Adaptive dropout for training deep neural networks. In: Advances in Neural Information Processing Systems, vol. 26 (2013)
4. Chen, C.P., Liu, Z.: Broad learning system: an effective and efficient incremental learning system without the need for deep architecture. IEEE Trans. Neural Netw. Learn. Syst. **29**(1), 10–24 (2017)

5. Yang, Q., et al.: Federated machine learning: concept and applications. ACM Trans. Intell. Syst. Technol. **10**(2), 1–19 (2019)

6. Zheng, Y., et al.: Broad learning system based on maximum correntropy criterion. IEEE Trans. Neural Netw. Learn. Syst. **32**(7), 3083–3097 (2020)

7. Li, Q., Diao, Y., Chen, Q., He, B.: Federated learning on non-IID data silos: an experimental study. In: 2022 IEEE 38th International Conference on Data Engineering (ICDE), pp. 965–978. IEEE (2022)

8. Igelnik, B., Pao, Y.H.: Stochastic choice of basis functions in adaptive function approximation and the functional-link net. IEEE Trans. Neural Netw. **6**(6), 1320–1329 (1995)

9. Zhang, L., et al.: Federated learning for non-IID data via unified feature learning and optimization objective alignment. In: Proceedings of the IEEE/CVF International Conference on Computer Vision, pp. 4420–4428 (2021)

10. Mishra, S.P., Dash, P.K.: Short term wind speed prediction using multiple kernel pseudo inverse neural network. Int. J. Autom. Comput. **15**, 66–83 (2018). https://doi.org/10.1007/s11633-017-1086-7

11. Howser, G., McMillin, B.: Using information-flow methods to analyze the security of cyber-physical systems. Computer **50**(4), 17–26 (2017)

12. Chen, D., Zhao, H.: Data security and privacy protection issues in cloud computing. In: 2012 International Conference on Computer Science and Electronics Engineering, vol. 1, pp. 647–651. IEEE (2012)

13. Kumar, M.K., Azam, S.M., Rasool, S.: Efficient digital encryption algorithm based on matrix scrambling technique (2010)

14. Mahmud, M., et al.: Applications of deep learning and reinforcement learning to biological data. IEEE Trans. Neural Netw. Learn. Syst. **29**(6), 2063–2079 (2018)

15. Shcherbatov, I., et al.: Power equipment defects prediction based on the joint solution of classification and regression problems using machine learning methods. Electronics **10**(24), 3145 (2021)

16. Arora, S., et al.: Stronger generalization bounds for deep nets via a compression approach. In: International Conference on Machine Learning, pp. 254–263. PMLR (2018)

PAMP: A New Atomic Multi-Path Payments Method with Higher Routing Efficiency

Jianan Guo[1], Lei Shang[2], Yilei Wang[1]($\boxtimes$), Tiancai Liang[3], Zhaojie Wang[1], and Hui An[1]

[1] School of Computer Science, Qufu Normal University, Rizhao, China
wang_yilei2019@qfnu.edu.cn
[2] Shandong University of Political Science and Law, Jinan, China
[3] Institute of Artificial Intelligence and Blockchain, Guangzhou University, Guangzhou, China

Abstract. The payment channel networks (PCN) technique effectively improves the transaction efficiency of a blockchain system, further promotes its practical application. Atomic Multi-Path Payments (AMP) are usually used, in payment channel networks, to divide transactions to improve routing efficiency, thereby improving the transaction throughput. Improper transaction division, however, may increase the occurrence of routing failure. Therefore, how to perform efficient transaction partitioning is an urgent problem to be solved. In this work, we propose an improved transaction partition method, named Proportional Atomic Multi-Path Payments (PAMP), which can enhance the efficiency of transaction routing. The key insight of PAMP is that, when a transaction is executed, the trade share can be well divided by the remaining capacity in multiple channels, which can greatly improve the routing efficiency and maintain the balance of channel capacity in the network. Simulation results show that, in contrast to traditional routing algorithms, the transaction success rate is increased by 2.3%, and the average execution time is reduced by 75.09 ms. PAMP improves the transaction routing efficiency, and also promotes the balance of network channel capacity.

Keywords: Blockchain · Payment channel networks · Atomic Multi-Path Payments

1 Introduction

In 2008, Nakamoto proposed a decentralized distributed platform and its accompanying cryptocurrency, named Bitcoin [1]. Then cryptocurrencies, as a new payment method, and the blockchains they rely on entered the public eyesight. However, the transaction processing performance of blockchain is far from that of traditional payment methods. For example, Bitcoin can only execute 7 transactions (Ethereum is 10–20) per second, while averages about 3500 transactions per second for VISA[1]. Therefore, the transaction processing performance of the blockchain must be enhanced, otherwise, the practical application of blockchain, as a payment fashion in the production environment, can only be in vain.

The key to enhancing blockchain transaction performance is to improve its scalability. The payment channel networks (PCN) [2–4] is the mainstream technology to improve the scalability of blockchain, currently[2]. For example, Lightning Network [8] is a typical application of payment channel networks on Bitcoin. The ideology of PCN is to place small transactions off-chain, and only two states/transactions of channel opening and channel closing are recorded on the blockchain. This approach is mutually beneficial for both blockchain and users: 1) The burden of bursting a large number of small-value transactions on the blockchain is alleviated, and users can enjoy faster payment services because they do not need to wait for transaction confirmation, e.g., 6 blocks should be appended in Bitcoin. On the flip side, 2) users can pay lower fees in off-chain transactions since no miners are needed to package transactions. Generally, in payment channel networks, the above idea/benefits are achieved by Atomic Multi-Path Payments [9]. By establishing a off-chain payment channel between two nodes, transactions between the two nodes can be proceed without taking up resources on the blockchain.

1.1 Related Works

Traditional payment channel networks use non-atomic payments [10] to implement transactions. This payment method is simple, suitable for small-value transaction networks, and users only need to confirm that the transaction amount is less than the minimum capacity on the payment path. However, this method has a drawback, that is, the transaction is likely to fail due to insufficient channel capacity, especially for large-value transactions. In order to eliminate this drawback, Atomic Multi-Path Payments (AMP) [2,11] came into being. As a key technology to improve the efficiency of off-chain payments, AMP enables transactions with the help of middlemen, even if there is no direct channel between users. Specifically, this method is to split a large transaction into multiple sub-transactions and conduct transactions on multiple payment paths. This payment method, however, introduces a new problem, that is, if a sub-transaction on some path fails, the entire transaction will be rolled back. If this case occurs, it not only consumes channel resources but also greatly increases the transaction latency. Sivaraman et al. [3,12] proposed a routing algorithm based on the packet forwarding mechanism, named spider. The idea of Spider is to split a transaction into fixed-size transaction units and append the temporarily unprocessable transaction units to the waiting buffer with the help of a queuing component. On average, the waiting time of a transaction is much less than the re-execution time after the transaction is rolled back, which is caused by the

---

[1] A credit card brand that is widely used around the world.

[2] In fact, sharding [5–7] is another way to scale a blockchain, but we do not focus on it since that is not the interest of this article.

failure of some sub-transaction unit, so the average transaction routing time can be greatly shortened and the routing efficiency can be improved. However, if the waiting time exceeds the preset threshold, the entire transaction will still be rolled back, which will consume more transaction resources and prolong the transaction time.

1.2 Our Contributions

In this paper, we propose an evolutive Atomic Multi-Path Payments method, named Proportional Atomic Multi-Path Payments (PAMP), which is mainly used to solve the uneven routing distribution of AMP in the off-chain payment network. Our main idea is to analyze the remaining path channel capacity on all available payment channels, divide the transaction amount of the current transfer transaction on multiple payment paths according to the remaining capacity, calculating the optimal weight by calculating the power ratio of all transactions. Finally, we divide the transactions on each payment channel according to the optimal weight. Experimental results show that our scheme increases the success rate significantly of the first transaction, and reduces the occurrence of transaction rollbacks caused by sub-transaction failures. An accompanying phenomenon is found, our scheme can make the channel capacity of the network in a relatively balanced state, which is beneficial to the execution of subsequent transactions.

2 Preliminary

2.1 How to Realize Off-Chain Payment?

Suppose there are two users Alice and Bob in the Bitcoin system. Alice wants to transfer 0.06 coin to Bob in the system. There are two ways to make payment off-chain. Either there is a direct payment channel between the payer and the payee. Alternatively, a transaction payment is made through an intermediary between the payer and the payee. Therefore, first, Alice needs to check whether exists a payment channel between Alice and Bob. As shown in Fig. 1, assuming that there is no direct payment channel between Alice and Bob, we can make transfer transactions with the help of other people who have payment channels. According to the friend topology in the network, as shown in Fig. 1, there are multiple friends who can complete the payment operation of 0.06 from Alice to Bob. Taking the transfer path through Friend a as an example, Alice can first transfer 0.06 to Friend a, and then Friend a will transfer the funds to bob.

2.2 How to Find an Optimal Transaction Payment Route?

The traditional payment process only ensures the success of a transaction payment by guarantee whether the bottleneck on each transaction path meets the transaction payment requirements. When Alice transfers 0.06 coin to Bob, obviously, all of the payment channels' capacity can meet this transfer requirement,

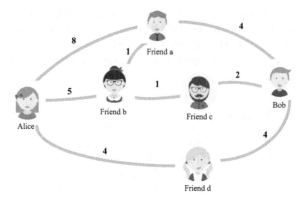

Fig. 1. Find an intermediary for payments between Alice and Bob.

and Alice can choose any channel for routing. However, When Alice transfers 6 coins to Bob, due to the limitation of channel capacity, there is no channel that can meet the transaction demand, and the transaction will be directly displayed as a transaction failure. Atomic Multi-Path Payments (AMP) can address this trouble due to insufficient channel capacity in off-chain payment. As shown in Fig. 2, Payer(Alice) splits the payment transaction into multiple transaction units and makes transfer attempts on multiple different routing channels, payee (Bob) only needs to check the total transaction volume and known whether the transaction on the different path is successful or not.

3   PAMP Design

In this paper, we analyze the causes of transaction errors in off-chain payment networks and find that although most networks use Atomic Multi-Path Payments (AMP) for routing pathfinding. However, there are problems such as low transaction success rate and unbalanced distribution of remaining capacity of off-chain channels during transactions. The root of this problem is that AMP technology splits a transaction into multiple transactions, so that the fund transfer from the payer to the payee is transmitted through multiple paths. Since the splitting of a transaction fund in the off-chain payment network is not based on the bottleneck requirements of the current path, the channel with small payment capacity may face huge transaction transfer tasks. However, the small payment capacity cannot meet the transfer task of large-value transactions, which eventually leads to the failure of the transaction. To solve this problem, we analyze all bottlenecks that satisfy the transaction needs after the sender's routing pathfinding. Calculate the proportion of the route to the capacity of all available routes according to the minimum bottleneck capacity that each route can pass through, and regard this proportion as an available weight of the route on all available routes. The weight is finally used to allocate the routing amount of the actual total payment demand on this path, thus solving the problem of transaction failure caused by uneven transaction splitting in the network. According to the different weight calculation methods in the network, the final route division method is also different. Therefore, we propose a power-based PAMP method.

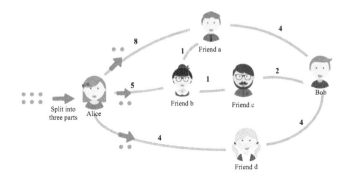

Fig. 2. First routing proportional division weight in PAMP

Network Construction. In an off-chain routed payment network G, suppose a transaction α represents the transfer β coins from the payer Alice (denoted by A below) to the payee Bob (denoted by B below).

$$\alpha : A \xrightarrow{\beta} B \tag{1}$$

There are M available paths satisfy transaction α in network G. If the routing weight is divided according to the same proportion (the power is one), then for any available path in the network, if the bottleneck on this path is In the case of a power of 1, the transaction amount allocated to it by transaction α is $m^{(1)}$:

$$m^{(1)} = \frac{c_m}{\sum_{m=1}^{M} c_m} \cdot \beta \tag{2}$$

Correspondingly, there are M available paths in network G that satisfy transaction α. If the routing weights are divided according to equal proportions (the power is one), then for any available path in the network, if the bottleneck on this path is 1, the power is equal to c_m. In the case of n times, the transfer amount allocated to it by transaction α is $m^{(n)}$:

$$m^{(n)} = \frac{c_m^n}{\sum_{m=1}^{M} c_m^n} \cdot \beta \tag{3}$$

The following is based on the transaction of Alice transferring 6 coins to Bob in Sect. 2, using the PAMP method for routing. Figure 3 shows the routing using First routing proportional in this method. The bottleneck in the path ALice -

Friend a - Bob is 4, so for this path, the amount that should be divided and paid in the First routing proportional is:

$$m^{(1)} = \frac{c_m}{\sum_{m=1}^{M} c_m} \cdot \beta = \frac{4}{4+4+2} \cdot 6 = 2.4. \tag{4}$$

That is, the route ALice - Friend a - Bob transfers 2.4 coins in this transaction.

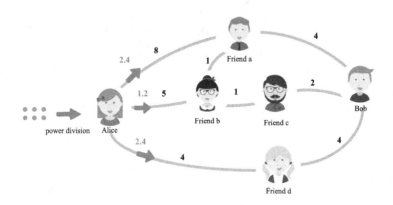

Fig. 3. First routing proportional division weight in PAMP

Correspondingly, under the squared proportional routing method, the amount is divided into

$$m^{(2)} = \frac{c_m^2}{\sum_{m=1}^{M} c_m^2} \cdot \beta = \frac{16}{4+4+2} \cdot 6 = 2.6. \tag{5}$$

Compared with First routing proportional, squared proportional routing magnifies the capacity advantage on this path. The reason is that the channel capacity of the channel meets the demand of the channel, which can further increase the routing on the route. This method helps to better allocate the remaining capacity of the entire network channel, thereby improving transaction efficiency for subsequent network routing.

4   Evaluation

Dataset. Our experiments use the data crawled in the ripple network by [8] as the original topology transaction network [13]. There are 67,149 nodes and 199,574 connection channels included in this dataset. This transaction network is a topology example of a certain transaction time in the ripple network in 2016. We randomly select 50,000 transactions as transaction examples. The original algorithm code is derived from the web page[3].

---

[3] https://crysp.uwaterloo.ca/software/speedymurmurs/.

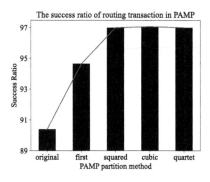
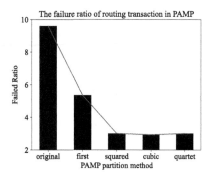

Fig. 4. Success ratio and failure ratio under different power divisions in PAMP

Experiment Analysis. We divide 50,000 transactions into power using different PAMP methods, and track the success ratio and average transaction running time. The experimental results show that the success ratio and average transaction running time are better than the original routing scheme regardless of the partitioning method. Among the parameters shown in Table 1, Squared proportional routing has the lowest total transaction execution times and the highest successful transaction rate. While the implementation efficiency of the Cubic proportional routing scheme is the lowest. Additionally, it should be noted that we also counted the number of transaction executions, and the total excused transactions in Table 1 is the total number of correctly executed transactions and incorrectly executed transactions. If the first transaction fails, the transaction is rolled back and the transaction is executed again. Therefore, there are fewer total excused transactions, which means that the number of required transaction executions is reduced and the transaction execution efficiency is improved. According to Fig. 4, we compare the transaction success rate and failure rate under different division methods. In this figure, the execution efficiency of the division mode above the square is basically the same, while the execution time

Table 1. Comparison of operating efficiency with the original routing algorithm when using PAMP for transaction partitioning.

Number of Txs (50000 times)	Original routing	First proportional routing	Squared proportional routing	Cubic proportional routing	Quartet proportional routing
Total excused Txs	65923	63240	**62822**	62867	62915
Successful Txs	33504	44197	**44457**	44317	44281
Failed Txs	22573	19061	18365	**16625**	16635
Average excused successful Txs period(ms)	3622.803	**3547.710**	3627.023	3604.907	3567.140

We use *Txs* denotes *transactions*, and *ms* denotes *microsecond*, for simplicity.

of the PAMP using the square division is shorter, and the execution efficiency is better. Therefore, we believe that the transaction execution efficiency using Squared proportional routing under this network is the best.

5   Summary and Future Work

The PAMP scheme proposed in this paper can well solve the impact of unbalanced channel capacity caused by uneven routing division in traditional AMP technology. Through the power division method, we can improve the transaction success rate and reduce the transaction running time, thereby effectively improving the transaction efficiency of off-chain payment. In the future work, we will analyze the failed transactions in the off-chain payment network, and further optimize the off-chain payment routing algorithm to improve transaction routing efficiency.

Acknowledgements. This study is supported by the Foundation of National Natural Science Foundation of China (Grant Number: 62072273, 72111530206, 61962009, 61873117, 61832012, 61771231, 61771289); Natural Science Foundation of Shandong Province (ZR2019MF062); Shandong University Science and Technology Program Project (J18A326); Guangxi Key Laboratory of Cryptography and Information Security (No: GCIS202112); The Major Basic Research Project of Natural Science Foundation of Shandong Province of China (ZR2018ZC0438); Major Scientific and Technological Special Project of Guizhou Province (20183001), Foundation of Guizhou Provincial Key Laboratory of Public Big Data (No. 2019BD-KFJJ009), Talent project of Guizhou Big Data Academy. Guizhou Provincial Key Laboratory of Public Big Data ([2018]01).

References

1. Nakamoto, S.: Bitcoin: a peer-to-peer electronic cash system. Decentralized Bus. Rev. 21260 (2008)
2. Prihodko, P., Zhigulin, S., Sahno, M., Ostrovskiy, A., Osuntokun, O.: Flare: an approach to routing in lightning network. White Paper, p. 144 (2016)
3. Sivaraman, V., et al.: High throughput cryptocurrency routing in payment channel networks. In: 17th USENIX Symposium on Networked Systems Design and Implementation (NSDI 2020), pp. 777–796 (2020)
4. Varma, S.M., Maguluri, S.T.: Throughput optimal routing in blockchain-based payment systems. IEEE Trans. Control Netw. Syst. 8(4), 1859–1868 (2021)
5. Luu, L., Narayanan, V., Zheng, C., Baweja, K., Gilbert, S., Saxena, P.: A secure sharding protocol for open blockchains. In: Proceedings of the 2016 ACM SIGSAC Conference on Computer and Communications Security, pp. 17–30 (2016)
6. Zamani, M., Movahedi, M., Raykova, M.: RapidChain: scaling blockchain via full sharding. In: Proceedings of the 2018 ACM SIGSAC Conference on Computer and Communications Security, pp. 931–948 (2018)
7. Dang, H., Dinh, T.T.A., Loghin, D., Chang, E.-C., Lin, Q., Ooi, B.C.: Towards scaling blockchain systems via sharding. In: Proceedings of the 2019 International Conference on Management of Data, pp. 123–140 (2019)

8. Poon, J., Dryja, T.: The bitcoin lightning network: Scalable off-chain instant payments (2016)
9. Mazumdar, S., Ruj, S.: CryptoMaze: atomic off-chain payments in payment channel network. arXiv preprint arXiv:2005.07574 (2020)
10. Dziembowski, S., et al.: Non atomic payment splitting in channel networks. Cryptology ePrint Archive (2020)
11. Rahimpour, S., Khabbazian, M.: Spear: fast multi-path payment with redundancy. In: Proceedings of the 3rd ACM Conference on Advances in Financial Technologies, pp. 183–191 (2021)
12. Sivaraman, V., Venkatakrishnan, S.B., Alizadeh, M., Fanti, G., Viswanath, P.: Routing cryptocurrency with the spider network. In: Proceedings of the 17th ACM Workshop on Hot Topics in Networks, pp. 29–35 (2018)
13. Armknecht, F., Karame, G.O., Mandal, A., Youssef, F., Zenner, E.: Ripple: overview and outlook. In: Conti, M., Schunter, M., Askoxylakis, I. (eds.) Trust 2015. LNCS, vol. 9229, pp. 163–180. Springer, Cham (2015). https://doi.org/10.1007/978-3-319-22846-4_10

Privacy-Preserving Searchable Encryption Scheme Based on Deep Structured Semantic Model over Cloud Application

Na Wang[1], Jian Jiao[2], Shangcheng Zhang[1], Jianwei Liu[1], Kaifa Zheng[1], Junsong Fu[3]([✉]), and Jiawen Qiao[1]

[1] School of Cyber Science and Technology, Beihang University, Beijing 100191, China
{nawang,zscbuaa,liujianwei,zhengkaifa,selina}@buaa.edu.cn
[2] School of Artificial Intelligence, Beijing University of Posts and Telecommunications, Beijing 100876, China
[3] School of Cyberspace Security, Beijing University of Posts and Telecommunications, Beijing 100876, China
fujs@bupt.edu.cn

Abstract. With the continuous development of cloud computing and storage, searchable encryption as a key technology has attracted wide attention. However, existing statistical-based models face long document feature vectors and can not fully catch the document semantics information. This leads to inefficient and unsatisfactory retrieval results. In this paper, we propose a deep structured semantic model of ranked search over encrypted data (DSRSE) based on a convolutional neural network for the first time. In this scheme, document index vectors and query trapdoors are generated by the convolutional neural network model (CNNM) and encrypted by the secure kNN algorithm. In order to protect documents' privacy security, we use private cloud servers to train the CNNM distributively. All parameters are updated constantly, and the CNNM is updated regularly. Furthermore, a clustering tree based index structure is proposed. Through inner product of document vectors, semantically similar files are clustered together for building a bottom-up index tree which enhances the retrieval efficiency. Analysis and experiments on real datasets illustrate that our schemes perform well in terms of privacy security, search efficiency and accuracy.

Keywords: Cloud computing · Ranked ciphertext retrieval · Convolutional neural network · Clustering tree

1 Introduction

In recent years, with the rapid development of cloud computing applications, data outsourcing has become a low-cost option for users, which involves privacy protection issues. To prevent cloud servers from obtaining privacy information, the outsourced data needs to be encrypted to protect privacy, but for

Y. Xu et al. (Eds.): ML4CS 2022, LNCS 13656, pp. 584–608, 2023.
https://doi.org/10.1007/978-3-031-20099-1_49

availability reasons, the retrievability of encrypted data is also required [24]. In general, privacy security is paramount in the design of searchable encryption algorithms. However, lower retrieval speed and query results that are less relevant to the query will significantly reduce the user experience. Therefore, a searchable encryption scheme that satisfies privacy protection, retrieval efficiency and retrieval accuracy should be proposed.

So far, many searchable encryption schemes, such as [1,22,47], have been proposed for privacy protection, retrieval efficiency and accuracy. However, existing schemes based on statistical semantic models such as TF-IDF have many potential risks. Wong et al. [35] proposed a secure kNN scheme based on kNN clustering, which can support multi keyword ranking retrieval. In addition, privacy disclosure may occur in partially damaged environments [3]. Li et al. circumvents this privacy risk and proposes a searchable encryption scheme for forward privacy protection. Nevertheless, the introduction of a large number of matrix operations can seriously slow down the retrieval speed and increase the user's local computing burden [47]. The LFGS scheme proposed by Miao et al. makes use of the fog computing idea, reduces the computing burden of users and improves the retrieval efficiency. However, this scheme can not support ranking retrieval, which will substantially affect the retrieval accuracy. In summary, the current statistical-based schemes have deficiencies in privacy protection, retrieval efficiency, and retrieval accuracy. Therefore, new technology needs to be introduced.

The continuous development of deep semantic models is a new way to solve these problems. Hua's research [16] shows that the deep learning model is unexplainable, which makes the adversary unable to obtain the privacy information even if he successfully obtains the extracted feature vector. This is instructive to improve the privacy protection of the scheme. Compared with the traditional words-bag method, the feature vector obtained by the deep learning model such as BERT [8] has a lower feature dimension, which will significantly improve the efficiency of the algorithm, especially those searchable encryption schemes with square order time complexity. Because the deep learning model exhibits superiority in privacy protection, retrieval efficiency, and retrieval accuracy, semantic models should be introduced in the design of searchable encryption schemes to improve performance.

In this paper, our scheme studies the deep structured semantic model of ranked search over encrypted data (DSRSE). First, the formal security analysis proves that our secure kNN-based scheme can effectively protect user privacy when the environment is partially damaged. Moreover, we construct query vectors and document vectors by using a latent semantic model of convolution-pooling neural network structure. The dimension of the constructed vector is much lower than that of the previous schemes, which greatly reduces computation time. In addition, the model takes both documents and queries as two points in the high-dimensional space where a more similar query and document have a shorter distance, so the documents with the same semantic are sorted together. Furthermore, a based-tree document indexes clustering structure is proposed. When searching top-k documents, the cloud server just needs to calculate relevance measurements of corresponding clustering-tree nodes and the query, which significantly reduces retrieval time. The comparison experiment proves that this scheme has the advantage in retrieval efficiency over FPMRSE. Finally, this scheme refers to the deep-level structural semantic model of [17, 27], retains maximum context information when generating vectors, and optimizes document ordering, thus it improves performance better. Analytical experiment shows that our proposed scheme has significant advantage over existing schemes in retrieval accuracy efficiency and accuracy, which are demonstrated through a large number of experimental evaluations.

Our main contribution are summarized as follows:

- We use convolutional neural networks to construct query vectors and document file vectors based on deep structural semantic information.
- Aiming at concealing document features, we propose the scheme with which the private cloud servers distributively train the convolutional neural network.
- Considering the higher the similarity of file vectors is, the shorter the spatial distance of high dimension gets, we design a bottom-up document index clustering tree structure to organize the documents vectors and improve the retrieval efficiency.
- Rigorous analysis and experimental results on real datasets demonstrate viability and feasibility of the proposed scheme.

The rest of this paper is organized as follows. We summarize related work in the field of encrypted document searchable in Sect. 2. Section 3 illustrates the notations, system model, threat model and design goal. Section 4 reveals the DSRSE framework and structure of the convolutional neural network CNNM. Section 5 describes the DSRSE scheme and the document index clustering tree in detail. Section 6 presents the security analysis of our scheme. Then we discuss the efficiency of our scheme in Sect. 7. At last, Sect. 8 concludes the paper.

2   Related Works

In recent years, cloud storage applications have developed continuously, and inexpensive data outsourcing services have attracted a large number of data users to put local data to the cloud [21]. However, since the cloud server is honest but curious, the data should be encrypted to protect privacy before being uploaded [42]. Moreover, the encrypted data should support retrieval to ensure availability, which derives the concept of searchable encryption. Since Song et al. [29] first proposed the scheme of reliable ciphertext retrieval, searchable encryption has been widely studied [28, 43, 44]. Among them, privacy security, retrieval efficiency and retrieval accuracy are the three core issues [31], which are highly related to the user experience. To protect user privacy and improve retrieval efficiency and accuracy, we propose DSRSE scheme. The superiority of our scheme is proved by theoretical analysis and comparative experiments.

Privacy security is the most important factor that determines the viability of a solution. Several searchable encryption frameworks [43] have been proposed for privacy protection in the field of searchable encryption. Wong et al. [35] proposed a ranking searchable encryption scheme security kNN, which enables the cloud to calculate the similarity between the document index and the query without gaining useful information from them. Since this scheme supports multi-keywords ranking retrieval, many subsequent schemes are based on this work [3,11,20]. However, Cao et al. found that the secure kNN scheme may disclose the document keyword information under the known background model [3]. Based on this, they proposed MRSE scheme, which can resist this attack. Yang et al. [38] constructed a new searchable encryption scheme based on the computational bilinear pairing assumption. Security analysis shows that their scheme can resist internal keyword guessing attack (IKGA) and ensure the indistinguishability of multiple ciphertexts. However, the above schemes [3,20,38] do not take the design of the retrieval structure into consideration. Cloud needs to traverse and calculate all document feature vectors for each query, which seriously affects the retrieval efficiency. Our scheme adopts MRSE framework, and the security analysis shows that this scheme can resist known background attacks.

On the premise of ensuring privacy and security, retrieval efficiency should also be fully considered [13]. To improve retrieval efficiency, a proper design of retrieval structure is essential. The BDMRS scheme proposed by Xia et al. [36] constructs a KBB retrieval tree structure, which can effectively reduce the retrieval delay compared with the traditional secure kNN algorithm. However, Yang et al. [41] found that due to the matrix multiplication required by the secure kNN algorithm, square order time complexity is introduced, which does not perform well in dealing with high-dimensional feature vectors. In view of the fact above, they proposed a searchable encryption scheme based on keyword encoding to overcome the shortcomings of secure kNN, but the performance is poor when the dimensions are low. In addition, in the traditional statistical-based feature vector extraction algorithm, the dimension of the feature vector is the same as the length of the keyword dictionary [3]. Therefore, when facing a large amount of data, the feature vector dimension is high and the security kNN is inefficient. It is worth noting that deep learning semantic models such as word2vec [34] and BERT [8], which produce low dimensionality of the feature vectors, is a feasible way to solve the low efficiency of the secure kNN algorithm in the face of high-dimensional feature vectors. Our scheme designs a convolution neural network model(CNNM), which has a low dimension of feature vectors and can effectively improve the retrieval efficiency.

Increasing retrieval efficiency cannot be achieved at the expense of reducing retrieval accuracy, which is also an important part of the user experience [31]. Existing searchable encryption schemes, such as the LFGS scheme proposed by Miao et al. [24], use the idea of fog computing to transfer the computing burden of users to fog nodes, which improves the retrieval efficiency. Although the analysis proves that their scheme is efficient and safe, the lack of ranking retrieval makes its retrieval accuracy poor. Compared with traditional methods such as

TF-IDF, semantic search was a significant research direction [33, 39, 40]. Semantic analysis addressed the language discrepancy between queries and documents [7, 23, 26, 30], which can improve retrieval accuracy. Fu *et al.* [9] built the user interest model with the support of semantic ontology WordNet to achieve personalized keyword exact search. In [18, 30, 37], mutual information model was used to build semantic expansion scheme. For example, Jadhav *et al.* utilized mutual information model to expand query keywords, then calculated the relevance scores of documents and all the semantically related keywords in [18]. Fu *et al.* [11] developed ranked multi-keyword fuzzy search scheme based on the uni-gram without the predefined fuzzy set. The deep learning semantic model has developed rapidly this year, which has significant advantage over traditional methods in the aspect of semantic expression [12]. In the light of this reason, we have designed a CNNM semantic model to extract the feature vectors of documents and queries. Experiments show that this model performs better in retrieval accuracy.

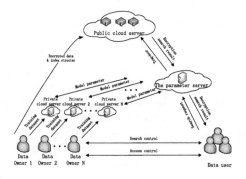

Fig. 1. Architecture of searching over outsourced encrypted cloud data.

3   Problem Formulation

3.1   Notations

The main notations used in this paper are shown as follows:

- $\mathcal{W}$: The plaintext query keywords.
- $\mathcal{D}$: The plaint document dataset, denoted as a collection of m documents $\mathcal{D} = \{D_1, D_2, \cdots, D_m\}$.
- $\mathcal{C}$: The encrypted document dataset, denoted as $\mathcal{C} = \{C_1, C_2, \cdots, C_m\}$.
- $\mathcal{P}$: The searchable index related with $\mathcal{D}$, denoted as $\mathcal{P} = \{P_1, P_2, \cdots, P_m\}$ where each index P_i is built for D_i.
- $\mathcal{I}$: The encrypted searchable index for documents, denoted as $\mathcal{I} = \{I_1, I_2, \cdots, I_m\}$.
- $\mathcal{Q}$: The query vector which is associated with $\mathcal{W}$.
- $\mathcal{T}$: The encrypted form of users' query $\mathcal{Q}$, called the trapdoor vector.

- $\mathcal{N}$: The number of the model learners.
- μ: The local mini-batch size.
- η: The learning rate.
- t: The weights timestamp, which is increased by 1 once the weights are updated.

3.2 System Model

As illustrated in Fig. 1, there are five entities in our designed system: data owner, data user, private cloud server, parameter server and public cloud server.

- *Data owner:* A data owner sends the plaintext document collection $\mathcal{D}$ to its private cloud server for training the convolutional neural network model (CNNM) together with other data owners. After receiving the trained neural network model, the data owner can generate the plaintext index vectors $\mathcal{I}$ and the document index clustering tree, which are encrypted separately with $\mathcal{D}$ and sent to the public cloud server.
- *Data user:* A data user communicates only with the parameter server. The data user sends the query $\mathcal{W}$ and receives the ordered top-k decrypted files from the parameter server.
- *Private cloud server:* A private cloud server belongs to a data owner. Every private cloud server is an "honest-and-reliable" entity with high security, good computing power and small storage space. Each private cloud server continuously optimizes the convolutional neural network model according to the query, clickthrough and the plaintext document set, then uploads the parameters to the parameter server.
- *Parameter server:* The parameter server is also a private cloud server which belongs to all the data owners. Hence, the parameter server is also considered as "honest-and-reliable". After receiving parameters trained in the private cloud servers, the parameter server performs updating iteration. The parameter server generates an encryption trapdoor $\mathcal{T}$ when acquiring a retrieval request from a data uer. During the search phase, the parameter server receives the related encrypted documents $\mathcal{C}$ from the public cloud server and sends the top-k decrypted files to the data user.
- *Public cloud server:* In principle, the honest public cloud is assumed to be a curious entity which is characterized by low security and large storage space. It is used to store ciphertext $\mathcal{C}$ and the encrypted document index clustering tree. Finally, the public cloud server calculates the relevance scores of the indexes and the received trapdoor $\mathcal{T}$ by the inner product and sends the ordered matched documents back to the parameter server.

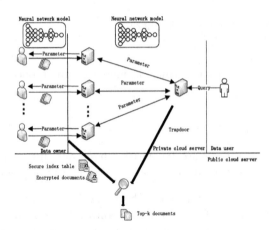

Fig. 2. Architecture of DSRSE scheme.

3.3 Threat Model

In our scheme, we assume the parameter server is trusted and the public cloud is an "honest-but-curious" server [3,5,32]. Based on the information known by the semi-honest public cloud server, we study two threat models [35] with the different threat level as follows.

Known Ciphertext Model. The public cloud only knows encrypted documents C, encrypted data index I, and secure query trapdoor T. In this situation, the public cloud server only attacks the model using the ciphertext only attack.

Known Background Model. The public cloud server is supposed to know more information than that in the known ciphertext model. The knowledge includes the correlation relationship of trapdoors as well as statistical information related to the data set. The public server uses the known trapdoor information to analyze the query keywords or the relationship between the trapdoor and documents.

3.4 Design Goal

To effectively utilize the outsourced cloud data for realizing ranked search under the aforementioned model, a proposed scheme needs to guarantee both security and performance.

- *Deep semantic:* Classical encrypted retrieval models using the statistical characteristics cannot capture contextual information of words and deep semantic of documents. Our scheme is aiming to investigate the semantics of the documents deeply, rather than to search based on word frequency.
- *Retrieval accuracy:* Instead of using the approach of statistical characteristics, our model is optimized by neural networks, and retrieval accuracy is higher than previous methods.

– *Efficiency:* Efficiency includes two aspects: search and storage. To reduce the dimension of the generated vectors is efficient, while it is significant to design an appropriate structure for managing document index vectors.

4   Framework for DSRSE and Structure of Neural Network

In this section, we provide the framework of deep semantic ranked search over encrypted cloud data (DSRSE). The convolutional neural network is trained by each private cloud server of data owners and the parameter server. In particular, the parameter server is the master private cloud server which manages the parameters of the CNNM. We input the query words $\mathcal{W}$ or the document D_i to the CNNM, then get the query vector $\mathcal{Q}$ or the document index vector P_i. In our solution, the correlation of the document and query is the score of their vectors inner product. Then, the public cloud server returns top-k files according to the relevant scores.

Efficiency of traditional retrieval methods decreases rapidly with the tremendous growth of the data volume in data center. In order to increase the retrieval efficiency, combining with the trained neural network model, we provide a tree-based searchable structure based on document vectors clustering. The clustering tree-based index structure is built from the leaf nodes to the root node by the data owners and used in the public cloud server. For finding out the related documents, the public cloud server applies the inner product to calculate the scores of query and nodes from top to bottom.

4.1   Framework

The architecture of DSRSE is depicted by Fig. 2. The data owner first work out the encrypted index from the convolutional neural network and the secret key. Then the neural network is trained distributively by the private cloud system. The data user inputs a query to the parameter cloud server to fetch the related files. After generating the trapdoor $\mathcal{T}$, the parameter cloud server sends $\mathcal{T}$ to the public cloud server. In the search phase, the public cloud server returns the parameter server top-k files. The parameter cloud decrypts the files and sends them to users. The DSRSE scheme consists of seven algorithms as follows:

– **Key** $(1^{l(n)}) \rightarrow \{SK, K\}$. A data owner outputs the secret key to encrypt documents and indexes by a stochastic secret key generation algorithm with an input a security parameter l. SK is a secret key set, including a $(n + u + 1)$ bit vector and two invertible $(n + u + 1) \times (n + u + 1)$ matrices $SK = \{M_1, M_2, S\}$. Moreover, K is a symmetric key.
– **Building** $(\mathcal{C}, \mathcal{W}, clickedhistory) \rightarrow CNNMDEL$. The distributed private cloud servers collect the documents $\mathcal{C}$, query words $\mathcal{W}$ and clicked history, then they train the distributed the deep convolutional neural networks model (CNNM) together with the parameter server. The parameter server updates and sends the CNNM parameters to each private cloud server intermittently.

- **Index** $(SK, \mathcal{D}) \rightarrow \{\mathcal{I}, \mathcal{I}'\}$. The searchable index $\mathcal{P}$ associated with $\mathcal{D}$ is generated by the CNNM. In the meantime, each data owner constructs a clustering tree based on the document indexes. By using the secret key SK, index $\mathcal{P}$ can be encrypted to the index $\mathcal{I}$. Then encryption vectors for non-leaf nodes $\mathcal{I}'$ are generated.
- **Enc** $(\mathcal{D}, K) \rightarrow \mathcal{C}$. Data users utilize secret key K to encrypt the document collection $\mathcal{D}$.
- **Trapdoor** $(\mathcal{W}, SK) \rightarrow \mathcal{T}$. With keywords $\mathcal{W}$ as input, the parameter server generates the query vector $\mathcal{Q}$ by using CNNM. And the encrypted vector $\mathcal{T}_\mathcal{W}$ is generated by using $\mathcal{Q}$ and secret key SK.
- **Search** $(\mathcal{T}, \mathcal{I}, \mathcal{I}', k_{top}) \rightarrow \mathcal{C}_\mathcal{W}$. The public cloud server computes the final measurement of $\mathcal{I}$ and $\mathcal{T}$, then it returns the top-k retrieval results $\mathcal{C}_\mathcal{W}$ based on the parameter k_{top}.
- **Dec** $(\mathcal{C}_\mathcal{W}, K) \rightarrow \mathcal{D}_\mathcal{W}$. The parameter cloud server decrypts encrypted documents $\mathcal{C}_\mathcal{W}$ returned and sends $\mathcal{D}_\mathcal{W}$ to the data user.

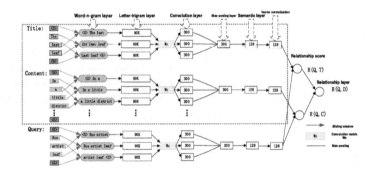

Fig. 3. Architecture of the CNNM

4.2 Deep Convolutional Neural Networks Model

Deep architecture has been applied successfully in the field of information retrieval [2,10,15,46]. To capture rich hidden structures, contextual relation and features in a document or a query, a neural network model based on [27] was recommended. The architecture of the CNNM is illustrated in Fig. 3. The input to the CNNM is a high-dimensional term document vector or query vector based on raw counts of terms, and the output of the CNNM is a 128 dimensions semantic vector. The structure of each layer of the model is described as follows:

Word-n-Gram Layer. We leverage a contextual sliding window to solve the problem of contextual structures [27]. In our scheme, it takes three words at a time for both queries and documents.

Letter-Trigram Layer. Word hashing technique [17] utilized here aims to solve effectively the problem of the dimensionality reduction in the bag-of-word term vector. Provided a word (e.g. leaf), we add symbols at the beginning and the end of the word (e.g. #leaf#). Then, we split this word into letter n-gram (e.g. letter trigrams: #le, lea, eaf, af#). Finally, a letter-trigram count vector represents the word.

Experiments show that about 30K letter-trigrams represent up to 500K different words. The dimensionality of the letter-trigram layer is $3 \times 30K$, where 3 is the size of the contextual sliding window. The k-th word-n-gram is represented as l_k.

Convolution Layer. The convolution operation applied in computer vision and natural language processing extracts local features of images and texts. To capture the contextual features, we resort a convolution matrix W_c in this layer. Each feature vector h_k is computed by

$$h_k = tanh(W_c \cdot l_k), k = 1, \cdots, k' \tag{4.1}$$

where k' is total number of word-n-gram. $tanh$ is activation function in this layer as

$$tanh(x) = \frac{1 - e^{-2x}}{1 + e^{-2x}} \tag{4.2}$$

Max-Pooling Layer. After using convolution layer to capture contextual features, we add a max pooling to save the most significant local features. Referring to the max-pooling layer of Fig. 3, with

$$v(j) = \max_{k=1,\ldots,k'} \{h_k(j)\}, j = 1,\ldots,300 \tag{4.3}$$

where $v(j)$ is the 300 numbers largest of the local feature vector h_k. Therefore, the max pooling layer has a dimensionality of 300.

Semantic Layer. Semantic layer is a fully connected layer, whose output is a low-dimensional semantic feature vector, with

$$Y = tanh(W_s \cdot v) \tag{4.4}$$

where the dimension of the Y is 128 in our scheme.

Vector Normalization. To simplify the calculation in ciphertext retrieval, the vectors Y generated by the previous layer are to be united as:

$$y = \frac{Y}{\|Y\|} \tag{4.5}$$

Relationship Score. For an article, a query may be included in the title or the content, and thus degree of relationship depends on two measurements. A semantic relevance scores about the title $\bar{T}$ or the content $\bar{C}$ is measured as:

$$\begin{cases} R(Q,\bar{T}) = y_Q^T \cdot y_{\bar{T}} \\ R(Q,\bar{C}) = y_Q^T \cdot y_{\bar{C}} \end{cases} \tag{4.6}$$

Relationship Layer. In a search phase, the relevance score $R(Q,\bar{T})$ and $R(Q,\bar{C})$ have different effects on ranked results. After calculating two related scores, the score of documents and a query at the relationship layer is calculated as

$$R(Q,\bar{D}) = w_{rt}R(Q,\bar{T}) + w_{rc}R(Q,\bar{C}) \tag{4.7}$$

where w_{rt} and w_{rc} are weights, they are initialized with a value in our experiment and constantly updated in the neural network.

Learning the CNNM. As the data for training the CNNM, the clickthrough logs which the private cloud servers collect are consist of queries and their clicked documents. Our objective is to optimize the likelihood of the clicked document given a query, equivalently, to minimize the following loss function:

$$L(\Lambda) = -log \prod_{(Q,\bar{D}^+)} P(\bar{D}^+|Q) \tag{4.8}$$

where Λ is the set of parameters in the CNNM. The loss function is also applied in speech recognition [14]. And the posterior probability of the relevance score between a positive document and a query $P(D^+|Q)$ is computed through a softmax function:

$$P(\bar{D}^+|Q) = \frac{exp(\gamma R(Q,\bar{D}^+))}{\sum_{\bar{D}'\in\bar{D}} exp(\gamma R(Q,\bar{D}'))} \tag{4.9}$$

where γ is a smoothing factor, which is set on a real-world data collection in our experiment. $\bar{D}$ denotes candidate document set, including a clicked document $\bar{D}^+$ and four unclicked documents $\bar{D}^-$. The parameters of the CNNM are randomly initialized as suggested in [25]. In our scheme, each private cloud server is used to achieve distributed training according to the stochastic gradient descent algorithm.

4.3 Distributed Convolutional Neural Network Training

In the DSRSE model, the CNNM is trained by using a plaintext data set and the private server is an "honest-and-reliable" entity. For these reasons, we assign the task of training the neural network to the private cloud servers. Causing the update of each private cloud server only reflects its own training data, we need a mechanism which shares the trained parameters and mixes the updates [6,45].

As shown in Fig. 4, a global view of the neural network weights is maintained by the parameter server. After receiving the gradients from the learners, the parameter server processes the data and updates the weights by the learning rate η (step length).

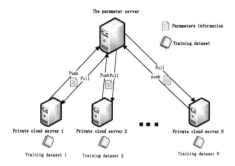

Fig. 4. Architecture of distributed server communicating

The private cloud servers train their own data according to the neural network model mentioned in Sect. 4.2. As shown in Algorithm 1 (In Appendix), When the parameter server receives each gradient $g_n^{(t)}$ which is pushed by each private cloud server, the new weights are computed as:

$$g^{(t)} = \frac{1}{N} \sum_{n=1}^{N} g_n^{(t)} \tag{4.10}$$

$$w^{(t+1)} = w^{(t)} - \eta g^{(t)} \tag{4.11}$$

where t is the timestamp which records update times and avoids sending data repeatedly. Each learner computes its own gradient $g_n^{(t)}$ using a mini-bathsize of μ. The distributed training is equivalent to training a neural network with batch size μN. The private cloud servers pull the new weights and start next training.

5   Proposed Scheme

To efficiently realise the encrypted documents ranked search, we use the inner product similarity to assess similarity scores. The document vectors $\mathcal{P}$ and the query vectors $\mathcal{Q}$ are generated by the CNNM which is described in the preceding section. The similarity score of P_i and $\mathcal{Q}$ is expressed as the inner product of two unite column vectors. For secure ciphertext retrieval, we adopt "secure inner product similarity" [35] where we generate the encrypted query vector $\mathcal{T}$ for $\mathcal{Q}$ and the encrypted searchable index $\mathcal{I}$ for $\mathcal{P}$. A bottom-up agglomerative hierarchical clustering approach is proposed to enhance the search efficiency. This strategy generates a hierarchical clustering tree whose leaf nodes are the encrypted document index vectors. The public cloud server calculates the related scores from the root node to the leaf nodes and the top-k related documents can be found without calculating the whole encrypted searchable vectors.

5.1   DSRSE Scheme

- **Key** $(1^{l(n)})$. Every data owner need to generate the secret key set SK, including a $(n + u + 1)$-bit key S whose entries are random integer 0 or 1 and two invertible random $(n + u + 1) \times (n + u + 1)$ matrices $\{M_1, M_2\}$. The secret key SK is 3-tuple $\{S, M_1, M_2\}$. Moreover, the symmetric secret keys in K are generated to encrypt the documents D independently.

- **Building**$(\mathcal{C}, \mathcal{W}, clickedhistory)$. The CNNM is trained by the private cloud servers and the parameter server in a distributed way. The specific steps are discussed in the previous section. Finally, every private cloud server and the parameter server has the same model parameters. Thus, the document vectors $\mathcal{P}$ and query vectors $\mathcal{Q}$ can be generated exactly in the same way.

- **Index** $(SK, \mathcal{D})$. The data owner uses the CNNM to build an index vector P_i for each document D_i whose dimension is 128. The data owner expands every vector from 128 dimensions to $(128 + u + 1)$ dimensions as $\boldsymbol{P}_i$, where the $(128 + u + 1)$-dimension value is 1, and other positions is set to a random number $\varepsilon^{(j)}$. Then, using the vector S, we slip the vector $\boldsymbol{P}_i$ into two $(128 + u + 1)$ dimensions vectors $\boldsymbol{P}'_i$, $\boldsymbol{P}''_i$. If $S[j]$ is 0, $\boldsymbol{P}'_i[j]$ and $\boldsymbol{P}''_i[j]$ are set as the same value as the $\boldsymbol{P}_i$; if $S[j]$ is 1, $\boldsymbol{P}'_i[j]$ and $\boldsymbol{P}''_i$ are set random values where $\boldsymbol{P}'_i + \boldsymbol{P}''_i = \boldsymbol{P}_i$. Then, index P_i is encrypted as $I_i = \{M_1^T \boldsymbol{P}'_i, M_2^T \boldsymbol{P}''_i\}$ and $\mathcal{I}'$ is built in the same way as I_i. The data owner eventually uploads $\mathcal{I}$, $\mathcal{I}'$ and $\mathcal{C}$ onto the public cloud server.

- **Enc** $(\mathcal{D}, K)$. The plaintext documents $\mathcal{D}$ are encrypted to $\mathcal{C}$ by the data owner, through a secure symmetric encryption algorithm using the symmetric secret keys in K.

- **Trapdoor** $(\bar{W}, SK)$. The data user uploads a query to the parameter cloud server which builds a query vector $\mathcal{Q}$ by using the CNNM. Then, the server expand the vector $\mathcal{Q}$ to be $(128 + u + 1)$ dimensions as $\boldsymbol{Q}$. We set randomly v positions as 1 from a range $(n, n+u]$ in $\boldsymbol{Q}$. A random number $t(t \neq 0)$ is set to the value of the last entry and all other positions are multiplied by $r(r \neq 0)$ at random. Following the similar splitting procedure above, two random vectors $\{Q', Q''\}$ are generated based on $\boldsymbol{Q}$. The difference is that Q' and Q'' are set random values where $Q' + Q'' = \boldsymbol{Q}$ on condition that $S[j]$ is 0; if $S[j]$ is 1, we have $Q' = Q'' = \boldsymbol{Q}$. The encrypted query vector is subsequently generated as the trapdoor $\mathcal{T} = \{M_1^{-1}Q', M_2^{-1}Q''\}$. Finally, the parameter server submits the encrypted trapdoor to the public cloud server.

- **Search** $(\mathcal{T}, \mathcal{I}, \mathcal{I}', k_{top})$. Once receiving the trapdoor $\mathcal{T}$ from the parameter server, the public cloud server calculates the relevance scores between $\mathcal{T}$ and node index $\mathcal{I}'$ and chooses the highest score of every level till the leaf node. Then, the public cloud server computes the relevance scores of $\mathcal{T}$ and document index $\mathcal{I}$. Finally, the top k_{top} documents are returned. At the whole search phase, the public cloud cannot get the plaintext keywords, document index vectors and trapdoors. k_{top} is the number that the date user intends to receive related files, which is discussed in Sect. 4. Specially, the cloud server computes the similarly result score between I_i and $\mathcal{T}$ as follow:

$$I_i \cdot \mathcal{T} = \{M_1^T P_i', M_2^T P_i''\} \cdot \{M_1^{-1}Q', M_2^{-1}Q''\}$$
$$= P_i' \cdot Q' + P_i'' \cdot Q'' = P_i \cdot Q \qquad (5.1)$$
$$= r(P_i \cdot Q + \sum \varepsilon^{(j)}) + t$$

– **Dec** $(\mathcal{C}_{\bar{W}}, K)$. The parameter server decrypts the returned ciphertext $\mathcal{C}_{\bar{W}}$ by using the symmetric secret key K and sends the documents to the data user.

5.2 Building the Document Index Clustering Tree

We propose a clustering tree structure based on the document index so as to improve the retrieval efficiency. As shown in Fig. 5, all the nodes are divided into two sets, one is leaf-node set and the other is cluster-node set. The value of a leaf node at leaf-node set is a document index vector. The cluster-node set includes all the non-leaf nodes.

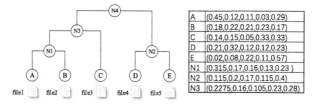

A	(0.45,0.12,0.11,0.03,0.29)
B	(0.18,0.22,0.21,0.23,0.17)
C	(0.14,0.15,0.05,0.33,0.33)
D	(0.21,0.32,0.12,0.12,0.23)
E	(0.02,0.08,0.22,0.11,0.57)
N1	(0.315,0.17,0.16,0.13,0.23)
N2	(0.115,0.2,0.17,0.115,0.4)
N3	(0.2275,0.16,0.105,0.23,0.28)

Fig. 5. Clustering tree.

Equation (5.2) defines the value of each non-leaf node. The count of leaf node is set as 1 and the count of each non-leaf node is equal to that of its child nodes. Moreover, the count of $node[i]$ represents the number of leaf nodes whose root is $node[i]$.

$$node[i].value = \frac{node[i].left.value + node[i].right.value}{2} \qquad (5.2)$$

Equation (5.3) quantifies the relevance score of two nodes. And a *node* represents a leaf node or a non-leaf node in our scheme. If "$node[i]$" is a leaf node, "$node[i].leafnode$" represents itself. If "$node[i]$" is a non-leaf, "$node[i].leafnode$" represents all the leaf nodes of the sub-tree whose root node is "$node[i]$".

$$Sco = \max(node[i].leafnode \cdot node[j].leafnode) \qquad (5.3)$$

The minimum relevance score of two nodes is defined as Eq. (5.4), where "$node1$" represents "$node[i]$" and "$node2$" represents "$node[j]$". Therefore, locating two nodes with minimum relevance score and taking two nodes as child nodes, we create a new non-leaf node to further build a clustering tree. As shown in Algorithm 2 (In Appendix), each data owner builds the clustering tree from the bottom to the top.

$$node1 \cdot node2 = \min(Sco(node[i] \cdot node[j])) \qquad (5.4)$$

5.3 Searching in the Document Index Clustering Tree

The value of every node in the clustering tree is encrypted using the same method as the encryption of P_i before sending to the public cloud server, and details are described in Sect. 5.1. Receiving the encrypted clustering tree and the trapdoor T with k_{top} sent by the parameter server, the public cloud calculates the relevance score from the root node and returns top-k ranked encrypted documents. The search strategy is shown in Algorithm 3 (In Appendix).

5.4 Updating the Document Index Clustering Tree

Once inserting, deleting, or modifying the document, we need to update the document index clustering tree. We provide a virtual node updating scheme. All the information of updating is generated by the data owner and uploaded to the public cloud server. The detail of insertion, deletion and modification is described as follows:

- **Insertion.** Considering the cost of frequently updating the tree is so high, we propose a strategy that data owner updates the clustering tree regularly. When time is not up to the specified period, we add the virtual node to the node where the relevance score of two nodes is minimum. The document index clustering tree is updated in the public cloud according to the insertion information. The updating information includes new node, encrypted document, $node[i]$ inserted, $node[i].value$ and the count of $node[i]$'s parent node.
- **Deletion.** The data owner sends the deletion information which includes the $node[i]$ to be deleted, the novel value and the count of $node[i]$'s parent node. The public cloud server updates the tree after receiving the information.
- **Modification.** Modification is equal to deleting one old node and inserting a new node. Therefore, the modification includes deletion information and insertion information as described above.

All the operations mentioned above are temporary updating operations within a time cycle TC. After a time cycle TC, the data owner updates the tree structure and sends it to the public cloud server. The time cycle TC is set according to the actual situation.

6 Security Analysis

As discussed in Sect. 3.3, we mainly consider the privacy security of documents, index and query. DSRSE schemes should ensure the above privacy even under a known background model with partially impaired environment.

6.1 Documents Privacy

In DSRSE, the AES symmetric encryption algorithm is used to encrypt the document set $\mathcal{D}$ to the ciphertext document set $\mathcal{C}$. The secret keys K for different documents and different data owners are different. Therefore, even the public server cloud gets a set of secret keys and all the encrypted documents, it cannot infer the other keys and decrypt the other ciphertexts. The ciphertext unlinkability of DSRSE effectively guarantees the security of document content and privacy for the known background threat model.

6.2   Privacy of Document Indexes and Trapdoors

In our scheme, document feature vectors $\mathcal{P} = \{P_1, P_2, \cdots, P_m\}$ and query $\mathcal{Q}$ are generated by convolutional neural network model (CNNM), which are 128-dimensional vectors. After that, they use the key SK to expand to $(128 + u + 1)$-dimensional vectors $\mathcal{I} = \{I_1, I_2, \cdots, I_m\}, \mathcal{T}$ via the secure kNN algorithm. According to the proof of Wong *et al.* [35], the number of equations obtained by the adversary under the known ciphertext model is less than the number of unknown quantities, and no information about the original plaintext feature vectors can be obtained from $\mathcal{I}, \mathcal{T}$.

In addition, because we add u random numbers to each feature vectors before kNN encryption, according to the analysis of Cao *et al.* [3], the privacy security of document index and query trapdoor can be guaranteed even under the known background model. If an adversary successfully decrypts a feature vector, due to the introduction of split indicator S in kNN, different index ciphertexts are unlinkable, which means he cannot obtain any information to attack other indexes. Further, even if the adversary breaks through the secure kNN scheme and obtains plaintext feature vectors, he still cannot access privacy information. This is because the unexplainability of the deep learning model and the keywords dictionary attack of statistics model. In fact, the plaintext vector obtained is still a random code for him, which further ensures privacy security under known background models.

7   Performance Evaluation

We implement the proposed scheme using python language on a computer with Intel Core CPU 2.9 GHz and Windows 10 server with a RAM of 4GB. The performance of our proposed system is contrasted with that of the MRSE scheme [3], PRSE scheme [9] and MRSE-HCI scheme [4]. In experiments, we evaluate the overall performance on a real-world data set, referred to as the evaluation data set henceforth. 20000 English queries sample is randomly selected from the one-year query-document log files. We conduct the performance analysis in terms of the trapdoor construction efficiency, retrieval efficiency and document retrieval accuracy. Each simulation is repeated 10 times and the average simulation results are presented and analyzed.

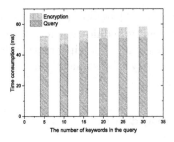
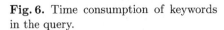
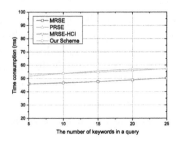

Fig. 6. Time consumption of keywords in the query.

Fig. 7. Time consumption of trapdoor generation.

7.1 Trapdoor Construction Efficiency

In DSRSE, the query is generated based on the CNNM, the time consumption of constructing the trapdoor includes the time of generating query and that of the encryption process. It can be observed from Fig. 6 that the time consumption slightly increases and remains the same with the growing of the number of keywords in a query. This is reasonable because the time consumption of encryption keeps stable and the time to generate query Q increases slightly. The main reasons for being stable is that the number of input neurons remains the same no matter how many keywords there are, so is the time of processing and calculation in CNNM. The time of trapdoor construction is between 52.355ms and 58.251ms. The time consumption of encryption is 6.993ms and it is about 12% of the total time consumption.

We further conduct the trapdoor construction efficiency comparison between our scheme and that of MRSE scheme, PRSE scheme and MRSE-HCI scheme. In Fig. 7, the time consumption of all four schemes linearly rises with the increasing of the number of search keywords in the query. Both MRSE and MRSE-HCI are better in performance, the time consumption of these two schemes is about 50ms. The time consumption of our scheme is higher than that of MRSE and MRSE-HCI and it is about 55ms on average. This is reasonable considering data preprocessing. It is noteworthy that the time consumption of encryption in our scheme is less than the other three schemes which given a shorter dimension query.

7.2 Document Retrieval Accuracy

In this paper, we measure document retrieval accuracy by the proportion of related documents in all the returned results. It is observed from Fig. 8 that the search accuracy of our scheme is always higher than 95% regardless of the number of documents compared to MRSE. In contrast, the retrieval effect of the MRSE scheme decreases sharply with the increasing of the number of documents, from nearly 90% to 80%. Therefore, our DSRSE scheme is superior to MRSE in retrieval accuracy and stability.

Furthermore, the performance of our scheme is measured by mean Normalized Discounted Cumulative Gain (NDCG) [19] comparing with that of MRSE.

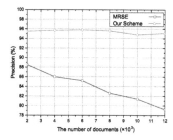
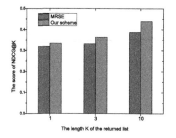

Fig. 8. A precision comparison of our scheme and MRSE.

Fig. 9. NDCG precision comparison of our scheme and MRSE.

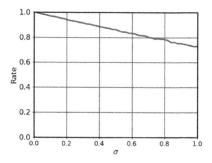

Fig. 10. Retrieval precision under different random factor settings.

In Fig. 9, we obtain significant 1.6% NDCG@1 improvement compared with that of MRSE. Under all possible return list lengths K, our scheme shows advantages over MRSE. In conclusion, the DSRSE scheme greatly improves the search accuracy in the encrypted cloud file system.

Moreover, considering that the random factor $\varepsilon^{(j)}$ is introduced into our scheme, it is necessary to discuss the effect of $\varepsilon^{(j)}$ on the retrieval accuracy. In our scheme, as shown in formula (5, 1), the similarity between the document index and the query trapdoor is affected by $\sum \varepsilon^{(j)}$. Let $\mathcal{X} = \sum \varepsilon^{(j)}$ be a random variable with a normal distribution. Then the mean of $\mathcal{X}$ should be 0, while the variance of $\mathcal{X}$ is set to σ. Different values of σ will represent the dispersion of $\mathcal{X}$, that is, the impact on the search results. As shown in Fig. 10, we calculate the change of the top 100 retrieval results under different σ values based on the results without adding random factors. We set the similarity of search results $\frac{\alpha}{100}$ as the accuracy retention $Rate$, where α is the number of times the same document appears in the top 100 search results. As can be seen from the figure, when σ is 0, we set the retrieval accuracy retention $Rate$ at this time to 1. With the increase of σ, the accuracy decreases gradually. Therefore, in order to ensure the retrieval accuracy, σ should not exceed 0.4.

7.3 Document Retrieval Efficiency

Time Complexity Analysis. As shown in Table 1, we have analyzed and compared the time complexity of the proposed DSRSE scheme with MRSE [3] and

Table 1. Time complexity analysis

Algorithm	Schemes		
	DSRSE	MRSE [3]	FPMRSE [47]
Key	$O(m) + O(d') +$ $O(2d'^2)$	$O(m) + O(d'') +$ $O(2d''^2)$	$O(m) + O(d'') +$ $O(2d''^2)$
Index & Enc	$m \cdot (O(T_{Enc}) + O(f)$ $+O(d') + O(2d'^2))$	$m \cdot (O(T_{Enc}) + O(f)$ $+ O(d'') + O(2d''^2))$	$m \cdot (O(T_{Enc}) + O(f) +$ $O(d'') + O(6d''^2))$
Update	$O(md' \cdot logm)$	$O(md'')$	$O(md''^2)$
Trapdoor	$O(f) + O(d') +$ $O(2d'^2)$	$O(f) +$ $O(d'') + O(2d''^2)$	$O(f) + O(d'')$ $+O(2d''^2)$
Search	$O(kd' \cdot logm)$	$O(md'' \cdot logk)$	$O(md'' \cdot logk)$
Dec	$O(kT_{Dec})$	$O(kT_{Dec})$	$O(kT_{Dec})$

FPMRSE [47] schemes. In which d' and d'' are the length of the document index or query trap, $d' = 128+u+1, d'' = d+u+1$ (d is the size of keywords dictionary). Considering that in the words-bag model, in order to extract document features, the size of dictionaries is often thousands [41]. Thus, $d' \ll d''$. In addition, T_{Enc} and T_{Dec} represent the time required for encryption and decryption of symmetric encryption algorithm, while $O(f)$ represets the generation time of feature vector. It can be noted that in Key, Index, Enc, Trapdoor and Dec algorithms, the three schemes have similar time complexity. However, due to $d' \ll d''$, our scheme has the advantage of time efficiency in these schemes. In Update and Search algorithms, our scheme has logarithmic time complexity, which is significantly superior to MRSE and FPMRSE due to the design of clustering tree search structure. Therefore, in general, our scheme is better than MRSE and FPMRSE in time complexity analysis.

Analysis of Simulation Experiment. In this part, we experimentally compare the document retrieval efficiency between our scheme and the above schemes (MRSE, MRSE-HCI and PRSE). As shown in Fig. 11(a), with the increasing of the number of documents from 1000 to 6000 in the collection, the retrieval time of all the four schemes grows. The search time of MRSE increases in an approximately linear manner with the linear growth of document set size. This is reasonable considering that the public cloud server need to scan all the document indexes in the search phase. The schemes of MRSE-HCI and PRSE perform better. However, the performance of our scheme DSRSE is tops all them above, and the retrieval time is no more than 6 ms at most, while the retrieval time of MRSE is up to 35 ms at most. The search process in DSRSE is based on the tree search and the vector dimension is low. Therefore, our scheme is more efficient when the document set has more files.

The search time, for each of the three: MRSE, PRSE and MRSE-HCI remains approximately unchanged no matter the number of keywords, which is shown in Fig. 11(b). This is rational considering that time of the process is constant. The search time of our scheme exhibits the similar trend with the number of keywords. On average, the retrieval time for the four schemes are: MRSE-30ms, PRSE-15ms, MRSE-HCI-11ms, DSRSE-5.1ms. Because generating the vectors by the CNNM structure, the vector dimension of DSRSE is low and it is more efficient to search related documents. Compared with the other three schemes, our scheme performs the best and it benefits from the novelty of the index structure.

7.4 Communication Overhead

Since multiple entities are introduced into our scheme, it is necessary to analyze the communication overhead of the scheme. Compared with the MRSE scheme [3], the DSRSE scheme proposed by us introduces a parameter server in order to improve the retrieval accuracy and reduce the computational burden of data users, which increases some communication overhead. Specifically, we transferred model training, query trapdoor generation and query result decryption from the data owners and data users to the parameter server and private cloud servers with more computing resources and storage resources, greatly reducing the local computing burden of users and improving the user experience.

For data communication overhead, we analyze the increase of our DSRSE scheme compared with MRSE scheme from two aspects. First, for the data owners and users of the main services of the scheme, the communication cost of the data users is not increased. Compared with the MRSE scheme, the data owner needs to send one more copy of the plaintext data to the private cloud server. However, it is worth noting that our scheme does not require the data owner to upload each plaintext data for training. Generally speaking, only when data

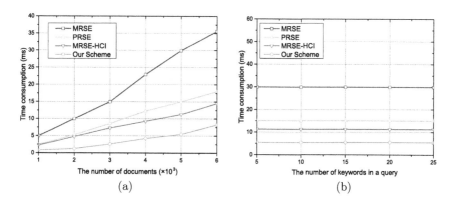

Fig. 11. Time consumption of document search with (a) different size of document set (b) different number of keywords in a query

users need to upload a relatively new type of document, they need to upload the corresponding training data set and update the parameters of CNNM. In general, the data owner does not need to constantly update the locally stored CNNM parameters. Therefore, our scheme only introduces a small amount of communication overhead to the data users and data owners, and does not affect the user experience.

In addition, our DSRSE scheme introduces the communication overhead of the private cloud server and the communication overhead of the parameter server. As we have analyzed above, the communication overhead of the private cloud server does not need to update the CNNM parameters at any time, so the introduction of this part of communication overhead has little impact. The communication cost between the parameter server and the cloud server is the same as that of the data user in MRSE. This part of communication cost takes into account that the parameter server has a very strong data bandwidth and will not cause data delay and thus affect the user's query experience. Therefore, in general, although our DSRSE scheme introduces some communication overhead, it will not affect the user experience.

8   Conclusion

In this paper, a privacy protected, efficient and accurate encrypted documents ranking retrieval scheme DSRSE based on the neural network and distributed private cloud servers is proposed. We utilize the convolutional neural network model to generate the document index vectors and query vectors. Theoretical analysis shows that our method reflects the semantic of files more accurately and the dimensions of vectors are far less than the existing schemes. Moreover, it is unnecessary to extract keywords from the document set, which reduces the computing burden on users. The convolutional neural network model is trained by the distributed credible private clouds. For each private cloud, the trained data set is independent, which enhances privacy protection. We employ the secure kNN algorithm to encrypt these document and query vectors. Therefore, the security of the vectors greatly increases while maintaining their ranking searchability. At last, a clustering tree structure is designed to improve retrieval efficiency. The security of our scheme is carefully analyzed from privacy protection, search efficiency and accuracy, revealing that our proposed DSRSE scheme can protect user privacy even under a known background model with partially impaired environment. Analysis and simulation results demonstrate that our proposed scheme provides secure, efficient and accuracy encrypted document search service to data users.

In our future work, we plan to optimize the neural network architecture or use a better model to explore the semantic of the documents in encrypted retrieval. Also, it is of significance to further improve retrieval efficiency.

Acknowledgments. This work was supported by the National Natural Science Foundation of China under Grant Numbers: 62001055, 62102017, 61932014, 61972018 and the Fundamental Research Funds for the Central Universities (YWF-22-L-1273).

A Appendix

Algorithm 1. Distributed Neural Network Training

Private Cloud Server $= 1, \cdots, N$:

function LOADDATA()
  1: load the training data $\{x_n, y_n\}$
  2: pull the weight $\varpi^{(t)}$ from the parameter server
end function
function TRAINING()

  1: compute the gradient $g_n^{(t)}$
  2: push the $g_n^{(t)}$ to the parameter server
end function
The Parameter server :
function UPDATEWEIGHT(t)

  1: $g^{(t)} = \frac{1}{N} \sum_{n=1}^{N} g_n^{(t)}$
  2: $w^{(t+1)} = w^{(t)} - \eta g^{(t)}$
  3: push the $g_n^{(t)}$ to the parameter server
end function

Algorithm 2. Building the Document Index Clustering Tree

Data Owner :
function LOADDATA()
  1: load the document index P_i as $node[i]$ $(0 \le i \le m)$
end function
function BUILDCLUTERTREE
  1: **for** $j = m; j \le 2m; j + +$ **do**
  2:   search two nodes $node1, node2$ in leaf-node set and cluster-node set whose relevance score Sco is minimum
  3:   $node[j].left = node1$
  4:   $node[j].right = node2$
  5:   **update** $node[j].value$ and $node[j].count$
end function

Algorithm 3. Searching in the Document Index Clustering Tree

The Public Cloud Server :
function SEARCH(CTNode)
1: $n = k_{top}$ and $Cnode$ initializes is root node
2: **if** $Cnode.count = k_{top}$
3:    **return** top-k documents
4: **if** $Cnode.count < k_{top}$
5:    compute the relevance scores between $\mathcal{T}$ and all the leafnode which root node is $Cnode$
6:    **return** top-k documents
7: **if** $Cnode.count > k_{top}$
8:    $Cnode = Cnode.left$ or $Cnode.right$, as a condition, the relevance score is minimum
9: $Search(Cnode)$
end function

References

1. Andola, N., Prakash, S., Yadav, V.K., Venkatesan, S., Verma, S., et al.: A secure searchable encryption scheme for cloud using hash-based indexing. J. Comput. Syst. Sci. **126**, 119–137 (2022)

2. Bao, Y., Qiu, W., Cheng, X.: Secure and lightweight fine-grained searchable data sharing for IoT-oriented and cloud-assisted smart healthcare system. IEEE Internet Things J. **9**(4), 2513–2526 (2021)

3. Cao, N., Wang, C., Li, M., Ren, K., Lou, W.: Privacy-preserving multi-keyword ranked search over encrypted cloud data. IEEE Trans. Parallel Distrib. Syst. **25**(1), 222–233 (2013)

4. Chen, C., Zhu, X., Shen, P., Guo, S., Tari, Z., Zomaya, A.Y.: An efficient privacy-preserving ranked keyword search method. IEEE Trans. Parallel Distrib. Syst. **27**(4), 951–963 (2015)

5. Chuah, M., Hu, W.: Privacy-aware bedtree based solution for fuzzy multi-keyword search over encrypted data. In: 2011 31st International Conference on Distributed Computing Systems Workshops, pp. 273–281. IEEE (2011)

6. Dean, J., Corrado, G.S., Monga, R., Chen, K., Ng, A.Y.: Large scale distributed deep networks. Adv. Neural Inf. Process. Syst. **25** (2012)

7. Deng, C., Yang, E., Liu, T., Li, J., Liu, W., Tao, D.: Unsupervised semantic-preserving adversarial hashing for image search. IEEE Trans. Image Process. **28**(8), 4032–4044 (2019)

8. Devlin, J., Chang, M.W., Lee, K., Toutanova, K.: BERT: pre-training of deep bidirectional transformers for language understanding. arXiv preprint arXiv:1810.04805 (2018)

9. Fu, Z., Ren, K., Shu, J., Sun, X., Huang, F.: Enabling personalized search over encrypted outsourced data with efficiency improvement. IEEE Trans. Parallel Distrib. Syst. **27**(9), 2546–2559 (2015)

10. Fu, Z., Wang, Y., Sun, X., Zhang, X.: Semantic and secure search over encrypted outsourcing cloud based on BERT. Front. Comput. Sci. **16**(2), 1–8 (2022). https://doi.org/10.1007/s11704-021-0277-0

11. Fu, Z., Wu, X., Guan, C., Sun, X., Ren, K.: Toward efficient multi-keyword fuzzy search over encrypted outsourced data with accuracy improvement. IEEE Trans. Inf. Forensics Secur. **11**(12), 2706–2716 (2016)

12. González-Carvajal, S., Garrido-Merchán, E.C.: Comparing BERT against traditional machine learning text classification. arXiv preprint arXiv:2005.13012 (2020)
13. He, W., Zhang, Y., Li, Y.: Fast, searchable, symmetric encryption scheme supporting ranked search. Symmetry 14(5), 1029 (2022)
14. He, X., Deng, L., Chou, W.: Discriminative learning in sequential pattern recognition. IEEE Signal Process. Mag. 25(5), 14–36 (2008)
15. Hu, Z., Dai, H., Yang, G., Yi, X., Sheng, W.: Semantic-based multi-keyword ranked search schemes over encrypted cloud data. Secur. Commun. Netw. 2022 (2022)
16. Hua, Y., Zhang, D., Ge, S.: Research progress in the interpretability of deep learning models. J. Cybersecur. 5(3), 1–12 (2020)
17. Huang, P.S., He, X., Gao, J., Deng, L., Acero, A., Heck, L.: Learning deep structured semantic models for web search using clickthrough data. In: Proceedings of the 22nd ACM International Conference on Information & Knowledge Management, pp. 2333–2338 (2013)
18. Jadhav, N., Nikam, J., Bahekar, S.: Semantic search supporting similarity ranking over encrypted private cloud data. Int. J. Emerg. Eng. Res. Technol. 2(7), 215–219 (2014)
19. Järvelin, K., Kekäläinen, J.: IR evaluation methods for retrieving highly relevant documents. In: ACM SIGIR Forum, vol. 51, pp. 243–250. ACM, NY (2017)
20. Li, H., Yang, Y., Luan, T.H., Liang, X., Zhou, L., Shen, X.S.: Enabling fine-grained multi-keyword search supporting classified sub-dictionaries over encrypted cloud data. IEEE Trans. Dependable Secure Comput. 13(3), 312–325 (2015)
21. Li, J., Yan, H., Zhang, Y.: Efficient identity-based provable multi-copy data possession in multi-cloud storage. IEEE Trans. Cloud Comput. (2019)
22. Li, X., Long, G., Li, S.: Encrypted medical records search with supporting of fuzzy multi-keyword and relevance ranking. In: Sun, X., Zhang, X., Xia, Z., Bertino, E. (eds.) ICAIS 2021. LNCS, vol. 12737, pp. 85–101. Springer, Cham (2021). https://doi.org/10.1007/978-3-030-78612-0_7
23. Liu, G., Guo, J.: Bidirectional LSTM with attention mechanism and convolutional layer for text classification. Neurocomputing 337, 325–338 (2019)
24. Miao, Y., Ma, J., Liu, X., Weng, J., Li, H., Li, H.: Lightweight fine-grained search over encrypted data in fog computing. IEEE Trans. Serv. Comput. 12(5), 772–785 (2018)
25. Montavon, G., Orr, G.B., Müller, K.-R. (eds.): Neural Networks: Tricks of the Trade. LNCS, vol. 7700. Springer, Heidelberg (2012). https://doi.org/10.1007/978-3-642-35289-8
26. Palangi, H., et al.: Deep sentence embedding using long short-term memory networks: analysis and application to information retrieval. IEEE/ACM Trans. Audio Speech Lang. Process. 24(4), 694–707 (2016)
27. Shen, Y., He, X., Gao, J., Deng, L., Mesnil, G.: A latent semantic model with convolutional-pooling structure for information retrieval. In: Proceedings of the 23rd ACM International Conference on Conference on Information and Knowledge Management, pp. 101–110 (2014)
28. Siva Kumar, D.V.N., Santhi Thilagam, P.: Searchable encryption approaches: attacks and challenges. Knowl. Inf. Syst. 61(3), 1179–1207 (2018). https://doi.org/10.1007/s10115-018-1309-4
29. Song, D.X., Wagner, D., Perrig, A.: Practical techniques for searches on encrypted data. In: Proceeding 2000 IEEE Symposium on Security and Privacy. S&P 2000, pp. 44–55. IEEE (2000)

30. Sousa, S., Kern, R.: How to keep text private? A systematic review of deep learning methods for privacy-preserving natural language processing. Artif. Intell. Rev. 1–66 (2022). https://doi.org/10.1007/s10462-022-10204-6

31. Tian, P., Guo, C., Choo, K.K.R., Liu, Y., Li, L., Yao, L.: EAFS: an efficient, accurate, and forward secure searchable encryption scheme supporting range search. IEEE Syst. J. (2021)

32. Wang, C., Cao, N., Ren, K., Lou, W.: Enabling secure and efficient ranked keyword search over outsourced cloud data. IEEE Trans. Parallel Distrib. Syst. **23**(8), 1467–1479 (2011)

33. Wang, C., et al.: Enriching query semantics for code search with reinforcement learning. Neural Netw. **145**, 22–32 (2022)

34. Wang, R., Li, Z., Cao, J., Chen, T.: Chinese text feature extraction and classification based on deep learning. In: Proceedings of the 3rd International Conference on Computer Science and Application Engineering, pp. 1–5 (2019)

35. Wong, W.K., Cheung, D.W., Kao, B., Mamoulis, N.: Secure kNN computation on encrypted databases. In: Proceedings of the 2009 ACM SIGMOD International Conference on Management of Data, pp. 139–152 (2009)

36. Xia, Z., Wang, X., Sun, X., Wang, Q.: A secure and dynamic multi-keyword ranked search scheme over encrypted cloud data. IEEE Trans. Parallel Distrib. Syst. **27**(2), 340–352 (2015)

37. Xia, Z., Zhu, Y., Sun, X., Chen, L.: Secure semantic expansion based search over encrypted cloud data supporting similarity ranking. J. Cloud Comput. **3**(1), 1–11 (2014)

38. Yang, G., Guo, J., Han, L., Liu, X., Tian, C.: An improved secure certificateless public-key searchable encryption scheme with multi-trapdoor privacy. Peer-to-Peer Netw. Appl. **15**(1), 503–515 (2022). https://doi.org/10.1007/s12083-021-01253-9

39. Yang, J., Zou, B., Qiu, H., Li, Z.: MLFNet-point cloud semantic segmentation convolution network based on multi-scale feature fusion. IEEE Access **9**, 44950–44962 (2021)

40. Yang, W., Sun, B., Ma, X., Zhu, Y.: A cross-lingual secure semantic searching scheme with semantic analysis on ciphertext. Electron. Lett. **58**(3), 103–105 (2022)

41. Yang, Y., Liu, X., Deng, R.H.: Multi-user multi-keyword rank search over encrypted data in arbitrary language. IEEE Trans. Dependable Secure Comput. **17**(2), 320–334 (2017)

42. Zeng, M., Qian, H.F., Chen, J., Zhang, K.: Forward secure public key encryption with keyword search for outsourced cloud storage. IEEE Trans. Cloud Comput. (2019)

43. Zhang, L., Xiong, H., Huang, Q., Li, J., Choo, K.K.R., Li, J.: Cryptographic solutions for cloud storage: challenges and research opportunities. IEEE Trans. Serv. Comput. (2019)

44. Zhang, M., Chen, Y., Huang, J.: SE-PPFM: a searchable encryption scheme supporting privacy-preserving fuzzy multikeyword in cloud systems. IEEE Syst. J. **15**(2), 2980–2988 (2020)

45. Zhang, W., Gupta, S., Lian, X., Liu, J.: Staleness-aware Async-SGD for distributed deep learning. arXiv preprint arXiv:1511.05950 (2015)

46. Zhang, X., Zhao, B., Qin, J., Hou, W., Su, Y., Yang, H.: Practical wildcard searchable encryption with tree-based index. Int. J. Intell. Syst. **36**(12), 7475–7499 (2021)

47. Zhao, S., Zhang, H., Zhang, X., Li, W., Gao, F., Wen, Q.: Forward privacy multi-keyword ranked search over encrypted database. Int. J. Intell. Syst. (2022)

A Event Extraction Method of Document-Level Based on the Self-attention Mechanism

Xueming Qiao[1], Yao Tang[1], Yanhong Liu[1], Maomao Su[1], Chao Wang[1],
Yansheng Fu[2], Xiaofang Li[3], Mingrui Wu[2], Qiang Fu[4], and Dongjie Zhu[2(✉)]

[1] State Grid Weihai Power Supply Company, No. 23, Kunming Road, Weihai, China
[2] School of Computer Science and Technology, Harbin Institute of Technology,
Weihai 204209, China
zhudongjie@hit.edu.cn
[3] Department of Mathematics, Harbin Institute of Technology, Weihai 264209, China
[4] Shandong Baimeng Information Technology Co., Ltd., Weihai, China

Abstract. Event extraction is an important task in the field of natural language processing. However, most of the existing event extraction techniques focus on sentence-level extraction, which inevitably ignores the contextual features of sentences and the occurrence of multiple event trigger words in the same sentence. Therefore, this paper mainly uses the multi-head self-attention mechanism to integrate text features from multiple dimensions and levels to achieve the task of event detection at the level of text. First, convolutional neural network combined with dynamic multi-pool strategy is used to extract sentence level features. Secondly, the discourse feature representation of full-text information fusion is obtained by multi-head self-attention mechanism model. Finally, using the classifier function to classify, and then detect the trigger word and category of the event. Experimental results show that the proposed method achieves good results in document-level event extraction.

Keywords: Document-level · Event extraction · Event detection

1 Introduction

1.1 A Subsection Sample

With the advent of the information age, mobile Internet has been developing rapidly, the information data is growing, the information knowledge is readily available, and the vast amount of hidden information that it contains is to be excavated. In fact, a large amount of data is generated on the network all the time depending on the occurrence of events [1]. Therefore, how to extract events from complex, redundant and difficult to integrate data is of great significance to the construction of knowledge graph [2], question answering system [3] and hot spot search. However, most of the current event extraction methods are for the sentence level, document level event extraction needs to be broken through.

Y. Xu et al. (Eds.): ML4CS 2022, LNCS 13656, pp. 609–619, 2023.
https://doi.org/10.1007/978-3-031-20099-1_50

An event is a change in one or more actions or states involving one or more actors at a particular time and place. Event extraction [4] is to extract the time, place, person and thing from the text describing event information, and present these event information in a structured form. Event extraction includes two sub-tasks. The first sub-task is event detection [5], which is used to discover trigger words in an event. Event trigger [6] words are the words that can best represent the occurrence of an event. It is usually a verb or gerund. Event detection is also called event discovery, which is to determine the category of events through the detection and classification of trigger words. The second sub-task is event parameter extraction [7]. Event elements are participants in the event and are the core components of the event, generally composed of entities, time and attributes (such as location, etc.). Events are represented structurally by extracting these elements and roles in the event. The traditional event extraction method with limited domain has a good extraction effect at present, but it lacks large-scale training data due to the influence of event types. The commonly used ACE2005 dataset [8] contains 33 event types, which cannot completely cover all events in the general field. The data scale is small, the distribution is uneven, and manual labeling is time-consuming and expensive. At present, although there are large-scale training data in general domain event extraction, the extraction effect still needs to be improved. Secondly, most of the current event extraction methods are sentence-level extraction methods, which aim to extract a single event in a single sentence, but ignore the existence of multiple event trigger words in the same sentence, and ignore the context association of the sentence in the whole text.

Therefore, this paper proposes a research method of document-level event extraction based on multi-head self-attention mechanism. Firstly, the dynamic multi-pool convolutional neural network (DMCNN) [9] is used to encode multiple features in sentences, and the most valuable sentence-level feature representation is dynamically output, when the sentence-level event detection ignores multiple trigger words in sentences. Secondly, each sentence-level feature in the sentence packet is input into the multi-head self-attention mechanism model [10] using the sentence packet strategy. Omni-directional and multi-dimensional enhancement vector representation, namely, discourse level feature representation, is obtained after the sentence is integrated with full-text semantic information in the whole text. Finally, the classifier function is used to classify the corresponding event categories.

2 Related Work

At present, the existing event extraction tasks are divided into four sub-tasks: event trigger word recognition, event type classification, argument recognition and argument role classification. The first two subtasks are merged into event detection tasks, and the last two tasks are merged into event parameter extraction tasks.

Event extraction can be divided into restricted domain event extraction [11] and open domain event extraction [12] according to the different methods of determining event categories in international evaluation and corpus. Open domain event extraction event types are unrestricted, the types of possible events and the structure of events are unknown prior to event extraction, and there is no need to annotate data. The idea behind open-domain event extraction is that two words have similar meanings if they occur in context and are used similarly. Similarly, in event extracts, if the candidate event triggers or the event trigger elements have a similar context, these event triggers tend to find the same type of event. The group average clustering method proposed by Yang et al. [13] sorted the texts to be clustered in chronological order, treated each document as a class, and made use of the timeliness and concentration of time to cluster each part to a certain size. Although the open domain event recognition can automatically discover new events, the discovered events often lack semantic information and are difficult to structure. In the event extraction method of limited domain, the type of the target event and the specific structure of each type should be defined before extraction, that is, the event elements contained in each type. At the same time, a small amount of annotation data should be provided so that each predefined event type has corresponding annotation samples. For example, ACE event extraction evaluation defines 8 event types, including 33 sub-event types, such as Business, Conflict and Transaction.

According to the different methods of event extraction, the event extraction methods of limited domain can be divided into pattern matching method and machine learning method. The method of pattern matching is to recognize and extract events under the guidance of some manually defined patterns. High-quality pattern constraints can achieve better results in specific fields. For example, the parallel automatic knowledge Acquisition (PALKA) mode extraction system proposed by Kim and Moldovan [14] uses semantic framework and phrase pattern structure to represent the mode of a specific domain. It uses the annotated corpus related to terrorism in MUC evaluation dataset for training to extract events, and has achieved good performance. However, the method based on pattern matching relies on the guidance of domain experts, is time-consuming and labor-intensive, has poor portability, low recall rate and is difficult to be reused. Researchers then turn to event extraction methods based on machine learning. The most representative one is event extraction based on supervised learning. This method models event extraction as a multi-classification problem. After feature vector extraction, supervised classifier is used for event extraction. For example, Support Vector Machine (SVM) [15], Naive Bayes Model (NBM) [16], Hidden Markov Model (HMM) [17], Maximum Entropy Model (ME) [18] et al. Although machine learning-based methods have achieved good results in event trigger word classification and event element classification, they need a large amount of annotated corpus, otherwise serious data sparsity will occur. And when extracting features, only sentence-level features are considered, while ignoring the background knowledge of the whole article.

According to the different process of event extraction, delimited domain event extraction methods can be divided into pipeline based extraction method and union based event extraction method. After 2015, with the development of deep learning, event extraction mainly develops into how to use neural network to automatically obtain features directly from text and then complete event extraction, so as to avoid the high cost of constructing features manually. The DMCNN model proposed by Chen et al. [9] is a typical pipe-based extraction method. In this method, event extraction is transformed into a two-stage multi-classification task, word vectors are obtained as basic features by unsupervised and trained methods, and a dynamic multi-pool strategy is proposed to process multiple trigger word features in sentences. Although this method considers multiple trigger words in a sentence, it still belongs to the sentence-level extraction method and has the problems of error propagation and long-distance dependence. To solve this problem, Trung et al. [19] proposed the joint extraction model of One for All in 2018, which uses EMD, ED and ARP joint modeling to share hidden layer representation across tasks to achieve communication between them, and achieved good results. Although the joint model can avoid error propagation, it cannot use the priori information of trigger words detected during event detection. Most of the above methods still remain in sentence-level event extraction.

According to the different granularity of event extraction, the event extraction method of limited domain can be divided into sentence level extraction method and document level extraction method. Feng et al. [20] proposed a hybrid neural network model for sentence-level event detection task, which combined BI-LSTM and CNN model to learn the continuous representation of each word in a sentence. The model also considered the importance of local context features in terms of event trigger words and event types. Although good detection effect is achieved, the case of multiple event trigger words in a sentence is not considered. Yang et al. [21] proposed DCFEE, a document-level Chinese financial event extraction system based on automatic labeling training data, which is divided into two parts: sentence-level event extraction and document-level event extraction. Sentence-level event extraction can extract event parameters and event trigger words from a sentence. Document-level event extraction aims to extract parameters of the entire document based on critical event detection model and parameter completion strategy. The system can quickly extract document-level events from Chinese financial statements, but it is still oriented to extracting Chinese events in a single domain.

Therefore, this paper proposed a document-level event extraction method based on multi-head self-attention mechanism, which takes into account both the existence of multiple trigger words in a sentence and the context relation of the sentence in the article. Based on DMCNN, this method is improved. It uses dynamic multi-pool strategy to consider the influence of multi-trigger words. Moreover, it integrates the features of sentences in articles with multi-head self-attention mechanism to obtain document-level feature representation, and then achieves document-level event detection extraction.

3   Methods

In this chapter, we first introduce the whole process of the text level event extraction method based on multi-head self-attention mechanism, and then introduce the specific algorithm implementation of each part.

The overall process of the text level event extraction method based on multiple self-attention mechanism realized in this paper is shown in Fig. 1, which mainly includes data preprocessing, feature extraction, classifier classification and other steps. In order to simultaneously consider the problem of multiple triggering words in a sentence and sentence context correlation in this paper, we designed the model structure as shown in Fig. 2. First, each sentence in the article is preprocessed and input into DMCNN model to obtain the sentence-level feature representation. Then, the sentence package strategy is used to input all sentence features into the multi-head self-attention model to obtain enhanced document-level feature representation. Finally, the trigger words and categories of the events are obtained by using softmax classifier to complete the task of detecting and extracting the event.

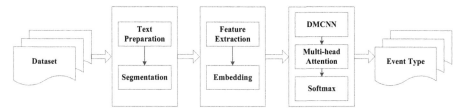

Fig. 1. Model frame diagram.

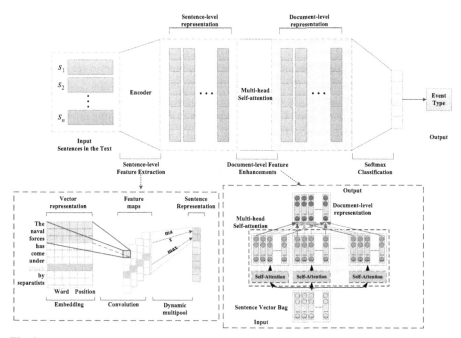

Fig. 2. Overall structure diagram of event detection model based on multi-head self-attention mechanism.

3.1 Sentence Level Feature Acquisition

DMCNN model is used to obtain the sentence-level feature representation to solve the problem of multiple event trigger words in a sentence. The model consists of five layers: input layer, convolution layer, pooling layer, full connection layer and output layer. The convolution layer is composed of multiple filters and feature graphs, and the pooling layer is composed of dynamic multi-pools. First, the pre-trained language model Skip-gram is used for word embedding representation, and word is used to represent each word marker vector transformed by searching word embedding, and each word is mapped to a d_w dimensional vector. Position is used to represent the distance between the current word and the trigger word, and the relative distance between the current word and the trigger word is converted into a real-value vector. As shown in Fig. 2, the word embedding size is assumed to be $d_w = 4$, the size of the position insert is $d_p = 1$. So the d dimensional vector corresponding to the i-th word in a sentence is shown in Eq. (1):

$$d = d_w + d_p * 2 \tag{1}$$

A sentence of length s can be expressed by the sequence $\{q_1, q_2, \cdots q_s\}$ as Eq. (2):

$$q_{1:s} = q_1 \oplus q_2 \oplus q_3 \oplus \cdots \oplus q_s \tag{2}$$

where $q_i \in R^d$, $\oplus$ represents the connection operation, $q_{i:j}$ represents the connection from q_i to q_j. Word embedding and position embedding together form the vector representation part of the instance, which is transformed into a matrix, and S is used as the input of the convolution operation.

The convolution operation aims to extract the combined semantic features of the whole sentence and compress these semantic features into feature maps. Convolution is the operation between the weight vector w and the input sequence q, and the convolution operation involves a convolution kernel ω. As shown in Fig. 2, assuming $\omega = 3$, it means that the context generates a new feature every 3 words of the sliding window, then $w \in R^{\omega * d}$. Feature sequence (feature graph) $c \in R^{s+\omega-1}$ is obtained by dot product operation of each ω-gram string in sequence q and weight matrix w, where the calculation formula of j-th feature c_j is as Eq. (3):

$$c_j = f(w \cdot q_{j-\omega+1:j} + b) \tag{3}$$

where b is the offset term, $b \in R$, $f(\cdot)$ is a nonlinear function, and the value range of j is $(1, s + \omega - 1)$. In order to extract multiple features, we assume that n convolution kernels are used for feature extraction, then the weight matrix can be represented by sequence, that is, the extracted features can be represented by Eq. (4):

$$c_{ij} = f(w_i \cdot q_{j-\omega+1:j} + b_i) \tag{4}$$

In order to capture the most important features in each feature graph dynamically, we use dynamic multi-pool strategy, which divides each feature map into two parts by using trigger words. Dynamic multi-pool returns the maximum value of each segment instead of a single maximum pool. As shown in Fig. 2, "attack" divides the sentence into two paragraphs $\{c_{i1}, c_{i2}\}$, and the operation process is shown in Eq. (5):

$$p_{ij} = \max(c_{ij}) \tag{5}$$

Therefore, the output of each convolution kernel is a two-dimensional vector $p_i = \{p_{i1}, p_{i2}\}$. Nonlinear functions such as hyperbolic tangent function tanh($\cdot$) are used to connect all output vectors $p_{1:n}$, and the output vectors of dynamic multi-pools are obtained. Then, the vector representation of a single sentence can be obtained, where g_i is the vector representation of the i-th sentence in the text.

3.2 Sentence Package Strategy

Assumption: If a text contains an event type, there is at least one sentence in the document that fully encapsulates the event type, treating all sentences in the same text as a sentence package. Assuming that there are m sentences in a sentence package, the expression of the sentence package can be obtained by using the method in Sect. 3.1.

3.3 Document-Level Feature Acquisition

Multi-head self-attention mechanism is used to extract document-level features, and multi-sub-feature space is used to fuse the contextual relationship of sentences in documents. The essence of multi-head self-attention is to carry out multiple self-attention operations, which can enable the model to obtain features of more scenes and levels from different representation subspaces, so as to capture more contextual features between sentences. This method adopts the strategy of multiplicative attention mechanism to realize the operation of highly optimized matrix multiplication, which can improve the feature expression ability of the model and reduce the calculation cost of the whole calculation.

Firstly, the expression $G = [g_1, g_2, \cdots, g_m]$ of the sentence package is input into the multi-head self-attention model. The calculation process of single-head self-attention is shown in Eq. (6) and Eq. (7), and r is used as the expression of the final output value of this layer:

$$\partial = \text{softmax}(a^m \tanh(G)) \tag{6}$$

$$r = G\partial^m \tag{7}$$

where $G \in R^{d^g \times m}$, d^g is the number of nodes in the hidden layer, a is a weight parameter vector, $a \in R^{d^g \times m}$, $\partial \in R^m$, $r \in R^{d^g \times m}$, , softmax($\cdot$) function is used to normalize the result of single-head calculation. The calculation process of multi-head self-attention is multiple calculation of single-head self-attention. Assume that the number of heads in the multi-head Attention model is H, that is, h single-head self-attention calculation is performed, and then the output is combined. The calculation process is as follows:

Before using sentence package to represent matrix G each time, in order to compress the dimension of G calculated by single self-attention and achieve the purpose of parallel execution of single-head Attention, a linear transformation of G should be performed first: $A_i^g G$, where $A_i^g \in R^{d^g/h \times d^g}$, $i \in \{1, 2, \cdots, h\}$. Use different weight a each time and calculate h times. Combine each self-attention result g^* and perform linear mapping to obtain the final multi-head self-attention calculation result g_c, as shown in Eq. (8):

$$g_c = A_c \otimes \text{concat}(g_1^*, g_2^*, \cdots, g_h^*) \tag{8}$$

where, $\otimes$ represents the dot product operation of element by element, the dimension of A_c is $h \times d^g$, and g_c represents the enhanced document-level vector representation integrating full text semantic information.

3.4 Classifier

Event detection is a multi-classification problem of event trigger words. Therefore, we use S function as a classifier in the output layer to calculate the conditional probability of each category, and then select the category corresponding to the maximum conditional probability as the event category of event detection output. The calculation process is shown in Eq. (9) and Eq. (10):

$$p(y'|S) = \text{softmax}(A_c g_c + b_c) \tag{9}$$

$$y = \underset{y'}{\text{argmax}}\, p(y'|S) \tag{10}$$

where $A_c \in R^{e \times hd_a}$, e is the number of event types. The objective function is the negative logarithmic likelihood function of regularized class y of L2, as shown in Eq. (11):

$$J(\theta) = -\frac{1}{k}\sum_{i=1}^{k} t_i \log(y_i') + \lambda \|\theta\|_2^2 \tag{11}$$

4 Experiment

4.1 Datasets

In this experiment, MAVEN [22] dataset annotated by Tsinghua University and Tencent's wechat AI was used. This dataset includes 168 generic event categories, 111611 events, 38853 event mentions, covering 4480 documents, 1276K tokens, and 49873 sentences. The experimental data set is much larger than ACE2005. Table 1 shows the top five event types in MAVEN.

Table 1. Five top-level event types and their percentages of MAVEN.

Top-level event type	Subtype examples	Percentage
Action	Telling, attack, building	46.9%
Change	Change event time, change of leadership	27.5%
Scenario	Emergency, catastrophe, incident	13.4%
Sentiment	Supporting, convincing, quarreling	6.4%
Possession	Commerce buy, giving, renting	5.7%

4.2 Evaluation Indicators

In this experiment, F1-measure, the official evaluation standard, is used as the evaluation index of the model. F1-measure adopts Precision (P) and Recall (R) to calculate. Precision is the ratio of the same number of detected trigger words and labeled trigger words to the total number of detected trigger words. Recall rate is the ratio of the number of the same detected trigger words and labeled trigger words to the total number of labeled trigger words.

4.3 Parameter Settings

Adam optimizer used by DMCNN model, except for the word embedding dimension and learning rate not mentioned in the original text, other parameters are the same as those set by Chen et al. [9]. The parameter Settings of hyperparameters refer to MAVEN.

The value of h of the parametric attention model in the multi-head layer refers to the experiment of Vaswani et al. [10] to select the best h value and take [1, 2, 4, 6, 10, 15], [30] as the candidate value, and adopt the five-fold cross-validation method to evaluate the model performance. When h value continues to increase, the model performance will decline. So the final value of h is 6.

4.4 Experimental Results

In order to compare this model with other models, all models were experimented with the same data set, with 168 event categories. Multi-head Attention layer was added to the DMCNN model, BiLSTM model, CRF model and BiLSTM_CRF model. The input word vector and position vector, the number of nodes in the hidden network layer, the network activation function and the model optimization method of these models were consistent with the parameter Settings of the experimental method in this paper. The experimental results are shown in Table 2.

Table 2. Experiment results.

Models	F1 (%)
Mul_ATT_CRF	66.4%
Mul_ATT_BiLSTM	67.5%
Mul_ATT_BiLSTM_CRF	62.1%
Mul_ATT_DMCNN	70.4%

Compared with the above four models, the final F1 value of the method proposed in this paper reaches 70.4%, which is higher than the above three models. This paper proposes a document-level event extraction method based on multi-head self-attention mechanism, which not only considers the actual scenario of multiple event trigger words in the same sentence, but also solves the long-distance dependency problem of convolutional neural network by using multi-head self-attention model. This method integrates document information from each self-feature space and takes into account the relationship between sentences in document context, which further improves the representation ability of the model. Therefore, experiments prove that the proposed method can be used to extract document-level events.

5 Conclusion

Based on existing models and sentence-level event extraction methods, this paper uses DMCNN and multi-head self-attention mechanism to model the text. First, sentence - level feature representation is obtained by DMCNN model. Then use the assumption that each document has at least one topic sentence that can fully represent the event category of the document. All sentence-level feature representations are input into multi-head Attention model, and semantic information is fused from multi-dimensional and multi-sub-feature space to obtain document-level feature representations. At last, the trigger word and category of the event are identified by classifier to complete the document level event detection and extraction task. Experiments show that the method is effective.

Acknowledgement. The authors would like to thank the associate editor and the reviewers for their time and effort provided to review the manuscript.

Funding Statement. This work is supported by State Grid Shandong Electric Power Company Science and Technology Project Funding under Grant no. 62061320C007, SGS-DWH00YXJS2000128, the Fundamental Research Funds for the Central Universities (Grant No. HIT. NSRIF.201714), Weihai Science and Technology Development Program (2016DX GJMS15), Weihai Scientific Research and Innovation Fund (2020) and Key Research and Development Program in Shandong Provincial (2017GGX90103).

Conflicts of Interest. The authors declare that they have no conflicts of interest to report regarding the present study.

References

1. Hoogenboom, F.P., Flavius, F., Uzay, K., Franciska, D.J., Caron, E.A.M.: A survey of event extraction methods from text for decision support systems. Decis. Support Syst. **85**(1), 12–22 (2016)
2. Ji, S., Pan, S., Cambria, E., Marttinen, P., Yu, P.S.: A survey on knowledge graphs: representation, acquisition, and applications. Trans. Neural Netw. Learn. Syst. **33**(2), 494–514 (2021)
3. Garg, S., Vu, T., Moschitti, A.: TANDA: transfer and adapt pre-trained transformer models for answer sentence selection. In: Proceedings of the AAAI Conference on Artificial Intelligence, vol. 34, no. 5, pp. 7780–7788 (2020)
4. Xiang, W., Wang, B.: A survey of event extraction from text. Access **7**, 173111–173137 (2019)
5. Gao, L.Z., Gang, Z., Luo, J.Y., Lan, M.J.: Survey on meta-event extraction. Comput. Sci. **46**(8), 9–15 (2019)
6. Wen, H.Y., Qu, Y.R., Ji, H., Han, J.W., et al.: Event time extraction and propagation via graph attention networks. In: Human Language Technologies, pp. 62–73 (2021)

7. Du, X.Y., Rush, A., Cardie, C.: GRIT: generative role-filler transformers for document-level event entity extraction (2020)
8. Walker, C., Strassel, S., Medero, J., Maeda, K.: ACE 2005 multilingual training corpus. Linguistic Data Consortium, Philadelphia (2006)
9. Chen, Y.B., Xu, L.H., Liu, K., Zeng, D.J., Zhao, J.: Event extraction via dynamic multi-pooling convolutional neural networks. In: Association for Computational Linguistics, pp. 167–176 (2015)
10. Vaswani, A., Shazeer, N., Parmar, M., Uszkoreit, J., Jones, L., et al.: Attention is all you need. In: Proceedings of the 31st International Conference on Neural Information Processing Systems, no. 11, pp. 6000–6010 (2017)
11. Davani, A.M., Yeh, L., et al.: Reporting the unreported: event extraction for analyzing the local representation of hate crimes. In: Proceedings of the 2019 Conference on Empirical Methods in Natural Language Processing and the 9th International Joint Conference on Natural Language Processing, pp. 5753–5757 (2019)
12. Liu, X., Huang, H.Y., Zhang, Y.: Open domain event extraction using neural latent variable models. In: Proceedings of the 57th Annual Meeting of the Association for Computational Linguistics, pp. 2860–2871 (2019)
13. Yang, Y.M., Pierce, T., Jaime, G.C.: A study of retrospective and online event detection. In: SIGIR, p. 98 (1998)
14. Kim, J.T., Moldovan, D.I.: PALKA: a system for lexical knowledge acquisition. In: Proceedings of the Second International Conference on Information and Knowledge Management, no. 8, pp. 124–131 (1993)
15. Suthaharan, S.: Support vector machine. In: Machine Learning Models and Algorithms for Big Data Classification Integrated Series in Information Systems, vol. 36 (2006)
16. Daniel, L., Pedro, D.: Naive Bayes models for probability estimation. In: Proceedings of the 22nd International Conference on Machine Learning, no. 8, pp. 529–536 (2005)
17. Eddy, S.R.: What is a hidden Markov model? Nat. Biotechnol. 22(10), 1315–1316 (2004)
18. Berger, A., Della Pietra, S.A., Della Pietra, V.J.: A maximum entropy approach to natural language processing. Comput. Linguist. 22(33), 39–71 (1996)
19. Nguyen, T.M., Nguyen, T.H.: One for all: neural joint modeling of entities and events. In: Proceedings of the AAAI Conference on Artificial Intelligence, vol. 33, no. 1, pp. 6851–6858 (2019)
20. Feng, X., Qin, B., Liu, T.: A language-independent neural network for event detection. SCIENCE CHINA Inf. Sci. 61(9), 1–12 (2018). https://doi.org/10.1007/s11432-017-9359-x
21. Yang, H., Chen, Y.B., Liu, K., Xiao, Y., Zhao, J.: DCFEE: a document-level Chinese financial event extraction system based on automatically labeled training data. In: Proceedings of ACL 2018 System Demonstrations, pp. 50–55 (2018)
22. Wang, X., Wang, Z., Han, X., et al.: MAVEN: a massive general domain event detection dataset. arXiv preprint. arXiv:2004.13590 (2020)

Author Index

Printed in the United States
by Baker & Taylor Publisher Services